Becoming an Effective Policy Advocate

From Policy Practice to Social Justice

FOURTH EDITION

Bruce S. Jansson
University of Southern California

THOMSON

BROOKS/COLE

Australia • Canada • Mexico • Singapore • Spain
United Kingdom • United States

THOMSON
™
BROOKS/COLE

Executive Editor: *Lisa Gebo*
Assistant Editor: *Alma Dea Michelena*
Editorial Assistant: *Sheila Walsh*
Technology Project Manager: *Barry Connolly*
Marketing Manager: *Caroline Concilla*
Advertising Project Manager: *Margaret Parks*
Project Manager, Editorial Production: *Kelsey McGee*

Print/Media Buyer: *Vena Dyer*
Permissions Editor: *Sue Ewing*
Production Service: *Carlisle Communications/Terry Routley*
Cover Designer: *Roger Knox*
Cover Images: *Photodisc/Getty Images*
Compositor: *Carlisle Communications*
Cover Printing, Printing and Binding: *Phoenix Color Corporation*

For more information about our products, contact us at:
Thomson Learning Academic Resource Center
1-800-423-0563

For permission to use material from this text, contact us by:
Phone: 1-800-730-2214
Fax: 1-800-730-2215
Web: http://www.thomsonrights.com

Brooks/Cole/Thomson Learning
511 Forest Lodge Road
Pacific Grove, CA 93950
USA

Asia
Thomson Learning
5 Shenton Way #01-01
UIC Building
Singapore 068808

Australia
Nelson Thomson Learning
102 Dodds Street
South Melbourne, Victoria 3205
Australia

Canada
Nelson Thomson Learning
1120 Birchmount Road
Toronto, Ontario M1K 5G4
Canada

Europe/Middle East/Africa
Thomson Learning
High Holborn House
50/51 Bedford Row
London WC1R 4LR
United Kingdom

Latin America
Thomson Learning
Seneca, 53
Colonia Polanco
11560 Mexico D.F.
Mexico

Spain
Paraninfo Thomson Learning
Calle/Magallanes, 25
28015 Madrid, Spain

Library of Congress Cataloging-in-Publication Data
Jansson, Bruce S.
  Becoming an effective policy advocate : from policy practice to social justice/Bruce S. Jansson. — 4th ed.
    p. cm.
  Includes bibliographical references and indexes.
  ISBN 0-534-52770-1
  1. Social service—United States. 2. United States—Social policy. I. Title.
HV40.J36 2002
  361.973—dc21   2002020071

To Jane Addams,
whose vision of a profession that prized social activism
stimulated me to write about policy practice

Contents

Special Features in this Edition

Policy Advocacy Challenges

Video Clips

Preface

When I first developed the concept, "policy practice," in the mid 1980s, I wondered if others would accept my argument that policy should be reconceptualized as a multifaceted intervention. I argued that policy should include analytic skills, political skills, value clarifying skills, and communication/organizing skills. It seemed an uphill battle because policy curriculum at the time focused on describing the many programs of the welfare state or upon analysis rather than policy as a means of intervention that would allow social workers to be change agents in specific settings.

I have been gratified by the extent that policy practice and policy advocacy have become fixtures in policy curriculum in the succeeding years. If social workers want to make a difference, they not only have to analyze policies and develop proposals, but work to secure their enactment in legislative, government, agency and community venues. They have to communicate their ideas effectively to others, organize or participate in coalitions, and develop links with advocacy groups. They must decide when to compromise and when not to compromise. It is this *combination* of skills, tasks, and competencies that makes policy a living discipline and that helps social workers to be participants in efforts to build a more humane society.

Our challenge is not merely to define social policy as an intervention, but to teach it in a way that encourages social workers to implement it during their careers. To encourage students to see policy as an intervention, I've added several Policy Advocacy Challenges, such as Professor Emanuel Gale's discussion of a living wage campaign in Sacramento, California, to the many that were included in the third edition. The text now contains 65.

I've added 14 video clips, each about ten minutes in length, in which distinguished social workers talk about using the media, lobbying, political campaigns, linking with advocacy groups, ideology, NASW's PACE, and political strategizing. A tape of these video clips is available to adopting professors. Simply request one from your local Wadsworth representative along with your request for this edition's revised instructor's manual/testbank, *Innovative Ways to Teach Policy Practice and Policy Advocacy,* ISBN 0-534-52771-X, to which I've added many contributions from faculty around the nation, including projects to involve social work students in realworld policy activities as they learn theoretical concepts. The instructor's video is ISBN 0-534-52775-2. Professors can access the instructor's manual by clicking the For Instructors tab at http: //info.wadsworth.com/jansson, but they will need a password, which they can obtain by calling the Wadsworth representative.

Students with adequate computer technology can access the video clips at http: //info.wadsworth.com/jansson where they should then click the For Students tab. They may also wish to visit and view these videos on the University of Southern California controlled site at www.usc.edu/socialwork/jansson.

With the help of librarian Stephanie Davis, I've inserted durable Internet sites in each of the chapters.

By discussing ideology and vested interests at many points in this edition, I've encouraged a realistic appreciation of the real barriers that policy advocates encounter as they seek policies that advance social justice.

In another change from the preceding edition, I now include informal policy within the rubric of social policy. I made this change because it became obvious to me that informal policy powerfully shapes the content of the formal policy choices of decision makers as well as the implementation of policies.

In a major change from the preceding edition, I've made "ballot-based advocacy" a central theme of this edition, discussing it in most chapters and adding an entirely new Chapter Twelve on this subject. No matter how skillful policy advocates may be in developing and seeking support for humane policies, our work comes to naught if we lack allies in legislatures and government agencies.

I identify four models of policy practice in this text: ballot-based advocacy, legislative advocacy, troubleshooting, and analytic. I contend that effective policy advocates should be knowledgeable about each model even if they typically meld elements of each into their work. (David Dempsey, Robert Schneider, and Jacqueline McCroskey helped me define three of the models in a jointly drafted chapter that is currently in press.)

I've completely rewritten Chapter One to provide a succinct introduction to policy practice and to identify specific challenges that policy advocates encounter.

I've streamlined this text in many ways, reducing the number of chapters from 15 to 14.

- I provide objectives for each chapter at its start and summarize each chapter's content at its conclusion.
- I've eliminated one chapter in the central part of the book and created a new Chapter Seven that focuses on developing policy proposals and a new Chapter Eight on presenting and defending policy proposals.
- I've consolidated materials about the nature of power and methods of developing power in a new Chapter Nine.
- I've placed materials on coalitions and task groups in a new Chapter Eleven on political strategy and action.

- I've created a new Chapter Twelve that focuses on ballot-based policy advocacy.
- I've moved some figures from the backs of chapters to the fronts of chapters and added some new figures.

A Web-based program (developed by librarian Stephanie Davis), which allows faculty to teach portions of this course on-line, is planned following publication of this edition. This WebTutor™ tool, which can be used with Blackboard or Web CT course management software for the professor, includes exercises, learning aids, and discussion topics. It will be available for order by faculty for their students. Contact your local representative for details and the date when this product will be available.

Policy practice and policy advocacy have now joined other social work interventions, such as administrative and community practice and direct-service. It allows social work to expand its horizons to embrace social reform in a way that returns us to the world view of some of the profession's founders. In ways both incremental and major, we can help our students and graduates move from the sidelines to center stage in battles to achieve greater social justice.

The coming decade will bring harsh challenges to the less fortunate of our society and our world. By viewing policy as a multiskilled intervention that emphasizes advocacy, social workers can strive to change the priorities of an affluent nation that seldom remembers the many people who do not share in the American dream.

Acknowledgments

People who generously contributed Policy Advocacy Challenges to this book, as well as innovative strategies for teaching policy advocacy to *Innovative Strategies for Teaching Policy Practice and Advocacy,* include the following:

Gail Abarbenel, Executive Director, Rape Treatment Center in Santa Monica

Mimi Abramowitz, Professor, School of Social Work, Hunter College of City University of New York

Gino Aisenberg, Assistant Professor School of Social Work, University of Washington

Tricia B. Bent-Goodley, Assistant Professor, School of Social Work, Howard University

Katherine Boland, graduate student, School of Social Work, Boston College

John Brekke, Professor, School of Social Work, University of Southern California

Stephen C. Burke, Associate Professor, School of Social Work, Marywood University

Sandra D. Butler, Associate Professor, School of Social Work, University of Maine

Theresa Clark, Assistant Professor, Social Work Program, Longwood College

Patrick Cunningham, Department of Social Work, University of Alaska

Anneka Davidson, Clinical Professor, School of Social Work, University of Southern California

Stephanie Davis, Research Librarian, University of California, Irvine

Ronald Dear, Emeritus Professor, School of Social Work, University of Washington

Bob Deaton, Professor, Social Work Department, University of Montana

Sarah-Jane Dodd, Assistant Professor, School of Social Work, Hunter College of City University of New York

Susan Einbinder, Assistant Professor, School of Social Work, University of Southern California

Marvin D. Feit, Professor and Director, School of Social Work, University of Akron

Emanuel Gale, Emeritus Professor of Social Work and Gerontology, School of Social Work, California State University at Sacramento

Nancy Gewirtz, Professor of Social Work, Rhode Island School of Social Work

George Haskett, Professor, School of Social Work, Marywood University

Catalina Herrerias, Associate Professor, School of Social Work, University of Oklahoma

Scott Henggeler, Director, Family Services Research Center in South Carolina

Gary Holden, Professor, Ehrenkranz School of Social Work, New York University

Michael Holosko, Professor, School of Social Work, University of Windsor, Canada

Deborah Franks Jacobs, Assistant Professor, Department of Social Work, Shippensburg University

Patsy Lane, Director, Department of Human Services, City of Pasadena

Shirley Lebovics, Clinical Social Worker and Adjunct Faculty, School of Social Work, University of Southern California

John McNutt, Associate Professor, School of Social Work, Boston College

Munira Merchant, Assistant Professor, Department of Social Work, Valparaiso University

Vince Ornelas, doctoral student at School of Social Work, University of Southern California

Tom Packard, Assistant Professor, School of Social Work, San Diego State University

John Potash, Founding Editor, *Social Justice Action Quarterly*

Matthew Ringenberg, Assistant Professor, School of Social Work, Valparaiso University

Lawrence Root, Professor, School of Social Work, University of Michigan

Ramon Salcido, Associate Professor, School of Social Work, University of Southern California

Susan M. Sanchirico, LaGuardia Community College

Robert Schneider, Professor, School of Social Work, Virginia Commonwealth University

Robert D. Schope, Assistant Professor, School of Social Work, University of Iowa

Essie Seck, Associate Professor, School of Social Work, University of Southern California

Jed Shafer, Adjunct Professor, School of Social Work, University of Southern California

Madeleine Stoner, Professor, School of Social Work, University of Southern California

Jolene Swain, Field Coordinator, School of Social Work, University of Southern California

Rita Takahashi, Professor, School of Social Work, San Francisco State University

Samuel Taylor, Emeritus Professor, School of Social Work, University of Southern California

Caroline Tice, Associate Professor and Chair, Department of Social Work, Ohio University

Thomas Watts, Professor and Director of B.S.W. Program, School of Social Work, University of Texas at Arlington

Katherine Wright, Adjunct Professor, School of Social Work, University of Southern California

Reviewers of the manuscripts that led to this final volume include the following: Janice Adams, Indiana Wesleyan University; Colette Brown, University of Hawaii–Honolulu; Hans G. Eriksson, Sor-Trondelag College; Christina Gringeri, University of Utah; Emma Gross, University of Utah; Joan Hashimi, University of Missouri–St. Louis; Richard Hoefer, University of Texas–Arlington; I. Sue Jackson, Bloomsburg University; Susan E. McDonald, DeSales University; John McNutt, Boston College; Pam Miller, Ball State University; John T. Pardeck, Southwest Missouri State University; Daniel Pollack, Yeshiva University; Dennis L. Poole, University of Central Florida; Susan B. Smith, Walla Walla College; and Charles H. Trent, Yeshiva University.

Of course, all errors of omission or commission rest on my shoulders alone.

Bruce S. Jansson

Becoming Motivated to Become a Policy Advocate: Policy Practice and Policy Advocacy as the Fourth Dimension of Social Work Practice

Many social problems beg creative solutions in the United States and in the world that require the determined work of social reformers.

Chapter One   argues that policy practice and policy advocacy are as important to social workers as their other three interventive disciplines: direct service, community, and administrative practice. Social workers must be conversant with social policies and must be able to seek changes in these policies, to advance such values as social justice and fairness and to advance the well-being of citizens and specific groups. They also need to work to change the composition of government to increase the likelihood that decision makers will seek policies that truly help citizens. We argue that policy advocates often encounter barriers, such as opposition from persons and groups with different values, entrenched interests, and mistaken beliefs about the causes and nature of specific social problems and issues. Since policy-changing work is often associated with controversy and conflict, policy advocates must obtain perspectives and skills that enable them to be effective change agents. By becoming

policy advocates, we join social-reform traditions not only in American society but in the social work profession—whether we work for policy reforms in communities, social agencies, local governments, state government, or the federal government, or through the courts. We discuss how electoral politics is pivotal to policy advocacy. We discuss key attributes that policy advocates need, such as a vision, persistence, and the ability to tolerate uncertainty.

Chapter Two   discusses moral, political, and ethical imperatives for policy practice and policy advocacy. Using the moral principles of beneficence, justice, and fairness, we argue that ethical professionals should supplement their one-on-one counseling by changing policy in agencies, communities, and legislatures. We also contend that social workers should use policy practice and policy advocacy to reform the human services system so that it incorporates findings from social science and medical research. Social workers should also engage in policy advocacy to counter other groups, politicians, and interests that support policies that do not advance citizens' well-being.

1

Joining a Tradition of Social Reform

We discuss in this chapter a tradition of social work advocacy that long has existed both within American society and within the social work profession and how policy advocates do the following:

- Seek changes in policies to improve the well-being of members of out-groups
- Seek policy reforms that are in the general interest
- Work from an ecological or systems perspective
- Change many kinds of policies including informal ones
- Prioritize policy changes that assist oppressed populations
- Encounter and surmount barriers to reform
- Join a tradition of social reform in American society and in the social work profession
- Develop attributes that support policy advocacy
- Try to change the composition of government by participating in electoral politics

Diversity and Policy Advocacy

When discussing diversity, most people focus on the unique cultures and perspectives of specific groups, such as women, African Americans, Asian Americans, Native Americans, gay men and lesbians, persons with physical and mental disabilities, older Americans, and children. Indeed, clinicians need extensive knowledge of different cultures and perspectives when working with members of various groups, lest they be insensitive to their needs and preferences.

But social workers risk ignoring many of the social and economic needs of these groups if they limit themselves to knowledge of their cultures and perspectives. Members of each group have experienced various kinds of discrimination and prejudice in American history, both in distant times and in recent history—discrimination and prejudice that remain active in contemporary society, even though civil rights and other protections have been enacted. Moreover, each of these groups experiences structural discrimination—a series of obstacles that, singly and together, interfere with the advancement of their members into the social and economic mainstream of American society.

American society has a variety of *out-groups* or subgroups, who have experienced discrimination and prejudice over an extended period—and whose members' well-being (as measured by economic and other criteria) often reflects the structural barriers they have encountered. These out-groups include *racial out-groups* such as African Americans, Latinos, and Native Americans. They have been subjected not only to overt racism in personal interactions with employers, teachers, physicians, the police, and people in other professions, but to policy discrimination as reflected in schools, training programs, housing, community amenities, and correctional and law enforcement programs that give poorer services or fewer resources to them than they give to caucasian populations. They include *sociological out-groups,* such as women, older persons, and people with disabilities, whose members are often expected to assume relatively dependent roles in society, whether in places of employment or in the broader society. They are often denied access to certain kinds of jobs, to promotions, and to roles within decision-making bodies because of widespread beliefs that they are incapable of moving beyond residual or lower-level roles within society. Disabled persons are often encouraged by the medical system to be dependent. They include *dependent out-groups,* such as children, who often must rely upon society for basic amenities such as financial assistance, health care, dental care, and adequate housing, but who are often given inadequate governmental support because they lack political clout. They include *non-conformist out-groups,* who are subjected to discrimination because they are widely viewed as violating important social norms, such as sexual norms (gay men and lesbians), social norms (criminal offenders and juvenile delinquents), or social expectations (persons with mental illness). They include *model out-groups,* such as Jewish Americans, Asian Americans, and some white ethnic Americans, who are denied resources and services because many Americans believe they have no social problems. They include *economic out-groups* including persons in low- and moderate-income groups who often lack sufficient resources, well-paying employment, or stable employment. Lack of resources, in turn, precludes them from some life options, such as safe neighborhoods, adequate housing, and economic security, that are available to more affluent persons. Discrimination against members of out-groups, whether expressed in personal encounters with others or through policy discrimination, often shows up in statistical measures of the economic and social well-being of members of specific out-groups. Members of racial out groups tend, for example, to have fewer resources, lower life expectancies, and poorer educational achievement than caucasian populations. Women are more likely to be poor than men, particularly when they are single heads of households. Persons with physical and mental disabilities are far more likely to be poor than other members of society. Gay youth are more likely than non-gay youth to commit suicide. Children are more likely than adults to live in poverty.

A critic might ask: "But don't these differences in economic, health, and other measures of well-being stem from the intrinsic problems of members of out-groups (such as medical problems in the case of the disabled) or from the cultural or work ethic of members of out-groups?" It is true; members of out-groups do sometimes contribute to their own problems. For example, a disabled person may simply choose not to seek employment because he has accepted norms of dependency widely ascribed to disabled persons or because he possesses a mental problem such as depression. Similarly, low-income persons of color sometimes exacerbate the problems of other persons in their communities by resorting to violent behavior or abusing drugs.

Yet efforts to generalize economic, social, educational, and other indicators of entire out-groups to the actions of specific persons are doomed to failure. When entire groups have economic, education, health, and other indicators of well-being that are sharply divergent from the dominant population, we rightly can surmise that external forces and policies impact them adversely and contribute to these outcomes. When a disproportionate percentage of single female heads of households are immersed in poverty, we can rightly ask what factors, singly and in tandem, affect or influence the economic outcomes of this population so that, as a group, its members suffer disproportionate poverty when compared to double-headed families or single females with no children.

When examining structural discrimination, we identify policies, familial factors, cultural factors, life experiences, community factors, and economic factors that *systematically* shape the lives of specific groups so they fall behind other groups that are not subject to structural discrimination. We can understand why such groups as low-income African Americans or single heads of household lag behind white males with college degrees in income only by examining a constellation of factors that systematically impinge on them. In the case of low-income, inner-city African Americans, such factors include the following:

- Overt discrimination on the basis of race
- Subtle discrimination that relegates African Americans to poorly paid positions and to education tracks that steer them away from college preparation
- Segregated communities that are distant from places of employment
- Lack of family and community role models who have secured higher levels of education
- Overcrowded schools
- Low expectations from school personnel, including excessive tracking
- Childhood poverty exacerbated by governmental policies such as the absence of family allowances
- Family stress stemming from poverty
- Lack of recreational programs
- Exposure to violence, such as from gangs
- High rates of mortality among adolescent males
- Lack of user-friendly health systems that provide preventive services
- Lack of well-paying, accessible, and stable employment
- Lack of access to the old-boy networks that give some people an inside track to jobs and educational opportunities

If we compare suburban white children whose parents have college educations with African American inner-city residents, the harsh workings of structural discrimination immediately become evident. These suburban children rarely confront these barriers—and if they do encounter specific ones, they rarely encounter a constellation of barriers. It is not surprising that suburban white residents are often unsympathetic to inner-city African Americans. Assuming from their own experiences that a level playing field does exist, many of them believe the inner-city residents lack personal characteristics, such as the work ethic, that would bring them out of poverty.

Consider single women who have high school diplomas or less. Regardless of their ethnicity, these women are likely to secure only relatively low-paying work because they cannot compete for the higher-paying jobs usually filled by persons with higher levels of education. As single parents, moreover, they must frequently support their children without financial assistance from another parent, even though governmental authorities have placed more emphasis in recent years on collecting funds from absent parents. Because the United States does not fund day care for many women for sustained periods, their meager paychecks are often depleted by day-care costs. Because employers are not required by law to provide fringe benefits, many low-wage-earning women do not have health insurance, so they must obtain health care for themselves or their children in crowded, difficult to access public clinics. Some of these women cannot afford cars, so they must use a time-consuming public transportation system that sometimes does not even have routes convenient to their workplaces. It is small wonder, then, that millions of poorly educated single mothers and their children remain mired in poverty for extended periods, no matter how hard they work to achieve a better economic standard. As with inner-city African Americans, poverty brings additional stresses to individuals and families who must struggle to make ends meet, who cannot afford amenities that others take for granted, and who often must live in blighted communities where rents are relatively low. (See Policy Advocacy Challenge 1.1.)

We should not merely take a short-term perspective when we examine the effects of external forces and policies. Most African Americans, for example, were deprived of land, civil liberties, and education in the 19th century—often relegated to rural areas of the South where they lived in appalling poverty. Unlike white immigrants from Italy, Ireland, and Eastern Europe, they were not allowed to participate in the emerging industrial order of northern cities in the 19th century. They only began moving to the North in large numbers well into the 20th century. They were consigned to play catch up under equally appalling conditions in northern cities, such as segregated communities, exclusion from trade unions, hiring and promotion prejudice in the workplace that consigned them to unskilled and uncertain jobs, poor health care, and poor schools—not to mention police brutality. It is hardly surprising that gangs and substance abuse festered in low-income African American areas, which further impeded upward mobility. Policy developments of preceding eras, then, impeded the ability of contemporary African Americans to achieve parity with caucasian Americans, whose upward economic assent was built upon generations of their children obtaining education, the accumulation of assets (such as savings and houses), and heightened expectations.

Policy advocates are sometimes not content merely with equalizing policies of out-groups and the dominant population. Because of the effects of long-term oppression on members of out-groups, we should sometimes favor *compensatory* strategies, such as extra tutoring or smaller classes in schools, outreach health services to encourage persons who do not usually use the health care system services to do so, or providing community-based services in areas where persons are particularly impoverished. Similary, affirmative action is sometimes needed to move out-groups' members more rapidly into employment and education—particularly when we conclude that out-groups' members would not otherwise achieve parity with the dominant population in the foreseeable future.

When identifying a variety of factors that lead certain out-groups to lag behind the population with respect to specific indicators of well-being, we must beware of several dangers. These include excessively stigmatizing groups, viewing them as excessively dependent, or relying on panaceas. Many individuals do make it up and out despite structural discrimination, such as African Americans who enter professions, single heads of households who successfully juggle raising children and careers, and paraplegics who use technology to care for themselves and enter the workforce. Nor should we view members of out-groups as passive victims of fate, since our challenge is to empower them to develop creative solutions for overcoming barriers they encounter. Indeed, we need to institute policies that provide incentives and avenues to help persons develop survival skills, improve their neighborhoods, establish helping networks, and develop advocacy groups—coupled with policies that give them resources, health benefits, and services. We should not succumb to the belief that specific policies will have a magical effect. To help single mothers improve their economic condition, for example, we need multiple, interacting policies that help them improve their lot, such as greater funding for child care, increases in the minimum wage, expansion of the earned-income tax credit (which gives low-income workers a tax rebate), increases in housing subsidies, more training and remedial education, expansion of food stamp subsidies, and expansion of health insurance for children and families. These policies should also help empower single mothers to develop their skills, education, coping mechanisms, and support systems.

POLICY ADVOCACY CHALLENGE 1.1 *MAPPING STRUCTURAL DISCRIMINATION*	Take any subgroup or out-group that lags behind the general population on specific social or economic indicators. Identify a constellation of factors that lead to structural discrimination against this subgroup by contrasting the subgroup with another group in the population that is not as subject to structural discrimination. Identify specific kinds of policy reforms that have been enacted to ameliorate such structural discrimination. What additional reforms would help the subgroup's members improve their economic and social status? Why do social workers need policy advocacy skills to address structural discrimination—and why are clinical skills not sufficient?

In policy practice and policy advocacy, then, social workers must consider diversity at more than just the cultural level. This allows social workers to address environmental factors that stack the deck against a subgroup's members and that powerfully shape their collective destinies. Social workers can use policy advocacy to remedy or address problems like the following:

- Inner-city poverty concentrations of African Americans, Latinos, Asian Americans, and Native Americans
- The feminization of poverty, with roughly one-fourth of American children living in impoverished households
- Extraordinary differences in educational attainment between white people and many people of color
- Large disparities between men and women in earnings and high-level positions in employment
- Extraordinary poverty among persons with physical and mental disabilities
- Discrimination against gay men and lesbians
- A dearth of services for people who abuse substances
- Problems of frail older people who need various kinds of tangible assistance but who are impoverished
- Inadequate safety-net programs to allow low-income persons to overt, excessive, economic problems
- Violence against women (See Policy Advocacy Challenge 1.2.)

POLICY ADVOCACY CHALLENGE 1.2

ENHANCING THE RIGHTS OF CHILDREN WHO ARE SEXUALLY ASSAULTED IN THEIR SCHOOL

Gail Abarbanel, M.S.W., L.C.S.W., Executive Director, Rape Treatment Center, Santa Monica–UCLA Medical Center

As a social worker, I view social policy reforms as a way to give meaning to the experiences of my clients, as well as a means to serve them better. The following case example illustrates these two functions:

Jennifer, a 12-year-old girl attending a Los Angeles middle school, was raped by another student—during the school day—on the school campus. After she reported the crime, she was revictimized by her eighth-grade classmates, who ridiculed and harassed her. Jennifer also was ostracized by some of her friends, who informed her that their parents had told them that they could no longer associate with her.

When the school district scheduled a disciplinary hearing, Jennifer received very little notice and no information about the procedures. When Jennifer and her parents arrived at the hearing, they were told that this 12-year-old child would have to go into the hearing room alone. No one was allowed to accompany her—no parent, no counsel, no support person—while she was subjected to cross-examination by the accused student's representative. The accused student, however, was allowed to have his parents and a legal representative present to support him during the entire proceeding.

Jennifer had been profoundly traumatized by the rape. She was too fragile psychologically, as most other 12-year-old children would be, to testify under the conditions set by the school district. However, she was informed by school officials that, without her testimony, there would be no disciplinary action. The hearing was postponed.

As a result of the Rape Treatment Center's efforts on the victim's behalf, when the hearing was finally held, Jennifer was allowed to be accompanied by an ACLU attorney. However, the attorney was required to remain silent. The school district officials seated Jennifer very close to, and directly opposite, the father of the boy who had raped her. The accused student's representative who questioned Jennifer insulted and taunted her. She also asked Jennifer to demonstrate some of the degrading things that had been done to her during the assault, an abusive practice called "reenactment" that would not be permitted in most legal proceedings involving either child or adult victims.

The hearing process was devastating for Jennifer. She was powerless, just as she had been during the rape. Again, she was revictimized—this time by the school district's disciplinary system.

As the founder and director of the Rape Treatment Center (RTC) at Santa Monica–UCLA Medical Center and a longtime advocate for victims of sexual assault, I intervened to protect this child, *and* I sought a remedy that would provide legal protection for other child victims and would prevent this kind of discriminatory treatment in the future. I turned to Assemblywoman Sheila Kuehl (D-Santa Monica), our representative in the state legislature. Together, we drafted legislation to establish rights for children who are sexually assaulted in their schools.

Under the new law, which became effective January 1, 1997, child victims are given many of the same rights afforded accused students in school disciplinary hearings, such as the right to have a support person accompany them during their testimony and to request a closed hearing. In addition, the victim's irrelevant sexual history is protected from disclosure. Sexual assault victims have had these rights in the criminal and civil justice systems for many years. However, in most states, the education codes recognize the rights only of accused students while overlooking the needs of victims. The new law corrects this inequity.

(continued)

(1.2   continued)

Passage of the legislation is only a first step. Students must be informed about the new rights and protections available to them if they are victimized. Schools must change their policies and procedures to implement the reforms required by the new law. The Rape Treatment Center has an established, school-based, sexual abuse prevention program that reaches thousands of students each year, as well as administrative personnel in schools throughout the community we serve. This program has enabled us to educate school personnel and students about the new law. Five years later, in 2002, its center educates new student cohorts and teachers.

Advancing the Public Interest at Home and Abroad

While policy advocates often focus on problems and issues affecting out-groups, they also tackle problems of citizens in general, which we call the public interest. They want child-care services, for example, that improve the developmental and cognitive well-being of any children who use them. They want schools that provide first-rate counseling services to children so that any children who develop mental-health or substance-abuse problems can obtain quality services. They want preventive services that diminish the incidence of major social problems that afflict citizens whether or not they are members of an out-group. For example, policy advocates might seek laws that disallow smoking in public places and require health-risk notifications on cigarette packages, seek antipollution measures, fight for better public transportation systems, or seek a living wage policy for all workers.

Policy advocates do not limit their activity to the United States. With the reduction of trade barriers, for example, many American corporations have relocated their operations abroad to escape high wages, antipollution regulations, and corporate taxes they confront in the United States. To the extent that they impose inhumane practices on other nations in a quest to expand their profits, policy advocates battle for international standards that govern wages and pollution—and seek to protect wages of American workers who often are given an ultimatum to accept lower wages to forestall their company from replacing their jobs with lower-wage workers abroad. Issues of immigration across national borders are germane, as well, to policy advocates who grapple with such issues as when immigrants should receive citizenship, and how immigrants' rights should be protected in the United States. Since policy advocates are interested in the well-being of persons no matter their location, some of them pursue issues of global social justice, such as how wealthy nations like the United States can assist third-world nations with poverty and such illnesses as AIDS.

Using an Ecological Perspective

An ecological, or systems, perspective is highly useful in policy advocacy. As our discussion of out-groups suggests, citizens' lives are impacted by multiple factors, including economic, cultural, social, community, and physiological, as well as discrimination or prejudice. Existing policies are part of their ecology: they limit resources, services, and opportunities that they receive, but also provide them. When developing policy proposals, advocates often examine the problems and populations that will be impacted by these proposals from an ecological perspective. They ask, for example, what forces and factors in the lives of welfare recipients influence whether they can secure and retain employment; then they seek policies that address these ecological factors. (We discuss an ecological perspective at greater length in Chapter 6.)

What Policy Practitioners and Advocates Seek to Change

Policy advocates aim to change social policies. This book uses a simple, problem-solving definition of *social policy* as "a collective strategy that addresses social problems." Our definition is similar to that of the late Richard Titmuss, an English social policy theorist.[1]

Defining social policy as goal-driven problem solving has several advantages. First, it makes clear that policies are established to address social problems that include the following:

- Victimization of persons by landlords, corporations, businesses, realtors, restaurant owners, and others—such as by providing them with unsafe rentals, providing unsafe products, not providing consumers with sanitary food, not paying employees sufficient resources to allow them to survive. These kinds of problems are often addressed by *regulations* such as the federal minimum wage, housing codes, regulations of the federal Food and Drug Administration, and local living wage regulations.

- Inability of citizens to meet their survival needs, thus imperiling their nutritional, housing, health, and other basic needs. These kinds of policies lead to *needs-meeting policies* that provide basic health and economic benefits to citizens, such as food stamps, Medicaid and Medicare health benefits, Supplemental Security Income (SSI), and rent-supplement programs.

- Inability of citizens to obtain skills and knowledge to find employment or to find employment that can meet their basic needs. These kinds of *opportunity-enhancing policies* include public education, job-training programs, and vocational education.

- Inability of citizens to cope with mental health, marital, substance abuse, and familial problems. These *social-service policies* include a wide range of mental health, child welfare, and substance abuse programs.

- Inability of citizens to navigate complex service-delivery systems. *Referral and linkage policies* establish case management, ombudsman, and outreach programs.

- Discriminatory treatment of members of specific out-groups by employers, schools, public facilities, transportation companies, landlords, and others. *Civil rights policies* prohibit specific infringements of the civil rights of out-groups' members, including the Civil Rights Acts of 1964 and 1965, local antihate laws prohibiting attacks on members of out-groups and defiling places of worship, and the Americans with Disabilities Act.

- Excessive inequality between low- and high-income persons. *Equality-enhancing policies* have targeted resources to low-income populations, such as the federal Earned Income Tax Credit; progressive features of federal, state, and local tax codes that tax affluent citizens more heavily than low-income citizens; and a host of programs that target services or resources to low-income populations, such as Medicaid, SSI, and food stamps.

- Inability of low-income Americans to accumulate assets such as savings accounts and real estate. *Asset accumulation policies,* such as federal legislation stimulating individual investment accounts, give citizens tax incentives and resources to initiate savings accounts and to purchase houses.
- Citizens lack public amenities necessary for recreation and commerce. Federal, state, and local governments enact *economic development policies* that promote construction of roads, parks, bridges, and public transportation.
- Certain portions of cities lack sufficient jobs to support their citizens. Various levels of government offer *economic development policies* such as tax incentives and loans to businesses that locate themselves in low-income areas.
- Low rates of participation in the political process by low-income persons that increases the disinclination of government to adequately fund programs to help them. Policies geared toward *facilitating political participation and increasing the political power of oppressed populations* include state and federal policies that prohibit excessive campaign contributions by special interests and that reapportion political districts so that they do not discriminate against persons of color.

We should note, as well, that many policies are geared toward improving defects in the operations of agencies that implement specific social policies. Imagine, for example, that a legislator succeeds in enacting legislation that provides prenatal services meant to decrease premature births and birth defects. Imagine, as well, that the person who sponsored the legislation finds, several years later, that it has had little impact on the rates of premature births or birth defects in an inner-city Latino area. Assume the legislator also discovers that neither bilingual nor outreach staff have been hired, that clinic hours are limited to daytime hours, and that programs are located at inconvenient sites for Latinas, such as at a distant public hospital. The following are problems in the human services system that are often the targets of policy reform in specific agencies, in specific service networks, or in legislation establishing new programs.

- *Fragmentation.* Barriers make it difficult for clients or consumers to obtain services from multiple programs.
- *Discontinuity.* Clients cannot obtain consistent, accessible services over a period of time.
- *Lack of access.* Barriers make services hard to use at specific sites.
- *Discrimination.* Service providers are hostile or indifferent to specific kinds of clients.
- *"Creaming."* Providers deliberately seek clients with less serious problems.
- *Wastage.* Different providers serve the same population for the same problem, or services are not provided efficiently.
- *Lack of outreach.* Providers make little effort to seek persons who do not currently use services.
- *Incompetent staff.* Staff are asked to perform tasks for which they have little training.
- *Lack of cultural sensitivity.* Providers make little effort to match their services to the cultural perspectives of the clients they serve such as by having bilingual staff or staff versed in specific cultures.
- *Inadquate funding.* Services are funded at such low levels that important activities are compromised or deleted.

Our definition of social policy as collective strategy to address social problems makes clear that policies are developed in many places, as the example of commitment procedures for people with mental illness illustrates. Policies may come down from the highest levels, including state mental health officials, county mental health departments, various courts, and even federal authorities. Although these *high-level policies* influence their work, staff in county mental health units may implement them in strikingly different ways. The staff at one county hospital may commit many more persons than the staff at another hospital, because each defines *imminent threat* differently.

It is useful to portray social policy as a kind of ladder extending from federal authorities to persons in the population who use services or programs. Policy advocates can intervene at any point in this policy ladder—or at several points. They sometimes seek to change the policies of individual agencies, such as specific not-for-profit, for-profit, or public agencies. They may seek to change the policies of higher-level agencies in counties, municipalities, or townships. They may seek redress in state or federal venues. Or they may seek court rulings that place restrictions on how local mental health agencies commit mental patients involuntarily to mental institutions.

Our definition of social policy eliminates the problem of establishing rigid boundaries between social policy and other kinds of policies. Most commentators agree that public welfare, child welfare, medical, and job-training policies are social policies, but they are less certain about income tax, environmental, economic, transportation, and other policies. Our definition suggests that specific policies become social policies whenever they influence social problems. For example, income tax proposals that increase or decrease the resources of poor persons become social policies when they affect poverty and unemployment. By the same token, tax policies that regulate how corporations depreciate their equipment are not social policies unless they can be shown to be relevant to such problems as poverty and unemployment.

Thus far, we have emphasized the content or substance of policies by focusing on the kind of social problems that specific policies address. These policies often are contained in statutes that are established when legislation is approved by local, state, and federal governments. We also can compare the form of different policies. *Policy objectives* (or mission statements) are a kind of policy because they shape the actions and choices of officials, executives, and staff. When a state mental health agency decides to drastically reduce the populations of mental institutions, its officials and staff are committed to this objective and to programs consonant with it. Imagine how services might change if, instead, top officials wanted to increase long-term institutional services for a range of mental conditions. (See Policy Advocacy Challenge 1.3.) By the

---

POLICY ADVOCACY CHALLENGE 1.3

THE IMPACT OF MISSIONS ON POLICIES AND SERVICES OF TWO CHILD WELFARE DEPARTMENTS

Develop two different child welfare departments based on very different sets of objectives or missions. Assume that one is concerned exclusively with taking severely abused or neglected children from families—a kind of policing and placing mission. Contrast this with another child welfare agency that views itself as a builder of community supports and strengths—and as primarily an agent of prevention. Develop a four to five sentence mission statement for each agency. Discuss how the two agencies would deploy their staffs of 50 social workers differently. Does this exercise help you understand the importance of informal policies?

same token, *rules and regulations* are a kind of policy because many social policies constrain the activities of officials, staff, and consumers. For example, rules and regulations place many restrictions on mental health personnel when they wish to commit someone involuntarily to a mental hospital. They must base their commitment on evidence that the person will harm self or others if not committed—and they must go through specific procedures, including holding hearings and providing legal counsel to the person being committed.

Budgets are a kind of policy since they determine what resources are devoted to specific, enacted policies—resources that determine whether a policy will be effective and who will receive it. Similarly, *eligibility policies* determine who will receive access to the programs established by policies. So-called means-tested programs, for example, are limited to persons who meet certain asset and income tests, as contrasted with so-called universal programs, such as Medicare, that are used by most people regardless of assets or income.

Formal or *written policies* can certainly be considered social policy, whether they are issued by legislation, or are court rulings, administrative guidelines, or budget documents. It is less immediately clear whether *informal* or *nonwritten policies* qualify. The issue requires some examination. When written policy contains relatively vague and ill-defined terms, officials must often develop informal policies to fill in the gaps. For example, some laws restrict involuntary commitment to persons who pose an imminent danger to themselves or others. Staff who require a strict standard may resist committing someone who has not actually attempted suicide, whereas other staff may believe that merely threatening suicide falls within this restriction. Though such standards have not been recorded in official policy, they are policies because they have the same effect as written policy. They are collectively defined rules that profoundly shape the actions of direct-service staff and their administrators.

Informal policies are absolutely critical to social policy because they cover a wide range of issues. For example, in a child welfare department, informal policies shape how staff conceptualize child welfare. Do they see their job exclusively as helping children who have been seriously abused or neglected, or do they also want to construct preventive programs to educate at-risk parents about parenting? Do they believe it is their job to link their services with schools, medical services, and job-training programs for parents, or do they see their work as isolated from other programs? Do they want to work with troubled families over an extended period, or do they see their responsibility primarily to remove children from such families?

Our definition of social policy, then, emphasizes both *formal* and *informal* policies. If the former includes rules, procedures, programs, and budgets that bind specific persons to specific courses of action, then subjective views of persons and groups constitute the latter. We cannot understand the workings of social agencies, legislators, or heads of governments without understanding both dimensions of social policy.

Without suggesting that any of them is more or less important than the others, we might distinguish four categories: (a) official, written policies; (b) informal, unwritten policies; (c) personal orientations toward policy, such as an aversion to specific rules or strong support of a specific policy; and (d) personal policy actions, such as obeying or disobeying a policy in a specific work setting. Bisno calls the fourth type "policy-in-action," whereas I have named it *actualized policy*.[2] All of these policy-related categories are important in social policy.

What Are Policy Practice and Policy Advocacy?

We define *policy practice* as efforts to change policies in legislative, agency, and community settings, whether by establishing new policies, improving existing ones, or defeating the policy initiatives of other people. By this definition, people of all ideological persuasions, including liberals, radicals, and conservatives, engage in policy practice. People who are skilled in policy practice increase the odds that their policy preferences will be advanced.

By *policy advocacy,* we mean policy practice that aims to help relatively powerless groups, such as women, children, poor people, African Americans, Asian Americans, Latinos, gay men and lesbians, and people with disabilities, improve their resources and opportunities. Thus, *policy practice* refers to efforts generally to change policies, and *policy advocacy* refers to efforts to help powerless groups improve their lot.

Because social workers usually work with people who are relatively powerless, their policy practice usually is policy advocacy. Therefore, we often refer to social workers' policy practice as *policy advocacy* in this book. Yet social workers as policy advocates need to ground their work in a range of tasks, skills, and competencies that also apply to policy practice. Sometimes we can even apply the tactics of skilled conservative policy practitioners to our policy advocacy. Because we focus on the policy-changing work of social reformers in this book, we frequently supplant the term *policy practice* with *policy advocacy.*

This distinction between policy practice and policy advocacy is important for several reasons. First, it allows us to discover the differences between the policy practice of social workers and, for example, that of the U.S. Chamber of Commerce, the National Association of Manufacturers, and the National Rifle Association. They are policy practitioners, but they are rarely policy advocates!

Second, this distinction allows us to develop a general framework for any policy-changing work (policy practice) that advocates can adapt to their own purposes. Were we to discuss only policy advocacy, we would be leaving out the general underlying principles of policy-changing work. Policy advocacy is hard work that requires its practitioners to use an underlying policy-changing framework, as well as specific tasks, skills, and competencies.

Finally, this distinction allows us to evaluate the results of policy-changing work in terms of its ultimate purpose. We might admire the National Rifle Association's ability to gain and use power to block gun control, but this tactical skill (the means) should not imply that the ends are praiseworthy.

Policies rarely emerge suddenly—but always during a developmental process. Policy advocates need both to understand this process and to be able to work skillfully within it. We discuss throughout this text the tasks and skills you will need to become an effective policy advocate. When presenting problems to agency, community, and legislative decision makers, advocates engage in *agenda-setting tasks.* When they use social science research that probes their causes and when they analyze how to present policy, practitioners perform *problem-analyzing tasks.* They also analyze social problems, such as homelessness, by classifying homeless persons, gauging the problem's prevalence in various communities, and seeking its causes.

Practitioners *develop proposals* when they create solutions to specific problems, whether legislation or proposals to improve agency services. Proposals may be relatively simple, such as those that change an agency's intake policies, or complex, such as those that establish major social programs.

Practitioners engage in *policy-enacting tasks* when they develop strategies to have a policy approved. When complex political processes are involved, strategy may consume major amounts of time and resources and demand frequent revisions. On other occasions, strategy may consist of one presentation at a critical meeting or personal discussions with highly placed decision makers.

Policy implementation involves identifying why a policy has not been adequately implemented and developing corrective strategies. *Policy-assessing tasks* require evaluating a policy and deciding what changes to make if the evaluation is negative.

Policy practitioners (and therefore policy advocates) use four basic skills as they engage in each of the stages of the policy-development process. They use *analytic skills* to obtain data, identify policy alternatives, compare their relative merits, and develop recommendations. (See Policy Advocacy Challenge 1.2.) *Political skills* help practitioners assess the policies' feasibility, identify power resources, and develop and implement political strategy. *Interactional skills* help practitioners make contacts, develop networks, build personal relationships, identify old-boy networks, and facilitate coalitions and committees.

Points made during the policymaking process require *value clarification* or *ethical reasoning.* Policy makers have to decide what objectives they favor when analyzing problems and developing policy proposals. Do they want drastic reforms or merely modest changes in existing policies? Values arise as well when policy makers define their motivations and loyalties. Do they identify with and seek to help certain powerless groups, the agency that employs them, or their particular work unit? Do they seek personal advancement through policy changes? Policy practitioners must also determine what risks they will take in questioning existing policies, such as the loss of their jobs in extreme cases. In addition, policy practitioners must wrestle with ethical issues related to procedural matters. Under what circumstances are deceptive, dishonest, or manipulative behaviors ethical? When is it ethical to undermine the credibility of another person or faction? When seeking support for a policy, is it ever ethical to make exaggerated claims about it? Ethical issues also arise about the substantive content of policies. For example, ethical principles are involved in involuntarily committing homeless persons with mental problems: Should laws protect homeless people's well-being or maximize their autonomy and self-determination?

Challenges Encountered by Policy Advocates

Policy advocacy is important—and challenging—work. By changing laws, rules, regulations, budgets, and objectives, policy advocates can positively impact the lives not just of specific individuals or families (as in direct-practice social work), but of large numbers of individuals and families. For example, prior to the enactment of the food stamp program millions of low-income families lacked the resources to provide proper nutrition to their members. Another example is a social worker who persuades an agency to hire a bilingual worker, thus allowing services to be provided to scores of families that otherwise might not have received them.

If policy advocacy is often rewarding, it is also challenging for several reasons. Indeed, policy advocates often encounter opposition or controversy when they try to change specific policies. Controversy or opposition is likely for several reasons, including a crowded field, divergent interests, divergent values and ideology, and different beliefs about whether a specific policy is, or will be, effective in addressing a specific social problem.

A crowded field   Unlike direct-service work, for example, the policy advocate rarely has the field to self. This is because social policies—and policies generally—commit or bind large groups of persons and organizations to specific courses of action by establishing ground rules that guide or direct their activity. Therefore, many groups, persons, and interests take an interest in specific policies—especially when someone wants to initiate a new one or change an existing one.

Influencing tangible interests of persons, groups, and corporations   When examining interests, policy advocates often ask, "Who benefits from the status quo, and who believes their practical interests would better be met by some or major reforms?" Since specific persons, interest groups, and corporations often benefit from specific policies, they often oppose changes in them—or only want changes that advance their own needs. As persons who have sought to reform American medical care have frequently discovered, for example, pharmaceutical companies, insurance companies, health plans, and the American Medical Association have often blocked needed reforms. Indeed, consumers are often the least represented in policy deliberations that can be dominated by persons and groups with resources to hire lobbyists and to give funds to politicians and political parties.

Divergent values and ideologies   People often support or oppose policies because they believe they impinge on their fundamental values. As developments in the United States during the 1980s, 1990s, and first portion of this century suggest, conservatives and liberals often battle over policies. Indeed, *ideology* is a shorthand way of summarizing persons' values, as can be seen in Table 1.1.

Conservatives prioritize such values as freedom (or liberty), localism in social policy, and individualism. Because conservatives also tend to believe that the private markets are relatively effective and humane in distributing societal resources, they are less inclined than liberals to favor regulations of corporations. Such persons as Ronald Reagan, Newt Gingrich, and George W. Bush share a world view that emphasizes policies that flow from these basic values. They favor relatively low taxes, believing that citizens' resources belong to themselves. They favor diminution of federal power, preferring to transfer to state and local governments many federal policy roles. They want to increase the role of private charity in American society while reducing public expenditures. They often oppose regulations of corporations, such as antipollution laws, increases in the minimum wage, work-safety regulations, and proposals to allow consumers to sue health maintenance organizations. Of course, not all conservatives are alike in their views. So-called moderate Republicans often want relatively more public spending, more government regulations, and less military spending than more conservative Republicans. Those drawn from fundamentalist churches often take positions on so-called social issues (such as abortion and regulations regarding pornographic literature) that differ from other Republicans.

One need only contrast the positions of Reagan, Gingrich, and Bush with those of Bill Clinton, Jesse Jackson, and Tom Daschle to see that significant ideological differences exist between conservatives and liberals. (See Table 1.1.) Liberals place somewhat

TABLE 1.1   Comparison of different ideologies

	Conservatives	Libertarians	Liberals	Radicals
Views of federal government	Negative, except in military and international policy and as source of subsidies for business	Negative	Relatively positive	Positive, unless it is under control of monied interests
Views of state and local government	Relatively positive	Negative	Divided, but federal government is often preferred	Less positive than views of federal government
Views of causes of social problems	Emphasis on personal and cultural factors	Unclear	More emphasis than conservatives on environmental factors	Environmental factors generated by monied interests
Views of capitalism	Positive	Positive	Positive, but regulations are favored	Negative, unless workers are empowered
Views of human nature	Relatively optimistic about affluent people, less optimistic about poor people	Favor policies that maximize the liberty of all people	Relatively optimistic about poor people but less optimistic about rich people	Pessimistic about monied interests, but optimistic about other people
Views of safety net	Want relatively meager safety net	Unclear	Want relatively generous safety net	Favor generous safety net
Attitudes toward abortion and other moral issues	Divided, but a significant faction favors government controls	Dislike government regulation of social matters	Usually oppose restrictions on abortion but favor restrictions on drugs	Often oppose restriction of social matters
Core value	Liberty, though some government incentives and regulations are favored	Liberty	Liberty, but social justice is also important	Social justice
Views of nongovernmental and governmental programs	Favor nongovernmental initiatives	Favor nongovernmental initiatives	Favor a mixture of both	Favor governmental programs, but often recommend worker or citizen inclusion in government decisions
Views of subgroups that lag behind others in economic status or that experience discrimination	Tend to deny their existence or minimize discrimination	Unclear	Favor some redistribution and strong civil rights	Emphasize oppression of out-groups and seek major corrective action

greater emphasis than conservatives on social justice, favoring somewhat more redistribution of resources to low-income persons. They have traditionally been in the forefront of efforts to secure social reforms that require greater expenditure of government resources or expansion of government regulations, even when these efforts require higher taxes. They are somewhat more critical of private markets in distributing resources or advancing other goals—making them more likely than conservatives to favor a minimum or living wage, work-safety regulations, antipollution measures, and proposals that would allow consumers to sue health maintenance organizations. Liberals have traditionally been somewhat less suspicious of the government than conservatives, often turning to the federal government to implement and fund an array of social programs. Even in state and local jurisdictions, liberals are more likely than conservatives to propose and support government programs. While many conservatives have favored civil rights legislation, liberals have often been even more supportive of efforts to assist persons of color, women, the disabled, and gay men and lesbians with regulations that curtail discrimination in employment and elsewhere.

Libertarians emphasize liberty or freedom. They oppose, for example, the so-called War on Drugs on grounds that citizens should be able to make their own lifestyle choices. They do not favor heavy taxation of personal income, believing citizens should be able to keep most of their resources. They oppose restrictions on abortion, censorship of pornographic literature, and most other policies that restrict individuals' liberty to make basic choices for themselves.

It is difficult to define radicalism with precision in an American society that lacks a strong socialist tradition. (See Table 1.1.) Yet we can find many persons in American history, such as the social-work leader Bertha Reynolds, who have been more insistent on equalizing wealth and power in the United States than liberals. They believe that capitalism, even when somewhat regulated by government, distributes wealth in an unfair manner. Radicals favor far higher taxation of private wealth than conservatives or liberals. They want government to redistribute resources aggressively to diminish economic inequality. They sometimes favor proposals to allow workers to acquire partial or complete ownership of corporations.

Different opinions about what works best   Policy advocates sometimes encounter opposition from persons and groups who contend that their proposals will not work or are too expensive. They might be told, "you can't solve problems by throwing money at them," or "*that* solution is too expensive," or "your solution will corrupt the work incentive of welfare recipients." Sometimes, they are told "we have tried that before and it didn't work."

In truth, it often is difficult to know precisely what policy solutions will ameliorate or solve social problems—especially complex ones like poverty, low school achievement, and some kinds of mental illness. It is difficult, as well, to know how to prevent some social problems, for instance high rates of cancer, heart disease, and mental illness or delinquency, substance abuse, and truancy. We know that diet and lifestyle changes would cut the rates of many health problems, but we do not know how to entice many people to make these changes.

The efforts of policy advocates to demonstrate that certain proposals will be effective and not too costly are made more difficult by disagreements about the proper goals or objectives of the policies. For example, advocates of welfare reform often want to know whether specific policies will allow female heads of households to increase their net income as they enter and remain in the workforce—and whether the well-being of their children will also be enhanced. So they are willing to spend considerable amounts of money on job training, child care, health care, social services, housing subsidies, and transportation to achieve these goals. By contrast, some conservatives consider the rapid movement of women and children off welfare rolls to be a priority so government saves considerable resources. With these objectives in mind, such conservatives do not give precedence to increasing the net income of women over time or even the well-being of children. They may assume that rapid movement into the labor force will improve women's and children's well-being just because the women are now working, no matter at what pay or in what job, or whether the children have adequate child care. In this example, then, policy advocates and conservatives talk at cross-purposes because they possess very different objectives. Advocates are likely to see conservatives' solutions as ineffective and conservatives are likely to see advocates' solutions as ineffective, partly because they emphasize different objectives.

Even when policy advocates share the same objectives with others, honest differences of opinion may exist about what policies will and will not be effective. Making different assumptions about human behavior, people sometimes disagree about the likely effects of a particular policy. In the case of welfare reform, for example, conservatives often believe that female single heads of households will not diligently seek and retain employment without a strong work requirement and economic incentives that make work more attractive than welfare. By contrast, some policy advocates may believe that such women will more likely respond to policies that they believe will enhance their future earnings and contribute to the well-being of their children.

Policy advocates can sometimes find and use research data to buttress their case that a specific policy will or will not work. Such data can be an invaluable tool for securing support for a policy recommendation, such as extensive research findings that followed the enactment of federal welfare reform legislation in 1996. To the extent considerable numbers of women have remained in or near poverty in the wake of welfare reform, policy advocates can cite research to support their case that new approaches are needed, that the minimum wage needs to be raised, that child-care subsidies need to be increased, or that living-wage legislation is needed in local jurisdictions. Policy advocates can use research data, as well, to make the case that certain social problems are serious, whether in terms of their incidence, their effects on people, or the costs they impose on society. Indeed, the Internet provides invaluable research data on myriad social problems and policies. (See Policy Advocacy Challenge 1.4.)

Joining a Tradition of Policy Advocacy

Policy advocates stand on the shoulders of many preceding reformers   An overview of recent American history shows that policy advocates have improved considerably the well-being of millions of Americans. Assume, for example, that Medicaid had not been created in the mid-1960s. Without Medicaid, the health care needs of low-income populations, already seriously underserved by public clinics, would have reached catastrophic proportions, because local and state governments lack the resources to

**POLICY
ADVOCACY
CHALLENGE 1.4**

*USING THE WEB
AS A POLICY
ADVOCATE*

*Stephanie Davis,
Research Librarian,
University of California,
Irvine*

As a MSW student, you have a wide range of resources you can use to learn more about policy issues and to stay informed about the issues relevant to your studies and/or clients.

Libraries

Libraries are the best source of information because their mission is to serve the people in their community by providing access to information. Your local public library or your university/college library is not only a place to find books on your topics, but it's the place to find librarians, who can help you form your research strategies and navigate the library system. Most libraries subscribe to electronic databases and catalogs that allow you to find citations and full text to articles, news, legislative information, political information, statistics, funding sources, and more. Before you start your research, visit your college or university library and talk to a librarian to get an overview of the databases your library subscribes to, and how to access those tools.

Government Depositories

Some university and college libraries are Government Depositories. This is a federal program that provides thousands of government documents for research and community purposes. If you're looking for any kind of federal government information, a government documents library is the place to start. Check with a librarian at your institution to see if there is a library in your area that collects government documents. The federal government is also publishing many documents on the Web. In the following chapters you'll learn more about how to find that information.

The Internet

The Web is, in general, a great tool for finding information. Searching the Web is easy, and the quality of search engines has improved greatly since the Internet became part of the public consciousness. A few recommendations for general information search engines are:

Google: Simple, easy to search, easy to navigate, and provides relevant results.

TeRespondo: Spanish metacrawler that searches on the more popular search engines. It also has a database of questions and answers that aid the user when searching, similar to Ask Jeeves.

FirstGov: The federal government's search engine, connecting you to government agencies, reports, statistics, and much more.

Local, state and federal governments have also been jumping on the Internet bandwagon. Many states and the federal government have mandates to make as much information accessible to citizens on the Web. The best place to start looking for information is usually your city or state Web site (for example, City of Los Angeles, Los Angeles County, California State Web site).

Exercise: Visit your library to investigate the information resources available to you at your university or college.

Are there any Government Depositories at the libraries in your area?

What kinds of databases are accessible at your library?

Find your city or state Web site, and write down the URL for future reference and exercises in this book.

address them. Older citizens who have exhausted their Medicare benefits would be unable to rely on the Medicaid program, and hundreds of thousands of them would be forced into nursing homes even worse than those they would have encountered in the 1970s. Many persons with AIDS, often financially devastated by the expense of medical procedures, would receive no services unless physicians and hospitals donated them.

Indeed, we can proceed through each of the major enactments of the 1960s and the succeeding decades and render a similar prognosis. Assume, for example, that Medicaid, SSI, and the food stamp program did not exist. Would that not have led to a homeless population many times the size of that existing in the 1980s and 1990s? Would economic inequality in the United States, already far greater than in European nations and Canada, not have become even worse? Considerable progress has also been made in addressing poverty among older persons; challenges to the civil rights of out-groups; unemployment and lack of services for persons with disabilities; malnutrition; the health needs of certain groups in the population, such as persons with kidney failure; the preschool needs of low-income children; and psychological conditions such as depression. Many persons of color markedly improved their economic and social situation in the decades following the 1960s, and many African Americans and Latinos entered the middle and upper-middle classes, partly as a result of affirmative action and civil rights laws that prohibited job-related discrimination.

We should not ignore the short-term humanitarian function of social programs. Even when they do not solve social problems, they provide resources and support to people who are experiencing such problems as unemployment, catastrophic health conditions, and mental trauma. Whether we are guided by specific religious teachings or by ethics, we realize that persons who experience hardship or trauma need assistance to diminish their suffering. This simple maxim guided the giving of alms to impoverished people in the Middle Ages, the providing of economic resources to impoverished people during recessions and the Great Depression in the United States, and the development of shelters for homeless people in contemporary society.

In many cases, problems that had seldom been recognized in prior eras were publicized and addressed by new policies because of the determined work of policy advocates. Rape, child abuse, Alzheimer's disease, spousal abuse, reading and learning disorders, discrimination against gay men and lesbians, and the needs of people with disabilities have existed throughout American history, but they have come to be widely recognized as important problems only recently. Victims of rape, for example, were subjected to punitive treatment, such as imputations of blame by judges and doctors, until many jurisdictions enacted laws that protected their rights. People with developmental disabilities often were placed in institutions in the 1950s instead of being mainstreamed in schools, communities, and employment. Children with reading difficulties routinely were dropped from school rolls in the 1950s, whereas now they often receive special services. Policy reforms emanated from a heightened public awareness of these problems and contributed to the public's knowledge of them, as individuals saw social programs' benefits to themselves, their relatives, and their friends. Moreover, social programs often have raised public expectations about the rights and needs of specific groups in the population. Americans in 1950 commonly assumed, for example, that people with paraplegia would be bedridden and institutionalized. By the 1990s many Americans were aware of these individuals' rights and capabilities, including access to mechanized wheelchairs, independent living arrangements, occupational therapy, and employment.

We can reasonably argue that the nation would have suffered harm in the absence of reforms enacted in the Progressive Era, the New Deal, and the Great Society; expansions of civil rights and entitlements in the 1970s; the Child Care and Development Block Grant of 1990; and the expansion of the Earned Income Tax Credit in the 1990s.

Reformers also have prevented the enactment of many reforms that would have harmed many Americans. Some conservatives have wanted, for example, to bar gay men and lesbians from teaching in public schools, to retain antisodomy laws of states that would allow gay men to be imprisoned for engaging in consensual sex with other men, to bar immigration of gay men and to deny them citizenship, to exclude gay men and lesbians from civil rights legislation prohibiting discrimination by employers, and to ban gay men and lesbians from the military. Only by assertive action through legislative and legal channels were advocates able to overturn or prevent most of these policies from remaining in place.

While specific policies have failed or have had mixed results, the combined effects of social reforms have transformed the lives of tens of millions of Americans in positive ways. Most contemporary Americans cannot remember and can barely comprehend the institution of slavery, imprisonment for indebtedness, capital punishment for relatively minor crimes, poorhouses, 14-hour workdays, unsafe working conditions, child labor, routine denial of civil rights, lynchings of African Americans, flagrant violations of the legal rights of radicals, the incarceration of people who publicly discussed birth control, the routine firing of gay men and lesbians, widespread malnutrition, and the denial of education to persons with disabilities.

Joining the Reform Tradition Within Social Work

Most professions are relatively conservative and are concerned mostly with licensure, training, and the enhancement of the remuneration of their members. Like public health, which also has had a strong activist tradition, social work has had a social reform tradition extending back to the formation of the social work profession. Such founders of social work as Jane Addams militantly supported an array of social reforms in the Progressive Era at the beginning of the 20th century, including housing codes to protect tenants, governmental inspection of food to avert illness, factory regulations to protect workers, and pensions for single mothers with children to avert dire poverty.[3]

In succeeding eras, many social workers joined this reform tradition by working for policy reforms in local, state, and federal jurisdictions. Their work was bolstered by numerous theorists who developed a systems or environmental perspective on human behavior, arguing that social inequality, blighted neighborhoods, inadequate resources, unemployment, environmental pollution, discrimination, and economic uncertainty cause human suffering and contributed to clinical conditions such as depression and poor health[4].

But narrower perspectives about social work coexisted with the reformist vision of Addams. Even at the profession's outset, such persons believed the profession should focus on casework, with scant involvement in social reform.[5] Myriad other theorists in succeeding decades adhered to this narrower view of the profession as they developed numerous clinical strategies that gave scant importance to environmental factors, discrimination, or poverty.[6]

Narrower perspectives are deficient on at least three grounds, however, as is discussed at more length in Chapter Two. By failing to address the societal factors that contribute to inequality, they neglect such values as social justice and fairness. With attention riveted exclusively on the problems of individuals, they do nothing to reform the human services delivery system so that it will provide services that are congruent with recent medical and social science findings. By abandoning the political arena, they allow other groups, with values and perspectives in opposition to the needs of clients, consumers, and citizens, to dominate public policy.

This book describes interventions, which I call *policy practice* and *policy advocacy*, that enable social workers to join the social reform tradition of the profession. They may seek changes in policies in social agencies or communities or in public arenas at local, state, and federal levels. They may integrate social reform work with other professional duties, such as clinical work, or they may specialize in it as planners, policy analysts, or organizers.

Policy Devolution, Technology, and Policy Advocacy

As the nation enters the 21st century, policy advocacy should become an even more vital component of social work practice. In a sweeping departure from the growth of policy powers of the federal government in the Great Society of the 1960s, many federal policies were devolved to state and local governments in the 1980s and 1990s. In the case of so-called block grants, the federal government provides funds to the states for social policy purposes and allows them to decide how to use these resources with minimal federal guidelines.[7] (For example, in Chapters Six and Seven we discuss how the federal government supplanted the AFDC program in 1996 with a block grant.)

This devolution of authority has meant that many policies influencing the lives of clients, consumers, and citizens are shaped by state legislatures, county boards of supervisors, and municipal governments. The social work profession used to be able to focus much of its reforming energies on the federal government; now it must establish a reforming presence in hundreds of locations around the nation.

In short, devolution has accentuated the need for policy-reforming work by dispersing key decisions to smaller units of government and disseminating many policies that used to be decided at the national level. If social workers do not actively lobby for policies that will help their clientele in numerous jurisdictions, other groups will dictate these policies, often with scant interest in the well-being of stigmatized or impoverished populations. Indeed, through policy practice and policy advocacy, the profession works to shape devolution so that it will help rather than harm clients, consumers, and citizens.

Policy advocacy also is needed to help equalize conditions and opportunities for tens of millions of Americans whose economic and social well-being have deteriorated in the wake of the technological revolution that has transformed the American economy. As recently as the 1960s, huge numbers of Americans earned good wages in union jobs in automobile, steel, and other manufacturing industries. As these basic industries relocated to other nations and were replaced by low-paying service industries, such as fast-food establishments, the wages of many Americans plummeted. An economic chasm has widened between persons with limited education and work experience and persons with college degrees and advanced skills.[8]

The social work profession has an ethical obligation to work to diminish this inequality. It needs to support social and economic opportunities that enable less affluent persons to better their lot through such programs as job training, remedial education, substance abuse counseling, preschool education, and family services. The profession also should work for redistributive programs that will provide resources and services to less affluent persons by such vehicles as an expanded Earned Income Tax Credit (EITC), housing subsidies, preventive medical care, and health insurance.

But social workers can work for these kinds of reforms only if they develop intervention skills that allow them to be effective policy advocates. This book's aim is to foster social reform work by discussing the specific tasks, skills, and competencies that social workers must master to become effective policy advocates.

Becoming an Effective Policy Advocate

Just as in direct-service, administrative, or community-organizing practice, we become *effective* policy advocates only as we learn key concepts and develop pivotal skills. Moreover, we need certain perspectives to deal with the uncertainties of changing policies. Let's discuss some concepts, skills, and perspectives as a prelude to examining them in greater detail in succeeding chapters.

Developing a Vision

Policy advocates need a vision of a preferred state of affairs, whether in specific agencies, communities, regions, states, or the nation. If we cannot envision an ideal state of affairs, we are unlikely to find fault with existing policies. This vision derives from our values, beliefs, and ideology, as well as from a desire to help vulnerable or oppressed people who receive inferior or negligible assistance. We do not attempt to define the vision in narrowly ideological terms because policy advocacy benefits from a variety of perspectives. The vision is nonetheless promoted and fueled by discontent with how existing policies and institutions measure up to an ideal.

Indeed, not only is a vision a driving force, but it can enhance a practitioner's political interests and build his or her credibility. A person has succeeded in communicating that vision when others describe him or her as someone who "has principles and really cares" or "is committed to changing things." By contrast, we tend to mistrust people who we feel are "only in it for themselves" or who "bend with the wind." Of course, inflexibility and dogmatism detract from policy practice, so people have to compromise between pragmatism and the beliefs or values that constitute their vision.

Social workers can create a vision by learning how policies have evolved in specific agencies and communities. They also should understand the policy implications of broad theoretical frameworks, such as an environmental approach. The vision may derive from identifying with the needs and aspirations of powerless or oppressed populations. Assuming that we have some empathy for the downtrodden, historical perspectives sensitize us to the discrimination, racism, inequality, and suffering that have prompted various policy reforms. We have inherited the missions of the reformers before us, including some of the profession's founders, such as Jane Addams, who devoted remarkable energy to policy practice in a society that lacked the policies that we now take for granted. In a compelling argument, Jerome Wakefield contends that "distributional justice" provides a central mission for the social work profession, distinguishing it from other professions and from traditional psychotherapy.[9]

Seeking Opportunities for Policy Advocacy

Social workers of all stripes can assertively seek opportunities for policy advocacy, whether as part of their employment or outside their work. To be effective advocates, social workers must ask: What systemic or environmental factors cause or exacerbate specific kinds of problems that my clients experience? (See Policy Advocacy Challenge 1.5.) We can try to change policies in the community or in our agencies, for instance, on task forces or committees. Within our agencies, as part of our employment, we can modify policies that we view as deficient, or develop new programs. In each case, we take a broader perspective that allows us to see more factors that adversely affect our clients and need to be remedied.

POLICY ADVOCACY CHALLENGE 1.5

CLINICAL SOCIAL WORKER ENGAGES IN CLASS ADVOCACY

Shirley Lebovics, M.S.W., L.C.S.W., Adjunct Faculty, School of Social Work, University of Southern California

I am a clinical social worker who fervently believes that social workers should serve as policy advocates. Even when we do not seek to change actual policies, we should often try to change the practices or attitudes of persons with whom our clients come into contact, i.e., informal policy.

As a social worker who specializes in counseling survivors of wife abuse, I found that many women from a specific religious community had received advice from their clergy that was misleading. Women were often encouraged to take equal responsibility for the abuse and/or to go home and simply resolve the conflict that had led to an abusive incident. Women were often not asked about physical violence or safety issues, since the clergyperson focused primarily on mediating the dispute that had led to the couple's crisis, rather than on addressing the larger issue of spouse abuse in the home.

This was understandable because (1) the women were not readily or openly disclosing the battering incidents, (2) the clergy may have been unaware of how to detect wife abuse in such instances, and (3) the role of clergy in counseling generally stresses restoring peace between the partners. Given the emphasis of religious values on the sanctity of marriage, the clergy may have felt reluctant to advise the woman in any direction that would ultimately lead the couple to divorce.

The battered women therefore were receiving mixed messages. While clergy would inadvertently ignore or minimize the abuse, the social worker would ask for detailed accounts of abusive incidents, discourage any self-blame on the part of the women, and emphasize the importance of safety and the use of a shelter. Instead of working in collaboration with one another, the social worker and the clergy were working with different goals in mind.

I addressed this dilemma by inviting all the local clergy to attend a workshop on spouse abuse. Individual phone calls were made explaining the rationale behind the workshop and personally inviting each clergy member to participate. The workshop was aimed at explaining the dynamics of abuse and suggesting ways to improve collaboration between clergy and social workers. Emphasis was placed on the importance of the clergy's role in identifying women who were battered, and on the necessity for them to interview women alone to encourage disclosure of the violence. Clergy were also shown how to discourage women from self-blame, and how to make use of local resources such as groups for men who batter, groups for survivors of abuse, and shelters. A question-and-answer period allowed discussion of difficult areas and case examples.

As a result of the workshop, clergy were sensitized to the prevalence and dynamics of spouse abuse, and an increased number of clergy made referrals to battered women's groups and specialized counseling. Clergy were also more inclined to speak about the issue of spouse abuse in the community, an effort that ultimately served to raise public consciousness. Enhancing awareness and education was an essential step toward assisting battered women to receive the support and guidance they needed on all levels.

By advocating the needs of abused women with clergy, I sought to help abused women in ways that went far beyond my interventions with specific clients. Similarly, social workers who are policy advocates try to enhance the general well-being of their clients by securing policies that provide them with resources, services, and opportunities.

Social workers can engage in policy advocacy outside their working hours by helping advocacy groups, working with their professional association, or participating in political campaigns. They can work to educate the public about important issues in their communities by participating in forums, writing letters to the editor or "op-ed" pieces, or working with the mass media to disseminate information.

Policy advocacy sometimes aims at ambitious changes such as the enactment of legislation. Other kinds of policy advocacy are more modest, such as changing a specific policy in an agency or even initiating an idea in a staff meeting.

Taking Sensible Risks

Policy advocates have to be sensible risk takers. Each of us has a finite amount of time and energy. It is unwise to squander them on trivial or hopeless causes, even though ethical considerations sometimes prompt us to participate in difficult battles. However, we also need to be willing to take risks. As we discuss in Chapter Eleven, some of us refrain from seeking policy changes because we underrate our own power (or that of our allies) or exaggerate the power of our opponents. (See Policy Advocacy Challenge 1.6.) Indeed, failures of omission are as important as errors of commission. In some cases, it is better to commit errors in trying to correct flawed policies than to avoid participating at all.

Balancing Flexibility with Planning

Policy advocates must develop plans to guide their work, but they must also be able to improvise during unexpected events. Planning helps organize their work into a purposeful, coherent pattern and clarifies which tasks to accomplish. Improvising allows them to seize unexpected opportunities, to counter their opponents' arguments, and to adopt new strategies that they did not anticipate in an earlier game plan. A policy practitioner makes plans by asking: "In light of the time and risk that I wish to take, what

**POLICY
ADVOCACY
CHALLENGE 1.6**

*A SOCIAL WORKER
ASSERTIVELY LOBBIES
A POLITICIAN*

*Anneka Davidson, M.S.W.,
D.P.A., Clinical Professor,
School of Social Work,
University of Southern
California*

I have lobbied State Assemblyman Steve Kuykendall on a wide range of issues, including planned parenthood, gun control, and income security. Recently, we focused on influencing Steve, a moderate Republican, about changing welfare policies. When I visited his office in Sacramento, I found him initially resistant to a liberal social welfare professor. However, we found common ground in the safety and care of children. After a whole hour of animated and increasingly friendly discussion, he openly endorsed expanded funding for child day care, medical coverage for uninsured kids, and job training for moms.

Subsequently, I arranged for Steve's minister (a friend of mine) to invite Steve to a private home to talk with lay leaders of that church who volunteer at local pantries and shelters. We thought this meeting would render him more sympathetic to the dire consequences of proposed cuts. We also hoped that Steve would agree to visit a food pantry supported by his church and would meet some of the clients. Although he did not agree to a site visit, Rep. Kuykendall did reaffirm his commitment to expanded nutritional, educational, and health care for young children.

Although I can't say that we altered Steve's votes, because welfare reform in California was ultimately decided by the "Big Five" (five white male leaders) behind closed doors, Steve's openness to at least discussing changes in Governor Wilson's original proposal gave us cause for hope that Republicans in the Assembly were not intractable.

For people who think they are too scared to talk to their legislator, I will share the story of my 9-year-old, who also met Rep. Steve Kuykendall. Brad visited Steve's office on a third-grade class trip to Sacramento. When Steve asked the class for questions, there was silence. Finally, Brad raised his hand and wondered, "Mr. Kuykendall, do you believe in smoking? Why did you take money from the tobacco company?"

Brad was challenging Steve's acceptance of $100,000 from R. J. Reynolds during the last week of his campaign. I was not even aware that Brad knew about this tainted contribution and certainly did not plot to have him pose this tough question. I was truly surprised to learn about his bold challenge weeks later. I share this story only to remind all of us that anyone (no matter how little) can ask his or her legislator a key question.

actions and arguments will help me obtain my objectives?" The advocate considers various strategies, either simple or more complex. The resultant plan then represents a decision that certain actions and arguments, rather than others, will yield an acceptable outcome. In light of the uncertainties of many situations, however, these hypotheses must often be guarded and subject to modification when circumstances dictate. Policy practice plans are made to be altered, because they reflect our best initial guesses.

Policy advocates need to be flexible enough to alter their style or approach situationally; like administrators, community workers, and direct-service practitioners, they need to improvise strategies as events unfold.

Developing Multiple Skills

Advocates who believe they can reduce policy practice to a simple set of recommended rules or a single style are likely to be disappointed when they discover that those rules or that style are not useful in some situations. Policy advocates need an array of analytic, political, interactional, and value clarification skills to use, singly or together, in specific situations and during extended policy deliberations. Because external realities require a combination of skills, a unidimensional policy advocate is likely to be frustrated.

Policy advocates, just like direct-service, community, and administrative practitioners, need several skills. Some skills are analytic; we need good ideas about the reforms we want in order to be effective advocates. Other skills are process and people oriented, as our discussion of political and interactional skills throughout this book suggests. Still others involve ethical reasoning, particularly when we confront moral dilemmas. To develop these skills into competencies, we need to work at them in the same way that we hone direct-service, administrative, or community-work skills.

Being Persistent

Policy advocates often need persistence, as the inspirational lives of such social reformers as Jane Addams and Martin Luther King, Jr., suggest. These people had an ability to persevere even in the face of repeated defeats and formidable obstacles. Unlike some of their colleagues who left reform causes after early battles, Addams and King maintained their devotion to social reform. Indeed, Jane Addams, who founded the pioneer social settlement Hull House in 1889, persevered not only during the Progressive Era, but also during the 1920s to support innumerable social reforms. If Martin Luther King, Jr., had not been assassinated, no doubt he would have been active in social reforms for decades more, because he had demonstrated that he was not inclined to rest on his laurels after any of his victories in the civil rights movement of the 1960s.

Of course, few of us have the persistence or the energy of these heroic figures. However, every community has particularly dedicated social workers who participate in many policy frays in their agencies and communities, and in broader arenas, even while they perform heavy direct-service, administrative, or community-work functions. We do not know why some people persevere while others cannot, but we can learn from people who have this ability, and we can seek to emulate them. Perhaps their persistence stems, in part, from a combination of their vision or moral purpose and an ability not to be deterred by personal attacks or policy defeats. A vision provides a rationale for policy practice, independent of the vagaries of particular moments or the defeats and recriminations that any policy advocate experiences.

Policy advocates need perspective to avoid pessimism and self-recrimination in the wake of defeats or partial successes. No single person or group is likely to prevail on the complex playing field of policy deliberations. Advocates must realize that defeats are more likely when people champion the needs of stigmatized and relatively powerless groups, which lack the clout of more powerful interests.

Tolerating Uncertainty

Policy advocates must be able to tolerate uncertainty, because policy practice often lacks structure and boundaries. While relatively few people participate in direct-service transactions, an open field often exists in policy practice, which continually draws new people into issues. Policy advocates often do not know what to expect when they initiate a proposal. Will it be associated with conflict, consensus, or apathy? And often, they cannot predict how much time and energy an issue will require.

Becoming a Policy Advocate

Policy practice can serve many purposes. In some cases, we want to advance our own interests or those of the profession, perhaps by seeking new licensing laws or better reimbursement from insurance companies. Using policy practice to advance personal or professional interests is not unethical if they have ethical merit. If professional social workers give persons counseling that elevates their well-being, then policy advocacy that seeks licensing and reimbursement for professional social workers is ethically sound.

At the same time, social workers should include policy advocacy in their policy practice, which means helping relatively powerless and oppressed populations. Ethical principles, such as social justice, fairness, and beneficence, which we discuss in Chapter Two, dictate that practitioners should engage in this work even if it brings no tangible return to them or to the profession.

When evaluating the outcome of policy advocacy, we should take into account the degree of difficulty encountered. People who undertake difficult tasks or encounter formidable opposition will lose relatively frequently, no matter how skilled they are. Conversely, people who work only on simple issues will probably emerge victorious on numerous occasions. If we were to evaluate policy practitioners solely on the basis of their policy victories, we would risk giving high marks to excessively cautious people.

Indeed, defeats do not necessarily suggest that policy practitioners have been unsuccessful. When people take the initiative to propose policies, they sensitize or educate other people who may not have been aware of specific issues. While this result brings no immediate successes, the defeated policy practitioner can reintroduce another proposal at a more propitious moment and hope that people who are now aware of the issue will change their position.

Combining Pragmatism with Principles

Policy advocates often must compromise for political reasons. With respect to controversial issues in organizational, community, and legislative settings, people rarely realize all of their goals. Yet there is a danger of making premature or excessive compromises that unnecessarily dilute a policy practitioner's goals. There is no simple way to resolve the tension between a pragmatic desire to achieve policy gains and a desire to retain provisions that a policy practitioner values. Indeed, policy advocates often encounter ethical dilemmas that they can resolve only by considering the merits of alternative courses of action and making difficult choices among them.

The Rewards of Policy Advocacy

Social workers who surmount barriers to policy practice, who bridge the various chasms discussed earlier in this chapter, and who develop policy-changing skills and competencies are often richly rewarded for their tenacity. Sometimes they attain notable successes when new programs are established, when funding is enhanced for a program, or when deficient policies are ended or modified. In such cases, social workers help entire populations and communities.

However, policy advocates who take on difficult challenges realize that they may not prevail in specific battles. Entrenched or conservative interests sometimes have the resources and power to circumvent or defeat policy advocates. Or when new policies have been enacted, they may receive inadequate resources or may be sabotaged by opponents during implementation. In such cases, advocates are still amply rewarded by the realization that they gave policy reform their best effort—and that they have joined legions of prior reformers who fearlessly tackled difficult issues. Some of these failures led to tangible victories farther down the road, educating citizens to the need for policy reforms and inspiring other reformers at some future point to resume the reforming effort.

Consider policy advocacy to be an adventure that expands the boundaries of professional practice in new and challenging areas. It can begin even during one's student career in a school of social work. (See Policy Advocacy Challenge 1.7.)

POLICY ADVOCACY CHALLENGE 1.7

HOW I STARTED THE SOCIAL JUSTICE ACTION QUARTERLY

John Potash, M.S.W.

I'd been out of college eight years and had sampled a few different social-work-related jobs. For the last six years, I had worked as a drug counselor. During that time, my hobbies were writing poetry and fiction, as well as one or two articles locally, and social activism.

As I was making a decision on which master's of social work program to enter, I had a bad car accident in Baltimore, Maryland. I decided on Columbia University in New York City, where I could attend part time while I recuperated. Rehabilitating faster than my doctors expected, I had a little extra time and explored activism at the school as well as helping an undergrad activist newspaper.

I quickly realized that my activist group could turn their expensively produced *Action Alert,* with its 8×11-inch pages, into a tabloid-sized newspaper. I proposed the idea, along with the seemingly grandiose idea of getting it to other schools around the country, to my activist group and received a mixed reception. Some were thrilled by the idea, some thought that my politics were "too radical" (in the "left" direction), and one opposed the idea for reasons I never quite comprehended.

That last voice of opposition seemed closely connected to an assistant dean who reportedly didn't have time to meet with me about monetary help from the school. He did let me talk to his assistant and relayed the information that if I got any help from the school, they would have to have editorial say over the newspaper's content. I was left figuring out ways to make the paper seem "official" enough to garner advertisements from neighborhood stores. I fought with the one administratively connected student to get $50 for my activist group and, with the neighborhood ad money, printed 3,000 copies of the first issue.

By the time it came out, I had helped form a New York City social-work-student activist group with activists from four other schools of social work, and they helped distribute it at their schools. The newspaper, which I titled *Social Justice Action Quarterly,* highlighted upcoming social actions as well as past actions, along with general articles on social activism related to social work. Other school students got some money from their schools to help me print out an extra 3,000 copies of the third issue. Then, at an annual Bertha Capen Reynolds progressive social work conference, I met many of the future distributors from around the country.

Getting more ads and starting to charge five cents a copy allowed me to print up to 6,000 copies, keep the paper at eight pages, and distribute it to an average of 20 schools. At more activist conferences, I met other interested students and professors in social work schools, for a larger network. Many of these distributors also submit articles or advertise about activist events.

(continued)

(1.7 continued)

When I got into school more full time, I had less time for gathering ads and had raised the price to ten cents a copy (not including postage) to keep me close to breaking even on the costs. I generally put at least 50 hours into each issue and get help with a total of about ten hours from Columbia and other New York City social work students.

I believe I have only one main ulterior motive for doing all this work, which is to have it help me publish an activist novel someday. I also feel less frustrated now that I can voice my feelings about the injustices in our society, in both journalism and poetry, to a wider audience. I further feel less alone in finding all the social work students, faculty, and practitioners around the country who feel as I do and express their feelings in the paper. And, of course, it would be nice if this activist paper helped create some positive changes in our social work community and society in general.

Changing the Composition of Decision Makers

No matter how skilled policy advocates are, they cannot obtain needed reforms in social policy unless they attract support from decision makers—whether legislators, mayors, members of county boards of supervisors, governors, presidents, or top appointees in government agencies. Even in agency settings, the composition of boards of directors, as well as persons in key administrative positions, powerfully shape what kinds of reforms are possible.

Policy advocates cannot, of course, easily change the composition of decision makers—but they are ethically derelict if they do not try. One vehicle is electoral politics, which is the nation's institutionalized method of selecting decision makers. It is true that electoral politics is often a corrupted process. Special interests often gain disproportionate power by contributing heavily to those candidates who represent their interests. Moreover, many poor people and members of some out-groups tend to vote less frequently than persons in the middle, upper-middle, and upper classes—an unfortunate tendency that tilts policy making away from those that would make the United States a more just society.

Yet policy advocates have had striking successes both in American history and in recent years. The Democratic Party, which has been somewhat more reformist than the Republican Party during and since the New Deal, has often controlled one or both chambers of Congress, as well as the presidency. Progressive governors and mayors have often been elected in state and local jurisdictions, and are frequently members of state assemblies and Senates, city councils, and boards of supervisors. Had this *not* been true, the many policy reforms of the 20th century would not have been enacted.

We will discuss in succeeding chapters many ways that policy advocates can participate in the electoral process, such as volunteering during campaigns, serving as official campaign aides, registering voters, initiating or working on propositions that are placed on the ballot, and donating (or raising) funds to and for specific candidates or parties. We will also discuss how policy advocates can actually build public-service careers by running for elective office themselves and by taking civil-service or appointive positions in government agencies. In the 2000 elections, for example, 14 social workers ran for elective office in federal elections—four social workers were members of the House of Representatives and two social workers were U.S. Senators. Many more held office at local and state levels, including many who were members of special government commissions, planning boards, and school boards.

Policy advocates can also seek administrative positions in social agencies, since these positions give them an inside track in shaping agency policies and implementing them.

Getting Started

Some readers of this text may think, "It is fine for others to participate in policy advocacy, but it isn't something I can do." For persons who envision careers limited to counseling, for example, the world of policy advocacy can sound daunting. It is more complex. Its outcomes are sometimes uncertain. It requires time commitments. It requires knowledge of new subjects like policy analysis and politics.

Do remember two things, however. Policy advocates seldom act alone—they usually work in tandem with existing advocacy groups or with persons who have experience in policy advocacy. Many of you will select an issue or policy that interests you while you are reading this book. You will soon discover that some persons and groups already have done policy-advocacy work with respect to it. In some cases, lobbyists for the National Association of Social Workers or other professional organizations closely linked to social workers will be quite familiar with your issue or policy. So you may be volunteering for them or working in concert with them—or, at the very least, learning about specific issues from them. In succeeding chapters, we will discuss how you can forge linkages with persons and groups familiar with your issue.

Remember, as well, that many social work students have not only read about policy advocacy, but have actually made a strong beginning, even during their professional training. Take the case of Vivian Clark, MSW student at the University of Houston School of Social Work, and Aimee Perron, MSW student at the Virginia Commonwealth University School of Social Work. Both were recipients of awards for innovative policy practice by social work students given by *Influencing State Policy* at a national conference in Charleston, South Carolina, in June 2001. Clark prepared at-risk youth to advocate on their own behalf at the Texas legislature by helping 10 youth attend a rally day to educate legislators about education issues. Working closely with Planned Parenthood's lobbyist, as well as a network of friends, classmates, and colleagues that she had organized, Perron lobbied and pressured for enactment of HB 2782 in the Virginia General Assembly. HB 2782 sought to allow wider access to emergency contraception (EC) by giving physicians, nurse practitioners, and physician assistants the right to dispense it and by allowing pharmacists to write prescriptions under certain protocols. (See Video Clip 1.1.)

VIDEO CLIP 1.1	**Projects During Their Professional Education**
PERSONAL ACCOUNTS BY TWO SOCIAL WORK STUDENTS ABOUT HOW THEY INITIATED POLICY ADVOCACY	In viewing Video Clip 1.1, consider the following. 1. Learn about Vivian Clark and her policy advocacy project in Texas. 2. Learn about Aimee Perron and her policy advocacy project in Virginia. 3. Discuss social work skills that you possess even before you begin studying policy practice and policy advocacy that are useful in policy-changing work.

Chapter Summary

What You Can Now Do

You are now equipped with an orienting perspective that will start you on the road to being a policy advocate. You can do the following:

- Articulate an ethical rationale for becoming a policy advocate from a social justice perspective
- Identify an array of policies, formal and informal, that shape human services and the well-being of specific out-groups, as well as the public interest
- Distinguish between policy practice and policy advocacy
- Identify specific barriers to policy advocacy
- Discuss different ideologies
- Identify social-reform traditions in the nation and in the profession
- Identify some attributes of effective policy advocates
- State why policy advocates often try to change the composition of government

The next chapter will equip you to articulate four central reasons why social workers should participate in policy advocacy.

Notes

1. Richard Titmuss, *Commitment to Welfare* (New York: Pantheon Press, 1968), p. 156.
2. Conversation with Wilbur Finch, who attributed this phrase to Herb Bisno.
3. Stanley Wenocur and Michael Reisch, *From Charity to Enterprise: The Development of American Social Work in a Market Economy* (Urbana: University of Illinois Press, 1989), pp. 47–60.
4. For example, see Carol Meyer, *Social Work Practice: A Response to the Urban Crisis* (New York: Free Press, 1970), and Carel Germain and Alex Gitterman, *The Life Model of Social Work Practice* (New York: Columbia University Press, 1980).
5. Mary Richmond, *Social Diagnosis* (New York: Russell Sage Foundation, 1917).
6. Harry Specht, "Social Work and the Popular Psychotherapies," *Social Service Review* 64 (September 1990): 345–347.
7. Bruce Jansson and Susan Smith, "Articulating a 'New Nationalism' in Social Policy," *Social Work* 41 (September 1996): 441–451.

8. For discussion of inequality in American society, see Claude Fischer et al., *Inequality by Design: Cracking the Bell Curve Myth* (Princeton, NJ: Princeton University Press, 1997).
9. Jerome Wakefield, "Psychotherapy, Distributive Justice, and Social Work, Parts 1 and 2," *Social Service Review* 62 (June & September 1988): 187–210, 353–384.

Suggested Readings

Definitions of Policy and Social Welfare Policy

Brian Hogwood and Lewis Gunn, *Policy Analysis for the Real World* (London: Oxford University Press, 1994), pp. 12–31.

Martin Rein, *Social Policy: Issues of Choice and Change* (New York: Random House, 1970), pp. 5–8.

Richard Titmuss, *Commitment to Welfare* (New York: Pantheon, 1968), p. 156.

Materials That Link Policy to Direct-Service Practice

Chauncy Alexander, "Professional Social Workers and Political Responsibility," in Maryann Mahaffey and John Hanks, eds., *Practical Politics: Social Work and Political Response* (Washington, DC: National Association of Social Workers, 1982), pp. 22–25.

Robert Goodin, *Reasons for Welfare: The Political Theory of the Welfare State* (Princeton, NJ: Princeton University Press, 1988), pp. 123–228.

Seymour Halleck, *Politics of Therapy* (New York: Science House, 1971), pp. 11–38.

Yeheskel Hasenfeld, "Power in Social Work Practice," *Social Service Review* 61 (September 1987).

Alvin Schorr, "Practice as Policy," *Social Service Review* 59 (June 1985): 178–196.

Michael Sosin and Sharon Caulum, "Advocacy: A Conceptualization for Social Work Practice," *Social Work* 28 (January–February 1983): 12–17.

Harold Weissman and Andrea Savage, *Agency-Based Social Work: Neglected Aspects of Clinical Practice* (Philadelphia: Temple University Press, 1983).

Overviews of Policy Deliberations

James Anderson, *Public Policy-Making* (New York: Praeger, 1975).

Bruce Jansson, *Theory and Practice of Social Welfare Policy: Analysis, Processes, and Current Issues* (Belmont, CA: Wadsworth, 1984), pp. 49–55.

Policy Practice and Policy Advocacy

Mimi Abramovitz, "Should All Social Work Students Be Educated for Social Change?" *Journal of Social Work Education* 29 (Winter 1993): 6–11, 17–18.

Josephina Figueira-McDonough, "Policy Practice: The Neglected Side of Social Work Intervention," *Social Work* 38: 179–188.

Norman Wyers, "Policy Practice in Social Work: Models and Issues," *Journal of Social Work Education* 27 (Fall 1991): 241–250.

Policy Practice and Policy Advocacy in Specific Settings

Ron Dear and Rino Patti, "Legislative Advocacy," in *Encyclopedia of Social Work,* 18th ed., vol. 2 (Washington, DC: National Association of Social Workers, 1987).

Karen Haynes and James Mikelson, *Affecting Change: Social Workers in the Political Arena* (New York: Longman, 1999).

Maryann Mahaffey and John Hanks, eds., *Practical Politics: Social Work and Political Response* (Silver Spring, MD: National Association of Social Workers, 1982).

Herman Resnick and Rino Patti, *Change from Within: Humanizing Social Welfare Organizations* (Philadelphia: Temple University Press, 1980).

Ramon Salcido and Essie Seck, "Political Participation among Social Work Chapters," *Social Work* 37 (November 1992): 563–564.

2

Articulating Four Rationales for Participating in Policy Advocacy

We discuss in this chapter four reasons social workers should engage in policy-reforming work:

- To promote the values that lie at the heart of social work and that are included in the profession's code of ethics, such as social justice, fairness, self-determination, and confidentiality
- To promote the well-being of clients, consumers, and citizens by shaping the human services system to conform to the latest findings of social science and medical research
- To create effective opposition to groups and citizens that run counter to the code of ethics and to the well-being of clients, consumers, and citizens, and to put pressure on decision makers to approve and retain policies that advance citizens' well-being
- To change the composition of government so that legislators and decision makers are more likely to advance such values as fairness and social justice, and promote the well-being of citizens

The Ethical Rationale for Policy Advocacy

We develop the ethical rationale for policy advocacy in two stages. First, we discuss why, in their direct-service interactions with clients, social workers should include policy-sensitive and policy-related activities. (These terms are defined later in this chapter.) Second, we discuss why social workers should engage directly in policy advocacy.

Beneficence and Professional Practice

Professionals of all kinds are bound by codes of ethics to place their clients' needs first. We describe this moral imperative to enhance clients' well-being as beneficence because it is a term widely used in moral philosophy.[1] Professionals, including social workers, act unethically when they knowingly harm clients, such as by providing them with unnecessary or inferior services. Professionals also are morally obligated to select interventions, diagnostic tests, and treatments that will most enhance their clients' well-being.

However, clients' well-being extends beyond the scope of the professionals they consult. A woman who cannot afford an adequate diet, for example, is unlikely to achieve physical well-being no matter how skillfully a physician treats her. The doctor who takes no interest in referring this patient to the food stamps program, to a social worker, or to someone else who can link her with this program is not acting beneficently toward the patient. Similarly, a lawyer is morally derelict if he or she helps a client obtain a divorce but has no interest in the client's economic fate after the divorce is final. (So many women have become mired in poverty when they must raise children single-handed that terms such as feminization of poverty have evolved.) Like the physician in the previous example, this lawyer should expand her or his professional work beyond mere technical responsibility.

Indeed, we can say that both the physician and the lawyer have two moral obligations: to make their professional recommendations with sensitivity to their clients' economic, social, and policy realities; and to engage in brokerage, liaison, and advocacy work for specific clients to improve these economic and policy realities.[2] The first moral obligation illustrates *policy-sensitive practice*, where professionals giving technical advice are aware that the client or patient may also confront negative policy-related consequences. Examples of professionals who are not policy sensitive abound: physicians who prescribe diets or medications that clients cannot afford, lawyers who obtain divorces for clients with no thought to the economic difficulties the clients are likely to face after the divorce is final, and teachers or school administrators who remain unaware of environmental factors, such as poor diet, that influence children's ability to learn. These professionals are morally obligated to shape even their technical advice to help their clients cope with external realities. Physicians must take the time to discuss patients' situational realities rather than merely saying, "Take this tablet three times daily for three weeks." Lawyers must speak with clients about the needs they will have during and after specific legal actions. Teachers must include parents in their teaching strategies. We call this policy-sensitive practice because it requires professionals to take into account their clients' economic and social realities, many of which derive from societal policies.

Professionals should also use brokerage, liaison, and advocacy services for specific clients. We call these *policy-related services* because they involve skills, such as mediation and conflict management, that resemble the skills used in policy practice. Brokerage is the negotiation of services for specific clients with other institutions and persons. A teacher, for example, may broker an agreement with a welfare office to obtain resources for a child with dyslexia.

Professionals need liaison skills to connect clients to related services. When a battered woman comes to a lawyer for divorce services, the lawyer may need to help her obtain access to a shelter. A physician should help low-income pregnant women obtain free food from the Women, Infants, and Children (WIC) program.

These professionals ought also to go to bat for their clients by engaging in case-based advocacy when they are unfairly denied services.[3]

We know, of course, that physicians, attorneys, and teachers often provide neither policy-sensitive nor policy-related services. Perhaps because they are unaware of the realities that affect their clients, they have been trained to provide only a technical, narrow range of services, or maybe they lack the resources to expand their work. These individuals may not want to take the time to discuss these external factors and, as a result, they may fail to address their clients' needs. Because we judge people's morality by both their omissions and their commissions, we can contend that professionals who do not engage in policy-sensitive and policy-related activities are morally deficient, even though they plead lack of time or knowledge.

Policy-Sensitive and Policy-Related Practice

We have deliberately begun this discussion with examples from professions other than social work to emphasize three things. First, all professionals are morally obligated to use beneficence to advance their clients' well-being. Second, they cannot do so without policy-sensitive and policy-related practice. Third, we can make moral judgments about all professionals' work on the basis of acts of both commission, such as lying to a client, and omission, such as not using policy-sensitive and policy-related practice. We are not holding social work to a standard and moral code different from those that apply to other professions.

We argue, however, that social workers are even more morally deficient than other professionals if they do not engage in policy-sensitive and policy-related practice, because they occupy a unique position in the human services system. Although surgeons should be concerned about their patients' welfare after they leave the hospital, their role in human services is relatively focused and specialized. They are primarily concerned with surgical procedures, are trained to perform them, and are reimbursed by insurance carriers exclusively to perform surgery. Notwithstanding our moral objections to a narrow scope, we often do not expect surgeons to go beyond their specific duties.

But beneficence takes on a broader meaning for social workers than for other professionals because of the profession's unusual nature. Many social work clients are trying to negotiate relationships not just with individuals, but with institutions. Social workers in child welfare agencies, hospitals, mental health clinics, homeless shelters, AIDS treatment programs, schools, or family courts do not merely address specialized needs, such as the need for medical treatment. They often deal with clients who have emotional trauma that cannot be resolved without negotiating interpersonal and institutional relations. Consider a patient who has been disabled by a car accident and who, after a year of intensive rehabilitation, is about to be released from the hospital. This patient will need assistance in renewing his family life, rekindling marital relations, obtaining disability benefits, seeking vocational assistance, and surmounting prejudice against people with disabilities as he reenters the job market. The ethical social worker has to engage in brokering, liaison, and case advocacy to help this client, rather than limiting self to narrow clinical services.[4]

Beneficence requires social workers to help clients resolve emotional trauma, such as the uneasiness of someone with a disability about his loss of physical abilities. He might feel inferior because he has internalized cultural images of persons with disabilities that emphasize their helplessness or inadequacies. Policies, services, and programs greatly influence clients' well-being. A person with a disability, for example, is likely to feel threatened by inadequate disability benefits, denial of those benefits by punitive bureaucrats, lack of governmental enforcement of the rights of people with disabilities, and inadequate homemaker aides during recovery.

Our discussion suggests that beneficence cannot easily be conceived of in narrow terms. No matter how skilled professionals are, they cannot help improve their clients' well-being without addressing the clients' dysfunctional relations with their environment. Nor can social workers improve clients' well-being if the clients are continually exposed to oppressive relationships in their families, communities, or jobs. Clients must grapple with any cultural images that demean them by examining how oppressive ideology affects their personal activities and self-esteem. In all of these cases, helpers have to supplement traditional direct-service interventions, which focus on intrapsychic matters, with other remedies. They might teach survival skills or assertiveness; help persons deal with discrimination; or use brokering, liaison, or advocacy interventions.

Ethical social workers also realize that they have limited time in which to help clients. Therefore, they need to teach clients skills to help them confront barriers, find resources, and manage their own cases. The social worker seeks to equip clients with the ability to take charge of their personal destinies in the future. The term *empowerment* is commonly used to describe these survival skills.[5]

While physicians can use their knowledge of physiology to declare an infection to be a pathology, social workers need to wrestle with the proper definition of pathology when they work with specific clients. Assume, for example, that a member of an oppressed minority appears paranoid—seeming to be excessively suspicious of other persons. Is this true paranoia or a reflection of actual encounters with oppressive persons and institutions? Assume that a client does not seem to know how to make and execute plans. Could this apparent pathology stem from living in an oppressive environment where planning is relatively futile because positive outcomes are unlikely? Does beating one's children reflect pathology or the common child rearing practices of a specific group? In each of these cases, social workers have to consider environmental and cultural realities even before making diagnoses, unlike the physician, who can diagnose an infected appendix without recourse to these realities. The social worker needs to educate oppressed people, such as battered women, about cultural forces, such as sexism, which they may have internalized. For example, many women return to oppressive spouses, not just for economic reasons, but because they believe they somehow caused abusive treatment.[6]

When social workers perform policy-sensitive activities, they should recognize the following:

- Some problems or pathologies reflect situational and environmental pressures rather than deep-seated characteristics.
- Some apparent problems or pathologies are functional adaptations to oppressive realities.
- Survival skills are often as important to people (particularly persons who have been excluded from mainstream institutions) as intrapsychic interventions.
- Some persons need help to overcome feelings of inferiority that stem from exposure to oppressive ideology and institutions.
- Some people need help to become more assertive.

- Empowerment, or learning skills that will counter oppressive realities, is often as important as purely intrapsychic interventions.

When social workers perform policy-related activities, they should realize the following:

- Often, they will need to negotiate service arrangements between clients and family members or institutions such as schools, welfare departments, child welfare departments, and clinics (brokerage).
- Often, they will need to connect persons to other persons, networks, or institutions (liaison).
- Often, they must be personal advocates for clients or must empower clients to become their own advocates (case advocacy).

POLICY

RELATED

Moving Toward Policy Advocacy

We have argued, thus far, that all professionals need to broaden their work to include policy-sensitive and policy-related practice in their interactions with clients. We also have argued that the unique role of social workers in child welfare, hospital, clinic, school, industrial, and other settings means that they in particular need to be attentive to environmental realities. We have made three related assertions: (a) benefits to clients are intimately linked to their relationships with institutions, oppressive relationships, and oppressive ideologies; (b) social workers have to address or be aware of these relationships if they want to improve the well-being of many of their clients; and (c) social workers' failure to acknowledge key elements of clients' personal predicaments can be criticized on moral grounds as not being beneficent to their clients.

We now move beyond direct-service practice to focus on changing policies in agency, legislative, and government settings. Possible activities include developing and working in coalitions, using power, developing tactics, lobbying, engaging in political campaigns, using persuading techniques, conducting policy-related research, drafting proposals, and reforming operating programs. (Recall that policy-sensitive and policy-related practices allow us to enrich and broaden our work with specific clients but do not emphasize interventions that will change policies in agencies or legislatures.) We make the moral case that *policy advocacy* seeking to advance ethical principles falls in the domain of all social workers, no matter what their role in the human services system.

To determine whether a moral imperative exists, let us again examine other professions, such as medicine, law, and teaching, before returning to social work. Assume that physicians know that people's health depends on regular access to primary health care and that millions of Americans currently lack this access because they have no health insurance. Given the importance of access to health care, we can clearly raise moral questions about physicians as a group and as individuals who do not invest extraordinary effort in changing the existing medical system. They also can be indicted if their profession does not lead the effort to educate others about AIDS and to distribute condoms. Similarly, attorneys can be criticized morally if they fail to support expansion of the government programs that provide legal aid to poor people. As Kozol's work suggests, many inner-city teachers must contend with staggering teaching loads in facilities that are far inferior to those in suburban districts,[7] and teachers can be lambasted on moral grounds if they fail to fight overcrowding in inner-city schools.

We know that physicians, attorneys, and teachers often overlook these policy defects. Moreover, the American Medical Association often has seemed more concerned about maintaining the fees and autonomy of physicians than about supporting reforms in the American medical system.[8]

But social work is in moral jeopardy equal to that of other professions if its members do not try to change policies. More than most other occupations, social work serves stigmatized populations. Because of their relative lack of power and because of societal discrimination, these groups most need assistance from government laws, regulations, and programs. However, their powerlessness makes them vulnerable to the whims of the broader electorate, government budget crunches, cuts in regulatory agencies' staff, and the backlash in the general public's attitude toward social programs. Were social workers not to serve as policy advocates for these populations, they would risk the moral charge of not caring about them. No matter how skillful, policy sensitive, and policy related, direct-service assistance cannot compensate for inadequacies in the broader society.

More often than many other professionals, moreover, social workers serve as salaried employees in organizations. Their ability to advance their clients' well-being depends largely on organizational matters, such as employee morale, organizational policies, staff members' ability to collaborate with one another and with other organizations, and adequate resources. While agency executives possess disproportionate influence, lower-level staff can participate in the deliberations and politics of organizations to enhance their ability to deliver quality services that advance the well-being of their clients. Staff who are wholly uninterested in organizational matters risk the moral accusation (as would social workers who never try to change societal policies) that they do not care about the well-being of their clients.

Far from constituting a distraction from ongoing social work practice, policy advocacy is integral to it. (See Video Clip 2.1.) An ethical social worker needs skills, concepts, and sensitivities drawn from policy advocacy to be a complete (and ethical) social worker. All social workers seeking to advance their clients' well-being should practice policy advocacy sometime in their careers at all levels: agency, community, and legislative.

Social workers can initiate social reform projects or work through chapters of the National Association of Social Workers or other professional organizations, or they can help existing advocacy and community groups. Indeed, empowerment, or helping

---

VIDEO CLIP 2.1 *POLICY ADVOCACY AND SOCIAL WORK*	In viewing Video Clip 2.1, consider the following. Learn an interesting perspective on the role of policy advocacy in the social work profession by the leading American expert on the history of the social work profession. Dr. Leslie Leighninger, Dean of the School of Social Work at Arizona State University, has written extensively on the history of the profession, as well as social welfare policy and services. After viewing her presentation, discuss these questions:

- Why did social work uniquely develop an interest in policy advocacy?
- Do all social workers emphasize policy advocacy? If not, why not?
- What does the code of ethics of the National Association of Social Workers say about policy advocacy?
- Can you see any barriers in your own career—and in your own thinking—to making policy advocacy a part of your professional life?

individuals assert their needs, extends to helping oppressed groups assert their rights collectively, whether through community-based organizations or broader advocacy groups.[9] Social workers can volunteer their services to these advocacy groups, serve as consultants to them, help them find resources, and conduct research for them.

Policy advocacy can realize fully the environmental approach to social work practice. If we change an agency's intake policy, develop a new program in an agency, or modify an existing law, we change the terms of service for many people, even if we initially engaged in our policy-changing work to help a single person or family. Clients' lives are powerfully shaped by societal and environmental factors that only policy practice can change, whether in agency, community, state, or national arenas. Without policy advocacy, the social work profession becomes, in effect, an apologist for existing institutions rather than a force for social reform.

Ethical social workers need to operate on several fronts during their careers. They must provide policy-sensitive direct-service practice, policy-related direct-service practice, and policy advocacy. They cannot engage in these disparate activities at all points in their careers; indeed, they are likely to engage only in episodes of policy practice. But these episodes ought to be a prized part of social work practice. Even relatively modest projects require social workers to possess skills and concepts not covered in direct-service literature and courses. We believe that policy practice curriculum should fill the gap by devoting considerable time to them.

Policy Advocacy and Powerless Groups

So far, we have justified policy advocacy in terms of individual clients' well-being. For example, we discussed helping persons with disabilities to obtain benefits, services, access to job training and jobs, transportation, homemaker aides, and other forms of assistance that derive from high-level policies. In this perspective, we engage in policy advocacy to enhance the well-being of individuals with disabilities by getting them more benefits, services, and rights.

But we can also justify policy advocacy from the vantage point of social justice, because we find inequalities in society morally objectionable, whether they exist among social classes or between mainstream society and a specific population, such as persons with disabilities. (See Policy Advocacy Challenge 2.1.) But should we be concerned about inequality in society? Let's discuss varieties of inequality, some reasons inequalities violate ethical standards, and the ways in which policy practitioners use policy practice to decrease inequality.

Varieties of inequality   If we were to analyze the current status of groups of American citizens on an array of dimensions, such as housing, income, neighborhood amenities, and health, we would find vast disparities among them. Social class provides a shorthand method of summarizing many of these disparities, because persons in the upper classes tend to possess more income (and therefore better housing, better neighborhood amenities, and better health) than those in the lower classes. We can also analyze disparities in current status between specific populations and the mainstream population. If we define white adult males as the mainstream population, for example, we can compare their average income with that of a specific other population, such as women, Latinos, African Americans, or children.[10]

**POLICY
ADVOCACY
CHALLENGE 2.1**

*EMPOWERING
CLIENTS OR
CITIZENS TO SEEK
SOCIAL JUSTICE*

*Anneka Davidson,
M.S.W., Ph.D.,
Clinical Professor,
School of Social Work,
University of Southern
California*

Harbor Interfaith Shelter, in San Pedro, established an ongoing support group for former residents. Most of the participating mothers, formerly homeless, were receiving welfare. In addition to providing emotional support and job guidance, the group offered an opportunity for empowerment.

Under the leadership of two vocal women, the group focused increasingly on policy advocacy. The staff social worker and the board (which I chaired) endorsed their campaign to influence their state legislators.

After twice visiting State Assemblywoman Betty Karnette, they went to lobby her on behalf of a bill they themselves had prepared. With a legal aid attorney, they proposed legislation that would provide a small amount of money for welfare children entering school in September. The mothers wanted their kids to have one set of new school clothes each year.

Betty Karnette carried their bill—although she made it a trial program for her district only. The bill passed, and Governor Pete Wilson signed it. The women felt tremendously empowered and vindicated.

How does this case illustrate how social workers can encourage ordinary citizens to engage in policy advocacy, lending them expertise and encouragement?

How does this case illustrate the extraordinary inequality that exists in the United States? (Remember that as these women were seeking funds for school clothing for their children, the U.S. Congress had recently voted $70 billion to replace F-15 fighter planes with a fleet of F-22s, even though an official report of the General Accounting Office, or GAO, had declared the F-15s to be sufficient against any known threat until the year 2014.)

We could also analyze the disparities among citizens not by current income and related indicators, but by access to opportunities, such as education, health services, assets (such as houses), networks (for example, acquaintances with clout), and rights (for instance, freedom from discrimination in jobs or promotions). Opportunity is, to some extent, the flip side of current status, since having opportunities allows us to obtain or improve our current status, such as in income. The feminists' complaint that women are often excluded from old-boy networks, for example, recognizes that promotions and jobs (current status) often depend on contacts that give persons an inside track; excluded from these networks, women often lose jobs and promotions to males. Indeed, current status and access to opportunities are reciprocal; people whose income increases, for example, can afford expensive housing, which tends to be near better schools and jobs, which gives them access to opportunities, which, in turn, allows their income to increase again.

When inequalities violate ethical standards   Inequalities of status and opportunity are inevitable in any society. Short of a fiat by someone with complete control over the economy who wants full equality, certain persons, classes, and populations will have greater current status and access to opportunities than others. Such inequalities exist even in noncapitalist societies, as illustrated by differences in wealth and status within

Native American tribes or between nobles and serfs in feudal society. But inequalities emerge in a particularly striking fashion in capitalistic societies, where those who control corporations or work in highly paid occupations such as law and medicine secure vastly greater income, assets, and access to opportunities than other people. Moreover, patterns of inheritance perpetuate these differences, and these discrepancies. The descendants of wealthy persons not only inherit wealth but also obtain access to opportunities by virtue of contacts, schooling, and other advantages.[11]

We confront formidable intellectual challenges when we ask, "What degrees and kinds of inequalities are morally objectionable?" We have to be clear, for example, whether we are questioning inequalities in status or access to opportunities. We need to discuss issues of threshold: At what threshold, or degree, is inequality morally objectionable? We also have to decide why inequality is objectionable, if at all. To the extent that we dislike inequalities, we must decide what kinds of policies should be used to reduce them.

We do not have the ethical field to ourselves. Many philosophers have wrestled with issues of equality. It is beyond the scope of this book to summarize and analyze their different conclusions and arguments, but to introduce the topic, we will briefly analyze some tenets of a leading contemporary philosopher, John Rawls. In his seminal work, *A Theory of Justice,* Rawls argues that we can best construct our moral vision of a good society by trying to imagine its internal arrangements from behind a "veil of ignorance," which obscures our own current status (such as income) or personal access to opportunities.[12] Rawls says that if we are aware of our current status and are, for example, relatively well off, we are likely to want a society that will perpetuate our economic well-being, even if others do not share in it. Therefore, we should retreat behind this veil, where our personal income and opportunities are not known to us. When conceptualizing the ideal society from this vantage point, we are likely to conclude that society should allow only those inequalities that will preserve or further the common good of society. We will reach this conclusion because we would not want to take a chance on being stuck in the lower reaches of a relatively inegalitarian society. We realize most people are in those lower reaches, whereas in egalitarian societies, people have similar statuses and opportunities. The rational person would, Rawls concludes, opt for an egalitarian society but would accept some inequalities. Occupations that require particular skills and training, such as brain surgery, would carry relatively high salaries to attract the most skilled and dedicated persons.

We can express Rawls's argument in simpler form by asking, "If you had the choice at the start of your existence—not yet favoring any specific society, and not knowing what social position you would hold—would you choose to live in the United States (with its relatively inegalitarian arrangements) or in a more egalitarian society such as Sweden, where discrepancies between the affluent and the less affluent classes are less marked, particularly when relatively equal access to health care and education are factored into the equation?" Rawls asserts that you would be likely to select Sweden because, on balance, you would not want to risk ending up in the American lower classes, many of whom live in blighted inner-city neighborhoods and lack health insurance.

Rawls's argument can be restated as the Golden Rule: Do unto others as you would have them do unto you. If you are not willing to experience the inequalities of the inner city, for example, you should not support policies that perpetuate such inequalities. This argument suggests that failure to engage in any social reform, whether as a private citizen or as part of one's professional role, is tantamount to violation of the Golden Rule.

If we do not want to live in inner-city areas without adequate health care and other amenities, we have a moral duty to try to improve the lot of inner-city residents and other persons who experience inequality.

We can also support efforts to reduce inequalities with economic arguments. Extreme inequalities produce undesirable economic effects on the nation.[13] At a time when Americans are competing with foreign nations, for example, they can ill afford vast reservoirs of relatively uneducated, unhealthy, and nonproductive citizens in the inner cities. But Americans have failed to invest in people, jobs, and infrastructure and have, in fact, decreased the productivity of inner-city residents. By supporting a relatively unproductive group of citizens, Americans place themselves at a competitive disadvantage with other nations that have more educated, healthier, and more contented citizens.

Similarly, vast disparities in status and opportunities produce undesirable social consequences. Persons in the lower reaches of relatively inegalitarian societies often despair of their chances to improve their lot. Such alienation often induces them to improve their lot through crime and drug dealing, which harms their neighborhoods and the broader society. If they despair of being able to work through the political system, they also may participate in violent collective uprisings at enormous cost to themselves, their neighborhoods, and the nation, as the domestic disturbances of the 1960s and the 1992 Los Angeles uprising suggest.[14]

We also can advocate reducing inequality in the name of the common good. (See Policy Advocacy Challenge 2.2.) In recent decades, it has been fashionable to argue that self-interested and individualistic behavior constitutes the highest or best activity. Society benefits, conservatives have often said, when persons work hard, take risks, and build businesses to improve their incomes. Carried to an extreme, however, self-serving behavior can yield unfortunate consequences. If society fails to fund quality schools and infrastructure, for example, it jeopardizes, economic growth—and alienates persons who believe they cannot improve their lot.[15] Conservatives' contention that "confiscatory taxes" will jeopardize economic growth are believed by satisfactory rates of economic growth in many European nations, whose level of taxation is often far higher than the U.S.[16]

POLICY ADVOCACY CHALLENGE 2.2 *IMAGINING A BETTER SOCIETY* *Anneka Scranton, M.S.W., Ph.D., Clinical Adjunct Professor, School of Social Work, University of Southern California*	All of us need to develop a vision of a better society as we aim to be policy advocates. (Policy advocacy is, after all, geared to improving society in some respect.) We can do this by a "dream exercise," where, singly or in groups, we try to imagine a better American society in ten or more years. • What is your dream of a more just society? • What is the most important change that would take place? • How might policy advocates begin working on this agenda? Alternatively, we can develop a vision by discussing the impact that specific policies have had upon members of our families, ourselves, or a specific client. (Select one of these persons as your point of reference.) • How have existing policies proven inadequate to redress some specific problems or issues of your family member, yourself, or a client • What is the most important change that needs to take place? • How might policy advocates begin working on this agenda?

One thing is certain: the United States currently has extraordinary rates of economic inequality. Millions of Americans live from paycheck to paycheck, possess no savings, have scant retirement accounts (save for Social Security), and do not have such assets as houses. A recent study of economic inequality in Los Angeles County, one of the most populous metropolitan areas of the United States, discovered that one in four workers was poor, including such diverse workers as janitors, maids, teachers, health practitioners, sewing machine operators, actors, parks and recreation workers, and parking lot attendants.[17] (The study defined poverty for the working poor as an annual income of $33,098 for a family of four based on the actual cost of living—or a higher threshold than federal poverty standards of $16,700 since the federal standard does not accurately measure survival needs of citizens in L.A. County.) They discovered that inequality between the top 20 percent and the middle 20 percent of earners in Los Angeles grew significantly in the 1990s—and nationally the net worth of the top 1 percent grew by 17 percent when adjusted for inflation while the bottom 40 percent lost an amazing 80 percent of their net worth. In the late 1990s, the top 1 percent of U.S. households owned 40 percent of the nation's wealth. Other findings included the following:

- The vast majority of the working poor—77 percent—work full time.
- Of persons in two-adult households with children where at least one adult reported income in the prior year, 45 percent were poor.
- Nearly 7 of 10 people in Los Angeles with no high school education were working poor.
- While Latinos make up 40 percent of the workforce, they account for 73 percent of the working poor.
- Thirty-three percent of persons in manufacturing and 51 percent of workers in the personal service sector were poor.
- Of the working poor, 59 percent lack health insurance, and half of these have children.

Policy Advocacy for Out-Groups

Rawls's approach to moral reasoning has considerable merit because his arguments force us to ponder ideal, or preferred, social and economic arrangements. But some readers may find Rawls's arguments relatively abstract. Why not proceed to social justice more directly by discussing specific groups who are clearly unequal to the dominant population? Why not seek to improve their lot on the grounds that it is unfair for such groups to be unequal? Our goal should be to move toward a situation where economic resources and opportunities are randomly distributed in society rather than existing disproportionately in specific out-groups. For example, all children should have access to preschool programs rather than tolerating (as now) a situation where many low-income children lack such access due to inadequate funding of the Head Start program.

Considerable evidence suggests that neither prized things nor inequalities are randomly distributed in the population. As we argued in Chapter One, American society has a variety of out-groups, or subgroups with a disproportionate share of social malaise, including *racial out-groups* (for example, African Americans, Latinos, and Native Americans); *sociological out-groups* (such as women, older people, and people with disabilities), which employers often expect to occupy relatively low positions or to leave the workforce entirely; *dependent out-groups* (for instance, children), which need other people's assistance but are often denied supportive programs because they lack political clout; *nonconformist out-groups,* which have different sexual orientations (such as gay men and lesbians), have violated social norms (for example, criminal offenders and juvenile delinquents), or have stigmatizing social problems (for example, persons diagnosed with mental illness); *model out-groups* (such as Asian Americans, white ethnic Americans, and Jewish Americans), which find it difficult to obtain support because society believes that they have no social problems, and *economic out-groups* (such as members of the lowest two economic quintiles) who often lack resources to meet important needs.

Professionals, and social workers in particular, should work to ameliorate such inequalities, both by getting these out-groups more and better services in specific agencies and by seeking changes in local, state, and federal policies. (See Policy Advocacy Challenge 2.3.)

POLICY ADVOCACY CHALLENGE 2.3

THINKING CRITICALLY WHEN USING THE WEB

Stephanie Davis, Research Librarian, University of California, Irvine

Many Web sites have been developed by groups that favor particular causes or populations. Many of these Web sites provide invaluable information—but others provide less reliable information. If you have experience doing research, you know that society is facing information overload. In the course of your research, you will access many different types of information using the resources above: Web sites, books, journal articles, magazine articles, think tank reports, agency reports, case studies, government documents, electronic journals, electronic books, and more.

So how do you know if information is credible or not? What is "good" information?

Throughout the research process, you will need to develop criteria for yourself to help you identify and best use the information you find. For starters, be aware that the purpose of every piece of information you find will be trying to convince you of something—they may be trying to sell you a product, persuade you to believe a certain idea or issue, influence you to vote a certain way, etc. Be a critical consumer whenever you are doing research, whether you're looking at Web sites or journal articles.

Exercise: On the Internet, go to the Checklist for an Advocacy Web Page at www2. widener.edu/Wolfgram-Memorial-Library/webevaluation/advoc.htm

Assess the following two sites based on the checklist criteria and the questions on the Advocacy Web Page.

- National Rifle Association

www.mynra.com/

- The Brady Campaign to Prevent Gun Violence

www.bradycampaign.org/

It is important to note that part of the evaluation is whether you agree with the ideas presented on each site. However, when doing research, especially if your ultimate goal is to persuade a group to agree with you, you need to be aware of what your opposition is saying so you can respond intelligently.

(continued)

(2.3   continued)

Many Web sites present information about out-groups and the advocacy groups that represent them. Here are several examples.

• The Center for Law and Social Policy. CLASP is a national nonprofit organization with expertise in both law and policy affecting the poor. Through education, policy research, and advocacy, CLASP seeks to improve the economic conditions of low-income families with children and to secure access for the poor to our civil justice system.

www.clasp.org

• The National Mental Health Association. The NMHA is "dedicated to improving the mental health of all individuals and achieving victory over mental illnesses." It is principally an advocacy organization comprising a large network of supporters. Resources, publications, activities, and a calendar of events are offered here.

www.nmha.org

• The National Organization for Women. The principal political organization for women in the United States, NOW is a progressive advocacy group seeking equality for all women. This site offers multiple and varied coverage of the policy agenda, including links to resources and an on-line newsletter.

www.now.org

• Institute for Women's Policy Research. The institute's Web site contains information about legislation or issues affecting women in general, as well as low income women.

www.wpr.org

• Center on Budget and Policy Priorities. The center is a leading advocate for legislative and budget reforms to help low- and moderate-income persons.

www.cbpp.org

• Children's Defense Fund. The leading advocacy group for children.

www.chldrensdefense.org

• American Public Health Association. A major player in health reform.

www.apha.org

We can use the principles of beneficence and social justice to support such efforts, but we also can draw on the doctrine of fairness when we try to decrease disproportionate inequality. Consider the case of expanding the Head Start program to serve all low-income African American children. We support the program because it enhances fairness by giving low-income African American children the educational, health, and child development services many white, middle-class families have long taken for granted. White, middle-class families send their children to nursery schools, have easy access to medical care, and purchase computers and other educational aides for their children. While expanding Head Start hardly reduces societal inequality on a grand scale, as implied by Rawls's framework, it reduces some of the inequalities of low-income African American children.

It is relatively simple for social workers to try to help members of the enumerated out-groups through policy practice. Advocacy groups have developed in local, state, and national jurisdictions to assist various out-groups; you can find these groups by word of mouth or by consulting directories in your local region. (See Box 2.1.) Social workers can participate in policy action by linking themselves to an advocacy group, whether as a volunteer, a member, a staff person, or a board member. (See Video Clip 2.2.) Other avenues exist, such as local and state chapters of the National Association of Social Workers. Social workers can also initiate their own projects, singly or together.

BOX 2.1   **Reference Works Listing Advocacy and Professional Groups**

> *Encyclopedia of Associations, 1993* (Detroit: Gale Research, 1993).
> *National Trade and Professional Associations of the United States* (Washington, DC: Columbia Books, 2001).
> *Regional, State, and Local Organizations, Encyclopedia of Associations,* 7 vols. (Detroit: Gale Research, 2001).
> *State and Regional Associations of the United States* (Washington, DC: Columbia Books, 2001).
> *Washington Information Directory: Guide to Government Agencies, Associations, Congressional Committees, Congressional Staff, and Congressional Caucuses* (Washington, DC: Congressional Quarterly, 2001).

VIDEO CLIP 2.2

LINKING TO AN ADVOCACY GROUP

In viewing Video Clip 2.2, consider the following. Dr. Anneka Scranton, Clinical Adjunct Professor at the School of Social Work of the University of Southern California, discusses advocacy groups and how to establish links with them in your local jurisdiction. Discuss the following:

1. Why individual policy advocates, operating by themselves, can rarely influence major policies singlehandedly
2. How you can find out about specific advocacy groups, whether through tapping key informants or using the Web
3. How you can learn more about a specific advocacy group
4. How you can work with a specific advocacy group

The doctrine of social justice, sometimes leads to painful predicaments, as with affirmative action. To decrease a specific out-group's inequalities, we sometimes must take away opportunities from a privileged group, such as white males. Say we have a limited number of positions in an organization and want to increase the number of women in those positions. We believe that women are underrepresented because of past discrimination. We can increase the number of female employees, at least in the short term, only by reducing the proportion of male employees. Does favoring female applicants (which our doctrine of social justice supports) deny social justice to male applicants? The answer depends partly on our time frame and our ultimate objectives. The doctrine of social justice dictates a random distribution of problems, such as unemployment or lower-paying jobs. Thus, positive discrimination for female applicants is justifiable because it makes men and women more equal (hence, it is fairer) with respect to jobs and higher positions, even if only within a particular organization. Were we to consider hiring women only when female applicants were better qualified than males, it would take decades to achieve parity. Affirmative discrimination for women was developed to move the clock ahead. From this perspective, it is hard to find an ethical alternative to affirmative action because any other policy would fail to redress historic patterns of inequality—at least until resources and opportunities are more randomly distributed in our population.[18]

Other Ethical Principles in Policy Advocacy

We have emphasized the ethical principles of beneficence, social justice, and fairness as rationales for policy advocacy. We have argued that these principles require ethical social workers to engage in policy practice. But what about other ethical principles, such as honesty, self-determination (or autonomy), confidentiality, and preservation of life; namely, the other ethical principles discussed widely in religious and philosophical literature?[19] When ethicists discuss various principles, they commonly refer to the following:

- *Autonomy.* The right to make critical decisions about one's own destiny
- *Freedom.* The right to hold and express personal opinions and to take personal actions
- *Preservation of life.* The right to continued existence
- *Honesty.* The right to correct and accurate information
- *Confidentiality.* The right to privacy
- *Equality.* The right of individuals to receive the same services, resources, or opportunities as other people
- *Due process.* The right to procedural safeguards when accused of crimes or when benefits or rights are withdrawn
- *Societal or collective rights.* The right of society to maintain and improve itself by safeguarding the public health and safety

Many philosophers have declared that right-living persons should adhere to these principles, as well as to the principles of beneficence and social justice we have already discussed. These principles often arise, of course, in professionals' interpersonal work, whether they are physicians, attorneys, teachers, or social workers. Professionals are urged by their codes of ethics to share information with their clients and not to deceive them (honesty); to let their clients make the important decisions that arise during their interaction with professionals (self-determination); to preserve clients' privacy by not divulging information about them to other people (confidentiality); and to act to advance clients' well-being (beneficence).[20] These ethical principles apply, as well, to policy advocacy, which often seeks to advance them.

Other Types of Ethical Reasoning

We have just discussed moral reasoning that relies on various ethical principles such as honesty—an approach philosophers call *deontology*. Another approach to ethical reasoning, known as *utilitarianism*, uses a different method of reasoning to formulate ethical recommendations. Utilitarians criticize reliance on ethical principles on the grounds that people often differ on the definitions or weighting of principles—or because the principles often conflict. When terminal patients want assistance in dying, for example, the principles of autonomy (or self-determination) and not killing conflict, so ethical resolution is difficult. Preferring to use empirical data to make ethical choices, utilitarians analyze the likely outcomes or consequences of specific choices, and choose the option that has the best outcomes.[21] When comparing two treatment options for people with depression, for example, they would select the option that was most effective as demonstrated by empirical data. Utilitarians examine not only the outcomes associated with specific options, but their relative cost. They might oppose a medical treatment that cost $2 million per patient even if it helped some patients recover, on grounds that the ratio of cost ($2 million per patient) to benefit (the numbers of patients cured) was too high. They would prefer a policy or treatment option with a relatively low cost-to-benefit ratio, such as prenatal care that is relatively inexpensive to provide but that averts serious health problems.

Utilitarians, in turn, are criticized by first-principle ethicists. Good data about the effects of a policy are often lacking. Even when we have them, people may disagree about what they mean or how to interpret them. Indeed, we sometimes support policies that do not have low cost-to-benefit ratios, such as providing expensive medical interventions to persons with relatively poor prospects of survival. In some cases, preoccupation with advancing the nation's well-being can lead us to flawed positions. In the infamous Tuskegee experiment, for example, African American men with syphilis were not treated deliberately so that researchers, able to study the unchecked course of the disease, could increase their knowledge of the disease.

Both utilitarians and first-principle ethicists are, in turn, criticized by *relativists* (sometimes called *intuitivists*), who contend that most people make ethical choices not through an extended process of reasoning, but through norms they derive from their culture.[22] When people in our colonial period placed wrongdoers on public display, they accepted a widely held norm that this punishment was morally acceptable. Some relativists also contend that ethical choices are often shaped by self-interest. When Congress debates health policy, for example, such groups as the American Medical Association, the American Hospital Association, and the American Association of Retired Persons often support policy options that will benefit the members of their associations. (See Policy Advocacy Challenge 2.4.)

It seems at first glance that choices based on self-interest must be morally flawed. In fact, however, moral people often couple their personal interests with ethical choices. Take the case of social workers who support expanded funding for mental health

---

<table>
<tr>
<td>

**POLICY
ADVOCACY
CHALLENGE 2.4**

*ETHICAL
REASONING
BY FIRING-LINE
SOCIAL WORKERS*

</td>
<td>

Take the example of Tenet Healthcare, a huge national healthcare corporation that was known until recently as National Medical Enterprises.* Assume that you worked as a social worker in one of their psychiatric hospitals, where patients were effectively imprisoned rather than being released once their treatment was finished. Wanting to exhaust patients' health insurance to enhance their revenues, some Tenet psychiatrists even sanctioned strapping down patients for months at a time, while making other patients remain silent for 12-hour stretches. Only when a task force of 600 federal agents investigated 20 facilities was the magnitude of this patient victimization made clear. (Eventually 700 claims were filed, and the corporation agreed to pay $100 million to settle them.) Had you seen these practices, which clearly reflected informal and formal policies of the corporation, and alerted federal authorities, you would have engaged in policy advocacy, since you would have sought not merely to redress the conditions for specific patients, but to change the formal and informal policies of the corporation itself.

What ethical principles did Tenet psychiatrists violate? Discuss why many Tenet staff did not report ethical violations to external authorities. How does this case illustrate how self-interest can sometimes lead people to make unethical choices?

*This case is discussed by Barry Meier in "For-Profit Care's Human Cost," *New York Times* (August 8, 1997), pp. C1, C4.

</td>
</tr>
</table>

---

programs. While they take this position partly to advance the well-being of persons with mental conditions, they also realize that enhanced funding would provide employment for more social workers. Likewise, advocates for specific populations, such as women, African Americans, or Latinos, try to advance the collective interests of these groups. If we contend that all self-interested choices are immoral, we wrongly call into question an array of meritorious policies.[23]

Yet relativists also draw criticism from other ethicists. Without any first-order principles or any consideration of consequences, ethical choices would have no basis. We could even justify the rampant discrimination against African Americans in the South in the 1950s on the grounds that it was consonant with the culture of the region.

We also cannot ignore practical matters when making ethical choices. Some choices may be ethically meritorious, but impossible to get approved by legislatures or other decision makers. In the case of health care reform in the United States, for example, a universal single-payer approach, such as is used in Canada, has considerable ethical merit, but American politicians are unlikely to enact such a plan in the foreseeable future.

Toward an Eclectic Approach to Ethical Reasoning

In light of the criticisms of each of the preceding approaches to ethical reasoning, a good case can be made that we should ask a variety of questions that reflect all of the philosophical stances considered here. We should consider first the principles that have a wide following in Western societies, whether derived from a reasoning process, as in the case of Rawls, or from religious sources. We should examine the likely consequences of specific choices, as suggested by utilitarians. We should realize that cultural norms as well as self-interest shape ethical choices, as argued by relativists. And we should not ignore practical considerations, such as the political feasibility of specific options.

BOX 2.2   **An Eclectic Approach to Ethical Reasoning**

Some Considerations Drawn from Deontologists
- Identify ethical principles that are relevant to an ethical dilemma and decide, on balance, which choices or actions best satisfy them.
- When ethical principles conflict—that is, point to different choices—seek a compromise solution that satisfies each to some degree.

Some Considerations Drawn from Utilitarians
- Conduct research to identify the likely consequences of specific options or actions, or when data are lacking, use knowledge about human behavior to infer the likely effects of specific policies.
- Select the option or choice that will maximize the positive consequences for society or for one (or more) of its subunits.

Some Considerations Drawn from Relativists
- Analyze cultural factors that shape the ethical choices of people in specific historical periods, while considering other factors, such as institutional and fiscal realities.
- Analyze how the interests of people—including ourselves—shape policy choices.

Practical Considerations
- Consider the practical implications of specific policies, such as their political feasibility and their cost, as well as administrative aspects.

As Box 2.2 shows, ethical reasoning forces us to consider many kinds of information when making ethical choices.[24] It requires us to integrate or synthesize this information in a process of ethical reasoning. In this process, we look for points of convergence and divergence. If deontological and utilitarian perspectives converge to suggest that a specific course of action or a specific policy choice is more meritorious than others, we can be fairly certain of our resulting decision. If these different perspectives lead us in diverging paths—that is, suggest different actions or choices—we have to devote more time and thought to seeking some resolution.

We may face an ethical dilemma when we have two or more options, each with some ethical merit.[25] We must then engage in a protracted process of ethical reasoning to decide which option, on balance, is preferable when principles, outcomes, self-interest, and practical considerations are entered into the balance. Reasonable people often come to different conclusions in such cases.

Returning to Ideology

Recall that we discussed conservative, libertarian, liberal, and radical ideologies in the first chapter. If conservatives and libertarians emphasize the value of liberty or freedom, liberals and radicals place somewhat (or considerably) more emphasis on social justice. (See Video Clip 2.3.) When we link ideologies with a discussion of ethics in this

VIDEO **CLIP 2.3** *CONSERVATIVES'* *BELIEFS*	In viewing Video Clip 2.3, consider the following. Professor Leon Ginsberg, a leading expert on conservatism, has written extensively on the subject. After viewing his presentation, ask yourself the following questions: • Why have conservatives been such a major force in American social policy during the last 25 years? • Do their policies help or assist specific classes or institutions in American society? • Do their policies give less help to other specific classes or institutions in American society?

POLICY
ADVOCACY
CHALLENGE 2.5
 	
USING DIFFERENT
IDEOLOGIES TO
FRAME ISSUES—AND
TAKING A POSITION
	Take any important social issue facing the United States, such as growing economic inequality, homelessness, or substance abuse. Frame conservative, libertarian, liberal, and radical approaches to it, using the differences among these ideologies found in Table 1.1.
	  Defend *one* of these approaches, using ethical arguments germane to social justice, and discuss in ethical terms why another approach is less preferable from a social justice point of view.
	  or
	  Discuss from an ethical perspective whether Ralph Nader resolved the ethical dilemma he confronted when he ran for the presidency on the Green Party ticket in 2000.

chapter, we can see that affiliation with an ideology is, at least in part, an ethical choice because one has to decide which value to emphasize. This choice, in turn, is not a trivial one because it has important consequences for the well-being of citizens. (See Policy Advocacy Challenge 2.5.)

  Let's begin with some consequences of conservatism and libertarianism. If society structures itself around the first principle of liberty, it maximizes the wealth and status of individual citizens as well as corporations. It taxes them relatively lightly. It issues relatively few regulations that circumscribe actions of corporations. It develops a relatively weak set of governments at local, state, and federal levels by limiting them to such housekeeping functions as funding the military, police and fire departments, sanitation, and infrastructure (such as roads). (Some conservatives concede that government should fund some things that private markets would not otherwise develop, such as parks, environmental clean-up programs and welfare programs that would provide a basic economic floor under the poorest members of society.) Both conservatives and libertarians contend that these relatively minimal government functions would suffice because private markets, if left alone, would take care of the economic affairs of the nation in an acceptable manner. Indeed, they contend that extensive regulations of private markets harms those markets. A relatively high minimum wage would, they argue, harm the natural efficiency of private markets, where labor is reimbursed at appropriate levels as determined by the automatic adjustment of supply to demand. (If some workers receive low wages, this is caused by their relative value in the natural workings of markets—and excessive subsidies merely make those markets inefficient.) Acceptance of a conservative or libertarian ideology is, then, a vote for maximizing the interests of individuals and corporations as they would exist in a relatively unregulated society with minimal government intrusion.

The key ethical problem confronted by conservatism is that its tenets often lead to policies that disproportionately assist relatively affluent persons while giving less or no help to less affluent persons. At any given point in time, society is divided into social and economic strata with different levels of resources, opportunities, and services. We have already discussed, for example, how white suburban Americans are relatively more affluent than inner-city African Americans—and how single female heads of households and their children are far more likely than Americans in families with two heads of household to be poor. Left to itself, moreover, labor markets do not reimburse many un-skilled and semiskilled workers at living wages, particularly when labor shortages do not exist domestically. While government cannot magically undo inequality or low wages, it does have some policy tools at its disposal. These include the following:

- Redistributing some resources to less affluent persons through the tax code, such as by lowering tax rates of the working poor or by expanding the size of the Earned Income Tax Credit
- Enhancing opportunities for low-income persons through job-training programs and enhanced education programs
- Giving low-income persons in-kind goods like food stamps, medical benefits, subsidized child care, and subsidized transportation
- Raising the minimum wage or requiring a living wage
- Helping low-income persons build up assets, such as helping them start savings accounts and buy houses

The problem with conservativism is that, carried to its full logic, it denies the use of these tools by government. Each of these tools runs counter to such conservative beliefs as minimizing the role of government, lowering taxes on all citizens, not interfering with private markets, and not tampering with the existing distribution of economic resources. Of course, few conservatives or libertarians fully comply with the tenets of their ideology. Many conservatives, for example, strongly support such programs as Medicare and Medicaid, even if they often opposed them when they were first enacted. (Conservative politicians also know that they will alienate those constituents who benefit from such programs as Medicare, possibly even threatening their reelection.)

Liberal and radical ideology pose less ethical risk to social justice in the sense that they do not rule out the use of government policy to redress inequalities. Yet liberals and radicals confront ethical issues, as well. While more inclined than conservatives to use government policies, they often do not know precisely what policies will solve specific problems—and they risk not increasing the well-being of citizens (or the ethical princi-ple of beneficence as well as utilitarian considerations) if they make wrong choices. A most obvious example was the flawed public housing programs established in the 1930s through the 1960s in major American cities. When low-income persons were segregated into huge public housing complexes, such as the infamous Robert Taylor Homes in Chicago, social mayhem occurred. The tenants were bedeviled by delinquency, sub-stance abuse, and violence—and received scant social services, much less police pro-tection. While liberals meant well when they developed public housing, they did not think through or anticipate social and economic consequences of segregating such large numbers of low-income persons in high-rise buildings. Only recently have most of these complexes been destroyed or converted into tenant-owned facilities that operate from an empowerment approach. Liberals can try to prevent the error of choosing an ineffective policy by drawing upon empirical research and social-science and medical research that allows them to select policies on the basis of hard evidence.

We should not forget that liberals often do not act on their ethical maxims. They, too, can be bought off by corporate contributions. They sometimes succumb to public opinion even when it runs counter to deeply held beliefs. Some people believe, for example, that some liberals acted against the maxims of social justice when they supported President George W. Bush's $1.3 trillion tax cut in 2001, because this huge tax cut meant the United States would have no extra resources for any social initiatives during the next decade.

Radicals encounter a major dilemma in the United States, as was illustrated by Ralph Nader's run for the presidency as the Green Party's candidate in 2000. The Green Party subscribed to such ethical principles as social justice more completely than the Democrats or the Republicans, wanting major new expenditures on domestic needs and favoring many measures to address poverty and disease in third-world nations. The Green Party alone wanted to cut military spending to free up additional resources for the domestic agenda. But the Green Party confronted an ethical dilemma: if its presidential candidate drew more votes from the Democratic candidate (Al Gore) than from the Republican candidate (George Bush), it might give the election to Bush—a self-announced conservative who probably gave less emphasis to social justice than Gore. Nader's decision to run for office, then, pitted his own ethical philosophy against the risk that he might cause many policy decisions after the election that would run strongly counter to his stated values. This risk came to fruition when Bush, possibly elected president because Nader did take more votes from Gore than from Bush, proceeded to push a conservative agenda of high tax cuts, high military spending, and scant focus on social-justice issues.

The Analytic Rationale for Policy Advocacy

We have discussed the ethical term *beneficence,* which is widely used in ethical literature to describe the duty to take actions to advance clients' and citizens' well-being. But how do we know what will advance their well-being when people often disagree? While research on social phenomena often is more complex to conduct and more difficult to interpret than laboratory research, it often yields useful information.

Without research, professionals often have taken actions or favored policies that actually harmed their clients or patients, even though they believed they were helping them. Take the case of schizophrenia—and the remarkable transformation that has occurred during the past 40 years in its treatment and in other mental health policies. It was widely believed in the 1950s that schizophrenia was caused by the controlling or coercive behaviors of the mothers of people with schizophrenia—and that the well-being of people with schizophrenia required them to be institutionalized for long periods, sometimes even for life, because they could not deal with the stresses of society. These two beliefs—held by legions of competent social workers, psychologists, and psychiatrists—led to treatments and policies that are hardly comprehensible to contemporary clinicians. Clinicians not only verbally chastised the mothers of people with schizophrenia for their controlling behavior but often advocated severing all ties between children and their mothers. Tens of thousands of people with schizophrenia were kept in the "chronic wards" of state mental institutions for decades, carefully segregated from the patients on "acute wards."[26]

A plethora of research after the 1960s suggested that these policies were misdirected and harmful to people with schizophrenia. Considerable research suggested that schizophrenia is a complex phenomenon that is not caused primarily (or, in some cases, at all) by mothers' behavior. If the mothers' behavior was its primary cause, why did many people with schizophrenia have siblings with no evidence of the malady? Considerable research implicated biological causes, suggesting that schizophrenia is a disease with genetic and physiological causes. Other research called into question the assumption that people with schizophrenia require institutionalization.[27] (See Policy Advocacy Challenge 2.6.)

While research strongly suggested that the long-term incarceration of people with schizophrenia was unnecessary, harmful, and wasteful, it did not demonstrate the kinds of care and supports they should receive in the community. Did they need intensive care or merely occasional contacts with clinicians? What kinds of therapy and what kinds of medication would be most useful? Because empirical data were lacking, people with

---

POLICY ADVOCACY CHALLENGE 2.6

AN EXAMPLE OF RESEARCH DURING BOTH POLICY AND PRACTICE

John Brekke, Ph.D., Professor, School of Social Work, University of Southern California

The hospitalization of people with psychiatric disorders changed dramatically beginning in the 1960s and 1970s. Three major streams of research spearheaded these changes. First, research led by Erving Goffman reported that the longer people stayed in the hospital, the sicker they got. As a consequence, the second stream of research centered on the impact of planned early discharge. Research by Glick et al. indicated that those individuals who were given planned early discharge (with intensive community services) did as well as those who remained hospitalized. Third, Stein and Test conducted a randomized research project to compare intensive community care with hospitalization. The results indicated that those receiving intensive community care actually did better. This combination of research has had an enormous impact on the institutionalization of people with psychiatric disorders and has resulted in increased funding for community care. Mental health systems and particularly state hospitals are changing across the United States and around the world. These changes are also driven by cost; the decisions are economically sound, humanitarian, and buttressed by research. The outcome paints a very favorable picture for policy makers. Unfortunately, there are some failures, especially among those who are homeless and mentally ill. However, research is continuing to try to help those who have not benefited from the changes in the system. Myself and many other researchers now turn our attention to how best to help persons with persistent mental illness in community-based settings.

I. D. Glick, W. A. Hargreaves, J. Drues, and J. A. Schowstack, "Short versus Long Hospitalization: A Prospective Controlled Study. 4: One Year Follow-Up Results from Schizophrenic Patients," *American Journal of Psychiatry,* 133 (1976): 509–514.

Erving Goffman, *Asylums: Essays on the Social Situation of Mental Patients and Other Inmates* (New York: Anchor Books, 1961).

L. Stein and M. Test, "Alternative to Mental Hospital Treatment," *Archives of General Psychiatry* 37 (1980): 392–397.

M. A. Test, W. H. Knoedler, D. J. Allness, S. S. Burke, R. L. Brown, and L. S. Wallisch, "Long-Term Community Care Through an Assertive Continuous Treatment Team," in C. Tamminga and S. Schultz, eds., *Advances in Neuropsychiatry and Psychopharmacology,* Vol. 1: Schizophrenia Research (New York: Raven Press, 1991).

schizophrenia were exposed to various arrangements. In light of the reluctance of politicians to fund outpatient services, many people with schizophrenia also lacked access to any supportive services. Some of them became homeless, living on the streets, in shelters, or in low-cost housing—often in unsafe neighborhoods where they were exposed to crime and violence. Some moved in with relatives or spouses in community settings.[28]

Our discussion of research on schizophrenia demonstrates the analytic rationale for policy advocates. If they wish to advance their clients' or patients' interests, social workers must change those policies and treatments that are harmful or ineffective. When less expensive approaches are found to be as effective as or more effective than more expensive approaches, they should favor them to save consumers' and taxpayers' resources.

Choosing Sides: Controversy and Research

It is incorrect to assume, however, that policy advocates, armed with the latest research, can easily modify all policies. Politicians, bureaucrats, and administrators often choose to ignore research findings that conflict with their ideology, their self-interest, or their customary practices.[29] Moreover, different researchers often reach divergent conclusions, which sometimes leads to conflict. In such cases, policy advocates must decide which researcher's data and conclusions are most meritorious.

The available research on social inequality provides an excellent example of conflicting research. Take the conflicting findings of two sets of researchers: Richard Herrnstein and Charles Murray's research was reported in *The Bell Curve: Intelligence and Class Structure in American Life;* and the findings of Claude Fischer, Michael Hout, et al., were reported in *Inequality by Design: Cracking the Bell Curve Myth.*[30] Both sets of researchers agree that American society is unequal and that African Americans are found disproportionately in the poorest classes, but they reach different conclusions about the reasons African Americans are disproportionately poorer than whites.

Publishing *The Bell Curve* in 1994, Herrnstein and Murray began their analysis by contending that scores on intelligence tests form a bell-shaped curve with a few people at the lower and upper ends, and most people falling in the middle. Drawing on data from a large national survey of 10,000 Americans who were followed from 1980 onward, they asserted that intelligence scores (as measured by the Armed Forces Qualifying Test, or AFQT) are strongly associated with life outcomes. Examining white non-Latinos, they contended that people with low IQ scores are more likely than those with high scores to be poor, high school dropouts, unemployed, unmarried, unwed mothers, or welfare recipients; neglectful mothers; and criminals. When comparing the effects of social class and intelligence, they concluded that intelligence scores were better predictors of life outcomes. Herrnstein and Murray then turned to their controversial assertions about connections between race, intelligence, and life outcomes. African Americans, they asserted, score, on average, 15 points lower than whites on intelligence tests—and they attributed African Americans' higher rates of poverty, school dropout, unemployment, single parent-headed families, use of welfare, and criminality to these lower intelligence scores.

The Bell Curve caused an immediate sensation, not just because it alleged that race and intelligence are associated, but because the authors contended that government can have little influence on social problems. If social problems are caused by personal factors like intelligence—and if intelligence is both unchanging and caused by genetic factors—then society cannot assume a major role in reducing poverty, curtailing school dropouts, or decreasing the use of welfare. Nor should society use affirmative action, since it contributes to the problem by stereotyping African Americans and reducing their self-esteem, as well as placing people in jobs for which they lack the needed skills and intelligence. These authors ended their book with the pessimistic conclusion that vast inequalities are inevitable, since they are caused primarily by differences in intelligence that cannot be influenced substantially by social remedies.

Claude Fischer and many of his sociology colleagues at the University of California at Berkeley (hereafter called the *Berkeley sociologists*) reexamined Herrnstein and Murray's data. The Berkeley sociologists had been perturbed by rising inequality in the United States, such as the marked increases in per capita income for the top 20 percent of the population compared with both the middle 60 percent and the bottom 20 percent from 1959 to 1989. They doubted that inequality is inevitable, pointing to smaller rates of inequality in other industrialized nations. And they doubted that inequality is caused primarily by personal characteristics such as intelligence, believing that persons' "social milieux" (family, neighborhood, school, and community) powerfully shape their economic destinies. These sociologists, then, suspected that inequality, rather than stemming from innate characteristics, is primarily a "social construction" that stems from specific policy choices of American society, compared with those of societies with lower levels of inequality. Why otherwise, they argue, would societies with the same or similar "genetic stocks," such as the United States, Canada, England, and Sweden, vary so much in their levels of inequality? And why would levels of inequality shift over time within a single country if individual characteristics like intelligence remain relatively constant?

The Berkeley sociologists used two major strategies: They analyzed the statistical procedures used by Herrnstein and Murray, and they asked fundamental questions about Herrnstein and Murray's assumptions, such as those concerning intelligence tests and the relative effects of individual talent and social environment on life outcomes. The Berkeley sociologists began by noting that even Herrnstein and Murray had conceded that only five to ten percent of the differences in life outcomes among their survey members had been caused by their intelligence scores, meaning that 90 to 95 percent of these differences had been caused by other factors. Put differently, even if all adults had identical intelligence scores, the inequality of household incomes would decrease by only ten percent. Intelligence scores assume only a modest role in shaping life outcomes—hardly the huge role suggested by Herrnstein and Murray.

The effects of intelligence on life outcomes become even more modest, the Berkeley sociologists contended, if intelligence is scrutinized more carefully. Scores on the AFQT test, they contended, are powerfully shaped by people's social environment, such as what they have been taught in high school, as well as by their response to the test itself (how seriously they take it and how hard they try). Moreover, people's success in employment is determined by many factors that have no relation to intelligence scores, such as creativity, persistence, and social skills. Indeed, when the Berkeley sociologists reanalyzed the data from the survey used by Herrnstein and Murray, they found that AFQT scores in 1980 did not accurately predict how the subjects had fared ten years later in employment markets.

The Berkeley sociologists also concluded that African Americans' lower scores on the AFQT did not suggest genetic causation. "Subordinate ethnic minorities" have often done more poorly in schools and on tests than dominant groups, "whether . . . Eastern European Jews in 1910 in New York, the Irish in England, Koreans in Japan, or

Afrikaaners in South Africa."[31] This historical perspective strongly suggests, they contended, that "it is not low intelligence that leads to inferior status; it is that inferior status leads to low intelligence test scores."[32]

If intelligence scores do not have a great effect on inequality—or on other life outcomes, such as criminality and welfare use—what factors do? The Berkeley sociologists discovered that a host of factors totally ignored by Herrnstein and Murray had significantly affected the life outcomes of the survey members, such as being female, unmarried, and a parent. Other factors associated with poverty included the attributes of persons' communities (such as the region of the country and the extent to which their communities were impoverished and had high dropout rates from high school), the number of years of schooling, and the academic track in high school. When these factors were included in the statistical analysis and when the technical errors made by Herrnstein and Murray were corrected, the Berkeley sociologists discovered that the AFQT scores had been eclipsed in explaining life outcomes by the combined effects of other community, economic, and social factors, including the survey members' likelihood of having out-of-wedlock births, of being incarcerated, of being on welfare, and of being divorced. They concluded that if all adults had the same family origins and environments (but still had different AFQT scores), inequality of household incomes would decrease by a whopping 37 percent. In short, the combined effects of familial and environmental factors, not AFQT scores, powerfully shape life outcomes. Moreover, AFQT test scores are themselves profoundly shaped by community and familial factors, a fact suggesting they are not intrinsic in one's nature but are artifacts of the social environment.

But the Berkeley sociologists were not content merely to criticize the statistical analysis of *The Bell Curve*. Moving beyond the survey findings of Herrnstein and Murray, they examined an array of social policies that influence income distribution. Some economic factors, such as the replacement of unionized and well-paying positions by service jobs in fast-food restaurants and other settings, had caused an economic deterioration in the wages of persons with high school or less education at the same time that the income of college graduates had increased.

These background economic factors, moreover, were supplemented by an array of American social policies that had also increased economic inequality during the previous 25 years. The Berkeley sociologists identified a system of inequality in the United States through "rules and rewards of the game" that had favored affluent persons, including the following: corporate decisions to pay well-educated and higher-level workers far more than less-educated and lower-level workers; reductions in the income tax rates for affluent Americans while the tax rates for less affluent Americans were raised or stayed the same; lack of public funding for child care (whose cost seriously depleted the incomes of less affluent Americans); affluent Americans' mortgage-interest tax deductions; linking health insurance to employment rather than providing national health insurance available to all Americans; and heavy subsidies to higher-education institutions that were used primarily by affluent Americans' children. Although Americans had made extraordinary progress in reducing poverty among elderly citizens by expanding Social Security and Medicare, they had constructed policies that had kept 20 percent of American children in poverty, compared with 9 percent of Canadian and Australian children, 7 percent of British children, and even smaller percentages of French, West German, and Swedish children. Americans had also exacerbated inequality by educational policies in secondary schools, such as having shorter school years than many other nations and tracking children from less affluent families away from college preparatory classes.

The Berkeley researchers' reexamination of the data used in *The Bell Curve,* as well as their use of findings from other social science research, suggests a causal framework radically different from that used by Herrnstein and Murray. In Herrnstein and Murray's model (see Figure 2.1), intelligence is strongly associated both with economic inequality (poverty and unemployment) and with such social problems as out-of-wedlock births, incarceration, divorce, injury, and idleness.[33] In the Berkeley sociologists' model (see Figure 2.2), "cognitive skills" (they used this term rather than intelligence) are caused by an array of environmental factors, such as the parental home environment and the adolescent community environment.[34] Although cognitive skills are associated with inequality, they share this distinction with many other factors, so their effects on inequality are diminished. Indeed, their association with inequality stems partly from their association with other variables that are also associated with inequality, such as the parental home environment and the adolescent community environment. But cognitive skills are not associated with social problems, as alleged by Herrnstein and Murray, and race bears no significant relationship to cognitive skills, inequality, or social problems.

Our discussion of these two research studies suggests that policy advocates must proceed carefully when basing their actions on empirical findings. Research can be misleading, simplistic, or erroneous for a variety of reasons and, as this example suggests, must be used with caution. Researchers may make technical errors in their collection and analysis of data, they may overestimate the effects of certain variables because they have excluded other factors they ought to have considered, or they may misinterpret their data. Nevertheless, policy advocates should try, to the extent possible, to base their actions on empirical findings.

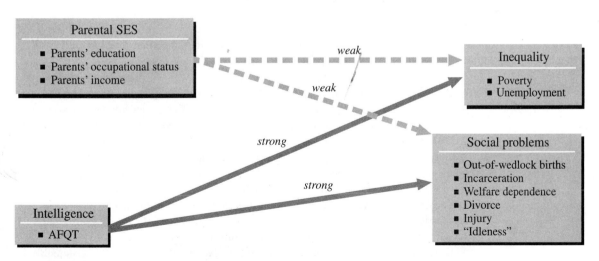

FIGURE 2.1   Herrnstein and Murray's model

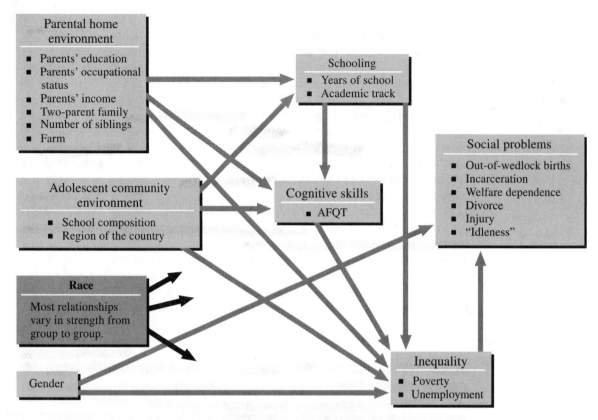

FIGURE 2.2   The Berkeley sociologists' model

The Political Rationale for Policy Advocacy

Policy choices that advance fairness and social justice in American society frequently do not receive a fair hearing because the political system is rigged against poor, oppressed, and powerless groups. Powerful interest groups, whether liquor interests, the National Rifle Association (NRA), pharmaceutical companies, or the U.S. Chamber of Commerce, often wish to sustain the status quo or even to roll back social reforms. Politicians who are pledged to restrict the role of government in American affairs, even when social programs and regulations are needed to redistribute wealth and to protect oppressed groups, often control pivotal offices or possess a majority in legislative chambers. Special interests and wealthy individuals usually provide the bulk of campaign funds for the legislators of both political parties—and often receive policy concessions in return for their contributions.

Public opinion is not necessarily receptive to needed reforms. Buying the myth that any individual can succeed merely through hard work, Americans often minimize the barriers—such as low-wage jobs, lack of subsidized child care, lack of health insurance, inadequate public transportation, and unfair systems of taxation—that impede upward mobility and that cast millions of Americans into poverty. Ostensibly a liberal, Bill Clinton often moved to the center or to the right in response to public opinion polls suggesting that Americans do not want major reforms or substantial increases in programs that invest in human capital. This moderate or conservative bias in public opinion is accentuated by the disinclination to vote of millions of poor people—a group so large that it could aptly be called the party of nonvoters. Whether this stems from procedural barriers to registration and voting or from cynicism about American politics, nonvoters make policy changes in American society more difficult.[35]

If Americans who favor social justice or fairness fail to participate in the political process, they risk increasing the extent to which the political process is skewed against social reforms. One thing is certain: persons opposed to social justice, such as some conservatives, love the political vacuum created when other people do not participate in the political process. Such defections merely allow them to realize their policy preferences more easily. Indeed, nonparticipation is a vote for the values of those who do participate, including more affluent members of society who vote at far higher rates than low-income persons or persons with relatively progressive viewpoints such as many youth.

The composition of government determines what kinds of social policies are (and are not) enacted in local, state, and federal jurisdictions. The political party that obtains a majority of the members of a legislative chamber gets an extraordinary advantage in shaping the legislation that is enacted by that chamber. It gets not only the majority of votes in that chamber, but it controls the chairs of all of its legislative committees, which allows it to determine what bills are given serious attention by the committees and when they are scheduled for votes. The political party that wins head-of-government positions like mayoralties, governorships, and presidencies also gets a huge advantage over other parties. These heads of government appoint the heads and top staff of key government agencies, allowing them to shape how specific programs are implemented. In addition, they can use the media more easily than other politicians to publicize policies that they favor and to attack opponents' policies.

Presidents and governors appoint many of the nation's judges, which allows them to have major influence over controversial court decisions on such topics as abortion and affirmative action. Majority parties in legislatures control how boundaries of political districts are established (so-called apportionment), allowing them to gain seats for themselves by drawing lines in ways that give them an advantage in certain districts.

The ethical stakes are high, as well, when propositions are placed on the ballot in local and state jurisdictions. Originally intended to allow voters to bypass corrupt politicians by placing legislative proposals directly on the ballot, the proposition process has often been used by special interests and conservatives to get their policies enacted. (See Policy Advocacy Challenge 2.7.)

Some social workers believe that political activity is antithetical to professionalism, viewing the development and use of power as unethical. This view is shortsighted, however, as Jane Addams realized in the early part of this century. If persons who are committed to social justice and fairness do not use power, they simply concede to persons who are not committed to these values.

Nor is it necessarily unethical to engage in self-interested activity. When social workers seek licensing laws, which now exist in all states, they want (among other things) access to reimbursements from insurance companies and Medicare. When they try to make certain positions in public agencies classified (that is, reserved for people with social work degrees), they seek to exclude other persons from these positions

POLICY ADVOCACY CHALLENGE 2.7

CONFRONTING POWERFUL INTERESTS

Anneka Scranton, M.S.W., D.P.A., Clinical Adjunct Professor, School of Social Work, University of Southern California

NRA supporters put "proposition E," a proposal to make permits to carry concealed weapons available on demand, on the ballot in Redondo Beach, California. The proposition, if passed, would have made it possible for citizens from anywhere in California to come to Redondo Beach to obtain a permit to carry a concealed gun: No background checks or questions would have been allowed.

Redondo Beach was chosen because of a Fundamentalist mayor and a conservative majority. A low voter turnout in a local election was anticipated. Spending probably $100,000, the NRA organized a downtown phone bank and called every registered voter.

A small group of local activists, including the League of Women Voters and the American Association of University Women, mobilized in response. Raising only $1,000 to print flyers, the 30 or so of us went door to door in pairs. In addition, we wrote letters to the editors of the local papers and contacted political reporters. The temporary coalition also reached out to the business community, warning business leaders that Redondo Beach would become the gun capital of California. The opposition of the police chief to Proposition E was reiterated on every possible occasion.

Emergent citizen outrage produced an extremely high voter turnout and defeated Proposition E by 2 to 1. The NRA supporters were chagrined, and we were elated—spending our last $50 on a victory party at my house.

How does this case illustrate the political imperative for social workers to engage in policy advocacy?

Had this "small group of local activists" not engaged in policy advocacy, what would have been the likely consequences—and who would ultimately have borne the brunt of these consequences?

What does this case tell us about the role of resources in policy advocacy? For example, are advocates destined to lose when they are outspent by powerful interests?

because they believe that social work education enhances the help available to vulnerable populations. To gauge the ethical merits of self-interested activity, we have to ask why people are seeking resources or power and how they plan to use their gains.

As Salcido and Seck argue, however, those who act only out of self-interest are morally derelict.[36] Legendary activists, such as Martin Luther King, Jr., risked their lives and ultimately lost them to advance social justice and fairness. Despite probable bad publicity, professionals should take positions on unpopular issues, such as the economic and social needs of AFDC women, the plight of prisoners on death row, and needle exchange programs to prevent AIDS among drug addicts. Disturbingly, Salcido and Seck found evidence that some chapters of the National Association of Social Workers engaged only in licensing issues and ignored broader issues.

Social workers need to engage in policy practice precisely because they often bring distinctive viewpoints into the policy-making process. An example is found in the comments (made during a personal conversation with the author) of Maurice Bischeff, who runs simulation games in the professional schools of the University of Southern California. He compared the tactics of business school students and social work students in a simulation game known as End of the Line, in which the participants assume the role of elderly people with limited resources, such as money and food, symbolized by paper clips; players "die" when they lose their stock of paper clips. Students in the business school usually created a win-lose situation that led to a few winners and many losers. Social workers, by contrast, often invited destitute players to join supportive groups that shared their dwindling supplies of paper clips. The social workers defined the game in win-win terms that emphasized cooperative rather than competitive strategies.

While Bischeff's observations do not provide definitive evidence, they suggest that social workers are somewhat more likely to identify with the underdogs, the downtrodden, and the oppressed. Of course, social workers with clinical interests need to move beyond empathy to policy advocacy if they want to diminish inequalities and injustices in American society.

Interlocking Rationales for Policy Advocacy

Ethical, analytic, and political rationales work together to buttress the case for policy practice and policy advocacy. (See Figure 2.3.)

Values like social justice and fairness, as well as identification with oppressed groups, prompt us to become policy advocates in the first place. Social research helps us discover effective ways of advancing these values and helping these groups, and allows us to choose among alternative remedies. No matter how meritorious our policy recommendations are on ethical or analytic grounds, we cannot have them implemented if we do not mobilize political support for them.

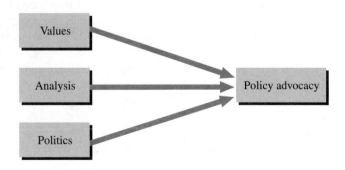

FIGURE 2.3   **Interlocking rationales**

Chapter Summary

What You Can Now Do

You are now equipped with skills in ethical reasoning that are needed for policy advocacy. You can do the following:

- Discuss differences between policy-senstive and policy-related practice—and how they differ from policy practice and policy advocacy
- Discuss Rawls's theory of social justice as it provides a rationale for working to help out-groups
- Develop an ethical position that draws together various kinds of ethical arguments
- Present an analytic rationale for policy advocacy
- Present a political rationale for policy advocacy
- Discuss why policy advocates often seek to change the composition of governments—and dangers that exist if they abandon the political arena and interests to others
- Understand how to use the Web intelligently to obtain information from specific advocacy groups

In the next chapter, we develop a framework for policy practice that sets the stage for discussing the skills, tasks, and competencies needed by policy advocates.

Notes

1. Robert Veatch, *A Theory of Medical Ethics* (New York: Basic Books, 1981).
2. For example, physicians are often implored to break down the barriers that patients encounter when seeking medical care; see Elizabeth Rosenthal, "Despite an Infusion of Public Funds, Women Find Barriers to Prenatal Care," *New York Times* (January 6, 1993), p. 6.
3. Ibid.
4. See Julie Kosterlitz, "Enablement, the Disability Movement after 1990 Victory," *National Journal* (August 31, 1991): 2092–2096.
5. Barbara Solomon, *Black Empowerment* (New York: Columbia University Press, 1976).
6. See Nancy Humphreys, "Integrating Policy and Practice," *Smith College Studies in Social Work* 63 (March 1993): 182–184.
7. Jonathan Kozol, *Savage Inequities* (New York: Crown, 1991).
8. The indifference of many physicians to the obstacles that poor people encounter when seeking medical services is discussed by Paul Starr, *The Social Transformation of American Medicine* (New York: Basic Books, 1982).
9. For a discussion of how policy practitioners can help advocacy and community groups, see Kim Bobo, Jackie Kendall, and Steve Max, *Organizing for Social Change: A Manual for Activists in the 1990s* (Washington, DC: Seven Locks Press, 1991).
10. Lester Thurow, *The Zero-Sum Society* (New York: Basic Books, 1980), pp. 155–190.
11. John Rawls, *A Theory of Justice* (Cambridge: Harvard University Press, 1971), pp. 83–90, 96–100.
12. Ibid.
13. Robert Reich, *Work of Nations: Preparing Ourselves for Twenty-First Century Capitalism* (New York: Knopf, 1991), pp. 171–261.

14. Ibid.
15. Robert Bellah et al., *Habits of the Heart* (Berkeley and Los Angeles: University of California Press, 1985), pp. 275–296.
16. Thurow, *The Zero-Sum Society,* pp. 155–190.
17. Paul Moore, et al., The Other Lost Angeles: The Working Poor in the City in the 21st Century (Los Angeles: Los Angeles Alliance for a New Economy, 2000).
18. A defense of affirmative action is provided by John Baker, *Arguing for Equality* (London: Verso, 1987), pp. 44–51.
19. Veatch, *Medical Ethics.*
20. Various authors discuss first-order ethical principles that are applicable to social work. See Frank Loewenberg and Ralph Dolgoff, *Ethical Decisions for Social Work Practice* (Itasca, IL: Peacock, 1988); Frederic Reamer, *Ethical Dilemmas in Social Service,* 2nd ed. (New York: Columbia University Press, 1990); Frederic Reamer, *The Philosophical Foundations of Social Work* (New York: Columbia University Press, 1993); and Margaret Rhodes, *Ethical Dilemmas in Social Work Practice* (Boston: Routledge & Kegan Paul, 1986).
21. The classic statement of utilitarianism is found in Jeremy Bentham, *An Introduction to the Principles of Morals and Legislation* (London: Athlone Press, 1970). For a critique of this approach, see Mackie, *Ethics,* pp. 126–134.
22. Ibid.
23. Ibid.
24. Bruce S. Jansson, *The Reluctant Welfare State,* 3rd ed. (Pacific Grove, CA: Brooks/Cole, 1997), pp. 22–23.
25. For a discussion of ethical dilemmas, see Tom Beauchamp and James Childress, *Principles of Biomedical Ethics,* 4th ed. (New York: Oxford University Press, 1994).
26. Bernard Bloom, *Community Mental Health* (Pacific Grove, CA: Brooks/Cole, 1977).
27. Erving Goffman, *Asylums: Essays on the Social Situation of Mental Patients and Other Inmates* (New York: Anchor Books, 1961).
28. Madeleine Stoner, *The Civil Rights of Homeless People* (New York: Aldine de Gruyter, 1995), pp. 79–97.
29. Thomas Mann and Norman Ornstein, *How Congress Shapes Health Policy* (Washington, DC: Brookings Institution, 1995).
30. Claude Fischer et al., *Inequality by Design: Cracking the Bell Curve Myth* (Princeton, NJ: Princeton University Press, 1997) and Richard Herrnstein and Charles Murray, *The Bell Curve: Intelligence and Class Structure in American Life* (New York: Free Press, 1994).
31. Fischer et al., Inequality by Design, p. 177.
32. Ibid., p. 172.
33. Ibid., p. 73.
34. Ibid., p. 74.
35. Frances Fox Piven and Richard Cloward, *Why Americans Don't Vote* (New York: Pantheon Books, 1988).
36. See Ramon Salcido and Essie Seck, "Political Participation Among Social Work Chapters," *Social Work* 37 (November 1992): 563–564, for a critique of NASW chapters that focus their political activities only on issues of licensure and reimbursement.

Suggested Readings

Understanding Moral Reasoning: Utilitarian Approaches

Jeremy Bentham, *An Introduction to the Principles of Morals and Legislation* (London: Athlone Press, 1970).

Understanding Moral Reasoning: Deontological Approaches

Tom Beauchamp and James Childress, *Principles of Biomedical Ethics,* 4th ed. (New York: Oxford University Press, 1994).

Understanding Moral Reasoning: Intuitionist Approaches

Ann Fleck-Henderson, "Moral Reasoning in Social Work Practice," *Social Service Review* (June 1991): 185–202.

J. L. Mackie, *Ethics: Inventing Right and Wrong* (London: Penguin Books, 1977).

Exploring Ethical Issues That Confront Social Workers

Frank Loewenberg and Ralph Dolgoff, *Ethical Decisions for Social Work Practice,* 3rd ed. (Itasca, IL: Peacock, 1988).

Frederic Reamer, *Ethical Dilemmas in Social Service,* 2nd ed. (New York: Columbia University Press, 1990).

Margaret Rhodes, *Ethical Dilemmas in Social Work Practice* (Boston: Routledge & Kegan Paul, 1986).

Exploring Ethical Issues About the Nature of the "Good Society"

John Baker, *Arguing for Equality* (London: Verso, 1987).

Robert Goodin, *Reasons for Welfare: The Political Theory of the Welfare State* (Princeton, NJ: Princeton University Press, 1988), pp. 227–359.

John Rawls, *A Theory of Justice* (Cambridge: Harvard University Press, 1971).

Frederic Reamer, *The Philosophical Foundations of Social Work* (New York: Columbia University Press, 1993).

2

SURMOUNTING CYNICISM BY DEVELOPING POLICY-ADVOCACY SKILLS

It is easy to succumb to cynicism when we view important social problems that have festered for decades or when we understand that legislators, presidents, and other leaders are often captive to special interests or have ideologies that make them disinterested in social justice. We can surmount cynicism, however, by gaining skills, knowledge, and perspectives that allow any of us to participate effectively in policy-changing work.

Chapter Three provides a framework for policy practice within a political and economic context, six policy practice tasks, four policy practice skills, and policy competencies. It discusses four styles of policy practice widely used by policy advocates. We argue that the concept of power must receive more attention in social work theory and curricula.

Because policy advocates need to understand the big picture that tells them how policy is made in legislatures, agencies, and communities—and how the composition of government can be changed—**Chapter Four** contains an overview of policy in these arenas.

3

Obtaining Skills and Competencies for Policy Advocacy

A POLICY PREDICAMENT	Policy advocates used to be able to focus much of their energy on lobbying in Washington, DC, because the federal government had often led the way in developing social reforms from the New Deal through the Great Society. But a process of devolution took place in the three decades following the 1960s where the federal government, while often providing some funds, gave states and localities greater power to determine actual policies. Accustomed to lobbying the Congress and federal bureaucracies, policy advocates now had to turn their attention to governors, legislators, and bureaucrats in each of the 50 state capitols. Wanting to get social workers involved in this huge lobbying and policy-making task, social work professor Robert Schneider organized a national organization to promote social work lobbying at the state level. At the end of this chapter, in Policy Advocacy Challenge 3.3, we discuss how he used an array of policy advocacy skills to develop this national organization.

This chapter provides a general framework for policy practice in any setting, whether legislative, organizational, or community. We discuss the following in this chapter:

- A policy practice framework that places policy deliberations in their contextual setting
- The policy practice tasks: agenda building, problem analyzing, proposal constructing, policy enacting, policy implementing, and policy assessing
- Four policy practice skills used to accomplish the policy tasks: value clarifying, political, interactional, and analytic
- The policy competencies used to operationalize each of the policy skills
- Four styles of policy practice that are used by policy practitioners, as well as hybrid styles
- The importance of power in policy practice

A Policy Practice Framework

To be useful to policy advocates, a policy practice framework must be multifaceted and must do the following:

- Place policy advocacy in its contextual setting because it never occurs in a vacuum
- Identify the values, ideology, interests, and goals of stakeholders in specific policy situations—including those of the policy advocate and his or her allies
- Discuss patterns of participation because an array of participants usually shape choices and outcomes
- Identify the key tasks that policy advocates undertake in their work
- Identify the fundamental skills that policy advocates should possess
- Identify the key competencies that policy advocates should possess

TASKS
SKILLS
COMPETENCIES

Such a framework is presented in Figure 3.1, which we will now discuss and illustrate with a case example.

The Policy Context

A framework (such as in Figure 3.1) that describes the context and tasks of policy making is useful because it provides an overview of the factors that affect policy deliberations. Indeed, it encourages us to ask important questions about how policy making works, both

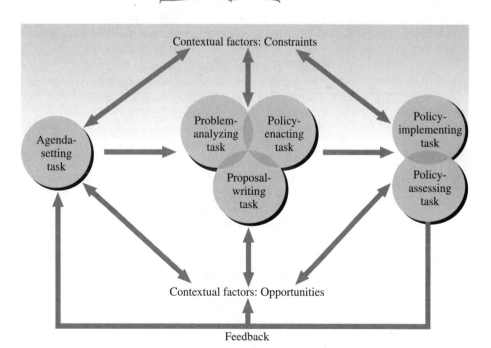

FIGURE 3.1   A dynamic model of policy practice and policy advocacy. Each task shown here involves participants' skills and competencies.

in general and in specific situations. We can ask, for example, whether political and economic forces determine the outcome of policy deliberations. In some cases, powerful interests have such clout that they can single-handedly shape the course of deliberations. Interest groups with large constituencies and many economic resources have developed extraordinary power through mass mailing, marketing, campaign underwriting, and vote-counting technology. This has been true of corporate groups like the American Association of Automobile Dealers or groups with mass membership like the American Association of Retired Persons.[1] Concerning other issues, however, powerful external interests do not exist or are locked in opposition to one another, giving policy advocates more latitude.

Moreover, the context shifts over time in response to both external events and policy deliberations. Proposals to enact major federal day-care programs, for example, would have faced certain defeat in the 1960s because few people believed women should work outside the home. By 1988, however, a determined group of children's advocates almost had a major day-care program enacted. They finally succeeded in 1990, partly because of massive increases in women's participation in the labor force.

Perspectives of Stakeholders and Policy Advocates

Policies are ultimately initiated, changed, or rejected by people—not by abstract forces. We can distinguish between stakeholders and policy initiators. *Stakeholders* are persons with a vested interest in a specific policy or issue being contested. These include the following:

- Leaders and members of interest groups
- Advocacy groups that have been active in seeking policy reforms in a progressive way
- Administrators and staff of existing programs
- Legislators (and their aides) who are members, or chairs, of committees that have been active with respect to the issue or policy under consideration
- Heads of government interested in a specific policy or issue, whether regarding its political importance to them or as they are charged with overseeing it
- Government agencies and funders who fund programs related to the policy—or who monitor or regulate them
- Consumers or beneficiaries of a specific policy or issue
- Regulatory bodies or courts associated with a policy or issue, such as state departments that inspect nursing homes and child-care centers
- Professional groups associated with a program or issue, such as the National Association of Social Workers regarding licensing issues related to social work
- Associations of agencies that focus on specific issues, such as the directors of child-care centers in a particular state
- Corporate interest groups such as the U.S. Chamber of Commerce or associations representing pharmaceutical companies (in the case of health legislation)
- Heads of political parties to the extent they believe a policy or issue has political ramifications for themselves

We call these persons and groups stakeholders because they have a stake in a policy or issue, whether political or economic, or because they are directly affected by it. Policy advocates need to discover at the outset who these people and groups are, because

POLICY
ADVOCACY
CHALLENGE 3.1

*CONDUCTING
RESEARCH TO
SUPPORT POLICY
ADVOCACY*

*Stephanie Davis,
Research Librarian,
University of Southern
California, Irvine*

On some levels, doing research to support policy practice is the same as doing research for a term paper. You still need to write clearly, state your arguments in a lucid and succinct manner, back up your position with other work in the same area or with statistics and other data, and you will need to cite any information that is not your idea.

However, in policy practice research, most likely you are casting a wider net in terms of the kind of information you want to find to support your case. In most cases, term paper research is based mostly in finding academic research articles and books. In policy practice research, your end goal is to persuade a certain group that you are right. You'll want to bring in other information such as legislation, new Congressional bills, case studies or reports from agencies or organizations.

A few research skills that will come in handy when starting your policy research:

- Know the extent of the resources in your community and make use of the expertise, such as other agencies, libraries, government departments, and educators.
- Search strategically: if you don't find the information you want at first, try searching with different keywords, in a different database, or on a different Web site.
- Inform yourself about your community, your city, and your state. This is as simple as reading a newspaper and watching the news.
- Remember that information that proves your point is just as important as information that disproves your point. You need to be aware of both.
- Familiarize yourself with the historical aspects of the problem you are trying to address in your work so you can learn how others have approached the problem in the past, how people have been impacted by the problem.
- Evaluate the information that you find, check your facts, and cite your sources.

they probably will become involved when advocates try to initiate, modify, or terminate a specific policy.

Not only do policy advocates need to identify these groups, they need to understand the likely positions and perspectives they possess. (See Policy Advocacy Challenge 3.1.) Of course, stakeholders do not always act consistently. Policy advocates should be careful not to assume that past actions and perspectives always predict future ones.

The sheer number and variety of stakeholders varies from issue to issue. In the case of relatively technical issues that affect relatively few people, relatively few stakeholders exist. Some minor technical change in laws that license social workers, for example, have import only to social workers. In contrast, any effort to reform national health care policies in major ways is relevant to scores of stakeholder groups and hundreds of politicians.

We want to know not only which stakeholders are likely to be involved, but the importance they attach to a policy initiative. Will the initiative be perceived in ideological terms; for example, will stakeholders believe that it is connected to deep-seated beliefs about society and how it should operate? Will key stakeholders see the policy initiative as affecting their basic economic and political interests, such as taking resources from them, giving them major additional resources, or impinging on their political base of support? We can ask, as well, if the policy intiative is likely to be perceived as costing a lot of money, which also raises the economic stakes to a range of persons since money is usually in short supply in legislatures and agencies. If any or all of these three factors are involved (ideology, key interests, or money), we can predict high interest by a number of stakeholders. Such interest could, in turn, suggest possible conflict or, at the very least, considerable maneuvering by stakeholders as they seek resolutions that will be consonant with their ideology, interests, and available resources.

Of course, the opposite also is true: initiatives seen as not impinging on ideology, interests, or budgets will likely attract less interest and controversy.

Policy initiators are persons or groups that initiate a change in existing policy. They may propose a new policy, or the modification or termination of an existing policy. Sometimes they are stakeholders themselves, such as a legislator or head of government who proposes new legislation. Sometimes they are advocacy groups. In rarer cases, policies are initiated by individual citizens, for example persons who want to change existing policies because they have had bad experiences with these programs or policies. Policy initiators bring their own perspectives, values, and ideologies to the table, as well as their own interests, which we need to understand to know why they have initiated a policy proposal and whether they will invest major resources in it. Is this an issue in which they have a longstanding interest? To what extent are they connected to other stakeholders in a positive way? Do they possess the expertise and resources to be effective advocates—and do they intend to invest major resources in this initiative, such as staff time and money? How are they viewed by other stakeholders—and will these perceptions affect their likely success in obtaining collaborators and allies? Are they likely to make a credible case for the initiative, such as by drawing on available data and research?

Patterns of Participation

Policy initiators usually do not have the field to themselves because other people participate in policy deliberations. Some are *bystanders* who take no part in policy deliberations, and others are *policy responders* who seek to modify or change the policy proposals of the initiators. *Opposers* decide to block or modify proposals. These groups rarely remain fixed; people change groups as policy deliberations proceed. Initiators often want to expand their ranks by attracting people from other groups, just as opposers want to convert people to their position.

Issues spark different levels of conflict during policy deliberations. Some issues create a great deal of disagreement, and others are resolved with minimal conflict. Participants' actions and rhetoric reflect the level of conflict. In high conflict, people use emotion-laden language, make vigorous efforts to outmaneuver other participants, use extraordinary tactics (such as filibusters), publicize the issue through the mass media, and try to enlist others to support their position. Conflict may result in the polarization of factions and groups, such as political parties, conservatives and liberals in legislatures, different factions in communities, or management and line staff in organizations. An absence of such conflict and alignments usually suggests consensual deliberations.

Policy deliberations often last a long time. A piece of legislation, for example, goes through subcommittees, committees, and floor debates before it is forwarded to elected officials, such as the president or the governor, for approval or veto. Policy initiatives sometimes take years to enact as their supporters work to educate others about the merits of their initiatives. Yet other issues are processed rapidly, as when heads of government place initiatives high on their agendas and successfully rally support for them. Proposals in agencies often proceed through sequences of deliberation in meetings and committees and with officials. Policy changes can be made quickly or slowly in agencies, as well. Some initiatives languish for years until a new executive decides to push them. Other issues, however, are resolved rapidly, such as decisions made in agency staff meetings to modify internal policies.

The Six Tasks of Policy Practitioners

To understand policy practice, we must review the recurring tasks that policy practitioners undertake, which we first discussed in Chapter One. In the *agenda-setting task,* practitioners gauge whether the context is favorable for a policy initiative, and they evolve early strategy to place it on policy makers' agendas. In the *problem-analyzing task,* practitioners analyze the causes, nature, and prevalence of specific problems. In the *proposal-writing task,* practitioners develop solutions to specific problems. Proposals may be relatively ambitious, such as a piece of legislation, or relatively modest, such as incremental changes in existing policies. In the *policy-enacting task,* practitioners try to have policies approved or enacted.

At some point, proposals are either enacted in their original or an amended form, or rejected. When analyzing these outcomes, we often ask: Who won and who lost? Those whose proposals are enacted with few changes are clear victors. Sometimes, however, apparent victors have actually lost because their proposals are so diluted as to be meaningless, as Peter Bachrach and Morton Baratz noted in discussing "decisionless decisions."[2] An example of a decisionless decision is enacting a new program when no resources are available. Clear losers are those whose proposals are rejected.

Policy practitioners continue to work even after policy enactment when they undertake the *policy-implementing task,* in which they try to carry out enacted policies. Once a policy has been enacted, policy deliberations focus on its implementation and assessment. (See Figure 3.1.) Considerable conflict may erupt during a policy's implementation as people and interest groups try to influence the priorities and directions of social programs. Unions, professionals, civil servants, and legislators, as well as heads of government, shape implementation.

Policy practitioners evaluate programs when they undertake the *policy-assessing task* by obtaining data about the implemented policy's performance. Policy practitioners frequently assess programs after policy enactment to see if they fulfill certain objectives. For example, researchers have assessed the food stamp program to see if it has decreased malnutrition in specific segments of the population, evaluated the Head Start program to decide whether it enhances children's cognitive development, and analyzed the Adoption Assistance and Child Welfare Act to determine whether it has shortened children's stays in foster care. Ultimately, we ask which segments of the population have benefited or have been harmed by a policy's enactment. If a new social program distributes resources exclusively to affluent persons, for example, we might declare that poor persons have lost.

When we discuss these policy tasks as separate entities, we suggest that they are easily distinguishable. In fact, persons often engage in several of these tasks at the same time. For example, legislators simultaneously engage in proposal-writing and policy-enacting tasks when they modify a proposal to enhance its prospects of enactment. They couple the problem-analyzing task with the proposal-writing task when they create a proposal that addresses the basic causes of a social problem or the needs of a specific group.

Moreover, policy practitioners rarely accomplish the various tasks sequentially and predictably. Legislators may draft a proposal before devoting much time to analyzing the presenting problem. They may revise the proposal in response to a social scientist's comments at a legislative committee hearing. In this case, they begin with the proposal-writing task, revert to the problem-analyzing task, and return to proposal writing. Similarly, a legislator may attempt to rally support for a vague and ill-defined proposal (the policy-enacting task), only to return to the problem-analyzing and proposal-writing tasks at a later time. Of course, this seemingly chaotic approach to policy making departs from the sequential process that some policy analysts describe, but events in the real world rarely correspond to any orderly approach. (To underscore the fluid nature of policymaking, we use overlapping circles in Figure 3.1 to characterize the relationships among the various roles.)

Our policy framework also poses interesting questions about the relationships among the phases of policy deliberations. The initial definition of an issue in deliberations (during the agenda-building and problem-analyzing tasks) often shapes people's perceptions and choices during the ensuing deliberations. In 1996, for example, many politicians were concerned about the size of the AFDC program. Framing the issue in this way led them to emphasize policy solutions that would reduce enrollment, such as providing training programs and requiring recipients to accept employment when it is available. Had the welfare reform issue been defined differently at the outset, policy makers might have emphasized other aspects of reform. Assume, for example, that legislators had focused on the relative poverty of unskilled single women with one or more children in their households. Had the issue been defined in these economic terms, legislators might have emphasized raising women's income by increasing the minimum wage, increasing tax incentives to their employers, decreasing the Social Security payroll deductions of low-paid workers, and increasing the AFDC benefits for those women who remained on the rolls.[3]

Similarly, activities in other phases of policy making also influence the outcome. Writing proposals and implementing policy are closely related. When policy makers establish lofty goals but their proposals allocate relatively few resources, for example, they decrease the likelihood that their proposals will be implemented.[4]

Four Skills That Policy Practitioners Need

When undertaking their various tasks, policy practitioners need at least four basic skills. They need *analytic skills* to evaluate social problems and develop policy proposals, to analyze the severity of specific problems, to identify the barriers to policy implementation, and to develop strategies for assessing programs. They need *political skills* to gain and use power and to develop and implement political strategy. They need *interactional skills* to participate in task groups, such as committees and coalitions, and to persuade other people to support specific policies. (See Policy Advocacy Challenge 3.2.) And they need *value-clarifying skills* to identify and rank relevant principles when engaging in policy practice. Just as many theorists have discussed the skills necessary for direct-service work, administration, and community organization, policy theorists need to discuss the skills needed in policy practice and policy advocacy.

POLICY
ADVOCACY
CHALLENGE 3.2

*FORMING A
COALITION TO
INFLUENCE A
STATE'S WELFARE
REFORM POLICIES*

*Emanuel Gale, Ph.D.,
Professor of Social Work,
California State
University at
Sacramento*

With the advent of the so-called welfare reform, some faculty at California State University at Sacramento (CSUS) and social workers in the community joined with some welfare mothers and others to organize the Community Action Coalition (CAC).

The Coalition's mission is to promote empowerment, self-sufficiency, and social justice through:

- Assuring strong support for families and children, in the face of a dramatic assault on the "safety net"
- Assisting communities in building and enhancing their assets and capacities

CAC has organized eight neighborhood chapters and is developing task forces on jobs, child care, and transportation. CAC has had meetings with representatives of the Department of Human Assistance (DHA) to identify the issues of concern and to provide recommendations as the county develops its plans.

The Division of Social Work at CSUS has assigned eight students to fieldwork with CAC, under the supervision of an M.S.W. who has retired from the County Department of Health and Human Services, with a faculty member in an advisory capacity.

The main responsibilities of the students will be to assist in strengthening neighborhood chapters through recruitment, leadership training, community organization, voter registration, advocacy, and ensuring neighborhood representation at appropriate forums.

The Child Care Task Force of the CAC has gathered data about the contradictions in the state's welfare goals. While pushing welfare mothers to work, the state has failed to provide adequate funding for child care. CAC has been documenting cases where the cost of child care is more than the mother can earn. Advocacy with the DHA has highlighted the potential crisis.

CAC will make special presentations to the city council and the board of supervisors about the critical issues concerning the implementation of welfare reform. Data will be presented with colored maps which graphically and dramatically document the zip codes most heavily affected. Neighborhood representatives will also address the issues of concern.

Future planning includes the possibility of contracts with CAC as a community-based organization and research projects with some faculty at the university.

Policy practice seems more complicated because it involves four skills, not one, but imagine if we argued that direct-service or administrative practice required only one skill! Although many policy theorists emphasize one or another of these skills, effective policy practitioners need all of them in many situations.

Policy Competencies

Policy practitioners must use the four policy skills when taking concrete actions in organizational, community, or legislative settings. We call these skills *policy competencies,* each of which is discussed on the pages indicated in Table 3.1. We can develop these competencies only by practicing them in agency, community, and legislative settings, much as we develop skills in direct service, community organization, and administration.

TABLE 3.1   **Policy competencies**

Political competencies	Organizational settings	Community settings	Legislative settings
Using the mass media (pp. 335–337)	Press releases and press conferences	Press releases and press conferences	Press releases and press conferences
Taking a personal position (pp. 296–298, 329–330)	Advocating a position in a staff meeting	Advocating a position with a community resident or official	Voting
Advocating a position with a decision maker (pp. 331–335)	Talking with an executive director about a policy	Talking to a school principal about a policy	Lobbying legislators or civil servants
Seeking positions of power (pp. 294, 345)	Seeking a high position in an agency	Running for the school board	Running for elective office
Empowering others (pp. 35–36, 172, 341–342)	Enhancing staff (or consumers') participation in agency policy making	Increasing citizens' participation in policy making of community institutions	Registering voters
Orchestrating pressure on decision makers (pp. 21–22, 55, 66, 84–86, 286–290)	Mobilizing protest within an agency	Mobilizing protest within a community	Mobilizing protest against legislators by phone trees, petitions, mass mailings, delega-tions, or protests
Finding resources to fund advocacy projects (pp. 340, 344)	Securing agency resources for coalitions and lobbying	Raising funds for advocacy groups	Raising funds for campaigns
Developing and using personal power resources (pp. 81–83, 173–175, 274–277, 285–298)	To mobilize support for a policy	To mobilize support for a policy	To mobilize support for a policy
Donating time/ resources to an advocacy group (pp. 339–345)	To an intra-agency coalition	To a community advocacy group	To an advocacy group focusing on legislative policy, a political campaign, or a political action committee like PACE
Advocating for the needs of a client (pp. 25–26, 31–33, 66, 297–298)	With agency officials	With community officials	With public officials
Participating in a demonstration (pp. 323, 335–336)	Protesting an agency policy	Protesting a community policy	Protesting a public policy

TABLE 3.1   *continued*

	Organizational settings	Community settings	Legislative settings
Initiating litigation to change policies (p. 91)	Of agencies	Of communities	Of public agencies and legislatures
Participating in a political campaign (pp. 340–345)	_____	_____	Working with a candidate for office
Voter registration (pp. 341–345)	_____	_____	Working with a political party or advocacy group
Analytic competencies			
Developing a proposal (pp. 16–17, 161, 179–205, 216–229)	Writing a grant proposal	Proposing an interagency consortium	Drafting legislation
Calculating trade-offs (pp. 210–220)	Examining program options	Examining program options	Examining legislative options
Doing force field analysis (pp. 314–320)	Before proposing an innovation in an agency	Before proposing a community innovation	Before proposing a legislative initiative
Using social science research (pp. 47–53, 134–135, 147–166)	Designing an intervention strategy	Designing an intervention strategy	Designing public policy
Conducting a marketing study (pp. 155, 157–161, 203–204)	Designing an agency program	Designing a community program	Designing a public program
Using the Internet (pp. 11–12, 40–41, 89–90, 148, 260, 313, 359, 370–371, 407–409)	Getting information germane to any policy task	Getting information germane to any policy task	Getting information germane to any policy task
Working with budgets (pp. 112, 183–185, 228)	Analyzing agency budgets	Analyzing the budget of a community institution	Analyzing a governmental budget
Finding funding sources for specific projects (pp. 222–223)	Researching foundations, private donors, or public donors	Researching foundations, private donors, or public donors	Researching foundations, private donors, or public donors
Diagnosing audiences (pp. 233–235, 240–243)	When making an agency presentation	When making a community presentation	When testifying
Designing a presentation (pp. 231–254, 335)	Before agency staff or officials	Before community representatives	Before public officials
Diagnosing barriers to implementation (pp. 13–15, 358–373)	When implementing agency programs	When implementing community programs	When implementing federally funded programs

(continued)

TABLE 3.1   (*continued*)

	Organizational settings	Community settings	Legislative settings
Designing strategy to improve implementation (pp. 370–372, 379–382)	In agency settings	In community settings	In public agencies
Developing political strategy (pp. 259–274, 320–354)	In agency settings	In community settings	In public agencies
Analyzing the context of policies and issues (pp. 62–63, 89–117, 134–137, 345–348)	In agency settings	In communities	In legislatures
Designing policy assessments (pp. 167–168, 389–404)	In agency settings	In communities	In legislatures
Selecting a policy practice style (pp. 69–70, 261)	In agency settings	In communities	In legislatures
Interactional competencies			
Coalition building (pp. 55, 66, 124–128, 173–175, 302–305)	Organizing a coalition in an agency	Organizing a coalition in the community to develop new programs	Organizing an advocacy group to pressure legislators
Making a presentation (pp. 231–251, 335)	Presenting to the board	Speaking at a community forum	Testifying before a legislative committee
Building personal power (pp. 81–83, 285–298)	Building networks and credibility	Building networks and credibility	Building networks and credibility
Task group formation and maintenance (pp. 84–86, 298–305)	Forming, staffing, and joining task groups	Forming, staffing, and joining task groups	Forming, staffing, and joining task groups
Managing conflict (pp. 250–254, 296–297)	Mediating disputes	Mediating disputes	Mediating disputes
Value-clarifying competency			
Engaging in ethical reasoning	In agency settings	In community settings	In public settings

Styles of Policy Practice

Just as different styles exist in direct-service practice (for example, cognitive versus psychodynamic approaches) and community organization practice (for example, social action versus community development approaches), different approaches exist in policy practice.[5] Let's contrast electoral, legislative advocacy, troubleshooting, and analytic

TABLE 3.2   Four styles of policy practice and policy advocacy

	Ballot-Based Advocacy	Legislative Advocacy	Analytic Advocacy	Troubleshooting Advocacy
GOAL	To change the composition of governments or to get a ballot initiative enacted or defeated	To secure the enactment of— or the defeat of— specific legislative proposals	To make policy choices that are based on hard data and structured analysis	To increase the effectiveness of operating programs
PIVOTAL ORGANI-ZATIONS TO WHICH ADVO-CATES ARE LINKED	Campaign organizations, political action committees, political parties	Advocacy groups, interest groups, community-based organizations, professional associations	Think tanks, academic centers, government agencies, funders	Planning or oversight groups composed of insiders, outsiders, consumers, and/or others
LEVELS OF CONFLICT	High conflict between contending campaigns in win-lose contests	Variable conflict, but usually moderate to high conflict	Conflict between stakeholders about technical issues and interpretive issues	Usually low to moderate conflict, unless outsiders protest specific implementing policies and actions
KEY SKILLS OF ADVO-CATES	Developing strategy, interacting with likely voters, raising funds, media relations, using polls and focus groups	Policy analysis, lobbying, knowledge of the legislative process, building and sustaining coalitions	Research and analytic skills, obtaining and processing data, making technical presentations	Diagnosing operating programs, understanding organizational dynamics, collaborative problem solving, managing conflict

models of policy advocacy (see Table 3.2). The *electoral style* is used when policy advocates want to get someone elected to office or when they want to initiate or contest a ballot initiative (also called a proposition). The goal is to change the composition of government by getting progressive candidates into office, and to defeat less progressive candidates, or to get a ballot initiative enacted or defeated, depending on whether they do or do not advance such ideas as social justice. Policy advocates work with campaign organizations, with political action committees (such as NASW's PACE), or with political parties. They can expect high conflict because elections and ballot initiatives are usually hotly contested. They need skills in talking with voters, framing issues, and working with campaign staff. Some policy advocates run for office themselves, as we discuss in more detail in Chapter 12.

Some policy advocates use a *legislative advocacy style* by which they hope to secure the enactment of meritorious legislation or defeat ill-conceived measures. They work with advocacy groups, community-based organizations, professional associations, and lobbyists as they try to convince legislators to adopt their measure or to defeat a measure that they dislike. Depending on the specific measure, the level of conflict can vary. (So-called hot button issues that polarize legislators by party or ideology are likely to be associated with high conflict, unlike more technical issues.) Policy advocates need skills in policy analysis, developing strategy, and working with coalitions; and knowledge of the legislative process and lobbying.

With an *analytic style* policy advocates use data to develop policy proposals or evaluate how existing policies are working. They often work in or with think tanks, academic units, funders, or government agencies. They need skills in conducting research, using data, and making recommendations.

Policy advocates sometimes use a *troubleshooting* style to increase the effectiveness of operating programs or to evaluate them with an eye to improving them. They need to work with planning groups that consist of members of the implementing team, sometimes, mixing insiders with outside consultants, government officials, funders, or consumers. In still other cases, they work with outside groups of consumers or others who bring pressure on the staff of a program to change it. In most cases, troubleshooting involves relatively low conflict because policy advocates engage in problem solving with staff and administrators to improve the workings of a particular program. Troubleshooters need skills in diagnosing why specific programs have flawed operations or outcomes, in obtaining data to assess them, and in working collaboratively with staff and administrators.

Not everyone is skilled in each of the styles—and tensions often exist among them. Some policy advocates like political maneuvering and excel in it, whether the electoral or legislative-advocacy style. They sometimes are critical of the analytic style, believing that proposals, no matter how meritorious on technical grounds, will come to naught absent political advocacy. Persons who like to use the analytic style are sometimes critical of persons who are excessively political. Some would like persons with technical skills to make key, objective choices. Some troubleshooters, excelling at using collaborative planning approaches to overcome such organizational problems as turf rivalries and fragmentation, are less comfortable with high-conflict strategies sometimes used by political activists.

The astute reader can see that the different styles correspond to the six tasks we have already discussed. Persons who use the analytic style often are most comfortable with the problem-defining, proposal-writing, and assessing tasks since these tasks often require the use of data and research. Those who use the legislative advocacy style often are most comfortable with the policy-enacting task, and persons who use the troubleshooting task are most comfortable with the policy-implementing task. The electoral style however, does not, correspond to any of the six tasks. It is unique because it focuses on campaigns, whether to elect candidates or to get ballot initiatives enacted. It neither aims to guide policy initiatives through the decision "making process" or troubleshoot existing programs, but to change the composition of government so that decision makers are more receptive to accepting humane policies and reforms in the implementation of social programs.

In the case of ballot initiatives, it aims to change policies by *circumventing* the regular legislative process.

In the real world, of course, the different styles often are combined in *hybrid styles*—with many persons moving among them. You cannot engage in legislative advocacy, for example, without doing at least some policy analysis, because your policy initiatives will not be credible if you use no data. You cannot be effective doing policy analysis if you are not looking ahead to political realities that you will confront in legislative arenas. If you draft a policy that makes sense in terms of data but that has no chance of adoption by legislators, you risk spinning your wheels. Both policy analysts and legislative advocates need to anticipate issues and problems during policy implementation lest they frame and enact policies that are poorly implemented because they failed to be forward looking. And all policy advocates, no matter their stylistic preferences, need to engage in ballot-based advocacy to enhance the chances that they will gain a hearing from the powers that be.

Quite apart from policy styles, effective advocates need a combination of each of the four skills to be effective. Someone who relies only on good values, does not develop and use power resources, and never uses analytic information ought to ponder whether this narrow approach to policy practice is effective in specific agency, community, or legislative settings. Similarly, people who are only political or only analytic risk not being effective in many situations. Policy practitioners who rely on a single skill are sometimes stereotyped: *opportunists* rely on political skills, *do-gooders* rely on values, and *policy wonks* rely on analytic data.

Applications of Policy Tasks and Skills

The four skills and six tasks intertwine during policy practice, as our discussion of the six policy tasks suggests.

Building Agendas

When they want to change existing policies, policy practitioners have to analyze the context to gauge whether it will support or oppose a specific policy initiative. If the situation is favorable, they may decide to proceed at once. If it is not favorable, they may devote time and effort to making the context more favorable, or they may decide to delay their policy-changing work until a more propitious moment. Policy practitioners encounter analytic, political, interactional, and value-based challenges when they try to make the context more favorable.[6] Their analytic challenge is to provide technical information to convince others that the problem deserves serious attention. They can argue that a problem, such as alcoholism, has sufficiently serious effects on society to warrant attention. Policy practitioners often use trend data to suggest that a problem is becoming more serious with time, a tactic that suggests that inaction will increase the severity of the problem.

Policy practitioners often use their analytic skills to create the impression that a crisis exists. When current data point to a problem's severity and trend data track the problem over time, decision makers are likely to believe that it demands immediate attention.[7] Policy practitioners use political skills to associate issues with political threats and opportunities in the minds of decision makers. Democrats got Congress to prioritize action on extending medicare coverage to prescription drugs in early 2001, for example, by threatening to use the issue to carry favor with millions of senior citizens, whose votes would be critical in forthcoming elections.

Policy practitioners have many ways of conveying the political importance of specific issues to decision makers. They can discuss important groups or funders who would like specific policy reforms in agency or legislative settings. They can imply to members of one party that members of another party may beat them to the punch if they fail to take interest in a specific issue.

Effective policy practitioners skillfully select propitious moments to inject issues into political deliberations. John Kingdon suggests that "windows of opportunity" exist when background factors are particularly favorable.[8] Perhaps a particularly scandalous condition has just been publicized, such as the neglect of someone with Alzheimer's disease. Maybe a recently elected city mayor, whose mother has Alzheimer's disease, supports funding a new initiative. Or perhaps a new research report documents the dearth of services to families of people with Alzheimer's. Alas, windows of opportunity often close quickly as the political situation changes. Democrats' desire to extend medicare to cover prescription drugs was frustrated by the tragic demolition of New York City's Twin Towers by terrorists on September 11, 2001, which diverted Congress's attention to military issues and "homeland defense."

Policy practitioners use interactional skills to place issues on the agendas of decision makers. Perhaps a committee chairperson agrees to address a specific issue at a forthcoming meeting, or an agency executive consents to form a task force to examine a problem. Perhaps the aide to an influential legislator agrees to discuss an issue with a powerful member of a legislative committee so that a bill will receive preferential treatment in the committee's deliberations.

To secure a privileged position for issues, then, policy practitioners need to use persuasive and coalition-building competencies. In personal discussions, they need to convince others that an issue is relevant to their beliefs, that important political threats or opportunities exist, or that credible people take an interest in the issue.

Policy practitioners confront value issues when they seek a preferred position for a specific problem in policy deliberations. To increase the prominence of an issue, practitioners sometimes inflate figures, exaggerate a problem's negative impact on the broader society, or magnify political threats or opportunities. These tactics pose ethical questions that practitioners must consider. In other cases, they may display undue caution by avoiding relatively unpopular but important issues, thus ignoring the needs of oppressed groups.

Analyzing Problems

People often analyze social problems, asking about their causes and developing typologies. When coupled with empirical research, these analytic tools help us define social problems and to develop proposals to address them.

Even analysis intersects with politics, however, because it must be framed to attract the attention of decision makers.[9] Words, titles, and explanations must be both comprehensible and palatable, as when advocates of AFDC reform in 1988 emphasized "family support" rather than "welfare reform" to make their measure more acceptable to conservative politicians.

When analyzing problems, policy practitioners often work with committees or advocacy groups that require them to use interactional skills. They often must make presentations to legislators, committees, or audiences to convince them that a specific course of action is needed to address a social problem.

Writing Proposals

People need analytic skills to choose between competing options in developing a proposal. Were writing proposals entirely analytic or technical, policy practitioners would hire experts, give them specific instructions, and use the finished product in policy deliberations. Because political realities usually intrude, however, policy practitioners need political, as well as analytic, skills to develop proposals. Many policies are shaped by extended deliberations, in which various amendments are made. As Ron Dear and Rino Patti note, the enactment of legislation often hinges on its advocates' willingness to accept amendments that may alter policies, such as a program's title, its administrative details, the services it offers, its eligibility standards, the type of agency that can deliver the services, or standards for the staff providing the services.[10] Policy practitioners use political and value-clarification skills to decide when to accept or oppose amendments. People who favor a proposal offer friendly amendments or relatively technical changes that improve the proposal's political prospects. The practitioner's task is more difficult when hostile amendments suggest scuttling the proposal or altering it fundamentally; for example, slashing it so profoundly that it no longer remains viable, or deleting or modifying the standards that govern staff qualifications. When faced with hostile amendments, the proponents of a proposal must weigh the advantages and disadvantages of accepting the amendments. Of course, such calculations are often complex; opposing a hostile amendment may feel principled, but it may cause regret if it leads to defeat of the proposal.

Believing that vagueness reduces controversy and conflict, policy practitioners often use political and value-clarification skills to decide whether to leave certain issues relatively vague in a proposal. Vagueness poses threats of its own, however, because vague proposals give implementers considerable latitude in filling in the gaps. If policy practitioners believe the implementers will have different perspectives from their own, they must dot all the *i*'s and cross all the *t*'s to limit the implementers' discretion.

Practitioners need interactional skills at many points in developing proposals. Committees may have a central position in fashioning proposals, whether in legislative or agency settings. Coalitions often play a prominent role in proposal writing; for example, they may mobilize opposition to hostile amendments or oppose efforts to make a proposal excessively vague, at least with the matters they deem particularly important. Personal discussions with a proposal's friends and foes will bolster friendly amendments and soften or avert hostile ones.

Enacting Policy

Practitioners use analytic skills when developing a political strategy to enact policy. They analyze the context, identify the power resources available to them, evolve a coherent political strategy, and use their political skills to implement the strategy.

Interactional skills help practitioners during the political process. They need access to people with inside information about the strategies their opponents are likely to use, and they use their persuasive skills to convert people to their side and to keep opponents on the defensive. Policy practitioners need group skills, such as the ability to work as leaders or staff in commitees, to develop and sustain coalitions, to diagnose why specific groups are not working, and to help task forces accomplish their work.

Policy practitioners confront some ethical issues during the political process. They must decide when tactics such as dishonesty are ill-advised and when they are necessary to defeat a well-organized opposition that is also playing hardball politics. It is difficult to establish inflexible ethical rules because realities, such as the opponents' tactics, often influence ethical choices. Moreover, political tactics often involve options that are not all bad, such as blatant lying, but only partly bad, such as withholding sensitive information from opponents.

Implementing Policy

Policy practitioners use analytic skills to decide what kinds of organizational arrangements will help implement specific policies; for example, hiring bilingual staff and establishing decentralized offices to help Spanish-speaking people obtain preventive health services.

At this stage, policy practitioners often must use political skills as well. Perhaps specific groups or individuals who wish to defend their turf decide to undermine a program's implementation or to preserve outmoded procedures; perhaps legislators who promised to support a program decide to allot it insufficient resources after it is enacted.

Implementing a social program requires collaborative relations among the program staff, and often with other agencies and programs that must provide referrals, consultation, and resources. To develop collaboration, policy practitioners often must use interactional skills, as in mediating disputes and forging interagency agreements.

Many issues arise during implementation that require the clarification of values. For example, because resources for social programs are scarce, staff members must decide which clients will receive priority. When policy advocates are themselves the implementers of a specific policy, whether in direct service or administration, they must decide whether to object to the failure of other staff to implement specific aspects of a program and when to do so.

Assessing Policy

Policy practitioners often participate in assessing operating programs to ascertain whether they meet specific objectives or criteria. When using analytic skills, practitioners must decide what kinds of data are needed, how to collect them, and how to interpret their findings. When assessing programs, policy practitioners often encounter political conflict. Some people may disagree about the criteria to be used; for example, whether a program's actual improvement of its users' well-being is more or less important than its efficiency. People may also disagree about how the collected data should be interpreted.

In conducting an evaluation, practitioners must use interactional skills to obtain the collaboration of many people. If high-level executives must grant permission to evaluate a program, for example, staff must share with researchers their insights about the program. Values intrude at many points during program assessments. For example, values shape the criteria selected to decide whether a program has been successful. That is, people might judge the success of a program for homeless people with mental illness by its effectiveness in removing homeless people from the streets, improving their self-esteem, or reducing the welfare expenditures of the county. The interpretations of research data are also shaped by values: One person might decide that the findings of a study justify the termination of a program, whereas another person might conclude that the data suggest enough success to merit continuation of the program.

Analyzing Policy Practice

Using the framework shown in Figure 3.1, we can describe policy practice during specific episodes; that is, relatively brief periods when practitioners perform one of the tasks. Or we can examine how policy practitioners perform a sequence of tasks; for example, an extended set of actions, verbal exchanges, and strategies. Indeed, we can envision a continuum extending from very brief episodes of policy practice, such as making a specific presentation, to a sequence that involves writing a policy proposal, seeking its enactment, and shaping its implementation.

We want to focus on certain episodes or extended sequences of specific people's policy practice to describe and evaluate actual instances of policy practice the same way direct-service and administrative practitioners and theorists describe and evaluate their work, by dividing it into specific episodes or sequences.

Our discussion of the six policy tasks and four policy skills helps us describe the episodic and sequential work of specific policy practitioners. As the following list shows, we can describe and evaluate someone's policy practice in ascending levels of generality: (a) using specific skills when working on specific tasks, or episodes; (b) using various skills when working on specific tasks, or episodes; and (c) accomplishing sequences of related tasks.

At the simplest level, we examine the use of a specific skill when a practitioner engages in a single policy task. We can evaluate the use of analytic skills (a single skill) in developing a policy proposal (a single task) by asking, for example, whether the practitioner became familiar with important social science research, consulted someone with technical expertise, and researched possible funding sources. We then can evaluate the practitioner's use of political skills by asking whether he or she examined the proposal's political feasibility and consulted with people who could secure support for it.

At a more general level, we can inquire about the practitioner's effectiveness in accomplishing a specific policy task that requires various skills. We can describe the combination of skills used to develop a policy proposal, whether there was an initial overall strategy, and whether the strategy changed as events unfolded. We might fault a practitioner who failed to supplement her or his analytic skills with political ones in a politically charged situation.

At an even more general level, we can examine the work of a practitioner who engages in several related tasks. We can ask how the practitioner not only constructed a specific proposal (one task) but also sought its enactment and implementation (two additional tasks). We might conclude, for example, that the practitioner exhibited technical expertise in writing the proposal but lacked the political skills to obtain its approval from decision makers.

Describing Policy Practice: A Case Example

A case from Edward Banfield's classic book *Political Influence* illustrates the policy practice framework presented in Figure 3.1.[11]

The Context

The staff of the Welfare Council of Chicago, directed by a social worker, believed that Cook County Hospital needed a new branch on the south side of Chicago, a large, low-income, primarily African American community. The massive Cook County Hospital was located on Chicago's west side, and many residents could reach it only by a long ride on public transportation. Some south-side African Americans obtained medical assistance from local nonprofit hospitals, such as Michael Reese Hospital or the Billings Hospital of the University of Chicago, but most had to travel a considerable distance to Cook County Hospital. Moreover, some African American leaders were angry that some south-side nonprofit hospitals dumped African American patients—that is, they told low-income African American residents to obtain medical assistance at the county hospital.

At the time of this case, the Democratic political machine and its leader, Mayor Richard J. Daley, Sr., dominated Chicago politics. Daley had tightly organized the city of Chicago, which was overwhelmingly Democratic, providing tens of thousands of city service positions in return for Chicagoans' support. Chicago was ringed by white and largely Republican suburbs, which provided a constituency for some Republicans on the Cook County Board of Supervisors. (The county includes both the city of Chicago and these white suburbs.) Democrats nonetheless firmly controlled the county board of supervisors under the leadership of Dan Ryan, himself a close political ally of Daley.

Constructing a branch hospital on the south side, which the Welfare Council strongly favored, would not be easy. The council would need county funds because public hospitals fell in the county's, not the city's, jurisdiction. Moreover, the council would need to find medical staff willing to work at the branch hospital and would have to make difficult decisions about which services the branch would provide. Should it, for example, provide only outpatient services, or should it provide surgical and diagnostic services as well? These logistic, financial, and planning challenges were small compared with the problem of securing political support for the branch hospital. Karl Meyer, the long-time director of Cook County Hospital, adamantly opposed building a branch hospital. Would it not be cost-effective, he asked, to expand the existing county hospital, rather than to invest funds in a new facility? He also contended that it would be difficult for a nonteaching hospital to obtain interns, residents, and top-notch physicians. (The county hospital was a teaching hospital). Some people believed that Meyer also feared that a branch hospital would dilute his power at the county hospital, which provided many jobs for Democratic Party supporters. Moreover, Meyer was a close friend of the powerful Dan Ryan. Thus, he had an important possible ally in the forthcoming battle over the branch hospital. It was not certain, however, where Ryan stood on the issue. By contrast, the Welfare Council was poorly connected to the power structures of city and county politics. Its large board consisted of businesspeople and professionals. These people sat on the boards of hundreds of Chicago social agencies, which the Welfare Council funded. They tended to be highly educated and affluent people, but they did not participate in the machine politics of the Daley administration.

Despite the seeming importance of the issue to the south-side African American community, no widespread support of the issue had developed there. The traditional spokespersons and interests on the south side included a powerful newspaper; an African American congressman affiliated with the Democratic machine; and some civil rights groups, such as the Urban League.

The Policy Tasks

Were we to analyze the policy practice of the Welfare Council leaders, we would describe how they addressed each of the specific policy tasks. (Because this is a complex and extended case, they addressed several tasks rather than merely one.) In building an agenda, the Welfare Council had to decide how to elevate interest in the issue by the county board of supervisors, which was preoccupied with countless other issues.

In analyzing the problem, the Welfare Council members established a rationale for constructing the branch hospital. Because the need for an additional facility seemed to be widely recognized, their primary strategy was technical: They asked their research and planning department, headed by Alexander Ropchan, to demonstrate the feasibility of constructing and staffing a branch hospital. They developed data that suggested it would be less expensive to build and staff the facility than some critics had suggested, and they obtained evidence that interns, residents, and physicians could be found to staff it.

The Welfare Council members undertook the proposal-writing task in which they estimated cost and staffing and described the kinds of services the branch would provide. They hoped, for example, that it would not be merely an outpatient hospital but would also provide family-practice, surgical, and specialty services. By contrast, others had suggested that it be only a feeder hospital to the county facility, offering relatively few outpatient services.

The council members assumed a policy-enacting task when they sought funds from the Cook County Board of Supervisors to build a full-service facility. When the county board eventually approved instead a bond issue to fund a major expansion of Cook County Hospital, the Welfare Council threatened to defeat the bond issue. As a result, the board made some concessions to the council. It dropped the bond issue and the plans for expanding Cook County Hospital and earmarked some funds for the eventual purchase of a site for a south-side hospital.

Had the branch hospital been constructed, the Welfare Council members might have assumed the policy-implementing and policy-assessing tasks. They would have participated in some deliberations regarding the policy's implementation; for instance, securing adequate annual funding from the county board, enhancing the hospital's outreach services to the surrounding community, and increasing its role in preventive programs, such as fighting the lead poisoning of children who ate lead-based paint in tenement houses. They could have helped assess the policy by examining whether the branch hospital had successfully prevented or treated specific kinds of illnesses, had met certain cost or efficiency objectives, and had fulfilled any other objective that had been established.

To understand the actions (or inactions) of the Welfare Council, we need to place its policy practice in the context of political, technical, value-clarification, and interactional factors. Indeed, we could not evaluate the council's work without taking into account the Democratic machine, Dan Ryan's power, Karl Meyer's strong preferences, and the lack of strong support by the south side for a branch hospital.

Using Skills to Accomplish Policy Tasks

To describe the Welfare Council's work in this case, we not only need to enumerate the policy tasks they undertook, but also to describe if and how they used analytic, political, interactional, and value-clarification skills.

To examine the use of various skills, let's look at the Welfare Council's work in analyzing problems, writing proposals, and enacting policy. When analyzing the problem of medical service on Chicago's south side, the council focused on the inaccessibility of traditional outpatient and surgical services to south-side citizens. Because they framed the issue this way, it was almost a foregone conclusion that they would advocate constructing a full-service public hospital on the south side. Indeed, they devoted much of their analytic work to proving that it was feasible to build and operate a large public hospital there. They used their political and interactional skills to try to convince decision makers such as Dan Ryan and Karl Meyer that they had framed the issue correctly. They issued a technical report and sent people to inform Ryan and Meyer of their conclusions.

In evaluating their problem analysis skills, then, we would conclude that they used analytic skills to document the lack of hospital facilities on the south side, and political and interactional skills to inform powerful decision makers of their position.

They also used analytic skills to develop a proposal for funding a south-side hospital, and they used interactional and political skills to inform high-level officials of their recommendations and to demand funds so construction could begin as soon as possible.

Convinced of the rectitude of their position, they saw no need to compromise or change their proposal to make it more acceptable to Ryan and Meyer and their followers and, indeed, maintained a relatively intransigent position during most of the policy deliberations. When Ryan sought Welfare Council participation in a task force he had established to study the issue, they maintained their righteous posture, at one point reading their position to the task force members with the clear implication that they would not accept amendments. They confined their interactional and political skills to enunciating their initial position.

When it became clear that those in power did not concur and, indeed, wanted instead to enlarge the existing hospital rather than build a south-side hospital, the Welfare Council quickly shifted strategy. Without amending or changing its own proposal, it sought to mobilize widespread opposition to Ryan's plan of enacting a bond issue to fund an expansion of Cook County Hospital.

When undertaking the policy-enacting task, the Welfare Council used its analytic skills to decipher political alignment on the issue. The council members apparently concluded that highly placed officials, such as Ryan and Meyer, were unlikely to favor a south-side hospital, but they seem also to have assumed that public opinion, particularly on the south side, would rally to their position and ultimately pressure the county to construct the new facility. Indeed, this optimism increased their intransigence with both Ryan and the task force he had established to examine the issue. They used their interactional skills during the policy-enacting task to convince Ryan and others that they would not negotiate.

When Ryan's task force recommended that the county vote on a bond issue to fund an expansion of the west-side facility instead of the construction of a new south-side branch, the council decided that the outcome was all up to public opinion. They assumed a negative or blocking role at this juncture as they sought to convince the county to withdraw the bond issue proposal. They organized a coalition of Chicago social agencies affiliated with the Welfare Council. They also allied with officials of Michael Reese Hospital, a nonprofit south-side hospital that wanted a public south-side hospital to ease the burden placed on its facilities by nonpaying patients. The council also obtained some coverage in a major local paper, which criticized the plan to expand the county hospital. Members of the coalition packed a public meeting on the issue and voiced their displeasure at the county's plans.

The Welfare Council was chagrined to discover that its campaign to defeat the proposal had not attracted the broad support of south-side African Americans. It had assumed that the major African American newspaper, politicians, and community groups would rally to its side, because, after all, it sought to build a major new medical facility in their district. The council was so optimistic that it would receive widespread support that it had not extensively consulted African American leaders or citizens. In fact, some African American leaders, who were concerned primarily about discrimination against African American patients by some south-side nonprofit hospitals, feared that constructing the public hospital might encourage even more dumping of indigent African American patients. Other African American politicians were beholden to the Democratic machine—and Ryan was a powerful member of that machine.

The Welfare Council eventually succeeded in forcing Ryan to change his position because he doubted that the bond issue would be approved if public opinion was divided. He agreed to give much less money to fund a relatively small outpatient clinic on the south side and a modest expansion of Cook County Hospital. It appeared in retrospect that neither side had prevailed: Ryan and Meyer had failed to secure a massive expansion of Cook County Hospital, and the Welfare Council had failed to secure a full-service south-side public hospital.

In characterizing its use of skills when trying to enact its proposal, we might conclude that the Welfare Council oscillated between a relatively optimistic posture early in the case, when it assumed most people would ultimately accept its position that a south-side facility was needed, and a relatively negative posture later in the case, when it assumed that Ryan would prevail without a determined public campaign to block his plan.

We have not yet evaluated the Welfare Council's policy practice in defining the problem, writing the proposal, and trying to enact policy. Was the council too dependent on its analytic skills during the problem-defining and proposal-writing tasks, excluding the use of political skills? Did it make erroneous judgments about political realities? Could it have made skillful advances to Ryan earlier in the case and acceded to some compromises that would have led to the construction of a south-side facility as well as an expansion of Cook County Hospital?

The Welfare Council's approach to policy deliberations was influenced by various personal, organizational, and situational factors. As officials of a charitable organization that stood outside Chicago's political system, the leaders of the Welfare Council did not know how to play Cook County's rough-and-tumble political game. The Welfare Council board members came from Chicago's affluent and well-educated corps of business and professional leaders and were disinclined to play ball with the political leaders of Chicago and Cook County. Accustomed to the detached position of providing technical reports on a variety of social problems in Chicago, the Welfare Council resorted predictably to a similar tactic in this situation.

Although there are explanations for the Welfare Council's lack of inventiveness in its strategy, we can nonetheless criticize the council. It committed a number of policy practice errors, such as relying excessively on a single skill and failing to assess the contextual realities.

Ballot-Based Advocacy

We have given an example of policy practice involving six tasks and four skills. But policy practice also includes the electoral style. We will not discuss specific political campaigns. That will be covered in Chapter Twelve. Suffice it to say that the six tasks and four skills also apply to developing and managing a political campaign. A candidate must decide when it is propitious to run for office in the context of background factors, her own track record, likely opponents, and likely assistance she will receive from funders and party officials *(agenda-building)*. She needs to decipher why her likely opponent is defeatable in the context of prior patterns of voting in the district and in public opinion polls *(problem-defining)*. She needs to make a case to contributors, volunteers, and party officials that her candidacy makes sense so that she stands a decent chance of winning *(proposal construction)*. She needs to actually wage the campaign by making correct strategy choices, mustering volunteers, raising funds, and using the mass media to her advantage *(policy enacting and policy implementing)*. Win or lose, she needs to assess her strategy and campaign organization so she can decide whether to run again, if she loses, or to develop strategy for the next campaign, if she wins.

Candidates need each of the four policy skills. They need political skills to devise strategy. They need value-clarifying skills to decide what tactics are ethical to use during the campaign, such as whether and how they would respond to (or initiate) hardball strategies like attacking opponents' records and integrity. They need analytic skills to initiate and debate campaign issues and to devise solutions to them. They need interactional skills to develop and maintain a campaign organization.

With the formation and expansion of PACE, the electoral style is becoming increasingly important to social workers. (See Video Clip 3.1.) Tens of thousands of members of NASW now contribute to PACE in connection with their annual dues. PACE carefully screens candidates across the nation, both in local and national races, to decide which of them will receive financial assistance from NASW.

VIDEO CLIP 3.1

HOW PACE WORKS

In viewing Video Clip 3.1, consider the following. David Dempsey, Director of Government Relations for the National Association of Social Workers, discusses the formation of PACE and how it works. Discuss these questions:

- What criteria should PACE use to decide whether a specific candidate merits financial support from PACE? (Try listing specific questions you might ask, drawing upon our discussion of ethics in Chapter Two.)

- With a limited pot to spend, should NASW also focus its resources on candidates seen to have a good chance of winning? How would you decide whether a particular candidate did have a chance of winning?

- Is it unethical for social workers not to give to PACE?

The Variety of Policies

Social workers confront policy issues at virtually every turn. The services they provide are dictated by policies from different sources: legislatures, government agencies, courts, funders such as United Way, contracts and grants that governmental authorities use to purchase services from agencies, professional associations such as the NASW, licensing and accrediting bodies, boards of directors of agencies, and administrative staff. We argued in Chapter One, as well, that some policies emanate from the informal culture of the staff who implement policies.

We do not suggest that these policies are restrictive, because they often provide implementing staff with considerable discretion. However, in many ways, they do shape the lives and work of citizens, clients, and implementing staff alike.

These policies vary in their effects and importance. Trivial policies have little importance, such as some of the detailed policies in agencies and programs. Others, however, have considerable impact on citizens and professionals; reformers should give these policies attention when they believe them to be dysfunctional.

Policies also vary in their malleability. Some are relatively simple to change because of their source, nature, and context. Practitioners find it much easier to modify a relatively simple, nonconflictual administrative agency policy than to change a controversial legislative policy that requires hundreds of legislators to concur.

Practitioners need not focus on a single kind of policy in their work; they can try to change simple or complex, agency or legislative, or controversial or noncontroversial policies. Our focus in this book, indeed, is on generic concepts that apply to any policy practice, no matter what the issue or the setting.

It would be possible, of course, to study policy practice in a more specialized way by focusing on specific settings like agencies or legislatures. We could also focus on a specific style of policy making like the analytic style. Alternatively, we could gear our discussion of policy to a specific sector, such as child welfare policy, rather than using a range of policy examples.

However, a broader treatment of policy practice has many advantages. Concentration on a single kind of policy, for example agency-based or legislative, would imply that that kind of policy should take precedence over other kinds. Concentration on policies that are relatively easy to change, such as some agency-based ones, would imply that social workers should not try to change more complex and controversial ones, such as legislative policies. Concentration on a single style of policy making, like the analytic style, would imply that this style is effective in all or most situations.

A generic approach to policy practice underscores the need for flexibility. Because policy practice occurs in many kinds of settings, takes many forms, and varies with the issue and the context, we believe it is better to understand concepts, skills, tasks, and frameworks that apply to a range of policy practice situations than it is to limit ourselves to a single style or situation.

The need for versatility in policy practice stems from the diversity of policy practices that social workers can undertake. Policy practice can occur inside and outside agencies, such as with line staff, supervisors, executives, community organizers who work with community groups and social movements, and lobbyists. Policy practice can occur in formally sanctioned or official projects, as when executives establish task forces to examine policy issues, or it can be informal, as when a direct-service worker decides to pursue an issue without the approval of higher officials. Policy practice can be planned or improvised, as when someone attends a meeting and decides on the spot to make a statement. Policy practitioners can assume affirming, blocking, or bystander roles. Practice can involve an extended sequence of actions or only one or two episodes. Policy practitioners may use only one skill suited to a specific situation, or they may use several skills at once. Policy practitioners may be leaders or initiators or followers regarding a specific issue.

A generic approach to policy practice, then, sensitizes us to the wide variety of policy practice situations and actions. It does not limit policy practice to specific styles, settings, or issues. It invites us to become participants in many ways and at different points in our professional work.

This generic approach offers no quick fixes or panaceas, however. Some issues are difficult to address, and some policies are relatively intractable. Policy making does not occur on a level playing field; some people bring more power resources to the game, some can invest more time, and some have more skill than others. Policy practitioners sometimes take some risks when they engage in practice, such as when employees try to change policies strongly favored by their employers. These cautionary notes should not, however, obscure the challenges and rewards associated with policy practice. Trying to change policies allows professionals to expand their boundaries and obtain the satisfaction that accompanies successful projects.

Overcoming Discomfort with Power

Many social workers do not participate in policy practice because they are disinclined to develop and use power. Powerless people sometimes enter a vicious circle: They are aware that they are powerless and avoid participating in policy practice, which makes them even more powerless. Social workers often work in programs that receive little support from the broader society or from the bureaucracies that they often must fight if they are to save programs. Moreover, most social workers are women. Rosabeth Kanter suggests that women are frequently excluded from the inner circles of power, which may erode the confidence they need to participate in policy practice.[12] This male-dominated society has also accorded background and supportive roles to women. When women and persons of color use power in ways that white males might, they are often perceived as aggressive and become the targets of animosity.

Although political skills are only one of four kinds of policy skills we have discussed in preceding chapters, they are essential to performing policy tasks. For example, people must use power resources, such as expertise and coalitions, to persuade highly placed officials to prioritize an agenda.

Using power is crucial in the policy-enacting task, to help enact or block proposals. It is also integral to implementing and assessing policy. Because of turf disputes, prestige questions, organizational hierarchies, and tradition, it is often as difficult to secure reforms during implementation as it is to enact policies to begin with. Selecting criteria, interpreting findings, and even deciding whether to undertake an evaluation are also strongly influenced by the power and interests of those who implement programs.

In addition to using power skillfully and assertively, effective policy practitioners must devote considerable time to developing power resources. They need to enhance their credibility by gaining access to networks of people who have information and power in specific settings.

Since developing and using power resources is integral to policy making, social workers severely jeopardize their ability to be policy practitioners if they are uncomfortable with power. Moreover, social workers need leadership skills so they can initiate and assume important policy-making roles.[13]

Social workers must realize that developing and using power are endemic in social work. Yeheskel Hasenfeld suggests the following:

1. Clinical social workers often use power.
2. They interpret their clients' problems in ways that conform to the mission of their agencies. They establish certain expectations about clients' roles during the helping process.
3. They use sanctions and penalties for clients whose responses to services fall outside specific norms or expectations.
4. They enforce (or choose not to enforce) agency procedures governing eligibility, referrals, and termination.
5. They proffer comments and suggestions that steer clients toward certain actions or decisions.
6. They take sides in family or other conflicts, sometimes in subtle ways.[14]

Indeed, if social workers did not use power in clinical transactions, clients would probably be disappointed. Clients expect their helpers, who presumably have considerable expertise, to guide them, offer informed suggestions, and establish realistic expectations. As agency employees, moreover, most social workers are instructed to enforce policies, procedures, and protocols. Certain ethical limits should be placed on the use of power; however, power is integral to the clinical roles of social workers and is not, as some imply, an unprofessional or unethical adjunct to social work. After all, administrators and community organizers often use power resources, and the literature of these disciplines is unlikely to deny it.

We need to demystify power and declare it a professional resource vital to both clinical work and policy practice. Like other professional skills, power needs to be observed, modeled, and practiced. Using simulations, role plays, videotapes, and films, and incorporating the concept of power into fieldwork, will help social workers learn about the use of power.

As the helpers of relatively stigmatized populations and as employees in chronically underfunded programs, social workers must grapple with such difficult questions as these: When is it futile to try to change specific policies or conditions? When can coalitions augment specific individual power? How does one overcome the vicious circle of helplessness that sometimes pulls in people with relatively little power?

We define *policy leadership* as "taking the initiative to develop new policies and to change existing ones to improve the human condition." People who initiate policy deliberations expose themselves to some risk, but they may also receive recognition and the psychological rewards of assuming a constructive, problem-solving role. We need to perceive leadership not as a burden but, like power, as an integral part of the professional role. When social workers fail to exert policy leadership, they allow other people with less commitment to clients' well-being and to oppressed minorities' needs to shape the human services delivery system.

Social Policy's Role in Ecological Frameworks

The importance of policy practice has always been merely implied in ecological, or environmental, frameworks, which continue to receive prominence in the social work literature that discusses direct service and human behavior. Perhaps because the writers of this literature tend to come from the direct-service segments of the profession, they usually fail to devote sufficient attention to policy practice.[15] The logic of environmental frameworks is clear; social workers who wish to help their clients have a professional duty to try to reform those factors that cause or exacerbate their clients' problems.

As we discussed in the preceding two chapters, changing existing policies provides one strategy for helping citizens and clients. Members of out-groups are subject to a variety of forces and policies (or the absence of policies) that make it difficult for them to improve their condition as compared to others. If social workers do not attempt to change these policies, they ignore key elements of the ecosystems of their clients.

Policy advocacy is, in short, a *professional* intervention because, like direct-service work, it is geared to improving the well-being of citizens and clients. We also argued in the preceding chapter that it is *unethical* not to engage in policy advocacy during one's career—and not to support efforts by the profession to lobby policy makers and to attempt to get progressive candidates elected to office.

Policy Practice as a Unifying Theme

As Phillip Popple suggests, it is a romantic idea to aspire to a profession that is wholly unified, when its members work in such different settings and undertake such different tasks. Indeed, he calls social work a "federated profession" that consists of various groups with different specializations and perspectives.[16] At the same time, however, if the profession lacks cohesion, it will fail to develop united positions and political clout on important issues like licensing and funding. Moreover, social workers will lack the strong professional organizations that can influence decision makers.

Perhaps policy practice and policy advocacy can serve as one unifying theme, because it is something that all social workers do, no matter what their specialization. It will allow social workers, singly and in groups, to shape the world to be more congruent with their values and to change those policies that profoundly affect the well-being of oppressed populations. Furthermore, it will infuse social workers with the broader vision of the profession's founders, as when Jane Addams tried to persuade decision makers to enact humane policies.

Chapter Summary

What You Can Now Do

Social policy has traditionally emphasized historical, philosophical, and descriptive content, but policy advocacy and policy practice are gaining prominence in professional literature. *Policy practice* refers to the skills and strategies of those who seek to modify policies, whereas *policy advocacy* describes efforts to change policies to gain greater resources and opportunities for powerless and oppressed out-groups. (See Policy Advocacy Challenge 3.3.)

POLICY ADVOCACY CHALLENGE 3.3

A SOCIAL WORK PROFESSOR ORGANIZES A NATIONAL COMMITTEE TO ADVOCATE FOR WELFARE RECIPIENTS

Robert Schneider, Professor, School of Social Work, Virginia Commonwealth University

In the summer of 1996, President Bill Clinton signed the "welfare reform" bill, and even though he said afterward that he did not like it and would work to change it, he and Congress had shifted the course of social policy in this country significantly. Not only did the bill radically change the entitlement programs, but the president's signing it clearly illustrated his commitment to the "new federalism" or "devolution" which transfers most of the responsibility for determining and implementing social policy to the 50 states.

As a social work educator, I watched these developments in August 1996 with frustration and a sense of futility. What would now be the fate of many vulnerable people whom social workers serve? Do the president and Congress really believe that the states will be equally caring and share their resources with their less powerful citizens? I could not accept doing nothing or going along with the new agenda. It was too much to ask, especially since I teach advocacy and policy practice to graduate students.

I asked myself what could be done to accept what had happened and then build a new direction that would be productive in the future. Living in Virginia's state capital, I have long used the state legislature as a laboratory for teaching students how the state policy process works and requiring them to participate each spring in the lawmaking session. Wouldn't it be potentially powerful, I thought, if all programs of social work located in state capitals required their students to become involved in the state policy-making process? I pondered this thought for a few weeks and expanded it. Even if a program in social work education is not located in a state capital, could faculty and students not learn how to influence state policy and legislation? Why not? After a few more weeks, I decided to try to organize a meeting to explore this idea with other social work educators. With support from my dean, I wrote to all 650 graduate and undergraduate programs in December 1996 and asked them to send a representative to a Saturday night meeting in Chicago during the Annual Program Meeting of the Council on Social Work Education (CSWE). In the interim, I decided to use my upcoming sabbatical semester to prepare for this meeting and organize a national network to promote an intensive campaign to convince students and faculty to learn how to influence state policy and legislation.

During the next two months, I did many things to launch my idea.

- I met with leaders of social work at the national level and asked for their feedback on my idea. I learned something from each one of them. I knew that I would need their support in the future.
- I personally invited key leaders or experts in social work policy education to our special session in Chicago.
- I wrote a draft set of papers: mission, goals, and objectives; rationale, potential student projects, and faculty assignments; bibliography; all 50 state legislatures' E-mail addresses; and potential resources that could be developed for faculty and students.
- I set an agenda for the meeting and brought copies of my draft documents and a sign-up sheet with me.

On March 8, 1997, on Saturday evening at 7:30 P.M., at the Chicago Sheraton Towers Hotel, I walked into the Colorado Room not knowing what to expect. Competing with the pleasures and food of a great city on a weekend night, I hoped for a few faces,

(continued)

(3.3   continued)

but I was not overly optimistic. To my surprise, approximately 30 people were waiting for me, including the president and executive director of the National Association of Social Workers. (Remember that I had sent out over 650 letters and special invitations and only 30 people came.) To me, it was a group large enough for a base of support and energy to move ahead. In the next hour and a half, I presented my vision of a national committee and, using my draft documents, highlighted current trends and issues and began suggesting future steps the group might consider. The members of the group were enthusiastic, and we informally approved our agenda for the next year. It consisted of the following:

1. Establishing a board of advisers from a list of prominent social work policy experts, leaders, and students.
2. Creating a Web site that would provide resources to students and faculty nationwide. One member offered to establish a temporary site the next week and succeeded in doing so.
3. Forming a national network of liaison faculty members. One liaison would be located in each of the 650 social work educational programs and would serve to communicate locally with students and faculty.
4. Identifying a variety of student projects and faculty assignments related to influencing state policy. These items could be shared with other faculty and students nationwide.
5. Initiating a survey of all social work educational programs to determine the extent to which state policy is emphasized in courses, field, and curricula.

At the close of the "Chicago meeting," some individuals contributed money and asked to be involved.

Of course, I returned to Richmond very heartened and filled with determination. I now believed that my plan to get social workers involved in state policy making was possible, even though much remained to be achieved.

After the March meeting, I immediately wrote to the 30 attendees and summarized our agreement. Eventually, I asked individuals to serve in various task groups reflecting our basic agenda above. I set August 15, 1997, as a target date to achieve our immediate goals. I wrote to all deans and directors again and asked them to assign a faculty member to be the liaison with our committee. I began organizing communication systems: E-mail networks, address labels, and phone/fax numbers. Within two months, I had recruited 19 outstanding social workers, educators, and students to serve on the board of advisers. Most of them were eager to support our mission—as long as there were not many meetings to attend!

I also based my planning and organizing on theoretical premises and data. Essentially, what our committee was attempting to do was to introduce a new idea and behavior into social work education. We were trying to "change" people's attitude toward policy, and *state* policy in particular. Old ways of doing things are never easy to modify, but researchers have uncovered some principles that will, if followed, increase one's chances of successfully introducing innovations. Information from the research literature on the "dissemination of innovation" and from "cognitive dissonance" theory formed the theoretical basis of our committee's activities.

By August 15, 1997, the national committee had achieved several goals and was contemplating the next six months' direction and planning:

1. A national network of liaison faculty members was forming, with 145 persons already assigned by their programs. An additional request was made to the programs in August.

2. A small grant application to cover immediate expenses was submitted to a national group.

3. A permanent Web site was designed and launched statepolicy.org.

4. *Influence,* a biannual newsletter of the committee, was published in August.

5. A national contest to identify the best student project and the best faculty assignment related to state policy was announced nationally. Winners would receive $100 cash, a free one-day pass to Disneyworld, and an engraved plaque and would be recognized at the next annual meeting of CSWE in Orlando in March 1998.

6. Long-range planning and funding became high priorities for the committee. New task groups will be formed and an agenda for three or four years is under discussion.

7. The committee had presentations at three national conferences of social workers accepted in 1997–1998, and speakers will inform their audiences of the committee's mission and goals.

Hopefully, there will be more to report in the future. The vision of this committee is to improve the efficacy of social workers in influencing state social policy, to involve faculty and students in learning about the state policy-making process, and to connect social work practice with policy practice. I believe the vision has been developed and initiated, but there is much implementation to do. Let's hope for the best.

"By July, 2001, this committee, now named 'Influencing State Policy (ISP),' had achieved other goals in its efforts to assist social work students and faculty:

1. A national contest, State Policy Plus, awarded cash prizes of over $4,800 and plaques for four years in a row to over 30 BSW, MSW, and Ph.D. students and faculty for projects and assignments that involved students in state legislative processes.

2. Over 90 percent of the MSW programs and 70 percent of the BSW programs had an official liaison serving ISP's mission across the country. There were 540 individual liaisons in the 163 MSW programs and 453 BSW program.

3. The website, had received over 12,000 visits since fall, 1997, and the monthly average had climbed to 500 during the academic year.

4. ISP received a grant to produce a 25 minute video, Making a Difference: Influencing State Policy, in 1999, and has distributed 960 copies of it nationwide.

5. Another goal of ISP was to encourage students to visit annually their state legislatures. 4,164 students in 2000 and 4,647 in 2001 made a personal visit to their legislatures.

6. In fall, 2001, ISP began offering a $2,000 stipend to Ph.D. students in social work who focused their dissertations on research or analysis of state-level policy.

(continued)

(3.3   continued)

7. Members of ISP analyzed current social work accreditation standards on policy in curricular guidelines of the national accrediting body and recommended several changes that were adopted.
8. ISP collaborated with The Urban Institute and Charity Lobbying in the Public Interest, both in Washington, DC, to disseminate research and materials on state welfare reform and lobbying.
9. In fall, 2001, ISP mounted a campaign to encourage social work programs to develop field placements for students directly with state legislators.
10. A video series, Legislative Advocacy, began production in 2001 with several 40 minute videos featuring social workers who were acting as lobbyists, coalition builders, and budget specialists.

After nearly five years in existence, Influencing State Policy, has developed an effective structure with active representation in most social work educational programs. Each liaison is a crucial link to faculty and students. Email and list servers assist in disseminating information quickly. Over 250 dues paying members provide funds along with an annual auction. Students who never imagined themselves in state policy and politics now realize that they are capable of introducing change at the legislative level on behalf of their clients. Clinicians and macro social workers all respond positively to ISP's slogan: "Policy affects practice; practitioners affect policy." (See Video Clip 3.2.)

VIDEO CLIP 3.2

***HOW* INFLUENCING STATE POLICY *WAS* FORMED**

In viewing Video Clip 3.2, consider the following. Professor Robert Schneider discusses the formation and operations of *Influencing State Policy*. After viewing the clip, discuss these questions:

- What policy practice tasks did Dr. Schneider undertake?
- What policy practice skills did he use?
- Can his work be characterized as *policy advocacy* as opposed to policy practice?
- How does this case illustrate the importance of persistence and risk taking in policy advocacy?
- What does the case demonstrate about social workers' power in influencing social policy?

You are now equipped to do the following:

- Diagram a policy-practice, policy-advocacy framework with a context and six tasks
- Discuss four policy-practice skills
- Identify stakeholders in specific policy-advocacy situations
- Identify four styles of policy advocacy
- Take a case study of policy advocacy and identify policy tasks, skills, and competencies used by participants
- Discuss why power is essential to policy advocacy

- Discuss why policy advocacy is an interventive discipline just as direct-service practice, administrative practice, and community organization are practice disciplines
- Discuss why policy advocacy can be a unifying theme for the social work profession

Policy advocates not only need a task- and skill-based framework, such as the one developed in this chapter, they also need knowledge about the way policies are developed in legislative, agency, community, and electoral situations—which we provide in the next chapter as a prelude to discussing the six policy-advocacy tasks in succeeding chapters.

Notes

1. See Hedrick Smith, *The Power Game: How Washington Works* (New York: Ballantine Books, 1988), pp. 215–269.
2. Peter Bachrach and Morton Baratz, *Power and Poverty* (New York: Oxford University Press, 1970), pp. 17–38.
3. Mary Jo Bane, "Welfare as We Might Know It," *American Prospect* (January–February 1997): 47–55.
4. Robert Montjoy and Laurence O'Toole, "Toward a Theory of Policy Implementation: An Organizational Perspective," *Public Administration Review* 39 (September–October 1979): 465–477.
5. Jack Rothman, "The Interweaving of Community Intervention Approaches," *Journal of Community Practice* 3 (3/4): 69–99.
6. For a discussion of building agendas, see Robert Eyestone, *From Social Issues to Public Policy* (New York: Wiley, 1978), and John Kingdon, *Agendas, Alternatives, and Public Policies* (Boston: Little, Brown, 1984).
7. Kingdon, *Agendas, Alternatives, and Public Policies,* pp. 95–105.
8. Ibid., pp. 182–184.
9. Smith, *The Power Game,* pp. 331–387.
10. Ron Dear and Rino Patti, "Legislative Advocacy," in *Encyclopedia of Social Work,* 18th ed., vol. 2 (Silver Spring, MD: National Association of Social Workers, 1987), p. 371.
11. Edward Banfield, *Political Influence* (New York: Free Press, 1996), pp. 15–56.
12. Rosabeth Kanter, *Men and Women of the Corporation* (New York: Basic Books, 1977).
13. Eleanor Brilliant, "Social Work Leadership: A Missing Ingredient," *Social Work* (September-October 1986): 327–328.
14. Yeheskel Hasenfeld, "Power in Social Work Practice," *Social Service Review* 61 (September 1987): 475–476.
15. For an exception, see Carel Germain's contribution to Samuel Taylor and Robert Roberts, *Theory and Practice of Community Work* (New York: Columbia University Press, 1985), pp. 30–58.
16. Phillip Popple, "The Social Work Profession: A Reconceptualization," *Social Service Review* 59 (December 1985): 560–577.

Suggested Readings

Value-Clarifying Skills

Robert Moroney, "Policy Analysis Within a Value Theoretical Framework," in Ron Haskins and James Gallagher, eds., *Models for Analysis of Social Policy* (Norwood, NJ: Ablex, 1981), pp. 78–102.

Martin Rein, "Value-Critical Policy Analysis," in Daniel Callahan and Bruce Jennings, eds., *Ethics, the Social Sciences, and Policy Analysis* (New York: Plenum Press, 1983), pp. 83–111.

Analytic Skills

Brian Hogwood and Lewis Gunn, *Policy Analysis for the Real World* (London: Oxford University Press, 1984).

Carl Patton and David Sawicki, *Basic Methods of Policy Analysis and Planning* (Englewood Cliffs, NJ: Prentice Hall, 1993).

Political Skills

Eugene Bardach, *The Skill Factor in Politics* (Berkeley and Los Angeles: University of California Press, 1972).

Charles Linblom and Edward Woodhouse, *The Policy-Making Process,* 3rd ed. (Englewood Cliffs, NJ: Prentice Hall, 1993).

Hedrick Smith, *The Power Game: How Washington Works* (New York: Ballantine Books, 1988).

Building Agendas

Joel Best, ed., *Images of Issues: Typifying Contemporary Social Problems* (New York: Aldine de Gruyter, 1989).

John Kingdon, *Agendas, Alternatives, and Public Policies* (Boston: Little, Brown, 1997).

Marc Ross and Roger Cobb, *The Cultural Strategy of Agenda Denial* (Lawrence: University of Kansas, 1997).

Smith, *The Power Game,* pp. 331–444.

Analyzing Problems

Hogwood and Gunn, *Policy Analysis for the Real World,* pp. 67–87, 108–127.

Patton and Sawicki, *Basic Methods of Policy Analysis and Planning.*

Enacting Policy

Donald deKieffer, *The Citizen's Guide to Lobbying Congress* (Chicago: Chicago Review Press, 1997).

Eric Redman, *The Dance of Legislation* (New York: Simon & Schuster, 1973).

Smith, *The Power Game.*

Implementing Policy

Yeheskel Hasenfeld, "Implementation of Social Policy Revisited," *Administration and Society* 22 (February 1991): 451–479.

Robert Montjoy and Laurence O'Toole, "Toward a Theory of Policy Implementation: An Organizational Perspective," *Public Administration Review* 39 (September–October 1979): 465–477.

Assessing Policy

Richard Nathan, *Social Science in Government: Uses and Misuses* (New York: Basic Books, 1988).

Patton and Sawicki, *Basic Methods of Policy Analysis and Planning,* pp. 300–328.

4

Understanding the Ecology of Policy in Governmental, Electoral, Community, and Agency Settings

This chapter provides a road map to legislatures, communities, agencies, and electoral politics in the United States. The map does not tell us what route to take or how fast to drive, but it orients us to the landscape so that we can better find our direction once we have started the trip.

To be effective, policy advocates must understand how decisions are made in each of these four arenas, how broader forces influence decision making, what rules or procedures are commonly used, who the key players are, and what the mindsets of key officials are.

We discuss the following in this chapter:
- The cast of players in governmental settings
- The mindsets of public officials
- The legislative process
- Social agencies in their political and economic context
- The players in organizational settings
- Community-based organizations that influence policies
- Electoral politics

The Players in Legislative and Governmental Settings

Anyone who conducts policy advocacy in the governmental sector must know who the key players are and what motivates them. (See Policy Advocacy Challenge 4.1.)

**POLICY
ADVOCACY
CHALLENGE 4.1**

*FINDING
INFORMATION
ABOUT POLITICAL
INSTITUTIONS ON
THE WEB*

*Stephanie Davis,
Research Librarian,
University of California,
Irvine*

Political institutions have an enormous impact on social policy. The importance of maintaining an awareness of the happenings of the political scene cannot be stated strongly enough. The sites below will help you to become knowledgeable about the structure of the government, how it works, and who the major players are.

• How our Laws are Made: A detailed description of the federal legislative process.
• THOMAS: Search engine for federal bills and laws, links to biographical information, and links to additional congressional Internet services.
• United States Senate: Links to Senators' Web sites, legislative agendas, votes, and more.
• United States House of Representatives: Links to Representatives' Web sites, legislative agendas, votes, and more.
• The White House.

Exercise: Using the search engines discussed in Chapter One, and the evaluation techniques discussed in Chapter Three, visit these Web sites and answer the following questions:

• Who are your state senator and your U.S. senator?
• What are their top legislative agenda items?
• Is there any information about their campaign finances on their Web sites?
• Who is their constituency?

Out-groups and Stakeholders
One of the best uses of the Web is to promote social justice. Organizations that represent out-groups and stakeholders often use the Web to focus on the issues and challenges faced by a specific population. One excellent example is the National Organization for Women. Another good example that focuses on an issue rather than a population is the National Mental Health Association.

Using the previously mentioned resources (do not forget the Checklist), find additional Web sites for out-groups or other stakeholders that measure up to your criteria standards.

Let's discuss elected officials (politicians), bureaucrats (unelected officials), lobbyists, and the interest groups with which they are affiliated. (See Figure 4.1.)

Elected Officials

We can distinguish three kinds of elected public officials: heads of government, such as mayors, governors, and the U.S. president; legislators, such as city councilpersons, members of county boards of supervisors, state legislators, and federal legislators; and officials elected to specialized public entities such as school boards.

Heads of government   The head of government (or chief executive) is the elected official charged with developing an administration. Thus, we name an administration after its leader, as in *the Bush administration.*

Although some local governments have nonpartisan elections, heads of government are often the titular heads of their political party in their specific jurisdictions.[1] Once he was inaugurated, for example, George W. Bush effectively became the national head of

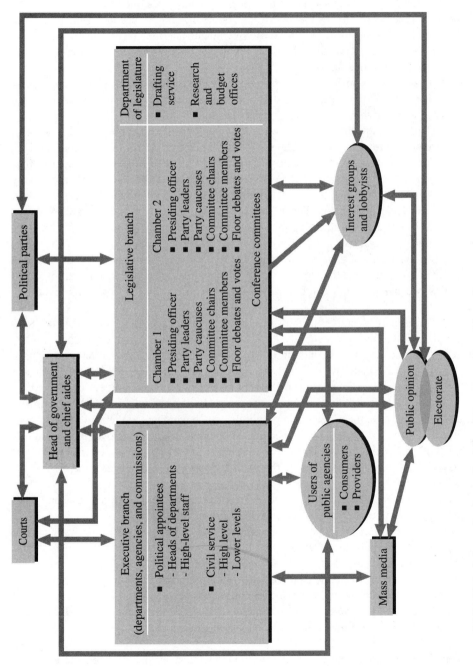

FIGURE 4.1   A schematic view of government and key players

the Republican Party, just as many mayors and governors head their political parties in their jurisdictions.

Heads of government usually have some guiding principles that shape their approach to the central issues they confront. As the differences between Ronald Reagan and Franklin Roosevelt show, a head of government can often be characterized as relatively liberal or conservative. Of course, ideology does not always predict how a politician will vote on specific issues.

Heads of government and other elected officials want to establish positive, popular records for their administrations that appeal to members of their own party as well as to other groups that they hope will enlarge their political base.

Their central position in government and their constitutional powers make heads of government pivotal in the unfolding of policy while they are in office. First, the U.S. president is in charge of the executive branch of government, which comprises the myriad agencies that implement federal governmental policies. These agencies are usually called *departments,* such as the Department of Health and Human Services (DHHS). State and local governments have similar organizations, with a head and executive branch. Heads of government appoint the high-level officials in the executive branch's departments or agencies.

Second, heads of government usually initiate a budget, even though the legislators make many of the final budgetary choices. This initiating role represents an important power because it allows chief executives to influence priorities within the executive branch.[2]

Third, chief executives usually develop a legislative agenda to which they often refer in general terms in speeches, such as the president's State of the Union speech. They have vast resources to help them fashion this legislative agenda. For instance, they have personal aides in their own office, their political appointees in the executive branch, and political allies who occupy powerful positions on legislative committees or in the party in the legislature.[3] Because heads of government have a central position in government and a high profile, their legislative proposals, which members of their own party or political allies introduce into the legislature, often have an advantage over individual legislators' proposals. Even with such power, the legislative proposals of many heads of government are defeated, particularly when the opposing party holds a majority in the legislature.

Fourth, chief executives often use their central position in government as a bully pulpit. Capitalizing on the extensive coverage the mass media usually accords them, heads of government often try to gain support for legislative measures, rally opposition against legislators who may block their policies, and educate the public about specific issues.[4]

Finally, heads of government can veto legislation that the legislature has approved, an important power since legislatures often cannot muster the votes (such as the two-thirds of each chamber required in the federal government) to override a veto. Some governors have line-item vetoes over the budgets that legislatures have approved; line-item vetoes allow heads of government to unilaterally change budget figures.

Legislators   Under the division of powers in federal, state, and local constitutions, legislatures have responsibilities and powers that often rival those of heads of government. Foremost, legislatures can develop, approve, and reject legislation. They use this power both to respond to legislation proposed by heads of government and to introduce their own legislation.

Legislators possess extraordinary powers over budgets. When they write legislation covering particular programs, for example, they often include the amount of the funds to be used for those programs in a specific year. Heads of government cannot exceed these sums when they make up their annual budget. In a separate process, legislators decide the total of the appropriations for a specific year and how to divide it among various programs. They usually begin with the budget proposed by the head of government but often make major changes in it.[5]

While not charged with actually implementing enacted legislation or writing the administrative regulations that will shape this implementation, legislatures engage in administrative oversight. Many of their standing committees hold hearings during which they ask high-level executive branch officials to discuss the operations of specific programs. Legislators also learn from their constituents about the operations of programs. When legislators believe they have found problems in programs, they have several remedies. First, they can amend the legislation that established the program. Second, they can convince executive branch officials to correct problems in programs by modifying their administration. For example, if legislators find that an existing program does not serve people with disabilities, even though they were intended to be part of the program when it was originally enacted, they might convince the program director to devote considerable resources to informing people with physical disabilities about the program. Third, legislators often use public hearings to expose issues, educate the public, hear feedback on proposed legislation, and put political pressure on heads of government and their appointees to correct problems. Indeed, as Hedrick Smith notes when discussing Congress, many legislators like to use the mass media to publicize specific issues, often in defiance of or without consulting senior legislators or party officials, whose power has diminished in the decades since Watergate.[6]

Legislatures seem formidably complex; in fact, they are all structured rather similarly. A diagram of the Wisconsin state legislature shows the essential structure of most legislatures. (See Figure 4.2.) Legislatures are usually divided into two houses, such as the House of Representatives and the Senate at the federal level, or the Senate and the Assembly at the state level, as in Wisconsin. Usually, both houses must assent to legislation or a budget before it can become operative. Many legislatures, like the U.S. Congress, convene annually, but some state legislatures convene only every two years. Moreover, the length of legislatures' sessions varies widely; Congress meets almost nonstop each year, but other legislatures convene only for several months.

The members of each house or chamber of a legislature, whether local, state, or federal, are elected by districts, whose precise shape changes over time. Districts are reapportioned as the population shifts and as the courts decide that existing district lines are unfair to specific groups, such as Latinos or African Americans. To understand specific legislators, then, we must analyze the characteristics of their constituents, whose preferences influence their positions on myriad issues. We might ask: Is the district relatively affluent or poor? Does it have a mix of ethnic and racial groups, or is it dominated by a single group? Is it urban, suburban, or rural? Is it dominated by a single party or evenly divided between two parties?[7] We can also ask whether specific legislators occupy relatively safe seats or whether they will face closely contested elections.

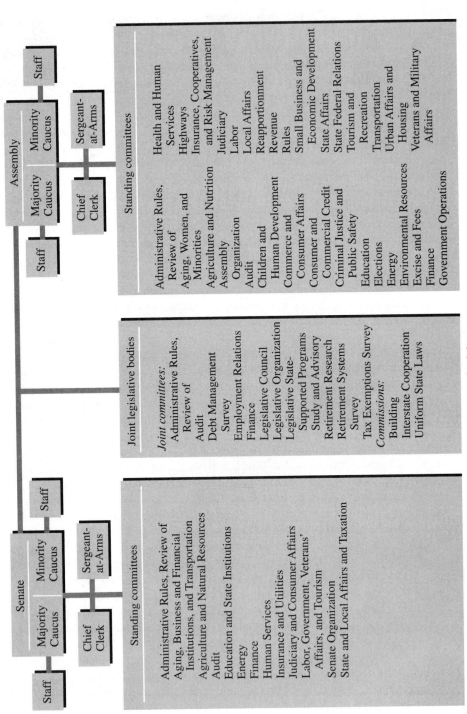

FIGURE 4.2   The structure of the Wisconsin state legislature

To understand how specific chambers of legislatures operate, we must first ask: Which party controls a majority of the legislature's members? The majority party appoints the chairs of all committees and has a majority of the members on each committee of that chamber. Moreover, the members of the majority party in each house elect the presiding officer of that chamber, such as the president of the U.S. Senate and the Speaker of the House. These high-level leaders have considerable power in determining when specific measures will be debated on the floor, in mobilizing support for or against measures, and in making important parliamentary decisions at critical junctures in floor debate. Presiding officers often have the authority to establish committees, assign members to committees, and appoint chairs of committees. In addition, they often have the power to decide where to route specific bills for deliberation. This power is critical because a presiding officer can often kill a bill by insisting that it go through specific committees that are known to be hostile to it.[8]

Each chamber has a second tier of powerful leaders: the floor leaders, who are also elected by caucuses and include the majority leader and the majority whip. Working in tandem with the presiding officer, these party leaders shepherd legislation through floor deliberations and decide which measures their party will support or oppose.[9]

A third tier of leaders, the chairs of the important committees of a chamber, are members of the majority party and have considerable power over the fate of legislation in their committees.[10]

Though at a disadvantage, a minority party often has considerable power in a specific chamber. It has its own leader, such as the U.S. House minority leader, who can mobilize support of or opposition to pieces of legislation. The minority party is allocated seats on all committees of a chamber in proportion to its share of the chamber's total membership, and its members sometimes obtain a majority vote on a committee by teaming with committee members of the majority party. Thus, in the era of Presidents Reagan and Bush, Republicans could defeat congressional legislation that the Democrats strongly favored by joining with southern Democrats, even though the Democratic Party had a majority in the House of Representatives throughout the period and controlled the Senate from November 1986 onward.

Because of their size and the myriad issues they consider, legislatures are divided into specialized committees. In the federal House of Representatives, for example, the Ways and Means Committee processes Social Security, Medicare, and tax legislation; and the Committee on Labor and Public Welfare processes social programs such as Head Start. (See Figure 4.2, which lists the committees in each chamber of Wisconsin's legislature, and Box 4.1, which lists the committees in each chamber of the U.S. Congress.)

As we have discussed, the presiding officers of each chamber often have considerable discretion in referring measures to committees. Many pieces of legislation go to multiple committees when they pose issues that cut across committee divisions. In other cases, certain kinds of legislation are automatically referred to a specific committee. Social Security and Medicare legislation, for example, are always considered by the House Ways and Means Committee and the Senate Finance Committee in the U.S. Congress.

Each legislative committee has its own internal structure. Its chairperson may be elected by the committee's members or appointed by the chamber's presiding officer. Committee chairs are usually powerful figures. Like presiding officers of the overall

BOX 4.1   **Standing Committees of the U.S. Congress**

Senate	House
Agriculture, Nutrition, and Forestry	Agriculture
Appropriations	Appropriations
Armed Services	Armed Services
Banking, Housing, and Urban Affairs	Banking, Housing, and Urban Affairs
Budget	Budget
Commerce, Science, and Transportation	District of Columbia
Energy and Natural Resources	Education and Labor
Environment and Public Works	Energy and Commerce
Finance	Foreign Affairs
Foreign Relations	Government Operations
Government Affairs	House Administration
Judiciary	Intelligence
Labor and Human Resources	Interior and Insular Affairs
Rules and Administration	Judiciary
Small Business	Merchant Marine and Fisheries
Veteran Affairs	Narcotics Abuse and Control
	Post Office and Civil Service
	Public Works and Transportation
	Rules
	Science and Technology
	Small Business
	Standards of Official Conduct
	Veteran Affairs
	Ways and Means

chamber, they can kill legislation by not placing it on the committee's agenda, by referring it to a hostile subcommittee, or by merely raising strong objections to it when the committee discusses it.[11] Each legislative committee has subcommittees that specialize in certain issues, within the whole committee's purview. Subcommittee chairs also have considerable power over issues that fall within their domain.

Legislation that presiding officers refer to a committee falls into two categories. Some of it is consigned, more or less at once, to the legislative junk heap because the committee, much less the full chamber, does not consider it seriously. The subcommittees and committees take other legislation seriously and mark it up in committee deliberations; that is, they amend it in various ways.

Most legislation, then, evolves in the course of deliberations that take weeks, months, or even years, and it can be amended on the floor of the chamber when the whole chamber decides whether to amend, accept, or defeat a bill.

Figure 4.3 shows the usual trajectory of legislative proposals, though many variations are possible. A bill usually starts in one chamber, progresses from committees to a floor debate and then a vote. It is then referred to the other chamber, where it follows a

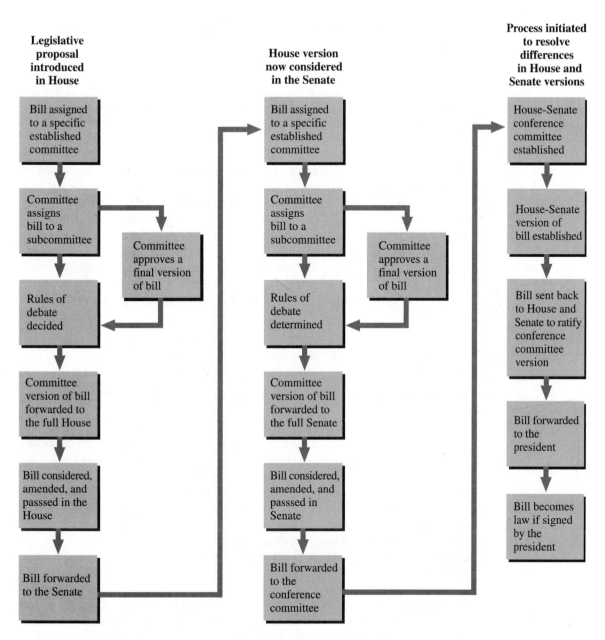

FIGURE 4.3   The route that a typical bill follows in the U.S. Congress

similar course. After the second chamber enacts its own version, representatives from each chamber seek a common version, which usually requires both chambers to make concessions. If the conference committee creates a joint version, each chamber must then ratify it before it goes to the president (or governor), who then signs it into law or vetoes it. Congress can override a veto if each chamber musters a two-thirds vote. Otherwise, the legislation dies.

Some legislative deliberations are relatively straightforward; relatively few amendments are offered and legislators move quickly to a decision. Other legislative deliberations, particularly those concerning controversial issues, are marked by various parliamentary maneuvers, such as the opponents' efforts to derail the legislation. In unusual cases, opponents in the Senate will even filibuster a bill by talking nonstop to prevent a concluding vote. Filibusters are not allowed in the House.[12]

Officials elected to special bodies   Officials elected to some special political bodies, such as school boards, wield considerable power within their areas. Other political bodies, such as county boards of supervisors and city councils, have markedly different structures from those of the state and federal legislatures. They consist of a single chamber, and the election of their members is often nonpartisan; that is, the candidates have no party affiliations on the ballot. Many differences exist among cities; for example, some have mayors elected by the public, and others elect their mayors on a rotating basis from the city council. It is beyond the scope of this discussion to elaborate on the differences in city governments, but policy practitioners need to be versed in them to participate in local politics.[13]

Unelected Officials or Bureaucrats

Legislators are far outnumbered by unelected public officials who work in government agencies in city, county, state, and federal jurisdictions. These public officials are either political appointees or civil servants.

Political appointees   Political appointees are high-level persons appointed to top jobs by heads of government, such as mayors, governors, or the president. They serve at the pleasure of the heads of government. They do not have long-term job security, because their mentor may dismiss them if they fall into disfavor, if they are considered to be a political liability, or when a new head of government comes into office. This new leader usually dismisses the prior staff and appoints his or her own nominees. Political appointees become spokespersons and representatives of their mentor, as when they discuss their administration's policy positions at press conferences. They are likely to have the same ideology as their mentor.[14]

Civil servants   Unlike political appointees, civil servants obtain their jobs through competitive exams. They are hired at a specific level or grade in the civil service hierarchy and then are promoted to higher grades based on annual job reviews by superiors. Those in higher grades have more power than those in lower grades, though there are many exceptions. Unlike political appointees, civil servants usually have job security, though they can be terminated as a result of funding cutbacks.[15]

Civil servants are the engines of government bureaucracies; they administer programs, draft regulations, collect data, and disburse funds to programs. Most civil servants outlast particular administrations. Indeed, civil servants are the permanent government, with real powers that equal or even exceed those of some political appointees.

Even though they receive their positions by competitive exam rather than by political appointment, some civil servants have close ties with legislators. They may have worked in the legislature as aides, and they may have developed relationships with other aides or with the staff of legislative committees.[16]

Lobbyists and Interest Groups

Lobbyists are professional advocates who represent interest groups or causes. Hired by corporations, trade associations, professional organizations, or groups representing specific populations or issues, they voice their perspectives to legislators and to officials in the executive branch of governments.[17]

We can distinguish between powerful lobbyists, who represent interest groups with considerable money and clout, and shoestring lobbyists, who represent groups with relatively little money and clout. Lobbyists' power depends on several factors. Truly powerful lobbyists not only have funds to make campaign contributions to the legislators they wish to woo, but also to entertain them by hosting special events, taking them out to meals, paying them to address special meetings or conferences, and even funding special trips for them. Powerful lobbyists often have considerable technical resources; their affluent interest groups can hire researchers and consultants to provide legislators with proposals and technical reports. Powerful interest groups in various states and in Washington, DC, such as the American Medical Association, do not hire single lobbyists; they often hire teams of lobbyists large enough to speak to most of the people in a specific legislature during a given period. They increase their clout further by forming coalitions with other lobbyists and interest groups with similar concerns. The American Medical Association, for example, may team with other medical interest groups and even with some corporations to support or oppose specific pieces of legislation.[18]

By contrast, shoestring lobbyists serve smaller and poorer groups. Often acting alone, they lack the resources to make even minimal contact with many legislators, to make large donations to campaign coffers, or to entertain legislators. Their relative poverty should not imply, of course, that they are powerless; they can shape public policy on certain issues by carefully using their resources, establishing coalitions with like-minded interest groups and lobbyists, and mobilizing their constituencies to pressure public officials—for example, by writing letters to them—on important occasions.

Lobbyists' character also shapes their effectiveness. While the general public widely views lobbyists as slippery and devious, they need reputations as straight shooters to be successful with legislators. Lobbyists who are caught telling lies, such as claiming someone supports a measure when she or he does not or giving deliberately misleading information, soon lose their credibility. Lobbyists must be persistent and must not let specific defeats deter them. They must like to engage in endless networking with legislators, civil servants, and interested citizens to form relationships that will help them achieve their goals.

Lobbyists' power hinges, of course, on the groups they represent. When we examine external pressures on legislators, then, we need to consider the power of specific interest groups. They obtain their power partly by hiring skilled lobbyists, but they also offer carrots (rewards and incentives) and sticks (implied or actual threats). The incentives include campaign contributions from political action committees (PACs) to specific politicians, volunteers to help with campaigns, and technical assistance on issues. The threats include withdrawal of these carrots, the endorsement of opponents in primaries and general elections, and the provision of funds and volunteers to opponents.[19]

Some interest groups that begin with relatively scant resources augment their power by building a reputation for the quality of the technical information they give legislators. The Children's Defense Fund and the Center for Budget and Policy Priorities in Washington have, for example, attained key positions concerning an array of issues, even though they lack the resources of the American Medical Association. By securing foundation funds, with which they have built a core of sophisticated researchers and have evolved a national constituency, these groups have developed credibility for their research and their principled positions.

Think tanks, which are institutions that conduct policy research and disseminate evaluations of specific policies, have also emerged to represent a range of perspectives. They issue periodic reports that carry considerable clout in Washington, as well as in the state capitals.[20]

Connections Among Interest Groups, Legislators, and Bureaucrats

Important relationships exist among lobbyists, legislators, and bureaucrats. Many lobbyists, for example, are former legislators, civil servants, or political appointees. Many civil servants are former aides to legislators, with whom they maintain important relationships, such as passing them "inside information."[21]

While commentators sometimes exaggerate their power, iron triangles link civil servants, legislators, and lobbyists (or interest groups) when the legislature considers specific issues. For instance, if legislation about child abuse goes through a state legislature, several people who know each other and have worked together in the past may become active. Such a collaboration may include lobbyists associated with children's advocacy groups; an association of the directors of public child welfare agencies around the state; professional associations, such as the state chapter of the National Association of Social Workers; a key civil servant in the state's welfare department; and an aide to a legislator with a long-standing interest in child abuse. Sharing similar points of view and past patterns of collaboration, these people may cooperate and bargain to develop a mutually acceptable policy and then may pool their resources to seek its enactment.

We do not want to imply that such relationships exist on all issues or that their power precludes important roles for other participants. But those who try to change policy in legislative settings need to be aware that these relationships exist and that they can be tapped into for technical advice or for the support of a specific measure.

Public Opinion

Politicians, bureaucrats, and lobbyists work in an environment of uncertainty. They realize that voters can end a politician's career and can bring down an administration.[22] Bureaucrats are also vulnerable to public opinion because scandals or unpopular decisions can ruin political appointees' and even civil servants' careers.[23] Legislators often try to implement programs in ways that will please their constituents, as illustrated by politicians who oppose placing mental health facilities and prisons in their districts.

However, measuring public opinion is an uncertain art. Politicians often read polls, but they realize that even accurate polls cannot predict future changes in public opinion. Politicians often gauge public opinion through mail from constituents and from talking to constituents in their legislative offices and in their home districts.[24]

The Electoral Process

To say the very least, the electoral process is highly competitive, because very few elections are uncontested at any level of government. The electoral process is the institutionalized guts of any democracy; it provides a nonviolent way of solving the problem of succession to office. It is competitive because it is a win-lose conflict where only one candidate can win.

The precise formats of elections are described in legal statutes and regulations that prescribe how candidates get on ballots, how votes are counted, how runoffs are held, how campaigns can be financed, and how long the terms of office are.

These precise rules vary widely not only between jurisdictions, but regarding specific kinds of offices. Rules that govern school board elections, for example, are very different from rules that govern federal elections.

Let's discuss the electoral process from a developmental perspective, from the early maneuvering by possible candidates through the actual elections.

Early Maneuvering

Long before most elections are held, potential candidates decide whether they want to make a run for a specific office. Potential candidates are sometimes approached by other persons, such as leaders of local, state, or national parties who want strong candidates who will have a chance at winning an office. Incumbents (persons already holding office) ponder whether they wish to run for office again—or whether they want to retire from public service, move into a government bureaucratic job, or seek yet another, often higher, office.

When deciding whether to run or rerun for a particular office, people consider various factors. Nonincumbents consider whether specific incumbents are vulnerable, whether because of their track record in office, weakness in public opinion polls, access to funds, or the extent that they are backed by other opinion setters or party officials. They consider, as well, which other nonincumbents might run for a specific office, because their chances diminish to the extent other formidable candidates enter the race. They take into account the degree of name recognition they already possess or might develop in the course of a campaign, because name recognition is crucial in many elections. They also think about whether they can develop grassroots support during a campaign, such as by eliciting support from community groups, local leaders, and volunteers. (Such successful candidates as Democratic Senators Debbie Stabenow and Barbara Mikulski gained early success in electoral politics by cultivating relationships with local community groups.)

Nonincumbents' motivation to run for office is often increased when their positions differ markedly from those of the incumbents. By winning, they not only gain office but substitute their positions for those maintained by specific incumbents. Candidates with a commitment to social justice often see their public service in ethical terms—not just as a way to advance their personal self-interest.

Nonincumbents face a hard reality: the overwhelming majority of incumbents win elections when they decide to rerun for office. This is so for several reasons. Incumbents tend to have relatively high name recognition because of media coverage of their prior elections and their actions while in office. They can often raise money relatively easily from special interests they have helped through their policy decisions while in office. They know the electoral ropes because they have already been through one or more prior campaigns, and they often have support from local, state, or federal party officials who do not want to lose the incumbents seats to the opposing party.

We should not overstate the difficulties faced by nonincumbents, however. Incumbents sometimes are vulnerable. A nonincumbent can run for an empty seat when an incumbent retires or runs for another office. Nonincumbents realize, moreover, that some races are less demanding than others in terms of the resources, name recognition, and time that they require. Nonpartisan elections, such as for school board, local planning councils, and positions on township or city councils, usually do not require the level of resources and name recognition required in partisan elections. Many nonincumbents begin their careers by not running for office at all: they get appointed to commissions in local jurisdictions or start their careers by obtaining jobs in government agencies or as aides to office holders. With a public-service base established, they can then scan the horizon for possible electoral races.

Seeking elective office is not for everybody. It takes time and effort, and it exposes persons to attacks from opposing candidates. Yet the rewards are numerous for persons who are elected to public office; they can make vitally important public-policy decisions because they are insiders whose votes count. Social workers possess characteristics that make many of them ideal candidates for public office. (See Video Clip 4.1.)

VIDEO **CLIP 4.1** *HOW POLICY* *ADVOCATES RUN* *FOR OFFICE*	In viewing Video Clip 4.1, consider the following. For a discussion of the way social workers can seek public office David Dempsey, Director of Government Relations for the National Association of Social Workers, discusses how social workers can run for office. Ask yourself the following questions: • What kinds of skills do social workers possess that are useful in running for office? • How does someone get started?

Running Campaigns

Once nonincumbents decide to run for specific offices, they must wage successful campaigns to secure those offices. Their first challenge is to get on the final ballot by prevailing in primaries or in nonpartisan races with more than two candidates. Primaries are partisan elections in which representatives of specific parties must defeat members of their own parties to get on the final ballot where they are pitted against the representatives of opposing parties. Al Gore and George W. Bush emerged on the final ballot in 2000, for example, by defeating such opponents as Bill Bradley and John McCain in primary contests. In nonpartisan contests with multiple entrants, the two candidates with the highest vote totals often appear on the final ballot if neither of them received more than 50 percent of the vote.

The key objective in any campaign is to get more votes than ones opponent. To accomplish this, candidates must find ways to persuade the voters who are already sympathetic to their positions to vote, and must get some undecided or swing votes as well. This requires them to engage in such tasks as the following:

- Develop positions on key issues that both speak to their natural constituency and appeal to some swing voters
- Make personal contact with many voters through campaign appearances and precinct walking
- Recruit and use volunteers to make personal contact with voters by phone and by precinct walking
- Reach voters through the mass media, such as through press conferences and debates with opponents
- Reach voters through advertisements in the mass media and mailings
- Increase the pool of sympathetic voters through voter registration, particularly in areas where public opinion is supportive

These activities, in turn, require candidates to raise campaign funds. These funds can come from friends, from political parties, from political action committees (see Video Clip 3.1 that discusses PACE on p. 90), and from personal resources. The amount of political resources required for a specific campaign varies widely depending on the competition for a particular office. In general, partisan races, hotly contested races, and races involving positions that imbue holders with great political power (such as races for state and federal offices) are more expensive than other races.

Once candidates face off, their ability to win partly depends on their skill in devising campaign strategy. They have to decide which issues to surface, what parts of the constituency to emphasize, how to respond to opponents' attacks, and how to get sufficient resources and volunteers to implement their campaigns. (We discuss campaigns in more detail in Chapter Twelve.)

Implementing public-service careers   Once candidates win their first election, they begin a public-service career. Some of them will be content to serve one or more terms in that office, but others will begin a decades-long public service career that takes them into multiple positions and offices. For example, Senator Debbie Stabenow, a social worker, became a U.S. Senator only after an extended career in which she held various lower-level offices. Some persons alternate between elected offices and offices in appointive positions in the government, as discussed in Video Clip 4.2.

The Mindsets of Elected Officials

Those who engage in policy practice in governmental settings need to understand the mindsets of heads of government, legislators, political appointees, and civil servants. Success in changing policy hinges on obtaining the help and support of these people.

VIDEO **CLIP 4.2** *HOW POLICY* *ADVOCATES* *DEVELOP PUBLIC-* *SERVICE CAREERS*	In viewing Video Clip 4.2, consider the following. David Dempsey, Director of Government Relations at the National Association of Social Workers, discusses how some social workers alternate between elected office and appointive or civil service positions. Ask yourself these questions: • Should some professionals envision a public-service career as opposed to more conventional careers? • What would motivate someone to select this option?

Policy practitioners can understand officials' mindsets only by examining the environment that shapes their choices.

The Environment of Public Servants: Elected Officials

Imagine that you have just spent two years planning, fund-raising, and campaigning to obtain your job. You have narrowly defeated a determined opponent who has already pledged to prevail in the next election, which is several years away. In response to this threat, you are likely to have reelection on your mind throughout your tenure. You will look at most issues with an eye to their effect on your reelection, and you will spend hours wondering about the general public's preferences. To deduce their views, you will study the following:

• Public opinion polls
• Recent outcomes of other elections in comparable districts
• The mail you receive
• The views of subgroups within your constituency, particularly those that you believe will support you in the next election
• The preferences of state or national organizations—for example, professional associations or groups such as the American Association of Retired Persons—that might contribute funds to your next campaign

Moreover, you will nervously eye the statements and positions of potential opponents in the next election. In some cases, you will support an issue to steal the thunder of your likely opponents, and in other cases you will openly support issues that they oppose to publicize your differences from them. In districts divided between liberals and conservatives, relatively liberal candidates often support liberal issues to solidify their support among liberals. They realize that without committed support from this constituency, they may lose to conservative opponents.[25]

This nonstop campaigning will make you sensitive to the political ramifications of certain choices. Some issues, such as increasing funds for city parks, will cause you little or no concern. However, issues seen as more controversial by important segments of your constituency will make you hesitate before committing yourself.

If elected officials often have their ears to the ground, they are also extraordinarily busy. Assume that you are a member of several major committees and subcommittees, each of which handles many issues on which you need to brief yourself before and during policy deliberations. As you hurriedly read technical reports and briefing papers, you simultaneously try to raise funds for your reelection bid. You make weekly trips back to your district to meet with its citizens and convene regularly with lobbyists from various interest groups. Constituents also come to your offices every day to speak with you. While a caseworker (this title is used even though these persons are not usually social workers) helps you process many constituent requests, you also devote some of your energies to specific requests, such as that of an older woman who wants help in coping with her husband's Alzheimer's disease.[26]

You also are concerned about your relationships with your legislative and party colleagues. Although at times you are a relatively independent legislator who wants to make a name for yourself, you also are part of larger systems that, much like an organization controls an employee, place some limits on your actions, such as pressuring you, decide in certain situations, to go along with policies and procedures you dislike. Because you want to increase your status within these systems, you must play by their rules. As a member of legislative committees and subcommittees, you know that the chairperson holds great power and can often determine which issues will receive a serious airing in the committee and which amendments will be enacted. You belong to a political party, as well, which meets regularly, agrees collectively to support or oppose certain measures, and parcels out rewards and penalties, such as committee assignments and campaign funds. If you are a complete renegade, you will suffer reprisals from high officials on your legislative committees and in your party.

Shortcuts: Aides, Lobbyists, and Priorities

With such a full agenda, you need to develop shortcuts. You have to rely heavily on aides to manage the bulk of your interactions with constituents, lobbyists, and others.[27] You are not afraid to delegate much of your work to these trusted aides, because without them, you cannot function. You create a division of labor by hiring specialists in legislative matters, in handling constituent demands (such as the woman who wants help with her husband's Alzheimer's disease), in fund-raising, and in public relations. In other cases, you rely heavily on lobbyists to do technical work for you, to do reconnaissance work with other legislators, to help you draft legislative proposals, and to help you write amendments to existing legislation.[28]

Early in your term, you decide that you have to develop priorities by taking some pieces of legislation seriously, and only giving glancing attention to others. Suppose a constituent wants you to sponsor a piece of legislation (by sponsoring it, you place your name at its head with those of other sponsoring legislators), but you decide the legislation is not a priority for you. Although you agree to sponsor it as a symbolic gesture to keep your constituent's goodwill, you know you will not invest energy in promoting it. You decide, instead, to expend your political capital (your power resources) liberally on issues that may bring you large political dividends when you come up for reelection, or that appeal to you for other reasons.

The Calculus of Choice

Any policy practitioner soon discovers that several factors shape legislators' choices. Indeed, precisely because so many factors intrude, policy practitioners should refrain from discounting legislators whose voting records make them appear unpromising. We can divide the determinants of choice into eight categories. We have already discussed the *electoral considerations* that lead politicians to support or oppose measures, based on the preferences of voters, interest groups, and campaign donors.

However, electoral calculations are not always easy to make, because politicians often have poor information on which to base predictions of how the public will respond to an issue in a future election. Politicians often try to gauge what positions *existing and potential opponents* will take on issues. Then, these politicians can upstage their rivals, take important issues from them, or take the opposite position.

Personal values and life experiences also shape politicians' positions; for example, many politicians who have had cancer show strong support for medical research.

Politicians sometimes support measures because they want to *obtain credit* for initiating a measure by going public before rival politicians take action. For this reason, politicians in the House of Representatives often vie with senators to develop legislative initiatives, and Democrats often try to develop a measure before Republicans take the initiative.

Some politicians support measures in areas where they hope to become known as *personal experts.* In the late 1980s, Senator Christopher Dodd (a Democrat) and Senator Orrin Hatch (a Republican) sought reputations as experts on day-care legislation by vigorously and publicly supporting the Act for Better Child Care.

Although they often focus on the needs of specific interest groups, politicians sometimes attend to the *public interest,* particularly when they believe voters will hold them accountable for decisions that hurt the public interest.[29] Indeed, politicians sometimes support budget cuts and corporate tax hikes, even in defiance of powerful special interests.

Politicians often base their choices on *political feasibility.* They do not want to invest effort in measures that have little or no chance of passage. In some cases, of course, politicians support measures that they believe will not be enacted. They do this to publicize their position to important parts of their constituencies.

Policy advocates must also remember that many issues have surfaced before in legislative settings. Like the rest of us, legislators often are creatures of habit; *habit* or *tradition* shapes their position on some issues. Of course, people often change their minds as they receive new information or as political realities shift.

Politicians have to decide not only how to vote, but whether to invest considerable energy in specific issues. When they want to avoid offending someone but are not really committed to a measure, they may give it only symbolic support. In other cases, when they personally favor an issue but fear negative consequences, they try to keep a low profile in their support. Sometimes, they openly campaign for an issue. At other times, they act as bystanders and may even absent themselves from the final voting to avoid offending either the supporters or the opponents of the legislation. In still other cases, they may openly oppose it.

Public advocates for an issue are aware, of course, that their measures are most likely to succeed if they have the support of especially powerful political leaders, such as committee chairs, the presiding officer of a chamber, and party leaders. These high-level leaders have extraordinary power, not merely in expediting measures through the legislative process, but also in attracting support for them from other, less powerful legislators. Policy practitioners' chances also increase as they obtain sponsors from both parties and from both relatively liberal and relatively conservative politicians. Of course, such breadth of sponsorship is not always possible.

Our discussion of the mind-sets of elected officials suggests that policy advocates need to exercise caution in making premature judgments about legislators' choices. Many factors can impel them to support or oppose a measure and to invest energy in it. For example, advocates of food stamp legislation were tempted to write off some conservatives who usually opposed social reforms. However, they soon found that many conservatives were becoming ardent supporters, whether because they were beholden to agricultural interests (who believed the food stamp program would enhance markets for farm products) or because they were genuinely troubled by the specter of malnutrition. Moreover, some Republicans did not want Democrats to get sole credit for enacting and expanding the food stamp program, which they believed would be politically popular. Liberal advocates for enacting and expanding the food stamp program, who would have faced an uphill political battle, found these conservative allies indispensable on numerous occasions.[30]

The Mindsets of Nonelected Officials

Policy practitioners frequently seek assistance from nonelected officials, whether political appointees or civil servants.

Political Appointees

When dealing with political appointees, one must always remember that they were appointed by high-level political allies, such as heads of government. Appointees will not usually support, at least openly, legislation that these mentors would not approve. Therefore, one can expect political appointees to seek permission from higher authorities before they commit themselves publicly to a measure.

In the real world, however, high-level political appointees, such as the U.S. Secretary of Health and Human Services, often make choices in a relatively ambiguous context. They may like a measure (or an amended version of it) but may fail to get a definite opinion about it from higher authorities who want the measure to evolve in the legislative process before they decide whether to support or oppose it. In this situation, a high-level appointee might have some aides work on the issue and might even give technical assistance to advocates of the measure. In other cases, political appointees receive word from their mentors, such as a governor or the president, that certain features of a measure are unacceptable to them and will elicit a veto, but other features are acceptable. In these cases, the head of government attempts to influence a measure by threatening to veto it if the final version contains certain provisions. In yet other cases, high-level appointees engage in a dangerous game of defiance; they quietly give background support to a proposal's advocates, even when they know that the head of government opposes the measure.[31]

Heads of government decide to support or oppose specific measures in much the same way legislators do. However, they are probably more attuned to a measure's budgetary implications than many legislators, because governors, mayors, and the president initiate budgets.

The political appointees in government agencies are likely to be interested in the facets of a measure that they will be called on to implement. They will attend to details such as what resources the measure will need, what relationships will exist between different levels of government, and what rules (such as eligibility procedures) will be left vague or will be defined. Like heads of government, political appointees will be interested in a measure's budgetary implications, because part of its funds may come from the department or agency.

Civil Servants

As nonelected officials who do not depend on politicians for their job tenure, civil servants often have a different perspective from that of politicians or political appointees. They commonly view themselves as professionals with specific expertise, and are not under the same compulsion to act political. Nor can they commit their bureaucracies to a specific measure, because that prerogative is reserved for political appointees who head agencies.[32]

At the same time, however, civil servants work in a political environment. They have to be sensitive to the desires of the high-level political appointees who administer their departments, because they work under them, and their job promotions and job assignments are influenced by these executives. As lower-level staff in the elaborate chain of command of government, they often receive directives from high officials and may receive reprimands if they do not heed them.

Policy advocates who approach lower-level civil servants about proposed legislation should not expect them to endorse it, because departmental or agency approval can come only from the director. However, lower-level civil servants can provide indispensable technical information, such as reports, studies, and data germane to writing a proposal.[33]

The degree of cooperation that a policy advocate receives from civil servants varies widely. Some civil servants are extraordinarily helpful to those who ask for technical assistance, but others are relatively cloistered and appear to be irritated by external requests. Their cooperativeness is often related to their personal disposition, their values (whether they like the proposed project), and their perceptions of the advocate (whether they trust him or her). Advocates must often be persistent when seeking help from civil servants, but they must also be aware that civil servants are responsible for numerous tasks.[34]

Like political appointees, civil servants sometimes give low-profile assistance to causes that they like, even without high-level departmental or agency approval. Advocacy groups sometimes find reliable contacts in government agencies who give them inside information that enhances their work.

Strategy in Legislative Settings

We have provided an overview of legislative and other governmental settings. With a knowledge of the procedures used in these settings and the mindsets of the legislators and officials who inhabit them, policy advocates have to devise strategy for having legislation enacted. They need to know how to obtain assistance in developing strategy, how to find sponsors for their legislation, how to testify before committees, and how to use phone calls and letters to pressure politicians. Moreover, practitioners often try to create favorable conditions for their policies in legislatures. A practitioner might, for example, participate in a politician's campaign, attend political club meetings or parties, and contribute resources and time to a political action committee (such as PACE, the political action committee of the National Association of Social Workers). Chapters Twelve and Thirteen are devoted to methods of developing and implementing political strategy.

The Political Economy of Social Agencies

Just as policy advocates need to understand the structure and operations of legislatures, they must also be familiar with organizational processes to understand how social agencies work. It is useful to analyze social agencies' political economy as a prelude to examining their policies.

To survive, social agencies require ongoing, regular resources to meet their payrolls and other overhead costs. A few lucky social agencies are massively endowed by private donors, but the officials of most social agencies must frequently interact with institutions, accrediting bodies, and clients to maintain a steady flow of resources. When social agencies stop receiving support from external sources or find these sources severely constricted, they go out of existence, downsize, merge with other agencies, or renegotiate their relations with the external world by changing their mission, their fund-raising strategies, or their marketing strategies.[35]

Social agencies, which have always been shaped by their political and economic context, were subjected to a particularly harsh set of realities in the 1980s and 1990s. Traditional sources of public funds were constricted during the budget cuts and tax revolts of those decades, when many citizens sought to reduce property taxes or objected to the budget levels of local, state, and federal governments. Agencies that receive funds from campaigns such as United Way and the United Jewish Communities, which raise funds for a coalition of agencies joined in a federation, often found their allocations diminished. The resources of federated campaigns have been depleted by competition from other fund-raising groups, national economic difficulties that have decreased corporations' contributions, and scandals (in the case of the national United Way, whose chief executive was accused of a misuse of funds).

The restricted flow of money from governmental agencies and federated campaigns has meant that larger numbers of social agencies have competed for the scarce resources of foundations, corporations, and private donors. Many social agencies have also found it difficult to maintain a large enough proportion of paying clients. (The clients of many agencies have become poorer and are beset by serious mental, economic, and other problems in an era of increasing inequality in the United States.)[36]

The revenues of social agencies come from a variety of sources. To survive, agencies need resources from fees, foundations, donors, and government. They also need clients.[37] Some clients come directly to agencies through word of mouth, advertising, and outreach programs. Others are referrals, as when one agency suggests that a client use another agency's services, or when courts or probation departments require people to obtain specific agency services. Interorganization exchanges often shape the flow of clients to an agency, as when the staffs of two organizations agree to enter a reciprocal relationship. Two organizations may negotiate an agreement whereby each agency focuses only on certain kinds of clients, while referring other clients to the second organization. Agencies may also develop joint programs funded by collaboration in writing a grant proposal or seeking a contract.

Demographic, cultural, social, and technological factors also affect agencies profoundly, as when the population shifts, public opinion changes, and new perceptions of social problems, such as family violence, evolve. These changes influence the extent to which people use agency services, the social problems they have, and the agencies they believe are relevant to their problems. While we usually think that agencies, once established, are permanent, many agencies cease to exist when their environment changes. For example, many agencies used to provide residences for pregnant teenagers, where they stayed before giving their newborns up for adoption. With legalized, safe abortions usually available and with many young women choosing to keep their babies, many of these agencies have disappeared or markedly changed their mission.

Various pieces of legislation impose procedural requirements on social agencies, such as the Americans with Disabilities Act of 1990, which requires agencies to accommodate people with chronic physical and mental disabilities. Various state laws require agencies to report certain social problems, such as child abuse; to inform patients or clients of the risks of certain procedures; to adhere to severe procedural limits when taking children from their natural parents; and to work within restrictions when committing people involuntarily to mental institutions. Federal legislation places restrictions on the use of restraints in nursing homes. Court rulings, such as those forbidding discrimination against members of specific ethnic or racial groups, also influence the procedures of many social agencies.

As we discussed earlier in this chapter, legislation that establishes and funds social programs often dictates the kinds of policies that agencies must follow in implementing them. Some program details that were left vague in the original legislation are defined later when the high-level government agency charged with implementing the program adds administrative regulations.

Some nongovernmental bodies issue regulations that agencies must follow to be accredited, and inspect the agencies regularly to ensure that these regulations are being followed. Because unaccredited agencies may have difficulty hiring staff or recruiting clients, such regulations powerfully shape agencies' choices.

Community pressures on social agencies include community groups, organized groups of clients, or individual clients who may request or demand policy changes. Citizens can place pressure on agencies, particularly governmental agencies, by complaining to government officials about specific services or policies they dislike. Pressure sometimes also emanates from the mass media, as in horror stories about services that clients have or have not received.

Competition within the broader community places pressure on organizations and undermines the security that agencies find in relatively stable streams of clients and resources. In the face of competition, agencies sometimes have to alter their programs or face retrenchment or termination. For example, by the 1970s, many YMCAs and

YWCAs were depending increasingly on fee-based recreation and exercise programs for middle-class people but found their resources imperiled by the rise of profit-oriented exercise centers.[38] Many Ys were forced to retrench when they were unable to develop alternative programs.

To secure resources in the harsh era of the 1980s and 1990s, organizations had to negotiate and manage relations with their political and economic environments by building relationships with existing and potential funders; by developing services that appealed to sufficient numbers of clients to provide revenues; by satisfying external funders that their services met specific evaluative criteria; by developing public relations campaigns to attract funders and clients to the agency; and by modifying their services as competitors encroached on their traditional sources of clients. Funders and clientele shape organizations' policies, as do agencies' adjustments to their turbulent environment. Although rarely reaching the levels described in Policy Advocacy Challenge 4.2, conflict can occur in agencies as people develop different positions in the context of their values and the agency.

POLICY ADVOCACY CHALLENGE 4.2

AGENCY IN POLICY TURMOIL

The Case of Dr. Breeze and the San Marcos Community Mental Health Center
Samuel H. Taylor, D.S.W.

Exactly one year ago, Dr. George Breeze came to San Marcos, a metropolitan suburb of Los Angeles with a population of 60,000 people, to direct the recently established San Marcos Community Mental Health Center. Dr. Breeze had previously worked in Philadelphia, where he had acquired a reputation as the innovative, inspiring, and flexible director of Manford University's Outreach Mental Health Services Department.

When Dr. Breeze initially interviewed for his position, several board members expressed some reservations about how he would fit in, since he did not wear a tie and seemed almost overconfident. Dr. Sedgwick, the retiring director, calmed the board by saying that, as a young psychoanalyst, he too had been fairly unconventional. The board had to keep in mind that this was no longer the San Marcos Clinic, it was a new mental health center, and it needed new ideas and the dedication of the youth. "He will work out," Dr. Sedgwick reassured them.

Shortly after George Breeze arrived at the San Marcos Community Mental Health Center, he made it clear to the staff that waiting lists, long-term therapy, and supervision were outdated. In the following months, he:

1. urged short-term, crisis-oriented management of cases
2. requested and received permission to establish an advisory board of citizens from the catchment area and another board composed of consumers
3. abolished the supervision system and established a flexible peer-consultation system
4. asked staff members to work evenings in order to see families
5. got into an argument with the Chief of Police about how officers were handling youngsters and emotionally ill persons
6. hired paraprofessionals from a human services program of a community college to serve as community aides
7. told the staff that he wanted to know personally about the service and disposition of each case that involved a racial or ethnic minority client because he suspected that the staff members were allowing biases to influence case management

(continued)

(4.2   continued)

Within six months, the staff in the agency had become deeply divided. Three major groups had formed and developed leadership. First, some of the original clinic staff members (who had helped Dr. Sedgwick prepare the mental health center application) resented Dr. Breeze's nontraditional ways and felt that they had no chance to introduce their ideas. They rallied behind Dr. Jones, met privately, and decided that they must take their case to other agencies, in San Marcos and to local civic leaders and then must present their complaints to the agency board with the support of these other groups and leaders.

The staff hired by Dr. Breeze (young activist professionals and community aides) learned of the strategy and immediately alerted Asian, black, and Chicano groups in San Marcos and rallied behind Dr. Smith, who contacted both the National Institute of Mental Health (the prime federal funder of the center) and the Citizen and Consumer Advisory Boards. They were ready to ask for termination of federal and state funds if Dr. Breeze was fired.

Finally, a number of agency supervisors formed a group behind Dr. Virtue that advocated "responsible change." They were not opposed to all the changes instituted by Dr. Breeze but particularly opposed to those that deprived "professionals" of their rightful positions of authority and prestige within the agency. They wanted restoration of the supervisory system and curtailment of hiring of new careerists.

The issue reached crisis proportions when a patient being cared for by a community aide committed suicide in a most sensational manner. A reporter from the newspaper interviewed a member of the original staff and was told that "this would never have happened if Dr. Sedgwick had been there; Dr. Breeze's ideas just don't work."

The board decided to hold a meeting to settle the issue, and they agreed to allow representatives of all sides to present their evidence. They felt that Dr. Breeze had introduced some good programs but also felt that he was unconventional. At this meeting, they hoped to reach a final decision as to whether Dr. Breeze should be fired, retained (but only after placing limits on the reforms he had issued), or given a vote of complete confidence.

"Traditionalists," then, rallied behind Dr. Jones and wanted to restore the traditional mission of the agency—long-term therapy with white and middle-class clients. "Insurgents" supported Dr. Breeze and his various reforms with no qualifications. "Advocates of responsible change" wanted some innovations but not at the expense of the traditional prerogatives of professionals. The board wished to bring unity to the agency as soon as possible to avoid further adverse publicity as well as possible loss of funds.

Source: This case was developed by Professor Samuel H. Taylor, Graduate School of Social Work, University of Southern California. Names and locations have been altered.

We do not mean to suggest that political and economic factors wholly determine organizations' actions. Not-for-profit agencies have latitude in deciding, for example, which public contracts or grants to seek. Governmental policies that descend on public and nonpublic agencies are often vague or ill defined on many points, so the staff in these agencies have considerable discretion in shaping many details of their services. While noncompliance with governmental policies poses legal and ethical questions, agencies sometimes disobey specific policies or bend the rules.

The description of the harsh atmosphere for social agencies in the 1980s and 1990s, such as funding restrictions, should not suggest that they cannot maintain humane, caring services. Even when such restrictions stretch staff resources to the limit, many agencies deliver effective services. Skilled leadership allows many agencies to keep up staff morale even in difficult circumstances.

As they manage and plan relations with their environment, agencies also must attend to their internal operations: They have to build and maintain a staff, design programs, mediate internal disputes and conflicts, develop decision-making processes, produce budgets, attend to logistical tasks, and maintain their facilities. Indeed, social agencies may be unable to obtain a steady flow of resources if they lack a reputation for delivering quality services. In the case of not-for-profit agencies, for example, foundations often ask community leaders about a specific agency's reputation in the community. This reputation depends on people's perceptions of the services and staff of the agencies they interact with or hear about.[39]

The executive of an agency, then, must juggle many tasks if the agency is to flourish, devoting attention to the agency's relations with its environment while trying to develop internal processes that enable the agency to maintain quality services. Of course, executives often delegate tasks, as when they use fund developers and planners for external relations and program directors for internal matters.

The Political Economy of Programs and Social Work Units

We have discussed social agencies' political economy, but many social workers operate in large organizations dominated by other professions, like hospitals, public welfare departments, corporations, and schools. Others work in specialized units within a broader social service organization, such as adoption units within child welfare departments, programs for homeless persons within mental health clinics, and programs to help single mothers within family counseling agencies.[40]

Our discussion of social agencies' political economy applies in double measure to these units or programs within larger organizations. They depend on their host organizations for resources and for permission to perform specific roles or functions. In turn, the political and economic factors that impinge on the host organization influence the subsidiary programs' ability to command resources and mandates from that host organization.

To illustrate, consider the case of a social work unit in a hospital. Such a unit must hire sufficient staff to help patients in many parts of the hospital, including the emergency room and the oncology and outpatient departments. It also needs permission from various units of the hospital, as well as the top management of the hospital, to assign personnel to these areas. To obtain these resources and permissions, the social work unit must be exceedingly adroit in managing its relationship with the hospital's officials and staff; indeed, the hospital is a key part of the social work unit's political economy. (A more detailed discussion of the political strategies the social work unit can use to obtain resources appears in Chapter Eleven.) In turn, the hospital's willingness to allocate resources to the social work unit hinges on factors in its political and economic environment, such as hospital accreditation standards and the extent to which Medicare and private insurance will or will not fund social work services.[41]

Some program units within larger agencies derive funds from both the host organization and special external funders. A project for homeless persons in a mental health clinic, for example, might receive funds from a governmental agency or a foundation and funds or supplies from the host organization. The directors and staff of such a program would need to be attentive to both sets of funders to ensure the program's survival. If the external funding ended or decreased, the program's staff would have to try to convince the clinic itself to increase its funding of the program.

Mapping Agencies' Policies

Our discussion of social agencies' political and economic context leads us to consider the nature, varieties, and content of agencies' social policies. To better understand the nature of agency policies, try to imagine a social agency without policies. In such an agency, the staff members would do their own thing without the guidance of agency rules, regulations, protocols, or priorities. There would be no written mission statement and no manual to define procedures. It would be impossible for the staff members to describe the agency's activities to outsiders, such as clients and funders. And how would clients using an agency with no policies know which services they could obtain and for how long? How would they know their rights, or what protections or safeguards were in place?[42]

Policies govern the relationships among agency staff members as well, so staff members in an agency lacking policies would find themselves in a chaotic and unpredictable environment. There would be no personnel policies to establish staff's duties and rights, rules for termination, or protection from arbitrary treatment. Nor would such an agency have clear priorities established by the agency budget, which is itself a kind of policy.

Although policies cannot shape every detail of an agency's internal organization or internal dynamics, they typically provide an agency with a central direction, priorities, guidance for its operating programs, and some protections for staff and clients.

Figure 4.4 maps the variety of agency policies. It is a complex diagram because of the wide range of policies, which cannot be easily summarized.

POLICY ADVOCACY CHALLENGE 4.3

MAP OF AGENCY POLICIES

Using Figure 4.4 as an orienting framework, select a specific program in a social agency. Trace the following:

- Its history
- What combination of policies exist within it or define it
- What money streams are relevant to it
- How it is (or is not) supported or shaped by informal policies in the agency
- Whether it has implications for relations between the agency and other agencies
- How it might be changed or reformed in the context of agency politics so that it provides better services

---

Some policies are originally external to agencies but are then internalized, like the policies agencies accept when they take funding from governmental programs. These

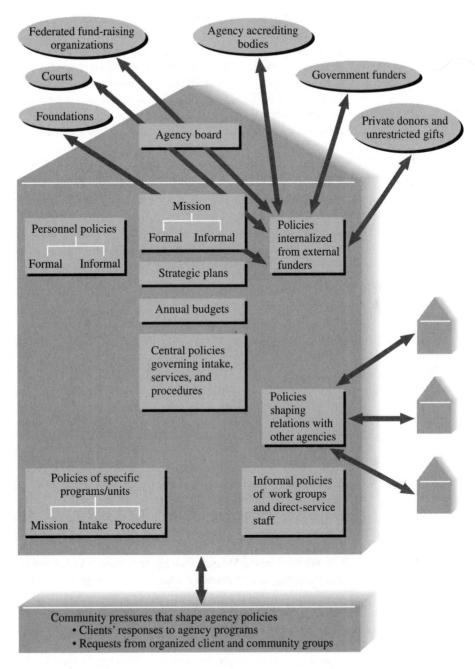

FIGURE 4.4   Map of agency policies

internalized policies establish specific rules, such as intake procedures, staffing requirements, content of services, reporting mechanisms, and a general statement about the program's purposes. An agency that has a number of externally funded programs (not-for-profit agencies now receive the majority of their funds from the government and from foundations) will have multiple sets, or clusters, of these externally established policies. Some details of funded programs are left relatively vague, so the agency's staff must fill the gaps with their own policies. (Of course, agency staff may ignore or even violate some of the funder's policies, though they run the risk that their omissions or violations will be detected during audits and monitoring.)

Court rulings shape agency policies as well, such as the *Tarasoff* decision, which requires social workers to inform intended victims when a client tells the worker that he or she intends to inflict bodily injury on them. Social workers who neglect to inform the threatened targets may be sued.[43]

The stipulations of nongovernmental agencies that purchase services that reimburse agencies (or their clientele) for specific kinds of services, such as health insurance companies, also affect agency policies.

Other agency policies are centrally established, even though external economic and social forces may influence their content. For example, most not-for-profit agencies have a mission statement that defines their priorities and direction.[44] One agency defines its mission as a career and job resource center created to serve a broad spectrum of women by helping them recognize and attain their employment and earnings potential in the work world through providing job and career resources in a supportive environment.

As you can see, mission statements are relatively vague; nonetheless, they establish the agency's general philosophy. In this example, the mission statement affirms certain activities, such as providing job and career resources, but not others, such as counseling services or mental health services. In addition to a mission statement, staff often have certain objectives, goals, or priorities in common. A staff member who says, "What makes us unique is that we like preventive services," or "We like to use outreach," suggests an overall approach to services that, she thinks, distinguishes her agency from other agencies.

Agencies' annual budgets also serve as policy statements, at least in part. They shape agencies' priorities by distributing resources to various programs, perhaps cutting funds for one program while increasing them for another. To fully understand an agency's policies, then, one must examine both its present and its previous budgets to determine its priorities and how they have changed.[45]

For services that it funds by itself, the agency must establish its own internal policies, such as intake procedures and the content of services. For example, a not-for-profit mental health clinic, might receive 50 percent of its annual operating funds from external funders (which shape the policies for those programs) and make up 50 percent of its budget from its own funds. The clinic would decide internally how to govern the intake, services, and other details of those programs funded with its own money.

Many nonprofit agencies receive funds from federated fund-raisers. Who then impose some of their own policies. They monitor the agency regularly and may make recommendations about the agency's internal priorities.[46]

In complex organizations, such as hospitals or government bureaucracies, many policies exist at the level of the unit, the bureau (or department), or the program. These smaller units often have their own mission statements. The following is the mission statement of one social work unit in a hospital:

> It is the mission of the Social Service Department to enhance the delivery of comprehensive health services by providing social services to the patients and their families of the University of Minnesota Hospitals and to assist in the resolution of social and emotional problems related to illness, medical services, and rehabilitation.[47]

These units usually have their own budgets, which the staff of the host organization review and approve, and their own policies. A social work department in a hospital may decide, for example, to fund social work services in one unit, such as the emergency room, but not in another, such as the neurology unit.

In addition to the budgets; mission statements; and official policies of agencies, units, or departments, many other policies are fashioned through informal systems and networks. While not documented, informal policies shape staff's actions and choices at many points in their work and deliberations. Informal policies may vary from official written policy, but they may also fill gaps when official policy is ambiguous.[48]

To illustrate the importance of informal policy even in the higher reaches of an agency, we will return to the discussion of an organization's mission. A written mission statement conveys a unity that is usually absent from organizations, because different staff members often have diverse and subjective notions concerning their organization's mission. While the official mission may, for example, stress services to families with single heads of households, some staff may want the agency to place more stress on serving intact families. Staff members may also disagree about the extent to which the agency should seek or accept governmental funds or about how intake policies should be structured. Sometimes, divergent notions of the agency's mission erupt into conflict, as when the organization selects a new director or when it deliberates over the agency's budget.[49] In other cases, however, staff may sublimate their differences and may even be unaware of some of them.

And on a very basic level, each agency employee will have a set of personal policies, or approaches, to his or her work. When confronting virtually identical client problems, for example, one staff member may provide services based on traditional psychotherapy, while another may emphasize survival skills, advocacy, and empowerment.

Personal policy preferences, as well as binding informal policies that many staff share, are neither good nor bad; they must be judged by their specific outcomes for the clients and the agency. If we decide that a worker's personal policy preferences or the informal policies of a group of staff result in prejudices against certain kinds of clients, such as gays, we will want to modify them. But sometimes these preferences and policies lead to positive outcomes, such as advocacy and outreach, constructive efforts to help clients, and extraordinary efforts to assist clients above and beyond the call of duty.[50] In addition, they sometimes help place legitimate limits on official policies, as when elderly patients are under pressure by hospital and Medicare administrators to leave the hospital as soon as possible after medical treatment. Disoriented by surgery and medications, such older persons often resist early discharge and find ready allies in social workers who help delay their discharge for one or more days. While operating in apparent violation of higher-level policy, these social workers can often justify their actions as being necessary for the well-being of their clients.

The Players in Organizational Settings

Anyone who seeks to change organizational policies encounters hierarchies and divisions of labor. These are the formal and structural characteristics of organizations that Max Weber emphasized in his classic writings.[51] A hierarchy is the chain of command that gives high-level executives such powers as creating high-level policies, hiring staff, and making budgets. The division of labor, or specialization, divides staff into units that focus on specific tasks, such as protective services, adoptions, and foster care in a child welfare office. While many organizational theorists have sought ways to soften hierarchy and specialization within organizations, they remain enduring, important features.

Some may associate these structural characteristics with control, rigidity, and fragmentation, but they also serve positive purposes. As productive collectives, organizations need powerful officials who focus on functions such as developing overarching policies, a mission, budgets, and planning. The complexities of the tasks in the modern welfare state often require specialization, both in the work of specific units or departments within the larger organization and in the work of the individuals within the units or departments.

Figure 4.5 provides useful clues to hierarchy and division of labor in a sample organization. The organizational units include those that provide specific kinds of services to clients and those that perform work for the larger organization, such as research and accounting. The figure also shows the distribution of power within the organization: The people toward the top of the hierarchy have certain formal powers.

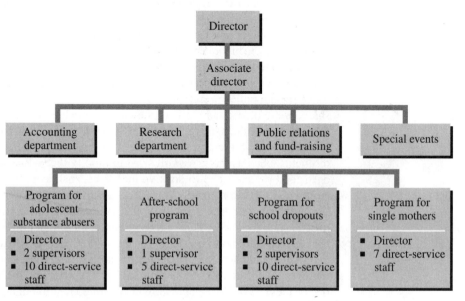

FIGURE 4.5   **Sample organizational chart**

Were we to attend only to the organizational chart, however, we would have an incomplete and distorted conception of the organization. Policy practitioners often want to know how power is distributed in organizations with respect to certain issues. While the organizational chart offers clues, it may overstate or understate the power of specific individuals.[52] The director of a relatively small unit, for example, may have considerable power with respect to certain issues and less power with respect to others.

To obtain a more complete understanding of organizational power, and other organizational dynamics and processes, we need to understand the interactions among the staff of an organization. We can conceptualize organizations as transparent overlays, placed on top of one another, that depict (a) the formal organizational chart, which displays the official hierarchy and division of labor; (b) the resources allocated to specific units, programs, or functions within the organization; (c) employees and internal programs that generate revenue, clientele, and prestige for an organization; and (d) informal relationships and patterns of consultation between members of the organization.[53] Of course, such overlays do not exist in the real world, but they provide a useful means of conceptualizing power and relationships within organizations. Together, these overlays provide useful, important information that allows us to build a fuller understanding of the dynamics of a specific agency.

Overlay 1: The Organizational Chart

Organizational charts tell us a great deal about the players in a specific organization. As we have discussed, people at high levels in the hierarchy, whether in specific units of the organization or in the broader organization, usually have powers and prerogatives that enable them to shape decisions. They help make budgets; participate in hiring, firing, promoting, and supervising lower-level staff; obtain access to information about the personnel, programs, and budgets of the agency; and have access to information about the resources and institutions in the agency's external environment.

We can sometimes infer a person's perspective from her or his position in an organization. Top executives are often concerned about the budget implications of specific choices, whereas lower-level professional staff often emphasize budget implications for clients and staff workloads. As intermediaries between management and direct-service staff, supervisors often share the perspectives of both higher-level and lower-level personnel. Those who direct or work in a specific program often view policy choices and agency budgets only from the perspective of that program.

The board of directors of nongovernmental agencies makes many important policy decisions. The board establishes an agency's high-level policies, such as its mission; hires its executive director; oversees the development of personnel policies; examines the agency's budget; and serves as the general overseer. Some public, or governmental, agencies also have advisory boards that offer suggestions to the top staff of the agency.[54] (The top executives of public agencies are ultimately responsible to those elected officials who appoint them, as discussed in the first portion of this chapter.)

An organizational chart, however, may be misleading. Some people in the higher ranks of organizations defer to persons who are horizontal to them or even below them in the formal chart. Organizational charts do not tell us which units or programs in an organization have considerable resources, and which ones the top executives favor. In addition, organizational charts imply that high-level persons make most general policy choices, but they do not tell us who has power with respect to specific issues. Many political scientists have observed that the distribution of power often varies with the issue; persons who are exceedingly powerful concerning certain issues may have little or no power regarding other issues.[55]

Overlay 2: Budget Priorities

We have noted that a budget is an important policy document because it establishes an organization's priorities. People who oversee program units with considerable resources, for example, often have more power than those who oversee units with relatively few resources. Examining budget trends in organizations can prove useful; if one unit has been losing staff positions while another has been gaining them, we can deduce that the power of each unit has changed. However, when considered individually, budgets may give us misleading impressions. Some persons who direct units with relatively small budgetary resources may have extraordinary power that derives, for example, from their close personal ties with other persons in the organization.

Overlay 3: Boundary Spanners and Mission Enhancers

Some persons are boundary spanners who have links with institutions, officials, and agencies that can bring substantial resources to an agency. They may have links to funders, such as staff in a foundation; a knowledge of funding sources or grant-writing skills; connections to elected officials (or their aides) who have power over the funds that go to the agency; a seat on an important committee in the host organization or in the community; or connections with key sources of referrals to an agency. Such people, who enhance agencies' resources and clientele, often derive power from these roles.[56]

Mission enhancers promote goals that highly placed persons in organizations favor. If the top officials in a hospital want to increase the number of older clients, they are likely to view with favor those units or officials within their hospital who they believe can advance this goal. Conversely, we can assume that units or staff whose activities are peripheral to the organization's central objectives are likely to have less power.

Overlay 4: Informal Relationships among Organizational Members

Some of the connections between persons in organizations are predicted by the organizational chart, but proximity in the organization's hierarchy does not tell us about patterns of friendship and trust, enmity, or social distance. Nor does it tell us about human contacts that span different units of an organization or that cut across levels of the hierarchy. Policy practitioners need to know about these relationships to understand processes and choices in organizations.

The formal organizational chart cannot tell us which persons will band together to enhance their power within an organization. Groupings take many forms. Some are ongoing informal clusters of persons who share knowledge and who support one another. Other groupings are constructed during specific controversies or crises, such as to oppose the termination of a program. Some groupings are relatively large; others consist of only a few staff members.

The Political Economy of Communities

Many kinds of communities exist. They may be so heterogeneous that they cannot easily be described, or they may be dominated by a specific group. Most neighborhoods within communities can be described by social class or economic variables, as well as by ethnic, racial, and age characteristics.[57]

As sociologists have long noted, communities have vertical and horizontal dimensions. When we discuss their vertical dimensions, we analyze the economic, political, and social institutions that descend on communities from the outside, such as supermarket chains, corporations, state or federal policies, the mass media, and social movements with local chapters or supporters. When we discuss their horizontal dimensions, we examine local civic associations (groups that advance a neighborhood's well-being), advocacy groups (local groups that promote specific causes), social agencies, public agencies, neighborhood groups, and churches. Moreover, social movements—that is, broad movements that foster social change, such as the civil rights movement of the 1960s and the Rainbow Coalition in the 1980s—sometimes develop local offshoots or chapters.[58]

When addressing specific issues in communities, such as where to place social service institutions or how to mobilize opposition to certain policies, policy advocates need to discover which community residents, leaders, politicians, and institutions have traditionally focused on this issue. Rather than a power elite that controls all issues, most communities have a series of elites that specialize in specific issues.

In seeking specific reforms in communities, policy advocates often affiliate with, consult, or enlist the support of community-based groups. These groups may include civic associations; advocacy groups; local chapters of national groups, such as NOW or the National Association for the Advancement of Colored People (NAACP); or local offshoots of social movements. Policy practitioners sometimes form coalitions representing social agencies and community groups when they want to oppose a specific measure, such as a cut in welfare benefits, or when they want to establish new programs, such as programs to help abused children.[59]

The mass media, including local papers, television stations, and radio stations, often assume a pivotal role in local communities. Of course, the mass media may be relatively conservative in local areas, so astute policy practitioners cultivate relationships with sympathetic reporters.

Many kinds of policy issues develop in communities. Some pertain to where buildings are or are, not, placed, such as whether a half-way house for persons with specific problems is placed in a certain neighborhood. Some pertain to the policies of institutions, such as local schools. Advocates might question, for example, whether a particular school provides sufficient tutoring to certain kinds of students, sufficient outreach to truants, or sufficient public health services. Some pertain to a local government's budget: should it allocate greater resources to specific programs or needs? Still other issues involve patterns of citizen participation in decision making, such as whether certain boards are representative of the jurisdiction's population. Advocates sometimes seek establishment of task forces to analyze problems such as inadequate child care, lack of after-school recreation programs, or gangs.

The community politics of many issues can be highly conflictual. For example, when a county welfare office wanted to establish a branch office in a certain community, remarkable conflict ensued that pitted policy advocates against persons and businesses who feared the office would lower property values and bring undesirable people into the area. Only after protracted conflict and some court rulings was the branch office finally established.

Chapter Summary

What You Can Now Do

You are now equipped to do the following:

- Understand how governments are structured
- Understand relations between legislators, lobbyists, interest groups, public opinion, and members of the executive branch
- Find names of key committees in state and federal jurisdictions
- Understand the mindsets of elected officials such as legislators and heads of government
- Know the mindsets of nonelected officials such as civil servants and political appointees
- Understand the political economy of social agencies
- Understand the political economy of programs and social work units within agencies
- Be able to map agencies' policies
- Be able to draw an organizational chart
- Use four overlays to develop a dynamic understanding of a specific social agency
- Understand the political economy of communities

Notes

1. See James McGregor Burns, *The Power to Lead* (New York: Simon & Schuster, 1984).
2. For discussion of the budget roles of the president, see Aaron Wildavsky, *The New Politics of the Budgetary Process* (Glenview, IL: Scott, Foresman, 1988), pp. 166–186.
3. Abraham Holtzman, *Legislative Liaison: Executive Leadership in the Congress* (Chicago: Rand McNally, 1970).
4. Hedrick Smith, *The Power Game: How Washington Works* (New York: Ballantine Books, 1988), pp. 388–428.
5. Wildavsky, *The New Politics,* pp. 165–212.
6. Smith, *The Power Game,* pp. 41–57.
7. Smith, *The Power Game,* pp. 145–150. For a classic discussion of the different orientations of conservative and liberal constituencies to social legislation, see Lewis Froman, "Interparty Constituency Differences and Congressional Voting Behavior," *American Political Science Review* 57 (March 1963): 57–61.
8. Marilyn Bagwell, *A Political Handbook for Health Professionals* (Boston: Little, Brown, 1985), pp. 63–64.
9. Ibid., pp. 64–66. See also Richard Cheney and Lynne Cheney, *Kings of the Hill* (New York: Continuum, 1983).
10. Bagwell, *Political Handbook,* pp. 67–68.
11. Judith Meredith, *Lobbying on a Shoestring* (Dover, MA: Auburn House, 1989), pp. 65–78.

12. Lewis Froman, *The Congressional Process: Strategies, Rules, and Procedures* (Boston: Little, Brown, 1967).
13. Glenn Abney and Thomas Lauth, *The Politics of State and City Administration* (Albany: State University of New York Press, 1986), pp. 130–212.
14. Laurence Lynn, *Managing Public Policy* (Boston: Little, Brown, 1987).
15. Smith, *The Power Game,* pp. 270–326.
16. For a discussion of links between legislatures and civil servants, see J. Weatherford McIver, *Tribes on the Hill* (New York: Rawson Wade, 1981), pp. 87–111.
17. Interactions between lobbyists and legislators are discussed throughout Jeffrey Birnbaum and Alan Murray, *Showdown at Gucci Gulch* (New York: Vintage Books, 1987).
18. See Policy Advocacy Challenge 11.1 in this book for a detailed discussion of the tactics used by lobbyists.
19. The role of funds from special interests and affluent Americans in campaigns and politics is discussed by Thomas Edsall, *The New Politics of Inequality* (New York: Norton, 1984).
20. See, for example, James Smith, *Brookings at Seventy-Five* (Washington, DC: Brookings Institution, 1991).
21. McIver, *Tribes on the Hill,* pp. 87–111.
22. See R. Douglas Brown, *The Logic of Congressional Action* (New Haven, CT: Yale University Press, 1990), pp. 1–87.
23. Lynn, *Managing Public Policy,* pp. 68–73.
24. Brown, *The Logic of Congressional Action,* pp. 60–87.
25. Ibid.
26. Smith, *The Power Game,* pp. 119–159.
27. Ibid., pp. 119–159; and Willard Richan, *Lobbying for Social Change* (New York: Haworth Press, 1991), pp. 53–54.
28. Smith, *The Power Game,* pp. 270–284.
29. Brown, *The Logic of Congressional Action,* pp. 141–144.
30. For a discussion of the need not to write off conservatives when developing coalitions, see Nancy Amidei, "How to Be an Advocate in Bad Times," *Public Welfare* 40 (Summer 1982): 41.
31. As an example of the ambiguous signals that high-level political appointees often receive from heads of government, see the roles of Elliot Richardson and Edward Zigler in my case study titled "An Extended Policy-Practice Case: Child Development and Daycare," in *Social Welfare Policy: From Theory to Practice* (Belmont, CA: Wadsworth, 1990), pp. 350–377.
32. Richan, *Lobbying for Social Change,* pp. 60–62.
33. See Ron Dear and Rino Patti, "Legislative Advocacy: Seven Effective Tactics," in Maryann Mahaffey and John Hanks, eds., *Practical Politics: Social Work and Political Responsibility* (Silver Spring, MD: National Association of Social Workers, 1982), pp. 107–108.
34. An example of a civil servant's resistance to a policy advocate is provided by William Bell and Budd Bell, "Monitoring the Bureaucracy: An Extension of Legislative Lobbying," in Mahaffey and Hanks, *Practical Politics,* pp. 128–130.
35. Yeheskel Hasenfeld, *Human Service Organizations* (Englewood Cliffs, NJ: Prentice Hall, 1983), pp. 43–49.

36. Economic pressures on human service organizations in the 1980s and 1990s are discussed by Stepen Webster and Mary Wylie, "Strategic Planning in a Competitive Environment," *Administration in Mental Health* 15 (Fall 1988): 25–44.

37. Hasenfeld, *Human Service Organizations,* pp. 50–83.

38. Mayer Zald, *Organizational Change: The Political Economy of the YMCA* (Chicago: University of Chicago Press, 1970).

39. Jean Potuchek, "The Context of Social Service Funding: The Funding Relationship," *Social Service Review* 60 (September 1986): 421–436.

40. Bruce Jansson and June Simmons, "The Survival of Social Work Departments," *Social Work* 31 (September 1986): 339–344.

41. Bruce Jansson and June Simmons, "The Ecology of Social Work Departments," *Social Work in Health Care* 11 (Winter 1985): 1–16, and Bruce Jansson and June Simmons, "Building Department or Unit Power within Human Service Organizations," *Administration in Social Work* 8 (Fall 1984): 41–56.

42. Robert Goodin, *Reasons for Welfare* (Princeton, NJ: Princeton University Press, 1988), pp. 190–193.

43. See *Tarasoff v. Regents of the University of California,* 1976. 17 Cal. 4d 425.

44. Hasenfeld, *Human Service Organizations,* pp. 84–109.

45. For a discussion of the politics of money in organizations, see Burton Gummer, *The Politics of Social Administration: Managing Organizational Politics in Social Agencies* (Englewood Cliffs, NJ: Prentice Hall, 1990), pp. 46–67.

46. For a critical view of federated fund raising, see Stanley Wenocur, "A Pluralistic Planning Model for United Way Organizations," *Social Service Review* 50 (December 1976): 586–600. See also Eleanor Brilliant, *The United Way: Dilemmas of Organized Charity* (New York: Columbia University Press, 1990).

47. Murray Gruber, ed., *Management Systems in the Human Services* (Philadelphia: Temple University Press, 1981), pp. 87–96.

48. A case study of the divergence between high-level official policy and the actual operative policies in agencies is provided by Franklin Chu and Sharland Trotter, *The Madness Establishment* (New York: Grossman, 1974).

49. Gummer, *The Politics of Social Administration,* pp. 10–11, 19–20, 162–163.

50. Goodin, *Reasons for Welfare,* pp. 190–193.

51. Hans Gerth and C. Wright Mills, eds., *From Max Weber: Essays in Sociology* (New York: Oxford University Press, 1946).

52. Gummer, *The Politics of Social Administration,* pp. 11–13.

53. Existing organizational theory, which presents a variety of factors that shape outcomes and behavior, is suggestive of the concept of overlays. Different authors emphasize different structural, political, and economic factors, as well as the informal culture of organizations. While placing organizational behavior in a political-economic framework, for example, Hasenfeld discusses these various factors in *Human Service Organizations.*

54. See, for example, Sheldon Gelman, "The Board of Directors and Agency Accountability," *Social Casework* 64 (February 1983): 83–91.

55. Robert Dahl, *Pluralist Democracy in the United States* (Chicago: Rand McNally, 1967).

56. Hasenfeld, *Human Service Organizations,* p. 8.

57. For a discussion of neighborhoods, see James Cunningham, "Are Neighborhoods Real? A Review Essay," *Urban Resources* 1 (Winter 1984): 19–22.

58. Roland Warren, *New Perspectives on the American Community* (Homewood, IL: Dorsey Press, 1977), pp. 260–365.

59. Milan Dluhy, *Building Coalitions in the Human Services* (Newbury Park, CA: Sage, 1990).

Suggested Readings

Legislatures

R. Douglas Arnold, *The Logic of Congressional Action* (New Haven, CT: Yale University Press, 1990).

J. Weatherford McIver, *Tribes on the Hill* (New York: Rawson, Wade, 1981).

Hedrick Smith, *The Power Game: How Washington Works* (New York: Ballantine Books, 1988), pp. 119–160, 270–326.

Government Bureaucracies

Laurence Lynn, *Managing Public Policy* (Boston: Little, Brown, 1987).

Interest Groups and Lobbyists

Marilyn Bagwell, *A Political Handbook for Health Professionals* (Boston: Little, Brown, 1985).

Hedrick Smith, *The Power Game: How Washington Works* (New York: Ballantine Books, 1988), pp. 215–269.

Policies of Social Agencies

Burton Gummer, *The Politics of Social Administration: Managing Organizational Politics in Social Agencies* (Englewood Cliffs, NJ: Prentice Hall, 1990).

Electoral Politics

The Political Economy of Services

Michael Fabricant and Steve Burghardt, *The Welfare State Crisis and the Transformation of Social Service Work* (Armonk, NY: Sharpe, 1992).

Yeheskel Hasenfeld, *Human Service Organizations* (Englewood Cliffs, NJ: Prentice Hall, 1983).

PART 3

COMMITTING TO PROBLEMS AND SOLUTIONS

Policy advocates are driven by the desire to improve society. As a prelude to their work, they need to identify specific problems or issues where they believe they can make a difference. Having committed to a problem or issue, they need to find solutions that appear meritorious—and that appear to have a reasonable chance of enactment.

Chapters Five through Eight discuss this preparatory work, which often determines whether policy advocates will succeed in changing existing policies. Chapter Five discusses how advocates place issues on agendas. Chapter Six covers how advocates analyze problems. Chapter Seven addresses how advocates develop proposals, and Chapter Eight discusses how they persuade others that their proposals have merit through debates, negotiations, oral presentations, and written documents such as policy memos and grant proposals.

chapter 5

Committing to an Issue: Building Agendas

As social work and public health advocates in Los Angeles looked around them in 1991, they saw carnage in the streets. With virtually no restrictions on gun selling and ownership, hundreds of thousands of citizens had armed themselves with an array of revolvers (often called Saturday night specials), shotguns, automatic rifles, and assault weapons. Gun dealers had brazenly established shops next to residential areas. Injuries and deaths from gunshots were particularly frequent in Latino and African American communities, where guns were widely used by gangs, drug dealers, and youth.

A coalition of social workers, public health officials, and other citizens formed a violence prevention coalition to address this carnage. The problem was how they were going to get the issue on the agenda of their elected officials, who had ignored it for years and who feared the political power of the National Rifle Association. A case study of agenda building, presented at the end of this chapter in Policy Advocacy Challenge 5.4, demonstrates that determined policy advocates can take on powerful groups like the National Rifle Association and emerge victorious, even when they cannot match their resources.

Experienced policy advocates realize that their first challenge is to get the policy issue on decision makers' agendas in agency, community, or legislative settings. Before an issue can advance into the later phases of policy practice, where proposals are actually refined and enacted, decision makers must decide that the issue is important enough to merit such serious consideration. It must compete with myriad other issues for the scarce time and resources of staff, executives, boards of directors, governmental officials, legislators, mayors, boards of supervisors, community leaders, and presidents. Policy advocates often have to use a combination of political, interactional, and analytic skills to place their issues on decision makers' agendas.

We discuss the following in this chapter:
- The importance of agenda-building processes to policy practice
- The three stages of agenda building: diagnosing, softening, and activating
- How social problems and solutions reach agendas
- How political processes shape agendas
- How windows of opportunity and policy entrepreneurs shape agendas
- How direct-service staff can build agendas
- The challenges policy advocates face in shaping agendas

How do we know when an issue is on the agenda? In legislative settings, this has happened when legislation has been introduced into the legislative process and referred to a committee, and has attracted the serious attention of some legislators—preferably ones with clout. In agency settings, an issue is on the agenda when it has become part of the agency's deliberations. Perhaps the executive director has formed a task force or committee to study it. Maybe the staff or the agency's board plans to discuss the issue in a meeting. A group in the agency may have decided to rally support for a policy change. In communities, an issue is on the agenda when community leaders and decision makers have decided to take it seriously enough to convene meetings to consider solutions.

Of course, placing issues or proposals on these agendas does not necessarily have a positive outcome; many factors, such as opposition, can defeat them. Indeed, many issues never reach the agenda because opposing groups successfully use tactics to keep them off the agenda.[1] And placement on the agenda does not tell us precisely what kind of proposal or solution will finally emerge, because proposals are finalized in the give-and-take of deliberations. But placement on the agenda does tell us that a proposal is well positioned to receive serious attention and that it has received an initial impetus, unlike many issues that do not even achieve this status. Were we not to discuss agenda building, it might seem that policy reforms can be easily initiated without any preliminary work, such as discussing the proposed reform, analyzing its feasibility, convincing others that it merits attention, considering who might get the ball rolling, and deciding on the right time to introduce the issue to others.

In this chapter, we discuss some policy practice skills that help get proposals onto agendas.

Taking the First Step

Assume that you work in an agency that provides job referrals and career assistance to women. You are perturbed because the agency provides little service to a specific client group, such as single teenage mothers. While some services are available to them, none of the services, you decide, focus on employment needs. While your distant challenge is to develop a proposal to help this population and perhaps secure funding for this help, your immediate challenge is to convince others, preferably decision makers at the agency, that the problem merits their serious attention. At this very moment, you are engaged in building an agenda. In this preliminary phase, you must place the issue on the agenda so that someone—perhaps an executive, a staff committee, or a committee of the agency's board—will examine the issue in more detail or delegate it to others for further exploration.

Agenda building is a critical phase of the policy development process. Skillful policy practitioners who are building an agenda try to create favorable conditions, interest, and support for a policy reform at the outset.

Why Agenda Building Is Needed

Legislatures

It is easy to see why most proposals fall by the wayside when we consider some simple realities that confront legislators and agency executives. Legislators must limit the number of issues they consider and must rank them in some order. Thousands of pieces of legislation are introduced into each session of state legislatures and Congress conceived by the legislators themselves, lobbyists, citizens, or professional associations. (See Policy Advocacy Challenge 5.1.)

Were legislators to debate even a large fraction of them, they would work themselves to exhaustion and not give careful attention to any of them. When many people with different perspectives and constituencies are involved, it takes time and effort to consider even simple pieces of legislation. In each chamber of Congress, for example, subcommittees consider the policies and forward them for further debate and votes to the full legislative committee, which forwards them to the full chamber for floor debates

---

POLICY ADVOCACY CHALLENGE 5.1

FINDING EMERGING LEGISLATION IN STATE AND FEDERAL JURISDICTIONS

Stephanie Davis, Research Librarian, University of California, Irvine

Federal Government Information

In 1995, a team of librarians and technologists from the Library of Congress created THOMAS under a federal mandate from the 104th Congress to make federal legislative information freely available to the public via the Internet. THOMAS, located online at thomas.loc.gov, is named for Thomas Jefferson, and provides access to many different types of political and government information:

- Legislation: text of bills and information about those bills introduced into the House and Senate, text of laws passed by Congress, record of how members of Congress vote on bills, motions and more (roll call votes)
- Congressional Record: an index to and full text of the official record of the speeches, remarks, issues, and other happenings in Congress
- House and Senate Committee information: membership, charges, schedules, text of hearings
- Senator/Representative directories: links to homepages with contact information, constituency information, profiles, legislative agendas; finding aids for locating a specific member by zip code and state.
- Other Congressional Internet Services such as the Government Printing Office, General Accounting Office, Congressional Budget Office, and others
- Links to guides on the legislative process in the House and Senate, database of historical documents, and more.

Your library may have access to a subscription database called *Congressional Universe,* which provides much of the same information as THOMAS. Both are excellent resources for finding federal legislative information

State Legislative Information

Finding State information is, in general, not as streamlined as finding federal information. States generally do not have the same mandate to place their legislative information on the Internet. There is a subscription database called *State Capital Universe* that provides access to state bills, regulations, statutes, policy and issue information, and biographical information about state senators and politicians.

Often the best way to find state information is to find your state's homepage on the Internet, and look for links to government, legislature, agencies, elected officials, and state libraries or archives. These are excellent starting points.

Exercises: First, spend some time getting acquainted with THOMAS at thomas.loc.gov. Select a topic of interest to you, and search for bills or laws on that topic (i.e., health care, welfare, children).

Next, using the search engines we discussed in Chapter One, find your state's homepage, and then find your state legislature's Web site. If the Web site allows for searching introduced and passed legislation, repeat the search you did in THOMAS.

- Compare the results of your searches—how are the bills or law similar? Do they address the same or similar problems? How is the state's approach different from the federal, and vice versa?
- Who introduced or sponsored each piece of legislation? Find their homepage and compare their legislative agendas.
- From your perspective, is the solution to the problem addressed in the legislation a good solution or a poor solution? Critique each piece of legislation as if you were a member of the state legislature faced with voting on that piece of legislation.

---

and votes. If each chamber enacts a different version, they may have to be sent to a conference committee composed of members of both chambers if each chamber has enacted a different version, and then to the president for his signature. Moreover, during this process, many legislators must spend endless hours with lobbyists and other citizens. It is no wonder, then, that leaders of legislatures decide not to put most measures on the legislative agenda, thus reserving their scarce time for those pieces of legislation they want to concentrate on.

Legislators often avoid issues that appear to give them little or no political advantage in reelection; politicians do not select issues that will not help them obtain or retain constituents' support. A particular issue may seem too controversial or may antagonize an important faction or interest group, even if it pleases other people.

Unlike agency executives, who often want to avoid contentious issues that could disrupt their agency, politicians are often attracted to issues associated with conflict if such issues can gain them support among their constituents. For example, liberal politicians may deliberately support an issue to anger conservatives and thus prove their ideological leanings to their liberal supporters. Legislators may opportunistically select issues that will give them media exposure and a resultant advantage over their opponents in an upcoming election battle. In addition, legislators often decide not to invest their limited time and resources in issues that stand little or no chance of success.

Agencies

Agency executives must manage organizations, raise funds, hire staff, adjudicate conflicts, and plan—tasks that occupy most of their working hours. Executives also confront myriad policy issues, such as deciding what kinds of clients to serve and which social problems fall within the purview of the agency, naming overarching objectives or goals, developing policies and procedures within specific grant proposals, deciding whether to be advocates for their clients in the broader community or in a legislature, determining what kind of staff to hire, and developing policies and procedures to guide the staff. Some of these policies concern internal, procedural matters, while others concern the goals or mission of the organization in its political and funding context.

In light of these many tasks, executives must ignore or defer many issues, even ones that seem important to a staff member, a board member, or a client. Were executives to try to examine each issue in considerable detail, they would become exhausted and frustrated.

Executives also ignore or defer certain issues because they would embroil the agency in conflict. Even seemingly mundane issues such as changing an agency's intake procedures may impassion people who want the issue left alone. Perhaps they like the existing policy because it furthers their own interests, as when they receive a steady flow of certain kinds of clients to their units. They may like the existing policy for ideological reasons; for instance, they may believe the agency should focus on the kind of clients it now predominantly serves. Perhaps they fear that some rival staff member has plotted the change in intake policy to gain some advantage over them or even to cause them harm. In this political context, then, it is understandable that executives leave most issues alone. Often, they act only when they are convinced that an issue merits attention in spite of possible political conflict and the time and effort it may take.

Executives are also likely to limit their attention to the most worthwhile issues and give preference to certain issues for several reasons. To increase agency resources amid funding cuts, they may select issues that will obtain greater funds for their agencies; they may feel pressured by certain persons to focus on an issue; or they may be more interested in certain kinds of issues than in others.[2] Executives, then, must limit the number of issues they consider and then rank them.

Policy advocates who want to bring their issues to the attention of executives and other agency personnel must upset the status quo. They must develop a strategy to convince agency executives that their issues merit attention.

The decision to give attention or prominence to an issue in the agenda phase of policymaking does not guarantee success at subsequent points. Even so, skillful policy advocates must devote considerable attention to building agendas. They realize that they have virtually no chance of long-term success if they cannot garner significant initial interest.

Communities

Agenda building also occurs in community settings as various issues vie for attention. Community activists may introduce ideas to community groups, the media, and community influentials, like blocking a freeway that will split the community, expanding a school, securing approval for a community park, or opening a counseling program for substance abusers. Activists may draw attention to a policy proposal by getting a story in the mass media, holding a community forum, or staging a protest. Or they may inject the issue into a campaign for city council or school board elections, with the ultimate objective of persuading community decision makers to prioritize it in their deliberations.

Three Challenges in Agenda Building

Agenda building can be conceptualized as a funnel. (See Figure 5.1.) We will discuss this agenda-building framework from the top down. Policy practitioners face three challenges when considering specific reforms: they (or their allies) must *diagnose* the context, *soften* the context, and *activate* change.

The top funnel illustrate the process that policy practitioners use to winnow a few issues from the multitude of issues that could be presented for active consideration. At the top of the funnel are the context and the practitioner's diagnosing role. Just beneath these are the modified context and the policy practitioner's softening role. The numbers *1* through *10* just above the funnel represent the many potential issues that exist in any setting. Policy entrepreneurs, who are discussed in more detail later, engage in the activating role when they pull a specific issue (in this case, number 8) into the funnel, where it is placed on the decision agenda when someone or some group prioritizes it for systematic deliberation. (See the decision agenda at the bottom of the top funnel in Figure 5.1.) After an issue is placed on the decision agenda, such as on to the agenda of a meeting or committee, it then enters policy deliberations where it is waylaid, defeated, or enacted. (See the bottom funnel in Figure 5.1.) This is a second winnowing process: relatively few policies are actually enacted after they enter policy deliberations. We can tell the stage of an issue in Figure 5.1 by asking several questions: Has the issue been floated with little or no discussion? If so, it is in the original context or the modified context. Has the issue been forwarded to a committee, a task force, or some other deliberative entity for further discussion? If so, it is on the decision agenda. Have systematic deliberations begun? If so, it is in policy deliberations. Has the issue been enacted by decision makers? If so, it is positioned for implementation at the bottom of the second funnel.

Policy advocates need to diagnose the context to identify contextual constraints and opportunities. If they decide that specific policies will be extremely difficult to change, they must do considerable work to change the context or to focus on alternative policy changes. When they decide that the contextual opportunities far outnumber constraints, they can initiate a policy-changing strategy at once. In some cases, the prognosis will be guarded or unclear.

Having diagnosed the context, policy advocates must soften it; that is, they must make it more amenable to a specific policy initiative. Even when the context appears bleak, they may discover that a few conversations with strategically placed persons will

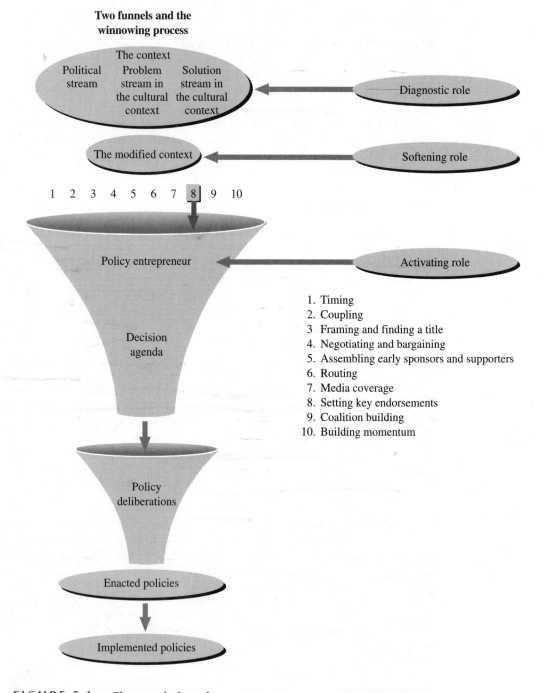

FIGURE 5.1   **The agenda funnel**

make the prognosis more optimistic or will indicate that their pessimistic forecast was unwarranted.

At some point, of course, policy advocates need to activate change. They need to get a decision maker or legislator to put an issue on the agenda of the other decision makers in the agency, community, or legislative setting. The chairperson might place the issue on the agenda of an agency committee or staff meeting. Perhaps a legislator drafts a piece of legislation and initiates a search for cosponsors. Or maybe a state's director of health and human services presents a detailed analysis of a particular problem in the administration of his or her program.

Agenda building is, then, the precursor to other policy practice tasks. Without it, most policy initiatives cannot proceed further. And, if policy advocates have successfully softened the context, they make ultimate success more likely.

We rely heavily on the pathbreaking work of political scientist John Kingdon in our discussion of agenda building. Before Kingdon wrote his classic work, *Agendas, Alternatives, and Public Policies,* many people ignored the agenda-building task altogether, conveying the misleading impression that policy reforms magically appear with no prior work by policy practitioners.[3] Or they used simplistic explanations. Some *rationalists* assumed, for example, that decision makers placed issues on agendas whenever they received technical reports or data that recommended a specific change. While this assumption is sometimes true, issues are often placed on agendas without empirical studies—and technical reports often gather dust in agency, community, and legislative settings. Indeed, legislators and even agency executives sometimes retain policies that they know to be ineffective if they are supported by powerful lobbyists or bring revenues to an agency. Some *incrementalists* assumed that administrators and legislators often introduced modest changes in existing policies in response to complaints or pressures, as when federal legislators expanded the Head Start program to include children with physical and mental disabilities in response to lobbying by groups representing these children. Kingdon rightly argues, however, that decision makers, in both agency and legislative settings, often support major changes in existing policy.[4] Legislators sometimes seek the major overhaul of a program or the enactment of a major social reform. Agencies sometimes launch new programs that diverge markedly from their existing programs.

Another theorist developed the *garbage can theory* of agenda building. Emphasizing organizations, he noted that many ideas bubble up regarding problems (e.g., social problems, service delivery problems, and administrative problems) and solutions (e.g., service delivery, program, or administrative innovations).[5] These problems or solutions may surface at staff or committee meetings, or at a retreat of the executives and the board. The executive director, alone or in deliberations with other high-level staff, may identify a problem. Even when agency members consider an issue fleetingly, problems and solutions often retain a place in their memories, remaining in a state of limbo—a figurative garbage can—until they are placed on the agendas of decision makers. Similarly, we can say that myriad problems and solutions exist in the "garbage cans" of legislatures. These problems and solutions derive from such sources as lobbyists, reform-minded legislators, think tanks, professional associations, and citizens. The garbage can theory suggests a more fluid and dynamic process than the rationalist or incrementalist theories, but it does not discuss in sufficient detail how certain issues are activated, or placed on policy agendas.

While we draw on Kingdon's theory, we also modify it. We include more factors in the context than he does, and we add the diagnosing, softening, and activating stages because they clarify the roles of policy advocates in bringing issues to the agenda.

As can be seen in Figure 5.1, agenda building is a precursor to actual deliberations. Agenda building merely gets specific issues or policies on the table to be followed by actual deliberations where they are processed by committees and legislatures. In this deliberative process, some of the issues and policies are also sifted out. Some are defeated. Some are cast aside. Some are tabled. What we have, then, are two funnels that each winnow issues and policies. What is actually enacted or approved—a small fraction of the issues and policies that began this trip at the top of the first funnel—comes out the bottom of the second funnel. Lest this sound too pessimistic, remember that many policies are enacted or approved by legislatures, communities, and agencies.

The Diagnosing Stage

When diagnosing the context, policy advocates must analyze streams of problems and solutions, recent professional decisions and trends, and political realities.

Streams of problems and solutions   When policy advocates begin their work, they must carefully consider the kinds of problems and solutions that have already been considered in a setting. Indeed, we can use Kingdon's language, as he refers to problem and solution "streams" in specific settings.[6]

In many agencies, one need merely examine developments in the agency during, say, the last five years to see that a problem stream exists. Take the earlier example of a small agency that provides job placement and career counseling services to women. The social worker who directs these services also founded the agency. In the beginning, the agency had a relatively narrow set of services, consisting mostly of posting job openings from area firms on a bulletin board and holding career-planning seminars for women. In the 10 years since its founding, the staff, the executive director, and the members of the board have identified problems that the agency could address. They initially discussed some of these ideas in meetings or in personal conversations, but over time, many of the ideas have led to new programs, funded grant proposals, and cooperative projects with other agencies. The agency has added special job placement and career planning services for Latinas, single teenage mothers, and displaced homemakers; a job placement program for unemployed women funded by the federal Job Training Partnership Act; and job fairs for high school women in a local school district. Each of these programs stemmed from a problem that someone placed in the agency's general problem stream in conversations or meetings. Of course, many other problems have been discussed that never reached solution. For example, the agency staff decided not to pursue a suggestion to provide a support group for unemployed women with a mental health orientation, because they believed it fell outside their mission, which emphasizes concrete services like job referral, job search, and career development services.

A stream of problems exists in legislative settings, too. Policy practitioners interested in reforming the child welfare system of a specific county, for example, would be likely to interview advocates and highly placed officials to find out what kinds of problems concerning the child welfare system have already been discussed. (See Policy Advocacy Challenge 5.2 for ways to search for legislative proposals that are in the hopper.)

POLICY
ADVOCACY
CHALLENGE 5.2

*USING THE MASS
MEDIA TO FIND
ISSUES ON THE
POLICY AGENDA*

Over a period of several weeks, collect stories in newspapers that suggest items likely to be placed on policy agendas. Group them under issues, problems, and solutions. Also analyze which political leaders or parties are likely to champion these issues—or is it difficult to predict what party or leader will take the lead? Are persons and parties with different ideologies likely to approach the issues differently?

Similarly, a stream of solutions exists in agency, community, and legislative settings. In our women's job placement agency, the staff, the board, and the executive director have considered decentralizing services, adopting a sliding-fee schedule, merging with a local YWCA, developing joint programs with a community college, and developing a computer lab to help job seekers find positions. In a specific county, the board of supervisors and child welfare officials may consider new management systems, new record-keeping systems, partnerships with local schools, and different ways of recruiting foster parents.

We can classify solutions into three broad groups. Some propose specific programs, such as interventions to help children, single mothers, or older people. Others aim to correct institutional problems, such as financing a program, changing an agency's fee structure, or enhancing the collaboration of different agencies in serving a specific client group. Still others propose methods of making decisions, such as setting up a task force, establishing a committee, or organizing an interagency planning committee.

We rarely begin policy practice with a blank slate. By examining streams of problems and solutions in specific settings, policy advocates discover where their issue fits into this larger picture. They might discover, for example, that others have already introduced the issue, but that it went nowhere because of budgetary implications. Or they might discover that their issue has never been discussed, but that related issues were the subject of initial discussion several years ago. As they piece together the recent history of streams of problems and solutions, policy advocates get a better sense of their issue's prognosis.

Recent professional developments and trends   Fads and trends can powerfully shape the prognosis of a policy reform. For example, partnerships and collaborations between agencies became widely popular in the mid-1990s, partly because many professionals, public officials, and funders came to believe that their clients required more intensive and complicated services than specific agencies could give. A policy reform encouraging collaboration would have fared better in this environment than if it had been introduced a decade earlier, when less attention was given to collaboration. Fads and trends can be discerned by examining professional journals, talking with professionals, and analyzing the kinds of innovations that funders (such as foundations and government agencies) prioritize.

Problem and solution streams exist in a cultural context whether in nations or in specific settings. "Problems" in one setting are not perceived to be problems in other settings. Americans are less likely to view great discrepancies in wealth as a problem as compared with many European nations. High levels of conflict between staff may be viewed as problematic in one agency but not another. Similarly, some solutions, such as national health insurance, are widely accepted in European nations but not the United States.

Political realities   Background political developments powerfully influence whether specific issues will be placed on policy agendas, as our discussion of the big picture in Chapter Four suggests. Let's start with legislative settings. When working on a policy issue or reform, policy advocates need to consider the viewpoint of important officials by finding out what position they have taken on similar issues or reforms in the past. This consideration should include the following:

- The viewpoints of heads of government or chief executives
- The viewpoints of legislators, particularly those who have official positions (like majority speaker or committee chairperson) or who have influential roles in specific caucuses such as a women's caucus
- The viewpoints of the legislators from one's own district, since they often support proposals made by their constituents
- The viewpoints of legislators who have assumed leadership on similar issues in the past, such as legislators who have taken a personal interest in child welfare issues
- The viewpoints of key members of government bureaucracy, whether political appointees or civil servants, particularly those who oversee programs and policies relevant to the present issue
- The viewpoints of lobbyists or the heads of interest groups that are active on the issue or policy
- The viewpoints of the public as reflected in polls or in recently contested elections
- The extent to which a policy reform is likely to receive sympathetic coverage in the mass media as reflected by media coverage of similar issues in the past

Policy advocates also need to consider court rulings that are germane to their issue. With respect to homeless people, for example, court rulings may have increased support for a specific policy reform, such as requiring local jurisdictions to provide shelters for homeless people.

In agency settings, policy advocates must consider a range of factors that shape the prognosis of a specific reform or issue, including the following:

- The extent to which a policy reform is consonant with the agency's mission
- The state of the agency's budget, such as whether it is running a deep deficit or is balanced
- The amount of interest that specific agency funders are likely to have in a specific issue or problem
- The viewpoints of the key agency officials, such as the director, top administrators, or members of the board of directors, and the directors of important agency programs, as surmised from their position in prior years on similar issues
- The viewpoints of the agency officials or staff who are likely to be most impacted by a reform or issue
- The viewpoints of union leaders (if staff are unionized)
- The likely effects of a specific reform on an agency's clientele
- The likely position of the agency's accrediting bodies

In community settings, policy advocates must consider the following:

- The viewpoints of key community leaders
- Local public opinion
- The perspectives of the local media

When considering the prognosis of policy changes in any setting, several factors often suggest that policy innovations will be relatively difficult to achieve:

- The sheer magnitude of a policy change (large changes are often more difficult to obtain than more modest changes)
- Whether an issue is already politicized (if the issue has already excited considerable political conflict, it is likely to be associated with political conflict when it is reintroduced)
- Whether persons with considerable power believe that specific policy changes will harm their economic, professional, or political self-interest (if they have this negative orientation, policy reform will be more difficult)
- Whether a specific reform will be expensive or difficult to implement (policies that present logistical or funding problems are often opposed by agency executives)

When engaging in diagnostic work, policy advocates should not prematurely abandon an issue even when they believe it has a negative prognosis. Reforms that will help powerless or oppressed populations, for example, are likely to encounter more difficulties. Had Martin Luther King, Jr., abandoned civil rights in the 1950s because of its poor prognosis, there would very likely have been no improvement in oppressive conditions suffered by African Americans. If advocates of welfare recipients had abandoned them as they encountered myriad problems in the wake of the welfare reform legislation of 1996, they would have consigned many of them to living standards even lower than when they had been on welfare.

The Softening Stage

Policy advocates can sometimes attempt to enhance the prognosis of a policy reform even before it enters policy deliberations by working in problem and solution streams and by building political support.

Working in problem and solution streams   As Kingdon suggests, those who want decision makers to take their problem seriously have to convince them that it is a problem and not merely a condition.[7] Unlike a condition, a problem poses a threat or danger to someone, whether a group in the population, an agency, or politicians. When a condition is perceived as a problem, legislators, agency officials, and others are more likely to view it as important—and even to believe that someone (or they themselves) will suffer dire consequences if it is not addressed. As advocates for welfare recipients convince others, for example, that failure to increase job training in the reauthorization of welfare reform in 2002 will harm many families with single heads of household, they will be better able to achieve reforms that will soften the harshness of that legislation. Similarly, if agency executives believe that their agency will suffer important consequences if they do not support a reform, they will be more likely to support it.

But how do we convince other people that certain conditions are problems? We can use data to argue that a condition is serious in its absolute numbers, that some subset of the population is afflicted far more than other portions of the population, or that the problem is becoming steadily worse.[8] Absolute numbers, such as the percentage of women with inadequate or no child care, can shock decision makers into believing that a condition is a problem. Someone with data indicating that Latinas lack adequate child care in far greater numbers than white women may be able to use these data to persuade legislators to fund day care for Spanish-speaking children. Data showing that a problem is worsening may convince legislators that it will reach crisis proportions without governmental intervention.

Advocates for corrective action often use words such as *crisis* to describe a condition. Because this word is overused, the advocate needs some evidence or rationale for its use. Take, for example, the dramatic spread of tuberculosis in the United States in the 1990s, which particularly affected AIDS patients and immigrants. When drug-resistant strains of the disease spread because many persons failed to take the prescribed medications long enough, advocates of greater funding for tuberculosis programs were able to convince federal, state, and local officials to prioritize funding for public health programs.

Policy advocates also need to demonstrate that a problem is not hopeless and can be ameliorated. For example, advocates have often found it difficult to secure support for inner cities, the underclass, and even people who are homeless because many legislators see these problems as unsolvable, in contrast to simpler ones. Advocates can buttress their cases by citing research or finding successful pilot projects that demonstrate that specific reforms will yield positive outcomes.

In addition, policy advocates can appeal to values such as the ethical principles of beneficence, social justice, and fairness by arguing that society (or a legislature) has a duty to address an issue.

Because politicians often consider how taking corrective action will affect their careers, advocates often try to state problems in relatively broad terms. They may stress the absence of child care for working women, the increased incidence of Alzheimer's disease among all social classes and races, or inadequate sex education in the schools. By presenting problems in general terms, advocates increase the likelihood that more politicians will see the problem as important to their constituencies.[9]

Terminology is important when describing problems. Hence, the contemporary tendency to refer to investment in human needs rather than spending. No practical difference exists between the two terms; both mean using public resources. However, investment appeals to many politicians, including relatively conservative ones, because it implies that society will receive a return on its expenditure of funds. Nomenclature can also appeal to socially acceptable symbols.[10] With the Family Support Act of 1986, Congressional advocates, such as Senator Patrick Moynihan, called their reforms "family support" rather than "welfare reforms," hoping that such words would attract more support from congressional conservatives.[11]

When faced with harsh fiscal realities, policy advocates try to show that a specific policy, such as increasing Head Start funding, will avert subsequent costly problems, such as welfare and crime. They may propose a pilot program and hope to expand it later.

Advocates encounter a double-edged sword when they use the word *prevention* to seek support for a problem. Prevention is, on the one hand, a culturally acceptable symbol because everyone prefers preventing a problem to fixing it afterward. On the other hand, decision makers often perceive preventive programs negatively. They may wonder if a specific problem, such as teenage pregnancy or drug use, can be prevented. They may want to prioritize services for persons who are already afflicted rather than fund prevention. Those advocating preventive programs, then, need to find evidence that they will successfully avert problems.[12]

Our discussion suggests that policy practitioners need to anticipate likely objections or opposition to a specific policy so they can diminish or rebut them. They should develop arguments to counter claims that a particular problem is not solvable or cannot be prevented, that a remedy is too expensive or too difficult to implement, that a particular issue does not fall within an agency's mission, that a specific problem is unimportant, or that voters will punish legislators who support a specific reform. As they successfully counter these objections, they soften the context, making it easier not only to get an issue placed on the agenda, but to get a reform enacted.

The media can serve as an important educational tool in policy practice. Stories in the press, on the radio, and on television about social problems can create powerful images in the minds of citizens and elected officials, who may decide to give them serious attention. A social worker in an agency found, for example, that a reporter from a local paper became a frequent ally.[13] When the social worker wanted the city to replace junkyards with low- and moderate-income housing, several stories in the newspaper about the blighted area prompted local politicians to take the neighborhood's problems seriously.

VIDEO CLIP 5.1

HOW POLICY ADVOCATES USE THE MEDIA

In viewing Video Clip 5.1, consider the following. Professor Ron Dear discusses the way social workers can use the media to educate the public about key issues and to elicit support for specific policies. Ask yourself these questions:

- Are social workers well situated to obtain media coverage?
- Why is it such a challenge to get media space?
- Why does the media insist on brief, to-the-point presentations, whether on the printed page or on the airways?

Social workers can help to shape agendas by using the mass media. This is not easy to do because the media ration their scarce time among many claimants. With their proximity to many social issues and problems, however, social workers increasingly should seek air time and print space in local and national media. (See Video Clip 5.1.)

As with social problems, only certain solutions make it to agency or legislative agendas. Those who examine solutions often test their fiscal, administrative, and political feasibility.[14] Assume that a staff person in a job-counseling agency for women is advocating not only referring women to jobs, but actually training them. Some staff may be skeptical about this idea's feasibility. They may ask whether the agency, which has emphasized job referrals and job search, can develop training programs in fields such as computer literacy. Can it find facilities to house these services, foundations or government funders to fund them, and the needed staff? Can it place the graduates in actual jobs? Since this program represents a marked departure from current programs, it is likely to encounter political opposition from some staff, as well as some board members, who will question whether the proposal falls within the agency's mission. Some staff may fear as well that the proposed service will detract from existing services. Decision makers also judge a solution's likely effectiveness and technical merits. Will a proposed program actually help clients, and will it be sufficiently inexpensive to prove feasible in light of the agency's budget? Policy advocates can counter such skepticism, of course, by citing evaluative research or by showing how a solution has been successfully used in model programs elsewhere.

Our discussion suggests that policy advocates must try to place a solution in a favorable light if they want it to get onto decision makers' agendas. They must accomplish this task, moreover, in settings where specific solutions vie with one another for the scarce space on agendas. They should also recognize that they may encounter opposition from persons or groups that do not like their solution and that want to cast it in an unfavorable light.

Political realities   Policy advocates can also soften the context by diminishing opposition to a specific reform. They can talk with persons in strategic positions to educate them about the need for a specific reform. They can directly address the concerns or objections these persons have, and they can correct erroneous information.

As Tip O'Neill, the late Democratic Speaker of the House, suggested, it is often effective to co-opt others by asking for their suggestions.[15] Policy practitioners can ask people to offer suggestions about getting a policy reform on the agenda. As these people offer guidance about how to proceed, they sometimes unwittingly become part of the change effort.

When softening the political context, it is important not to prematurely dismiss some people on the basis of their ideology or prior positions. To the extent they can, policy advocates want to construct a "big tent" that contains an array of persons, even those with divergent perspectives, to build a coalition that can support a policy reform. To achieve this objective, they must be open to input from a variety of people, have good listening skills to understand various perspectives, and be willing to compromise.[16]

Of course, this approach is not always feasible in highly polarized situations, where policy advocates sometimes have to rely on the support of a specific faction. Indeed, in some situations, policy advocates have to create a ruckus to get decision makers to pay attention to an issue, such as organizing demonstrations, picketing, or sit-ins. Disruptive activities sometimes backfire by hardening decision makers against a proposal or issue, but they can also mobilize popular opinion.

Even though specific proposals have not been constructed yet to address a specific problem or issue, people often wrongly anticipate their likely content. Someone may think, for example, that a costly remedy is inevitable or that a proposal will require major changes in existing policies. Policy advocates sometimes allay opposition by noting that nothing is set in concrete, that is, a proposal will emerge only after the viewpoints of many persons are solicited. People may anticipate, as well, a decision-making scenario that predisposes them to oppose a policy initiative, such as its domination by persons with specific viewpoints, by members of a specific political party, or by members of a specific faction. To the extent that multiple points of view will be sought, a policy advocate can emphasize an inclusive decision-making process that draws on multiple perspectives.

When an agency staff member wants to make the political context more favorable to a problem or solution, he or she can point to funding trends, court rulings, or professional developments that support a specific change in agency policy.

The Activating Stage

Now we turn our attention to the activating stage, which appears inside the funnel in Figure 5.1. A policy entrepreneur is a decision maker, a legislator, a chairperson, an executive, or another person who has the power to pull an issue onto an agenda so that it will receive serious consideration.[17]

To pull an issue into the decision funnel, policy entrepreneurs use tactics that often include timing, coupling, negotiating, assembling early sponsors and supporters, and routing.

Timing and windows of opportunity   Calling key times "windows of opportunity," Kingdon suggests that they represent relatively brief moments when "the time is ripe" for specific initiatives. In legislative settings, key events often sensitize legislators to a specific issue. Dramatic and publicized stories, such as a homeless person's death from exposure or a flagrant example of child abuse, may make them suddenly aware of specific needs. A task force may issue a report that alerts people to a problem, such as the one issued in 1993 that described the amount of elder abuse in California. When the media cover such events extensively, public opinion may encourage legislators to consider a legislative proposal.

Pivotal events in the political stream stir up support for a specific problem or solution. With Bill Clinton's victory in November 1992, after 12 years of Republican rule, many people hoped that issues that had lain dormant would now reach congressional agendas, such as national health care reforms, parental leave bills, expanded programs for children, job-training initiatives, changes in military policies concerning gay men and lesbians, and pro-choice issues. With renewed hope that their issues would now reach decision or choice agendas, people invested time and resources in publicizing and championing them. As this example suggests, though, the placement of issues on decision agendas does not mean they will be successfully resolved. Political opposition and budget deficits stopped many of Clinton's reforms. This example also illustrates how windows of opportunity often close rapidly. When the Republicans captured control of both houses of the Congress in 1994 and retained this control in 1996, they aborted many of Clinton's reforms.

Similarly, Republicans hoped when George W. Bush won the White House in 2000, that many issues that conservatives had suggested during the preceding eight years would come to the surface. They hoped that large tax cuts would be enacted particularly for middle-, upper-middle, and upper-class Americans. Some of them wanted large increases in military spending. Even during the presidential campaign, Bush had discussed "faith-based initiatives" to give religious institutions federal dollars to provide services to poor people, the homeless, and others. Conservatives hoped that proposals to privatize Social Security—letting citizens invest their own resources rather than turning over their payroll taxes—would soon be enacted. They favored vouchers for schools so citizens could select whatever schools they wanted with vouchers funded by the government.

Here, too, fast-moving events shifted the agenda. The tragic demolition of Twin Towers in New York City on September 11, 2001 propelled issues of national and domestic security to the forefront while putting domestic policy issues on the backburners.

Regular, predictable windows of opportunity exist in legislative settings during annual budget preparations, when advocates can seek a discussion of expanded resources for specific programs.[18] When legislation is being reauthorized—that is, renewed—advocates sometimes obtain reforms in the legislation.

Pivotal events in social agencies also create opportunities for changing policy. A governor, mayor, or large foundation might announce a new program for dealing with a problem related to an agency's mission, thereby creating a positive milieu for policy changes. Dramatic events may sensitize an agency's executive director or board members to a problem that the agency does not currently address, as when enactment of federal welfare reform in 1996 provided a positive climate for developing programs to help women leave the welfare rolls. An affluent person may bequeath unexpected funds to an agency, enabling it to start a new program. Fiscal crises sometimes force an agency to reconsider its priorities or to search frantically for resources from new funding sources. Perhaps an accrediting agency is about to make a visit, causing the agency to make some changes that will guarantee a favorable report.

New tides in an agency's politics also create opportunity, such as the arrival of a new executive director or other high-level staff.[19] While executives are not omnipotent, their critical position allows them to chart new directions for agencies. Changes in the leadership of an agency's board of directors may also create a positive milieu for policy changes. When agencies engage in systematic planning about their mission and programs—often called *strategic planning*—their staff and boards are often open to program and policy reforms. Indeed, strategic planning is a formal planning approach to finding issues, problems, and solutions that should be placed on agendas. (See Policy Advocacy Challenge 5.3.)

POLICY ADVOCACY CHALLENGE 5.3 *ANALYZING AN AGENCY'S STRATEGIC PLAN*	Find the most recent strategic plan that was conducted in a social agency. 1. What issues, problems, and policies were highlighted? 2. Which of them were actually implemented? 3. What political, budget, or other factors favored some issues and problems, but not others?

Timing allows policy entrepreneurs to capitalize on windows of opportunity. Their strategy involves (a) preparing for an opportunity by analyzing an issue or problem, (b) recognizing when a window of opportunity augurs well for it, and (c) seizing the moment by seeking support for placing it on the decision agenda.[20] In government settings, the policy entrepreneur is often an enterprising legislator with persistence, creativity, respectability, and good timing, or a creative lobbyist or advocate who convinces a legislator that the time is ripe to draft and introduce legislation on a specific issue before the window of opportunity closes. In agency settings, policy entrepreneurs can come from anywhere within the organization, recognizing a window of opportunity for a specific issue and persuading others to place it on the decision agenda.

Alas, windows of opportunity usually close, and often in a relatively short time. Participants change, people think that a problem has been adequately addressed by some other measure, and new issues supplant older ones. The momentum of policy change may also be lost as persons haggle over the details of a suggested reform, as opposition emerges, as budget exigencies intervene, or as other issues surface.

Coupling

Policy practitioners sometimes try to make imaginative connections between elements of the context. Perhaps someone in an agency has discussed decentralizing services (a solution) while someone else has noted the relative lack of services to the Latino population (a problem). A policy entrepreneur in the agency may suggest writing a grant proposal to develop outreach stations for the Latino population, a proposal that would couple the problem with the solution.[21]

Framing and Finding Titles

Policy entrepreneurs put a twist on proposals to make them appealing to decision makers. For example, they may portray a benefit as an *earned* benefit to make it difficult for opponents to argue that it is a *welfare* benefit. This strategy is illustrated by arguments used to support the enactment of a tax credit given to families with working parents in 1973. Policy advocates also found a *Title* that supported this interpretation, calling the legislation in this case the Earned Income Tax Credit. Had this program been framed as a *welfare* program, it probably would not have been enacted in light of widespread political opposition to welfare.

Negotiating and Bargaining

Even before an issue appears on the decision agenda, policy entrepreneurs need to accommodate different points of view. Even though policy proposals are not developed until an issue has entered policy deliberations (see the bottom of the funnel in Figure 5.1), policy entrepreneurs can develop a tentative proposal that draws on different perspectives. Even at the outset, they should, if possible, create a win-win atmosphere that allows different people and factions to believe they will each have a piece of the action. If a win-lose atmosphere exists at the outset, a combative mood guarantees that intense opposition will exist when policy deliberations begin.[22]

Assembling Early Sponsors and Supporters

In legislative arenas, policy entrepreneurs actually enlist people to sponsor a legislative proposal by placing their names on it. The characteristics of these sponsors is very important: If they are powerful politicians who also represent an array of perspectives, the chances of the legislation passing are much better than if the legislation is sponsored by only a narrow range of politicians who lack power.[23] Even in agency settings, policy entrepreneurs enlist an array of persons during the agenda-building process by soliciting their advice, for example. If highly placed and well-regarded officials want to resolve an issue—and if they agree on broad directions—the likelihood of a successful resolution increases.

Routing

Policy entrepreneurs must find a home base for their issue by routing it to decision makers who want to resolve it in ways that the entrepreneurs find acceptable. When a choice exists in legislative settings, they have to decide which committee should get jurisdiction. Naturally, a policy entrepreneur does not want an issue routed to a committee whose chairperson or members do not want to act on it or have contrary views. By discussing the routing with highly placed politicians and members of a special committee (called the Rules Committee in the U.S. House of Representatives), policy entrepreneurs can sometimes influence routing decisions.[24] Policy entrepreneurs influence routing decisions in agency settings as well; they may seek jurisdiction by a specific committee, the general staff, the agency's board, an ad hoc committee, or the executive director. Of course, some issues, such as fundamental changes in agency policies, have to be considered by the agency board.

Media Coverage

Timely coverage of proposals are often critical in projecting them into decision agendas. Getting key endorsements policy entrepreneurs need to obtain the support of important decision makers. They often want supporters who hold prominent positions in legislation on agency settings coalition building policy entrepreneurs need to develop an array of supporters and link them into a formal or informal coalition. Building Momentum policy entrepreneurs want to develop the perception that their issue or proposal is rapidly obtaining support—and that it will move rapidly toward policy deliberation.

Can Direct-Service Staff Help to Build Agendas?

Our discussion suggests that policy advocates in agency and legislative settings can diagnose and soften the context, as well as search for a policy entrepreneur.

Is agenda building restricted to legislators and high-level agency staff, such as executive directors? To be sure, these persons are best situated to assume pivotal roles in building agendas, but direct-service staff can participate in agenda building in both agency and legislative settings, doing the following to soften the context:

- Discuss and publicize unmet needs in the human services system
- Obtain information to gauge the seriousness of specific problems
- Frame specific issues to make them appeal to executives or legislators
- Establish a coalition or action group to publicize a specific problem, such as elder abuse, whether in an agency or in the community
- Seek high-level support to establish a task force to study the issue
- Discuss or publicize a promising approach to a social problem
- Document how this approach or solution has been used successfully elsewhere
- Find information about the solution's feasibility, such as information about its cost and administrative requirements
- Establish an action group to obtain support for a specific solution, whether in an agency or in the community
- Seek high-level support to establish a task force to study the solution
- Publicize specific problems or solutions in the mass media
- Work on or support the campaigns of candidates who advocate specific social reforms
- Lobby legislators or agency officials to sensitize them to specific problems or solutions

To find windows of opportunity, staff can identify strategic times in the workings of agencies or legislatures when conditions will favor advancing specific initiatives. Finally, staff can search for policy entrepreneurs who can place a specific issue on the agency's or legislature's agenda.

Policy Advocacy for Powerless Populations and Unpopular Issues

Thus far, our discussion about agenda building has emphasized how agenda processes work and how a pragmatic policy practitioner can use these processes to reach policy goals. When we discuss how agenda processes actually work, however, it is important to remember that they are often skewed against unpopular issues and powerless groups. For example, the Children's Defense Fund, established in 1973, sought for more than 15 years to convince Congress to place day care on its agenda, finally succeeding in 1989. Advocates of massive programs for homeless persons have not yet succeeded, despite more than a decade of lobbying and activism. Others have sought national health insurance since the 1930s, still unsuccessfully despite a resurgence of hope in 1993. Those who want to change the American federal tax structure to truly reduce economic inequality have been relatively unsuccessful for decades.

Were we to promote only those issues that are likely to achieve prominence on agendas, we would ignore some issues that need support even though short-term successes are unlikely. Recall our discussion in Chapter Two of the ethical principles of social justice and fairness, which stimulate policy practitioners to address the inequalities experienced by groups such as African-Americans, Latinos, Native Americans, women, gay men and lesbians, children, and persons with stigmatized conditions—even when the short-term prospects are bleak.

Groups that plug away for unpopular issues and populations may be laying the groundwork for subsequent policy changes. In the case of day care and the Children's Defense Fund, advocates' diligent and sustained lobbying, as well as their assistance to grass-roots reform groups throughout the United States, doubtless educated many politicians about the specific problems and needs of children. When pressure from feminist groups and corporations that hired large numbers of women finally placed day care on Congress's decision agenda in the 1980s, the Children's Defense Fund spearheaded a coalition to seek specific legislation. Had they not promoted the issue in the preceding two decades, however, they might not have been successful in the 1980s, or the final legislation, which was hardly adequate in its funding and scope, might have been even more limited.

Militant groups, such as Act-Up, whose members engage in nonviolent protests and disrupt public functions to seek better care for people with AIDS, sometimes educate the public about desperate, unmet needs even if they do not work for direct influence on the legislative process. Abolitionists in the 1850s, suffrage workers in the early part of this century, and civil rights advocates in the 1950s and 1960s used militant strategies to force neglected issues onto public officials' agendas. They persisted despite criticism that their tactics were unethical or unwarranted. These kinds of groups sometimes soften up the electorate and decision makers so they will contemplate ideas they had not seriously considered before.[25]

Electoral Processes

Agenda setting is applicable, as well, to electoral politics. Politicians, parties, and activists always try to find issues that can be used to distinguish themselves from their opposition. They want issues that will appeal to their natural constituencies while also allowing them to appeal to swing voters. If they do not find new issues and their opponents do, they lose a strategic advantage in upcoming elections.

The search for new issues is particularly intense after a party loses an election. When George W. Bush won the White House in 2000, for example, Democrats wondered where they should go next in terms of issues. Liberals in their ranks wanted Democrats to focus on health care reform, policies to help working families (such as child care, college tuition subsidies, increasing the Earned Income Tax Credit), and upgrading caring work by increasing wages of persons who work in nursing homes and homeless shelters, teachers, and others. Other Democrats urged even more liberal policies for fear the Green Party, which already took many votes from Al Gore in 2000, would erode Democrats' base of support in the 2004 presidential elections. They favored substantial shifts in national priorities, including significant increases in domestic spending and cuts in military spending. Conservative Democrats favored large tax cuts and increases in military spending.

Republicans, in turn, wanted issues that would appeal to their natural constituencies while also retaining support of swing suburban votes. While most followed the lead of president Bush, some moderate Republicans wondered by the end of 2001 if the president's issues would allow them to win in their districts in forthcoming elections. Some of them, such as Jim Jefferds who actually left the Republican Party in summer 2001 to become an independent, feared that the president's policies were too conservative. Some of them favored more domestic spending, were less enamored with school vouchers and privatizing Social Security, and were more critical of the antimissile defense program.

Partisan politics, then, is intensely concerned with setting political agendas at the party and presidential level. Agenda setting happens in local constituencies, as well. Potential candidates scan the horizon to see if they can find issues that will put incumbents on the defensive. Indeed, decisions about whether to run for office often hinge on whether nonincumbents believe they can find defining issues that set themselves apart from incumbents. Incumbents, in turn, constantly seek new issues to enable them to ward off challenges.

In this nonstop process of agenda setting, ideology assumes a key role partly because the two major parties have somewhat different bases of political support. A large segment of Republicans' constituencies derives from relatively affluent segments of the population, farmers, and Southerners—in contrast to the more urban, Northern, and working-class base of support for Democrats. Republicans' natural base of support is relatively more conservative than Democrats'—so the two parties gravitate toward somewhat different ideologies and, therefore, positions on issues.

But ideological differences between the two parties ought not be overstated. Both parties often compete for swing votes, such as in the suburbs, where citizens are somewhere in the middle. If Democrats have some conservative voters, Republicans have a moderate faction that resists staunch conservatism. So both parties often battle for the center, seeking issues and policies that will appeal to centrist voters so they can gain a winning edge.

Developing Links with Advocacy Groups

Policy advocates who wish to build agendas in the broader community, but who do not know how to get started, should consider connecting with an established advocacy group. (See Box 2.1.) Effective advocacy groups try to shape public officials' agendas by pressuring them to consider solutions or problems, presenting research that underlines the importance of addressing specific social needs, and publicizing stories in the mass media that dramatize certain issues. Would-be advocates can join a local group or a local chapter of a national group, meet the director of the advocacy group, subscribe to its newsletters and other materials, volunteer to work on its outreach and education projects, help its staff conduct research, and help the group lobby public officials. Those who want to be involved can work with local and state chapters of the National Association of Social Workers (NASW), whose leaders and lobbyists pressure legislators. Both advocacy groups and the NASW not only generate ideas for the general agenda, such as specific pieces of legislation, but also put pressure on politicians to move these ideas toward choice or decision agendas. They often try to convince the chairpersons of pivotal legislative committees, for example, to hold hearings and seriously discuss proposals, rather than let them slip into oblivion.

Policy advocates can also campaign for politicians they believe will put certain issues on policy agendas. For example, PACE, the political action arm of NASW that backs politicians who support issues favored by NASW, regularly canvasses NASW members to work for the candidates it supports.

Using Multiple Skills in Agenda Building

We can see in Policy Advocacy Challenge 5.4 how policy advocates use the four skills that we discussed in Chapter Three. They use political skills to analyze and engage in the political stream; analytic skills to develop and use data in the problem and solution streams; interactional skills to help problems and solutions reach policy deliberations in agency and legislative settings, persuade people to take specific problems and solutions seriously, participate on committees and task forces, and organize coalitions; and value-clarifying skills to decide whether to invest energy in promoting an issue in the first place.

POLICY ADVOCACY CHALLENGE 5.4

FIGHTING THE GUN LOBBY: A COALITION WORKS TO PLACE GUN CONTROL ON THE POLITICAL AGENDA

Eugene Aisenberg, Ph.D., School of Social Work, University of Washington

Preparatory Work

The Greater Los Angeles Violence Prevention Coalition (VPC) is a grass-roots volunteer coalition which began in 1991. Five citizens from the Los Angeles area became concerned about the escalation of violence and its destructive effects. Led by Billie Weiss, they agreed to form the VPC as a means of promoting the prevention of violence. Currently, the coalition's membership comes from all segments of the community, including the legal and medical community, law enforcement, social work, public health, mothers who have lost children to violence, and other concerned citizens. The general mission of VPC is to reduce violence and injury in Los Angeles County. As a result of VPC's policy efforts, on March 11, 1997, the Los Angeles County Board of Supervisors passed an ordinance calling for the elimination of the state preemption of local firearms regulation; establishing a surveillance system for the ongoing collection, sharing, and

(continued)

(5.4   continued)

analysis of data and information relative to the incidence of violence and weapon-related injury; imposing new restrictions on gun dealers and other requirements related to the location of their business; requiring the implementation of certain security measures in the storage of guns; and instructing the county counsel to draft for the board's consideration a county ordinance banning the sale of so-called junk guns or Saturday night specials.

Diagnosing the Context

In 1992, the Policy and Planning Committee of the Violence Prevention Coalition began looking at the epidemic of gun violence from a public health perspective. This model views injury as preventable and stresses the collection of data and the evaluation of outcomes. The committee examined firearm legislation at the local and national level and also networked with other public health advocates. In addition, it collaborated with public health investigators from across the country who had experience in researching gun manufacturers. Also, the committee conducted research which revealed that firearms were the leading cause of death of people under 35 years of age in Los Angeles County. As a result of these findings, the policy committee proposed a policy statement to the VPC general membership later that year. This statement declared that VPC would focus its efforts on three principal fronts: (1) reducing the accessibility and availability of firearms in L.A. County; (2) promoting nonviolence as a desirable way to address conflict; and (3) promoting violence prevention programs and activities. This statement was passed and enacted. Subsequently, the VPC began to gather additional information and epidemiological data regarding the manufacture and accessibility of firearms and the types of guns used to inflict injuries.

By 1994, the VPC's investigation into the types of guns that were responsible for fatalities and the types of guns that had been confiscated by police following crimes revealed that six police departments were reselling these confiscated weapons at auctions. VPC provided this information to legislators. In 1994, Carla Hill served as vice chair of the coalition. In 1995, she was chair of the Policy and Planning Committee of VPC. During these two years, in response to the data, legislation was introduced at the state level seeking to restrict law enforcement agencies from reselling confiscated weapons. Both efforts failed and have never passed. At the same time, California assemblyman Louis Caldera and state senator John Vasconselos introduced legislation to prohibit the sale of Saturday night specials. These proposed bills failed the first time.

From these early experiences in the political arena the coalition learned many valuable lessons, including that their work does not cease with placing their issues on the agenda of decision makers. Taking into account these failed efforts to restrict the sale of handguns and those of others across the country led the VPC to shift its focus from the state to the local level and to move away from trying to tackle the specific issue of banning the sale of guns. This decision also took into account the contextual constraint of California's state law of preemption prohibiting local governments from passing legislation to control the sale of guns. Previous legal efforts by other entities had not been successful in overturning this state preemption.

Working within these constraints, VPC began to collaborate with numerous other coalitions in looking at national policy with an eye to what would be effective locally.

During this time, Contra Costa County in California was successful in restricting the number of federally licensed firearm dealers doing business in residential areas. This success provided a window of opportunity that shaped VPC's targeting these so-called kitchen table dealers. This was viewed as the best chance to succeed and pass in the face of formidable barriers to enactment.

Local communities and legislators began to enlist technical assistance and advocacy support from VPC. For instance, the coalition provided critical data and support that were instrumental in the efforts of the cities of West Hollywood, Pasadena, Compton, Santa Monica, Los Angeles, and others to restrict the sale of firearms within their boundaries by prohibiting firearm dealers from selling guns in residential areas, banning the sale of Saturday night specials, and requiring the registration of ammunition. The assistance provided by VPC and its successes have enhanced the reputation of the coalition in the legal, legislative, and public services arena. Empowered by the success of local ordinances and by data that these specific reforms had withstood legal challenges and had yielded positive outcomes, the VPC targeted the County of Los Angeles. As part of its agenda building, Billie Weiss and other members of the coalition initiated contact with County Supervisor Yvonne Brathwaite Burke and dialogued with her and her staff for over a year regarding the issue of firearms and the feasibility of passing a county ordinance restricting the sale of guns. Later during this period, Supervisor Zev Yaroslavsky and his aide also participated in these discussions. Together, they began crafting the wording of a possible ordinance.

In this process, opposition and barriers to enactment were identified. Barriers to reform included the NRA gun lobby. It is well funded, well organized, and able to mobilize large numbers of people. It also supports financially a number of legislators to ensure their reelection. Another barrier was the young people living in high-risk neighborhoods, who were reluctant to give up their guns. The public's belief that having a gun will serve as protection was another barrier, as was the concern that business would be lost since the region of Southern California is the largest U.S. manufacturer of weapons. In addition, negotiation and compromise entered into the drafting of the ordinance. Threats of legal challenge and questions regarding constitutionality were also considered.

Softening the Context

Instrumental in pulling the issue into the agenda funnel was the fact that Supervisor Yaroslavsky agreed to assume the lead regarding the proposed ordinance. He felt that this issue was significantly important. To be sure, he incurred the political risk of alienating a portion of his conservative constituency. However, he also gained support from a broader base of the citizens of his district. In addition, his leadership on this issue enabled him to gain valuable publicity, as the media portrayed him as an advocate of safety. VPC's educational efforts helped promote a shift in the public's perception of the issue. The ordinance, instead of being framed as seeking gun control, was successfully framed as an issue of safety.

Obtaining data from the Bureau of Alcohol, Tobacco, and Firearms, VPC mapped the location of firearm dealers throughout the county. The facts revealed that dealers

(continued)

(5.4   continued)

were overwhelmingly conducting business in residential areas, many of them selling guns less then 1,000 feet from schools. The coalition also gathered information on gun dealers who, in response to the City of Los Angeles ordinance, had moved their operations out of the city but continued to sell guns. These gun dealers circumvented the ordinance by illegally selling weapons out of their cars on roads outside the city limit. They did so without punishment.

Activation Stage

The coalition exposed this information to the L.A. County Board of Supervisors at a public hearing in October 1996. The information not only softened the context but also garnered valuable support. On seeing the map, one supervisor recognized that a gun dealer with the license to import, to sell, and to manufacture guns and explosives lived only three doors from his own home. This discovery proved fortuitous as it persuaded the supervisor to lend support to the county ordinance proposed by VPC. Supervisor Yaroslavsky's leadership position as chairman of the Board of Supervisors provided additional leverage and weight during the deliberations on the ordinance.

At this hearing, testimony was given by various members of VPC who represented a broad base of the community. Indeed, all segments of the community were represented, in sharp contrast to the representation of the opposition, the NRA, which clearly reflected only a segment of the population. The broad representation by VPC strongly demonstrated to the Board of Supervisors that the community, not just one segment, supported the ordinance.

The version of the ordinance submitted to the Board of Supervisors at this October hearing sought (1) to restrict the selling of guns to nonresidential districts, (2) to criminally cite dealers who continued to sell guns in residential neighborhoods, and (3) to require trigger locks to be installed on all new guns and to require special security measures regarding the storage of firearms in gun shops and stores. These items were chosen for their feasibility; they were considered achievable. They did not present possible conflict with the Second Amendment, nor did they interfere with the state's preemption law. In general, they were seen as small but effective steps that would have significant impact.

At this hearing, the Board of Supervisors asked that further work be done on the proposed legislation to address lingering concerns regarding the wording of the ordinance and its ability to withstand legal challenges. The board assigned the county counsel to work with VPC to address these issues. In the drafting of the final ordinance, negotiation and compromise came into play.

During these ensuing months, support for the ordinance was sought from the members of the Board of Supervisors. Knowing the members' voting records on similar issues, the VPC focused on those supervisors considered receptive to the ordinance. The Violence Prevention Coalition also gathered data on the number of gun deaths and the number of weapons dealers in each local community of Los Angeles County. This information was widely disseminated among its membership. VPC members used this information to address their own local supervisors through personal visits and other communication in order to sensitize them and educate them about the nature of the problem, its scope, the reason why guns were significantly responsible, the need to address the issue, and the concern for safety. Such contact was ongoing and helped convince the supervisors that the number of firearm dealers was indeed a problem to address, not merely a condition to tolerate and endure. Political pressure was also exerted as VPC skillfully used the media through press conferences and press releases to keep the issue at the forefront of the agenda of the board.

The progress of the ordinance was due in large part to the shift in the political and social climate in recent years. Gun violence is no longer seen strictly as a law enforcement issue. Rather, it is seen as a public health issue. Thus, it evokes less controversy and garners more acceptance. Local efforts to address the sale of firearms are more and more successful. Thirty-nine local communities have now passed ordinances. This progress has softened the climate for legislators to tackle the issue. Indeed, the local successes have diminished the fear of the NRA and have enabled legislators to take a more courageous stand on the issue. For example, at the last national election in 1996, for the first time representatives throughout the country were voted out of office for voting against gun control measures. The local communities' successes in California have also been instrumental in turning the tide at the state level. In California, both houses of the legislature have recently passed bills regarding restriction of the sale of Saturday night specials. Work is now under way to reconcile differences between the two versions and present a unified bill to the governor for signing. Without the local efforts, this legislation would probably never have occurred. Such efforts have shaped awareness of the problem as well as demonstrated that such a problem is solvable.

On March 11, 1997, Carla Hill, Chairperson of VPC, gave testimony to the L.A. County Board of Supervisors. Again, VPC members were present at the hearing. The Board of Supervisors passed the ordinance with the exception of the prohibition of the sale of Saturday night specials. The passage of the ordinance was due in part to the legislative efforts being conducted at the state level. The board, however, mandated the L.A. County Health Department, in collaboration with other county agencies, to gather surveillance data on the use and sales of guns, the types of injuries they inflict, and the costs related to gun violence. In addition, for the first time, the Board of Supervisors allotted funding to the Department of Health Services toward establishing this surveillance data system.

The passage of this ordinance reflects a tremendous amount of work, perseverance, skillful analysis, political and interactional skill, and collaborative effort. It also reflects the success of policy practitioners in effecting reform.

Exercise:

- How does this case illustrate how grass-roots citizens' groups can place issues on the agenda?
- How did the VPC change its strategy during the case as circumstances changed?
- What kinds of power did this coalition have that allowed it to succeed even when pitted against a gun lobby that had vastly greater resources?
- How does this case illustrate that policy advocates must often make compromises in order to succeed?

Chapter Summary

What You Can Now Do

You are now equipped with skills to do the following:

- Diagnose agendas in legislative, agency, and community settings
- Enhance support for a problem or solution by softening the context
- Develop support for a problem or solution by using such tactics as timing, coupling, negotiating, finding sponsors, and routing
- Place items on the agenda as a direct-service worker

We discuss methods of analyzing problems in the next chapter.

Notes

1. Marc Ross and Roger Cobb, *The Cultural Strategies of Agenda Denial* (Kansas City: University of Kansas, 1997).
2. Robert Eyestone, *From Social Issues to Public Policy* (New York: Wiley, 1978), pp. 20–21, and Frank Baumgartner and Bryan Jones, *Agendas and Instability in American Politics* (Chicago: University of Chicago Press, 1993), pp. 250–251.
3. John Kingdon, *Agendas, Alternatives, and Public Policies* (Boston: Little, Brown, 1984).
4. Ibid., pp. 83–88.
5. Michael Cohen, James March, and Johan Olsen, "A Garbage Can Model of Organizational Choice," *Administrative Science Quarterly* 17 (March 1972): 1–25.
6. Ibid., pp. 95–121.
7. Kingdon, *Agendas, Alternatives, and Public Policies,* p. 115.
8. Ibid., pp. 95–108.
9. The work of advocates to place Alzheimer's disease on national policy agendas illustrates how advocates seek to dramatize the severity or pervasiveness of a social problem—even when precise data are lacking. See Julie Kosterlitz, "Anguish and Opportunity: Alzheimer's Disease," *National Journal* 23 (March 9, 1991): 2728–2732.
10. See Reich's use of the term *investment* rather than *spending* in Robert Reich, *The Work of Nations: Preparing Ourselves for 21st-Century Capitalism* (New York: Knopf, 1991), pp. 252–261.
11. Bruce Jansson, *The Reluctant Welfare State,* 2nd ed. (Pacific Grove, CA: Brooks/Cole, 1993), p. 293.
12. The political problem of securing funds for prevention is illustrated by the AIDS epidemic; see Julie Kosterlitz, "AIDS Wars," *National Journal* 24 (July 25, 1992): 1727–1732.
13. For uses of the media to place issues on an agenda, see Hedrick Smith, *The Power Game: How Washington Works,* (New York: Ballantine Books, 1988), pp. 331–387; and Baumgartner and Jones, *Agendas and Instability in American Politics,* pp. 103–125.
14. Ibid., pp. 138–139.
15. Chris Matthews, *Hardball: How Politics Is Played* (New York: Summit Books, 1988).
16. Donald deKieffer, *The Citizen's Guide to Lobbying Congress* (Chicago: Chicago Review Press, 1997), pp. 19–20.

17. Kingdon, *Agendas, Alternatives, and Public Policies,* pp. 174–193.
18. Ibid., pp. 110–115.
19. Ibid., pp. 160–162.
20. Ibid., pp. 188–193.
21. Ibid., pp. 181–188.
22. Clinton decided not to use the single-payer Canadian system not only because health provider groups opposed it, but because the federal government would have been required to fund the entire package of benefits just as Clinton was trying to reduce the federal deficit. Ibid., pp. 1, 9.
23. Ron Dear and Rino Patti, "Legislative Advocacy: Seven Effective Tactics," *Social Work* 26 (July 1981): 289–297.
24. Ibid.
25. Kingdon, *Agendas, Alternatives, and Public Policies,* pp. 134–138.

Suggested Readings

Joel Best, ed., *Images of Issues: Typifying Contemporary Social Problems* (New York: Aldine de Gruyter, 1989).

John Kingdon, *Agendas, Alternatives, and Public Policies* (Boston: Little, Brown, 1997).

Julie Kosterlitz, "Anguish and Opportunity: Alzheimer's Disease," *National Journal* (April 28, 1990), pp. 1008–1015.

Marc Ross and Roger Cobb, *The Cultural Strategies of Agenda Denial* (Lawrence: University of Kansas, 1997).

Jeffrey Schmalz, "Whatever Happened to AIDS?" *New York Times Magazine* (November 28, 1993), pp. 55–86.

Hedrick Smith, *The Power Game: How Washington Really Works* (New York: Ballantine Books, 1988), pp. 331–387.

Rochelle Stanford, "Child Care Quagmire," *National Journal* (February 27, 1993), pp. 55–86.

chapter  6

Committing to a Solution: Analyzing Problems

POLICY PREDICAMENT

Bill Clinton promised in his presidential campaign of 1992 to "end welfare as we know it" and to limit welfare to "two years and you're off," intending to introduce legislation to place most welfare recipients in jobs. To develop his plan, Clinton established a 32-person task force in 1993. But Clinton did not have the field to himself. Such conservative theorists as Charles Murray had contended even in the mid-1980s that AFDC ought to be eliminated because it gave "perverse incentives" to single heads of households to have children and to depend on the government for AFDC, Medicaid, and food stamp benefits.[1]

Faced with the enactment of welfare reform legislation in 1996 that gave state governments the primary role in shaping welfare policies, social work professor Nancy Gewirtz developed a coalition to seek humanistic policies in Rhode Island. How did she use policy advocacy skills to seek these policies, particularly when many conservatives had pressured the governor to adopt punitive strategies? How did she develop strategy from 1996 through 2001 to make certain that the humanistic policies were not cast aside during the actual implementation of welfare reform in Rhode Island? We discuss her strategies in Policy Advocacy Challenge 6.7 at the end of this chapter.

Developing and Defending Policy Proposals

We now enter a pivotal of the policy-practice process: identifying and analyzing social problems or issues, developing policy proposals, and defending policy proposals. In a way, we can compare this part of the process to the rudder on a boat; it gives us direction and purpose. This chapter discusses the following:

- Cultural and political factors that shape perceptions of social problems

- Analytic approaches to classifying problems as to prevalence, location, severity, and causes
- Qualitative approaches to analyzing social problems
- How social problems vary in different populations
- How to contest definitions, measurements, and perceptions of social problems of oppressed populations
- How social problems are slippery concepts

Putting It All Together

Figure 6.1, a circle made up of the six tasks, is a conceptualization of this process. The first task for policy advocates, and the focus of this chapter, is to familiarize themselves with a social problem or issue and develop an analytic approach to it. (See the oval at the top of Figure 6.1.) The second task, and a focus of Chapter Seven, is to identify an array of relevant options that might address the problem or issue. (See the second oval, clockwise from the first.) The third and fourth tasks (see the third and fourth ovals, clockwise) are to compare the relative merits of competing options and draft a proposal (again, in Chapter Seven). And the fifth and sixth tasks (see the fifth and sixth ovals, clockwise) are to seek supporters or funders for specific proposals and make oral or written defenses of them, the focus of Chapter Eight.

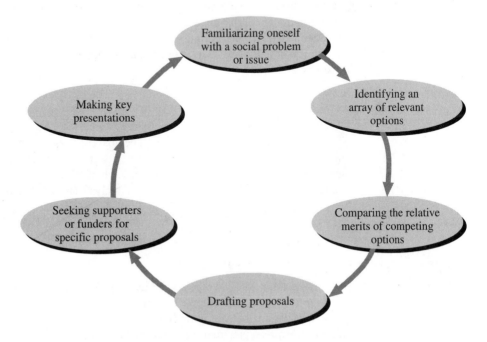

FIGURE 6.1   **Developing and defending policy proposals**

Policy advocacy is not always, of course, the neat, orderly process suggested by Figure 6.1. Sometimes advocates skip some of the points, such as hurriedly devising a proposal when they face time deadlines rather than devoting enough time to analyzing a problem. Sometimes they have to rule out certain options because they are not politically or fiscally feasible even if they are attractive on technical grounds. Sometimes they do things out of order, such as finding supporters or funders for specific proposals before analyzing a problem or issue extensively. Policy advocates need to be able to improvise as the situation dictates rather than follow a rigid format. Remember, policies are fashioned in the real world where many people and groups often participate in a fluid and changing process.

Do Policy Advocates Have to Analyze Problems?

Some people may believe that policy advocates do not have to analyze problems because their work is driven by their progressive values, such as their commitment to social justice and fairness. In fact, advocates must analyze problems for several reasons. Were they not to base their recommendations (at least in part) on hardheaded analysis of specific problems, including the use of up-to-date research, they would often find their proposals dismissed as lacking a substantive base. (See Policy Advocacy Challenge 6.1.) Moreover, a candid assessment of the social reforms of prior eras suggests that they often have not worked, partly because their advocates lacked sufficient knowledge of specific problems when they proposed specific reforms. The classic example is public housing for low-income persons. Believing they were providing a long-term solution, reformers in the late 1930s and the next two decades obtained federal funding for huge public housing projects, not fully realizing they would become segregated by class and by race—and bedeviled by high rates of crime and drug use.

POLICY ADVOCACY CHALLENGE 6.1

USING THE WEB AS A TOOL IN POLICY ANALYSIS

Stephanie Davis, Research Librarian, University of California, Irvine

Analysis is an essential part of policy work and advocacy. Analysis can take many forms, i.e. statistics, reports, case studies, etc. The goals of analysis (in part) establish a definition for the problem, investigate the causes, history and impacts of the problem, and determine who the problem affects. Your research will lead you to ask these questions and more. A few examples of sites that present analysis are listed below:

- Center on Budget and Policy Priorities www.cbpp.org
- Fedstats www.fedstats.gov
- John F. Kennedy School of Government at Harvard University ksgwww.harvard.edu

Using these sites and others you find for your specific issue or problem, assess how well the sites address your topic or issue.

Web sites are also useful for finding statistics. Why are statistics important? First of all, they provide a picture of our country—information about our population, pastimes, habits, how we spend our money, where we work, and the problems we face as a nation.

Using statistics to back up your words or to show the impact of a specific problem on a population can be powerful.

As part of your research you may be asked to find statistics, such as the number of children in foster care, or the percentage of women without health care. There are many places to find statistics, online and in print sources such as books and journal articles. Here are a few resources to get you started:

- *Dictionary of U.S. Government Statistical Terms.* Alfred N. Garwood and Louise Hornor. 1991.
- *Historical Statistics of the United States: Colonial Times to 1970.* 2 vols. 1975.
- *Social Work Almanac.* Leon Ginsberg. 1995.
- *Statistical Abstract of the United States.* U.S. Bureau of the Census. 1878–.
- *The World Almanac and Book of Facts.* 1923–.

There are also three indexes that provide comprehensive access to statistical information, available in print and through the subscription database *Statistical Universe:*

- *American Statistics Index* (United States Federal Government statistics)
- *Index to International Statistics* (International statistics from inter-governmental organizations, including the United Nations)
- *Statistical Reference Index.* (Statistics collected by states, private agencies, non-profit organizations, and research organizations)

Online Sources:
- FirstGov, the Federal Government Search Engine www.firstgov.gov
- Fedstats, One-Stop Shopping for Federal Statistics www.fedstats.gov
- University of Michigan Documents Center Statistical Resources www.lib.umich.edu/govdocs/stats.html
- United States Census Bureau www.census.gov

Evaluating Statistics:
Locating your statistics is only the first step. You need to evaluate this information critically as you would a journal article, report or book.

Here are criteria to consider when evaluating statistics:

- Where does the information come from—the government, corporation, private agency, state or regional agency?
- Did the government pay for the study that produced the statistics? If not, who paid?
- How old is the statistical information? Is it based on the current census, or the previous census?
- What was the sampling size and sampling error?

Exercise:
Go to the library and find the most recent edition of *Statistical Abstract of the United States* (it's published every year). Find statistics about your research topic or an issue that interests you. Then look at the Appendix titled "Limitations of the Data" (usually Appendix III). Do these limitations have a possible impact on the data you found? Give three reasons how the data you found could be incorrect or inconsistent.

When searching for new solutions to problems, policy advocates must realize that persons, groups, and institutions often select policies that will enhance their prestige, revenue, and power, sometimes with scant regard for citizens who need assistance. Tradition often shapes policies, even when existing policies are obviously outmoded and ineffective. Professional wisdom, which often fosters effective services, sometimes promotes dysfunctional policies, such as many surgeons' excessive reliance on radical mastectomies, hysterectomies, and heart bypass operations. Policy makers are not immune to societal prejudices and misconceptions, as well as fads and presumed panaceas. So policy advocates must subject their policy choices to careful deliberation to minimize the effects of power, tradition, fuzzy intentions, and intuition.

Indeed, a school of policy theorists emerged in the 1960s known as *policy analysts*. Why not establish decision-making rules in advance, they asked, so that only policy options that have obtained positive evaluations will be chosen? Why not make extensive use of research so that objective information guides policy choices?

As the definition of *analysis* in *Webster's New World Dictionary* states, the analytic approach emphasizes the "breaking up of a whole into its parts to find out their nature."[2] Most analytic frameworks suggest a careful four-step process in defining policy problems, collecting information, and reaching policy solutions after extended deliberation.[3] In the first task, policy advocates identify stakeholders, that is, persons and groups that have a legitimate interest in a policy issue. In the case of welfare reform, such groups include service staff, welfare recipients, governors, county welfare directors, and federal legislators. Realizing that these stakeholders have different vantage points, policy advocates often elicit these stakeholders' perspectives as they proceed with their work. In the second task, policy advocates analyze the problem at hand by asking the following questions:

- Can we establish a typology that defines subvarieties of the problem?
- How do we measure the problem's prevalence?
- How do we locate persons or institutions who have the specific problem, or who might develop it?
- How do we locate people who will develop the problem?
- How do we assess the relative importance of the problem to society, to some group in the population, or to specific institutions?
- How do we determine what causes the problem?

In the third task, after comparing alternative remedies, policy advocates develop a proposal that addresses the problem. As we discuss in Chapter Seven, they ask such questions as these:

- What policy options should be considered?
- What criteria and measures should be used to compare the options?
- Which policy option is preferable?
- What policy remedy will most effectively prevent or redress the problem?

In the fourth task, policy advocates disseminate technical data and policy recommendations to decision makers, hoping they will agree about the proposed remedy.

We can now return to an ecological or systems perspective. Most social problems involve not just individuals, but individuals enmeshed in relationships with families, peers, community institutions, and economic forces. To understand why they occur and how to redress them, we should often use broader perspectives that place these problems in their context. As we shall see in succeeding discussion, we stress this ecological perspective throughout this chapter.

Using a Flowchart to Analyze Problems

It is useful to diagram social problems so that we can develop solutions or ameliorating policies. Let's begin with an overarching diagram that can be used, in whole or part, to analyze any social problem. Then let's develop a diagram specifically geared to the welfare-to-work problem to show how to apply the overarching diagram to a specific problem.

Five Cells in a Flowchart Format

Our overarching diagram has five cells placed in a context that includes familial, community, and economic factors. (See Figure 6.2.) Let's begin with the context, because human services always exist in a context.

Family members, peers, and social networks powerfully shape how people address their needs, whether they seek organized services, how they respond to organized services, and whether they develop specific problems and how they deal with them. Persons in affluent communities with outstanding schools and services, for example, have a head start compared with persons in low-income communities with poor schools, poor housing, and high rates of crime. We also should not forget cultural factors that influence how people define specific problems and whether they seek help from organized institutions and programs.

The cell at the far left of Figure 6.2 represents the prevention arena which describes persons who have not yet developed a problem like substance abuse, mental illness, poverty, or diabetes. The prevention arena shows interventions we can use to stop persons from developing specific problems. We can sometimes identify at-risk factors that allow us to target interventions that decrease the odds of a specific person developing a specific problem. In some cases, we find out by luck that specific interventions prevent certain problems, such as when medical researchers discovered that the daily intake of small amounts of aspirin lessened persons' likelihood of contracting colon cancer. In other cases, we have no idea how to prevent certain problems, and sometimes considerable controversy exists about the effectiveness of specific interventions. Preventive strategies sometimes require the active involvement of people, for example, changing their lifestyles (such as diet) in an effort to avert a specific social problem. In addition, society sometimes attempts to prevent certain social problems, by instituting changes in peoples' environment, such as decreasing pollutants, improving the safety of automobiles, or preventing cigarette sales to youth.

If we are successful in preventing specific problems—or if some people simply do not develop them—they stay within the preventive arena. People who do develop specific problems move into one of the three cells in the middle of the diagram.

- the top-middle cell describes persons who remain outside the orbit of all organized systems of care. To the extent they get help from others, it is from family and neighborhood members, persons at their place of employment, the clergy, and others in their support systems.

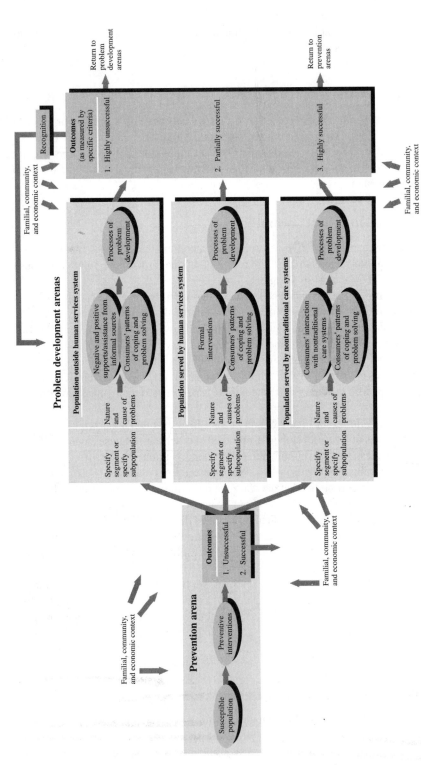

FIGURE 6.2 An ecological model of social problems

• the middle-middle cell describes organized systems of care, such as social agencies, hospitals, clinics, schools, job-training programs, and professionals.
• the middle-bottom cell describes programs that operate on an empowerment or self-help perspective such as Alcoholics Anonymous, programs for persons who are physically challenged, and community-based programs for persons with persistent mental problems.

This distinction between those who remain outside institutions and programs and those who remain in them is critical to understanding social policy. In many cases, only a small percentage of persons with specific problems actually seek organized services for them. For example, huge numbers of persons with mental illness, medical problems, poverty, reading disorders, and delinquency are not helped by organized institutions and programs—whether because they do not know about them, they believe they are not eligible, they do not want to present a stigmatized condition to others, they drop out of services, or they do not perceive themselves as having a problem.

We should not prematurely conclude that persons outside the orbit of organized programs do not cope with or even solve their problems. Many people solve problems on their own or with help from support networks in their own communities, and a certain number, such as substance abusers, mature out of their problems over the course of time.

Yet some persons clearly harm themselves by not using organized programs. People with diabetes or cancer, for example, may die from their malady if they do not get medical help—as may persons with clinical depression. Persons with severe reading disorders are unlikely to deal with their condition without assistance. It is important to ask why some people do not avail themselves of organized programs. Some people lack the resources needed to use organized programs as in the case of medically uninsured Americans. Some may not know about organized services, and others may be given services that they perceive to be intrusive, demeaning, or ineffective. Finally, organized services may be so severely underfunded that people cannot gain access to them, as is true with substance abuse counseling.

Other people do use organized services and programs to address specific problems, whether voluntarily or because they are required or coerced into using them. Voluntary entrants enter organized services because they want assistance with specific problems and believe that organized services can help them. To understand how they fare during such service transactions, we need to understand not only what is provided to them, but how other factors (such as family and support networks, economic conditions, and peer factors) shape how they perceive and benefit from services.

Involuntary entrants are forced to get certain services, often by the courts, who require persons to use them to avoid incarceration or other penalties. Implied, stated, or perceived threats can also lead some persons to seek services, such as a parent who fears she will lose custody of her children if she does not solve a substance abuse problem or accept services from a child welfare agency.

Some people turn not to organized programs, but to programs or activities that use a self-help or empowerment paradigm. Examples include community-based programs to help physically, mentally, or developmentally challenged persons, Alcoholics Anonymous, and community-based programs that help people purchase their own houses. In each of these cases, people have problems, whether physical disabilities, substance abuse, or poverty, but these programs focus on persons' strengths in dealing with them. (Many programs that help physically challenged persons do not even use words like disability, clients, or diagnosis.) They want to mobilize peoples' existing skills and motivation or help develop them. For example asset-building programs operate under the assumption that poverty can best be averted by helping persons obtain assets, like houses or savings accounts, that middle-class and upper-class people commonly use to advance their well-being. These empowerment programs not only use different language and different strategies, but they are not structured like traditional social agencies. They are more likely to have informal organizational structures and less likely to have charts on their clients. In addition, their staff are less likely to be credentialed professionals.

Consider the case of a self-help agency that assists persons with persistent mental problems such as schizophrenia. Psychiatrists, mental institutions, and counseling by professionals comprise the central thrust of traditional mental health services. By contrast, community-based programs with an empowerment perspective aim to inculcate problem-solving skills in persons with persistent mental problems. They may provide them with low-cost housing, encourage them to seek employment while providing job training and referral services, and give them skills to develop social supports such as going to specific organized activities. They are taught to monitor their medications so they can seek technical assistance when certain symptoms emerge. The community-based program establishes an advisory council, comprised of persons with persistent mental problems, to develop additional empowerment strategies.

Typologies within the middle cells   It is important to remember that populations with specific problems are not homogeneous in the prevention. Indeed, considerable evidence suggests that specific interventions often do not work for many people, who may respond to different approaches. Later we discuss in more detail, using welfare reform as our example, how policy advocates need to develop typologies identifying subgroups within a larger population that possesses a specific problem.

Relationships among the cells   People move among the three cells in the middle of Figure 6.2 in interesting and complex ways. For example, someone may begin in organized services, drop out of them, and then be helped by a community-based empowerment program. Someone else may solve a problem with the assistance of family members and move back into the prevention arena. Or people can use organized institutions and empowerment programs simultaneously, such as when a physically challenged person uses traditional health services while getting help from a community-based organization run by physically challenged people. (See Policy Advocacy Challenge 6.2.)

An important issue in social policy is whether the organized system of services can successfully draw upon family and neighborhood resources (the top-middle cell in Figure 6.2) or the work of agencies using an empowerment paradigm (the bottom-middle cell). It would seem advisable for social agencies, for example, to use community leaders and caregivers, such as barbers and beauticians, to refer cases (such

POLICY ADVOCACY CHALLENGE 6.2	Take a social problem that interests you-and diagram it following the format of Figure 6.2. Be certain to include the prevention arena, persons who are not part of the organized service-delivery system, and persons who do receive help from the organized service-delivery system. What does this exercise teach about the following?
DIAGRAMMING A SOCIAL PROBLEM	• The relative numbers of persons who remain outside the human services system • The role of families, communities, and self-help groups • The potential promise of preventive strategies • The sheer number of outcomes that are possible for clients, patients, and consumers of service • The sheer number of policies that influence whether and how persons move through and access the organized human services system

as depressed persons) to trained professionals working in agencies—and even to use them to give therapeutic services that supplement professional ones. It would also seem logical for organized systems of care to organize support networks for persons with mental and other problems, since considerable research suggests that persons with social supports fare better than many others in addressing their problems.

However, these courses of action need to be taken with the awareness of certain risks, as a number of researchers and theorists suggest. Social supports are not always helpful to clients, such as when dysfunctional relationships exist within them that may even exacerbate someone's problems. When family and neighborhood persons relate to professionals, they may lose their natural way of relating to a client. It takes time for professionals to organize and relate to community and family supports—and it is not always clear how to do it.

Nor is it easy for organized systems of care to relate to empowerment-focused programs such as those for persons who are physically challenged. Empowerment-focused groups are often suspicious of professionals, such as physicians, who they believe label them and treat them paternalistically. They may fear overmedication and excessive use of surgery. In some cases, traditional organized systems of care incorporate units or programs with an empowerment perspective, such as a birthing clinic in a hospital that uses midwives and places less emphasis on traditional medical ways of delivering babies.

Outcomes   On the far right side of Figure 6.2, outcomes are depicted. Successful outcomes can include eradicating a problem or lessening its severity or impact. If we use an empowerment approach, successful outcomes would include mobilizing persons' personal strengths to allow them to cope with specific issues in their lives or to overcome such challenges as physical disability. Unsuccessful outcomes can include failure to solve or redress a problem or to develop personal coping strategies. However, neither successful nor unsuccessful outcome measures are objective phenomena, but invented measures that vary widely. We sometimes try to assess the effectiveness of specific programs by using techniques of program evaluation—whether quantitative or qualitative approaches.

Illustrating a Flow Chart with Welfare Reform

We will illustrate the use of a flow chart with the welfare-to-work issue. We do not have to use all of the cells in Figure 6.2 because we focus on organized systems of care in this case—we use only the prevention arena, the center-middle cell, and the right-hand cell. (See Figure 6.3.)

By way of background, recall that President Bill Clinton and the Congress revolutionized the American welfare system when they approved the Personal Responsibility and Work Opportunity Reconciliation Act in 1996. It replaced AFDC with state-run welfare programs to be funded by a combination of federal block-grant funds and state resources. (Grants under the new state-run program were called Temporary Assistance for Needy Families, or TANF, grants.) The legislation ceded virtually all decisions to the states. Only prohibiting them from reducing their current spending on welfare more than 20 percent, it even allowed them not to fund welfare for specific families if the state's allotted funds ran out, to replace cash payments with in-kind assistance (such as food items), and not to provide fair hearings if recipients believed their rights had been violated.[4]

Rather than establishing statewide rules, as under the AFDC program, states could let each of their counties establish their own programs drawing on state block-grant funds. The federal government did not add significant training and day-care funds to the federal block-grant funds. The legislation also cut food stamp allotments deeply, ended welfare payments under the Supplementary Security Income program (SSI) for legal immigrants, and proposed the removal of many disabled children from SSI rolls. This welfare reform legislation set in motion developments that would profoundly shape the well-being of millions of women and their children, requiring 50 percent of single-parent recipients to be participating in work or work-related activities by the year 2002.

Welfare reform is an excellent example of how policymakers analyze social problems, using such methods as quantitative research. Yet it also demonstrates that perceptions of social problems, as well as proposed solutions, are profoundly shaped by such nonrational factors as values, culture, and politics. Indeed, persons with radical, liberal, and conservative perspectives disagreed sharply about the advisability of the welfare reform legislation. Indeed, these divergent perspectives will come into play when congress decides whether to reauthorize welfare legislation in 2002 (the 1996 legislation lets welfare reform, including federal payments to states, expire unless congress reauthorizes it).

We use welfare reform throughout this chapter as a case example of policymaking in the United States. It demonstrates that policy advocates must assert their analyses of social problems, lest other analyses prevail.

Figure 6.3 presents a flowchart of single heads of households who are susceptible to joining welfare rolls, who currently use welfare, or who have left welfare rolls. It includes various *stages of development,* as seen from an analysis of the model from the left to the right, moving from a susceptible population not yet using welfare to an array of users of welfare to former users who have left the rolls. Policy advocates are also interested in understanding the *dynamics* of a problem, such as patterns of movement between the different phases as depicted in Figure 6.3 by arrows between the different stages. They might ask, for example, what percentage of susceptible persons actually seek and obtain welfare benefits; what percentage of recipients obtain jobs and for how long; how many recipients leave the welfare rolls permanently; what percentage of

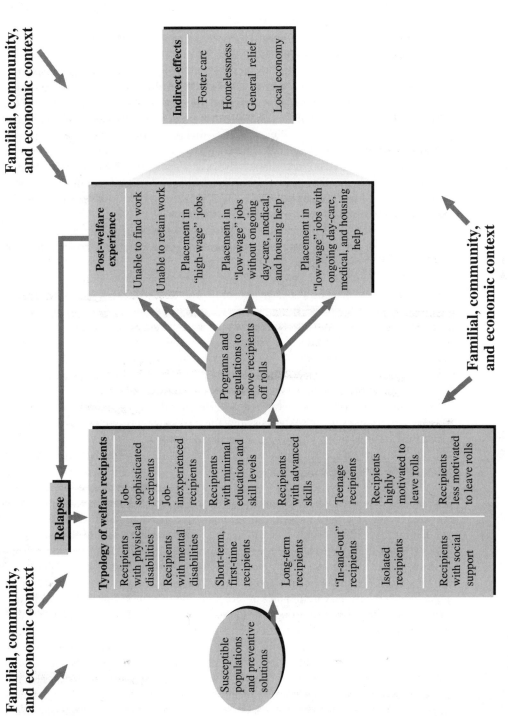

Familial, community, and economic context

Familial, community, and economic context

Familial, community, and economic context

Relapse

Susceptible populations and preventive solutions

Typology of welfare recipients

Recipients with physical disabilities	Job-sophisticated recipients
Recipients with mental disabilities	Job-inexperienced recipients
Short-term, first-time recipients	Recipients with minimal education and skill levels
Long-term recipients	Recipients with advanced skills
"In-and-out" recipients	Teenage recipients
Isolated recipients	Recipients highly motivated to leave rolls
Recipients with social support	Recipients less motivated to leave rolls

Programs and regulations to move recipients off rolls

Post-welfare experience

Unable to find work

Unable to retain work

Placement in "high-wage" jobs

Placement in "low-wage" jobs without ongoing day-care, medical, and housing help

Placement in "low-wage" jobs with ongoing day-care, medical, and housing help

Indirect effects

Foster care

Homelessness

General relief

Local economy

FIGURE 6.3   A dynamic flowchart of single heads of household who become welfare recipients

former recipients find themselves with a net income lower or higher than when they were on the welfare rolls; and how many recipients move repeatedly between welfare and work during a brief period.

A typology of welfare recipients can classify them with respect to their manifestations, chronicity, and demographic characteristics (see the center portion of Figure 6.3, titled "Typology of welfare recipients"). *Manifestations* are outward behaviors, symptoms, or characteristics that differentiate people with specific problems. They are widely used to establish typologies of illness in medicine and mental health, as illustrated by the diseases and illnesses listed in any medical encyclopedia or in the *DSM-IV.*[5] For example, a typology for epilepsy would contain a listing of symptoms or behaviors, as well as physiological characteristics such as brain-wave patterns. We can establish types of welfare recipients, based on such characteristics as whether they have extensive or little job experience, whether they possess job-related skills, and the extent of their education. Or we could establish categories based on recipients' views about job seeking, such as "discouraged job seekers versus optimistic job seekers."[6]

Policy advocates often examine the *chronicity* of problems. For example, welfare recipients can be classified as chronic users, in-and-out or oscillating users, brief one-time users, and occasional users.

By using manifestations, chronicity, and demographic factors, policy analysts develop typologies of persons who have a specific problem. Typologies are useful because they make clear that populations with a specific problem are not homogeneous and consist of specific subgroups with distinguishing characteristics. Some single heads of household who receive welfare, for example, have had extensive working experience, and others have never been employed. Some of them are teenagers, and others are considerably older. Some have physical or mental disabilities; others have no disabilities. Some are highly educated; others have not completed the eighth grade.

Typologies are useful for several reasons. Because they divide people with specific social problems into smaller subgroups, they force policy practitioners to develop an array of interventions rather than relying on a single approach.[7]

Indeed, many theorists in social marketing contend that policy advocates must segment populations into smaller groups, much as we have done in Figure 6.3.[8] As these theorists identify smaller groups, they can use so-called focus groups to find out what kinds of services or resources the members of these groups believe they need. A policy advocate forms a focus group of five to eight people who fit into a subgroup like those in Figure 6.3, choosing people who are likely to articulate the needs of this subgroup. She develops five or six broad questions framed to capture their definitions of their problems and the interventions that they believe will be effective. She poses the questions, allowing 15 to 25 minutes' discussion per question, carefully eliciting the views of all group members. Taking careful notes or recording the session, she analyzes the group's responses at a later time to develop policies and programs geared to this group's needs.[9] (See Policy Advocacy Challenge 6.3.)

Typologies facilitate evaluations of programs and policies as well. A welfare-to-work program may be highly successful with a specific subgroup, such as highly educated recipients who have had prior work experience, but may have poor rates of success with less educated recipients with scant work experience. Were policy practitioners to rely on global evaluations of welfare-to-work recipients, they would fail to detect variations between subgroups, thwarting efforts to design strategies designed to address

POLICY ADVOCACY CHALLENGE 6.3

A FOCUS GROUP IN ACTION

A social worker wants to establish outpatient services for older citizens in a major hospital but wants to obtain their perspectives. She segments this population into ambulatory but relatively healthy older people and those with more acute or chronic conditions. Realizing that older people in her hospital's service area are Caucasian and Asian, she draws from these two groups to form two focus groups of well older people. She develops the following broad questions:

1. What kinds of medical problems or issues do well older people have?
2. Where do you currently receive outpatient medical services?
3. What problems do you experience with the services that you currently receive?
4. If you could establish the ideal outpatient agency for well older people, what would it be like?
5. What dangers or pitfalls would you advise the staff of this outpatient agency to avoid?

The policy advocate gains important insights from the older people she has consulted. For example, she finds that they value continuity of care (i.e., having a regular doctor) more than promptness of service.

Armed with insights from her use of focus groups, she develops a proposal for outpatient services that she hopes will be accepted by the hospital's board of directors.

Exercise: Using this example, develop questions for a focus group that you might establish concerning issues confronting single heads of household trying to survive in the wake of welfare reform. Decide what kinds of mothers by age, ethnicity, and work experience you wish to invite to your focus group, remembering that you want to focus on specific kinds of women.

their specific needs. Typologies also allow policy practitioners to establish priorities. If research suggests that certain subgroups are most likely to become long-term users of welfare, for example, state authorities can prioritize programs to assist them. Typologies help us understand not only welfare populations, but also people who have other social problems, such as mental illness, poverty, child abuse, and marital discord.

Of course, typologies are not a panacea, as we discuss at more length later. Critics may ask, for example, whether the subgroups in Figure 6.3 are mutually exclusive, since welfare recipients often fall into several of them. Persons who construct typologies often encounter a dilemma regarding the breadth of their categories. If relatively few categories are used, it is difficult to develop specialized programs that focus on the needs of specific subgroups. If too many categories are used, policy practitioners may fail to see the commonalities of persons in different subgroups, such as the common problems that welfare recipients confront as they enter job markets.[10] In the case of mental health typologies, such as the DSM-IV, many critics wonder whether some of the categories have been invented by psychiatrists or actually describe existing mental conditions.[11]

The Causes of Social Problems

Problems are caused by physiological, personal, familial, community, and societal factors. (See Box 6.1 for various causes of welfare dependency.) Welfare dependency is linked to such personal and familial factors as levels of education; job-related experiences; family size; whether a woman has been divorced or widowed or has had children out of wedlock; how much child support a woman receives; personal orientations toward welfare; the physical or mental disabilities of a head of household; and whether a woman has a child or children with disabilities.[12] These personal factors operate not only singly but together to cause welfare dependency. A woman's risk of dependency increases, for example, if she is the single head of a household, does not receive child support, and has a child with disabilities.

Welfare is also shaped by a host of community factors, such as rates of unemployment, wage levels, the availability of child care, the receptivity of employers to hiring welfare recipients, the availability of transportation, and the availability of job-training programs.[13] The likelihood of high rates of welfare in a community increase as multiple factors interact, such as low-wage employment, unavailability of day care, and high rates of unemployment.

BOX 6.1   **Some Causes of Welfare Dependency**

1. Physiological causes
   a. Physical disabilities
   b. Developmental disabilities
   c. Mental disabilities
2. Personal and familial causes
   a. Age (e.g., teenage mothers)
   b. Educational deficits
   c. Skill deficits
   d. Lack of work experience
   e. Lack of role models that facilitate job entry
   f. Lack of child support
   g. Subjection to abuse by spouse or others
3. Environmental causes
   a. Lack of jobs in local area
   b. Lack of jobs in local area that pay sufficiently to allow economic independence
   c. Lack of job placement and training programs
   d. Lack of public or subsidized transportation to job sites
   e. Discrimination by employers against welfare recipients
   f. Competition for scarce jobs from other people, such as unemployed persons, new job entrants, persons reentering the labor force, and immigrants
4. Interacting causes placing some people at higher risk of welfare dependency
   a. Persons associated with two of the preceding at-risk factors
   b. Persons associated with three of the preceding at-risk factors
   c. Persons associated with four or more of the preceding at-risk factors

Various personal, familial, and environmental factors often act together to place some people in higher risk categories than persons who are exposed to only one factor. A woman may experience short-term risk, for example, when her husband leaves, rendering her economically dependent on government programs. But her chances of securing employment that pays enough to allow her to leave the welfare rolls increase if she has prior work experience, has a college degree, lives in a neighborhood with expanding economic opportunities, and has access to affordable transportation and child care. By contrast, a woman who lacks all of these advantages and who is also left by her husband is less likely to find employment that pays enough to make her economically independent.

Policy advocates use both quantitative and qualitative research to analyze the causes of specific problems. Four approaches are common. First, they compare persons with a social problem with persons who do not have it, to infer from their differences why certain persons develop the problem. Because welfare dependency is strongly associated with single-parent families, for example, we can infer that persons in families that are supported by a single wage are more vulnerable to poverty—and welfare—than persons in families with dual wages.[14] Second, they follow people through time to discover why they develop a problem, such as following teen women to discern why some of them become pregnant and join welfare rolls. It is more difficult to conduct this second kind of research, because it requires gathering data at many intervals from participants who must agree to participate for an extended period.[15] Third, they evaluate existing programs to find clues to a problem's causes. If recipients who received ongoing and substantial day-care subsidies after they left the rolls have lower rates of recidivism than recipients who did not receive them, policy practitioners can surmise that day-care expenses force many women onto the rolls.[16] Fourth, they get information directly from persons who are experiencing a specific problem, by observing them (as in anthropological studies) or by interviewing them.[17]

Rather than limiting ourselves to examining the immediate causes of welfare dependency, we can analyze a sequence of factors that causes dependency. If low wages cause welfare dependency for many single mothers, for example, we can ask what causes low wages. If many poverty-stricken inner-city persons do not live near job sites, what caused residential segregation by race and social class? The answers to these kinds of questions force us to consider social reforms that might address the economic and social forces that ultimately cause welfare dependency, such as raising the minimum wage or securing housing for low-income persons in suburban areas, where jobs are increasingly located.[18]

When researchers examine the causes of social problems, their perspectives influence their work, such as whether they emphasize personal, psychological, economic, biological, or environmental causes. Researchers with *public health* or *ecological perspectives* emphasize occupational, economic, familial, peer, and neighborhood factors.[19] When examining the causes of welfare, for example, these researchers implicate low-wage industries, the sheer cost of day care, the lack of transportation, and the placement of many jobs in suburban areas that are distant from inner-city residents. They also cite discrimination against welfare recipients by many employers.

Persons with *radical perspectives* implicate economic and social inequalities, the reduced economic opportunities of certain populations, and the practices of corporations as causes of specific social problems.[20] With the globalizing of the economy, for example, corporations often place their factories in low-wage nations in the developing world, thereby eliminating jobs in the United States that might have employed some welfare recipients. In addition corporations have often relocated their plants to suburban sites, making it difficult for inner-city residents to get to them. Corporations stand to benefit, moreover, from welfare reforms that force hundreds of thousands of people into the competition for jobs, allowing them to depress wages even further for relatively un-skilled persons.

Analysts who use *medical* or *disease models* explore the physiological factors as-sociated with specific problems.[21] Considerable numbers of welfare recipients are dis-abled or must care for children with disabilities. Medical or disease models dominate the medical and increasingly, the mental health fields, where physiological and pharmaceu-tical causes and solutions dominate.

Persons who emphasize *intrapsychic factors* explore personal and familial causes of social problems. Some researchers contend, for example, that teen pregnancy is often caused by a constellation of personal and familial dynamics, such as abusive parents, truancy, and poor school performance.

In a departure from traditional approaches, some persons adhere to *behavioral frame-works,* contending that certain social problems can be redressed only by providing rewards and disincentives that make welfare less attractive than employment. Persons who favor disincentives advocate reducing the levels of welfare grants or requiring teen mothers to live with their parents except when they are abused by them. Persons who favor rewards often favor allowing recipients to retain some assistance from the government even after they leave welfare so their post-welfare income will exceed their welfare income.

Some people emphasize *deterrent strategies* that penalize persons with social prob-lems. Deterrents might include time limits for welfare or ending welfare altogether for certain groups of persons, like legal immigrants.

These different approaches often cause vigorous debates among theorists, analysts, and researchers. Persons who implicate economic and environmental factors often con-tend that counseling is an ineffective strategy. Radicals contend that, without remedying the inequalities in American society and the stress that poverty causes, many social prob-lems cannot be significantly alleviated. Contending groups often selectively cite re-search evidence to support specific remedies and to attack the proposals of persons who use different paradigms.

These various frameworks and causal factors are not mutually exclusive, because var-ious causes interact. Sophisticated policy practitioners and theorists believe that social problems are caused by an array of factors that combine the traditional approaches.[22] The risk of dependency increases when someone has not completed high school, has had no prior work experience, lives in a geographic area with high unemployment, has been sub-jected to parental abuse, and is sexually victimized by an older male. Such theorists as William Julius Wilson analyze these kinds of intersecting factors that shape complex phe-nomena like welfare dependency.[23] Indeed, policy advocates should take leading roles in critiquing social policies that are premised on simplistic analyses of social problems.

Developing Interventions and Programs

Having established a typology and analyzed causation, policy advocates devise interven-tions to solve specific social problems. They develop curative strategies and preventive programs, measure the prevalence of specific problems, and conduct research to locate persons with specific problems.

Some policy initiatives emphasize a deterrent approach, but many policy advocates favor a public health and radical approach. Single women have children for many reasons, including coerced sex, lack of knowledge of contraception, a desire for companionship, and a desire to form a family unit. (In many cases, women believe that the father of the children will remain part of the family, only to find that he deserts, divorces, or fails to marry the mother of his children.) Research does not suggest that a diminution of welfare benefits markedly diminishes the number of single-headed families because women do not base childbirth decisions primarily on economic calculations.[24]

Once women do have children and once they are single heads of households, economic realities force them into poverty when they confront low-wage jobs and the sheer cost of day care, transportation, health care, and housing. Many of them realize from personal experience or from discussions with other women who have tried that they cannot support their families with income from low-wage jobs. So, many women stay on the rolls for extended periods or resort to on-and-off patterns as they enter and leave jobs that cannot finance their basic needs. Indeed, the decision to seek welfare in these economic circumstances is often a meritorious strategy used by women who care about their children enough to want them to have sufficient food, clothing, medical care, and housing.[25]

What is needed, then, is not deterrence but a constructive approach to make work pay enough to (at least) bring families to a poverty standard. This can be accomplished by giving all families in the lowest economic quintile in-kind help through day care, health care, and housing subsidies that continues as long as families remain below the poverty level. These in-kind subsidies need to be supplemented by direct income subsidies, such as an expanded earned-income tax credit (EITC) that gives families tax rebates as long as they remain below the poverty level.

Also needed are programs to help people employed at low wages to upgrade their earning potential. Persons with minimal skills and limited education must be prepared for jobs that are geared to their abilities and must receive sophisticated job placement services. To the extent that their skills and education can be enhanced to improve their long-term prospects, they should receive extended services, education, and job training. Some recipients need help moving to areas with less unemployment and those with disabilities might need jobs geared to their capabilities.

Even these remedies, however, ignore the reality of growing inequality in the wage structure of the United States. Dramatic increases in the minimum wage, as well as an increase in the power of American trade unions, are needed to raise wage levels for low-wage workers whose economic status has been eclipsed by the dramatic growth of wages for highly skilled and educated workers. Many advocates participate in a movement to require "living wages" in jobs that flow from government contracts.

Another set of interventions must be directed to employers in the private and public sectors. It is tempting to portray private employers as villains, but it is understandable that they would try to fill specific slots with job seekers who already have the requisite skills and job experience, which many welfare recipients do not possess. Without economic incentives for employers to hire them, many welfare recipients will not get jobs except during booming economic periods—and they are likely to be the first persons to be laid off when the nation enters a recession.[26] Moreover, federal, state, and local governments must create large numbers of public service jobs and retain them as long as the private sector does not absorb welfare recipients. These public service positions are needed particularly by recipients who are physically or mentally challenged. The government ought also to offer massive tax incentives to corporations that locate in low-wage areas, rather than the minor incentives offered under the current tax code.

Of course, booming economic growth will reduce the welfare rolls in some states even without these ameliorative policies. It will make deterrent strategies appear successful in the short term because employers, facing labor shortages, will hire many welfare recipients into low-wage jobs and will even promote some of them into moderate-paying ones. In the long term, however, the deterrent approach to welfare is not likely to be effective because it does not upgrade the skills and education of recipients; consequently, they will be vulnerable to layoffs when economic growth slows. Services and policies tailored to the needs of specific subgroups are needed rather than a single set of policies. (See Policy Advocacy Challenge 6.4.)

To protect the rights of single heads of households and to safeguard their children, the welfare reforms of 1996 should have included a *bill of rights* for welfare recipients. If they participate in activities that prepare them for work, diligently seek employment, and secure employment, they should not fall beneath poverty standards or beneath the combined AFDC, food stamp, housing, and health benefits that welfare recipients received just before the enactment of welfare reforms. This bill of rights is needed to prevent the victimization of recipients by states that push recipients into poverty by insisting they take low-wage jobs, while cutting off the child-care, health, housing, and transportation

---

POLICY **ADVOCACY** **CHALLENGE 6.4** *DESIGNING* *SERVICES FOR* *WELFARE* *RECIPIENTS*	A policy advocate who wishes to design services for welfare recipients might use focus groups, as well as research, to develop different interventions for the following: 1. Recipients who have never worked and who have not completed high school 2. Recipients with some or considerable college education and with prior work experience 3. Latino recipients in rural areas with seasonal labor 4. African American recipients in inner-city areas 5. Recipients who have physical disabilities 6. Recipients who have mental disabilities

Take a stab at writing several hypotheses for one of these specific groups or for one of your choosing. For example, an hypothesis might read: "On-the-job training, as opposed to classroom training, will be most effective in helping welfare recipients who have not completed high school to get and retain jobs."

Try to identify policies and services that would be useful to these six subgroups if they were able to establish ideal programs. How might provisions of the federal welfare reform as reauthorized in 2002—or your state's approach to welfare reform—help you to meet the needs of some of these groups, and how might they impede efforts to meet the needs of other groups? Can you identify any policy changes you might recommend to allow federal legislation-or your state's approach to welfare reform—to better meet the needs of any of these groups?

subsidies needed to keep them above the standards that existed before the enactment of welfare reform.

A bill of rights is also needed to protect recipients from the so-called workfare programs in some localities that place recipients in public jobs for extended periods that pay wages beneath poverty standards. Without these protections, many states will engage in a race to the bottom, implementing punitive policies to prevent the migration of recipients from other states.[27] This bill of rights ought to be enacted by the federal government, because its protections should be national in scope and binding on the various states. Of course, many conservatives would oppose a bill of rights, whether because it interferes with the rights of the states or because they believe that subpoverty income acts as an incentive to work hard.

Our discussion of welfare suggests, then, a variety of interventions that address the economic, environmental, familial, and personal factors that foster dependency. (See Box 6.2.) A deterrent approach to welfare lacks the rich mixture of programs, regulations, and resources that a humane welfare system should provide its citizens, whether it is administered federally (as in the case of the defunct AFDC program) or by the states (as in the wake of the welfare reforms of 1996).

Preventive Programs

Both Figures 6.2 and 6.3 show prevention arenas at their left edges. Prevention is akin to apple pie and motherhood, yet Americans devote scant resources to the prevention of most social problems, including the need for welfare. The challenge is to find preventive strategies that are sufficiently effective for funders to devote resources to them.

BOX 6.2   **An Array of Interventions to Increase the Resources of Low-Wage Earners**

1. Direct economic assistance
   a. Expanded EITC
2. In-kind economic assistance
   a. Child-care, health, transportation, and housing subsidies
   b. Food stamps
3. Indirect strategies to elevate wages for low-wage employees
   a. Increases in the minimum wage and enactment of a living wage
   b. Encouragement of trade unions
4. Job creation
   a. Public subsidies of private wages
   b. Public service jobs
   c. Expanded tax concessions to industries that locate in areas with high unemployment
5. Encouragement of mobility
   a. Relocation assistance to promote migration from areas of high unemployment
6. Tailoring of services to the needs of subgroups
7. A bill of rights for welfare recipients

The promise of prevention   We should make a distinction at the outset among primary, secondary, and tertiary prevention. We emphasize primary prevention in Figures 6.2 and 6.3 because it prevents persons from experiencing important problems in the first place. Were we to prevent some people from ever getting cancer by cutting use of pesticides, for example, we would achieve *primary* prevention. In *secondary* prevention, persons with a specific problem are given assistance in its early stages, thus averting a full-blown or serious problem. When medical and mental-health screening problems locate persons with early-stage cancer or early-stage depression, for example, they can avert life-threatening cancer and depression through early interventions even though they failed to prevent cancer and depression altogether. *Tertiary* prevention aims to arrest a well-developed problem by using interventions that stop it from evolving further into a catastrophic condition. For example, the progression of clinical depression can often be stopped in persons treated with new medications as compared with persons who only receive counseling. (We can now update Figures 6.2 and 6.3 by noting that, although primary prevention occurs in the left-most circle, secondary and tertiary prevention occur in the middle circles of the diagram as persons are engaged with organized services or with community-based empowerment programs.)

Many preventive strategies have been shown to be effective at primary, secondary, and tertiary levels. With respect to primary prevention, for example, we know that lifestyle changes such as exercise, reduction of fat intake, reduction of alcohol consumption beneath certain thresholds, and weight control can markedly change health and mental health outcomes. We know that the requirement that automobile riders use seat belts and that bicycle and motorcycle riders use helmets have saved tens of thousands of lives. We have good evidence that Head Start improves school performance years after children have graduated from it. We know that educational credentials, such as a community college or college degree, markedly increase earnings (and therefore reduce poverty) in succeeding years. With respect to secondary and tertiary prevention, we have good evidence that early treatment stops the progression of an array of medical, mental health school, and job performance problems.

All of these examples share certain characteristics. Research had established links between specific causal factors and specific problems. Prevention interventions could be targeted to persons with identifiable at-risk factors, such as obesity, sedentary lifestyles, poor diets, and lack of educational credentials—thus allowing society to focus its interventions on persons with these at-risk characteristics. Or, in the case of seat belts society targeted everyone who rides in cars, with clear evidence that the preventive intervention, seat belts, would increase the percentage of persons who survive car accidents. In each case, the cost of prevention was not so prohibitive that opponents could contend that society could not afford it.

Yet the promise of prevention is often unfulfilled. Certain interventions are poorly funded and implemented even when data suggests their effectiveness. Relatively few resources are devoted to helping persons make lifestyle changes; for example, even when sedentary lifestyles and obesity are strongly linked to various diseases and shortened life expectancy. We often invest too little money in programs that might prevent poverty, such as tutoring and preschool programs.

We lack good research on some preventive strategies, such as whether we can prevent many mental health problems from occurring in the first place. We do not yet know whether certain asset-building strategies actually work in the long term, such as helping low-income persons to establish savings accounts or to own their own homes, though early results are promising. Therefore, we need to examine an array of factors that impede greater emphasis on prevention.

Factors that impede prevention   A series of barriers discourage prevention, including the problem of efficiency, difficulties in marshaling evidence of the effectiveness of preventive programs, the power of special interests, and competition with curative programs.

The problem of efficiency   To understand the problem of efficiency, let's assume that we know precisely which persons will develop social problems, such as which teenage women will have out-of-wedlock births in high school and enter the welfare rolls. Our knowledge would be based on research about at-risk indicators, such as the various causes of welfare dependency listed in Box 6.1. Assume that this research allows us to predict with complete accuracy *true positives* (women who will join the rolls) and *true negatives* (women who will not join the rolls). Under these circumstances, we will direct our prevention efforts exclusively to the true positives, excluding true negatives from our project because we have accurately predicted they will not join the welfare rolls. Were policy advocates able to predict accurately which women would become welfare recipients and which would not, they could develop a highly efficient prevention program that targeted its preventive services and resources only to true positives and provided no preventive services to true negatives.

In the real world, however, our ability to predict which people will and will not develop a specific problem is imperfect.[28] Some women have characteristics that are frequently associated with pregnancy in high school, such as low school achievement, abusive parents, and sexual victimization by an older male, but defy the odds and do not become pregnant. These women are *false positives* because they do not become welfare recipients, even though they have at-risk characteristics. Conversely, some women do not have these at-risk characteristics and do become pregnant. These women are *false negatives*. To the extent that a prevention program makes incorrect predictions about who will and who will not develop a problem, it wrongly directs some of its resources to false positives and wrongly fails to direct its resources to some persons who will develop a problem. As it wastes resources in this manner, the prevention program's efficiency declines. (See Figure 6.4 for examples of a relatively inefficient prevention program—Program B—and a relatively efficient prevention program—Program A.)

Prevention programs further decline in efficiency, moreover, if they cannot help persons actually avert a problem. Assume, for example, that a program asks teenagers in a high school who the school staff believe are at high risk of becoming pregnant to take a pledge to be abstinent. Also assume that the staff later discovers that this intervention is relatively ineffective in averting teen pregnancy. Even if this program had correctly predicted which teens would become pregnant, it would be inefficient because its intervention—getting teens to pledge abstinence—is relatively ineffective in averting teen pregnancy. This situation is not unusual: Prevention programs must both direct resources to true positives *and* develop effective interventions.

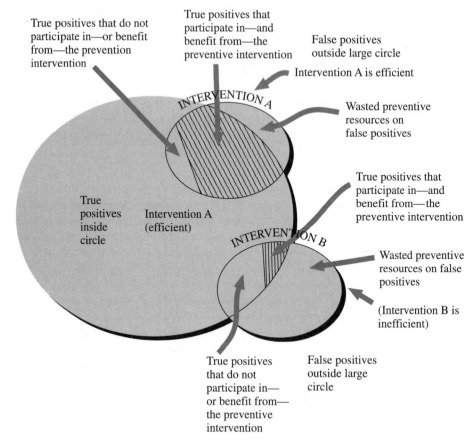

True positives that do not participate in—or benefit from—the prevention intervention

True positives that participate in—and benefit from—the preventive intervention

False positives outside large circle

Intervention A is efficient

Wasted preventive resources on false positives

True positives inside circle

Intervention A (efficient)

True positives that participate in—and benefit from—the preventive intervention

Wasted preventive resources on false positives

(Intervention B is inefficient)

True positives that do not participate in—or benefit from—the preventive intervention

False positives outside large circle

FIGURE 6.4   An efficient and inefficient preventive intervention

Problems in getting people to participate   Efficiency also declines when prevention programs cannot persuade people who are at risk to participate. Some teens refuse to participate because they do not want to make the effort, dislike the intervention, fear the motives of its staff, or are persuaded by peers not to participate.

We need not be excessively pessimistic: Some prevention programs are highly efficient and effective. (See Figure 6.4.) For example, the Ford Foundation funded a system of mentoring for high school students deemed to be at high risk of truancy and dropping out. High school graduates were assigned students to whom they were mentors for at least three years, aggressively monitoring the attendance and performance of these students, immediately finding them when they were truant, and getting them tutorial assistance when they received failing grades. The mentors visited the homes of their students frequently to secure the cooperation of parents and to address familial factors that impeded school attendance. In schools with dropout rates exceeding 50 percent, the mentoring program reduced dropout rates to less than 10 percent.[29]

It is useful to discuss as well the importance of passive prevention in social policy, as it is distinguished from active prevention. If active prevention helps people make corrective lifestyle changes or personal decisions to forestall a disease or problem (such as changing diets, engaging in exercise, using birth control, or stopping smoking), passive prevention changes the environments of people to diminish the likelihood that they will develop a problem. Examples of such changes are installing seat belts in cars (to prevent injuries or deaths from crashes), removing pollution from the air (to prevent lung diseases), and persuading food manufacturers to reduce the saturated fat in certain foods (to prevent heart disease). In each of these cases, people passively receive the benefits of these environmental changes without having to alter their lifestyle or to make different choices.[30] As in the case of active prevention, however, advocates must convince decision makers that the cost of these measures will be balanced by the benefits to society. For example, many advocates had to pressure legislators for years before convincing them that the cost of seat belts would be offset by the number of deaths they would prevent.

Many prevention measures fall between the active and passive poles. Banning smoking advertisements from billboards near schools, for example, is effective only if teenagers decide not to smoke.

Difficulties in marshaling evidence of the effectiveness of preventive programs   It is often difficult to marshal the empirical evidence that specific programs actually prevent specific problems. Researchers must follow subjects over a significant period of time to demonstrate that preventive interventions actually reduce such problems as teen pregnancy or alcoholism. They also have to rule out the effects of other factors that have affected the lives of their subjects during this period. And they must demonstrate a magnitude of prevention that justifies the costs of the preventive program. The problems in demonstrating the effects of preventive programs are well illustrated by the controversy in the health field over the efficacy of dietary supplements like vitamin C; researchers remain uncertain despite myriad studies. Yet some interventions have been demonstrated to have remarkable success, such as the aforementioned mentoring program for students at risk of not finishing high school.

The unproven efficacy of genetic testing   Genetic testing has enormous promise for conditions linked to genetic factors, such as many health problems and possibly some mental health problems. If researchers can identify genetic predispositions to certain problems, they can involve persons with them in preventive programs, such as lifestyle changes for persons with a disposition for heart disease. But the efficacy of genetic testing is now limited to relatively few conditions—and it remains to be seen if persons with genetic predispositions will commit themselves to prevention programs that could allow them to avert certain problems.

The power of special interests   Special interests often oppose meritorious prevention projects. Cigarette companies have successfully thwarted efforts to prevent teenagers from smoking because cigarette manufacturers consider teenagers a lucrative and growing market. Automobile manufacturers fought the installation of seat belts for years because of the cost. Right-to-life and moral majority groups have prevented many schools from providing effective sex education programs, as well as birth control services. Professionals who are socialized to medical models tend to focus on curative rather than preventive remedies.

Yet determined reformers often overcome the power of special interests. Laws requiring the use of helmets by motorcyclists and bicyclists have saved thousands of lives, even though they were strenuously opposed by motorcyclists. Even cigarette companies, despite opposition, have been required to comply with many governmental regulations.

Competition between curative and preventive programs   Preventive programs must compete for funds with programs that help people who already have specific problems. In the case of welfare programs, for example, states and localities must expend vast resources to sustain dependent families, whether providing them with welfare benefits, helping them get jobs, subsidizing child care, or providing health care. Advocates who want significant resources to prevent teenage girls from joining the rolls have to convince legislators to divert scarce resources from curative to preventive programs.

We should not be deterred from developing preventive programs just because they are often inefficient, are difficult to evaluate, are opposed by special interests, or compete with curative programs. To the extent that we can prevent problems, we not only forestall human suffering but also avoid future costs. (See Policy Advocacy Challenge 6.5.)

Measuring the Magnitude of Problems

It is relatively simple to measure the magnitude of welfare dependency among single women with children because public authorities issue data about the number of persons who receive welfare checks. Other problems, such as homelessness and substance abuse, are more difficult to measure because people who have these problems often do not seek public services. Policy advocates often have to demonstrate that specific problems are

---

POLICY ADVOCACY CHALLENGE 6.5

DEVELOPING A PREVENTION PROGRAM AND CONVINCING DECISION MAKERS TO ADOPT IT

Try to develop an intervention program for an inner-city school that seeks to diminish teen pregnancy. As you plan the program, discuss whether it should do the following:

- Try to increase teenagers' self-esteem
- Emphasize career and employment planning in hopes that teenagers who believe they have an economic future will be less likely to have children
- Seek to change behaviors of teenagers or attempt to change behaviors of males, to the extent that teenagers become pregnant because they are raped or pressured to have sex by older men
- Include the parents of teenagers in their project in hopes that improvements in family functioning will avert pregnancies
- Provide birth-control information and devices

Assuming that you lack resources to provide your intervention to all teenagers in the school, what at-risk factors might you use to decide whom you would try to reach?

Once you have developed a tentative strategy, discuss what strategies you might use to persuade teenagers to participate in your intervention.

Discuss some problems you might face in trying to convince the local school board to adopt your intervention for the entire school district. Discuss the problem of efficiency in this context.

---

sufficiently important to merit the attention of agency staff, funders, government officials, and legislators.

Legislators, funders, and agency executives are likely to invest scarce resources in programs that they believe address widespread problems. Rates, prevalence, and incidence are commonly used to measure the relative magnitude of social problems.[31] *Rates* (expressed as percentages), for example, measure the ratio of a group of persons, such as white males between the ages of 18 and 25 who were arrested for drunk driving in a specific year, to a larger reference group, such as the total number of white males in this age bracket in the population that year. *Incidence* (also expressed as a percentage) measures the ratio of new cases—for example, the number of new arrests in 2001 of white males aged 18 to 25—to a larger reference group, such as the total number of white males in the population that year in that age bracket. *Prevalence* (again, expressed as a percentage) measures the ratio of persons who are currently experiencing a social problem to the total population. A policy practitioner might want to compare the number of persons currently being prosecuted for drunk driving to the total number of drivers on a specific day. Each measure provides a somewhat different estimate of the problem's seriousness. These kinds of data are often available from city, county, state, or federal agencies or from research literature in the social and health sciences.

Practitioners can use a variety of technical approaches when measuring the magnitude of social problems. When data are not available from government agencies or the research literature, policy practitioners measure social problems in other ways. Jonathan Bradshaw contrasts measures of felt need, expressed need, expert need, and comparative need.[32] *Felt need* measures persons' belief that they have a problem. An agency might interview a sample of working mothers with preschool children, for example, to assess their belief that they cannot afford day care. Of course, persons sometimes exaggerate their actual needs or, in the case of stigmatized conditions such as substance abuse, underreport them.

Expressed need measures persons' actual search for specific services. A policy practitioner might examine the length of the waiting lists at drug treatment centers, for example, or the number of calls that a hot line receives about substance abuse. Although a knowledge of clients' service-related behaviors is useful, these behaviors may not accurately reflect people's actual needs. Some persons do not seek services, for example, because they believe they cannot afford them, do not like social agencies, are unaware of the services, think they will receive ineffective services, fear they will be prosecuted, or fear they will be subjected to punitive services because of their stigmatized condition.

Policy advocates sometimes assess *expert needs* by asking experts, such as social scientists, social work practitioners, local agency executives, or government officials, for their estimates of the severity of specific problems. Experts can draw convincing evidence from current research, such as the extent of alcoholism among women. Of course, experts' biases and values may influence their position and credibility; someone who defines alcoholism as consuming many drinks each day will provide a lower estimate of the problem's seriousness than someone who uses a more stringent standard, such as consuming only several drinks a day.

A *comparative need* approach measures unmet needs by comparing the services offered in different communities. Assume, for example, that certain neighborhoods have many drug treatment programs, but others with similar demographic characteristics have few. We can infer a larger unmet need for drug treatment services in the neighborhoods with fewer treatment programs. One should interpret comparative need measures with caution, however, because they rely on inference rather than a direct measure of need. For example, a neighborhood with few drug treatment programs will appear to have a shortage of services when compared with neighborhoods that have too many such programs.

Using several or all of these means of assessing needs helps us gauge the importance of specific social problems. If we were trying to promote drug treatment programs in a specific neighborhood, for example, we might look into the length of the existing programs' waiting lists (expressed need), ask high school students for their perceptions of the seriousness of adolescent substance abuse (felt need), discover whether similar neighborhoods have more programs (comparative need), and get information from selected experts (expert need).

Measurements of social problems become more dramatic when they include trend data suggesting that a specific problem is becoming more serious. Such data may come from felt-need, expressed-need, comparative-need, or expert-need sources, or from rising rates, prevalence, or incidence of specific problems. A dramatic increase in a community's substance abuse problems, for example, would be documented by a rising rate of deaths from overdose and longer waiting lists for drug treatment programs (felt need).

Policy decision makers, however, do not spring into action merely because policy advocates present them with data about the prevalence of a problem or the need for specific services. Legislators often ignore overwhelming data about a problem, particularly when they are not subjected to strong pressure by voters and interest groups or when powerful interests oppose ameliorating measures. Despite large numbers of deaths and injuries from guns in inner-city areas, for example, politicians in most jurisdictions have not enacted stringent measures to control guns because of opposition by the National Rifle Association. Politicians sometimes take action not when a problem is becoming more serious, but when the public believes it is becoming more important or when party leaders believe they can improve their political fortunes by taking action. In the case of welfare reform in 1996, for example, the cost of AFDC had risen from $15.5 billion in 1970 to $22.3 billion in 1993—not a marked increase after adjusting for inflation. Yet a welfare crisis was proclaimed, leading the Congress and the president to rescind the AFDC program and to devolve welfare assistance to the states.[33]

Locating Problems Spatially

It does little good to determine that a problem is relatively widespread if we cannot locate and reach its victims or, in the case of preventive programs, its potential victims. Social science tools are one way to locate people with certain problems. The U.S. Census, done every ten years, does not collect data about social problems such as substance abuse and mental illness but instead states demographic, economic, and housing data in aggregate terms for specific geographic regions.[34] Nonetheless its data are important to social workers because social scientists have linked demographic and economic factors with social problems. For example, poor persons are more likely than affluent persons to experience specific medical problems, to be unemployed, to have poor housing, and to be pressured by dealers to use illegal drugs. Members of certain ethnic groups are more likely than others to have some medical conditions, such as sickle cell anemia and Tay-Sachs disease. By using economic, housing, demographic, and ethnic data, policy practitioners can infer high rates of certain social problems in specific geographic areas.

Policy advocates need not confine themselves to census material. Local public health offices, various state agencies, municipal and county authorities, and some federal agencies, such as the National Institute of Mental Health, regularly collect and compile various kinds of population-based data.[35]

Census and other public data can also shape marketing, outreach, and advertising strategies. An agency could publicize its services in certain neighborhoods with a high concentration of specific groups. For example, the agency could market its services to areas with working women (day care), adolescents (substance abuse), or elderly people (home health care services). Policy advocates can even inspect neighborhoods to decide where persons with specific kinds of problems live. As a tenant organizer, for example, I discovered that I could easily locate substandard housing by observing the window frames in specific neighborhoods; from flaking paint and the absence of putty, I could often predict the overall condition of the rental unit.

When trying to understand why certain communities have higher rates of certain kinds of problems than other communities, policy advocates need to consider causation. Welfare dependency is not distributed randomly, for example, but clusters in certain communities as personal and familial factors interact with community factors. (See Policy Advocacy Challenge 6.6.) For instance, the South Central and East Los Angeles portions of Los Angeles County have high rates of welfare dependency compared with such areas as the San Fernando Valley and communities in the western end of Los Angeles County.[36] Both South Central and East Los Angeles have a high incidence of single-headed families and low-wage jobs—factors strongly associated with welfare dependency. Policy advocates for welfare recipients in the wake of welfare reform clearly need to concentrate their efforts on areas such as these, demanding expanded child care, job training, public service jobs, and job creation for these areas.

It should not be surprising that South Central and East Los Angeles are heavily populated by Latinos and African Americans. Though a majority of American welfare recipients are white, a significantly higher percentage of Latino and African American citizens than whites receive welfare. This association is, in turn, linked to personal, familial, and community factors. People of color have, on average, lower levels of education than whites, are more likely to live in households with a single head, and are more likely to live in neighborhoods with high rates of unemployment and low wage scales. We cannot ignore the effects of discrimination either; although employers often discriminate against welfare recipients generally, they are most likely to discriminate against welfare recipients who are also members of racial out-groups.[37]

POLICY ADVOCACY CHALLENGE 6.6 *USING DEMOGRAPHIC DATA TO LOCATE POPULATIONS AT RISK*	Assume that you are a high-level official planning strategies for preventing welfare dependency in Nashville, Tennessee. You know that people living in low-income areas are at greater risk of joining welfare rolls than are people who live in more affluent districts, so you decide to use census data to construct a map that shows the areas where relatively large numbers of people with low incomes reside. (See Figure 6.5.) What other kinds of maps might you construct based on risk factors for welfare?

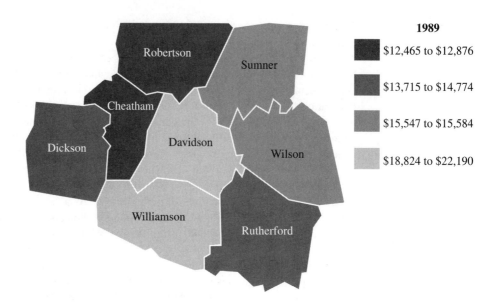

1989

■	$12,465 to $12,876
■	$13,715 to $14,774
■	$15,547 to $15,584
■	$18,824 to $22,190

FIGURE 6.5   **Per capita income by county for Nashville**

Assessing Policy Reforms

When policy reforms have been enacted, policy advocates gather evidence to decide whether they have been effective. (We introduce the topic of policy assessment at this juncture but discuss it in more detail in Chapter Fourteen.) Before evidence can be gathered, however, policy advocates must identify the criteria that define effectiveness. In the case of welfare reform, an array of possible criteria can be chosen, some of them emphasizing the well-being of the heads of household, children, and families.

- Has the economic well-being of heads of household deteriorated, remained the same, or improved?
- Has their well-being changed when measured by other indicators, such as substance abuse, family violence, or mental health status? Has the housing of recipients and former recipients deteriorated, remained the same, or improved as measured not only by the quality of housing but by the incidence of homelessness and overcrowding as people doubled up in housing?
- Has the well-being of children deteriorated, remained the same, or improved as measured by medical, educational, and developmental measures?
- Have more (or fewer) mothers had their children placed in foster care as they lost or increased their economic resources? Has family functioning deteriorated, remained the same, or improved as measured by the extent of family violence, the quality of parenting, and the incidence of children running away?
- Have absentee parents diminished or increased their interactions with family members—and have these interactions been constructive or harmful? Have absentee parents become more or less likely to contribute child support?

Policy advocates might also use criteria that focus on the cost to society of specific policy reforms. Policies sometimes are given favorable evaluations when their benefits to society greatly outweigh their costs. Benefits may include reductions in welfare costs as TANF rolls diminish, greater income tax revenues stemming from workforce participation by former recipients, and decreased costs of food stamp and Medicaid subsidies, as well as diminished day-care subsidies as some heads of household gain employment with wages sufficient to cover the cost of day care. But these benefits may be offset by various costs, including the diversion of some families to other welfare rolls, such as local general relief (GR) that subsidizes nonworking women who have exhausted their time limits on the TANF rolls. Other costs may include training, job placement, and day-care subsidies associated with helping recipients find and retain jobs; subsidies to private employers; and the cost of public service jobs. Some costs may rise because former recipients develop personal and familial problems due to welfare reform. Examples are the cost of expanding foster care rolls and the cost of police and prisons, mental health institutions, substance abuse programs, and homeless shelters. Were these various costs to be relatively small compared to the benefits, welfare reforms would have a high benefit-to-cost ratio, leading some policy practitioners to declare them effective. Conversely, were these various costs to be relatively high compared to benefits, welfare reform would have a low benefit-to-cost ratio, bringing negative assessments by some policy practitioners.[38]

The assessment of some policies becomes enveloped in controversy because people often disagree about which criteria are most important. Some conservatives insist that welfare reforms be assessed primarily on their ability to reduce the size of the welfare rolls regardless of their effects on the well-being of heads of household, children, or families. They would maintain that these reforms had been effective, even if net family income diminished when families left the welfare rolls, because they view economic hardship as a prod to promote the work ethic even among women who are already working full time. [39] Though they want to diminish the welfare rolls, many policy advocates insist that the well-being of heads of household, children, and families is most important, thereby regarding welfare reform as a failure if it scores poorly on measures of well-being even if it reduces the size of the welfare rolls. They would contend that welfare reform is not successful that takes women off the rolls but envelops them and their children in grinding poverty and economic uncertainty. They also point to evidence that substance abuse, crime, mental distress, family violence, and the removal of children from their natural homes by child welfare workers increases as families live in extreme poverty.

Even if policy advocates could persuade conservatives to stress the well-being of heads of household and children when assessing welfare reforms, they would rarely agree with them about how to measure well-being. Nutritional and housing experts would tell us, for example, that a family of three needs a specific level of resources to meet its basic nutritional and housing needs. Were many ex-recipients to lack these resources, many radicals and liberals would declare welfare reform to have failed—or they would insist on higher subsidies to the working poor. But some conservatives would assail the opinions of these experts, insisting that lower levels of nutrition and housing will suffice. Worried about reducing incentives to work, many conservatives would adopt lower absolute standards than radicals and liberals.

In addition, some conservatives and policy advocates would not agree about the interpretation of benefit-to-cost ratios. Some conservatives assess welfare reform in terms of its ability to reduce monetary costs to society. Therefore, they favor spartan job-training and educational programs to help recipients, on grounds that these programs diminish benefit-to-cost ratios because they are expensive. (Since many welfare recipients have no education beyond high school—and many have not even finished high school—remedial education could cost hundreds of millions of dollars if given for protracted periods to hundreds of thousands of recipients.) Nor do some conservatives favor ongoing day-care, housing, transportation, and medical subsidies to working single heads of household, even those in low-wage jobs who will descend into poverty without these subsidies. Expensive even if limited to the first six months of employment, these subsidies would require huge sums of money to be made permanent or to be given for extended periods, thus reducing benefit-to-cost ratios. Policy advocates would say that, without long-term or permanent subsidies, single heads of household in low-wage jobs cannot meet even the bare survival needs of their families. Those earning $6 an hour (roughly the minimum wage) earn only $960 a month—a sum not even sufficient to meet housing expenses in many urban areas, much less to cover food, housing, health care, and day care. Because of their limited education and low skill levels, many former welfare recipients are unlikely to graduate into high-paying jobs. Because low-wage jobs rarely pay health insurance or day-care subsidies, many former recipients will not be able to escape poverty unless given permanent subsidies.

Social Problems as Slippery Concepts

Flowcharts like the ones in Figures 6.2 and 6.3 are useful, but they do not reveal the subtle distinctions and philosophical issues that confront policy advocates. Social problems are human constructs, not purely objective phenomena. Indeed, by referring to social phenomena as social problems, people define them as requiring human intervention to be solved. They invent terms and classification systems, sometimes even when demonstrable problems do not exist or when it is unclear how many people have them. Part of the subject of this chapter, then—the analysis of problems—is a consideration of the basic concept of *social problem*. Let's analyze some ambiguities and philosophical issues that most social workers will confront during their careers.

When Are Social Problems Real, and When Are They Invented?

Because social problems are social conditions invested with human meaning, all of them are "invented."[40] Pestilence and famine were regarded in medieval times as inevitable and not solvable, but they are widely regarded in contemporary society as problems that demand solutions—at least in developed nations where the resources and technology exist to address them. Myriad conditions have only recently been called problems, such as dyslexia, many mental disorders, and such physiological conditions as menopause. (Successive versions of the *DSM,* which describes mental conditions for mental health professionals, have included scores of additional conditions, often with no credible evidence that they are important mental problems.)[41]

Most of us would agree, however, that we can be relatively confident in declaring some conditions to be problems. Such conditions as malnutrition, heart disease, cancer, and severe mental depression bring demonstrable suffering and death to their victims. Moreover, human service workers and health workers diagnose these conditions with high levels of reliability by using diagnostic tests that have been perfected through decades of research. But other social conditions are called problems without evidence that they are regular and identifiable phenomena in the real world. Critics of *DSM-IV* contend, for example, that research demonstrates that qualified clinicians cannot reliably make distinctions among many of the disorders listed.[42]

Social workers should view problems with healthy skepticism. As they proliferate with scant evidence that they are truly problems, human service workers are likely to treat subjects unnecessarily, to label them, and to apply remedies to conditions that do not require treatment. Indeed, the attitude toward some problems must be reversed, as is illustrated in the medical field by childbirth. For centuries, when childbirth was viewed as a normal condition rather than as a problem, women delivered their babies at home with the help of a midwife—a practice still prevalent in some European nations. Once childbirth was declared a medical problem by American obstetricians, women were taken to hospitals for delivery, drugged heavily, and subjected to extraordinarily high rates of cesarean section—policies that vastly increased the cost of childbirth without lowering the infant death rate.[43] Only recently has the pendulum reversed, as increasing numbers of women use midwives, either in hospitals or in their own homes.

Some social conditions are so complex that it is difficult to know when they are problems. Take the case of teen pregnancy, which is widely viewed as a problem. Considerable medical evidence suggests that when girls of 12 or 13 give birth, they imperil themselves and their infants, who experience high rates of birth defects. Such risks diminish sharply, however, as girls enter their mid and late teens. One researcher contends, moreover, that on a variety of indicators, including wages and amount of schooling, low-income women who have children in their mid to late teens are not worse off than women who wait to have children.[44] (The researcher contended that because they do not have to interrupt their careers with pregnancies and child rearing, women who have children early may be more able than women who wait to concentrate continuously on work and careers.) Even this cursory discussion suggests that teen pregnancy may not always be a problem. Indeed, we might well ask whether the decision of some teen mothers to have children is a legitimate lifestyle choice, particularly in light of evidence that some of them do not harm themselves or their children.

Many Social Problems Defy Simple Solutions, But Many People Favor Panaceas

Most social problems are complex phenomena that do not lend themselves to simple solutions. Yet people frequently demand panaceas, as American history amply suggests.[45] This familiar pattern reasserted itself with respect to welfare reform in the mid and late 1990s with the adoption of a deterrent strategy to deal with a complicated problem. Because of its roots in the social and economic fabric of American society, welfare dependency cannot be solved by deterrence; it is caused by such factors as low-wage jobs; residential segregation; and the high cost of day care, housing, medical care, and transportation.

Moreover, solving problems requires persistence rather than time-limited crusades. As existing welfare recipients enter the job market, additional women will require job-seeking assistance or welfare when they have children and can find only low-wage jobs. Many women who secure jobs will lose them during recessions. When welfare recipients do receive jobs, they will displace some current workers (male and female) from the labor force, particularly in areas that do not have high rates of economic growth. As even this brief discussion suggests, many social problems cannot be solved but merely ameliorated through continuing efforts.

The panaceas are sometimes promoted by class and racial prejudice. Because they have not experienced the actual circumstances of living in many inner-city and rural areas—and are not subject to the structural factors that cause and sustain social problems like high levels of crime, unemployment, disease, delinquency, welfare dependency, bad housing, homelessness, and dropping out of school—many affluent Americans seek simple solutions aimed at changing the values and viewpoints of low-income persons. Some believe that sex education programs preaching abstinence will eradicate teen pregnancy. Some favor the widespread use of volunteers to teach children to read or to offer middle-class models to impoverished children. Some support deterrent policies to diminish crime rates and welfare dependency in inner-city communities. These solutions do not take into account the realities of living in these communities.

Priorities Are Not Chosen Rationally

The literature on policy analysts sometimes conveys the misleading impression that decision makers rely on research to shape public priorities. We already have mentioned, for example, that policy analysts often try to gauge the costs to society of specific problems, such as the work absenteeism, death, and lost wages that derive from alcoholism. However, the reality that politics ultimately shapes the selection of priorities can be shown by two examples: antismoking policies and the magnitude of the resources devoted to children's programs. An extraordinary body of research has implicated smoking in hundreds of thousands of deaths annually, yet strong gains were made in regulating tobacco as a drug only in the late 1990s. Many researchers have argued that interventions directed at children, such as children's health programs, have a high benefit-to-cost ratio. Yet the United States devotes only a small fraction of its domestic budget to children—and continues not to fund medical coverage for many of them.

Solving One Problem Can Create Others

Even if some problems can be solved, others often emerge in their wake, as in the case of welfare reform. While saving money by paying reduced welfare costs, society incurs new costs as some (or many) former recipients receive lower resources from employment or from general relief. As some become homeless, they require shelter care and develop health problems that local authorities have to fund. Foster care costs rise as some mothers become unable to provide adequately for their children. Economic desperation is likely to bring increases in family violence, crime, and substance abuse. As some recipients exceed their allotted time on welfare and still are unemployed, counties and cities will have to expend more funds for general relief.[46]

The precise amount of these new costs to society will depend partly on rates of economic growth. In parts of the country with robust growth, job creation will absorb large numbers of former welfare recipients, but they will compete with other unemployed people, new job seekers (such as recent graduates from high school), and immigrants for scarce jobs in other areas. When former recipients do find jobs, some other job seekers will not find work and will be forced onto general relief. Were a recession to occur, moreover, the relief and unemployment rolls would vastly expand.

Variations in Problems

When pointing to the issues in defining, measuring, and conceptualizing social problems, many policy advocates stress the differences between groups in the population. Alcoholism appears, for example, to have different causes and to take different forms in men and women.[47] Unlike men, whose alcoholism often stems from occupational stress and peer pressure, many women develop alcoholism during times of family crisis, such as marital discord, divorce, or a child's death. Unlike alcoholic men, who tend to drink in public—in bars or with friends—many alcoholic women drink secretly. These differences in both the causes and manifestations of alcoholism suggest that men and women need different kinds of treatment, as well as different kinds of preventive services.

Moreover, cultural differences affect people's responses to services. Spanish-speaking families, for example, often defer to male heads of household before seeking assistance for specific problems. In white families, women often take the initiative in seeking services for specific problems. If they want to be successful, social service agencies that serve Latinos must try to include male heads of household in service transactions.[48] Some ethnic groups require bilingual and bicultural staff who can interpret nuances of expression and probe for the meaning of verbal and nonverbal cues that would escape staff from the dominant culture. Some persons respond favorably to one approach, such as a specific kind of counseling, whereas others respond to behavior modification or to membership in support groups, such as Alcoholics Anonymous. Deterrent measures, such as increasing the cost of alcohol or cigarettes, appear to decrease some people's use, but they may be even more effective when supplemented with counseling programs and reductions in advertising.

The vast literature that has recently evolved on "culturally sensitive practice" and "multidiversity" stresses the need to adapt programs to specific populations.[49] This sensitivity must occur on two related levels. First, we need to examine the differences in specific social problems in different populations, as our discussion of alcoholism among males and females suggests. Second, services must be adapted to the culture and norms of specific ethnic and racial groups.

We should remember as well that the problems of oppressed populations are often caused or exacerbated by the hostile environments and extreme poverty that many of their members encounter, particularly in inner-city communities. The rules of mental health, for example, whether in diagnosis or treatment, must be modified when social workers are helping persons who live in areas that look like bombed-out cities, who are exposed to violence daily, who cannot obtain secure jobs that will allow them to escape poverty, and who can obtain amenities such as health care only by waiting for days in clinics. Terms such as *paranoia, inability to make long-term plans,* and *flight,* which can be used in the diagnosis and treatment of mental conditions or problem-solving deficits in middle-class citizens, must be used cautiously in labeling persons in these high-stress environments, where trust, planning, and permanent social arrangements are less feasible.

The term *empowerment* helps us reconceptualize some of the services that social workers provide to persons in high-stress environments. (While empowerment is not limited to persons in high-stress environments, it may have particular relevance for them.) When seeking to empower persons, social workers often emphasize survival skills, such as helping persons cope with the fragmentation of services, understaffed services, and hostile bureaucrats. Rather than focusing on pathology, empowerment helps people develop personal plans to improve their lives. Indeed, some people favor terms like *consumers of service* rather than *patient* or *client* to avoid labeling people. Some social workers advocate placing less reliance on mental health diagnostic categories, such as those in *DSM-IV,* that label persons on the basis of deficits rather than strengths.[50]

Challenges for Policy Advocates

We have noted that policy advocates who help oppressed populations encounter particular challenges in policy arenas because their issues are frequently unpopular. Certain kinds of issues and populations have a relatively privileged position in American culture, as can be seen by their success in securing a disproportionate share of resources. Fund-raisers for hospitals, certain cultural undertakings, and privileged educational organizations such as private schools have an enviable job in raising funds compared to shoestring organizations that help stigmatized populations.[51]

Moreover, the broader population views the problems of stigmatized conditions, such as homelessness or AIDS, through prejudiced lenses. Rather than viewing homelessness as stemming from an absence of halfway houses, decent social services, and affordable housing, many persons stress the personal failings of those who are homeless as the major, even the sole, cause of this condition. Rather than viewing AIDS as an epidemic, similar to cholera in prior eras, some persons view many who have this disease through the lens of homophobia, seeing it as stemming from an aberrant lifestyle choice. Problems of oppressed populations are, moreover, often viewed as relatively hopeless and unsolvable, unlike those of more powerful populations.

When policy advocates suggest that inequalities in American society, such as discrepancies in the incomes and opportunities of the social classes, should be rectified, they are often dismissed as left-leaning radicals. In a society that lacks a strong radical tradition, the rhetoric of social equality is often dismissed. But advocates for powerless populations and unpopular issues often realize that without a fundamental redistribution of resources and opportunities, specific groups, such as inner-city African Americans, will remain on the periphery of American society. They will be unable even to imagine themselves significantly improving their lives.

These common perceptions of the problems of oppressed populations underline the need for their advocates to educate people, whether through the mass media or through personal discussions with highly placed officials. They must contest the definitions and conceptualizations of specific social problems, such as equating welfare with bad character rather than with limited, low-paying jobs. They have to resist people's stereotypes by arguing that certain groups do, in fact, have different needs and problems.

Chapter Summary

What You Can Now Do

Policy advocates need considerable sophistication in thinking about social problems, which are complex phenomena. Yet they also need to use political, value-clarifying, and interactional skills even as they use analytic skills in the problem-analyzing task. (See Policy Advocacy Challenge 6.7.)

POLICY ADVOCACY CHALLENGE 6.7

A BROAD-BASED COALITION TAKES THE INITIATIVE IN THE WAKE OF WELFARE REFORM

Nancy Gewirtz, M.S.W., M.P.A., Ph.D., Professor, Rhode Island College School of Social Work

I first became involved with welfare as a student. My first M.S.W. field placement was working "inside" the system—in a welfare department. Then, there was a major philosophical shake-up in my M.S.W. program, resulting in the alienation of "inside-the-system" placements, so I spent my second-year placement working on the "outside" with a welfare rights organization. I decided that both experiences together gave a much clearer view of how to engage in effective policy practice. I vowed that if I ever got to lead an M.S.W. program, I'd try to make sure all students had both opportunities. And luckily, that's what I've been trying to do these last 20 years.

I am cofounder and volunteer chair of the Rhode Island Campaign to Eliminate Childhood Poverty, where students, along with volunteers and staff, have been proposing and advocating for progressive welfare legislation and regulations for a number of years. We have routinely worked with like-minded organizations like the local chapter of NASW and grass-roots groups composed of recipients of welfare, as well as with sympathetic legislators.

But 1995 was shaping up to be a very different year. The Republicans had just swept Congress, and they "meant business." The president was also talking about "ending welfare as we know it." The national mood, influenced by persistent economic recessions, had most Americans feeling afraid. As a result, they were opposed to federal programs that they perceived as handouts when they were working hard and still falling further behind.

I knew that the same old coalitions, strategies, and tactics would simply not be enough to stave off the tidal wave of change about to occur. I knew that any chance of protecting poor children and their families from this onslaught would require brave new strategies which had to involve groups with a lot more power and influence than we had previously enjoyed.

While I was frantically pondering how to expand our influence, I serendipitously attended a forum on the Republican Contract with America. At that event, the director of an influential business-sponsored organization that monitors government spending spoke. After the meeting, I went up to him and introduced myself. I told him of my concerns about the impact that massive welfare changes might have on this state's economy. He was interested!

We set up a meeting and decided it would be politically effective, given our widely different perspectives, for us to put together a broad-based coalition including groups like the United Way, the Urban League, the Council of Churches, key Republican and Democratic legislators, his business "watchdog" group, and my policy advocacy organization in order to obtain a wide range of input on what welfare reform should look like and to get a fair and effective program passed by our state legislature. We agreed it was

(continued)

(6.7   continued)

important to invite the governor and welfare administrators to participate in the development of this comprehensive plan. While the governor respectfully declined, indicating he was going to develop his own plan, he did allow staff people to provide us with critical information we needed to proceed with our planning.

Our diverse Family Independence Coalition met for 18 months learning about the current system as well as each others' perspectives. The result was the drafting of legislation for a new state system. We were not far into the process when it became very clear that, given our disparate perspectives, we had to establish clear, measurable principles or goals that we all could support. We hammered out the three guiding principles that focused our deliberations over the next many months. They were that children should not be further impoverished by welfare reform; the new state plan should move people from welfare to work as quickly as feasible; and given our state's deep economic troubles, should, at least for the first year, be revenue-neutral.

Meanwhile, early in the process, the governor submitted his own legislation, which among other things would have cut benefits, violating our first principle. However, the governor's proposal did include some positive aspects, such as an entitlement to child care and medical coverage for children up to 18 for families whose income was at or below 250 percent of the poverty line.

Over the course of many months, we were able to use our respective influence with the local media to follow the competing proposals with a vengeance, giving the issue high visibility. Finally, after months of deliberation and compromise, the Family Independence Act was signed into law by the governor.

Just a few weeks later, the federal government passed the Temporary Assistance to Needy Families Act, which ended the six-decade guarantee of cash assistance to poor children and their families. But our new state law maintained the entitlement to cash assistance for children, allowed for the training and education critical to successful entry into the job market, increased dramatically the amount of earned income parents could keep before reductions in their welfare benefits until they were no longer eligible for assistance, allowed two-parent families to receive assistance, included a strong case management component, and incorporated the governor's entitlements into child and health care.

There were some very scary times during the process when those of us involved in the negotiating were afraid we might not be doing the right thing. After all, we were keeping company with those who hadn't been seen as friendly to our issues. The fact that we met regularly with our traditional allies, who frequently reminded us that we were "playing with the enemy," didn't help either. Yet, ultimately, the lesson learned was that if you clearly know what your "bottom line" is and you don't compromise it in any major way, ad hoc coalitions such as the Family Independence Coalition can be very effective for specific, time-limited projects. In addition to constantly reviewing our guiding principles or goals, we found that our ability to bring together influential and divergent interests in the state was critically important to our success. As I'm fond of telling my students, you have to strain to think outside "the box." First, you have to assess the problem carefully, and then you have to allow yourself to imagine different strategies that might also benefit those with power and credibility, who often appear to be your adversaries. And absolutely key to success is always using your clinical skills to develop relationships with all involved in the policy practice process.

The five years since the passage of federal and state welfare reform laws have been filled with challenges and rewards as we moved from policy-making to policy implementation. Three of the policy-practice activities we have engaged in provide useful policy-practice teaching tools.

First, some of the advocates, engaged in negotiating the Family Independence Act, established a new policy-practice organization. The Poverty Institute at Rhode Island College School of Social Work allows us to focus less on organizing and more directly on policy research, analysis, and advocacy. It also provides field placements for many students interested in experiences or careers in policy-practice.

Second, The Poverty Institute has been co-chairing, with the state Department of Human Services (DHS), a unique Welfare Reform Implementation Task Force. The twice a month, two hour meetings are open to the public and are consistently attended by representatives of DHS, other state departments that work with welfare recipients, non-profit providers, recipients, and community advocates. There have been about 13 sub-committees that have submitted implementation recommendations to DHS. These sub-committees include but are not limited to domestic violence, housing, education and training, transportation, staff training, research, etc. Many of the recommendations have been implemented by DHS. "Co-optation" is always a danger when policy-practice advocates work intimately with an organization that is often the target of change, in this case DHS. But, the Poverty Institute believes through this process we have improved our "watch-dog" capacity, broadened the community of active participants in welfare reform, built more trusting working relationships with the DHS staff, and have learned a lot about why bureaucracies can be so dysfunctional!

Third, during the summer of 2000, the business-backed government spending "watch dog" organization, that was so crucial to the passage of our state welfare reform law, sent a letter to the director of DHS. They wanted to know why our state had the slowest rate of welfare caseload reduction in the country! The Poverty Institute, which has continued to work with the business-backed group on other projects, was contacted immediately by DHS to determine what strategies we should use to deal with this potentially threatening situation. We knew that a host of provisions in our law were designed, not just to get families off of welfare but out of poverty. For example, the Family Independence Act allows 24 months of education and training before work, an increased income-disregard, a 5-year state time limit begun only after a full work-readiness and family assessment is completed, etc. It is possible that our business benefactor had forgotten about these provisions, all of which can cause families to remain on welfare longer. However, the more likely reason for the letter is the unfortunate reality that state and national politicians now judge welfare reform success solely on caseload reduction, not family well being. Therefore, our former business coalition member probably was concerned our state was spending too much money with little short-term success.

The Poverty Institute ended up brokering the relationship between DHS and the business-backed organization, resulting in the research and publication of an analysis of Rhode Island's caseload reduction. DHS staff and an MSW intern at the Poverty Institute

(continued)

(6.7   continued)

conducted the research for the eight state comparison study. After many meetings and much negotiation the largely positive outcomes were published in a report released by the business-backed group and the Poverty Institute. The report was distributed to the governor, legislators and other policy "influencers" and covered on the front page of the state's major newspaper. Unfortunately, the headlines reinforced the state's slow case-load decline but ultimately the shared goals of the Poverty Institute and DHS was achieved. We had an opportunity to re-educate our business-oriented friends about the details of our state law, demonstrate that the state seemed to be making progress, and most importantly there have been no deleterious changes to our original law this leg-islative session. One lesson learned is that politically driven ad hoc coalitions serve a purpose at the time they are formed. It is very difficult to re-engage them down the road for a host of reasons.

Exercise:

Using this case as your focus, discuss how members of the Family Independence Coalition developed specific analytic approaches to the problem of welfare dependency and how it should be addressed by the state government of Rhode Island.

- What are the differences between policy making and policy implementation?
- What policy practice skills are necessary for policy making? For policy imple-mentation? What skills are necessary for both?
- What kind of organizing do policy practitioners undertake? What is the difference between organizing and policy practice?
- What is co-optation? How can you recognize when it is happening?
- Why is it important to "broaden the community of active participants in welfare reform"?
- What factors might have led the Poverty Institute to be in a brokering role with DHS and the business-backed group? What skills were necessary to accomplish this task?
- What is an ad hoc coalition, and why is it difficult to reconvene politically moti-vated ad hoc coalitions?
- How must policy advocates often compromise in the problem-analyzing task, perhaps not seeking their ideal solutions, in order to obtain allies?
- How must analytic skills be coupled with political skills What political strategies did the coalition develop?
- How must analytic skills be coupled with value-clarifying skills What ethical dilemmas did Professor Gewirtz confront, and how did she resolve them?
- How must analytic skills be coupled with interactional skills What interactional challenges did Professor Gewirtz and the coalition encounter?
- How does this case demonstrate that determined policy advocates can make a dif-ference, even when they have scant resources?

(continued)

You are now equipped with skills to do the following:
- Develop flowcharts of social problems that include several stages of development
- Develop typologies
- Identify causes of specific social problems
- Articulate curative interventions
- Analyze some issues in getting the organized service system to work with informal systems
- Develop preventive solutions
- Measure the magnitude of problems, as well as their spatial location
- Analyze why social problems are slippery concepts

Having analyzed problems, we discuss in the next two chapters how to develop proposals to address them.

Notes

1. For an overview of the politics of welfare reform, see David Elwood, "Welfare Reform as I Knew It," *American Prospect* 25 (May–June 1996): 22–29.
2. Webster's *New World Dictionary* (New York: Simon & Schuster, 1982), p. 16.
3. Robert Mayer and Ernest Greenwood, *The Design of Social Policy Research* (Englewood Cliffs, NJ: Prentice-Hall, 1980).
4. Mary Jo Bane, "Welfare as We Might Know It," *American Prospect* 30 (January–February 1997): 47–53.
5. The *DSM-IV* is the fourth edition of the *Diagnostic and Statistical Manual of Mental Disorders,* published in 1994 by The American Psychiatric Association.
6. See the testimony of David Ellwood in the U.S. Senate, *Hearings,* Subcommittee on Social Security and Family Policy of Committee on Finance (March 2, 1987), pp. 105–111.
7. See J. K. Wing, *Reasoning about Mental Illness* (London: Oxford University Press, 1978), Chap. 2.
8. Phillip Kotler, *Principles of Marketing,* 4th ed. (Englewood Cliffs, NJ: Prentice Hall, 1989), pp. 42–46.
9. Richard Krueger, *Focus Groups: A Practical Guide for Applied Research* (Newbury Park, CA: Sage, 1990).
10. See David Mechanic, *Mental Health and Social Policy,* 3rd ed. (Englewood Cliffs, NJ: Prentice Hall, 1989), pp. 16–44.
11. Stuart Kirk and Herb Hutchins, *The Selling of DSM: The Rhetoric of Science in Psychiatry* (New York: Aldine de Gruyter, 1992).
12. Bane, "Welfare as We Might Know It."
13. Claude Fischer et al., *Inequality by Design: Cracking the Bell Curve Myth* (Princeton, NJ: Princeton University Press, 1996), pp. 102–128.
14. David Ellwood, *Poor Support: Poverty in the American Family* (New York: Basic Books, 1988).
15. Irving Piliavin et al., "The Duration of Homeless Careers: An Exploratory Study," *Social Service Review* (December 1993): 57–69.

16. Richard Berk et al., "Social Policy Experimentation," *Evaluation Review* 9 (August 1985): 387–431.

17. Claire Renzetti and Raymond Lee, eds., *Researching Sensitive Topics* (Newbury Park, CA: Sage, 1993).

18. Bane, "Welfare as We Might Know It."

19. U.S. Department of Health and Human Services, *Alcohol and Health: Report to U.S. Congress* (Washington, DC: Government Printing Office, 1987), pp. 97–119.

20. Steven Wineman, *The Politics of Human Services: A Radical Alternative to the Welfare State* (Boston: South End Press, 1984).

21. For a critique of the medical model in substance abuse, see Dorothy Nelkin, *Methadone Maintenance: A Technological Fix* (New York: Braziller, 1973).

22. William Miller and Hester Reid, "Matching Problem Drinkers with Optimal Treatments," in William Miller and Nick Heather, eds., *Treating Addictive Behaviors: Processes of Change* (New York: Plenum Press, 1986), pp. 175–204.

23. William Julius Wilson, *When Work Disappears: The World of the New Urban Poor* (New York: Knopf, 1996).

24. Melissa Healy, "Welfare 'Family Cap' Fails to Cut Birthrate in New Jersey," *Los Angeles Times* (September 12, 1997), pp. 1, 16.

25. David Zucchino, *Myth of the Welfare Queen* (New York: Scribner, 1997).

26. Louis Uchitelle, "Welfare Recipients Taking Jobs Often Held by the Working Poor," *New York Times* (April 1, 1997), pp. 1, 10.

27. Paul Peterson, "State Response to Welfare Reform: A Race to the Bottom?" in Isabell Sawhill, ed., *Welfare Reform: An Analysis of the Issues* (Washington, DC: Urban Institute, 1995), pp. 7–10.

28. Martin Bloom, *Primary Prevention: The Possible Science* (Englewood Cliffs, NJ: Prentice Hall, 1981).

29. Jonathan Smith, "Quantum Opportunities Program," *New York Times* (March 9, 1995), pp. 1, 2.

30. Bloom, *Primary Prevention.*

31. Ibid., pp. 173–174.

32. Jonathan Bradshaw, "The Concept of Social Need," *New Society* 30 (March 1972): 640–643.

33. Mary Ellen Hombs, *Welfare Reform: A Reference Handbook* (Santa Barbara, CA: ABC-CLIO, 1996), p. 54.

34. See National Institute of Mental Health, *A Working Manual of Simple Evaluation Techniques for Community Mental Health Centers* (Washington, DC: Government Printing Office, 1976), pp. 99–146.

35. Ibid.

36. Jennifer Wolch and Heidi Sommer, *Los Angeles in an Era of Welfare Reform* (Los Angeles: Southern California Inter-University Consortium on Homelessness and Poverty, 1997), p. xxiv.

37. Fischer et al., *Inequality by Design,* pp. 129–157.

38. Carl Patton and David Sawicki, *Basic Methods of Policy Analysis and Planning* (Englewood Cliffs, NJ: Prentice Hall, 1993).

39. Ellwood, "Welfare Reform as I Knew It," pp. 27–28.

40. Arnold Green, *Social Problems: Arena of Conflict* (New York: McGraw-Hill, 1975), pp. 67–115.

41. Kirk and Hutchins, *The Selling of DSM,* pp. 199–218.

42. Ibid.

43. Barbara Ehrenreich and Deirdre English, *For Her Own Good: 150 Years of the Experts' Advice to Women* (New York: Anchor Books, 1979).

44. See the discussion of Joseph Hotz's work in Richard Cooper, "Contrary Message on Teenage Pregnancy," *Los Angeles Times* (May 24, 1997), pp. 1, 14.

45. Bruce S. Jansson, *The Reluctant Welfare State,* 3rd ed. (Pacific Grove, CA: Brooks/Cole, 1997), pp. 352–353.

46. Wolch and Sommer, *Los Angeles in an Era,* pp. 78–80.

47. Vasanti Burtle, ed., *Women Who Drink: Experience and Psychotherapy* (Springfield, IL: Charles C Thomas, 1979).

48. Vicente Abad, "Mental Health Delivery Systems for Hispanics in the United States: Issues and Dilemmas," in Moises Gaviria and Jose Arana, eds., *Health and Behavior: Research Agenda for Hispanics* (Chicago: Simon Bolivar Hispanic American Psychiatric Research and Training Program, 1987).

49. See, for example, Wynetta Devore and Elfrieda Schlesinger, *Ethnic-Sensitive Social Work* (St. Louis: Mosby, 1981), and Donna Ferullo, *Cultural Diversity in Social Work Practice* (Boston: Social Work Library at Boston College, 1991).

50. Barbara Solomon, *Black Empowerment* (New York: Columbia University Press, 1976).

51. Jean Potuchek, "The Context of Social Service Funding: The Funding Relationship," *Social Service Review* 60 (September 1986): 421–436.

Suggested Readings

Developing Typologies

David Ellwood, *Poor Support: Poverty in the American Family* (New York: Basic Books, 1988).

Controversies in Defining and Conceptualizing Social Problems

Mary Jo Bane, "Welfare as We Might Know It," *American Prospect* 30 (January–February 1997): 47–53.

David Ellwood, "Welfare Reform as I Knew It," *American Prospect* 25 (May–June 1996): 22–29.

Claude Fischer et al., *Inequality by Design: Cracking the Bell Curve Myth* (Princeton, NJ: Princeton University Press, 1996).

Stuart Kirk and Herb Hutchins, *The Selling of DSM: The Rhetoric of Science in Psychiatry* (New York: Aldine de Gruyter, 1992).

How Culture and Values Influence Definitions of Social Problems

Joel Best, ed., *Images of Issues* (New York: Aldine de Gruyter, 1989).

Malcolm Spector and John Kitsuse, *Constructing Social Problems* (Menlo Park, CA: Cummings, 1977).

Technical Approaches to Analyzing and Measuring Social Problems

Jonathan Bradshaw, "The Concept of Social Need," in Neil Gilbert and Harry Specht, eds., *Planning for Social Welfare* (Englewood Cliffs, NJ: Prentice Hall, 1977), pp. 290–297.

Christopher Jencks, *The Homeless* (Cambridge: Harvard University Press, 1994).

Irving Piliavin, Michael Sosin, Alex Westerfelt, and Ross Matsueda, "The Duration of Homeless Careers: An Exploratory Study," *Social Service Review* (December 1993): 57–69.

7

Developing Policy Proposals

POLICY PREDICAMENT	When the U.S. Congress enacted the Personal Responsibility and Work Opportunity Reconciliation Act of 1996, it established a deadline of August 2002 for Congress to "reauthorize" (i.e., extend) the legislation. Many advocacy groups, including the National Association of Social Workers, submitted policy recommendations in 2002 to the Department of Health and Human Services regarding the content of its reauthorized legislation. (See Policy Advocacy Challenge 7.5 at the end of this chapter.)

    We discussed some methods of analyzing social problems in Chapter Six, but our attention now shifts to—what do we do about the problems? How do we develop *policy proposals* that will address them? (See the second, third, and fourth tasks of Figure 6.1 on p. 169.) Any policy proposal contains *policy options,* therefore we discuss them in this chapter as a prelude to comparing their relative merits and to drafting proposals in the next chapter. We discuss the following in this chapter:
  - How vantage point shapes the views of stakeholders
  - Policy options that recur in the American welfare state
  - How to map a policy proposal by linking policy options into a coherent proposal
  - How to link analytic, political, interactional, and value-clarifying skills to develop policy proposals

Intersecting Arenas and Stakeholders

Before we discuss policy options, we need to make clear that proposals are fashioned through deliberations and discussions of stakeholders—key persons, groups, and institutions with an interest in a particular policy issue. They include administrators, consumers, advocacy groups, government officials, persons from the private sector (such as business leaders), and persons from so-called NGOs (nongovernment organizations). Which stakeholders play a role in policy deliberations varies from issue to issue.

For example, welfare-to-work issues are currently a matter of policy deliberations in every state. Welfare reform illustrates the phenomenon of intersecting arenas and different stakeholders. If the term *intersecting arenas* describes links between the federal, state, county, and municipal arenas as well as governmental and nongovernmental sectors, *stakeholders* are the officials and advocates who operate in specific arenas. (See Figure 7.1.)

Welfare reform is like an intricate dance in which the moves of each of these stakeholders are profoundly influenced by the moves of the others. When the president or Congress make specific legislative choices at the national level, state and local officials are profoundly affected. Within specific states, governors and state officials, county officials, corporate leaders, advocacy groups, nongovernmental agencies (NGOs), current and former recipients, federal authorities, and the courts engage in a kind of dance where each of them assumes a key role in making choices about states' policies. Governors often set the agenda on welfare-to-work issues because of their pivotal position. Because corporations provide many jobs to former recipients, they are important players in welfare reform. County officials often are given key implementing roles of states, so they enter policy deliberations. Courts oversee the legality of policies in each state, so other players often ask whether specific choices might be challenged in court. The federal government, somewhat quiet since passage of the landmark welfare reform legislation in 1996, will reenter the picture when it decides whether to reauthorize the 1996 legislation in 2002. At that time, it could leave the 1996 reforms largely intact or it could completely change them. Community-based and university-based advocates and researchers

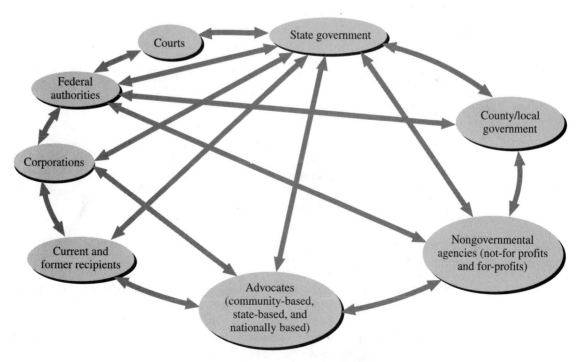

FIGURE 7.1   **Intersecting arenas and stakeholders**

often pressure state and local governments to modify policies that harm the economic well-being of impoverished families, as was discussed by Professor Nancy Gewirtz in Policy Advocacy Challenge 6.6 on pp. 195.

Stakeholders have various motivations and perspectives as they consider the merits of specific policies. We have discussed ideology at many points. Some stakeholders bring their ideological preferences to the table, such as when conservatives insist that welfare-to-work programs ought to emphasize deterrence and ought not include government resources. Policy advocates, in turn, are often somewhat more likely to support spending on child care, transportation, health care, and job subsidies for former recipients—and to want a longer period of transition during which they can get these benefits.

Other factors also shape positions, such as economic interests. (See Policy Advocacy Challenge 7.1.) Some corporations, for example, may want relatively unskilled workers—and so may favor public subsidies of work slots and spending on child care and other survival needs of working low-income women.

POLICY ADVOCACY CHALLENGE 7.1

STAKEHOLDERS AND THE WHEEL OF INTERACTION

We can use the wheel of interaction shown in Figure 7.1 to understand the proposal preferences of specific stakeholders by placing them in the center of the wheel. In the politics of welfare reform in your state or local jurisdiction, for example, place community-based advocates representing current and former welfare recipients in the center of the wheel. What demands or requests might they make of other stakeholders with respect to the following:

- Childcare
- Medical care
- Subsidies to employers to entice them to hire relatively unskilled women
- Transportation
- Job training
- Whether working women can still get some welfare payments
- The length of the transition period during which former recipients are still eligible for various benefits
- Other policies

Then take one or two of the other stakeholders and discuss their likely positions, realizing that vantage point, ideology, political interests, and economic interests powerfully shape perspectives. Which stakeholders would advocates most fear? What coalitions might they establish with specific stakeholders in hopes of advancing their mutual policy preferences? Why would unlikely bedfellows sometimes exist?

Political considerations also intrude, such as when a governor wants to demonstrate to voters that she has reduced welfare rolls faster than many other states. We should not forget that electoral politics is often on the minds of governmental stakeholders. They often anticipate that an issue like welfare could become a campaign issue—and take positions on key issues with this in mind.

Unfortunately, current and former welfare recipients are often the least likely to participate in deliberations about policies governing welfare-to-work programs. Unlike in the 1960s when welfare recipients were often powerful participants, former and present recipients are usually poorly organized—and often fear that they will experience retaliation from public authorities if they are critical of current policies.

Recurring Policy Issues and Policy Options

When designing policy proposals, policy advocates must consider a range of issues. They can be placed in nine groups that establish the following:

1. A mission for a proposal
2. How a proposal's services will be structured
3. The resource path of a proposal
4. The content of a proposal's services
5. How a proposal's resources will be rationed
6. How agencies associated with a proposal will be linked
7. How a proposal's services will be linked to communities
8. How the implementation of a proposal will be overseen
9. How a proposal's services will be assessed

As they encounter each of these nine issues, policy advocates must choose among competing alternatives or options.

To illustrate our discussion, we will consider a hypothetical policy advocate in Washington, DC, who wants to develop a federally funded program for victims of spousal abuse.[1] She thinks abused women need the immediate protection that shelters afford and realizes that many women lack the resources to find alternative sources of safe shelter. She works for a shelter in Baltimore and is connected with a coalition of service providers, feminists, victims of spousal abuse, and professionals who want the federal government to take a more active role in addressing this problem. (The group is called the Stop Wife-Battering Coalition.) This policy advocate knows that several local programs have been initiated for this purpose, mostly by underfunded nonprofit agencies that have sought assistance from foundations, private benefactors, and public sources, such as the U.S. Department of Housing and Urban Development. Despite their founders' determined efforts, these centers have proved woefully inadequate to help the rising number of women who seek relief from spousal abuse. The coalition tentatively calls its proposed program the Federal Shelter Program.

Establishing a Mission

While developing this program, the policy advocate must create some objectives for the Federal Shelter Program. We have noted that policies usually contain explicit or implicit objectives that provide programs with an overarching direction. Often, the preambles of legislation also provide such a rationale.

When discussing the shelters with legislators' aides, she finds no consensus on the federal government's mission in responding to spousal abuse. Some legislators are uninterested in the issue, believing that advocates grossly exaggerate its importance and magnitude; indeed, one aide contends that battering is a "figment of the imagination of do-gooder social workers, who want to create more jobs for themselves." Other legislators favor a "get-tough" strategy that would provide federal funds and policy requirements to local governmental units to find, prosecute, and imprison offenders. However, they object to direct federal assistance to shelters, which they think local jurisdictions should fund. Still other legislators want to provide federal assistance to a national network of shelters for battered women and their children.

While believing that better law enforcement is also needed, our policy advocate and other participants in the Stop Wife-Battering Coalition decide to emphasize federal assistance to shelters. The coalition also wants the shelter program to offer a service to help women cope with their predicament and link them to legal, welfare, job placement, and other services.

Their objectives, then, emphasize federal funding to establish shelters and to serve the women who seek protection there. This mission has important consequences for the policies they will develop; had they adopted a mission that emphasized prosecuting spouse abusers, their proposal would have taken an entirely different form.

Designing the Structure of Service

Having established a general direction, this policy advocate and her allies encounter some practice questions: Who should ultimately oversee the new program? What kinds of agencies should receive funds for the program?

Fixing ultimate responsibility   Programs and agencies are typically classified into policy sectors, such as mental health, health, child welfare, public welfare, and gerontology. Assigning a specific program to a sector is often arbitrary and sometimes contentious. For example the federal Office of Education and the federal Office of Economic Opportunity (OEO) vied for the Head Start program at its inception. In truth, it could have been placed in either of them because it has educational components as well as the parent and community participation that OEO emphasized.[2] Ultimately, it was placed in OEO because its key founders feared that placing it in the Office of Education would render it a mere educational program that lacked advocacy, parent-participation, and child-development dimensions.

Returning to our example, the policy advocate has to decide who should have ultimate responsibility for the program. If the Federal Shelter Program were assigned to the National Institute of Mental Health, for example, its major focus might become providing counseling services, with less emphasis on providing shelter services. If it were assigned to the Department of Housing and Urban Development, social services might be eliminated. Of course, the policy advocate could try to make it an independent agency that reports directly to the president and is possibly linked to other programs that assist victims of violence.

She not only needs to decide which governmental department should receive ultimate jurisdiction, but must also develop policies about implementation. In doing so, she must ask the following questions: Should state officials (perhaps from a state agency) or federal authorities oversee the program and who should choose which agencies are to receive federal funds? Who should collect statistics about how the shelters use their funds, to keep legislators informed? Who should attend to program problems, such as misuse of funds or failure to comply with local building codes? Who should determine the shelters' eligibility policies within a specific state? Should these policies be contained within the federal legislation, be defined by federal officials after the legislation has been enacted, or be left to the discretion of state officials?

In the 1960s, legislators made federal officials responsible for many funding and operational decisions. Indeed, in many federally funded programs in the War on Poverty, local agencies applied directly to federal authorities for funds, and federal officials inspected and audited local projects. Since then, authority increasingly has been vested in state, regional, or county officials, who ultimately report some details of local programs, such as program statistics, to federal funders. (In the Reagan administration, even this reporting was minimized because he wanted to eliminate federal roles in favor of state and local ones.)

The policy advocate must weigh the advantages of using the various levels of government.[3] If she believes that many local units will be particularly unreceptive to the needs of battered women, she can vest responsibility in the federal government. However, it is difficult for federal officials to superintend the operational details of thousands of shelters—and the political climate bodes ill for policies that propose augmenting federal power. Alternatively, she can choose a middle course by directing the federal funds to state authorities, but requiring them to follow specific standards and report specific information to federal authorities.

Kinds of agencies receiving funds   The policy advocate has to decide which kinds of agencies can receive federal funds. Should not-for-profit, public, or profit-oriented agencies, or some combination of these receive funds?[4] Not-for-profit agencies have boards of directors, but their members are not allowed to have a financial stake in the agency, nor do the boards have shareholders or other investors who receive dividends. (Agency surpluses must be reinvested in the agency, whose staff receive fixed salaries.) Not-for-profit agencies are exempt from state and federal taxes, and contributors can usually deduct donations from their income, provided the agencies have a tax-exempt status with the Internal Revenue Service and with the state authorities that oversee nonprofit agencies. Profit-oriented agencies are owned by private investors, whether owners or stockholders, who expect a financial return on their investment. (Owners may assume a major role in overseeing their agencies or may cede management to outside managers who work under their general direction.) Public agencies are usually funded exclusively by public authorities and clients' payments. In actual practice, though, complex hybrids exist. Virtually all not-for-profit agencies and some profit-oriented agencies receive contracts from public authorities; indeed, most not-for-profits receive more than 60% of their revenues from public contracts and grants. Some nonprofits even have profit-oriented subsidiaries.

The policy advocate has to compare these kinds of agencies when deciding whether to give them funds. Because public agencies lack a profit motive, they have no economic incentive to deceive or shortchange clients. Many critics have assailed public agencies, however, because they are often bedeviled by red tape, and by civil service and unionized employees who cannot be easily removed if they are ineffective. Although ultimately accountable to elected officials, many public agencies do not make extensive use of community resources, such as volunteers and support groups. Because public agencies often have emphasized services to poor persons, they often are shunned by working- and middle-class citizens, who also may believe them to be excessively bureaucratic.[5]

Not-for-profit agencies are perceived as more innovative than public agencies because fewer regulations constrain their programs.[6] As they tend to be smaller than public agencies and have boards composed of residents, some of them are probably more responsive to the needs of specific communities. Some critics nonetheless question whether not-for-profit agencies are actually more innovative than public agencies and note that their boards are often dominated by community elites, with scant participation by ordinary citizens.[7] Some of them engage so aggressively in marketing and fund-raising that they are indistinguishable from profit-oriented agencies, which also have their defenders and detractors. Many persons advocate privatizing the human services by giving profit-oriented organizations an expanded role in delivering services. They contend that private markets enhance the efficiency of human services and the gearing of services to clients' needs. Wanting to instill market efficiency into the human services, they content that public agencies that are inefficient or unreponsive to consumers should be supplanted by for-profit or not-for-profit agencies.[8] Many critics vigorously challenge this positive portrayal of for-profit agencies. They point out that profit-oriented nursing homes and day-care centers sometimes attract clients with deceptive advertising, cut the quality of their services to increase their profits, and refrain from serving persons who cannot pay their fees.[9]

Planning the Extent of Devolution and the Resource Path

The policy advocate realizes that fiscal resources are the lifeblood of the human services system and that shelters desperately need funds to survive. She must choose a funding source for social programs, determine how much money to give specific programs, and select a funding channel—and she must make these choices in the context of existing policy realities.

Extent of devolution   Intense controversy exists about the respective roles of federal and state governments. Indeed, a movement to devolve federal programs and policies to state and local levels has taken place during the last three decades. After establishing federal social insurance and welfare programs during the Great Depression, the United States vastly enlarged a federally directed welfare state in the next four decades; federal domestic spending rose from a paltry two percent of the gross national product (GNP) in 1930 (before the depression) to 17 percent by 1979.[10] This growth in the federal government was a result of widespread cynicism about the ability of state and local governments to address social problems. Even as liberals took the lead in developing this welfare state, conservatives chafed at the rise in federal power and launched three successive assaults on it. Richard Nixon, Ronald Reagan, and Newt Gingrich attempted in the early 1970s, the 1980s, and the mid-1990s, respectively, to cut federal spending and to devolve federal programs to state and local governments using so-called block grants. (Unlike categorical programs such as Head Start, which the federal government funds, defines, and regulates, block grants distribute funds to states or localities with relatively few restrictions.) Reagan succeeded in establishing nine block grants in 1981 that redirected the funds for 77 categorical programs into block grants, and Gingrich and his allies, with some cooperation from Bill Clinton, ended AFDC as a federal program and entitlement and converted it to a block grant.

While conservatives have often framed relationships between federal and nonfederal governments in either-or terms, many permutations are not only possible but desirable, as can be seen in Table 7.1. Where programs should be placed on a continuum extending from sole federal to sole state or local depends, I contend, on how the programs rank on eight criteria.[11] (Of course, many people might disagree with my recommendations, such as some conservatives who would like to turn virtually all social programs over to the state and local governments.)

TABLE 7.1 Orienting framework criteria for placing social policies on the federal-to-state continuum

Criteria	Sole federal	Devolved with federal tilt	Devolved with state/local tilt	Sole state or local
Extent to which federal tax code is used	X			
Extent to which program addresses survival needs	X	X		
Likelihood that states will discriminate	X	X		
Extent to which problem requires large resources	X	X	X	
Extent to which economic competition between states inhibits socially responsive policies	X	X	X	
Extent to which problem is linked to global competitiveness	X	X	X	
Extent to which local inputs and partnerships are needed		X	X	X
Service-intensive programs		X	X	X

National authorities should fund programs that meet survival needs, such as SSI, the food stamp program, social insurances, and the now-devolved AFDC program. Not only do these programs require huge resources, but they are unlikely to be funded sufficiently by state and local governments for several reasons. The nationwide total of state and local tax revenues is only half the total of federal tax revenues; thus, state and local governments lack the resources for large programs, particularly as they also must fund schools, highways, prisons, and the local share of such federal programs as Medicaid. Moreover, many policy experts fear a "race to the bottom" as states compete to cut their safety net programs.[12] Fearing that low-income persons will immigrate if they offer safety net programs that are more munificent than those of other states, some states offer miserly benefits. Many states restrict their tax revenues, moreover, by keeping their tax rates lower to entice corporations that like low-tax states, and these constrictions of their tax revenues diminish their resources for social programs.

Many other programs can be devolved with a federal tilt so the federal government provides some funds and considerable oversight and regulations, or they can be devolved with a state/local tilt so the government provides fewer resources, less oversight, and fewer regulations. Many social service programs that require local input and partnerships and that need to be tailored to local needs fit into these two models. But many of these programs should not be completely devolved because they will be poorly funded. Moreover, the nation has a stake in many state and local services, such as job training, that keep American citizens competitive in job markets as the economy globalizes.

Some programs should continue to be funded and administered by local and state governments, such as large components of secondary education and correctional institutions. States and localities can and should fund many social programs that fill the gaps in federal and state programs.

Sources of funds for social programs   Policy advocates must choose from a variety of funding options.[13] The extensive general revenues of local, county, state, and federal governments fund many programs. Since the 1930s, the federal government has emerged as the major funder of social welfare programs, because it raises roughly two times the combined tax revenues of state and local governments, which include state income taxes, state (or local) property taxes, and state (or local) sales, excise, and license taxes. General revenues provide a useful source of funds for social programs because they are generally unrestricted. However, fierce competition exists over general revenues, as many groups, thousands of existing social programs, and the Department of Defense all seek them. When taxes are periodically cut, access to general revenues becomes even more difficult.

Payroll taxes fund Social Security and Medicare programs. These taxes take a certain percentage of employees' or employers' payrolls, or both. While payroll taxes are a predictable and stable source of revenues, it is virtually impossible to develop new payroll taxes because Social Security and Medicare already preempt a considerable share of people's income.

Clients' payments for services fund a significant share of the nation's social programs that are run by agencies or private practitioners. Requiring payment discourages clients from the unnecessary use of social and medical services. In the case of sliding fees, relatively affluent persons shoulder a substantial part of programs' operating costs. However, charging fees often deters poor persons from seeking needed services.

Special taxes, such as on marriage licenses, auto licenses, and alcoholic beverages, are often earmarked for specific programs, as when states use taxes on marriage licenses to fund shelters for battered women. Like payroll taxes, special taxes provide a stable source of revenues for specific programs, but political interests, such as liquor companies, often oppose them, fearing the taxes will raise the cost of their products and erode their markets.

Private philanthropy, including federated community fund-raising drives (such as United Way and appeals for Jewish and Catholic agencies), corporations, foundations, and individual donors, remains a major funding source for social programs, even though it has been eclipsed by governmental funding since the late 1950s.[14] Private philanthropy provides funds that are often less restricted than government funds because they are not usually earmarked for specific programs. As with general government revenues, however, agencies and programs compete fiercely for scarce philanthropic funds, particularly since the cuts in government funding in the 1980s and 1990s. The bulk of private philanthropic dollars is, moreover, given to educational, medical, and cultural groups rather than to agencies serving persons with stigmatized conditions or from low-income groups.

Determining levels of funds   Euphoric after the enactment of legislation, policy advocates often discover that the programs they have championed have received inadequate funding. The funding of public programs usually follows a two-step procedure.[15] First, legislatures authorize funds by stipulating how much money (an upper limit) a specific program can receive in a given year. Second, the legislature appropriates—that is, actually commits—a specific amount of money to the program for a specific year. As illustrated by Medicare, Medicaid, and Social Security, legislatures provide open-ended funding for some programs, in which they agree to fund whatever costs those programs incur in a specific year. However, most programs must battle for their funds in the appropriations process, often receiving far less money than was authorized for them, because of competing demands for the available funds.

We should realize that choices about the funding of social policies occur in a broader context, whether at county, state, or federal levels. Using the federal level as an example, assume that you wanted federal resources for a so-called discretionary program. (The funding of discretionary programs is determined annually in the push-and-pull of the budget process, unlike interest on the federal debt and entitlements—or mandatory spending—like Medicare, Medicaid, Food Stamps, SSI, the Earned Income Tax Credit, and Social Security, which are automatically funded to the level of claimed benefits in a given year.) When mandatory spending is subtracted from budget totals, about 36 percent of federal budget revenues remain. In turn, more than one-half of these revenues are absorbed by military spending, meaning that about 13 percent of the entire federal budget is available for domestic discretionary spending. Many claimants that are not social programs vie for these discretionary dollars, including transportation, the National Park Service, environmental clean-up, road and bridge construction, public works programs, and foreign policy. About five percent of the total federal budget exists for discretionary social programs of the Department of Health and Human Services, so advocates of increased funding for specific programs must realize that they play in a crowded field—and they must use considerable pressure and lobbying to convince legislators to increase funding for the program they favor. Even in agency settings, policy advocates who want greater resources for a specific program must understand the agency's budget so they can make a good case for shifting resources from existing programs to one that they favor—assuming they cannot find new resources, such as by writing a grant proposal.

Some legislative committees are authorizing committees that, essentially, decide the maximum amount of resources that can be expended on a particular program in a given year. (An example is the House Committee on Economic and Educational Opportunities that authorizes resources for the Social Services Block Grant.) Appropriations committees decide how much money will actually be given to a specific program in a given year. So advocates need to get both sufficient authorizations and sufficient appropriations for specific programs.

Funding channels   Once funds exist for a social program and some combination of public, nonprofit, and profit-oriented agencies has been chosen to receive the money, funding channels need to be devised to distribute these resources. We can visualize the funds as flowing through channels, or routes, from various levels of government to agencies or consumers. (See Figure 7.2.)

Federal funders often provide money directly to agencies, as shown in Route 1. Funding may take the form of *project grants,* in which the federal government gives funds to a shelter to provide services to battered women. If project grants usually give agencies considerable latitude, government *contracts* specify the precise services the government wishes to provide, such as "5,000 days of residential services, for battered women in Fargo, North Dakota."[16]

Alternatively, some persons argue that federal funders should provide resources directly to consumers (Route 5). For example, some persons favor the use of *vouchers,* that is, funds consumers can use to purchase specific services, such as day care. Government may place limits on the kinds of commodities that can be purchased and may require providers to meet certain licensing standards. Government funds may also take the form of *vendor payments* that reimburse providers for their services to specific clients.[17] For

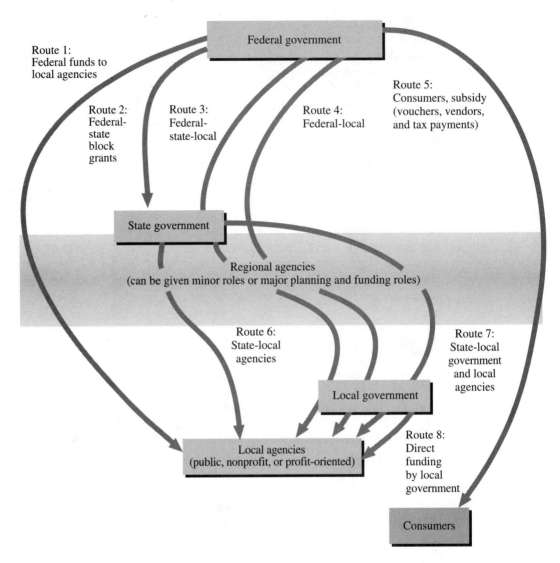

FIGURE 7.2   Possible funding channels

example, the Medicaid program directly reimburses hospitals and physicians for the medical services they provide to low-income patients.

In the federal-to-state channel (Route 2), the federal government distributes funds to the states, which then distribute the funds to specific agencies. Advocates of state government support this policy because it gives the states an enhanced role in the human services system. Indeed, advocates of block grants, which are relatively unrestricted funds that the federal government gives states or local units of government, argue that they give recipients the flexibility to use the funds as they wish and to adapt their programs to local need. Opponents of block grants contend that they provide local jurisdictions with carte blanche use of federal funds for trivial or misdirected programs, and might allow them to underserve specific groups.[18] These opponents favor the federal funding of specific programs that requires the recipient to use the money for specific purposes and to adhere to numerous federal regulations. These programs, such as the Head Start program, are often called *categorical programs.* In the Reagan administration, a number of large block-grant programs were established, including ones for maternal and child health and for social services. While the federal government placed some restrictions on how the states could use these funds, there were fewer constraints than in the 57 categorical programs that these two replaced. (As we discussed in the last chapter, welfare reform legislation in 1996 replaced the categorical AFDC program with a federal block grant.)

Alternatively, the federal government can fund local governments directly (Route 4), a tactic favored by some mayors and county supervisors who chafe at the extraordinary power of the federal government. In this case, local governments would use federal funds to fund shelters for battered women within their jurisdictions.

Similarly, the states use many channels when they distribute their funds to local programs. They may distribute the funds directly to agencies (Route 6) or they may use local governments to distribute funds to agencies (Route 7).

Each funding channel has its critics and defenders. Those who favor the use of vouchers contend, for example, that it promotes healthy competition among agencies for clientele and decreases the need for government bureaucracy. Critics, however, point to many defects in market schemes. Although armed with vouchers, many low-income consumers cannot find quality providers because relatively few of them have agencies or practices in low-income areas.[19]

Indirect financing   We have focused on how federal and state governments finance social welfare programs directly. Social welfare services can also be financed indirectly through the tax system, as when clients are given *tax deductions* that allow them to deduct specific health, housing, or social welfare expenditures from their pretax income. In the case of interest payments on their mortgages, for example, millions of Americans receive tax deductions for their housing. *Tax credits* are direct cash rebates from the U.S. Department of the Treasury to taxpayers who meet specific eligibility standards after they have filed their taxes, such as cash received by low-income families through the EITC. Some taxpayers receive tax credits by subtracting payments for specific programs from their federal taxes; for example, many working women fund part of their day-care expenditures by subtracting a child-care credit from the taxes they would otherwise pay. *Tax exemptions* allow taxpayers not to pay taxes on part of their income. For instance, people can subtract from their taxable income an exemption for each dependent, which lowers their taxable income.

By these indirect methods of financing social welfare, then, citizens receive money not by direct government appropriations, but through tax concessions.[20] The advantage of using the tax system to finance social welfare is that it does not require appropriations and thus avoids political uncertainties. However, tax concessions often benefit wealthy persons and corporations disproportionately. (See Policy Advocacy Challenge 7.2.) For instance, the tax deductions for mortgage interest payments on expensive homes vastly exceed the deductions for modest homes, and tenants generally receive no assistance from the tax codes. Although the government gives persons with tax-subsidized benefits a free hand in choosing their services, it does not usually regulate or monitor them. For example, persons who receive day-care credits may use services that do not meet basic standards.

POLICY
ADVOCACY
CHALLENGE 7.2

*THE UPSIDE DOWN
WELFARE STATE[1]*

Mimi Abramovitz, DSW,
Professor, School of
Social Work, Hunter
College School of Social
Work, Director of Social
Welfare Program, The
Graduate Center, City
University of New York

It is commonly accepted that government tax and spending policies create more equality because they cushion the blows of the market economy for the poor. But a broader look at spending levels, benefit amounts, and vulnerability to budget cuts reveal, by and large, government programs favor the haves over the have-nots. Contrary to popular wisdom, as it is currently configured social policy reinforces inequality.

Social Welfare Spending for the Middle Class. In 2000 the federal government spent more than one trillion dollars on social welfare programs or 61 percent of all federal spending including Welfare, Food Stamps, Supplemental Security Income (SSI), the Earned Income Tax Credit, Social Security Medicare among numerous other programs. Paradoxically, the majority of these dollars ended in the pockets of the well-to-do. While $235.9 billion dollars went to means-tested public assistance program for the poor, we spent a much larger $793.9 billion for programs that do not use poverty or need as a criterion for receiving aid. Programs for the have-nots absorbed 23 percent of all entitlement spending compared to 77 percent for the more affluent.[2] While the latter comprise more of the U.S. population, they profit from less restrictive and more generous programs and from the belief that they are more worthy of aid.

Tax Expenditures for the Affluent. When tax expenditures are factored into the equality calculation, it turns out that the government spends even more on the more well-to-do. Tax expenditures—revenue losses stemming from provisions of Federal Tax laws which reduce income taxes that people pay[3]—represent taxes the government chooses not to collect. Few people think of the tax code as a social welfare system, yet these dollars address the same common human needs as social welfare spending including family support, retirement, health care, housing, child care, and education but are targeted to the needs of the middle and upper class.

Between 1965 and the late 1990s, the number of tax expenditures grew from 50 to 166. The cost to government in lost revenues rose from $36.6 billion in 1967 to an estimated $587 billion in 2000—$292 billion more than the $295 billion allocated to the military that year. Projections indicate that from 1996 through 2002, taxes not collected will amount to $3.7 trillion—more than enough to have paid off the $3.4 trillion national debt in 2000.[4] This tax spending on the gilded welfare state for upper class often exceeds similar program for the poor. The US Joint Committee on Taxation[5] projected that in 1998 the federal government would spend some $72.2 billion on housing subsidies for the rich (mortgage interest tax deductions, property taxes and capital gains on home). This contrasts sharply with the $24 billion spent by Department of Housing and Urban Development on low-income housing and rental subsidies for the poor. On a larger scale, the $587 billion tax expenditure bill for 2000 was $352 billion more than the $235 allocated to means-tested programs for poor people; $118 billion more than the $406 billion for Social Security and just $378 billion less than the total $966 billion spent on entitlement benefits.[6]

The benefit levels of both the social welfare and tax benefit systems also favor the affluent over the poor. Tied to the cost of living, social insurance programs serving the middle class pay significantly higher benefits than the public assistance programs for poor people that lack this built-in protection against erosion from inflation.[7] Tax benefits are even more class-biased. The 1999 tax cut amounted to nearly $32,000 more a year for the wealthiest one percent of the U.S. households while the bottom 60 percent suffered a $166 cut.[8] The 2001 Bush administration's $1.3 trillion, ten year, tax cut continued this uneven pattern.[9]

The differential vulnerability to budget cuts furthers the systemic inequalities resulting from government policies. The nation's leaders readily cut spending for the needy—who lack political clout and who are deemed unworthy of government aid—while protecting programs used by the better-off middle class. In the mid-1990s, low-income programs received 23 percent of all mandatory funds but suffered 93 percent of the cuts. Low-income programs received 21 percent of discretionary spending but absorbed 43 percent of the cuts.[10] Tax expenditures are particularly *in*vulnerable to the budget ax. Less visible to the wider public than direct social spending and less subject to the perils of the budget process, they win Congressional approval more easily and remain on the books longer than direct spending programs.

Corporate Welfare. Government aid to business and industry intensifies the upward bias of social policy. As reported by the conservative Cato Institute every major government department is a repository for government funding of private industry.[11] The editors of *TIME Magazine* estimated that the government dispenses about $125 billion a year to companies to help them advertise their products, build new facilities, train their workers, and write off the cost of perks.[12] Corporate welfare also includes direct government grants, tax reductions, support for research and development, discounted user fees for public resources among others. But the vast bulk of government largesse to big business appears in special tax abatements which in fiscal 2000 cost the government approximately $195 billion—far, far larger than direct-spending business subsidies.[13]

In sum, everyone is on welfare but the class biases of both the highly visible social welfare system and the hidden welfare state embedded in the tax code, ensure that government tax and spending policies do not benefit everyone equally. To make government a better deal for ordinary Americans in the United States—whose gap between the rich and the poor exceeds that of any other industrialized nation—social workers can help expose the gilded welfare state as undemocratic and unfair and call for a system based on real distributive justice for all.

[1]Title adapted from HUFF, D. (1992, Winter). Upside-Down Welfare, *Public Welfare*, pp. 36–40. See also Abramovitz, M. (2001, October). Everyone Is Still on Welfare: The Role of Redistribution in Social Policy. *Social Work* 46 (4): 297–308.

[2]CONGRESSIONAL BUDGET OFFICE (2001, January). *The Economic and Budget Outlook: Fiscal Years 2002–2011.* Washington, DC: U.S. Government Printing Office.

[3]U.S. JOINT COMMITTEE ON TAXATION (2001, April 6). *Estimates of Federal Tax Expenditures for the Fiscal Years 2001—2005.* Washington, DC: U.S. Government Printing Office, pp. 2–3.

[4]CONGRESSIONAL BUDGET OFFICE (2001, January). *The Economic and Budget Outlook: Fiscal Years 2002–2011.* Washington, DC: U.S. Government Printing Office.

[5]U.S. JOINT COMMITTEE ON TAXATION (1998, December 14). *Estimates of Federal Tax Expenditures for the Fiscal Years 1999–2003.* Washington, DC: U.S. Government Printing Office, Table 1, pp. 17–18.

[6]CONGRESSIONAL BUDGET OFFICE (2001, January). *The Economic and Budget Outlook: Fiscal Years 2002–2011.* Washington, DC: U.S. Government Printing Office.

[7]HOUSE COMMITTEE ON HOUSE WAYS AND MEANS (2000). *Overview of Entitlement Programs* (2000 Green Book). Washington, DC: Government Printing Office.

[8]LAV, I. J. & GREENSTEIN, R. (1999, August 29). *Tax Bill Contains Only Modest Benefits for Middle Class Despite Its High Cost.* Washington, DC: Center on Budget and Policy Priorities, p. 1.

(continued)

(7.2   continued)

[9]SHAPIRO, L. & SLY, J. (2001). *Bush Tax Cut and House Rate Cuts Widen Record after Tax Income Disparities.* Washington, DC: Center on Budget and Policy Priorities.

[10]GREENSTEIN, R., KOGAN, R., & NICHOLS, M. (1996). *Bearing Most of the Burden: How Deficit Reduction During the 104th Congress Concentrated on Programs for the Poor.* Washington, DC: Center on Budget and Policy Priorities.

[11]HERSHEY, R. D., JR. (1995, March 7). A Hard Look at Corporate Welfare. *New York Times,* p. D1.

[12]BARTLETT, D. L. & STEEL, J. B. (1998, November 8). Corporate Welfare, *Time Magazine,* p. 38.

[13]STATEMENT OF ROBERT S. MCINTYRE, DIRECTOR, CITIZENS FOR TAX JUSTICE. Before the House Committee on the Budget Regarding Unnecessary Business Subsidies, June 30, 1999.

Some funding choices   The policy practitioner has to state in her legislative proposal how much funding she is requesting, to what extent the states should match federal funds, whether the states should receive funds with relatively few restrictions, and whether in some states taxes on marriage licenses should be used to fund shelters.

When examining funding channels, she has to review her attitudes toward the various levels of government. If she decides to emphasize the states' role in superintending the program, she will propose that federal authorities direct funds to states, which will then fund the shelters. If, by contrast, she wants to emphasize the role of the federal government, she will have federal authorities directly fund local agencies, or she will develop a categorical program providing funds to states, which follow specific guidelines in using the funds.

She decides to ask for an authorization level of $450 million in the first year, with authorizations to rise to $600 million within three years. Although she wants more funds than this for the program, she realizes that conservatives, as well as some moderates and liberals, will object to a larger program during a period of federal budgetary deficits. She selects Route 2 from the funding channels; that is, the federal government is to give funds to the states, which then fund local shelters. She would have preferred direct federal funding of shelters, but decides that this alternative is not politically feasible.

Defining Services

As she develops an initial outline of the Federal Shelter Program, the policy practitioner must provide direction for the shelters' services, decide what mix of preventive and curative services to offer, and determine how to ration scarce resources.

Establishing an orienting framework   We can return now to our discussion of conceptual frameworks in Chapter Six, where we contrasted public health, intrapsychic, deterrent, and other paradigms frequently used in social policy. The policy practitioner has to articulate an orienting framework on which to base her services.

The policy advocate realizes that women who have been subjected to abusive behavior often have multiple problems, such as legal, psychological, familial, medical, and economic issues. Many of them contend with divorce and police protection, suffer from anxiety and depression, have children traumatized by family violence and disruption, have serious physical injuries from the violence, and face a loss of income after separating from their spouses. These considerations prompt the policy practitioner to favor multifaceted services integrated with residential services. As she struggles to define the services, she decides she wants some combination of advocacy, crisis intervention, and referral services, integrated by a case management system.

She is certain, however, that some shelters will not provide any social services, because they will lack the funds or will be preoccupied with the residential services. Therefore, she decides to specify in the legislation the services that shelters receiving federal subsidies will need, including crisis intervention, referral services, and case management services, to attend to battered women's multiple needs.

She does not want the shelters to become mere places of residence for battered women; indeed, she wants to link the shelters to their surrounding community and local feminist organizations. Moreover, she wants them to be advocates, not only for individuals, but also for battered women in general. She wants the shelters to support policies that increase the prosecution of spousal abusers and that include battered women in the existing state programs that provide financial reimbursement to the victims of violent crimes. Besides case management and other services, she decides to require advocacy for battered women, the use of volunteers, and battered women's participation on the shelters' governing or advisory boards (to be discussed later). Even with these stipulations, she realizes that many shelters will seem to offer only a residence, not a multiservice center, because it is far simpler to define facilities' formal attributes than it is to shape their informal qualities, such as sensitivity, advocacy, or responsiveness to community needs.

Staff and licensing   The policy advocate realizes that implementing these plans requires competent staff. She also knows, however, that considerable competition may develop among social service professionals if she favors certain kinds of professionals, such as social workers, in her legislation.

Before we can understand her predicament, we need to discuss how professions, including social work, develop their power and credibility.[21] Professions develop out of both altruism and self-interest. Members of specific professions want to protect consumers from incompetent persons (altruism), but they also want to reserve certain jobs and private practices for persons who meet certain requirements (self-interest). Both altruism and self-interest encourage monopolies from which professionals exclude outsiders who have not received specific training.

Professions must establish minimal education and training requirements, both to be certain that their members have certain competencies and to distinguish their members from the general public and from other professionals. (If no minimum requirements existed, anyone could use the title of the profession and pose as a member of it. This would undermine the profession's credibility because consumers and employers would be likely to believe the title meant nothing.) To protect their members, then, professions specify minimal training and education and develop methods for monitoring them. In the case of social work, graduate schools, whose graduates receive an M.S.W. degree, cannot be accredited by the Council on Social Work Education (CSWE) unless they follow minimal classroom and fieldwork requirements.[22] Similarly, persons who claim they have the B.S.W. degree must have completed specified undergraduate education and fieldwork requirements that CSWE specifies. Programs not accredited by CSWE can graduate students, but they would have difficulty recruiting faculty, and their graduates might have trouble finding jobs.

However, professional organizations are rarely content, again for reasons of altruism and self-interest, to rely exclusively on accreditation to enhance their status. They also want government to use its licensing powers to reserve certain titles, tasks, and positions for their members.[23] Licensing of titles means that by state law, people can use titles such as licensed clinical social worker, physician, or attorney at law only when they have met certain training requirements, including graduating from an accredited program and engaging in postgraduate training. For example, in some states, the requirements for the title licensed clinical social worker (L.C.S.W.) include working for a specified number of hours under a licensed clinical social worker's supervision.

Licensing of tasks or functions requires people to complete certain training before performing specified tasks, such as surgery or prescribing drugs. This kind of licensing represents an even more potent form of protection for a profession because—unlike the licensing of titles, which merely regulates the terms that persons use to describe themselves—it limits certain tasks to members of a profession.[24] Imagine the power that licensed clinical social workers would suddenly gain if all counseling were limited to them, just as surgery is limited to physicians!

Professions often try to keep certain positions in government agencies to themselves by having them *classified.* When government authorities require certain credentials for a civil service position, such as a master's degree in social work, they prevent members of other professions from competing for that position. It is small wonder that professional social workers have been perturbed by declassification, which removes the requirement that one must have a master's degree, or even a bachelor's degree, in social work for many positions in child welfare agencies, welfare programs, and other programs. Licensing and classification are often controversial because rival professions vie to reserve certain positions for themselves or to prevent other professions from monopolizing them.[25]

Our policy advocate must decide whether to require the shelters that receive federal funds to hire certain kinds of professionals. The legislation could stipulate, for example, that each shelter's director of social services must have an M.S.W. degree and that only members of specific professions with a supervised practicum in clinical work can provide certain counseling and case management services. Such requirements may enhance the quality of the shelters' social services and make their services billable to insurance. But the policy practitioner realizes that such staffing requirements have some disadvantages. They will substantially increase the cost of maintaining the shelters, because the shelters will have to pay the higher salaries that professionals command. Professionals excluded from directing the shelters, such as marriage and family counselors and psychologists, may oppose the legislation. Some people may even argue that professionalizing the shelters will detract from their use of volunteer and community support; many feminists seek to increase the contributions of nonpaid women to programs that help women. The policy advocate decides to require that the shelter directors have an M.S.W. degree and that the direct-service staff have had a supervised practicum, but not to specify their professional affiliation.

Preventive versus curative services   When contemplating whether to incorporate a major preventive component, the policy advocate confronts difficult dilemmas (see Chapter Six). The number of women on waiting lists for shelters makes it difficult to justify spending large sums on prevention, and it is difficult to know how to prevent abusive behavior in light of the complexity of the problem and the absence of definitive research. Abusive behaviors probably stem from some combination of exposure to abuse as a child, marital discord, substance abuse, cultural factors, sexism, situational stressors such as unemployment and poverty, ownership of a gun, a national culture that promotes violence, and possibly a genetic predisposition toward violence. While large-scale national reforms could address some of these causes, the policy practitioner cannot easily address them in her legislative proposal. If *primary prevention*, which is directed to persons not yet having a social problem, is difficult to accomplish, she nonetheless wonders whether her legislation could engage in *secondary prevention*, which aims at averting the further progression of problems that are in their early stages. As members of her coalition brainstorm the issue, they decide that properly advertised local hot lines would encourage women to seek early assistance. Thus, the policy advocate includes in her proposal a section qualifying shelters to apply for funds to set up a hot line.

Rationing Scarce Resources

There are always many people who need assistance, so every social agency and social program must engage in some form of rationing.[26] Our policy practitioner must grapple with this issue as she plans the legislation, because the resources that Congress might authorize will not be sufficient to address the large demand for services by battered women, who have formed long waiting lists for the existing shelters. Moreover, if the Federal Shelter Program is enacted and advertised, it is likely that many women who do not currently use services will seek them.

Formal or direct methods of rationing   One of the most common methods of restricting access is giving free services only to those who fall beneath a minimum level, such as the official poverty line. This method is called *means testing*. Using income measures poses some problems, however.[27] Means testing requires shelter staff to check applicants' financial records, a time-consuming task. Many abused women are, moreover, in a chaotic financial situation in the wake of leaving their spouses or partners, losing access to joint banking accounts, and lacking independent sources of income. Can shelter staff accurately identify actual available income, as opposed to total family income, in these circumstances? Income-based eligibility, however, has some advantages. It allows social agencies to focus scarce resources on those who are least able to purchase services.

In addition to, or instead of, basing eligibility on income, the policy advocate can use diagnostic criteria, such as the level of danger, the frequency or severity of the abuse, or the extent of the applicants' personal trauma. Like mental health institutions, which often limit access or at least involuntary commitment to persons who are a danger to themselves or others, the policy practitioner can limit use of the shelters to women who have actually been abused rather than those who have only received verbal threats. Diagnostic criteria have the advantage of limiting the programs to the persons who appear to have the most serious problems. This is an important consideration when dealing with battered women, whose lives are sometimes in danger. However, these criteria place applicants at the mercy of intake staff, who may misread the seriousness of a woman's problem or who may allow their own preferences to shape their judgments.[28] Indeed, intake staff may be more sympathetic to certain persons, such as members of their own racial or ethnic group or women with certain kinds of problems. When analyzing her options, the policy advocate might choose to use a number of eligibility criteria. She could, for example, limit free service to persons earning less than a certain amount and require shelter staff to give priority to women in danger of serious injury.

The policy advocate cannot resolve rationing issues without considering certain values and her original mission. If she wants a national network of federally subsidized shelters that will serve most battered women, she may establish eligibility policies that are relatively nonexclusionary. She could even aim to make the shelters an entitlement, much like Medicare or Social Security, that will receive automatic funding for whatever services they provide to abused women during a given year. This option would have bleak political prospects, however, because of its high cost.

We should note that buck passing is common with respect to eligibility. In order not to make difficult and sometimes controversial choices, federal legislators, for example, may yield eligibility decisions to states or agencies, as in some block-granted programs. Such ceding of decisions on eligibility standards has some merit because standards of living and demand for services vary in different parts of the nation. Critics contend, however, that more conservative and poorer states restrict eligibility excessively when given this power.

Indirect methods of restricting access   Social agencies and programs devise policies that indirectly influence clients' access. One method of rationing is to place upper limits on the intensity or duration of services. To allow more persons to receive assistance, a program administrator may decide, for example, to limit residence in a shelter to a certain number of months. When placing limits on services, policy practitioners must balance effectiveness with equity. If the intensity, duration, or number of services or benefits is markedly reduced, more consumers will receive program benefits (equity is increased), but the services may be distributed so thinly that they are ineffective or inadequate. Policy practitioners must make difficult choices when considering the relative intensity or number of program benefits.

Another common method of rationing resources in social agencies and programs is to adopt a first-come, first-served policy, in which consumers receive services in the order of their application. This approach appears at first glance to be equitable because no favoritism is possible. However, this policy has its own liabilities. People with serious problems may need preferential access, and certain kinds of clients may drop off waiting lists.

Some critics argue that social agencies should reserve resources for underserved populations, much as affirmative action has reserved employment slots for women and racial minorities. According to this argument, social agencies should also develop outreach to these populations and examine service utilization patterns in order to reach consumers who leave the service prematurely.

Some social agencies ration services by discouraging specific populations from using them. Overt discrimination is probably less serious than subtler forms.[29] Low-income populations that want tangible assistance with economic and social problems will probably not use some service approaches, such as extended talking therapies. Similarly, a lack of bilingual and ethnic minority staff will deter ethnic minorities from using services. Agency personnel may not fully realize that their forms of service or their staffing patterns powerfully influence who does or does not use the program.

Agencies ration services indirectly in many other ways, including the location of facilities, the use of specific program titles, and the selective use of outreach. Facilities located in low-income areas promote use by poor persons, just as facilities in many suburban areas favor affluent populations. The importance of titles becomes obvious when one examines the difference between "free clinic" and "women's free clinic": the latter clearly would encourage female users and discourage male users. Patterns of outreach and advertising also influence access; if an agency advertises its program to relatively affluent populations, for example, it biases access toward these persons and away from other populations.

Charging fees is another way to restrict access. As fees increase, low-income consumers are less likely to seek services and more likely to terminate as soon as possible. Some policies, such as restricting services to regular hours, impose a hidden but substantial burden on working persons and poor persons who must, in effect, pay a fee by taking time from their employment.

Our policy advocate reluctantly decides that she has to ration the services financed by the Federal Shelter Program because of the enormity of the unmet needs. She decides to restrict access to three months of residence in the shelters unless a woman remains in imminent danger of physical abuse. She also decides to require the shelters to disseminate information about their services to a broad range of community groups, and she establishes a sliding-fee schedule that can be waived when family finances are disrupted by dislocation.

Addressing Agency Network Issues

It was customary in the 1950s to conceptualize a social agency as an autonomous entity providing services more or less in isolation from other agencies. But in the succeeding decades, many policy theorists came to realize that agencies had to develop links with one another if they were to provide quality services. Child welfare agencies maintain hundreds of thousands of children in foster care, while serving the natural families of many of these children and the dysfunctional families whose children have not been removed.

No matter how dedicated its staff, the child welfare agency cannot provide quality services unless it links these children and families to schools, mental health agencies, job-training agencies, job search agencies, substance abuse clinics, adult education agencies, health providers, Social Security offices, and government welfare agencies. Indeed, linkage must occur on several levels simultaneously. At a case management level, child welfare staff need to develop individualized plans for children and families that identify an array of services, make referrals, and monitor referrals to be certain that children and families actually receive them. If a child welfare agency lacks funds to purchase services, moreover, children and families will sometimes fail to receive them from referral agencies that are overwhelmed by current demands on their services. So case management has to be supplemented with purchase-of-service resources.

At a more ambitious level, however, a child welfare agency must develop partnerships and collaborations with other agencies. In some cases, it must subcontract with other agencies to help specific kinds of families and children. A child welfare agency might subcontract with a family-counseling agency, for example, to provide family support and empowerment services for dysfunctional families that show promise of improving their parenting sufficiently so that children can remain in the family. Or a child welfare agency might establish a *collaborative project* with other agencies to which each contributes staff and resources. It might, for example, establish a collaboration with a substance abuse agency and a job-training agency, creating a new program that combines substance-abuse, job-training, job-referral, and family-counseling services. The substance-abuse, job-training, and family-counseling staff would not only meet separately with families but have frequent case conferences, both among themselves and with the families.

Links among agencies were also fostered by a *managed-care* revolution in the 1990s. It began in the health service industry in response to the double-digit annual increases in costs that confronted government funders, corporations, and insurance companies.[30] By 2002, the United States was spending about 16 percent of its gross domestic product, or GDP, on health care—far more than any other industrialized nation. Before the advent of managed care, autonomous physicians were reimbursed for each test or service, such as $1,000 for removing an appendix. Few limits were placed on their fees, and insurance companies usually reimbursed physicians and hospitals for whatever fees they charged. Such *fee-for-service* reimbursement was very costly because it encouraged physicians to do excessive surgeries and diagnostic tests, as their incomes were based on the number of services they provided. Determined to establish limits on these costs, insurance companies formed managed-care organizations and placed physicians and hospitals under tight controls. To participate in managed care and to get reimbursed, physicians and hospitals had to agree to limit their charges and to get approval for diagnostic tests and surgeries. Variously called *preferred-provider organizations* or *health maintenance organizations,* these managed-care organizations sharply restricted the autonomy of physicians and hospitals.

It seemed at first that managed care, which began with health services, would not affect social workers, but it was soon extended to mental health services, which employ tens of thousands of social workers. Because, originally, they had provided some mental health benefits, health insurance companies placed mental health practitioners under controls similar to those on physicians: If they wanted to be reimbursed, mental health practitioners had to agree to certain fee levels and had to get approval if they wanted to provide treatment that exceeded, in many cases, 10 sessions.[31] This trend toward managed care in the mental health services was accelerated by federal legislation in 1996 that required health insurance plans to include mental health coverage. Managed care in mental health quickly spread to the public sector as well. For example, the Los Angeles County Mental Health Department, which is charged with caring for persons with chronic conditions who receive SSI, decided to subcontract its services to not-for-profit and for-profit agencies, giving them specific payment amounts per patient. This method of financing care, called *capitation,* differs markedly from fee-for-service. Whereas mental health providers had often billed insurance companies and public authorities by the hour for the clinical services they provided, capitation meant that they received a flat amount per year for each patient in their care, say, $1,500 per patient. As with managed care generally, capitation removes any incentive to overextend services, because the more treatment provided, the less return on the time expended.

As clients soon discovered, the movement toward managed care had both positive and negative consequences. By placing providers under the control of insurance administrators and by setting limits on their fees and services, it fostered greater efficiency in health and mental health. Some managed-care health facilities, however, chose to underserve their patients and clients, increasing their revenues per capita, for example, by deciding to deny diagnostic tests, surgeries, and mental health services even to patients and clients who clearly needed them.[32]

Indeed, policy advocates in many states introduced legislation that placed restrictions on managed-care insurance companies, such as diminishing the power of their administrators to force providers to restrict their services excessively, or that gave consumers the right to appeal treatment decisions that denied them services or tests.

In some cases, policy advocates work to create regional organizations to fund local agencies and shape policy choices. For example, the Ryan White legislation provides federal funds for AIDS treatment and prevention programs.[33] This legislation created regional boards across the nation that distribute funds to agencies in their area, monitor these agencies' services, and create new programs when gaps or omissions exist. While critics view these regional organizations as yet another layer of bureaucracy, their advocates note their ability to locate unserved needs, promote joint programs, and advocate for the needs of underserved populations.

Addressing Community Factors

We noted earlier that our policy advocate wants to embed the shelters in her program in the community. She inserts provisions in the legislation to encourage shelters to spread word of their services to local self-help groups; local professionals who have extensive contact with women (such as hair stylists); female community leaders; and agencies that link women to schools, job placement, medical services, free clinics, and other social agencies. She also requires the shelters to provide advocacy services, such as seeking greater protection by local police departments for women who have been abused.

Because shelters' staff and boards will define priorities and objectives, the policy advocate requires the boards to select 51 percent of their membership from currently or previously battered women, female leaders in the community, and local professionals who work in self-help and other agencies. These kinds of board members should be more sympathetic to her objectives than the businesspeople and professionals who usually dominate agencies' boards. To give the boards even greater powers, the policy practitioner also requires them to review programs and budgets in the hope that they will promote the full range of services in the legislation, including advocacy and outreach.

Guiding and Overseeing Policy Implementation

As we discuss in more detail in Chapter Thirteen, implementation is a critical part of the policy process. Were policy advocates not to consider implementation in their proposals, they would ignore a vital aspect of the policy-making process. They must consider two issues: Who will establish the detailed policies that will guide the implementation of their proposal, and who will monitor their proposal's implementation?

Most proposals do not attempt to define the myriad administrative policies that will shape their implementation. While they may discuss a broad strategy for determining eligibility, for example, they may not describe detailed policies, such as how current income will be calculated if a means-tested sliding-fee approach is used. These kinds of details are frequently decided through *administrative regulations* that a high-level agency establishes. Our policy practitioner decides to give the responsibility for establishing these detailed policies to the states rather than vesting them with the federal government, partly because she fears that conservatives will oppose her Federal Shelter Program if it gives the federal government this role.

She must also decide whether the programs of specific shelters will be monitored by higher authorities to see if their services are in compliance with the policies in the legislation and the states' administrative regulations.[34] She also must decide whether shelters will be given technical assistance to help them implement these federal and state policies. She decides they will and gives state agencies the task of monitoring the shelters and providing them with technical assistance. Realizing that monitoring and technical assistance can be costly because staff must be hired and reimbursed to travel widely, she decides to earmark some of the Federal Shelter Program's resources for these two functions.

Assessing Implemented Policies

Policy proposals often discuss how programs or services they establish will be assessed. In the case of the Federal Shelter Program, the policy advocate must decide who will perform these assessments and how they will be funded. As with monitoring and technical assistance, she decides to give this responsibility to the state agency that oversees the shelters.

An Overview of the Proposal to Fund Shelters for Battered Women

We have watched our policy advocate face a number of policy options and make some tentative choices. Here is an overview of her decisions.

She has established a mission by proposing a nationwide system of shelters for battered women. The shelters will provide these women with a range of social services. She has designed the structure of service to place the Federal Shelter Program in the U.S. Department of Health and Human Services, to use only nonprofit agencies, and to set some standards at the federal level, but requires each state to appoint a lead agency to administer the funds to the local shelters. She has planned the disbursement and circulation of resources by establishing an authorization level of $450 million, which will increase to $600 million within three years, using Route 2 from Figure 7.1. She has defined the services to be offered by using an ecological paradigm and requiring that they include referral, crisis management, case management, advocacy, legal help, and outreach; proposing a regional hot line in designated regional areas; and requiring the shelter directors to have an M.S.W. degree and direct-service staff to have had a supervised practicum.

She has rationed scarce resources by establishing a sliding fee that can be waived when family finances are disrupted by dislocation; by limiting residence to a period of three months, which can be extended when the resident remains in imminent danger of physical abuse; and by giving admittance priority to women in imminent danger of physical abuse. She has included local coordinating boards to link the work of different shelters. The proposal addresses community factors by requiring outreach to underserved segments of the population, links with community support systems, and advocacy; and by requiring 51 percent of the board to consist of currently or previously battered women, staff in agencies or support groups for this population, or community leaders. Finally, she has arranged for overseeing policy implementation by earmarking 3 percent of funds for state agencies to monitor the shelter programs.

As we will see in the next chapter, it is relatively simple to list policy options and to make preliminary choices, as our practitioner has done. But she and other members of her coalition have not yet encountered the difficulties of the political process or persons who are not favorably disposed to the proposal. At that point, she will have to make some agonizing choices.

The Anatomy of Policy Proposals

We can conceptualize proposal writing as choosing from the competing options on various policy issues. The policy advocate maps a proposal by drawing lines between alternative options on a diagram that displays the issues and the competing options. (See Figure 7.3, which illustrates the choices made by the policy practitioner who has constructed the Federal Shelter Program. The shaded items are the options she has chosen.)

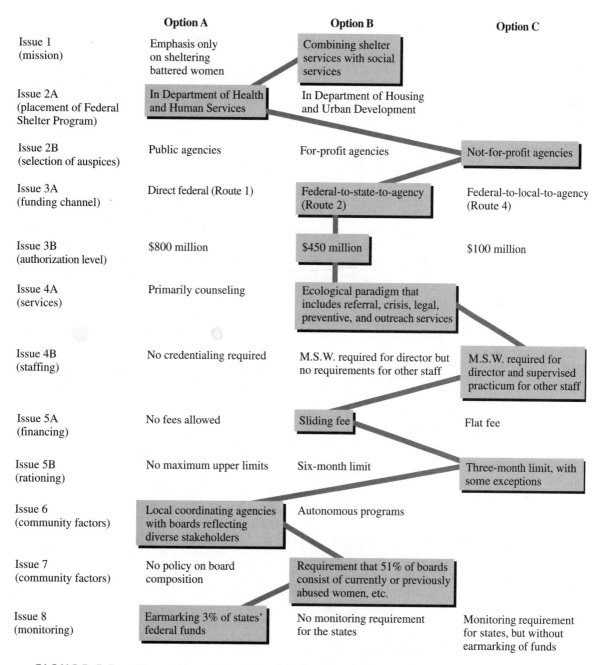

	Option A	**Option B**	**Option C**
Issue 1 (mission)	Emphasis only on sheltering battered women	Combining shelter services with social services	
Issue 2A (placement of Federal Shelter Program)	In Department of Health and Human Services	In Department of Housing and Urban Development	
Issue 2B (selection of auspices)	Public agencies	For-profit agencies	Not-for-profit agencies
Issue 3A (funding channel)	Direct federal (Route 1)	Federal-to-state-to-agency (Route 2)	Federal-to-local-to-agency (Route 4)
Issue 3B (authorization level)	$800 million	$450 million	$100 million
Issue 4A (services)	Primarily counseling	Ecological paradigm that includes referral, crisis, legal, preventive, and outreach services	
Issue 4B (staffing)	No credentialing required	M.S.W. required for director but no requirements for other staff	M.S.W. required for director and supervised practicum for other staff
Issue 5A (financing)	No fees allowed	Sliding fee	Flat fee
Issue 5B (rationing)	No maximum upper limits	Six-month limit	Three-month limit, with some exceptions
Issue 6 (community factors)	Local coordinating agencies with boards reflecting diverse stakeholders	Autonomous programs	
Issue 7 (community factors)	No policy on board composition	Requirement that 51% of boards consist of currently or previously abused women, etc.	
Issue 8 (monitoring)	Earmarking 3% of states' federal funds	No monitoring requirement for the states	Monitoring requirement for states, but without earmarking of funds

FIGURE 7.3   **The anatomy of the Federal Shelter Program proposal**

Policy advocates had to devise policy proposals for welfare reform in each state after the Personal Responsibility and Work Opportunity Reconciliation Act was enacted in 1996. This is an ongoing process with many states changing their policies as they approached 2002 when the federal government would decide whether to rewrite the 1996 legislation. As with the Federal Shelter Program, choices had to be made about a number of issues. (See Policy Advocacy Challenge 7.3.)

POLICY ADVOCACY CHALLENGE 7.3 *PORTRAYING YOUR SOLUTION TO WELFARE REFORM*	As the date for reauthorization (or extension) of the Personal Responsibility and Work Opportunity Reconciliation Act neared in 2002, advocates in many states developed proposals regarding how the act might be rewritten—and how their state welfare programs might also be altered. Advocates realized that programs funded by the Temporary Assistance for Needy Families block grant (TANF) had often succeeded in markedly reducing welfare rolls in the years since 1996 when the act was enacted. But they also realized that TANF programs had failed miserably in elevating many women above poverty levels or in helping them to get into a career trajectory that would allow them to better their condition in coming years. They also realized that child care was often inadequate and that health care benefits were sometimes terminated when women left welfare rolls. We can construct a welfare reform matrix that lists key issues that advocates had to address as they sought reforms in welfare programs. (See Table 7.2.) Fill in alternative options on this diagram as you develop an "ideal" welfare proposal for your state. Identify possible compromise positions that you might consider if you had to reach an accord with persons holding different positions. Then find whether your plan, in either its ideal or compromised form, bears a resemblance to its actual welfare proposal enacted by Congress in 2002 or implemented by your state legislature in the wake of congressional reauthorization.

TABLE 7.2   **The anatomy of a welfare reform proposal in one state**

	Option A	Option B	Option C
Issue 1 (emphasis on child care, training, and services)			
Issue 2 (extent of speed of reduction in rolls)			
Issue 3 (emphasis on public service jobs)			
Issue 4 (extent of state provision of employer subsidies or other incentives to employers)			
Issue 5 (extent of state cession of power to counties)			
Issue 6 (organizational relations between welfare, employment, community college, and social service agencies)			
Issue 7 (specify another issue)			
Issue 8 (specify another issue)			

Trade-Offs: Systematically Comparing Policy Options

Policy advocates sometimes use a **systematic process** to compare the relative merits of competing options like the ones discussed in the previous chapter. To make systematic comparisons of policy options, policy advocates often proceed deliberately; they identify options, select and weigh criteria, rank options, and develop a decision-making matrix.[35] You should know about this analytic style of reasoning because it is often used in policy deliberations.

Identifying Options

Policy analysts rarely feel comfortable with a single policy approach, wanting to compare and contrast alternative policies before making a final selection. Someone seeking to end malnutrition in certain segments of the population, for example, might examine the merits of distributing food directly to certain persons, changing the food stamp program, and changing existing welfare programs to give low-income persons more funds to purchase food. These three policy choices might be contrasted with expanding income tax credits to poor persons to allow them to purchase more food. By identifying these four options, the policy analyst hopes to avoid being prematurely committed to a specific policy.

Let's consider the systematic process of examining trade-offs by using as our example an M.S.W. student intern who discovered that Spanish-speaking patients in her hospital placement had very few translation services available to them. She observed that some newly admitted patients had been hospitalized for as long as 24 hours without receiving any explanation of their medical condition or treatment. Many hospital staff were not informed about nuances of Latino culture, moreover, that powerfully shaped patients' responses to medical treatments. For example, a Latina signed an informed-consent form for a hysterectomy. Her physician, knowing that her bilingual son had served as her interpreter, assumed that she favored the treatment plan, only to discover the next day that she was so irate that a hysterectomy had been performed that she was threatening to sue the hospital. Only later was the physician informed that it is culturally inappropriate for a Latino son to discuss private parts with his mother—and that the embarrassed son had told his mother that a tumor would be removed from her abdomen! In turn, the mother was furious, not only because she had not been informed about the procedure, but because hysterectomies are considered taboo procedures by some segments of the Latino community.

The intern's challenge was to develop a proposal to address this situation. To do so, she had to compare alternative strategies and gauge which one would be most effective in getting translation services to Latinos. She did not take this task lightly; she realized that the well-being of many Latinos depended on getting translation services.

The social work intern identified four options:

1. Develop a cultural awareness course for new medical residents to instill a sensitivity to the culture and language of Spanish-speaking patients. In particular, the course would help the residents understand the need to engage these patients in extended discussions and caring services to offset their fear of the medical system and their inability to express their needs in English.

2. Develop a computerized list of all hospital employees and residents who speak Spanish, allowing them to be paged by medical staff when translations are needed, thus easing the burden on the seven full-time interpreters employed by the hospital.
3. Hire more interpreters.
4. Recruit 40 bilingual Latino undergraduate students to serve as volunteer interpreters two hours per week, assigning them to the nurses' station in each unit of the hospital.

Selecting and Weighing Criteria

In order to select an optimal policy, policy advocates must first identify the criteria to use as a basis of comparison. In simple cases, a single criterion suffices; given three policy options, for example, with the single criterion being cost, the cheapest policy option would be selected. In most cases, however, advocates identify several criteria. For example, they might consider costs, administrative feasibility, and effectiveness in addressing consumers' needs.

Policy advocates can select a variety of criteria. As was discussed in Chapter Two, *value-based criteria* are reflected in such terms as equality, equity, social justice, and various freedoms, such as the right to free speech, the right to privacy, the right to receive accurate and honest information, and the right to self-determination. (Moral philosophers, religious leaders, the due process clause of the Fifth and Fourteenth Amendments to the U.S. Constitution and the Bill of Rights discuss these value-based criteria.)

Consumer-outcome criteria define specific policies' effectiveness in ameliorating social problems. In the social services, for example, people often scrutinize how various policy options will affect clients' well-being.

Terms such as efficiency and cost reflect *economic criteria*. Having limited resources, policy advocates must assess the relative cost of competing options. *Feasibility criteria* pertain to the political and administrative practicality of specific policy options. An option may seem quite attractive but may be rejected because it cannot be implemented or is not politically feasible. For example, some people believe we should decriminalize certain drugs, such as cocaine, by selling them at cheap prices in state-regulated stores. However, many practical details confound the administration of this policy. If cocaine were legalized, what about countless other substances, including some that have not even been invented? If cocaine were legalized, the state-regulated stores might offer a wide assortment of mood-altering substances. Who would pay for growing or manufacturing the currently illegal drugs? Should poor persons be allowed to use their food stamps to purchase them? Could federal authorities easily override state laws that declare mood-altering substances illegal? Would authorities have to limit the amount of a drug someone could purchase, or could persons obtain unlimited quantities? Could drugs in such an open market be kept from adolescents or schoolchildren, or would older friends, siblings, or even some parents supply them? Some politicians would very likely assail this policy for threatening to corrode our youths' morals by making drugs too accessible.

Externalities criteria are used to assess how a policy option would affect institutions or persons who initially appear to be unrelated to the policy. If drugs, including hallucinogens, were decriminalized, policy analysts would have to ask whether driving accidents would markedly increase. This externality could not be dismissed as trivial because as many as 35,000 Americans die each year from accidents caused by driving while under the influence of alcohol, a decriminalized and accessible drug. However, some positive externalities might offset these negative ones. The reduced price of drugs and their increased availability in state-regulated stores would drive criminal elements, gangs, and foreign profiteers out of drug dealing and would make it unnecessary for addicts to steal to support their habit.

Terms such as cost-effectiveness reflect how we can combine several criteria into single measures.[36] In cost-effectiveness studies, analysts want to know which policy will most benefit consumers at the lowest cost. One policy option may yield considerable benefit to consumers, but at a prohibitive cost; another option may yield few benefits, but at a low cost; and a third option may provide considerable benefits at a relatively modest cost. A policy analyst who wants a cost-effective policy would probably select the third option because it balances cost and effectiveness.

When selecting more than one criterion, policy advocates need to weigh their relative importance. This is not a scientific undertaking; it reflects the values of the policy practitioner. When discussing alternative criteria for evaluating welfare reform (see Chapter Six), many policy advocates would be more likely than conservatives to emphasize welfare reform's effects on the economic well-being of former recipients, whereas many conservatives would emphasize its effects in reducing the welfare rolls.

The social work intern decided to select four criteria, assigning a numerical value to each of them. To force herself to determine the relative importance of these four criteria, she decided to make the four scores add up to 1.0. She gave the most weight to cost and effectiveness in helping patients with translation needs, wanting to help patients immediately but realizing that funds were short in her hospital. (Each of these criteria was scored as 0.3.) She included the criteria of political feasibility and ease of implementation, realizing she would need high-level approval that would stem partly from the administrators' belief that the project could be easily implemented. (Each of these criteria was scored as 0.2, so the total score for the four criteria was 1.0.) Of course, someone else might have weighted the criteria differently.

Creating a Decision-Making Matrix

To help them select policies, advocates often construct a decision-making matrix that graphically portrays the options and the criteria.[37] The social work intern placed her four options and her four criteria on a decision-making matrix that organized her options and criteria into a table. (See Table 7.3.)

Recall that she had already rated the criteria by giving scores of 0.3 to cost and effectiveness and scores of 0.2 to political feasibility and ease of implementation. (See the criteria at the top of Table 7.4, which shows how she rated the criteria and the options.)

She then rated the policy options by the criteria (Table 7.4). She decided to rank each of the options from 1 (poor) to 10 (outstanding), using information gleaned from physicians and administrators, as well as her own best guesses. She rated the cultural course as 6 with respect to cost because it would require the development of curriculum and staff to teach it. Since the computerized list would be relatively inexpensive to produce, she gave it a ranking of 8. She ranked the hiring of more interpreters as 1 because it would require more paid hospital staff. The recruiting of undergraduate volunteers was

TABLE 7.3   A decision-making matrix

	Criteria			
Policy options	Cost	Effectiveness in helping patients with translations	Political feasibility	Ease of implementation
Cultural course for new residents				
Computerized list of Spanish-speaking employees				
Hiring more interpreters				
Recruiting 40 bilingual undergraduate volunteers				

TABLE 7.4   Scoring policy options by using policy criteria

	Criteria				
Policy options	Cost (0.3)	Effectiveness in helping patients with translations (0.3)	Political feasibility (0.2)	Ease of implementation (0.2)	Total
Cultural course for new residents	$6_{1.8}$	$3_{.9}$	$8_{1.6}$	$6_{1.2}$	5.5
Computerized list of Spanish-speaking employees	$8_{2.4}$	$7_{2.1}$	$8_{1.6}$	$6_{1.2}$	7.3
Hiring more interpreters	$1_{.3}$	$9_{2.7}$	$3_{.6}$	$8_{1.6}$	5.2
Recruiting 40 bilingual undergraduate volunteers	$7_{2.1}$	$9_{2.7}$	$9_{1.8}$	$6_{1.2}$	7.8

ranked 7; while they would provide free labor, staff time would be needed to recruit, train, and coordinate them. She then ranked the four policy options by the remaining three criteria. As shown in Table 7.4, she gave the lowest score on effectiveness in helping patients with translations to the cultural course (3) on the grounds that it might sensitize residents to the culture of Latinos, but it would not provide new translation services. Regarding political feasibility, she ranked the option of hiring new translators the lowest, giving it only a score of 3 because she doubted that the hospital administrators would fund this proposal. All of the options were relatively easy to implement, she decided, not giving any of them a score lower than 6.

She discovered that each option had at least one weakness: The cultural course would not make an immediate impact on the translation needs of patients; the computerized list would not prove easy to implement since bilingual staff could not interrupt their regular assignments and become translators on the spur of the moment; hiring new translators was too costly; and training and coordinating undergraduate volunteers might prove difficult to implement.

The student intern now had to calculate scores that combined her ranking of the options for each criterion and the relative importance of each criterion (the numbers in parentheses under each criterion in Table 7.4). She multiplied the option rating in each cell by each criterion score, arriving at a final score for each cell (the subscript number in italics). To score the recruiting of undergraduate volunteers by the cost criterion, for example, she multiplied 0.3 times 7, arriving at a score of 2.1 in the lower-left-hand cell.

Then, she added the scores for each option across the table to discover the total score for each option. She concluded that using undergraduate volunteers was the best solution, because it received a total score of 7.8, compared with the next closest option, the computerized list, which received a score of 7.3. (See the total scores for each option in the right-hand column of Table 7.4.) She hoped she could get a local foundation to provide funds for a part-time coordinator to recruit and train these volunteers. She was excited about this option for educational reasons as well: It would provide an excellent opportunity for the students to learn about the health care system.

The term *trade-off* refers to assessing the comparative advantages of policy options. The policy practitioner seeks to discover which option has the most weight, that is, the greatest net score on the criteria that the policy analyst has identified and ranked.[38] Thus, the student intern selected the fourth policy option, even though other options had received higher scores on specific criteria.

When reviewing this example of a decision-making matrix, it is important to dwell not on the details of the scoring rules, but on the style of analytic reasoning. Other approaches to scoring could easily have been used to rank the criteria and the various options and to compute the final scores. When using an analytic style of reasoning, the policy analyst breaks the selection process into a series of sequential steps that eventually lead to an overall score for specific options.

Using a policy matrix like Table 7.4 does not necessarily eliminate conflict; persons may disagree about the criteria selected, their relative importance, and specific options' scores for those criteria. When policy analysis occurs before a policy is enacted, as in this hospital case, policy practitioners must predict the outcomes, costs, and consequences of options. Such predictions often turn out to be partially inaccurate; in this case, the student intern might later discover that she had underestimated the costs of a policy option or its effectiveness in solving a social problem.

Qualitative Rankings

Had the student intern not been quantitatively inclined, she could have ranked her four policy options qualitatively. Some critics of quantitative techniques would readily support this tactic on the grounds that the existing data do not allow accurate quantitative rankings. However, persons making qualitative rankings (such as high, medium, and low) would still have to develop options and criteria and weigh the criteria to judge the relative merits of the two policy options.

Table 7.5 portrays some trade-offs that social workers in agencies often encounter. Indeed, the policy advocate discussed earlier in the chapter who developed legislation to help battered women would have encountered each of the trade-offs in Table 7.5 when designing shelter programs at the local level. (See Policy Advocacy Challenge 7.4.)

TABLE 7.5   Trade-offs in policy options

Policy options	Advantages	Disadvantages
Using intensive rather than extensive services	Provides in-depth services with greater impact	Denies services to large numbers of consumers
Developing community-based rather than institutional services	Decreases stigma of service; helps integrate consumers into mainstream	Is difficult to orchestrate several community services and involve transient populations
Using generalist rather than specialized services or staff	Focuses on client as a whole person	Staff members lack specialized expertise relevant to consumers' specific needs
Providing preventive rather than curative services	Allows early detection and treatment of social problems and educates consumers to forestall development of problems	May neglect the needs of people who already have a serious problem
Using universal rather than selective eligibility	Allows staff to serve all applicants; makes imposing means tests unnecessary	Makes it difficult to target scarce resources on those with particularly serious problems
Using decentralized rather than centralized services	Makes outreach to consumers possible; improves access to services and use of community networks	Is more expensive to operate than centralized facilities
Using multiprofessional teams rather than single professions	Allows many professions to contribute to service	May promote interprofessional conflict

POLICY ADVOCACY CHALLENGE 7.4

MICRO-LEVEL POLICY: EXAMINING POLICY TRADE-OFFS IN AGENCIES

Take any social agency with which you are familiar and any of the policy options listed in Table 7.3. Discuss how the administrators and staff of the agency have wrestled with that option and what solutions they have chosen in the context of trade-offs. If possible, interview some agency staff about their choices concerning the option; otherwise, use your knowledge of the agency to speculate about the possible trade-offs they had to consider when they made their choices.

Linking Policy Skills

The evolution of the Federal Shelter Program proposal demonstrates that effective policy advocates combine analytic skills in identifying, comparing, and selecting policy options with other policy practice skills. Our policy advocate had to develop and maintain a coalition and make ethical choices as she (and her allies) decided whether to make compromises to get the proposal enacted.

As our example of the proposed legislation to fund shelters for battered women suggests, policy advocates must be acutely aware of political realities as they construct proposals. In drafting the legislation, our policy advocate decided at several critical junctures to modify some of the provisions to accommodate political realities. She chose, for example, to propose a fiscal authorization at the rather limited sum of $450 million in the first year. She also chose to use the states to administer the funds (Route 2), rather than to give federal authorities a more expansive role. In making these concessions to conservative and moderate politicians, she had to wrestle with an ethical dilemma: Is half a loaf better than none? Recall our Chapter Two discussion of ethical dilemmas that arise when ethical principles, such as social justice, are pitted against pragmatic factors, such as political realities. (See Policy Advocacy Challenge 7.5.)

The proposal-making process is illustrated by the reauthorization of its Personal Responsibility and Work Opportunity Reconciliation Act in 2002. Policy advocates had to identify specific policy options that could be included in revised legislation that would better address the economic and familial needs of low-income women and their children. Choosing these policy options is, of course, a precursor to social action. Advocates realized, for example, that their preferred policies would be strongly opposed by many conservatives. Advocates would have to build coalitions and devise political strategies if they were to be successful in the nation's capital as well as in state legislatures.

POLICY ADVOCACY CHALLENGE 7.5

WELFARE OVERHAUL ADVISED: NASW SAYS AIM SHOULD BE POVERTY REDUCTION

John O'Neill, M.S.W., Staff for NASW NEWS, *February 2002, Vol. 42, No. 2, pp. 1, 10. Reprinted by permission.*

In November, NASW submitted to the Department of Health and Human Services a comprehensive list of recommendations for shaping legislation to reauthorize the welfare reform act passed in 1996.

Facing a congressionally imposed deadline for reauthorization by August 2002, the Bush administration has been holding "listening sessions" for governors, state legislators, state welfare department staff and welfare administrators, and gave interested parties like NASW an opportunity to analyze the consequences of the 1996 law and suggest improved ways to aid the nation's poor.

"NASW believes significant improvements can and should be made to the Personal Responsibility and Work Opportunity Reconciliation Act of 1996, P. L. 104-193," said NASW President Terry Mizrahi and Executive Director Elizabeth J. Clark in a cover letter for the 35-page NASW comments and analysis.

It was the 1996 act that, among other things, eliminated welfare benefits as an entitlement, created the Temporary Assistance for Needy Families (TANF) block grant, established a federal time limit of five years for direct cash benefits, fostered a work-first mentality rather than focusing on training and education, placed much emphasis on getting people off welfare roles and gave states great latitude in establishing programs.

The time limits for benefits to expire, many of them set by states for periods shorter than the federal five-year limit, have begun and will accelerate in the future. In New York State, about 50,000 people were scheduled to lose many benefits at the first of the year.

(continued)

(7.5   continued)

The law presents many opportunities for improvement, said Mizrahi and Clark, but NASW generally restricted its recommendations to three areas:

- Reducing the number of families living in poverty.
- Improving assistance to recipients with multiple barriers to self-sufficiency.
- Enhancing the capacity of the welfare system infrastructure.

NASW also addressed funding, benefit levels, services for immigrants and research. Its comments were based on previous positions policy statements, the work of a special task force before passage of the 1996 law, and research on welfare reform since 1996 by social workers, NASW members and others, said Cynthia Woodside, senior government relations associate, who wrote the comments.

"At this point, few national organizations are advocating a return to welfare as an entitlement," said Woodside. "Our efforts will be in areas like trying to eliminate or modify time limits and allowing counseling or other kinds of services that a recipient participates in to count as working toward self-sufficiency."

NASW's far-reaching comments begin by asking that Congress and the Bush administration make a dramatic shift in national policy: to move the emphasis of TANF from reducing the welfare rolls to reducing child and family poverty.

Under current law, "states can reduce their required work participation rates and avoid federal financial penalties by focusing their energies on caseload-reduction efforts, without regard to the economic well-being of families who leave the welfare rolls," says the NASW analysis.

One option would be to reduce states' need for caseload reduction in years in which the states' child and family poverty rates increase. Another, according to NASW's comments, would be to award bonuses to states for moving children and families out of poverty, especially those in deep poverty.

Other recommendations under the first broad heading of poverty reduction include:

- Allowing education and training to count toward state work participation rates.
- Evaluating state welfare performance on training and placement of women in nontraditional jobs that pay high wages.
- Expanding asset-development programs, including streamlining rules for individual development accounts.
- Changing child-support rules so substantial portions of child-support payments and arrearages go to families whether they are receiving TANF benefits or have left the rolls.
- Guaranteeing a minimum benefit for all families legally entitled to private child support.
- Creating new federal incentives to reward states that improve access to other benefits and services such as food stamps, Medicaid and child care through improvements like better administrative procedures, evening and weekend office hours, and improved outreach.

Under the broad heading of improving assistance to recipients with multiple barriers to self-sufficiency, NASW said that as welfare caseloads have fallen, more families still on the rolls have severe or multiple barriers to employment. The comments contain an array of recommendations to assist those with mental health and substance abuse problems and those subjected to domestic violence and racial and ethnic discrimination.

Among many recommendations are:

- Expanding allowable "work" activities to include treatment and counseling for mental illness, substance abuse and domestic violence.
- Requiring use of intensive case management for families with multiple barriers.
- Funding training for frontline staff on identifying the basic signs and symptoms of the more common mental health disorders, substance abuse problems and signs of domestic violence.

Under the broad heading of enhancing the capacity of the welfare system infrastructure, NASW's comments say that contrary to public perception, very few frontline welfare caseworkers are trained social workers. Rather, most have little or no professional social work training, even as the clients remaining on the rolls have more barriers to self-sufficiency and need more assistance from their caseworkers.

Among recommendations in the infrastructure area are:

- Requiring states to invest in comprehensive training for frontline staff and supervisors, lower workloads of case managers, hire more highly skilled staff and improve consultation with professionals in other fields.
- Revising federal benefit programs to facilitate service integration.

For a summary analysis and listing of recommendations: www.socialworkers.org/advocacy/positions/tanf.htm.

Chapter Summary

What You Can Now Do

You are now equipped to do the following:

- Identify stakeholders and understand how their vantage point affects their perspectives
- Identify a range of policy options that often recur in policy-advocacy work
- Diagram a proposal in the context of alternative options that occur with respect to specific issues
- Examine trade-offs using both quantitative and qualitative approaches
- Understand how analytic skills must often be coupled with political, interactional, and value-clarifying skills

Having discussed how we meld an array of options together to form a policy proposal, we discuss how we write policy proposals in the next chapter.

Notes

1. For an overview of one effort to secure federal legislation to fund shelters for abused women, see the *Congressional Quarterly Almanac,* vol. 35 (Washington, DC: Congressional Quarterly Service, 1979), pp. 508–509. Also see Liane Davis and Jan Hagen, "Services for Battered Women: The Public Policy Response," *Social Service Review* 62 (December 1988): 649–667.
2. Bruce Jansson, "The History and Politics of Selected Children's Programs and Related Legislation" (Ph.D. dissertation, University of Chicago, 1975), pp. 66–67, 76–77.

3. See Paul Gorman, "Block Grants: Theoretical and Practical Issues in Federal/State/Local Revenue Sharing," *New England Journal of Human Services* 4 (Spring 1984): 19–23; Robert Fulton and Ray Scott, "What Happened to the Federal/State Partnerships?" *New England Journal of Human Services* 4 (Fall 1984): 38–39; and Allen Imersheim, "The Influence of Reagan's New Federalism on Human Services in Florida," *New England Journal of Human Services* 5 (Spring 1985): 17–24.

4. Some overview literature on auspices includes Ralph Kramer, *Voluntary Agencies in the Welfare State* (Berkeley and Los Angeles: University of California Press, 1981), and Bruce Jansson, "Public Monitoring of Contracts with Nonprofit Organizations: Organizational Mission in Two Sectors," *Journal of Sociology and Social Welfare* 6 (May 1979): 362–374.

5. For an overview of some criticisms of public agencies, see Ralph Kramer, "From Voluntarism to Vendorism: An Organizational Perspective on Contracting," in Harold Demone and Margaret Gibelman, eds., *Services for Sale* (New Brunswick, NJ: Rutgers University Press, 1989), pp. 101–102.

6. For a critical overview of the emergence and roles of nonprofit agencies in the federally funded welfare state, see Eleanor Brilliant, "Private or Public: A Model of Ambiguities," *Social Service Review* 47 (September 1973): 384–396.

7. For criticisms of voluntary agencies, see Kramer, "From Voluntarism to Vendorism," pp. 102–103.

8. For a defense of profit-oriented agencies, see Emanuel Savas, *Privatizing the Public Sector: How to Shrink Government* (Chatham, NJ: Chatham House, 1982).

9. For criticism of profit-oriented agencies, see Harold Demone and Margaret Gibelman, "Privatizing the Acute Care General Hospital," in Barry Carroll, Ralph Conant, and Thomas Easton, eds., *Private Means—Public Ends: Private Business and Social Service Delivery* (New York: Praeger, 1987), pp. 50–75.

10. Alice Rivlin, *Reviving the American Dream: The Economy, the States, and the Federal Government* (Washington, DC: Brookings Institution, 1992).

11. Bruce Jansson and Susan Smith, "Articulating a 'New Nationalism' in American Social Policy," *Social Work* 41 (September 1996): 441–451.

12. Paul Peterson, "State Response to Welfare Reform: A Race to the Bottom?" in Isabel Sawhill, ed., *Welfare Reform: An Analysis of the Issues* (Washington, DC: Urban Institute, 1995), pp. 7–10.

13. For an overview of funding options, see Paul Terrel, "Financing Social Welfare Services," in Neil Gilbert and Harry Specht, eds., *Handbook of the Social Services* (Englewood Cliffs, NJ: Prentice Hall, 1981), pp. 392–394.

14. Ibid., pp. 398–399.

15. Classic accounts of the authorizations and appropriations processes are found in Richard Fenno, *Power of the Purse* (Boston: Little, Brown, 1966), and Aaron Wildavsky, *Politics of the Budgetary Process* (Boston: Little, Brown, 1964).

16. See Demone and Gibelman, *Services for Sale.*

17. John Coons and Stephen Sugarman defend voucher and vendor payments in *Education by Choice: The Case for Family Control* (Berkeley and Los Angeles: University of California Press, 1978). Frederick Thayer criticizes them in "Privatization: Carnage, Chaos, and Corruption," in Carroll, Conant, and Easton, *Private Means—Public Ends,* pp. 146–170.

18. Various points of view on block grants appear in Richard Nathan and Fred Doolittle, "Federal Grants: Giving and Taking Away," *Political Science Quarterly* 100 (Spring 1985): 53–74, and Richard Williamson, "The 1982 New Federalism Negotiations," *Publius* 13 (Spring 1983): 11–33.

19. Thayer, "Privatization."

20. Herman Leonard, *Checks Unbalanced: the Quiet Side of Public Spending* (New York: Basic Books, 1986).

21. Bruce Fretz and David Mills, *Licensing and Certification of Psychologists and Counselors* (San Francisco: Jossey-Bass, 1980).

22. David Hardcastle, "The Profession: Professional Organizations, Licensing, and Private Practice," in Neil Gilbert and Harry Specht, eds., *Handbook of the Social Services* (Englewood Cliffs, NJ: Prentice Hall, 1981), p. 677.

23. Ibid., pp. 679–683.

24. Ibid., pp. 666–687.

25. S. K. Khinduka, "Social Work and the Human Services," *Encyclopedia of Social Work,* 18th ed., vol. 2 (Silver Spring, MD: National Association of Social Workers, 1987), p. 691.

26. For a discussion of rationing, see Richard Frank, "Rationing of Mental Health Services: Simple Observations on the Current Approach and Future Prospects," *Administration in Mental Health* 13 (Fall 1985): 22–29.

27. A general discussion of means tests appears in Neil Gilbert and Harry Specht, *Dimensions of Social Welfare Policy,* 2nd ed. (Englewood Cliffs, NJ: Prentice Hall, 1986), pp. 82–84.

28. For a discussion of staff discretion, see Robert Goodin, *Reasons for Welfare: The Political Theory of the Welfare State* (Princeton, NJ: Princeton University Press, 1988), pp. 184–228.

29. For subtle forms of discrimination and rationing, see Sharon Sepulveda-Hassell, *An Assessment of the Mental Health Treatment Process: Eliminating Service Barriers to Mexican Americans* (San Antonio, TX: Intercultural Development Research Association, 1980), and David Ramirez, *A Review of Literature on Underutilization of Mental Health Services by Mexican Americans: Implications for Future Research and Service Delivery* (San Antonio, TX: Intercultural Development Research Association, 1980).

30. John Inglehart, "The Struggle between Managed Care and Fee-for-Service Practice," *New England Journal of Medicine* (July 7, 1994): 63–67.

31. Wes Shera, "Managed Care and People with Severe Mental Illness: Challenges and Opportunities for Social Work," *Health and Social Work* 21 (August 1996): 196–201, and Susan Rose and Sharon Keigher, "Managing Mental Health: Whose Responsibility?" *Health and Social Work* 21 (February 1996): 76–80.

32. Marc Rodwin, "Conflicts in Managed Care," *New England Journal of Medicine* (March 2, 1995), pp. 604–606.

33. John Fleishman et al., "Organizing AIDS Service Consortia: Lead Agency Identity and Consortium Cohesion," *Social Service Review* (December 1992): 547–560.

34. For a discussion of monitoring, see Bruce Jansson, "The Political Economy of Monitoring: A Contingency Perspective," in Demone and Gibelman, *Services for Sale,* pp. 343–359, and Kenneth Wedel and Nancy Chess, "Monitoring Strategies in Purchase of Service Contracting," in Demone and Gibelman, *Services for Sale,* pp. 360–370.

35. The analytic process of identifying and selecting options is discussed by Eugene Bardach, *The Eight-Step Path of Policy Analysis* (Berkeley, CA.: Berkeley Academic Press, 1996).
36. Ibid., p. 27.
37. See, for example, Robert Francoeur's "decision making matrix" in *Biomedical Ethics: A Guide to Decision Making* (New York: Wiley, 1983), pp. 127–137.
38. Bardach, the *Eight-Step Path,* pp. 49–54.

Suggested Readings

Federal, State, and Local Relationships

Bruce Jansson and Susan Smith, "Articulating a 'New Nationalism' in American Social Policy," *Social Work* 41 (September 1996): 441–451.

Paul Peterson, *The Price of Federalism* (Washington, DC: Brookings Institution, 1995).

Alice Rivlin, *Reviving the American Dream: The Economy, the States, and the Federal Government* (Washington, DC: Brookings Institution, 1992).

Profit-Oriented, Not-for-Profit, and Public Agency Relationships

Barry Carroll, Ralph Conant, and Thomas Easton, eds., *Private Means—Public Ends: Private Business and Social Service Delivery* (New York: Praeger, 1987).

Harold Demone and Margaret Gibelman, eds., *Services for Sale* (New Brunswick, NJ: Rutgers University Press, 1989).

Sheila Kamerman and Alfred Kahn, *Privatization and the American Welfare State* (Princeton, NJ: Princeton University Press, 1984).

Lester Salamon and Alan Abramson, *The Nonprofit Sector and the New Federal Budget* (Washington, DC: Urban Institute Press, 1986).

Stan Smith and Deborah Stone, "The Unexpected Consequences of Privatization," in Michael Brown, ed., *Remaking the Welfare State* (Philadelphia: Temple University Press, 1988), pp. 232–252.

Organizational Issues in the American Welfare State

Darlyne Bailey and Kelly Koney, "Interorganizational Community-Based Collectives: A Strategic Response to Shape the Social Work Agenda," *Social Work* 41 (November 1996): 602–611.

John Fleishman et al., "Organizing AIDS Service Consortia: Lead Agency Identity and Consortium Cohesion," *Social Service Review* (December 1992): 547–560.

John O'Looney, "Beyond Privatization and Service Integration," *Social Service Review* (December 1993): 501–534.

Fiscal Issues

Harold Demone and Margaret Gibelman, *Services for Sale* (New Brunswick, NJ: Rutgers University Press, 1989), pp. 101–102.

Herman Leonard, *Checks Unbalanced: The Quiet Side of Public Spending* (New York: Basic Books, 1986).

Paul Terrel, "Financing Social Welfare Services," in Neil Gilbert and Harry Specht, eds., *Handbook of the Social Services* (Englewood Cliffs, NJ: Prentice Hall, 1981), pp. 380–410.

Professional and Staffing Issues

Bruce Fretz and David Mills, *Licensing and Certification of Psychologists and Counselors* (San Francisco: Jossey-Bass, 1980), pp. 9–29.

David Hardcastle, "The Profession: Professional Organizations, Licensing, and Private Practice," in Gilbert and Specht, *Handbook of the Social Services,* pp. 666–688.

Allocation Issues

Richard Frank, "Rationing of Mental Health Services: Simple Observations on the Current Approach and Future Prospects," *Administration in Mental Health* 13 (Fall 1985): 22–29.

Prevention

Thomas Frieden et al., "Tuberculosis in New York City: Turning the Tide," *New England Journal of Medicine* (July 27, 1995): 229–233.

Dennis Poole, "Achieving National Health Goals in Prevention with Community Organization: The Bottom-Up Approach," *Journal of Community Practice* 4 (Nov. 2, 1997): 77–92.

P. J. Porter, "Ways and Means of Providing Primary and Preventive Health Services," *Journal of Health Care for the Poor* 6 (1991): 167–173.

Staff Discretion

Robert Goodin, *Reasons for Welfare: The Political Theory of the Welfare State* (Princeton, NJ: Princeton University Press, 1988), pp. 184–228.

Michael Lipsky, *Street-Level Bureaucracy* (New York: Russell Sage Foundation, 1980).

Policy Analysis

Eugene Bardach, *The Eight-Step Path of Policy Analysis* (Berkeley, CA.: Berkeley Academic Press, 1996).

chapter  **8**

Presenting and Defending Policy Proposals

We will help you become an effective policy advocate by discussing the following in this chapter:

- Combative persuasion like debates and hardball negotiations
- Establishing specific objectives with specific audiences
- Diagnosing audiences
- Developing a persuading strategy
- Tactics for apathetic, hostile, and expert audiences
- Friendly communication strategies in debates and mediation
- Writing policy memos
- Writing grant proposals

Having developed meritorious proposals, policy advocates also need to defend them, whether in one-on-one discussions, presentations to larger audiences, or debates. Without policy persuasion skills, they cannot attract sufficient support for their ideas to be effective. (See steps 5 and 6 of Figure 6.1 on p. 169 and Policy Advocacy Challenge 8.1.)

POLICY ADVOCACY CHALLENGE 8.1

READING ABOUT PERSUASIVE SPEAKING

Stephanie Davis, Research Librarian, University of California, Irvine

The following books may be informative and helpful in learning more about persuasive speaking:

Aubuchon, Norbert. *The Anatomy of Persuasion.* (New York: Amacom, 1997).

Mutz, Diana C., Paul M. Sniderman, Richard A. Brody. *Political Persuasion and Attitude Change.* (Ann Arbor: University of Michigan Press, 1996).

Rybacki, Donald Jay, Karyn Charles Rybacki. *Advocacy and Opposition: an Introduction to Argumentation.* (Boston, MA: Allyn & Bacon, 1999).

Stettner, Morey. *The Art of Winning Conversation.* (Englewood Cliffs, N.J.: Prentice Hall, 1995).
Tannen, Deborah. *The Argument Culture.* (New York: Random House, 1998).

We distinguish here between friendly and adversarial communications. In friendly communications, policy advocates try to decrease opposition to a proposal with conflict-reducing techniques. For example, they stress commonalities with the audience or engage in win-win negotiations that emphasize shared interests. In adversarial communications, a policy advocate tries to best a person or group with opposing points of view through debates or hardball negotiations. Naturally, most of us would like to use friendly communications, but adversarial ones are sometimes needed.

It would be difficult to overstate the role persuasion plays in policy advocacy. In order to enact policies, advocates often face significant challenges from people who are deeply opposed to their position or who are apathetic. No matter how loudly persuaders shout or how articulately they make their case, their efforts will come to naught unless the audience sees merit in the message and decides to heed its prescriptions. People highly skilled in the art of persuasion tailor their messages to specific audiences and situations.[1]

Policy advocates try to influence people through interpersonal discussions, proposals, speeches to large audiences, memoranda, formal reports, debates or arguments, messages (such as editorials), or the mass media.

The social context is often important. One persuader may be successful in interacting with people in relative isolation. However, she may find her work frustrated by external noise, such as peer pressure or competing messages from other senders. For instance, political campaigners seldom have the luxury of engaging in extended personal discussion with voters. Because of opposing candidates' messages, pressure from families and friends, and people's traditional political loyalties, politicians often fail to secure votes from those who might otherwise be sympathetic to their candidacy.[2]

Ideology and Policy Positions

Proposals and Ideology

Ideology powerfully shapes proposals in legislative settings. In 2000 through 2002, for example, Democrats and Republicans proposed markedly different versions of gun control legislation, patient-rights legislation, federal tax-cut legislation, and school-reform legislation; their different proposals emanated from their different ideologies and their different political constituencies.[3] Republicans tended to favor lower federal expenditures, corporate interests (in the case of gun manufacturers and HMOs), lower taxes, and greater consumer choice (school vouchers) whereas Democrats tended in the opposite direction in each of these areas.

Legislators from both parties realize that the "devil is in the details." It is in legislative details that broader ideologies are often manifested. In the case of complex legislation, conservatives, moderates, and liberals may battle over scores of legislative details, as they did concerning welfare reform legislation of 1996—and as they will again in 2002 when this legislation is reauthorized. Points of ideological conflict may include the following:

- How much federal money to expend on the proposal
- How much child care, transportation funds, and health care to include

- How long to make the transition period during which former recipients can qualify for supplemental welfare payments, child care, transportation, and health care
- Whether to define many or few policies governing welfare-to-work at the federal level—or whether to let the states make most or all of these choices
- Whether to include federal monies for subsidizing employment of former recipients so their total wages bring them near or above poverty levels
- Whether to keep or relax the five-year lifetime limits on welfare—and the kinds of exceptions that will be allowed if lifetime limits are established

The political context strongly influences the outcomes of grand debates like this one. If the recession of 2001 is replaced by rapid economic growth and reduction of welfare rolls as occurred from 1997 to 2001, conservatives' case that the federal government can devote relatively little money to welfare is buttressed. If the contrary occurs, liberals' case that increased spending on welfare is needed is strengthened.

Unless one party has a huge majority in legislative chambers, compromise versions of legislation usually emerge in the course of negotiations. One party or faction will make concessions on specific points in return for concessions from another party or faction on other points. Each party or faction will want to convey the impression to their constituents that, on balance, they won or at least received major concessions from opponents. Sometimes a party or faction will want to delay the outcome if they think that delay will strengthen their position, such as when public opinion polls or trips to their home districts suggest widespread support for their positions. On other occasions, a party or faction may decide to resolve the conflict so they are not seen as sabotaging an eventual solution. They also may decide to do so if they think opponents are besting them in the polls or with their constituents.

The effects of ideology on policy debates are sometimes muted by other factors. We should not forget that legislators often get tangible benefits from specific policies or programs. Even the most ardent conservative, for example, may favor certain big spending programs because her or his constituents benefit from them, such as when conservatives support major increases in food stamps because they benefit farmers in their districts. Similarly, many liberals vote for huge and sometimes unnecessary weapon systems, because they provide jobs to their constituents. Personal experiences often assume a major role, such as when a conservative supports large increases for mental health programs because a close relative has a serious mental problem. So policy advocates should not assume that they cannot find allies even among legislators who they might expect to be ideologically opposed to specific proposals.

Electoral Politics and Proposals

Proposals lie at the heart of political campaigns as opposing candidates try to assemble a winning strategy. Candidates need to identify which issues will resonate positively with their natural constituents, as well as with sufficient numbers of swing voters to give them a winning margin.

So various possibilities ensue. In some cases, candidates avoid issues they perceive as no-win, such as the issue of military spending in the 2000 presidential contest. They may decide that the issue will polarize their potential supporters and, therefore, decide to avoid it. Both liberal and conservative candidates avoid certain hot-button issues for this reason.

In other cases, candidates address issues but only take fuzzy positions, fearing that highly specific positions would antagonize key groups of their intended supporters. For this reason, debates between candidates are often disappointing to listeners who believe that no one took a strong position on major issues.

Candidates sometimes take contradictory positions on specific issues, emphasizing different points to different audiences. This can backfire, of course, if opponents charge them with waffling on the issues.

Of course, candidates often do take highly detailed positions on some issues. A Democratic candidate, for example, may favor a specific increase in the minimum wage.

Candidates have to decide not just what they support, but what they oppose. Indeed, both are important in electoral campaigns; opposition to opponents' issues allows candidates to draw distinctions to the electorate between themselves and their opponents. In some cases, candidates misstate opponents actual views to magnify distinctions, often drawing the retort that they are distorting the record.

Combative Persuasion

In *combative persuasion,* presenters use confrontive strategies to modify the opinions and actions of those who oppose them.[4] Two kinds of combative situations exist. In the first type, persuaders use coercive, one-on-one confrontation to change an adversary's position. For example, the presenter might demand that an agency executive make the agency's services more responsive to a specific population's needs. In the second type, persuaders debate an adversary hoping to convince observers to choose their point of view over that of the adversary. In a staff meeting, for example, a presenter might argue with another person to win over staff members. Coercive messages and negotiations are forms of combative persuasion.

Adversarial Debates

Three parties exist in adversarial debates: the persuader, the adversary, and an audience of observers. Debates rarely follow a structured format (except when school debate teams meet), and arguments often arise.[5] For instance, a staff member presents a proposal in an agency meeting, one or more persons criticize it, and its initiator then defends it; for example someone testifies to a legislative committee to oppose mandatory HIV testing for prostitutes. Persuaders sometimes hope to change the minds of both their immediate adversary and the audience that hears their argument.

Harry Johnson, a lobbyist for an AIDS advocacy group, is attacking a conservative legislator's proposal to require all testing services, both public and private, to give state public health officials the names of all persons who test positive for HIV. He is debating the legislator before a student audience. To illustrate the array of arguments that debaters can use, Policy Advocacy Challenge 8.2 presents 12 arguments Johnson can use.

POLICY
ADVOCACY
CHALLENGE 8.2

*ATTACKING
SOMEONE ELSE'S
PROPOSAL*

Johnson can do the following:

- *Attack the values implicit or explicit in the proposal.* A debater can contrast any value premise with an alternative value premise. While the legislator values control to protect the public's health, Johnson favors protecting the privacy and freedom of people who test positive for HIV. Such privacy, he contends, conforms with traditions embedded in the Bill of Rights. Persons who are HIV-positive but might remain free of AIDS symptoms for many years particularly need privacy to protect them from discrimination.

- *Attack the proposal's feasibility.* Public health departments would ask HIV-positive individuals to list persons with whom they have had sexual relations. Department officials would then alert each of those partners to their possible infection with HIV. However, it is extremely time-consuming to develop these lists and to contact the persons on them, and health departments lack sufficient staff. "If public health officials lack the staff to adequately accomplish their existing functions, how can we expect them to assume these added functions?" Johnson might ask.

- *Attack the legislator's motives* by saying, "He wants a witch hunt, not humanistic services for those who are HIV-positive."

- *Attack some unanticipated or adverse consequences of the proposal.* People who fear they carry the virus may avoid testing if the results are not confidential. Many people would forgo testing, fearing that their identity would be revealed to employers, landlords, and others.

- *Attack the legislator's use of specific analogies.* The legislator contends that public health departments have long required divulging the names of persons with syphilis and gonorrhea. The legislator says this information has led to successful efforts to alert sexual partners to their possible infection. To attack this analogy to other sexually transmitted diseases, Johnson notes that syphilis and gonorrhea are currently epidemics despite these practices. Moreover, discrimination against people with these treatable diseases is not nearly as marked, he might argue, as against persons who are HIV-positive. Unlike syphilis and gonorrhea, the initial infection with HIV is often followed by a lengthy period—sometimes more than 10 years—when the person has no serious symptoms, much less AIDS. "If we breach the confidentiality of persons with a disease of such duration," Johnson argues, "we risk extended damage to their careers and reputations that does not occur with treatable diseases, such as syphilis."

- *Attack the legislator's uses of data and analytic assumptions.* The legislator contends that such action has already been successful in Colorado. Johnson criticizes specific quantitative studies that the legislator uses to buttress this claim. Johnson attacks the methods used to collect the data, the applicability of the Colorado data to his state, and the way the legislator has interpreted the data. (We discuss methods of criticizing quantitative studies in more detail in Chapter Fourteen.)

- *Attack implicit models of human motivation* in the legislator's rationale for the proposal. Requiring that testing centers report HIV-positive persons' names to the public health department implies that most HIV-positive persons will not voluntarily cooperate with public health officials. This assumption suggests that most HIV-positive persons lack a strong sense of social responsibility. Johnson asserts that many HIV-positive individuals are (or can become) concerned about former and current sexual partners if given access to high-quality counseling that does not infringe on their confidentiality. When they receive their test results, for example, they can be told about voluntary counseling and the need to inform current and prior sexual partners of their risks. Johnson also reframes the issue, moving away from forcing HIV-positive persons to assume social responsibility to providing assistance to HIV-positive persons to help them arouse their inherent altruism. The gay men's community's remarkable generosity to people with AIDS and the proliferation of support networks they have established support this contention.

- *Attack the legislator's conception of the chain of events that would follow the enactment of his proposal.* The legislator assumes that testing centers will provide the names of HIV-positive people to the state's public health department; this department will contact HIV-positive people; HIV-positive people will agree to provide the names of previous sexual partners or persons with whom they shared needles when using drugs; public officials will contact these partners; and the partners will agree to be tested for HIV, will practice safe sex, and, if they test positive, will provide public officials with the names of their partners. Johnson contends that this chain of events will often be broken at one, two, or more points. We have noted that public health departments often lack the staff to make these contacts. When forced to divulge names, some HIV-positive persons may decline to be cooperative because of the violation of their privacy and the imposition of mandatory procedures. In the case of casual sexual encounters or needle sharing, HIV-positive persons may be unable to supply names. Because of the population's mobility, it will be difficult to locate some of the partners, even if authorities have their names.
- *Expose the vagueness in the legislator's proposal,* which may make it seem less attractive to other people. Perhaps his proposal fails to describe how the testing services, some of them private ones, will be linked to the state's public health department. Perhaps the proposal fails to discuss how the mandatory reporting policy will be evaluated for its effectiveness in slowing the spread of HIV.
- *Attack unacceptable trade-offs in the legislator's proposal.* Johnson commends the legislator for wanting to stem the spread of HIV (a desirable objective) but argues that, noble as it may be, this objective should not cost tens of thousands of individuals their privacy (a valued objective) or cost the government exorbitant amounts. When making this kind of argument, the lobbyist says, in effect, that we need to stem the spread of HIV with methods that do not violate personal privacy and that are not so costly.
- *Argue that the legislator's proposal will be rendered ineffective by other events.* Argue, for example, that technology that allows individuals to test themselves for HIV in the privacy of their homes renders moot the mandatory reporting law, because many people bypass public or private testing centers.
- *Offer a counterproposal.* Because tracking partners is expensive, Johnson argues that scarce public resources ought instead to be invested in public education projects, such as efforts to promote safe sex by the use of condoms. Perhaps scarce resources should be invested in teaching addicts and prostitutes how not to become infected and how

(continued)

(8.2   continued)

not to spread the disease to other people. The lobbyist might conclude that the state will get a far better return on funds invested in an educational program than in a mandatory reporting program.

As an exercise in attacking someone else's policy proposal, attack Johnson's arguments in light of the extraordinary progress that had been made against AIDS by mid-1998. New drug therapies had appeared that markedly cut death rates from AIDS. Strong legal protections had lessened discrimination against people with AIDS. In early 1997, New York began a program to test newborns for AIDS and to tell mothers of the results, rather than (as previously) telling the mothers only when they asked. Many public health officials around the nation had begun to urge the reporting of HIV to public health officials. Colorado and New York State had begun more aggressively to implement a partner notification system even in 1998 so that partners of persons with HIV could get testing. By 2002, many AIDS advocacy groups came to support partner notification systems.

To hone your debating skills, assume you now are debating against Johnson's position in the preceding debate—from the vantage point of someone deeply committed to eradicating this cruel disease. What arguments would you use—and where would you attack Johnson's positions?

Coercive Messages

Policy advocates may use coercive messages when they believe that decision makers will oppose their position and that cooperative messages will not work because of decision makers' political and ideological stance, discriminatory attitudes, and tradition. In addition, decision makers may feel that existing resources are already so committed to other programs that they cannot support a new program.[6]

At the outset, practitioners may make a formal demand that includes a threat, for example, to take further steps, such as litigation, protests, sending delegations to even higher authorities, or publicizing the issue through the mass media.[7]

Policy advocates often try to influence the social context through coercive messages. They may insist that the decision maker listen to a delegation, rather than to one person. They may physically surround the decision maker with members of their group. In some cases, persuaders inform the mass media of the encounter before it has occurred to place even more pressure on decision makers.

Coercive messages are effective in some situations, but they also carry the danger of retaliation.[8] For example, staff in an agency who use coercive messages with their executive director may be fired or demoted. Moreover, once coercive messages have been initiated by one side in a dispute, a vicious circle of escalating intransigency and reprisal often begins that makes it increasingly difficult for the opposing sides to cooperate. Both sides then begin to view the conflict as win-lose, rather than win-win, so that any concession to the other side becomes a personal defeat.[9]

Negotiations: Hardball and Win-Win Options

We have discussed both friendly and adversarial approaches to communication. Either approach—or some combination of the two—can be used in negotiations. Let's start with a friendly approach.[10] Directors of two different programs in an agency must decide which of them will administer a new program that will bring considerable prestige and revenue to the person who wins. Rather than staking out a position at the outset, Mary Jones (who wants an amicable solution) encourages mutual discussion of the situation. She encourages Jack Hoopes, the other administrator, to acknowledge that he would benefit from the added revenues and the challenge of running a new program, just as she would. Rather than moving toward rapid closure and a hardening of positions, Mary moves the discussion toward brainstorming, in which each of them imagines alternative solutions:

1. The new program goes to only one director.
2. The two directors jointly administer the new program.
3. One director receives basic authority for the program but gives the other director key roles in the new program, while retaining the program's revenue for his or her unit.
4. A rotational system is devised to give each of the directors a chance to administer the program.

To Jones's delight, Hoopes's initially adversarial stance has diminished by their third meeting. Already overburdened by other programs, he wants responsibility for only one facet of the new program. To underscore her desire to reach a conciliatory solution, Jones offers to cede to Hoopes one of her current programs that closely resembles other programs that he directs—and she makes this concession without a request by Hoopes. After only five meetings, Jones and Hoopes have concluded this win-win negotiation with heightened respect for one another.

This win-win approach can be contrasted with a hardball or win-lose approach.[11] Assume that Jones and Hoopes strongly dislike one another, have already had repeated battles over turf and revenue, and want jurisdiction over the new program. Both believe that they will lose significant prestige to the other party if he or she gets control of the new program. In their first meeting, both of them state that they want control of the new program because it fits in with their existing programs and, fearing to appear weak, stick to this position during the next four meetings. The agency director then tells them that she will decide if they cannot reach an agreement, and Jones reluctantly implies that she will consider ceding the program to Hoopes, but only if she receives some of his existing programs in return. Convinced he has Jones at a disadvantage, Hoopes makes no concessions during the next three meetings, finally agreeing to cede a small program. Unsatisfied with this concession, Jones demands a larger program instead. Only after several additional stalemated meetings and another threat by the agency director to intercede, Hoopes agrees to Jones's request. Both parties leave the negotiations with renewed animus toward one another, determined not to yield any ground in future negotiations.

Hardball negotiations usually begin with each side presenting an initial position. As the negotiations proceed, each side decides whether and when to grant concessions to the other side—as a means of testing their intentions, as a sign of good faith, or as a quid pro quo for a concession the other side has made. As the negotiations proceed, each side has to decide how tolerable a stalemate would be, whether the other side will match its concessions, and when to make concessions. If both sides believe it is necessary to resolve the conflict, each party will gradually reveal where it is willing to make concessions. The two sides often use delays, veiled or open threats, and inducements to persuade the other side to make concessions.

We should not forget the role of mediator, who operates between contending factions. Assume that two opposing factions in your agency have been embroiled in conflict for a sustained period. They want to resolve the conflict but do not know how to achieve this resolution. You approach both parties with an offer to mediate the dispute, and they accept. After talking with both sides to better understand their position, you set up a meeting where you will act as mediator. During this meeting, your role is not to suggest solutions, but to facilitate a discussion in which both sides state their concerns and wishes, brainstorm possible solutions, and move toward a settlement. Several meetings may be needed. In more complex mediations, such as between members of a union and those of management in a social service agency, the two parties may meet separately and communicate only through the mediator. For mediation to be successful, each party to a conflict has to believe that the mediator will not manipulate the situation to the other's advantage, but will merely help the two sides to come to a settlement.[12]

In both adversarial and friendly negotiations, a positive outcome is not guaranteed. Even after a friendly start, two parties may become sufficiently stalemated so that no solution emerges. Or a solution may have to be imposed by a higher-level person or by an official *arbitrator* who is appointed to reach a solution. Arbitrators are frequently used in stalemated negotiations between labor and management.

Adversarial or Friendly Communication: Which Is Preferable?

Let there be no doubt: friendly communications and negotiations are preferable to adversarial ones. Parties to conflict can usually settle issues more rapidly when they accommodate one another, are more likely to emerge from friendly communications with respect for one another, and are more likely to develop creative solutions. Indeed, an extensive literature urges policy practitioners to make greater use of collaborative techniques.[13]

Yet friendly communications are not always possible. The relations between Newt Gingrich and Bill Clinton during the budget and tax negotiations in 1995 and 1996 illustrates this. If even one party is determined to stake out a position and maintain it, the other party cannot naively assume that conciliation will work. Indeed, Clinton would have risked being steamrollered had he not staked out his position and adhered to it, at least until he could pressure Gingrich to make some concessions.[14]

In Table 8.1, we identify some situations where friendly and adversarial approaches are used. Policy advocates should first attempt conciliation to see if the opposing party will engage in collaborative problem solving. But if their conciliation fails and their opponent tries to steamroller them, they may have to use hardball strategies. (See Policy Advocacy Challenge 8.3.)

TABLE 8.1   Situations favoring friendly and adversarial approaches

Situation	Friendly approaches	Adversarial approaches
Relations between parties	Amicable	Hostile
How this issue has been discussed in the past	With low conflict and mutual concessions	With high conflict and few concessions
Extent to which one or both parties have a rigid position based on ideology or self-interest	Neither party has a fixed position at the outset	Both parties have fixed positions at the outset
Extent to which parties attach symbolic importance to issue (e.g., view a loss or victory as having extraordinary consequences)	Neither party attaches symbolic meaning to the outcome	Both parties believe a victory is vital to their well-being, to advance their self-interest or their ideology
Role of onlookers or followers	Onlookers do not pressure the parties to best each other	Onlookers pressure each party to best the other side
Extent to which parties value conciliation	Both parties value conciliation	Both parties value hardball tactics
The effects of the negotiating style	Low conflict and mutual concessions reinforce a win-win style	High conflict fosters more conflict and reinforces a win-lose style

POLICY ADVOCACY CHALLENGE 8.3

USING HARDBALL AND SOFTBALL STYLES OF NEGOTIATION

Try out conciliatory and hardball negotiating strategies on a controversial issue in your particular area by simulating a negotiating situation with another person. (You can find a policy issue by looking at a newspaper, or you can pick an issue in your field placement or in your school.)

Create the negotiating situation by assigning different sides to two parties, such as union versus management, students versus school administration, clients versus administration, or citizens versus bureaucrats. Address the issue first in a hardball manner and negotiate for, say, 30 minutes. Then try negotiating it in a softball manner for 30 minutes. Discuss which style would have worked best in different situations. Was it difficult to shift styles in midstream? What interpersonal skills are needed for each style?

Persuading Specific Audiences

We have mostly emphasized combative persuasion thus far. Now we turn to *friendly persuasion,* presenting techniques for changing an audience's beliefs and actions by engaging it in a cooperative transaction rather than by confronting it. When such persuasion is used skillfully, audiences are hardly aware that their perspective has changed or that the persuader has been using a carefully developed strategy.

Determining Objectives

Before persuaders can decide how to fashion a message, they have to establish objectives. Objectives can be ranked on a continuum extending from ambitious to modest. At the most ambitious level, persuaders hope both to markedly modify the audience's beliefs and to convince them to take specific actions, such as helping change a policy, performing specific tasks, or pressuring decision makers to support a proposed policy. At a somewhat more modest level, a persuader may be content, at least in the short term, merely to modify others' beliefs, perhaps as a precursor to having them take action. (As we will discuss later, changing people's beliefs does not necessarily cause them to change their actions.) Hoping eventually to convince an agency executive to support a new policy, a staff member might send him information about an unmet need in the community or a promising pilot project in another agency.

Efforts to maintain an audience's beliefs and actions fall between the ambitious and the modest ends of the continuum. Assume that agency members fear that someone will soon question a favored program, and they want to head off this attack by maintaining, or even strengthening, their director's support for the program. Assume as well that the director has funded the program relatively generously. The agency members need to send messages that reinforce the program's importance so the director will not be unduly influenced by the impending attack.[15] While this endeavor sounds relatively modest, it is more ambitious than merely educating others, because its aim is to influence beliefs and actions.

We also need to distinguish between the short- and long-term objectives of persuasion. When planning a message on one occasion, a policy advocate may have a relatively modest objective, such as sensitizing an audience to an issue. However, he or she may anticipate relaying a series of messages to an audience that will ultimately change their beliefs and rally their support of a new policy. Indeed, policy advocates often hope to persuade people bit by bit. A campaign might consist of interpersonal discussions, a memorandum, and a formal presentation, each planned to move an audience toward support of a policy.

It is more difficult to develop a series of presentations, of course, than to make a single presentation. In a series of presentations, the policy advocate must decide when to proceed beyond educating the audience to seeking their support for new policies and beliefs. The policy advocate does not want to proceed too cautiously or too rapidly from modest to ambitious objectives.

Diagnosing Audiences

Policy advocates often try to diagnose audiences. They want to know the audience's beliefs, degree of motivation on an issue, fears and hopes, and the extent to which situational or historical factors may influence their response to a message.[16]

When examining audiences' beliefs, policy advocates gauge the degree of opposition to their message. Audiences are most hostile to a message when they oppose both its value premises and its fundamental argument. When policy advocates seek to persuade a conservative audience to support softening some of the deterrent provisions of welfare reforms, for example, the audience is likely to disagree with their value premises that society is obliged to help impoverished people, that it should expand its social welfare roles, and that unemployment and low-paying jobs, rather than the size of the existing welfare grants, are the primary causes of expanding welfare rolls.

Audiences are less hostile when the value premises and logic of the message approximate their own beliefs or when they have a flexible or undefined position. When an audience has a broad zone of tolerance, it is open to new ideas, values, or perspectives. Advocates encounter a difficult challenge when the audience's zone of tolerance is relatively narrow.[17]

When an audience is hostile to a policy, persuaders have to try to figure out why. Indeed, theorists suggest that audiences are most receptive to messages relevant to their own fears and hopes. When a new agency program is proposed, for example, some staff may fear it will jeopardize their current responsibilities; divert funds from favored projects; or cause new burdens that they do not wish to shoulder, such as learning new skills or working longer hours. Skillful persuaders carefully allay these kinds of fears in their messages.[18]

Audiences also differ in their levels of involvement in specific topics. All of us have been part of audiences that could not care less about a message. Perhaps we have been inundated with boring messages about the same subject or do not perceive its relevance to us. In such cases, a novel or unusual argument is sometimes effective. (See Policy Advocacy Challenge 8.4.)

POLICY ADVOCACY CHALLENGE 8.4

USING A NOVEL MESSAGE

Patsy Lane, M. S. W., Director, Department of Human Services, City of Pasadena

During the time I was a member of the statewide Child Development Policy Board, state legislators and administrators were considering "loosening" the regulations for licensing child-care centers, as a cost-saving measure. One proposed change was to reduce child-care licensing staff by decreasing the required number of licensing staff's on-site visits to child-care programs. Such site visits were already perceived as dangerously few by the social service and child-care providers—in many cases, only once every few years. Various child and family advocacy groups tried to educate state decision makers that any reduction in such regulations would be detrimental to the quality of child care and would place children at risk. It was a challenge to find an effective way to communicate to legislators how problematic such a regulatory change would be: Often, the objections were dismissed as overly protective of children.

Finally, a staff person of the Child Development Policy Board submitted a very effective one-page chart: a comparison of inspection requirements for child-care facilities with those for dog kennels. Dog kennels, it seemed, averaged a regulatory site visit every six months, while child-care facilities averaged one such visit every two years. This comparison created a dilemma for elected state officials and administrators: Would they be perceived as valuing the safety and care of dogs in kennels much higher than those of children in licensed child care?

Outcome   Shortly thereafter, the proposed reduction in regulatory visits to child-care facilities was dropped.

Lessons learned   A key lesson in this case was the importance of how a message is communicated. Sometimes, the logical, professional, well-researched, well-documented approach (i.e., "regular site visits prevent problems and promote good child-care practice") does not succeed in advancing good policy and practice, so look for other creative ways to frame and illustrate the issue.

Similarly, policy advocates often identify positive factors that might motivate some audience members to support a policy. A new program in an agency, for example, might allow staff members to develop new skills, increase their job security by bringing in new revenue, and enhance the agency's prestige and that of its staff members. Moreover, many professionals respond favorably to policy initiatives that address important or unmet client needs.[19]

The social context may influence the audience's response to a particular measure. If a social agency is cutting costs, for example, its staff members are unlikely to support a costly new program. Audiences' responses also are influenced by prior events. If, for example, a specific issue has been presented previously to some members of an audience, their recollections of prior discussions, which they may communicate to those who were not present, can powerfully shape the whole audience's responses. If an issue was divisive, it may generate extensive conflict when it is reintroduced. By contrast, policy issues associated with positive traditions often have a good chance of being met with a positive audience response.[20]

Until now, we have assumed that audiences' viewpoints are relatively homogeneous. In fact, audiences usually contain a range of perspectives; one faction may support a new policy, while another faction may be opposed. Practitioners must identify a mixed audience's factions.[21] They should decide how to address the subgroups in their messages, perhaps appealing first to one segment of the audience ("Some of you fear that . . .") and then to another ("Others of you believe that . . ."). Even when audiences have divergent perspectives, policy advocates can identify and appeal to common values, hopes, or aspirations, saying, for example, "Despite our differences on this issue, we all agree that this agency needs to diversify its services."

Tailoring Objectives to the Audience   Policy advocates often establish objectives that are either too modest or too ambitious. Persuaders may falsely believe that an audience is so hostile to their message that they can hope to achieve only minor changes. By contrast, persuaders establish unrealistic expectations if they falsely believe that their audience is similar to themselves. Those with liberal perspectives, for example, may unrealistically expect to make an extremely conservative audience accept a policy that stems from liberal premises, only to find that the message merely unites the audience in its preexisting opposition to knee-jerk liberals.

Strategies of Persuasion

With objectives, audience, and situation in mind, policy advocates must develop a persuading strategy by selecting a medium, a sequence of presentations, a format, and a presentation style. After discussing these components, we will discuss tactics for specific audiences.

Selecting a Medium

Persuaders rely on symbols, such as words and visual aids, to influence audiences' ideas and actions, but they can present these symbols in many ways: through speech, documents, graphic aids, or some combination of these methods. Because these modes of communication are so familiar, we often do not consider their relative merits.

Public speaking allows presenters to interact with the audience. Oral communication allows persuaders to be flexible; if they are skilled at thinking on their feet, they can change their message midway through to respond to perceived fears and hopes that will impede or facilitate a positive response. When persuaders want an audience to become emotionally involved in an issue, they often use arguments that culminate in a call to audience members to support a cause actively.[22]

Written communications, such as memoranda, letters, and reports, allow precision, unlike spoken communication, where definitions and details are often relatively vague. When presenters want audiences to commit themselves to a course of action, they can elicit relatively binding agreements with documents; a memo, for example, may ask people to check a specific category, such as "agree or support," "disagree," or "undecided." Written communications are useful in explaining technical subjects, such as the implementation details for a specific policy or a summary of existing research; it is difficult to convey technical subjects in brief addresses.[23]

Graphic materials, such as graphs and slides, simplify complex materials and often help capture the attention of a hostile or indifferent audience. Someone seeking support for vulnerable populations, for example, can use pictures or slides to promote sympathy or interest. If used to excess, however, graphic materials can lose an audience's attention.[24]

Using a Sequence of Presentations

When we envision presentations, we customarily think of one effort to convince an audience to take a specific position on an issue. In fact, skilled persuaders realize that they will be more effective if they use a sequence of persuasive encounters—a variety of written, interpersonal, and other communications, perhaps culminating in a formal presentation. A persuader might first use some informal personal encounters to discover where people stand on an issue and what they fear or dislike to initiate the process of changing the audience's knowledge or beliefs.[25] She might then plan a meeting to educate her audience about an issue as a prelude to a meeting to take action.

Selecting a Format

When you get to the formal presentation, the format is critical. Every speech has a beginning, a middle, and an end. Your challenge is to command your audience's attention at the outset, impart important substantive information in the middle, and conclude with the presentation's essential purpose (such as persuading the audience to take action, set up a committee, or take a specific problem seriously).

It is essential to decide what you want the audience to do as a result of your presentation, for example, to set up a committee to study an issue, to take a condition very seriously, or to gain new knowledge. Once you have decided on your objective, you can develop a format that will achieve it.

Do not lock yourself into a single format prematurely. Try different versions of your speech. Think about novel points you can make at the outset or in the conclusion that will appeal to your audience. Brainstorm to develop alternative outlines.

Skilled policy advocates use basic formats tailored to specific kinds of communications. These formats establish an integrating logic for a presentation. Seven such formats are given in Box 8.1.[26]

BOX 8.1   Alternative Formats for Policy Advocates

To discuss how a problem developed, you can use a *time* structure of the sequence of events that caused the problem. Such a speech might begin, "I want to discuss how the problem with our agency's intake procedures developed by taking you through a sequence of events."

    A. Intake procedures in 1985.
    B. Revisions of intake procedures in 1986.
        1. Why revisions were made.
        2. The nature of the revisions.
    C. Changes in the composition of our agency's clients between 1987 and 1991.
    D. Intake problems caused by these changes in clientele.
    E. Options we should consider in revising our intake procedures again.
        1. Option 1.
        2. Option 2.
    F. Call for a task force or committee to make recommendations.

To explain a problem, you can use a *topical* structure that discusses a problem's components. Such a speech might begin, "I want to discuss operating problems in our agency as a prelude to some policy recommendations."

    A. We are experiencing a number of problems in our agency's program for school dropouts.
        1. Problem 1.
        2. Problem 2.
        3. Problem 3.
    B. Relationships among these three problems.
    C. Options we should consider to address these problems.
        1. Option 1.
        2. Option 2.
        3. Option 3.

To establish that a problem exists and needs attention, you can use a *criticism* structure to describe the problem and the criteria for demonstrating that it is a problem. For example, you might say, "Our intake procedures are faulty because clients with serious problems do not receive prompt attention and because the procedures are unfair."

    A. An overview of our intake procedures.
    B. Why our intake procedures need to be overhauled.
        1. Problems of fairness.
        2. Problems encountered by clients who are denied immediate service.
        3. Administrative problems.
        4. Staffing problems.
    C. The need to collect more information about Problems 2 and 4.

B O X 8.1   *(continued)*

> D. Call for a committee to collect the information and make some recom-
>   mendations.
>
> *To show a cause-effect relationship,* use an *association* structure. Say, "I want to
> discuss how the problem with our intake procedures stems from the rapid in-
> crease in our waiting list."
>
> A. Discuss problems with the intake policy.
> B. Discuss specific changes in the nature of the clientele using the agency
>   during the past five years.
> C. Link the problems with the changes in clientele.
> D. Discuss possible implications for changing intake policy.
>
> *To gain acceptance of a plan,* use an *argument* structure, where you present the
> elements of the problem and the central features of your corrective plan. Begin,
> "I want to discuss why our intake policies are faulty and then present a five-part
> plan to deal with the situation."
>
> A. Discuss problems with the intake policy.
> B. Provide solutions.
> C. Discuss how the solutions address specific criteria.
>   1. Administrative feasibility.
>   2. Fairness.
>   3. Cost.
>
> *To criticize someone else's statement of a problem or plan,* use a *refutation*
> structure, where you state his or her central tenets and then present your argu-
> ments about why they are flawed. Say, "I want to discuss why the plan Susan
> Smith offered to correct our intake system is flawed."
>
> A. Provide an overview of the intake problems.
> B. Describe the central elements of Smith's plan.
> C. Discuss how it fails to address certain criteria.
>   1. It is not administratively feasible.
>   2. It is not fair to certain kinds of clients.
>   3. It would be too costly.
> D. Discuss an alternative approach and why it is better.
>
> *To influence people to take action,* use a *directive* structure, where you state the
> reasons why immediate emergency action is needed. You might say, "This situa-
> tion is urgent. We should send a delegation at once to see the head of the welfare
> agency."
>
> A. Why this problem has taken on urgency.
>   1. Effects on clients.
>   2. Possible political ramifications.
>   3. Implications for our funding.
>
> *(continued)*

BOX 8.1   *(continued)*

B. Why a delay in addressing it would be calamitous.
C. Alternative courses of action.
   1. Write a letter.
   2. Contact the head of the welfare agency by telephone.
   3. Send a delegation.
   4. Other actions.
D. A call to action.
   1. Send a delegation.
   2. Have the delegation make the following arguments.
   3. Supplement the delegation with other actions.
      a. Call the mayor.
      b. Contact a member of the county board of supervisors.

Our discussion suggests that policy presenters should tailor their outline to the subject they are discussing. While outlines can take different forms, they need to include a logical sequence of topics that structures the presentation for both the presenter and the audience.

Fine-tuning a presentation   Once presenters have developed a medium, analyzed the audience, and developed an outline, they can fine-tune the presentation in numerous ways and, in the process, revise the outline. Presenters often use specific techniques to make a presentation more interesting to the audience. They may add case examples to capture the audience's attention. They may elicit audience participation during part of the presentation by asking, "Which of these options do you prefer?" or "Can you think of an option I have not considered?" They may use a particular visual aid, such as a chart distributed to the audience or presented by overhead projector.

The following is an illustrative presentation to the staff of an agency about its flawed intake procedures. The speech is based on an outline and uses a criticism structure.

I. Initial statement, an overview of the presentation: "I will discuss three reasons why I think our intake policies are flawed."
II. Supporting arguments: "Why do I think they are flawed?"
      A. Certain clients with serious conditions have to wait long periods. (Discuss Client A as an example.)
      B. Certain kinds of people drop off the waiting list disproportionately. (Discuss Client B as an example.)
      C. Our waiting-list procedures frustrate certain clients. (Discuss Client C as an example.)
III. Ask the audience to share any experiences they have had with the intake procedures.
IV. Recommendation: Establish a committee to find alternative ways to structure our intake procedures.

Developing an Effective Presentation Style

Your effectiveness as a presenter is based not only on the substantive content of your presentation, but also on your *delivery style,* including your relationship with the audience, your speech patterns, and your use of gestures.[27]

You have to feel comfortable with your basic outline before you begin your presentation, and you need to have rehearsed it so that you need only to look at the bold headings from time to time as you make the presentation. Most audiences like presenters to make eye contact with them.

To offset the fear that you will ramble, you may start by explaining the presentation's basic logic, that is, the basic points you will cover. Select an interesting case example, visual image, or analogy to gain the audience's attention at once. Make clear transitions as you move from topic to topic with statements like, "Having discussed why intake procedures are flawed, we can now move to possible remedies." Wrap things up with a thoughtful conclusion that draws on the preceding sections of your presentation.

Try to avoid distracting habits, such as fumbling with papers, using excessively rapid or slow speech patterns, or pacing back and forth. Some experts in presentation videotape themselves before making presentations to discern the unconscious, distracting mannerisms that all of us have.

What do you do if you are frightened about making speeches? Most important, try not to run away from public speaking opportunities, difficult as they may seem. Some of us develop fright instincts when making speeches and we can break these patterns only with practice. Many people find it useful to pause momentarily before speaking to gain equilibrium, to collect their thoughts, and to remind themselves of the presentation's outline.

Tactics for Specific Audiences

You will want to modify your outline as you consider the likely nature of your audience, which may be hostile, apathetic, or expert.

Policy advocates sometimes encounter *hostile audiences* with values or beliefs that predispose them to oppose a specific message. Various techniques can decrease hostility. You can identify common values, perspectives, and practical concerns that link you to the audience. These links may be common group memberships, educational affiliations, or demographic traits. Or you can appeal to higher values that you share with the audience, by saying, for example, "All of us share concern for the homeless people we see on the streets." Some policy advocates seek conservatives' support for social programs by appealing to their patriotism; if Americans want the nation to remain competitive in international markets, these advocates may argue, they need to address the high dropout rate in schools.[28]

You can establish your credibility with hostile audiences by citing authorities or experts the audience is likely to respect and by discussing credentials or experiences of your own that increase your credibility. To seem reasonable, you can present both sides of complex issues and freely admit that alternative viewpoints are inevitable. Rather than beginning with your conclusion, you can build a case, hoping that your evidence will gradually change the audience's view of an issue. You might reach your eventual proposal only after rejecting or refuting alternative positions.[29]

Humor often defuses tense situations. Some persuaders make fun of themselves so the audience perceives them as unceremonious and unpretentious. If told with skill, anecdotes at the start of a presentation may ease audiences into subjects they find difficult or stressful.

Apathetic audiences present similar challenges. It is important not to overwhelm apathetic audiences with complex arguments or data, which will intensify their apathy. Nor is it wise to tell the audience that they should care about an issue, an intrusive technique likely to make them retreat even further into apathy. The skillful persuader makes the presentation interesting and lively, stresses few themes or arguments, presents a simple argument, and offers interesting and unusual evidence that the audience has not heard before.[30]

The members of *expert audiences* perceive themselves to be well versed in the presentation topic. Presenters need to offer an array of perspectives and evidence to such audiences, admitting that the existing knowledge is imperfect and that choices are difficult. They need to discuss the merits of alternative options and not move quickly to a single solution. The presenter should pay tribute to the audience's expertise by recognizing that they have thought extensively about the subject and, perhaps, by eliciting their opinions or suggestions.[31]

Other Tactical Choices

Additional tactics help presenters modify their outlines.

Single-sided or two-sided arguments?   Should persuaders present the strongest possible argument for a specific policy (a single-sided argument), or should they consider both sides of an issue (a two-sided argument)? Some social psychologists suggest two-sided arguments for critical or hostile audiences because the persuader anticipates and defuses some criticisms and therefore appears reasonable and open-minded. Single-sided arguments are more effective with audiences that share the values of the speaker.[32]

How much dissonance?   All persuaders want to change their audience's beliefs, but they have to decide how much dissonance, or discrepancy between the audience's beliefs and the proposal, to introduce. If they ask for massive changes, they risk alienating the audience. If they ask for minor changes, they risk undermining possible support for more extensive change.

When persuaders anticipate hostility, they should probably not begin by suggesting massive changes. Several presentations should be scheduled, the first one seeking to educate the audience, rather than to secure a commitment to major change. A sympathetic audience is more immediately open to a commitment to major change.[33]

Climax or anticlimax?   Social psychologists' findings on whether the beginning of a presentation or the end makes the strongest impression are contradictory, but either the introductory or the concluding portion of a speech is the strongest, and the weakest points should be inserted in the middle sections.[34]

Who should present?   When a choice exists, persuaders need to ponder carefully who should present information to a specific audience. Presenters to hostile or apathetic audiences should have either high credibility with them or styles of communication suited to overcoming hostility and apathy. It is sometimes useful for multiple presenters to give different portions of a presentation.[35]

Adapting the setting   Skillful persuaders sometimes find or create a setting conducive to reaching a specific audience. Intimate settings may be chosen over formal settings to increase rapport. Seating arrangements may be devised to facilitate exchanges between the presenter and the audience. Graphic aids, such as slides, may overcome an audience's apathy. Sometimes, an audience is broken into smaller groups that later reconvene to share their solutions to a specific problem.[36]

Honoring protocols and expectations   Audiences often have specific expectations about a presentation. Legislators, for example, expect testimony to legislative committees to be relatively brief—not more than 10 or 15 minutes.[37] (Detailed materials and the text of the presenter's comments are submitted separately.) An audience may have certain expectations regarding the formality, tenor, and style of a presentation. An audience of persons who consider themselves experts on a subject expect the presenter to offer alternative viewpoints, whereas an audience of activists often expects a call to action. To understand these expectations, presenters need to speak with audience members before their presentation or with people familiar with the audience.

Assembling a Strategy

To illustrate persuading strategy, let's examine how Harry Johnson, our lobbyist for an AIDS advocacy group who was introduced in Policy Advocacy Challenge 8.2, develops strategy to secure support for legislative reforms for people with AIDS.

The Hostile Audience

Suppose that Harry wants to convince some conservative Republicans—the people most likely to be critical of the gay community and to believe that people with AIDS "brought it on themselves"—to support a major legislative initiative. The legislation would expand the state's funding of home health care programs to serve people with AIDS. It would cover homemaker, visiting-nurse, and physical therapy services. Both Medicaid recipients and people considerably above the poverty line would receive these services. (Currently, counties fund most state home-health services, but only for individuals who meet restrictive income standards.) Admittedly, the new program will be expensive, because many people with AIDS who are not eligible for existing county programs will need extended home-health services.

Harry decides to make two presentations to this skeptical and hostile audience. The first will capture his audience's interest and cut through their stereotypes, and the second will obtain their suggestions for legislative strategy.

Even before the first presentation, Harry enlists the assistance of several sympathetic Republican legislators, who agree to moderate the sessions and expedite discussion. He wants his introduction to make at least some of the conservative legislators perceive the problem in human, personal terms rather than abstract, ideological ones. He decides to present several case histories of HIV-positive people who have encountered difficulty when seeking home-based services. To decrease the audience's perception of the problem as belonging only to gay radicals, he relates several cases of conservative Republicans who have contracted the disease. He also makes analogies with older people and people with disabilities to communicate that the AIDS population's home-health needs and problems are similar to those of other, more accepted populations. He concludes the first presentation with a question-and-answer session about the dimensions of the problem.

During the second presentation, Johnson uses a format with a two-sided argument. After quickly summarizing some factual information from the first session regarding the problem's dimensions, he lists some alternative remedies: the cost-effectiveness of establishing different levels of eligibility for home-health services, the merits of working through local nonprofit agencies rather than through the counties' home-health programs, and the benefits of focusing the services on specific subgroups of people with AIDS. After discussing the merits of these various options, he provides a legislative proposal that a bipartisan group has tentatively drafted but not yet introduced into the legislative process.

The Sympathetic Audience with Some Hostile Members

The legislative proposal is introduced into a legislative committee with many sympathetic members but some hostile ones. Johnson, who hopes to intensify support for the proposal, encounters the dilemma of addressing a mixed audience. Should he write off the minority and direct his comments to the sympathetic members, or should he target his comments to the hostile minority because he already expects the majority to support the proposal?

Johnson decides to focus his comments on those who are sympathetic but to include points in his presentation that will attract some votes from those who are hostile. (The sympathetic do not need an extended argument and want only a brief, dramatic message to energize them to support the proposal.) Indeed, he focuses his presentation on a particularly poignant case. To appeal to the hostile members, however, he selects a case that illustrates how providing a homemaker and other services will allow some people with AIDS to remain productive workers (and hence taxpayers) for a longer period than if these services are unavailable.

The Expert Audience

Johnson also seeks support for the proposal from hospital administrators, whose professional association wields power within the state. Unlike most legislators, who have scant knowledge of the intricacies of health care programs, hospital administrators are familiar with the existing programs. Therefore, Johnson decides to emphasize practical cost and administrative issues, such as how the proposal will be implemented, how the state will monitor it, and how it will affect the duration of hospitalization of people with AIDS.

To enhance his rapport with this audience, Johnson cites evidence and arguments obtained from a hospital administrator and some hospital social workers who specialize in discharge planning. Because the proposal's funds will be funneled through nonprofit agencies, he discusses how these agencies will coordinate their services with hospitals.

Throughout his presentation, Johnson elicits input from the experts, both to obtain their insights and to make it clear that he respects their expertise.

Interpersonal Discussions

As this legislation progresses from initial proposal to drafted legislation to (it is hoped) enacted legislation, Johnson will have countless discussions with foes and friends of the legislation, officials in the state's bureaucracies, local officials, and community activists. These discussions will take many forms. In some of them, Johnson will solicit information about people's positions, biases, and perspectives, thus maintaining a fact-finding posture. Of course, his patience will be tested when individuals are hostile toward people with AIDS, like the legislator who maintains that "the solution to the AIDS problem is to require all testing centers to turn over the names of HIV-positive persons to public health officials." As Lewis Dexter suggests, the lobbyist should remain "benevolently neutral" in some of these hostile discussions.[38] While he need not agree with these legislators, he need not attack them either. Indeed, he might say, "We share a desire to bring this epidemic under control. What are your ideas about how to help people with AIDS remain productive members of society in the interim?"

In some of these discussions, Johnson uses a directive format, seeking support for the proposal. He asks the leader of an advocacy group to mobilize support for the legislation by obtaining letters and phone calls from key legislators' constituents. He also uses a combination of flattery and emotional language: "We've turned to you many times in the past, and you have never let us down. How do you think we can place pressure on these five legislators who are possible swing votes?"

Other discussions follow a substantive format, such as those with health experts. In these conversations, Johnson seeks assistance in defining the home-health needs of people with AIDS, the potential cost of specific provisions in the legislation, and the administrative considerations.

We can often improve our presentation skills by studying the work of successful presenters. An example is Jesse Jackson's speech to the Democratic National Convention on August 27, 1996. (See Policy Advocacy Challenge 8.5.)

POLICY ADVOCACY CHALLENGE 8.5

WHY A PRESENTATION WAS SUCCESSFUL

Jesse Jackson, Founder of the Rainbow Coalition

We Must Seek a New Moral Center

Thirty-three years ago tonight, a young preacher about the same age as my son was putting the final touches on one of the great prophetic messages of our age.

On August 28, 1963, Dr. King projected a vision of peace and equality that could heal our nation, and a troubled world.

His vision touched America's conscience. The Republicans in San Diego put forward the image, the vision, of a big tent.

Remember, America, you can't judge a book by its cover.

On the cover, Powell and Kemp.

But inside, the book was written by Newt Gingrich and Ralph Reed and Pat Buchanan.

What is our vision tonight? Just look around.

(continued)

(8.5   continued)

This publicly financed United Center is a new Chicago mountain top. To the South,
Comiskey Park, another mountain. To the west, Cook County Jail, with its
11,000 mostly youthful inmates.

Between these three mountains lies the canyon.

Once Campbell's Soup was in this canyon. Sears was there, and Zenith, Sunbeam,
the stockyards. There were jobs and industry where now there is a canyon of
welfare and despair.

This canyon exists in virtually every city in America.

As we gather here tonight:

one-fifth of all American children will go to bed in poverty;

one-half of all African American children, growing up amidst broken sidewalks,
broken families, broken cities, broken dreams;

the No. 1 growth industry in urban America, jails;

one-half of all the public housing built in this nation during the last decade, jails;

the top 1 percent wealthiest Americans own as much as the bottom 95 percent—the
greatest inequality since the 1920's.

As corporations downsize jobs, outsource contracts, scab on workers' rights, a class
crisis emerges as a race problem. The strawberry pickers in California, the
chicken workers in North Carolina, deserve a hearing and justice.

We must seek a new moral center.

We have been here before.

The last time we gathered in Chicago, high winds ripped our tent apart. We could
not bridge the gap. We lost to Nixon by the margin of our despair.

In 1968, the tension within our party was over warfare.

In 1996, it's welfare. Last week, over the objections of many Democratic Party leaders, and the opposition of millions of Americans, Franklin Roosevelt's six-
decade guarantee of support for women and children was abandoned.

On this issue, many of us differ with the President. Patricia Ireland and I even picketed the White House.

But we can disagree and debate, and still work together. Diversity is the measure of
this party's strength; how we handle adversity, the measure of our character.

We must find the bridge, keep our tent intact. And we must make the commitment
to right the wrongs in this bill.

Now that we have ended welfare as we know it, we must provide jobs and job training and education and day care as we ought to know it.

The fight was never about welfare, but always about jobs and opportunity. Welfare
is the exhaust pipe of a failed economic engine. We want to be a part of the engine of growth.

The passage of the welfare bill creates a moral imperative to provide a job with a
living wage for every man and woman in America. That was Roosevelt's
dream, and Dr. King's.

What is our obligation to the people in the canyon?

First, we must claim and reclaim our children.

We must lift our children up, not lock them up.

Instead of three strikes and you're out, we must have four balls and you're on:
in prenatal care and Head Start, ball one;
an adequately funded education, ball two;
access to a marketable skill or a college education, ball three;
a good job at a living wage, ball four.
Eleven thousand youthful inmates to our West, without treatment, most return sicker and slicker.
We need a trade policy that works for working people.
Right now, we subsidize corporate welfare to take jobs out of the canyon.
I recently visited Indonesia, and I am clear on this: When corporations can downsize and outsource to nations which pay 30 cents an hour, our workers cannot compete nor should they have to.
And tonight, labor leader Muchtar Pakpahan and opposition leader Mrs. Megawati face government interrogation and harassment.
Respect for human rights must remain a nonnegotiable part of fair trade.
In the canyon, we must have a plan to rebuild and redeem our cities, to reinvest in America.
I suggest we have at least as much sense as the honey bee, which knows enough to repollinate her flower.
When the Berlin Wall came down, we offered Poland a development bank, 40 year loans, three-fourths of 1 percent, first payment due in 10 years.
America has $6 trillion in private and public pension funds. We could take 5 percent of the workers' money, with workers' consent, government secured, to rebuild our infrastructure.
It will not increase taxes.
After World War II, we helped rebuild Germany, the Marshall Plan. We helped rebuild Japan, the MacArthur Plan.
Now we must rebuild America.
Sometimes, though, you have to play good defense before you get back on offense.
President Clinton has been our first line of defense against the Newt Gingrich Contract-on-America right wing assault on our elderly, our students, our civil rights.
We must maintain that line of defense and protect the First Lady, too, from their mean-spirited attacks.
We must re-elect the President and take back the Congress, and stop the right wing train in its track.
In 1994, the Gingrich tidal wave was not so high; our sea walls were too low. With only 40,000 more voters, Newt Gingrich would never have taken power.
This low turnout cannot repeat itself in 1996; we must inspire and mobilize our base vote, the margin of our hope.
The stakes are so very high.
This year, for the first time in our lives, the right-wing extremists Dole, Gingrich, Lott, Armey, Helms, and Scalia-Thomas have a chance to take over all three branches of government. This would be an unparalleled disaster for our people.

(continued)

(8.5   continued)

Our job is to win in November.

Our mission is to lift America up with a higher vision, to redeem the canyon, to find the moral center.

In this season of high stakes and critical choices, if you don't vote, you are irrelevant to the process. If you go along to get along, you're a coward. Only by principled engagement can you be a force for change and hope.

Remember our history: Progress comes through an enlightened President, in coalition with an energized people.

In 1932, F.D.R. did not run on a New Deal platform. The people mobilized around their economic plan, and F.D.R. responded with the New Deal.

F.D.R. was the option. The people provided the answer.

In 1960, neither Kennedy nor Nixon ran for President on the promise of a public accommodations bill. But Dr. King supported Kennedy; J. F. K. was the best option.

Desegregated public accommodations came from Greensboro and Birmingham, from the sit-ins and marches and street heat. From we, the people, in motion.

In 1964, neither Goldwater nor Johnson campaigned on the Voting Rights Act. But Dr. King supported L.B.J.; he was the best option. We won voting rights on the bridge at Selma.

We, the people, provided the answer.

In 1996, Bill Clinton is our best option. The cross is on his shoulders. But burdens shared are easier to bear.

We, the people, must organize and mobilize to help the President provide a better answer for America.

In Tracy Chapman's words, we must "start all over, make a new beginning . . . make new symbols . . . redefine the world."

After November, we, the people, must hold on to the moral center, and continue to fight for expansive, inclusive, humane politics in America.

This is our mission.

It is a vision worth struggling for.

Keep hope alive.

To understand why this speech was a notable success, analyze the following:

What goal or objective did Jackson set for himself in this speech? (Remember that Clinton was running against a conservative Republican, Bob Dole, and that Jackson wanted desperately to bring Democratic liberals on board, even though many of them were disenchanted with Clinton, who had just signed welfare legislation that many of them opposed.)

What overarching theme did he develop?

Why did he use the title "We Must Seek a New Moral Center"?

How is the speech organized?

Why is the speech relatively brief?

Even without hearing this particular speech, judging from other speeches you have heard Jackson deliver, how did he prove the adage that a speech's effectiveness is due as much to the presentation skills of the speech maker as to its formal content?

Writing Succinct Policy Memos

Until now, we have discussed mainly oral presentations designed to present and defend policies. Now we turn to tactics for seeking approval of policies in written documents: succinct policy memos and grant proposals. A good way to articulate the comparison and choice of options is to write a succinct memo. Succinct memos are often effective because decision makers, pressed for time, need concise summaries of policy issues and recommendations. Of course, more extensive materials can be appended to a succinct memo or supplied later if needed.

Policy Advocacy Challenge 8.6 is a good example of a succinct policy memo that delineates a number of options, examines their advantages and disadvantages, ranks them qualitatively, and reaches a conclusion at the end. This memo is for the commissioner of a social worker's states department of mental health (DMH). The social worker examines policy options regarding her state's services for persons who are mentally ill, comparing (1) deinstitutionalization, (2) the liquidation of the existing state schools, and (3) the implementation of a purchase-of-service (POS) system of community care, in which public authorities reimburse nongovernmental agencies for providing specific community-based services. She recommends deinstitutionalization coupled with retaining smaller hospitals.

POLICY ADVOCACY CHALLENGE 8.6

CONSTRUCTING POLICY MEMOS

Memorandum to the Commissioner

1. Policy issue In the context of the next five-year plans, what should be the role of state hospitals for people with mental illness? Specifically, should DMH care for its remaining institutionalized clients completely within existing institutions, completely within the community by purchase of services (POS), or somewhere in between? How can the department shape its personnel policy accordingly?

Recommendations: The goal for clients who are mentally ill should be to liquidate existing state hospitals, leaving one small institution in each of the seven regions to serve violent patients. The proposed facilities would be operated under private auspices under state contract. Community care services should be completely POS. DMH's personnel policy should be, implicitly, one of attrition, where civil servants in DMH are trained and transferred to other state positions and to community service settings under public auspices in settings like municipal hospitals. Explicitly, DMH should work closely with unions to arrange for three options: early retirement, training and transfer to other state positions, and training and transfer to community service settings under public auspices

(continued)

(8.6   continued)

to preserve vesting but not civil service protections. These places might be municipal hospitals, state-university-sponsored settings, and so forth.

2. Summary and analysis of issues   The impetus for deinstitutionalization stems from a belief, buttressed by research findings, that large institutions inhibit and discourage the potential of those who are mentally ill to function independently. Prevalent in the past 20 years, this belief underlies passage of the Community Mental Health Centers Act of 1963. Legal developments, especially several Supreme Court decisions, have hastened deinstitutionalization by prohibiting involuntary commitment without provision of treatment. Social programs, such as Medicaid, Medicare, Title XX, and SSI, have provided heretofore absent funding for community services. These developments took 370,000 people out of public mental hospitals from 1955 to 1975. In Massachusetts, 7,000 people left state hospitals between 1971 and 1978.

Current situation: These deinstitutionalized clients have frequently been placed in nursing homes that lack the resources and the inclination to meet the needs of residents who are mentally ill. Many other individuals reside in substandard boarding houses, do not receive rehabilitation or treatment services, frequently decompensate, and are readmitted to state hospitals. Still other individuals are simply lost to follow-up treatment.

This situation stems from gaps in community services for the deinstitutionalized population, the availability of services not tailored to the needs of the individual who is mentally ill but offering a protective environment, and pressure to deinstitutionalize quickly because of mounting costs and a desire to avoid legal suits. This urgency precludes planning to fill service gaps and to foster receptive community attitudes.

What should the optimal community care system look like? What is needed? The literature abounds in descriptions of successful and unsuccessful community care programs for deinstitutionalized people who are mentally ill. The same essential program elements emerge again and again as keys to success or failure. They are targeting patients who are chronic, which is a priority; links to other resources, for example, vocational rehabilitation; community provision of the full range of functions associated with institutional care; individually tailored treatment; culturally relevant programs tailored to local communities; specially trained staff attuned to the survival problems of clients who are mentally ill and living in noninstitutional settings; public or private beds; and internal evaluation of these resources.

The problem at hand is how to move states such as Massachusetts from having half-filled institutions and underserved deinstitutionalized clients to a fully community-based model that incorporates these eight program elements.

3. Available options   The following options are available to us:

Option 1: Discontinue deinstitutionalization. Devote scarce resources to upgrading institutions.

• Pro: This option appeals to those who doubt the potential of individuals who are mentally ill for growth and who, because of concern or contempt, want them off community streets. It is administratively simpler, leaving the state in complete control.

However, it is likely to be more costly than using community services, because community-based programs have federal funding sources, such as SSI and Medicaid.

- Con: Research offers strong evidence that large institutions reduce individualization, thereby discouraging the ego development necessary for independent functioning. Current concern for civil liberties will not tolerate this option, particularly with regard to those who are mentally ill.

Option 2: Develop a complete community care system, incorporating the eight program elements. Fund the services with POS.

- Pro: Critics of POS say that providers dominate the state, which loses control. However, this has been due largely to a lack of state planning; an abundance of personnel trained in direct service, rather than management; and a state inferiority complex. These deficiencies can be altered. State legislatures must be persuaded to keep providing funds to support institutional care and new funds to develop community services. Once community settings are in place, institutional expenditures can be converted to community expenditures, and new funds can be discontinued. This interim support of two systems is vital to planning efforts. Administrative personnel can be retrained and direct-service personnel phased out. Liquidating property assets and converting direct-service expenditures into POS money provide the state with buying power it need not be afraid to exercise. Community mental health centers and other financially distressed community service settings will welcome state funding.
- Con: As exemplified by community mental health centers, community programs reject people who are mentally ill as "unrewarding." Community residents reject people who are mentally ill out of fear, disgust, and concerns about property devaluation. Although some programs may welcome state funding, delayed payment creates prohibitive cash flow problems.

Option 3: Develop a community care system incorporating the eight key elements using POS, but maintain small, regionally located state institutions to treat people who are mentally ill and violent. The proposed facilities would be privately managed and staffed. Develop a limited number of direct-service community programs under other public auspices, such as municipal hospitals and state-university-sponsored settings. Staff them with transferred institutional personnel.

- Pro: This option is particularly suited to people who are mentally ill. Patients who are violent frequently cannot be treated safely in community hospital settings. Small, secure institutions in each region will provide more humane, cost-effective care than will large institutions preserved for this purpose. The rationale for private administration, as for POS versus direct services, rests on the assumption that personnel currently serving in state institutions would re-create in the proposed small institutions the negative institutional practices that suppress client development. As institutional personnel are moved into community settings, they can be purged of their institutional ways; the literature describes how this has been done successfully. Most of the best personnel have now left the state systems. Private community programs are fiercely resisting incorporating the remaining state personnel, even the professionals. However,

(continued)

(8.6   continued)

because unions are strong and influence state legislators, and out of a sense of fairness, employee concerns about jobs and retirement benefits must be considered. Three options may meet state personnel's needs, while preserving the state's policy of attrition: early retirement benefits, training and transfer to other state positions, and training and transfer to community settings under other public auspices.

- Con: Any residual institutional role is dangerous, because it will be overutilized. The incentives needed to attract private management and professional staff for the proposed facilities would outweigh any cost-effectiveness the facilities would provide.

4. Recommendation   Choose Option 3.   *Rationale:* People who are mentally ill have few, if any, advocates (families are often nonexistent for one reason or another) and suffer from a fluctuating disease requiring several treatment methods. As a result, inpatient beds must be available, and some of these beds must be in a secure setting to protect others from patients who are violent and patients who are suicidal from themselves.

5. Implementation factors   *How can legislators be persuaded both to keep supporting an institutional system and to develop community-based services?* They must be impressed with the horrors of a poorly planned deinstitutionalization process. Plenty of examples exist, probably even locally. Use them to gain crucial planning time.

How can unions be persuaded to comply with an implicit attrition policy that will no doubt be perfectly explicit to them? The state administration must convince local legislators—that is, those whose areas are most affected by deinstitutionalization—that institutions are inhumane, anachronistic relics that must be abolished (the state can point out that Senator Backman has been vocal in this regard), but that the state wishes to be fair to employees caught in the middle.

DMH management should be sure to broaden the base when dealing with unions. They should meet not only with union leaders but also with the rank and file and with respected professionals. DMH should be sensitive to employee anxieties and committed to retraining and relocation efforts. New York State has been successful in this area and offers a good model.

What about the future? Should the state aim to dismantle all direct-care services permanently? No. Once the current system has been dismantled and POS has been in operation for a while, DMH should evaluate the cost-effectiveness of direct-care services versus POS, especially for outpatient services.

Exercise: As you read this case, try outlining a memo on another issue. If you want practice in writing succinct policy memos, also try making this memo even more concise, such as by reducing its length by one-half. Sometimes, even one- or two-page memos can be highly effective in generating interest in a policy issue.

<small>SOURCE: This case is a modified version of one by Dr. Marcia Mabee.</small>

As with any policy choice, others may take issue with her analysis and conclusions by questioning her criteria or ranking of the options, or by proposing options not even presented in her memo. The importance of this memo for our purposes lies not in its specific conclusions on a policy issue at a particular point in her state's history, but in its style of reasoning about options, criteria, trade-offs, and conclusions. All social workers can similarly analyze issues and problems, even those that arise in the agencies where they work.

Gaining Support for Grant Proposals

When constructing proposals, such as legislative proposals, proposals to establish new programs in agencies, and grant proposals, policy advocates find that specific strategies often make their proposals more enticing to decision makers and funders. We focus here on a grant proposal written from an agency site. At first glance, some readers may wonder whether grant proposals are policy proposals, since they do not involve legislation. In fact, grant proposals are part of policy advocacy. They seek resources, after all, to fund innovative policies of agencies and agency networks. In many cases, they allow expansion of services to underserved populations. They often establish new programs. They are, in fact, agency counterparts to legislative proposals. Let's return to our discussion from the preceding chapter of the social work intern who wanted resources to expand translation services for Latinos in the hospital where she had her internship.

Writing an Imaginative Title

Policy advocates should develop creative, eye-catching titles for their proposals—titles that will attract support from a wide range of persons. In naming her proposal in a foundation grant, for example, the student intern could select a purely descriptive title, such as "Increasing Translating Services to Latinos in XYZ Hospital." Alternatively, she could select a more imaginative title, such as "Linking the University with a Hospital to Help Latinos Navigate the Health System."

Giving a Compelling Rationale

Proposal writers have to provide a compelling rationale, or decision makers and funders will perceive their proposal as addressing trivial problems.[39] Bear in mind that most proposals must compete with many others, and in the winnowing process, proposals that are perceived to be unimportant are likely to be discarded.

The student intern should provide dramatic instances of harm to Latino patients caused by the lack of translation services. She should present data that show the desperate shortage of translating services, as well as the likelihood that this shortage will not be redressed by the hospital in the near term. She could provide quotations from physicians, nurses, and social workers that confirm the shortage of translators, as well as the adverse effects of this shortage on patients.

Drawing on Research Findings

Some innovative policies hinge on the research and conceptual work we discussed in Chapter Six. The student intern might find data demonstrating that Latino patients without adequate translation services suffer specific consequences in medical transactions. Or she might find data from a pilot project in another setting where student volunteers have successfully served as interpreters.

Setting Clear Objectives

Proposals fare best when they contain clear objectives.[40] The student intern ought to estimate the number of patients who would be helped annually by her student volunteers, both overall and on specific units. She should estimate how many students would be recruited to be volunteers. Objectives are often made clearer when they are linked to specific time lines. Perhaps the intern would allow three months to recruit and train her 40 students as a prelude to moving ahead with the translation services.

Including an Evaluation Component

Policy advocates often include an evaluation component in their proposals to gauge whether their innovation has been successful.[41] The student intern might propose gathering data directly from Latino patients who have used the volunteer students. Or she might propose gathering data from medical staff, nurses, and social workers. She might also ask the students to evaluate the project, asking whether they have received adequate training and whether they have expanded their knowledge of the health care system.

Demonstrating Feasibility

Laudatory as a proposal may be, decision makers and funders must believe that it is feasible.[42] The student intern would need to answer such questions as the following: Do top hospital and university administrators favor the proposal, and will they cooperate with it? Who will be in charge of the program's implementation? Has the student intern already located a competent coordinator whose qualifications are included in her proposal? Where will the project be housed? How will the volunteer students be trained? In what accounts will the project's funds be kept? Who will audit or oversee the budget? And how long will it take to get the program up and running?

Establishing Partnerships

Many policy innovations are not accepted by legislatures or private funding sources because they are not clearly linked to other programs, whether through joint planning, referral networks, joint programs, or shared facilities. These partnership links must be clearly articulated. The student intern should discuss how she would gain the cooperation of local colleges and hospital administrators in her project and how she would get these administrators to work together.

Demonstrating Support

Proposals rarely are approved if they lack substantial support.[43] The student intern should attach letters of support for her project from top college and hospital administrators, as well as from community leaders. When people introduce legislative proposals, they often try to get a range of legislators to be cosponsors.

Proposals are strengthened, moreover, if they demonstrate tangible support. Perhaps the hospital and university will agree to provide some funding for the project, and to make in-kind contributions such as donating office space, equipment, supplies, and staff time.

Many foundations also want evidence that other institutions will contribute to a project once foundation or government funding ceases. Perhaps the student intern could obtain assurances from university and hospital staff that they will assume a larger share of the project's funding after several years.

Developing a Realistic Budget

Policy advocates must develop realistic budgets that clearly state what magnitude of resources are needed and how they will be used. If advocates seek excessive funding, foundations and legislators may see their proposals as wasteful. If they seek funding that is clearly inadequate, funders may regard the proposal as unrealistic. The student intern would need to write a so-called line item budget that shows the precise funds needed for different categories of expenditures, such as salaries, supplies, transportation, rent, mailings, and telephone.[44]

Finding Funders

The student intern has to search for potential foundation funders for her proposal. These foundations include corporate foundations, small family foundations, large foundations, and community foundations. Corporate foundations typically give small grants to projects where their corporate headquarters (or major installations) are located. They are particularly fond of sponsoring events, like luncheons, and giving in-kind contributions, like supplies or copy machines. Small family foundations are established by wealthy individuals who typically give relatively few grants each year compared with large foundations. Some large foundations, like the Ford and Rockefeller Foundations, usually fund ambitious proposals with national implications, unlike other large foundations that emphasize grants to specific parts of the country. Community foundations, such as the Rhode Island Foundation, the Milwaukee Foundation, or the California Community Foundation, are quasi-public entities that have some public officials, as well as community leaders, on their boards. (See Policy Advocacy Challenge 8.7.) Their charters require them to make grants exclusively in their local jurisdictions.[45]

POLICY ADVOCACY CHALLENGE 8.7 **FINDING FUNDERS VIA THE WEB**	Following are some useful references for fundraising and grant writing in the human services: Cheryl Clarke, *Storytelling for Grantseekers: The Guide to Creative Nonprofit Fundraising* (San Francisco: Jossey-Bass, 2001). Kim Klein, *Fundraising for Social Change,* 4th ed. (San Francisco: Jossey-Bass, 2001). Mal Marwick and Stephen Hitchcock, *Ten Steps to Fundraising Success: Choosing the Right Strategy for Your Organization* (San Francisco: Jossey Bass, 2002). Mal Marwick, Ted Hart, and Nick Allen, eds., *Fundraising on the Internet: The e-Philanthropy Foundation.org's Guide to Success Online* (San Francisco: Jossey-Bass, 2002). Flexibility is critical in finding funding sources, as discussed in Policy Advocacy Challenge 8.8.

POLICY
ADVOCACY
CHALLENGE 8.8

*CREATIVELY SEEKING
FUNDING SOURCES*

*Patsy Lane, M.S.W.,
Director, Department of
Human Services of the
City of Pasadena*

While serving as an administrator for VOALA (a large nonprofit organization), we were seeking funds to rehabilitate an old, deteriorated skid-row hotel and convert it to a new alcohol detoxification, recovery, and support service site. Funding specifically for such a project was very limited, but in our search, we learned that the federal Department of Housing and Urban Development had something called an Urban Development Action Grant (UDAG). At first glance, UDAG funding did not seem relevant to our proposed creation of an alcohol recovery and social service site, but as we reviewed the category called "Neighborhood Revitalization," we began to rethink our project. It seemed apparent that to rehab a deteriorated skid-row hotel and create a new hub offering a range of social and health services (including addressing local problems with public inebriates) would eliminate an area of "urban blight" and revitalize a neighborhood—key criteria for UDAG funding. We redesigned the concept, broadening the range of health, housing, and social services and including information and education activities to further enhance the neighborhood.

Outcome   Our organization submitted the grant proposal, and the project was awarded $1.6 million in UDAG funds.

Lessons learned   Most human service programs have multiple outcomes, address multiple issues, and fit into more than one funding category. Flexibility and creative design are keys to making a project fundable by a variety of potential sources. If you view a potential project from a limited perspective, or as a single-category item, you may miss out on key opportunities for funding, partnerships, collaboration, and other resources.

Revising the Proposal

Proposals rarely emerge full-blown from first drafts; they are gradually developed in an evolutionary process. Amendments to bills are written in successive committee deliberations during the legislative process. Grant proposals to foundations, government authorities, and other funding bodies also are extensively revised as they are drafted. In some cases, the framer will write a one-page version and circulate it to other persons, including a staff member in a foundation or a government agency. A later version, which may be four or five pages long, will be circulated for comments again as a prelude to a more lengthy final version.

Translating complex ideas into fluent prose requires considerable skill. Excessive jargon, long-windedness, complex sentences, and poor syntax diminish interest in a proposal. Many decision makers, such as legislators, who lack technical understanding are disinclined to read dense, lengthy materials. Policy practitioners sometimes err, of course, in the opposite direction; if their proposal is too brief and fails to address important issues, their work may be discarded as superficial.

We provide an example of a grant proposal in Policy Advocacy Challenge 8.9 that social worker Katrina Gould developed while she interned in an AIDS program.

<table>
<tr><td>

POLICY
ADVOCACY
CHALLENGE 8.9

*WRITING A GRANT
PROPOSAL: THE
AIDS PREVENTIVE
EDUCATION
PROJECT*

Katrina Gould, M.S.W.

</td><td>

Problem Statement

The City Council of Pasadena received a report from the City Health Officer on "The Status of AIDS in Pasadena." As a result, the City Council appointed the Pasadena AIDS Strategic Planning Task Force. The task force was charged with developing a proactive plan to determine what Pasadena and public and private organizations could do to address the AIDS crisis.

The task force consisted of Pasadenans, including AIDS service providers, politicians, persons with HIV, doctors, school board members, religious leaders, and public health officials. They formulated the following mission statement: "No member of our community will be newly infected by HIV and those infected will get appropriate care."

To begin to assess AIDS-related needs in Pasadena, the task force developed a continuum-of-care model. It consisted of four major categories into which all educational and treatment services would fall. The continuum included preventive education, early intervention, symptomatic intervention, and extended care.

Recognizing that preventive education is the best "cure" we have for HIV, the task force focused much of their attention on it and dedicated nearly four times as many recommendations to it as to other sections of the continuum of care. Several recommendations focused on guidelines for HIV preventive education in relation to substance abuse, calling for educational materials and programs. The plan urged community groups and institutions to become involved in preventive education.

These recommendations gave rise to this proposal, which aims to train the staff of drug treatment facilities to teach its clients behaviors that will decrease their chances of becoming infected with HIV.

Agency Description

The mission of the All Saints AIDS Service Center (ASASC) is "to serve people whose lives are affected by HIV and AIDS by providing service, preventive education, and advocacy for an appropriate community and government response." It is a nondenominational, not-for-profit agency established in 1988 that has offered direct services to 750 persons with AIDS, as well as preventive outreach programs to thousands in the San Gabriel Valley region of Los Angeles County, including Pasadena. Currently registered with the center are 400 clients, and 60 new clients register for these services each month. More than 300 people attend one of the center's 13 support groups, which are conducted in English and Spanish. The center's health education team provides outreach services to public agencies, local corporations, prisons, parole officers, Head Start programs, Planned Parenthood, schools, colleges, and other health-care agencies. The staff has 25 members and 600 volunteers. ASASC implements its education and prevention programs in its education and prevention section. The programs mentioned in this section are described in an attached appendix.

</td></tr>
</table>

(continued)

(8.9   continued)

Proposed Program

Goals   The primary goal of the preventive education plan is to teach the staffs of six to eight Pasadena agencies facts about HIV/AIDS, information about the relationship between addiction and HIV, and training in behaviors that reduce the risk of acquiring the disease. It is hoped that, by focusing on the staffs of these agencies rather than on their clients, community preventive education will continue, even after this grant's 12-month period.

Objectives   To achieve these goals, the proposed project will meet these objectives:

1. ASASC will develop a training curriculum in collaboration with a representative from the Public Health Department. This curriculum will build on ASASC's existing AIDS 101 curriculum to change the attitudes and behaviors that place the substance-abusing population at risk. This curriculum will be developed by the end of the first six weeks of the project.
2. ASASC will conduct four intensive sessions per agency for the staff of six to eight agencies. These sessions will occur between the 3rd and 9th months of the 12-month period.
3. Two months after the final education session, ASASC will conduct one follow-up session for each agency to address successes and challenges specific to that agency. ASASC will conduct two follow-up evaluative sessions during the 10th and 12th months for all involved agencies.
4. ASASC will seek specific levels of demonstrated competence from the staff of drug treatment centers at specific points in this project:

   • Of the trained drug treatment staff, 80 percent will meet specific criteria during teach-back presentations at each agency's fourth intensive session.
   • Of the trained drug treatment staff, 80 percent will exhibit a 90 percent rate of knowledge at the end of the project, imparted to them between the first and the final sessions.
   • Of the trained drug treatment staff, 50 percent will demonstrate that they have disseminated HIV/AIDS information by making formal presentations during the 12 months of the project.

Proposed Plan

ASASC will train the staff of at least six to eight Pasadena agencies that treat users of drugs, including alcohol and intravenous drugs. The training will include four intensive sessions with direct-service personnel the agency has chosen to participate in the training.

The training will consist of a pretest to gauge the level of knowledge with which participants enter the program; information addressing interconnections between low self-esteem, risky behavior, and substance abuse, and discussions of the possible origins of addictive and risky behavior; role playing about safe sex, in which drug treatment staff will deepen their understanding of the discomfort and difficulties in making behavior changes; basic information on HIV/AIDS, such as how infection occurs, how infection spreads, and the biology of AIDS; a list of community resources and discussion about how to access them; information about psychodynamic issues that emerge when substance abusers become aware that they have been at risk and want to be tested; and discussion of homophobia and how it shapes the views many persons have of HIV and AIDS.

Month-by-month time line   The first 2 months of this 12-month project will focus on setup tasks, including recruiting a health educator to implement the program, having the health educator and Public Health Department collaborate to build a curriculum for training drug treatment center staff, contacting drug treatment agencies that might participate in the project, and assembling reading material for the educational project.

In the next 6 months (Months 3 through 9), the health educator will conduct training, sometimes in conjunction with other staff of ASASC's education and prevention section.

The final 3 months (months 10 through 12) will emphasize discussions among the trainees of the various drug treatment centers. They will meet at ASASC offices to explore problems they have encountered in helping their substance abuse clients modify their risky behaviors. These meetings will provide ASASC with feedback about its training strategies. They will also help the trainees see ASASC as an ongoing resource.

Staffing and evaluation   The health educator will be hired by and report to ASASC's coordinator of the education and prevention program. ASASC already has an Education Advisory Committee, including experts on immunology, psychology, child abuse prevention, nursing, legal issues specific to HIV and AIDS, social work, and education. Members of this committee, in liaison with the Public Health Department and the health educator, will develop instruments and materials to evaluate this project at various intervals. Methods of evaluating the "teach-backs," where trainees teach clients through role play, will also be developed.

Budget

Personnel Costs	
Coordinator of Education and Training (1/5 FTE* @ $32,000)	$ 6,400
Health educator (1 FTE* @ $28,000)	28,000
Fringe benefits @ 18%	6,192
Subtotal for personnel	$ 40,592
Travel	
100 miles per month of local travel (@ $ 28/mile for 12 months)	$ 336
Airfare to project meeting in Washington, D.C.	300
Conference costs	550
Subtotal for travel	$ 1,186
Direct costs	
Educational materials	$ 1,750
Printing/copying	575
Postage	75

(continued)

(8.9   continued)

Direct costs (*continued*)	
Advertising	75
Supplies	75
Software support	75
Equipment repairs	75
Books and publications	125
Refreshments	50
Subtotal for direct costs	$ 2,875
Indirect costs	
Rent	$ 5,750
Telephone	1,150
Insurance	500
Janitorial	1,300
Audit	375
Copier maintenance	250
Miscellaneous	125
Administration	840
Subtotal for indirect costs	$ 10,290
Total cost of project	$ 54,943

*Full-time equivalent

SOURCE: This is part of a proposal prepared by Katrina Gould, M.S.W., in collaboration with staff at the All Saints AIDS Service Center, Pasadena, California.

Exercise: Pretend that you are a grant officer at a foundation that has just received this proposal. Imagine that you have a pile of 200 other grant proposals on your desk and that you can pick only 20 of them for funding. Having a skeptical orientation, ask tough questions about this proposal.

To get yourself into the mind-set of a foundation staff person, make a list of key questions that you would be likely to ask about all grant proposals. (*Hint:* Draw on the discussion of qualities of good policy proposals in the preceding section of this chapter—but feel free to add other questions that may be germane to your foundation.) How does this proposal stack up on these questions? Would you fund it?

Chapter Summary

What You Can Now Do

Our discussion in this chapter suggests that communication skills are a key part of policy advocacy—whether oral presentations (such as debates, negotiations, or speeches) or written presentations (such as succinct policy memos or grant proposals). You are now equipped to do the following:

- Engage in debates on affirmative or negative sides
- Use hardball and win-win options in negotiations

- Develop strategy for making presentations to audiences, such as diagnosing them, setting objectives, selecting a medium, and developing a format
- Improve your presentation style
- Write succinct policy memos
- Write grant proposals

In the next three chapters we turn to tactics for developing and using power resources in policy advocacy—as well as tactics for participating in electoral politics.

Notes

1. Willard Richan, "A Common Language for Social Work," *Social Work* 17 (November 1972): 14–22.
2. Herbert Simons, *Persuasion,* 2nd ed. (New York: Random House, 1986), pp. 18–21, and Donald Cegala, *Persuasive Communication: Theory and Practice,* 3rd ed. (Edina, MN: Bellwether, 1987), pp. 13–15.
3. Michael Barone, "The 49 Percent Nation," *National Journal* (June 9, 2001): 1710–1716.
4. Simons, *Persuasion,* pp. 253–254.
5. Ibid., pp. 190–192.
6. George Brager, Harry Specht, and James Torczyner, *Community Organizing,* 2nd ed. (New York: Columbia University Press), pp. 355–357.
7. Simons, *Persuasion,* pp. 253–256.
8. Ibid., pp. 259–261.
9. Ibid., pp. 253–256.
10. Roger Fisher and William Ury, *Getting to Yes: Negotiating Agreement without Giving In* (New York: Penguin Books, 1991).
11. Ibid. Also see Herb Bisno, *Managing Conflict* (Newbury Park, CA: Sage, 1988), pp. 99–147.
12. See Jay Folberg and Alison Taylor, *Mediation* (San Francisco: Jossey-Bass, 1984).
13. Fisher and Ury, *Getting to Yes.*
14. Bruce Jansson, *Reluctant Welfare State,* 3rd ed. (Pacific Grove, CA: Brooks/Cole, 1997), pp. 327–341.
15. Simons, *Persuasion,* pp. 23–24, 141–142.
16. Karlyn Campbell, *The Rhetorical Act* (Belmont, CA: Wadsworth, 1982), pp. 69–118.
17. Ibid., pp. 101–116.
18. Ibid., pp. 69–118.
19. Stan Paine, G. Thomas Bellamy, and Barbara Wilcox, *Human Services That Work* (Baltimore: Paul Brooks, 1984), pp. 42–44.
20. Morton Deutsch, *The Resolution of Conflict: Constructive and Destructive Processes* (New Haven, CT: Yale University Press, 1973), pp. 124–152.
21. Segmentation is discussed extensively in marketing literature; see Phillip Kotler, *Principles of Marketing,* 4th ed. (Englewood Cliffs, NJ: Prentice Hall, 1989), pp. 42–46. Also see Simons, *Persuasion,* pp. 143–146.
22. George Brager and Stephen Holloway, *Changing Human Service Organizations* (New York: Free Press, 1978), pp. 199–203.
23. Ibid.

24. See Marya Holcombe and Judith Stein, *Presentations for Decision Makers* (New York: Van Nostrand Reinhold, 1983).

25. Ibid., pp. 16–25.

26. Ibid., pp. 11–13.

27. Simons, *Persuasion,* pp. 124–129, and Robert Reid, *Work of Nations: Preparing Ourselves for the 21st Century* (New York: Knopf, 1991), pp. 154–168.

28. Hedrick Smith, *Rethinking America* (New York: Random House, 1995).

29. Simons, *Persuasion,* pp. 148–154.

30. Ibid., pp. 153–154.

31. Ibid., p. 153.

32. Cegala, *Persuasive Communication,* p. 136.

33. Simons, *Persuasion,* p. 153.

34. Cegala, *Persuasive Communication,* p. 134.

35. See Brager et al., *Community Organizing,* pp. 342–343.

36. Paul Ephross and Thomas Vassil, *Groups That Work* (New York: Columbia University Press, 1988), p. 157.

37. George Sharwell, "How to Testify before a Legislative Committee," in Maryann Mahaffey and John Hanks, eds., *Practical Politics: Social Work and Political Response* (Silver Spring, MD: National Association of Social Workers, 1982), pp. 85–98.

38. Lewis Dexter, "Role Relationships and Conception of Neutrality in Interviewing," *American Journal of Sociology* 62 (September 1956): 153–157.

39. Craig Smith and Eric Skjei, *Getting Grants* (New York: Harper & Row, 1980), pp. 173–181.

40. Armand Lauffer, *Grantsmanship and fund raising* (Beverly Hills, CA: Sage, 1983), pp. 238–246.

41. Ibid., pp. 80–84.

42. Ibid., pp. 236–246.

43. Smith and Skjei, Getting Grants, p. 152.

44. Soraya Coley and Cynthia Scheinberg, *Proposal Writing* (Newbury Park, CA: Sage, 1992).

45. Ibid.

Suggested Readings

Policy-Persuading Strategies

Austin Freeley, *Argumentation and Debate,* 6th ed. (Belmont, CA: Wadsworth, 1986).

Willard Richan, "A Common Language for Social Work," *Social Work* 17 (November 1972): 14–22.

Herbert Simons, *Persuasion,* 2nd ed. (New York: Random House, 1986).

Negotiations and Mediation

Herb Bisno, *Managing Conflict* (Newbury Park, CA: Sage, 1988), pp. 98–147.

Roger Fisher and William Ury, *Getting to Yes: Negotiating Agreement without Giving In* (New York: Penguin Books, 1991).

Jay Folberg and Alison Taylor, *Mediation* (San Francisco: Jossey-Bass, 1984).

Margaret Gibelman and Harold Demone, "Negotiating a Contract: Practical Considerations," in Harold Demone and Margaret Gibelman, eds., *Services for Sale* (New Brunswick, NJ: Rutgers University Press, 1989), pp. 131–148.

Developing Grant Proposals

Soraya Coley and Cynthia Scheinberg, *Proposal Writing* (Newbury Park, CA: Sage, 1992).

Jean Potuchek, "The Context of Social Service Funding: The Funding Relationship," *Social Service Review* (September 1986): 421–436.

ADVOCATING FOR CHANGE

No matter how skilled policy advocates are in accomplishing agenda building, problem analyzing, and proposal writing, their work comes to naught if they cannot get their recommendations enacted, whether in agencies, communities, or legislatures. Therefore the discussions of power and strategy in the next four chapters are critically important to policy advocates.

Chapter Nine discusses how to develop and use power. **Chapter Ten** covers how to develop political strategy. **Chapter Eleven** addresses how to develop and implement political strategy in legislative, community, and agency settings. **Chapter Twelve** discusses how to change the composition of government by participating in electoral politics.

Developing and Using Power

POLICY PREDICAMENT	A social work intern in a mental health agency discovers that no mental health services are provided to children whose parents have been institutionalized for psychiatric problems. She soon discovers numerous political obstacles to the development of such services. What political tactics would she devise? (We present this case in Policy Advocacy Challenge 9.2 after briefly discussing politics.)

Power and politics have a bad reputation among some professionals, who regard them as unseemly—even unethical. However, power and politics can often be used for ethical purposes, and each of us can develop and use power resources to help stigmatized groups and unpopular causes. To help you become an effective policy advocate, this chapter discusses the following:

- The positive functions of politics in policy deliberations
- The transactional nature of power relationships
- Person-to-person and substantive power resources
- Ways to shape policy outcomes indirectly
- Personal characteristics that enhance political effectiveness
- Issues of autonomy, discretion, compliance, and whistle-blowing
- The importance of power differentials
- External and internal vantage points when making policy changes
- Ways that policy practitioners develop power resources
- Ways that members of out-groups encounter challenges when seeking and using power
- The psychology of power as illustrated by intimidation and assertiveness
- The dynamics of task groups, including coalitions and networks

In Defense of Politics

People sometimes call those who are preoccupied with political realities opportunistic, power-hungry, or wedded to special interests. Some truth exists in these assertions, but they obscure how important politics are to policy advocacy. Before discussing some of these functions, we define the word *politics* more precisely. Some people equate politics with government policy making; indeed, one part of Webster's definition declares it "the politics and aims of a government [and] the conduct and contests of political parties."[1] Certainly, these government and party functions belong in a definition of politics, but what about politics in other settings, such as social agencies, professional associations, and communities? Webster's comes to our aid by including in its definition, "the political connections or beliefs of a person [and] the plotting or scheming of those seeking personal power, glory, position, or the like."[2] Webster's choice of *plotting* and *scheming* suggests a disdain for political activity, though the definition includes power-related struggles in any setting. We need a definition that does not cast aspersions on persons who develop and use power, because leaders such as Franklin Roosevelt, Robert Kennedy, Jesse Jackson, and Marian Wright Edelman have used power for noble ends.

At the risk of rewriting the dictionary, let us hazard our own definition. Politics represents efforts by people in governmental and nongovernmental settings to secure their policy wishes by developing and using power resources. When defined in this manner, politics becomes relevant not only to highly placed officials, but to anyone who tries to influence policy making.

It is difficult to imagine a world where politics does not exist, because political processes are endemic in social discourse. (See Policy Advocacy Challenge 9.1.)

POLICY ADVOCACY CHALLENGE 9.1

FAMILIARIZING YOURSELF WITH POLITICAL INSTITUTIONS

Information about politics can be found in many places, such as C-SPAN on cable television, on the Web, and the Internet at an array of Web sites like the following:

The U.S. Senate   This site gives the name and state of each U.S. senator, along with links to their offices to view what issues they are currently focused on. It details what the Senate as a whole is working on, and it offers an opportunity to contact your state's senators via E-mail and to voice your own opinion.

www.senate.gov

The U.S. House of Representatives   This site gives the name and state of each U.S. representative, along with links to their offices to view what issues they are currently working on. It also details what the House as a whole is considering. It offers an opportunity to contact your representative via E-mail and to voice your own opinions.

www.house.gov

(continued)

(9.1   continued)

The White House   Home page for the president and the vice president. This site gives you the opportunity to visit the press room and see what daily activities are occurring at the White House. It also offers an E-mail link for writing to the president or the vice president on issues of importance to you.

www.whitehouse.gov

To access information about your state legislature and your governor, you need to find Web sites specific to your state by consulting your librarian.

Without political recourse, people who lack formal authority would have to obey existing policies or seek remedies through other means, such as force.

The political process in a democracy provides a way for people with conflicting values or opposing positions to resolve their differences. Some policy analysts claim to be purely objective and scientific in their approach, but even they make many value-laden choices in their analyses.[3] Therefore, even an analytic position often requires negotiation through the political process.

Analytic and Political Approaches to Policy Advocacy

The political model differs markedly from the analytic approaches we discussed in the preceding chapters. The analyst wants to discover technically superior solutions to a problem by using quantitative and qualitative techniques, but the adherent of the political approach wants to understand existing political realities to select feasible options and develop an effective political strategy to outmaneuver likely opponents.[4] If the analyst assumes that the truth will win out, the politician assumes that might will prevail. If analysts devote most of their time to technical tasks, political practitioners devote their time to gauging patterns of support for and opposition to specific issues, to developing power, and to implementing political strategy. (Of course, sophisticated policy practitioners can creatively couple analytic and political approaches in specific situations, as we discussed in Chapter Three.) Policy advocates who use a political approach ask questions like those presented in Box 9.1.

BOX 9.1   A Political Model

Distribution of power
- What persons, interests, and factions are likely to participate in certain policy deliberations?
- What are their power resources?
- What are their likely positions on a proposal?
- How strongly do they hold these positions?

Political stakes in an issue
- What political benefits and risks will I encounter if I participate in certain policy deliberations?

BOX 9.1   *(continued)*

- Should I be a leader, a follower, or a bystander?

Political feasibility
- What patterns of opposition and support are likely to be associated with specific policy options?
- Which position, on balance, should I support?

Political strategy
- What power resources do I (or my allies) currently have that are relevant to these deliberations?
- What power resources might I (or my allies) develop that will be relevant to these deliberations?
- What strategies will we use as the deliberations proceed?

Revising strategy
- How should I change my strategy in light of evolving political realities, including my opponents' likely moves?
- As the political realities change, how should my role change?

Let us now consider the policy predicament encountered by the social work intern who wanted to develop innovative services for the children of parents who have been institutionalized for psychiatric reasons. (See Policy Advocacy Challenge 9.2.)

POLICY ADVOCACY CHALLENGE 9.2

DEVELOPING AN INNOVATIVE PROGRAM IN AN INHOSPITABLE SETTING

In this case, a social work intern tries to develop an innovative program in a mental health agency. She notes that the agency, which considers itself an advocate for children's mental health needs, lacks a program to help children whose parents have been institutionalized for psychiatric problems. She hopes to obtain approval for an eight-week crisis model of services to these children but soon realizes that she has encountered numerous political barriers.

It is curious that the Mountain View Child Guidance Clinic considers itself an advocate for children's mental health needs when it neglects children of the psychiatrically hospitalized parent. Such children are in crisis and experiencing extreme family disequilibrium. They need immediate assistance in understanding and dealing constructively with feelings and thoughts associated with this experience. It is preferable that this intervention occur at or near the time of the crisis, when defenses are most fluid and before maladaptive patterns of functioning have solidified. To meet this need, I am trying to develop, in addition to the brief services offered by the clinic, a crisis group for the children of psychiatrically hospitalized parents.

The coordination and cooperation necessary for such a program would be a landmark in the clinic's history. Its success would depend on the referrals of psychiatrists who assist patients admitted to local public and private psychiatric hospitals. If the clinic bypasses the physician's authority and accepts referrals directly from hospitals' social

(continued)

(9.2   continued)

service departments, we would alienate some physicians, who might imperil the program by boycotting it.

Announcements could be sent to the hospitals, their social service departments, and specific physicians. The service must offer support to both the physician and the hospital.

The politics of this agency dictates that the new program not be called preventive, lest funders and policy makers not favor it. Because they believe that no room exists in the budget for prevention, this program will be called crisis intervention.

We could approach four local hospitals with announcements of the new clinic program. A follow-up phone call would add a personal touch and hopefully clinch the process. As a staff member, I would persuade physician friends of its merit, while soliciting their support.

There are a number of barriers to change in this agency. The clinic focuses its energy on the quantity rather than the quality of services. Of primary importance to the executive director is avoiding a waiting list. To this end, he mobilizes all forces and automatically shelves any program change that would conflict with this aim. Further, staff are usually inundated with work and have little time to create innovative services. Similarly, the agency values efficiency in programming and expenditures. Clinic executives believe that they cannot afford to risk any revenue by applying funds to areas other than those directly funded and approved. Another barrier to innovation is the agency staff's disinclination to participate in program development, which deprives the agency of new program ideas. Staff members seek what fulfillment is available through the clients themselves and leave the business of the clinic to the bureaucracy.

I am only a student intern in this agency, but I want to get this innovation off the ground before my field experience ends. Considering the nature of the agency, it is essential to introduce the change in an administratively sanctioned way through approved channels. Therefore, I initially broached the idea of the innovation to the director of outpatient services, Mr. Jones, who is my preceptor for short-term and intake cases. On first mentioning the plan, I was careful to make it appear to be an idea that I had developed in the course of discussions with him. I told him I saw the idea as consistent with comprehensive mental health care for children, an ideal he often espouses. Underscoring that the services would take only eight weeks, which he likes, and stressing its efficiency in terms of the waiting list, I ventured to actually propose a pilot plan. He groaned and suggested that I "write it up," with no explanation of what that meant. Rather than irritate him further, I did not mention the project for several weeks. I then told my regular field instructor that I was discussing with Mr. Jones a new program for the children of hospitalized patients, and I received her approval to use this project as a learning experience in program design.

Several weeks later, I found that Mr. Jones had completely forgotten my plan. But in further discussion, he expressed strong interest and even brainstormed an initial strategy with me that would help the innovation gain gradual support in the Mountain View Child Guidance Clinic. He argued that we should develop a two-phase strategy. In phase one, I would develop a pilot project. Because I am a student intern, it would not need formal clearance by high-level executives or the agency board. He would simply notify the executive that a student intern was establishing a pilot group for children of institutionalized parents. He urged a low profile during this initial period. After we initiated the project, he would develop a strategy for a formal proposal that would go to the executive director and hopefully eventually to the board. That would be phase two. If all went well, the agency would formally earmark funds for the program. He hoped that my experience with the pilot project would provide useful information for writing the formal proposal and presenting it orally to the executive and the board. He concluded our meeting by saying, "You know you will have to do the entire program in the pilot phase. All the screening and everything." He seemed tantalized by the idea of obtaining increased service with no additional expenditure of staff time.

To date, I have succeeded in involving Mr. Jones in planning sufficiently to encourage his sense of investment in the program. I have abided by the rules in recognizing his authority and decision-making powers and deemphasizing my own initiative. My short-term strategy, then, is to begin the program myself. But a number of obstacles could still interfere with program acceptance by key decision makers, even during the pilot phase.

One obstacle is the issue of community coordination. Currently, the clinic has superficial coordination with local mental health agencies, exchanging cases only sporadically. No clear plan exists for coordination of services. This program necessitates an intermediate type of coordination, a case-planning coordination organized into a whole-family approach. The current fragmentation in the treatment of families with a disturbed member would be a danger to this program, because it would undermine the purpose of comprehensive care. What factors are involved in this coordination process?

First, there is the issue of goal conflict. On the surface, there appears to be little; both the psychiatric hospitals and the clinic serve and are concerned with families' mental health needs. But is that really the case? In fact, the hospitals view the treatment of the parent-patient from a pathology rather than a family systems perspective. Therefore, they may choose to refer the child not for group, but for individual treatment as an "impaired" family member. It will be important to impress on these staff members that the groups help the child in crisis, rather than provide long-term therapy. With regard to the power relationships between agencies, the major snare seems to be the physicians' autonomy. The administrators of local psychiatric hospitals may perceive the children's group as highlighting their own program deficiencies and therefore may choose to provide a similar service themselves.

At present, the agencies do not consider themselves interdependent. Instead, they coexist in separate realms of the psychiatric community and rarely communicate. More positively, though, they may cooperate with this project, not only because of the children's emotional needs, but also because child and adult agencies are complementary community services that do not usually compete for the same clientele.

To alleviate some of the tension between agencies and to facilitate the common goal of improved community mental health, I will plan individual visits to each hospital's social services department. I may be invited to present this program to the monthly meeting of hospital psychiatrists, an opportunity for a direct encounter with most of the staff physicians. In addition, I will invite representatives of each hospital to the clinic for an orientation and open house, which should improve relationships between clinic and hospital and emphasize the community nature of the project.

Within the clinic itself, a political process will follow the initiation of this program. When Mr. Jones seeks its official approval, he must submit it to the medical director for

(continued)

(9.2   continued)

confirmation; he in turn will take it to the executive committee for approval, and they will then present it to the board of directors for final approval. However, because Mr. Jones is the most powerful person in the agency, his approval should lead to its acceptance.

A complicating factor is the director of training, Ida Brown. To be candid, she does not particularly like Mr. Jones and often opposes any proposals he initiates. She may interfere in the decision-making process by pushing for a nondecision; that is, she may suggest that the plan be initiated only after lengthy study or pending the location of special sources of external funding. Another problem may arise because many in the agency focus on the child of an institutionalized adult as a patient, a view that clashes with the program's preventive mission.

I also see several other groups developing in relation to the program. One consists of the senior administrator and the chief of program development (also the director of support services). These two men are allied in their unstated mission to increase clinic prestige and influence in the community. They will probably support the program from their stated position of commitment to enriching the quality of the services available to the community. This position would appear reasonable and would underscore the senior administrator's interest in the efficient business operation of the clinic.

The executive director himself will probably support the program in deference to Mr. Jones, to whom he defers on all issues pertaining to the outpatient services of the agency. The outpatient service functions virtually independently of the day-treatment and other components of the agency.

The medical director is also a figurehead, whose medical degree is valued by the agency. He will most assuredly remain neutral lest he find himself in the middle of a political battle. He appears to have little power in the agency.

The board of directors also has little power in this agency. The members are most concerned about what mural is painted on which wall and how chairs are grouped in the waiting room. Program development is not their expertise, and they usually abide agreeably by decisions made by the executive director.

In the future, I see this program as an integral part of the clinic's services, if it can survive the pilot and approval stages. The children served during their first experience with a parent's hospitalization may choose to return to us if the parent is rehospitalized. Children who have experienced numerous parental hospitalizations will be able to compare previous episodes with the one eased by clinic services. We may then see self-referrals by children and families, reducing the need for physician referrals.

Mr. Jones wants me to assist him in writing the formal proposal after my pilot project has been in operation for five months. The project has made me realize that good clinical skills need to be supplemented by program design and political skills. How else can social workers develop and institute innovative services?

Exercise   List both barriers to this innovation and potential sources of support. Remember, of course, that some barriers can be eliminated or partly addressed by the strategy of the social work intern.

If you had encountered this situation and had wanted to obtain this mental health innovation, would you have persevered, or would you have decided not to proceed because too many political barriers existed? Does a danger exist of prematurely deciding that the "glass is half empty"? In the case of the children who needed help while a parent was institutionalized, what ethical implications might the intern have faced had she decided to discontinue her effort?

How does this case illustrate the adage that many people fail to secure their policy objectives because they prematurely discount their power resources? What power resources did this intern have?[5]

SOURCE: This case is adapted from one by Stacy Stern, M.S.W. Names and locations have been altered.

The Nature of Power

If politics is both inevitable and, at least in some cases, beneficial, policy advocates have to understand political power and develop skill in using it. We will first discuss the transactional nature of power relationships and then analyze the power resources that people use in these relationships. We will use the case presented in Policy Advocacy Challenge 9.2 to illustrate power and how it is used.

When the social work intern wanted to develop an innovative program to help children, she realized at once that various barriers to preventive programs existed in the agency. In this simple two-person situation, where X "sends" power and Y "receives" it, X succeeds in exercising power by convincing Y to take an action that he would not otherwise have taken. The social work intern has exercised power with her preceptor, Mr. Jones, if he assents to a program that he would not otherwise have supported.[6] (The intern has not exercised power if Mr. Jones would have initiated the innovation anyway.)

If X uses physical coercion, Y has virtually no choice—for example, when a criminal suspect is forced to enter a police car at gunpoint. In some situations, it is difficult to determine the line between voluntariness and coercion; for example, people in desperate economic straits may feel forced to accede to requests if they fear the loss of their jobs. However, some people do leave jobs to follow the dictates of their conscience.[7] Were the intern to make Mr. Jones support the innovation by holding a gun to his head, she would be forcing him to make this decision. We agree with Peter Bachrach and Morton Baratz that force is not power, because it gives people little or no choice.[8]

Real power involves transactional rather than unilateral relationships and choices.[9] The receiver in a power transaction (Y) can choose whether to accede to the sender's (X's) suggestions. Y has many options; for example, he or she could refuse to follow X's suggestions, voice indecision, agree but not really mean it, agree enthusiastically, or respond ambiguously. The social work intern had to discuss the program innovation with Mr. Jones on two occasions before he formally committed himself to her project. He gave only symbolic support on the first occasion (probably not wishing to discourage the intern), having completely forgotten the plan when the intern reintroduced the idea several weeks later. However, he seemed to support the idea enthusiastically on the second occasion, even initiating ideas about strategy. If the exercise of power is transactional, the actions of both partners must be examined. We can portray power relationships graphically by placing arrows between X and Y, as in Figure 9.1.

Power's transactional nature has important consequences for political strategy. Even in this simple two-person example, success in using power hinges on a number of considerations. X first has to decide that a particular issue warrants the expenditure of power. The intern's commitment to children's well-being, as well as to preventive mental health, led her to put effort into securing the innovation. (We discuss the intern's power resources later.)

Power often enters into transactions that involve more than two persons. (See Figure 9.2.) We first discuss the transactional nature of power to provide an overview and then move on to power resources. As a person with little formal power, the intern realized that officials in the upper reaches of the organization ultimately would have to approve the plan. Because she could not shape their actions directly, she had to work through Mr. Jones, hoping that he would convince them to support the innovation.[10] In this case, two sets of transactional relationships exist; the intern (X) tries to convince Mr. Jones (now Z) so that he will persuade, say, the director of medical services (Y). See Figure 9.2, where the dashed line signifies the intern's exerting power over the medical director by using Mr. Jones as an intermediary. (Intermediaries are commonly used in legislatures and agencies.) We will now discuss the various power resources people use with other people in power relationships, including person-to-person power, substantive power, and indirect power.

Person-to-Person Power

Policy advocates sometimes exert power in personal discussions with others. We call this *person-to-person power.* In their classic article, John French and Bertram Craven discuss expertise, coercion, rewards, charisma, and authority as power resources.[11] When using *expertise,* senders display their personal credentials and knowledge to convince others. For such entreaties to be effective, of course, the receivers have to believe that the senders are experts. The student intern in Policy Advocacy Challenge 9.2 realized that high-level officials would be more likely to approve her innovation after its successful implementation as a pilot project. After this success, they could argue, as experts, "We know how to implement this kind of innovation."

Policy advocates use *coercive power* when they threaten penalties, for instance, by hinting at the loss of a job, a promotion, or a desirable position if another person does not support a specific policy. Politicians may threaten to punish opponents by opposing legislation they want, cutting programs or funds from their districts, or not granting them

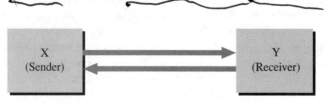

FIGURE 9.1   Direct power transactions

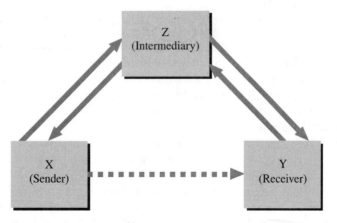

FIGURE 9.2   Indirect power transactions

positions on key committees. Threats may backfire as well, because they may alienate people.

When using *reward power,* policy advocates promise inducements, such as promotions, pay increases, financial or other support in upcoming campaigns, and bribes. They may also promise a quid pro quo. They will support someone's policy request in return for that person's support.[12] Like coercive power, reward power backfires if people believe they have been unfairly pressured to adopt a position that offends their ethical sensibilities.

Charismatic power derives from personal qualities of leadership, moral authority, and persuasiveness and is used to stimulate others to follow their wishes. The *power of authority* stems from one's position in an organization's hierarchy: Followers hope to receive rewards and avoid sanctions by following their superiors' suggestions. Persons who use the power of authority try to influence the actions of subordinates in several ways. They may imply that it is the duty of employees to follow the wishes of persons with higher rank. They may suggest that persons who deviate from their wishes will suffer repercussions, such as demotion or loss of employment. Or they may reward persons who accede to their wishes. In practice, then, power that derives from the organizational hierarchy is often coupled with coercive and reward power.

We have discussed person-to-person power in dyads, but it is also used when a sender gives presentations to groups. An executive might say to his or her whole staff, for example, "Support this policy or our agency will suffer severe financial repercussions" (coercive power), or a politician might say to a neighborhood group, "Have people vote for me if you want this neighborhood improvement" (reward power).

Person-to-person power also can extend to third parties. One person may ask another to intervene with a third person, as when a politician asks an ally to persuade a fellow legislator to support specific legislation. Even a third party's possible intentions are a source of person-to-person power, as in the suggestion that a funder may harm an agency if it fails to adopt certain policies. A person also might invoke a third party's expertise by citing the research findings of a respected academician.

Person-to-person power is most effective when the sender selects the kind of power that the receiver is likely to honor. The receiver may respond to expertise, for example, but not to coercion. Effective users of power learn as much as they can about the predispositions of the people they seek to influence.

We have already noted the importance of selecting power resources carefully and applying them skillfully. Practitioners who use expertise as a power resource, for example, have to marshal persuasive evidence and make the receiver believe that the expert really is an expert.[13]

Power resources can be used singly or in tandem. An advocate may use both a carrot (reward power) and a stick (coercive power) in persuasion and may try different power resources over time; if one fails, another may work.

People sometimes ask those they fear will oppose their views for advice on a difficult issue. Persons are often flattered to be consulted and are less likely to oppose a proposal when they have contributed some of its features. We sometimes call this method of increasing power *co-optation*. For example, the student intern solicited Mr. Jones's advice and intimated that the innovation had evolved in her discussions with him.

Substantive Power

People often form opinions about a policy, not because they have been encouraged to support or oppose it, but because of how they view its substantive content. Policy practitioners exercise *substantive power* when they shape the content of policies to elicit support from specific persons. For example, two persons favor providing low-income housing subsidies in a government program, but one wants the subsidies to go only to people below poverty standards, while the other also wants the subsidies to go to people with moderate incomes. The initiator of the housing-subsidy proposal might decide against a precise definition of the income levels, hoping that both persons will vote for it. Indeed, vagueness is often an effective tactic when persons disagree about the specific details of a proposal.[14] Of course, vagueness also can be counterproductive because an excessively vague proposal will arouse the opposition of those who strongly favor specific measures. Moreover, when key points of legislation are not defined, the implementers of the legislation have more leeway. If one party believes the other party will control the presidency (and thus the top appointive positions in implementing agencies), they will want to make key points specific so their political foes cannot implement the legislation contrary to their wishes. For example, in 1988, some Democrats, fearing that Republicans would not insist on minimum child-to-staff ratios when implementing a national day-care proposal, tried to place specific ratios in the federal legislation.[15]

Policy advocates exercise substantive power when they change a policy's content to enhance specific decision makers' support for it. In the aforementioned day-care proposal, its advocates inserted many provisions to counter conservatives' opposition, such as putting a modest ceiling on the program's costs and giving the states a significant role in shaping the programs within their boundaries. These changes may be made when a proposal is initially drafted, during deliberations, or when the proposal goes before a legislature or other decision-making body. Substantive power often involves compromises; one faction may modify one provision in exchange for another faction's changing another provision.

Policy advocates encounter, dilemmas when using substantive power. They may change a policy proposal to obtain one person's support, only to find that they have alienated someone else. When they make numerous concessions to obtain opponents' support, proposals may become so diluted as to be, in the words of Bachrach and Baratz, "decisionless decisions" or merely symbolic measures.[16]

For example, Senator Hubert Humphrey and Representative Augustus Hawkins initiated a legislative proposal in the 1970s requiring the federal government to create jobs whenever the national unemployment rate exceeded 3%. By the time the legislation was enacted, it was only a vague statement that the federal government would seek full employment. It required no specific actions, such as developing public works when considerable unemployment existed.[17] Skillful policy practitioners often refrain from offering changes in a proposal until they are certain that compromises are needed for its passage.

A policy advocate using substantive power also may couple a relatively unpopular proposal with more popular ones. In "Christmas-tree legislation" (so named because of the "gifts" many legislators place in it for certain persons or interest groups) in Congress, politicians insert various previously unenacted proposals in a larger piece of legislation just before the yearly congressional session finishes at the end of December. Politicians who oppose these inserted measures nonetheless vote for the legislation because it contains some of their own measures.[18] A controversial proposal may be swept to victory when it is attached to a popular proposal. Foes of abortion, for example, won prohibition of the use of Medicaid funds for abortions when they attached it to the appropriations bill for the Department of Health and Human Services.[19]

Proponents have many ways to shape a proposal so that it is nonthreatening to potential opponents. A program may be designed and portrayed as a pilot project to defuse opposition.[20] Proponents may place a proposed program under a specific government unit's jurisdiction to make it more appealing to potential opponents. Proponents enhanced support for the Supplementary Security Income (SSI) program, which provides income to destitute older people and people who are disabled, by proposing that it be placed under the jurisdiction of the Social Security Administration, because that unit of government was more acceptable to conservatives than units that administer welfare programs.[21] Proposals titles are often selected to make them more acceptable to conservative politicians. Senator Moynihan emphasized family support payments rather than welfare payments when discussing a welfare reform initiative in 1988.[22]

Christopher Matthews contends that many successful politicians avoid discussing basic principles when considering legislation.[23] Realizing that mentioning fundamental principles often alienates valuable allies with different perspectives from their own, they focus instead on the precise details of the legislation. It is better, they reason, to win battles over the content of legislation than to have shouting matches about ultimate purposes. On the other hand, an enunciation of basic principles is needed in some cases to rally support for a measure.

Using Indirect Power

Until now, we have discussed the use of power in direct transactional relationships. However, people also can use power indirectly by influencing decision-making procedures and the process and context of deliberations.

Power in Decision–Making Procedures

Policy is often fashioned by *decision-making* or *procedural power* during deliberations. In legislatures, for example, numerous people and committees, and finally the full body must assent to a policy before it can be enacted.[24] (Recall Figure 4.3 depicting the normal course of legislation through both chambers of the Congress.)

There are many parliamentary techniques and strategies for increasing a proposal's chances of enactment, or for blocking a proposal: bypassing persons, committees, and meetings unfavorable to the proposal, while routing the proposal to those more favorable; persuading party officials to steer a proposal to the committee most favorably disposed or to leapfrog a meeting or procedure; and using person-to-person power with key decision makers, such as chairs of important committees, not only to obtain their support, but also to secure their assistance with logistic details. A committee chair can place a proposal in a preferred position on a meeting agenda, insist that policies undergo further subcommittee deliberations, or abbreviate lengthy deliberations to help or prevent a specific measure's enactment. Clever strategists are well versed in such tactics.[25]

Procedural tactics are sometimes counterproductive, however, provoking accusations of unfairly stifling dissent by rushing a proposal through a legislature, stacking the cards for or against a proposal, or bypassing normal channels. Ethical objections may also be raised when concerned persons are excluded from policy deliberations.

When initiating proposals, it is necessary to know who the key decision makers are, whether they favor a proposal, and whether the opposition can be overcome. In the early years of the Reagan administration, Republicans chaired the U.S. Senate committees because their party had a majority in the Senate. White House staff members and these Republican chairs mobilized party support for bills that Republicans favored. Disgruntled Democrats discovered that many of their legislative initiatives never made it beyond these committee chairs, even when they had considerable support in the House, where the Democrats were in the majority. When the Democrats regained control of the Senate in the 1986 elections, they, in turn, used their control of the Senate committee chairs to scuttle many of the legislative proposals of the Reagan administration.[26]

Decision-making procedures also exist in agencies. A staff member, committee, or executive may propose a new agency program, which is then developed by a staff committee and brought to the full staff for consideration. The executive then may take it to the board of directors, which may refer it to a board committee before taking a final vote. Or simpler procedures might be used: A hospital social services director wants to develop social work services on the neurology ward and only seeks the agreement of the medical director of neurology. After the services have been in effect for some time, the staff member obtains formal approval from a higher hospital official, perhaps when he needs additional funding from the hospital's budget.

In Policy Advocacy Challenge 9.2, the social work intern carefully considered procedural options as she developed a strategy for her program innovation. Because of barriers to this innovation in the agency, such as tight budgets, the intern and her preceptor decided the innovation would be doomed if they began with a formal proposal to the executive director. Therefore, they planned a two-phase strategy: first to develop a pilot project without securing formal high-level clearance, and then, after proving the program workable, to develop a formal program proposal that would go through the executive director to the board for approval. The intern and the preceptor improved their proposal's chances not through efforts to convince other people of its merits, but by shaping the decision-making process.

Process Power

Policies are shaped in the give-and-take of deliberations, which are characterized by their tenor, tempo, and scope of conflict. The *tenor* is the level of conflict; the *tempo* is the timing, pace, and duration of deliberations; and the *scope of conflict* is the number and kind of people who participate in them. Policy advocates use *process power* when they influence the tenor, tempo, or scope of conflict of deliberations in order to get a specific proposal enacted.

Let's begin with the crude analogy of a schoolyard dispute to illustrate process power. After the two parties have developed their positions in the dispute, they must decide how to resolve it. First, they shape the tenor of deliberations: Will they use brute strength (a fight), have an amicable discussion, or take some middle course in which they shout at each other but do not fight? Next, each must decide what tempo of deliberations will help their cause: Will they seek a speedy settlement or protracted deliberations? Finally, they determine who should participate in the conflict: Do they want a narrow scope of conflict that will exclude outsiders from their interaction or will they invite others to join the fray, in the belief that a broad scope of conflict will help their cause.[27]

A bully with physical superiority might decide to initiate a fight, whereas the proverbial 90-pound weakling might want to expand the scope of conflict to include powerful allies. One side might want to resolve the issue speedily so the opponents won't have time to organize an attack. The opponents might decide that their cause will benefit from relatively low conflict and the use of behind-the-scenes deliberations from which the other side is effectively screened.[28] The social work intern in Policy Advocacy Challenge 9.2 wanted to keep her innovation low profile during its pilot phase so it would not create controversy.

We can usefully contrast win-lose politics with win-win politics. In win-lose politics, each side in the contest believes that it loses each time the other side wins and therefore wants to contest every point. In win-win politics, the two sides believe they will obtain mutually beneficial concessions. While they do not want to concede all points, they are open to compromise so they will both emerge better off than before deliberations. It would be a more pleasant world if people perceived win-win possibilities in more conflicts and transformed these conflicts into win-win situations. In many cases, however, this approach is not feasible. Parties may have conflicting values, may not trust their opponents, and may believe they will suffer severe losses if they make concessions.

Individuals can influence the level of conflict. People who wish to intensify discord, for example, can use emotion-laden words; refer to conflicts in the fundamental values at stake; enlarge the scope of conflict by publicizing the issue; use unusual tactics, such as the filibuster in the U.S. Senate; or clearly state that they do not want amicable resolution: "We plan to fight to the finish," or "We will accept no significant changes in our proposal!"[29] People who believe that conflict will be detrimental to their cause will try to diminish conflict, for example, by emphasizing a proposal's technical features, identifying the common interests of all the parties, and discouraging the participation of those who will raise the level of conflict.

Timing is another kind of process power. The timing of a disputed proposal often favors a specific side. If someone introduces a proposal at an inopportune moment, its chances may be imperiled, no matter how skillful its defenders or how great its merits. Whether in agency or legislative settings, such background factors as budgetary deficits, a crowded agenda, or an unsympathetic executive provide a harsh environment for a policy proposal. When a favorable context exists, a proposal defeated earlier may suddenly sail through the political process.[30]

Unfortunately, policy advocates often have limited power to influence the political process because of limited control over the actions of their opponents. Someone who wants to limit conflict, for example, may find that goal sabotaged by opponents who succeed in escalating conflict or enlarging the scope of conflict by publicizing it in the mass media—as the frequent leaks to the press about government business suggest. Even skillful policy advocates miscalculate. Someone who introduces a proposal at a seemingly opportune moment may later become aware of background factors that will scuttle it. Moreover, policy processes often develop a momentum that cannot be slowed, no matter what advocates do.[31] Tradition also frustrates policy advocacy: Issues that have previously generated high conflict, such as national health insurance, are sure to stir up conflict if reintroduced.[32] The dimensions of a proposed change also shape the course of conflict; proposals for massive changes are more likely to polarize liberals and conservatives than more modest proposals.[33]

Shaping Contexts

We have already noted that power transactions occur within a context that includes public opinion and interest groups.

We have focused on the tactics of individuals in power relationships, but power relationships are profoundly influenced by the affiliations of policy advocates with advocacy groups (sometimes called *interest groups*) and coalitions. Politicians are more likely to take the advice of an advocate who is backed up by affiliation with a recognized group or coalition. Such affiliations give advocates several advantages. Recognized groups or coalitions can mobilize external pressure by activating their members and those of affiliated organizations. As a result, they are more likely than solo advocates to get attention from the mass media, particularly as they develop long-standing associations with reporters and officials in television and the print media. Because they can obtain funds from foundations and other sources more easily than solo advocates can, advocacy groups and coalitions can conduct more sophisticated research than solo advocates—research that enhances their standing with legislators and government officials. And because advocacy groups are long-standing organizations, their staff can develop ongoing associations with government officials and legislators, as well as close working relationships with the staff of other advocacy groups that allow them to pool resources, share contacts, and form coalitions around specific issues. It is not sufficient only to develop advocacy groups and coalitions, however; policy advocates need also to enlist them in well-conceived campaigns to secure policy reforms.

Sometimes policy advocates can use a low scope of conflict, relying on personal relationships with policy makers to bring policy changes. In such cases, advocates do not mobilize external pressure on legislators because they believe they can secure policy reforms without it. In other cases, however, they do need to mobilize external pressure in a well-coordinated campaign that includes letter writing, coverage by the mass media, and even demonstrations.

Policy advocates should try, then, to work with and through advocacy groups and coalitions whenever possible. If such groups do not exist, policy advocates should form them. (We discuss strategies for organizing coalitions in the next chapter.)

External pressure can also be placed on social agencies. As Yeheskel Hasenfeld and other organizational theorists with a political economy perspective note, organizational policies are shaped by many forces.[34] Funders, courts, community groups, and community leaders all can shape organizations' internal policies. Just as policy advocates sometimes pressure legislators, they sometimes pressure social agencies to modify specific policies or to consider program innovations. For example, in the 1960s, local chapters of the National Welfare Rights Organization frequently picketed or sent delegations to local welfare offices to challenge discriminatory practices.

Hedrick Smith argues that television has revolutionized political tactics in Congress, especially since the decline in power of political party leaders and legislative committees. The committees have lost power because of procedural changes and an increase in party members' power to choose their committee memberships.[35] Viewing themselves as quasi-independent of their party and seeking a national as well as a local constituency, many politicians regularly make videotapes that they forward to the media in their constituencies. Through the mass media, then, politicians increase public support for issues they believe will enhance their popularity. Advocacy groups and coalitions also need to make skillful use of the mass media, as we discuss in Chapter 13, by having press conferences, writing editorials, briefing reporters, and staging media events.

Successful Power Users

Personal characteristics—*persistence,* for example—increase some persons' ability to shape policy outcomes. (See Video Clip 10.1.) Jane Addams and Martin Luther King, Jr., persevered over decades despite repeated failures in their quest for social justice. Even our student intern, who might have been discouraged by her preceptor's initial irritation about her proposed innovation, brought up the issue again several weeks later and secured a positive response. As we noted in Chapter Five when discussing agenda building, some issues float for years and then resurface when someone is sufficiently persistent to reintroduce the measure.

VIDEO CLIP 9.1

SUCCESSFUL CHANGE AGENTS

In viewing Video Clip 9.1, consider the following. Dr. Anneka Scranton, Clinical Professor, School of Social Work, University of Southern California, discusses her perspectives about power and assertiveness.

Policy advocates who focus on an issue's content and avoid attacking the motivations or character of their opponents are often viewed more positively than those who make personal attacks.[36] As we point out in the next chapter, even though we often have to respond to unfair attacks on our intentions or motivations, we do not usually enhance our personal power by initiating such attacks.

Although skillful policy advocates are flexible, they do not bend with every breeze. Personal credibility, which is essential to the effective use of power, will be eroded if they seem excessively opportunistic. They must be able to stick to their basic convictions, even in the face of opposition.

However, successful policy advocates also are skilled in fashioning compromises, which are frequently needed to obtain support in agency and legislative settings.[37] A fine line sometimes exists between having convictions and being able to compromise.

Power in Organizations

We have discussed power relationships and power resources, using many examples from legislative settings. As our example of the social work intern suggests, power relationships and power resources also are used extensively in social agencies as advocates try to improve services for clients. We now discuss a special kind of policy issue that many social workers confront at some point in their professional work: when to challenge policies or practices that they believe to be unethical and that are supported by higher level staff and officials.

Discretion, Compliance, and Whistle-Blowing

The interrelationship of discretion, compliance, and whistle-blowing confronts direct-service and other social service staff throughout their careers. Considerable controversy may exist in an agency about how much discretion, or autonomy, policy makers and administrators should grant human service workers. Under what circumstances should social workers be able to disobey policies they believe are unethical? When should social workers take their disagreements about internal agency matters to external parties, such as the mass media?

Defining Zones of Discretion

When analyzing policy implementation, we often think in broad terms, such as agency budgets and leadership, taking a top-down perspective. We also can take a bottom-up perspective by beginning with the line worker, who translates policy into action.

High-level policies may seem to dictate virtually all the actions of direct-service staff. However, much of their work occurs within zones of discretion, where their own judgments and choices shape their actions.[38]

Why do agencies cede so much discretion to their direct-service staff? Assume that you are a high-level administrator and are quite certain about the intake policies you want in your agency's program for children with learning disorders. You can write some definitive admission standards, such as "Only children from families with XYZ income shall obtain admittance to this program." Because this kind of policy is quantitative, it is clear-cut and allows no exceptions. However, when you come to "learning disorders," you despair of writing an exact definition, and you must cede to those who will implement this policy considerable discretion in selecting children with learning disorders.

Moreover, you must let professional workers determine when a child has reached sufficient learning competence to make her or him ineligible for continuing service. Realizing that some people will need extended help and others may overcome their problems quickly, you decide against a blanket rule that establishes a maximum period of service.

Our discussion suggests that professionals are given so much discretion because they often are required to use their own judgment on complex social problems, human motivation, and clients' progress. High-level officials may also decide that professionals need the latitude to make exceptions to policies. Assume, for example, that legislators are aware that some psychotic patients need to be committed to institutions even though they are not suicidal and have not physically threatened other persons, the criteria usually used for involuntary commitment. Legislators may add professional judgment to those criteria, even though such discretion may sometimes lead to unnecessary commitment.

In connection with the autonomy of direct-service workers, we must note as well that the location and nature of their work precludes detailed oversight. Direct-service workers conduct much of their work in private interactions with clients. Moreover, many human services agencies do not conform to the bureaucratic models discussed by Max Weber; rather than having tight controls in centralized structures, many of them are "loosely coupled" organizations with several quasi-independent programs, units, and branches. In such organizations, it is difficult for top administrators to regulate the work of direct-service staff.[39]

Ceding discretion to professionals bears some risks and may lead to discrimination against certain clients in the name of professional judgment. A professional may decide that people with specific learning disorders should not be allowed into a program, because he or she is prejudiced against them has erroneous perceptions of their condition.[40]

Some professionals take advantage of the discretion allowed them to further their own material interests or their own narrow approach to service delivery. Franklin Chu and Sharland Trotter discovered that many mental health professionals failed to implement federally legislated policies because they were uninterested in working with psychotic or low-income persons.[41] A few social workers have even siphoned clients from their public agency for their private practice, despite the widely held ethical norms that prohibit this practice.

There is a constant tension between maximizing professional discretion and making binding rules to prevent discrimination against particular clients and to protect the public interest. If professionals often want to expand their discretion, policy makers often want to constrict it.

Issues of Compliance

A social worker in a public welfare setting dislikes specific, punitive policies. A social worker in a child welfare office objects to pressures to reunify families that have not been adequately analyzed or helped. Social workers who do not want to implement specific policies can adopt several strategies. First, they can keep their noncompliance secret even from their supervisors by bending or ignoring rules, by enforcing rules halfheartedly, or by counseling clients in ways that circumvent specific policies. Second, they can comply with official policy but use every available means to seek exemptions for specific persons. For example, to help an older person avoid early discharge from a hospital, they might claim that no nursing home beds can be found, after a half-hearted look for a bed, or they may even even lie about a bed's availability. (Such deception returns us to the first strategy.) Third, they may comply with official policy in every respect, even while believing it to be defective. Fourth, they may comply with official policies while trying to change them.

No easy answers exist for such dilemmas. The duty to obey official policy cannot be dismissed lightly; professionals' credibility would be severely jeopardized if they routinely flouted the rules. Yet some policies are unethical or harmful to clients, whether to all clients or just to those with idiosyncratic needs. Beneficence requires us to consider disobeying policies that appear to be inimical to clients' needs or to be in violation of professional ethics. However, it is difficult to protest policies when high-level officials strongly promote them or when agency officials fear that higher authorities, such as legislators, will retaliate if they discover noncompliance.

By the same token, direct-service social workers sometimes find that their colleagues do not implement good policies. (Social workers may fail to implement meritorious policies because they have narrow helping philosophies that deemphasize such activities as outreach, they believe they lack the necessary expertise or resources, they feel burned out, or they are prejudiced against certain kinds of clients.) In such cases, social workers should try to change their colleagues' behavior through educational techniques or technical assistance, or even by alerting higher management to the noncompliance. Changing peers' behavior can pose a formidable challenge, however, particularly when the agency atmosphere is not conducive to challenging the norms.

Whistle-Blowing

Individual staff members should try to work through normal channels, but what if they find specific policies or other staff members' actions (such as corruption) so morally flawed that they cannot abide their continuation? And what if they fear that open opposition will cause their dismissal or other penalties? An emerging literature suggests that staff members can ethically publicize flawed policies and actions by divulging information to persons outside the organization, such as members of the mass media, legislators, state authorities, regulators, or funders.[42] They can reveal this information to outsiders, either using their own names or speaking on condition of anonymity in order to prevent personal reprisals. However, whistle-blowers who make their names public are sometimes perceived as more credible than those who leak charges anonymously. They also can give the information to the National Association of Social Workers (NASW), which will protect their identity while making the information public.

Whistle-blowing is an attempt to correct lapses by calling external parties into the conflict. It is ethical if the policies or actions are major, not trivial, violations of ethics or professional standards; if the whistle-blower has extremely good evidence that he or she cannot modify policies by conventional means; and if the whistle-blower has excellent evidence that he or she will be subjected to serious penalties as a result of raising questions about the policies or conduct. (Despite recent legislation in some states that protects whistle-blowers, as well as sanctions that the NASW can exact against employers who fire whistle-blowers, persons sometimes have justifiable reason to believe that they will be in jeopardy if they engage in whistle-blowing.) At the same time, whistle-blowing is abused when persons raise trivial issues, such as minor indiscretions in an agency, or when they have not fully considered alternative means of changing policies.[43]

Our prior discussion of discretion suggests that social workers often encounter not objectionable high-level policies, but vague policies that require them to develop means of filling the policy vacuum.

Exerting External Pressure

We have discussed power that policy advocates use within agency and legislative settings, but they may also try to influence policy makers from outside, whether from community groups, external agencies, coalitions, interest groups, or professional associations.

As we have discussed, legislators often respond to pressure from lobbyists, interest groups, experts, officials within the government, and constituents. These people may exert pressure during personal interactions in legislators' offices, at social gatherings, during legislative hearings, or by correspondence. In some cases, legislators themselves bear the brunt of the pressure, while on other occasions, lobbyists and constituents try to persuade legislators' aides.[44]

Policy advocates often encourage these sources of external pressure to convince legislators that they will suffer severe repercussions from opposition to a measure. But pressure must be carefully timed, focused, and planned so that it contributes to support for a specific proposal.[45] Unfocused pressure is sometimes counterproductive; for example, letter-writing campaigns that use form letters (politicians like individualized expressions of support) or conflicting testimony by coalition members at legislative hearings. Pressure is particularly effective when it is carefully timed to precede important votes.

Supporters of a proposal often form coalitions of diverse groups and institutions to exert pressure on politicians. (We discuss coalitions in more detail in the next chapter.)

Power Differentials

So far, our discussion may falsely suggest that all of us have an equal opportunity to wield power, and that if we just put our minds to the task, we will succeed in having policy proposals enacted. This optimistic conclusion ignores harsh realities, such as the power differentials that give some people a significant advantage over others.

Legislators and high-level government officials have *formal authority*, which gives them the power to approve or disapprove certain policy initiatives; to make proposals; and to obtain access to program, budget, and technical information. They have access to other highly placed people who yield information and assistance that are not available to others, and they often command obedience from others when they issue directives or make recommendations. Executives of agencies and government bureaucracies have considerable power over their subordinates, as well as experience and knowledge. Technical experts on specific topics often have extraordinary power in governmental and agency settings.

The leaders, staff members, and lobbyists of groups that have large constituencies, such as interest groups, professional associations, and social movements, derive power from these constituencies that can exert influence on decision makers who do not heed policy suggestions. These leaders, staff members, and lobbyists also have useful expertise that helps them cultivate personal relationships with decision makers that further enhance their power. Some interest groups increase their power by making large campaign contributions to politicians who support their position. In a compelling account of how the mass media and large interest groups (such as the American Association of Retired Persons and political action committees) influence policies, Hedrick Smith contends that well-organized, grass-roots constituencies with extraordinary resources and access to the mass media are wielding increasing power in legislative settings.[46]

Individuals who help shape and enact budgets, such as legislators on appropriations committees and officials who control budgets in bureaucracies, often have extraordinary power because "those who pay the piper call the tune." A professor of mine once lamented social workers' tendency to seek jobs in organizations' personnel sections when the staff in the fiscal departments usually have more power to shape the policies and programs of bureaucracies. Officials in the federal Office of Management and Budget (OMB) are key players in establishing the nation's domestic policy because they shape the president's budgetary recommendations.

In some cases, authority figures command obedience even when their suggestions are ethically flawed.[47] The impulse to obey authority figures may stem from peer pressure, loyalty to the organization, lack of information about specific issues, or fear of sanctions.

We should not overlook the role cultural symbols play in giving certain persons and groups more power than others. Officials affiliated with socially acceptable issues, such as children, health, and education, are often more influential than people associated with socially stigmatized groups, such as people who are mentally ill, welfare recipients, or ex-offenders.[48]

Discrimination patterns in the broader society influence power transactions. Rosabeth Kanter suggests that women are often excluded from decision making in large organizations because of gender-based prejudice and because they lack access to old-boy networks. Members of minority groups often encounter similar problems.[49]

Although few people would deny that power differentials exist, some theorists, such as C. Wright Mills, have suggested the existence of a power elite, such as the leaders of well-financed interest groups, that monopolizes power and consigns other people and interests to marginal roles.[50] On the other hand, "pluralist" theorists, such as Robert Dahl, have suggested that many interests and people shape policy choices.[51] These theorists point to the multiple interest groups that shape policies in municipal, county, state, and federal jurisdictions.

Who is right? Each theory applies in some situations. In some areas, specific people and interests have the power to dominate policy making, whereas in others, policy choices stem from a political process in which almost anyone can participate. In still other situations, certain people and interests have the power to set agendas and shape choices, but determined and well-organized groups can force them into important concessions. As we discuss in the next chapter, policy practitioners need to be realistic in assessing the distribution of power in specific settings.

The case of the student intern illustrates how persons with little formal power can be surprisingly successful. By taking the initiative, working through an intermediary (Mr. Jones), developing an effective innovation, and securing support for the innovation from psychiatric hospitals, the intern mapped a sophisticated strategy to secure a major policy change in her agency.

Ethical Issues

Some social workers believe that developing and using power is unprofessional. We argued in Chapter Three, however, that although they may be unaware of it, social workers use power frequently in their work, including their direct-service work. Whenever they guide, direct, or suggest options to clients, they use power. When they make recommendations to supervisors or external authorities, such as the courts, they use power. Indeed, we argued in Chapter Two that it may be unethical not to use power in certain situations, such as questioning defective policies or seeking policy changes. In such cases, we said, social workers (and other professionals, such as teachers, attorneys, and physicians) may fail to advance beneficence, social justice, and fairness.

Power can be used unethically—dishonestly or manipulatively—but we cannot make simple, easy-to-follow ethical rules. Someone who is blatantly dishonest to gain a strategic advantage is clearly behaving unethically, but there are grayer areas in ethics. For example, should someone volunteer to an opponent that she will attack his position in a forthcoming meeting? Is withholding this information the same as lying? As discussed in Chapter Two, we may also encounter ethical dilemmas when we use power, as when honesty and social justice conflict. For example, what if enacting a measure to help low-income persons hinges on your telling a falsehood to an opponent of that measure? Faced with this ethical dilemma, you would certainly want to reflect carefully and seek consultation before acting.

The use of manipulation is also an ethical issue. Assume that you want to win and are convinced that you cannot unless you use a devious parliamentary maneuver that will place your opponent at a disadvantage, use a threat to gain an opponent's support, or suppress data that would make your position appear less tenable. All of these behaviors are manipulative because they will give you an advantage at the expense of open discourse and free choices. Such tactics are usually unethical and even counterproductive because they may cause others to distrust you and even oppose your position. However, certain manipulative behaviors, like some forms of dishonesty, can be justified in limited situations. You might rightly decide that ethical principles, such as social justice and beneficence, are at stake; that your opponents are using hardball tactics, so you must use them, too; and that you will lose without some form of manipulation. Here, too, you will want to reflect and seek consultation.

Developing and Using Power

We have discussed the nature of power and different kinds of power. Now we examine in more detail some interactional dimensions of power: how policy advocates obtain it, how they decide when and whether to use it, and how they use power in groups or coalitions.

Moreover, what special obstacles do members of oppressed outgroups, such as women, gay men and lesbians, and racial minorities, confront as they seek to obtain and use power in specific settings?

In contrast to their well-heeled counterparts, lobbyists for powerless or stigmatized groups must often work with scant resources. What tactics do they use to influence legislation, and how do they sometimes achieve surprising successes? We discuss the tactics of low-budget lobbyists in Policy Advocacy Challenge 9.3.

POLICY ADVOCACY CHALLENGE 9.3

HOW LOW-BUDGET LOBBYISTS GET POWER

The phone rang a dozen times before a harried Rand Martin could grab it. He disconnected the caller when he tried to put the line on hold so he could finish another call. Such is life when you are between secretaries and cursed with a cheap, quirky phone system.

He would probably receive little sympathy from Sherry Skelly, who lacks not only a secretary but, until recently, a desk, a typewriter, and an office. Until she managed to scrape up the money, she had been using a donated hallway as her headquarters. She still makes do with a single phone line and an answering machine.

Martin and Skelly are lobbyists, Martin for the AIDS-oriented Lobby for Individual Freedom and Equality (LIFE), and Skelly for the California Children's Lobby. You can tell they are lobbyists because they work bills, meet with legislators and consultants, and testify at hearings. Their pictures are also in the Secretary of State's *Directory of Lobbyists.*

But if you look for other signs that signify "lobbyist" to most of the public, you will not find any. The organizations they represent never show up on the lists of heavy campaign contributors. They keep their fingers crossed when they send their cards to legislators on the floor, hoping to speak with them, for, unlike their heavyweight counterparts, Martin and Skelly are unable to command an audience. They do not have legions of staff to keep them posted on the dozens of bills they must track. If they hit the Sacramento hot spots at night, it is to relax and enjoy themselves; their budgets do not allow for the drinks or dinner that might further connections with lawmakers and legislative staff. In short, what these two lack is money.

Of course, they are not alone. The Fair Political Practices Commission lists 762 registered lobbyists. Ranking lobbyists by affluence, there are only eleven big operators at the top. Those eleven receive in excess of $500,000 in client fees and spread around hundreds of thousands of dollars more in campaign contributions.

Much lower in the rankings are the lobbyists for public interest groups—California Common Cause, Consumers Union, American Civil Liberties Union—along with lobbyists for state agencies, departments, and commissions. Although they have no money to grease the wheels of power, they usually have enough resources to track bills, produce position papers, and rally the public.

Scraping dead bottom are a subgroup of public interest entities, such as LIFE and California Children's Lobby, whose annual budgets detail how many stamps may be used and how many photocopies may be made in one month. Martin runs his operation on a budget of $80,000, including office rent, his salary and that of a secretary. Skelly makes it on $63,000. Clearly neither of them is in it for the money. If it is true that money turns the wheels in the capital, then one would expect Martin's and Skelly's work to be mostly futile. So who are these penny-pinching lobbyists, how do they get by, and what can they possibly accomplish?

"A lobbyist is a be-all," says the twenty-seven-year-old Skelly. "I feel like I'm a mediator and a resource who can provide expertise on an issue. If you have no money, you end up working closely with consultants, and consultants are very detail-oriented."

Expertise, a flair for detail, credibility—these are the tools a low-budget lobbyist brings to work every day. Some of the weight such a lobbyist carries is personal, earned over years of consistently giving good advice and testimony; some of it comes from the organization he or she represents.

California Children's Lobby, for instance, is an umbrella group for child-care providers, child-care educators, and parent groups around the state. Skelly says the lobby has a twenty-year track record of grass-roots activism that makes it an effective advocate on children's issues.

"It's a very sophisticated network," she says. "With the phone tree we have, we can get forty calls into a member's office on a particular bill within an hour. These people know the [legislative] members in their areas; they write letters, make phone calls, and involve the parent groups. This committed network has been developing for the past ten or twenty years, and now it's primed and ready to go."

Skelly, who has been with California Children's Lobby for almost a year, says she is the only full-time lobbyist for children's issues in Sacramento. Although that has the drawback of spreading one person too thinly over hundreds of bills, it does mean that Skelly has become a focal point for children's issues and a natural funnel for information, studies, and trends.

But beyond the clout of her organization, Skelly works on developing her own ties and credibility. She knows about one-quarter of the members of both houses. "When I meet a member, I don't just talk about my bills," she says. "Education bills, minimum wage—if I know a certain member is interested in something this year, then I talk about that. Then they know I'm interested in their concerns and views and not just pushing my agenda." Just as important are her consultant contacts. "Consultants tap into [lobbyists] as a resource. You have to prepare good amendments for bills and make good suggestions well in advance of hearings if you are going to influence the outcome."

The 34-year-old Martin, who has been a lobbyist on health issues for three years, says he is always working on his recognition and credibility with both legislators and consultants. Unlike Skelly's organization, Martin's group is still learning to flex its political muscles.

While children's issues may be simmering on a front burner this year, Martin's issue has been boiling at high speed for a couple of years.

Martin was instrumental in forming the Lobby for Individual Freedom and Equality, an umbrella organization for 42 California organizations concerned about AIDS. He has been its sole lobbyist since it began.

The first full year of operation, he felt swamped, working out of his living room to track 65 bills. Confronted with 142 bills this year, last year is beginning to look calm in retrospect.

(continued)

(9.3   continued)

"The number of bills, so many legislators and staff to get to know, plus keeping a fledgling organization afloat—it's been difficult," Martin says.

The difficulties are not just in the part of the job that deals with bills. He has learned quickly that a discount lobbyist not only needs to keep an eye on developments in the capital but also needs to educate, guide, and cajole the groups he represents. One of his biggest tasks is forming his backers into a cohesive, effective voice.

"Gays and lesbians have always been very adept at turning people out on a single issue, but they've been unable to do it on a consistent basis," Martin says. "LIFE has been working to build that kind of network. LIFE illustrates a new political maturity that acknowledges the need for a group to have continuous visibility."

Networking and consensus-building are slow processes, however, and the AIDS epidemic is moving very quickly. "Building a network takes longer than gaining personal access to an individual legislator, but it's every bit as important," Martin says.

Important, yes; comfortable, no. Martin is often caught between a legislative agenda that threatens to move ahead without LIFE and purists on his board who believe compromise is synonymous with evil. "It puts us in a tough position, because we have liberal legislators who want to side with us telling us we have to give on some things," Martin says. "But then we have those who believe LIFE needs to maintain a pure image in the gay-lesbian community. And there's a need for those kinds of people: they create such a pure position, we look like moderates in comparison."

So Martin frequently finds himself in the role of an educator, not just to consultants and legislators, but to his own group members, who need to understand how the process works and what is probable, feasible, and impossible.

Skelly agrees with the vision of a lobbyist as an educator. She conducts seminars and attends the monthly meetings of a half-dozen child-oriented organizations. It's important for the folks back home to understand how Sacramento works and how they can affect what comes out of the capital.

"The Children's Lobby network can produce a teen parent and her partner, holding a baby, to give testimony at a hearing," Skelly says. "We can call on experts in the field and find out anything a legislator might want to know. These people are on the scene where state programs are actually working, so they are in a good position to know what's wrong and what needs to be done. They need to be able to convey that information to the legislature."

Skelly says that such personal testimony at hearings can have a "significance beyond dollars."

But dollars do count, no matter how optimistic or well-armed with statistics a lobbyist may be.

"A lobbyist without money just doesn't have the access," Martin says. "It's most visible when lobbyists are giving testimony. The committee members sit up and listen when it's someone with clout or money; they pay attention."

Martin says this matter-of-factly, with little bitterness in his voice. He regretfully accepts reality; lobbyists without the big bucks have to be more diligent in preparing arguments, supplying statistics, and proposing improvements—sometimes to no avail.

"You take a lot of frustration home. But then there have been people we've turned around on a particular issue," Martin says. "I think we've had a lot of impact on Dr. Filante [Assemblyman William Filante] and helped build his leadership on the AIDS issue among Republicans."

Skelly says her biggest victory came last year when she helped secure $500,000 in the state budget for California State University child care. The governor had already vetoed a $1.2 million expenditure, so getting the partial funding past his blue pencil was a plus. "These campus centers had been struggling along for twenty years without any state funding, and many of them were on the verge of closing," she says. "So this was the first time general-fund money was ever committed to campus child care, and I was very excited about it."

The upbeat Skelly cannot remember a defeat that left her depressed in the past, but even an optimistic nature will not block reality this year. California Children's Lobby's top priority is a statutory cost-of-living adjustment for child care. The governor has already vetoed similar legislation in the past. The governor also placed an equitable cost-of-living adjustment in his budget proposal this year, cutting the ground out from under Skelly's arguments by removing the need for immediate action. "I have to admit I'm beginning to anticipate a problem," she says.

Like all lobbyists, Martin has experienced both victories and defeats. His biggest victories have been killing two of GOP State Senator John Doolittle's ten-bill AIDS packages, and his worst defeat was the passage of a bill to test prostitutes for AIDS.

Victories that come by defeating bills are often fleeting. One of Doolittle's bills would have substantially relaxed AIDS test confidentiality laws, including turning results over to public health officials, and the other would have allowed widespread testing in psychiatric institutions. Those two are dead, but other measures this year are likely to accomplish at least some of Doolittle's goals.

The prostitute bill's passage was the type of fluke that leaves lobbyists with nightmares. The bill swept out of the Assembly, not as a well-reasoned policy decision, but on a Gang-of-Five tidal wave while Martin watched helplessly. "It happened so fast, and most of it was behind closed doors," Martin says, "so we really couldn't do much about it."

Had the Gang of Five, a group of dissident Democrats, not been trying to find common ground with Republicans so they could successfully challenge Speaker Willie Brown, the prostitute bill would have stayed buried or at least could have been modified to be less objectionable to LIFE, Martin says. But it is just one of several bills on which Martin expects defeat, leaving him feeling stressed and making his shoestring-budget operation all the more depressing.

"Burnout is common with public interest lobbyists," Martin says. "The ones you see around the building who have been here for 20 or 30 years work for industries, big-buck clients."

So if Martin received an offer from a big-time lobbying firm, would he switch?

"I couldn't leave LIFE dangling in midsession," says Martin, who is gay and deeply committed to the fight against AIDS. "But in the longer term, yes, I'd probably move on. You can have a deep personal commitment to an issue, but it only lasts until burnout hits."

(continued)

(9.3   continued)

Martin, whose father is a Washington, DC, lobbyist, is already well sidetracked from the theater career he had planned. He keeps his hand in acting and directing with a Davis community theater group, but his future is in the capital. "It's in my blood," he says simply. "The more I've been involved in government activities, the more I've been fascinated with what is going on in Sacramento."

The fascination is still there for Skelly, as well. "I really enjoy lobbying. It's exciting and stimulating."

Skelly didn't start out as a lobbyist. An active role in starting a child-care program at UC Santa Barbara put her in the limelight when the university's student association needed a lobbyist. Two years there and another year with the Children's Lobby have satisfied her itch to do something professionally that focuses on children.

"I have a bottom-line commitment to education and children's issues. I might move on to something else in the future. But I'm pretty dedicated to children's issues and, right now, I couldn't imagine doing anything else."

❖ ❖ ❖

How do policy advocates compensate for their meager resources in state capitals, where well-heeled lobbyists, with many times their resources, compete with them for the attention of legislators? What kinds of power resources do they have? How can they achieve some successes even when they cannot wine-and-dine legislators extravagantly? Do they have any advantages when contrasted with well-heeled lobbyists?

Obtaining Power Resources

The successful use of power resources in transactional relationships depends on several factors. Policy advocates must build their personal credibility, learn how to network, and create links with groups that can help them in their policy practice.

Building Personal Credibility

Whether they are attorneys, physicians, or social workers, professionals require personal credibility to be effective with their clients. Similarly, the personal credibility of policy advocates influences the degree to which others will listen to them.[52] (See Policy Advocacy Challenge 9.3.)

Several tactics can enhance individuals' personal credibility. They can emphasize that they are reasonable and pragmatic team players affiliated with successful institutions, who have integrity and authoritativeness and a positive track record. People often use Machiavellian tactics as well to enhance their personal credibility, although not without ethical and practical risks.

Appearing reasonable and pragmatic   Policy advocates sometimes increase their credibility with decision makers who have different values by not emphasizing a proposal's underlying principles and by focusing instead on its substantive provisions.[53] Assume, for example, that a policy advocate who has a radical perspective wants to redistribute resources to poor people by substantially increasing the benefits of the food stamp program. When dealing with the aide of a conservative legislator, this policy advocate will downplay his radical ideology and emphasize instead both the details of the reform and the objective of increasing distressed farmers' revenues. By downplaying his ideology, which is dissonant with the ideology of conservative politicians, the policy advocate will seem more credible to the aide.[54]

Policy advocates who sacrifice their preferences excessively in their zeal to appear reasonable and pragmatic may find this strategy counterproductive if other people perceive them as disingenuous.

Appearing to be a team player   Adherents of power-dependence theory suggest that others view us as credible when they depend on us.[55] Let us consider the social work units in two hospitals. The unit in Hospital 1 contents itself with providing crisis intervention services to patients, whereas the unit in Hospital 2 fills several functions besides traditional counseling. The staff members assume a highly visible role in discharge planning, providing financial counseling for patients, providing social services to rape victims, serving as intermediaries between the hospital and the state's department of children's services in suspected cases of child abuse and neglect, operating a substance abuse clinic, and providing home-based services to frail, older persons. Top decision makers in Hospital 2 depend on the social work staff for these services. Indeed, they cannot imagine how their hospital would function without this unit. By contrast, top decision makers in Hospital 1 hardly know that the social work unit exists, much less that it is vital to the hospital. According to power-dependence theory, decision makers are more likely to heed suggestions of the director or other staff of the expansive social work unit at Hospital 2 than at Hospital 1.[56]

Power-dependence theory suggests, then, that policy advocates can increase their stature by assuming multiple functions beyond their narrow job descriptions. As the director of a social work unit once said to me, "I might even consider washing windows!" These expanded functions serve several purposes; they make high-level administrators feel beholden to the units and individuals who perform these many positive tasks for the institution, and they make these units and individuals appear to be team players who care about the institution's broader interests.

Policy advocates also can enhance their credibility by taking the initiative to make changes within an organization. Assume, for example, that in a casual conversation with a social worker, a hospital administrator remarks on "the turnover of nursing and social work staff in the pediatrics unit during the past five years, which has severely jeopardized the quality of services and staff morale." If the social worker seizes the initiative and offers to survey the staff before discussing possible causes of the turnover, she makes the administrator dependent on her by performing a necessary task. Volunteering this service makes her appear to be a team player. If she assumes additional roles on this project, such as chairing a committee, she continues this proactive and positive role. We can imagine that these assertive actions would enhance her credibility on this issue.

People can also increase their image as team players, and thus their credibility, by shaping policy proposals germane to an organization's mission.[57] Of course, ethical concerns limit the use of this tactic because we should not make proposals based on morally objectionable values. If a hospital does not wish to serve any poor patients who lack insurance, even those with emergency conditions, a social work unit should not seek funds for additional staff to screen out such people.[58]

Personal integrity   Some people may rightly wonder whether some of these tactics for increasing personal credibility will imperil practitioners' integrity. If we constantly appear to be reasonable and to be team players, when should we speak out for specific causes or not be team players when we think the team needs fundamental reforms?

Policy advocates may take as models many effective legislators who have combined moderate approaches with principled and outspoken positions on certain issues. Hubert Humphrey, Phillip Hart, and Claude Pepper often championed social causes before they became popular or fashionable, and with some risk to their political well-being. Yet these men were highly successful legislators, were reelected overwhelmingly and often, and enjoyed immense popularity among their legislative peers. Perhaps one reason for their credibility was that many people perceived them as having integrity, as being able to draw the line when their most fundamental beliefs were challenged.[59] Humphrey became a determined advocate for civil rights legislation, as did Pepper for Social Security. Even people who disagree with others' values often admire them for taking risks to defend their values. People who bend like willows with every passing breeze do not command this respect. Of course, even Humphrey, Hart, and Pepper had to decide when to invest their energies and take risks; on many issues, they were more willing to accommodate others.

Authoritativeness   When we want to change a policy in an agency, community, or legislative setting, opposition may arise from people who say the change is not warranted. The policy advocate often can diminish such inertia by demonstrating authoritativeness on the subject and offering evidence that supports the policy change, whether by citing important research, documenting similar changes in other settings, or quoting reputable experts.[60] In the case mentioned previously of the high rate of staff turnover in the hospital's pediatrics service, the social worker might conduct her survey of the situation by using a well-known standardized instrument that measures staff morale. As individuals appear to be authoritative on a specific issue, they increase the likelihood that they will be perceived as authoritative on future occasions.

Developing a positive track record   One cannot develop credibility merely by using rhetoric; people have to observe firsthand, or hear secondhand, that someone is competent, trustworthy, or authoritative, or that a department performs indispensable services.

Secondhand reports may be quite helpful in establishing credibility. As people initiate useful policies and try to change existing policies, they obtain a good reputation not only with those they encounter directly but also with those who hear positive feedback about them.

Affiliating oneself with successful institutions   Credibility stems not only from individuals' actions and attributes, but also from their affiliations. Assume that a hospital administrator receives requests for additional funding from the directors of two units. The first director's unit has been marked by chronic and repeated turmoil, and the administrator does not perceive it as providing quality services. The second director's unit is widely viewed as outstanding; the hospital administrator has received many positive reports about its services and staff. Although the directors may have similar personal characteristics, we can guess whose request the hospital administrator is more likely to heed.

The lesson for social workers who work in bureaucracies is simple. Personal credibility stems in part from being associated with a well-regarded and effective unit. That unit, in turn, derives its reputation from the quality of its work and its staff.[61] Practitioners can enhance their credibility indirectly by improving the services of the unit that employs them.

Using Machiavellian tactics   Some individuals try to enhance their credibility by using negative tactics, such as harming others' reputations, buck-passing, sandbagging, and turf or empire building. Those who use Machiavellian tactics often assume that they can enhance their own reputation only by diminishing the reputations of their colleagues. Buck-passing means blaming others for one's own failures,[62] and sandbagging means diminishing another's accomplishment by contending that others, perhaps even oneself, were really responsible for it.[63] As any participant in bureaucratic politics can confirm, many people excel in turf or empire building, which means accumulating power and responsibility by wrestling them from others.[64] People malign colleagues to diminish their initiatives by suggesting that the proposals reflect ulterior and evil motivations, such as a desire for status or power.[65]

These negative tactics are quite effective in some political campaigns, and some administrators obtain power by using them. But the credibility of those who use them suffers, because they are perceived as immoral.

Illustrations from Policy Advocacy Challenge 9.3   Policy Advocacy Challenge 9.3 illustrates how many interactional skills low-budget lobbyists need to develop power resources. Rand Martin tells us that his power depends on his being reasonable and pragmatic in dealing with legislators, though he finds it is difficult to make concessions that he and his allies do not want to make. He discusses building a reputation for personal integrity and authoritativeness by providing well-researched, accurate information to legislators. Both he and Sherry Skelly mention the need to develop a track record of timely and responsible contributions to legislators.

Networking

A network is the number and range of supportive relationships a person has.[66] Networks are important to policy practitioners in several ways. Individuals with broad networks develop early-information systems through which they learn about issues, problems, and trends relevant to their work, and they have many sources of advice as they develop policies and strategies.

There are many kinds of networks. *Lateral networks* consist of relationships with colleagues; *vertical* and *subordinate networks* consist, respectively, of persons who are superior to and beneath a person in an organization's hierarchy. People have *heterogeneous networks* when they have supportive relationships with others in a range of positions both within and outside their work. A social worker in a hospital has a heterogeneous network, for example, when it includes members of different units or departments and different professions. Some relationships in networks are short-term, perhaps fashioned in response to a specific problem, while others are long-standing.

Strategies that help expand a person's networks include enhancing visibility, seeking inclusion in decision-making bodies, cultivating mentors, obtaining access to informal groups, and developing links with social movements.

Enhancing personal visibility   Some people develop networks by increasing their visibility in bureaucratic, community, legislative, and social settings.[67] An example is the young Lyndon Johnson, who lived in a boardinghouse when he first arrived in Washington, DC, as an aide to a legislator. To meet other aides who lived in the same boardinghouse, he brushed his teeth three or four times each morning and took several showers. In these encounters, he asked the other aides about their jobs and their interests, a tactic that convinced each aide that Johnson cared about him.[68]

Indeed, politicians often employ a tactic that others can use. Although exchanging information is important, both as an end in itself and as a method of establishing a relationship, it should be supplemented by actively seeking advice, support, or suggestions from others. As Christopher Matthews notes, people like to be asked for advice; it makes them feel important and wanted.[69]

Obtaining inclusion in decision-making bodies   To examine specific problems, agencies often establish either ongoing committees or time-limited ad hoc committees.

Membership on these committees is sometimes controlled by top officials in the organization. However, individuals can seek membership by showing interest or by suggesting the formation of a committee to examine a problem. Committee membership is an excellent opportunity to obtain an inside position on important issues, improve one's credibility, and extend one's network.

Seeking mentors and inclusion in informal groups   In her research on why women have difficulty obtaining promotions in corporations, Rosabeth Kanter implicates their exclusion from mentoring relationships and old-boy networks.[70] Males, she observes, develop informal relationships with high-level male officials, who become their mentors, giving advice and information about the internal workings of the corporation, its politics, taboo subjects, informal factions, upcoming policy issues, and strategies for obtaining promotion. Mentors also introduce these neophytes to important officers of the corporation and into informal cliques and relationships, and go to bat for them when they need high-level assistance.

As J. McIver Weatherford notes with respect to legislatures, old-boy networks span the legislative, bureaucratic, and lobbying spheres of government as people move among them in their employment.[71] In both state and federal capitals, powerful legislators have an intricate network of acquaintances, many of them former aides, in lobbying and the bureaucracy. They tap into these rich networks at many points in their work—when contemplating whether to introduce legislation, when seeking to help a constituent with a specific problem, and when searching for issues that will enhance his or her reputation as an initiator of new legislation.

These old-boy networks contain a wide-ranging set of contacts that provide their members with assistance, information, business connections, and job possibilities. Many high-level decisions are made during social encounters among the people in these networks; those outside such networks are not consulted about these decisions and therefore have no advance notice of future policy changes.[72]

The workings of the mentor system and the old-boy network are manifestly unfair to those not included in them. Lacking allies within such networks, many women and racial minorities are excluded, as are loners, or those disinclined to maintain a network of relationships.[73] Declarations about the evil nature of these networks, however, will not make them disappear, nor will the moral victories of those who avoid them erase the disadvantages this exclusion brings.

Illustrations from Policy Advocacy Challenge 9.3   Both Rand Martin and Sherry Skelly make clear that low-budget lobbyists depend on contacts within the state's legislature and governmental agencies. While lacking money to entertain legislators and their aides, they can nonetheless develop a range of connections by increasing their visibility in an arena filled with other lobbyists with greater resources.

Developing links with social movements   Some policy advocates develop links with groups that take interest in issues such as AIDS, reforms for children, and persons with physical or mental disabilities. The members of such groups, who often have minimal resources, are highly knowledgeable about specific issues and deeply committed to them. Other people become active in local chapters of professional organizations, such as the National Association of Social Workers, or form relationships with politicians or civil servants.

Such connections increase a person's power within her or his own organizations because those who have them are often viewed as more credible than those who lack them. They bring into an organization ideas and information from these external contacts.[74] In turn, to help these external groups or movements, the members sometimes recruit other staff or even clients as volunteers, though they must be certain that their clients do not believe they must participate to receive services.[75]

Illustration from Policy Advocacy Challenge 9.3   Sherry Skelly tells us that maintaining external allies is critical to a low-budget lobbyist's success. She inherited and helped maintain a sophisticated network of children's advocates throughout the state. She uses the network to increase her expertise on myriad issues and to place pressure on legislators at pivotal points.

Out-Group Members' Problems

We have already alluded to Rosabeth Kanter's pioneering work on problems that female executives confront when seeking power in organizations. Her observations apply as well to persons of color, gay men and lesbians, people with disabilities, and members of any groups that confront prejudice.[76]

Members of these groups use the techniques we have already discussed, such as networking, but they must be even more diligent and persistent. They can also develop relationships with other members of their own group in their workplace, such as women who have attained positions of power, to provide special assistance, support, and advice. When such contacts are lacking, they should seek help from mentors outside the organization, in similar or related organizations.

Members of out-groups can also find allies among mainstream persons, who may, for example, take the lead in diversifying an agency's staff or including a broader range of staff in supervisory positions.

The case of the low-budget lobbyists illustrates how persons with marginal power resources can gain significant power with careful strategy.

Developing Assertiveness

Policy advocates sometimes fail to seize strategic opportunities to shape policies because they assume they cannot win. In some cases, as our discussion of power differentials suggests, the deck is stacked against them. In many other cases, however, individuals undermine their own effectiveness by becoming fatalistic.

To use power effectively, people must first decide that they possess power resources, that they can use them successfully, and that they want to use them. The word *assertiveness* describes this proclivity to test the waters, rather than to be excessively fatalistic.

Assertiveness is undermined, however, by two dispositions. The first is a victim mentality that disposes people to believe that others will conspire to defeat their preferences.[77] A director of a hospital's social work department might believe, for example, that the nurses and physicians will systematically oppose any proposals by social workers. The second is fatalism about using power in a more general sense; some people believe that only high-level persons or powerful interests can wield power successfully, and that people outside these exalted categories cannot effectively participate in policy deliberations.

Both the victim mentality and fatalism create self-fulfilling prophecies. People who believe that others will conspire against them and that only a restricted group can use power effectively will fail to use their personal power resources; those who see them as disinclined to participate in policy deliberations are likely to ignore their occasional suggestions and to exclude them from policy deliberations, further reinforcing the victim mentality and fatalism.[78] Fatalistic practitioners ignore the diversity of potential power resources and assume that they cannot increase theirs even by enhancing their credibility, finding allies, establishing networks, developing expertise, and obtaining information.

To understand this problem, recall our discussion of the sender of power (X) and the receiver of power (Y), as illustrated in Figure 9.1. Assume that you are Y, that you work in an agency, and that your program director intimidates you. Through his demeanor toward you, his intimidating remarks, and even his veiled threats, your director seeks to dissuade you from trying to make changes in the program.

What can you do? You can realistically assess both the risks and the benefits of trying to change defective policies. Those who intimidate others derive power from convincing them that they have no recourse but to follow the intimidator's suggestions that he or she has won. Ask yourself, "Is my program director's power as extensive as he suggests, or can I use my own power resources without incurring unacceptable penalties, such as losing my job?" Ask other people how they perceive a specific policy to see if your perceptions have merit, and find out whether they also feel intimidated or whether your director is singling you out. You can try direct communication with your program director, focusing on substantive issues and the specific issues on which you differ with him to see if he is more bark than bite. Accusing someone of seeking to intimidate you usually makes the situation even worse.[79]

If you are truly subject to intimidation, you should not expect easy answers. An assertive person does not passively accept a situation but tries to diagnose it, identifying possible strategies and then trying several options in search of one that works.

Here is an example of assertiveness. The director of a hospital's social work department requested a budgetary increase for her department but was denied. She noticed, however, that even unsuccessful entreaties served to educate top officials about social work programs and that some officials actually felt guilty about denying well-presented and justified requests. She decided not to be intimidated and to make further requests for funds for her department. She discovered that skillfully and frequently requesting funds brought increases in her unit's budget. Unlike departments with more timid executives, her department gained size and stature as she assertively sought resources, even after a number of unsuccessful requests.[80]

Illustration from Policy Advocacy Challenge 9.3   Policy advocates with minimal resources must combat burnout and fatalism. Despite the overwhelming advantage of the lobbyists with munificent resources, these two low-budget lobbyists have asserted themselves, persevered, and obtained notable successes.

Can Direct-Service Staff Use Power Resources?

Our discussion of out-group members' special problems and of assertiveness leads naturally to the question: Can people at the bottom of the heap, like direct-service staff members, use power resources, or does their subordinate position in the organizational hierarchy make them powerless? Organizations vary considerably; some executives elicit and even expect input from direct-service staff, and other executives are authoritarian.[81]

Direct-service staff already have considerable power stemming from their personal knowledge of an agency's problems. Many supervisors and executives value suggestions from direct-service staff about a range of agency matters and respond readily to well-conceived suggestions for changing existing services. Executives depend on direct-service staff for the agency's reputation, efficiency, revenues (when the agency charges for services), and public relations with clients and other agencies. Most agencies would cease to exist if they lacked competent front-line staff.

Direct-service staff members who belong to unions can imply or state that their work will be disrupted if certain demands are not met; such demands usually involve salary and workload, but unions sometimes also seek changes in policy. Even without union backing, direct-service staff can vigorously protest some policies by taking their case directly to high-level staff.

Direct-service staff often have access to at least some agency decision-making processes, such as staff meetings, retreats, unit meetings, and meetings with supervisors. Developing their power through the strategies we discussed earlier in this chapter (such as enhancing personal credibility and visibility, networking, and developing relationships with external groups) is likely to increase their power in these agency deliberations. Moreover, they can seek membership on specific agency committees or even suggest that a committee be formed to examine a specific issue.

Direct-service staff can also wield power indirectly as in Policy Advocacy Challenge 9.1 by influencing a supervisor to initiate a suggestion. They can also form coalitions within the agency to pressure administrators to modify specific policies. However, staff members should be realistic about the limits on such power.

Direct-service staff members often derive power from their autonomy.[82] Although regulations may govern the length and intensity of services, recommend procedures, and establish priorities, they are difficult to enforce because the details of direct-service work are hard to supervise. Moreover, it is possible to bend some rules without technically violating them. Carried to an extreme, autonomy brings anarchy, but in moderation, represents an important kind of power.

In addition to their participation in decision making, direct-service staff members can shape outcomes by helping to build agendas, define problems, and construct proposals, as discussed in Chapters Five through Eight.

Direct-service staff do not, of course, have the power resources of executives, funders, or legislators, so they must enhance their power resources imaginatively and select the issues on which they will use their influence.

Chapter Summary

What You Can Now Do

You are now equipped to do the following:

- Define power and politics
- Engage in power relationships
- Use an array of power resources including direct and indirect ones
- Use power in organizational settings through normal channels and, rarely, through whistle-blowing
- Surmount power differentials in certain circumstances
- Grapple with ethical issues when using power resources
- Develop power resources
- Network
- Develop skills in assertiveness

In the succeeding chapter, we discuss how we use our power resources to develop political strategy, whether in legislative, agency, or community settings.

Notes

1. *Living Webster Encyclopedic Dictionary of the English Language* (Chicago: English Language Institute of America, 1977), p. 737.
2. Ibid., p. 737.
3. Martin Rein, "Value-Critical Policy Analysis," in Daniel Callahan and Bruce Jennings, eds., *Ethics, the Social Sciences, and Policy Analysis* (New York: Plenum Press, 1983), pp. 96–100.
4. William Coplin and Michael O'Leary, *Everyman's Prince* (North Scituate, MA: Duxbury, 1976).
5. Tom Burns, "Micro-Politics, Mechanisms of Institutional Change," *Administrative Science Quarterly* 6 (September 1961): 257–281.
6. Peter Bachrach and Morton Baratz, *Power and Poverty* (New York: Oxford University Press, 1970), pp. 17–38.
7. For a discussion of the dilemmas of those who receive power resources, see Stanley Milgram, *Obedience to Authority* (New York: Harper & Row, 1975).

8. Bachrach and Baratz, *Power and Poverty,* pp. 17–38.

9. Ibid.

10. Edward Banfield, *Political Influence* (New York: Free Press, 1961), pp. 307–314.

11. John French and Bertram Craven, "The Bases of Social Power," in Dorwin Cartwright and Alvin Zander, eds., *Group Dynamics: Research and Theory* (New York: Harper & Row, 1968), pp. 259–269.

12. Doris Kearns, *Lyndon Johnson and the American Dream* (New York: Harper & Row, 1976), pp. 190, 224–227.

13. See Christopher Matthews, *Hardball: How Politics Is Played* (New York: Summit Books, 1988), pp. 21–43.

14. Bruce Jansson, *Theory and Practice of Social Welfare Policy: Analysis, Processes, and Current Issues* (Belmont, CA: Wadsworth, 1984), p. 184.

15. Julie Rovner, "Daycare Package Clears First Hurdle in House," *Congressional Quarterly Weekly Report* 46 (July 2, 1988): 1833–1836.

16. See Bachrach and Baratz, *Power and Poverty,* pp. 17–38.

17. *Congressional Quarterly Almanac,* vol. 34 (Washington, DC: Congressional Quarterly Service, 1978), pp. 272–279.

18. Jansson, *Theory and Practice,* p. 184.

19. Joseph Califano, *Governing America* (New York: Simon & Schuster, 1971), p. 67.

20. Gerald Zaltman and Robert Duncan, *Strategies for Planned Change* (New York: Wiley Interscience, 1977), p. 100.

21. Vincent Burke and Vee Burke, *Nixon's Good Deed: Welfare Reform* (New York: Columbia University Press, 1974), pp. 195–204.

22. Congress, Senate, Committee on Finance, *Hearings before the Subcommittee on Social Security and Family Policy,* pp. 2–14 (January 23, 1987).

23. Matthews, *Hardball,* pp. 144–154.

24. Lewis Froman, *The Congressional Process: Strategies, Rules, and Procedures* (Boston: Little, Brown, 1967).

25. Eugene Bardach, *The Skill Factor in Politics* (Berkeley and Los Angeles: University of California Press, 1972), pp. 234–240.

26. Bruce Jansson, *Reluctant Welfare State: A History of American Social Welfare Policies,* 1st ed. (Belmont, CA: Wadsworth, 1988), pp. 212–214, 222.

27. Eric Schattschneider, *The Semisovereign People* (New York: Holt, Rinehart & Winston, 1980), pp. 20–46.

28. Jansson, *Reluctant Welfare State,* p. 217.

29. Morton Deutsch, *The Resolution of Conflict: Constructive and Destructive Processes* (New Haven, CT: Yale University Press, 1973), pp. 124–152.

30. John Kingdon, *Agendas, Alternatives, and Public Policies* (Boston: Little, Brown, 1984), pp. 1–22.

31. Deutsch, *The Resolution of Conflict,* pp. 124–152.

32. Ibid., p. 368.

33. See Theodore Lowi's discussion of the politics of redistributive measures in "American Business, Public Policy, Case Studies, and Political Theory," *World Politics* 16 (July 1964): 677–715.

34. Yeheskel Hasenfeld, *Human Service Organizations* (Englewood Cliffs, NJ: Prentice Hall, 1983).

35. Hedrick Smith, *The Power Game: How Washington Works* (New York: Ballantine Books, 1988), pp. 388–444.
36. Matthews, *Hardball,* pp. 144–154.
37. Ron Dear and Rino Patti, "Legislative Advocacy," in *Encyclopedia of Social Workers,* vol. 2 (Silver Spring, MD: National Association of Social Workers, 1987), p. 37.
38. Michael Lipsky, *Street-Level Bureaucrats: Dilemmas of the Individual and Public Service* (New York: Russell Sage Foundation, 1980), pp. 16–18.
39. Kenneth Weick, "Educational Organizations as Loosely Coupled Systems," *Administrative Science Quarterly* 21 (March 1976): 1–9.
40. Robert Goodin, *Reasons for Welfare* (Princeton, NJ: Princeton University Press, 1988), pp. 184–228.
41. Franklin Chu and Sharland Trotter, *The Madness Establishment* (New York: Grossman, 1974).
42. Sissela Bok, "Blowing the Whistle," in Joel Fleishman, Lance Liebman, and Mark Moore, eds., *Public Duties: The Moral Obligations of Government Officials* (Cambridge: Harvard University Press, 1981), pp. 200–215.
43. Ibid.
44. George Sharwell, "How to Testify before a Legislative Committee," in Maryann Mahaffey and John Hanks, eds., *Practical Politics: Social Work and Political Response* (Silver Spring, MD: National Association of Social Workers, 1982), pp. 85–98.
45. Ibid., pp. 81–84.
46. Smith, *The Power Game.*
47. Milgram, *Obedience to Authority.*
48. Richard Fenno, *The Power of the Purse* (Boston: Little, Brown, 1966), pp. 366–390.
49. Rosabeth Kanter, *Men and Women of the Corporation* (New York: Basic Books, 1977), pp. 129–163.
50. C. Wright Mills, *The Power Elite* (New York: Oxford University Press, 1956).
51. Robert Dahl, *Pluralist Democracy in the United States* (Chicago: Rand McNally, 1967).
52. See Herbert Simons, *Persuasion,* 2nd ed. (New York: Random House, 1986), p. 130. Also see discussion of credibility by George Brager, Harry Specht, and James Torczyner, *Community Organizing,* 2nd ed. (New York: Columbia University Press, 1987), pp. 342–347.
53. Matthews, *Hardball,* pp. 144–352.
54. Rochelle Stanford, "Beleaguered Lobbyists for the Poor—Taking Allies Where They Can Find Them," *National Journal* 12 (September 20, 1980): 1556–1560.
55. Richard Emerson, "Power-Dependence Relations," *American Sociological Review* 27 (February 1962): 31–40, and D. J. Hickson et al., "A Strategic Contingencies Theory of Organizational Power," *Administrative Science Quarterly* 16 (June 1971): 216–229.
56. For research findings on power-dependence theory in hospital settings with social work departments, see Bruce Jansson and June Simmons, "Building Department or Unit Power within Human Service Organizations: Empirical Findings and Theory Building," *Administration in Social Work* 8 (Fall 1984): 41–44, 49–50.

57. See Bruce Jansson and June Simmons, "The Ecology of Social Work Departments: Empirical Findings and Strategy Implications," *Social Work in Health Care* 11 (Winter 1985): 1–16.

58. Bruce Jansson and June Simmons, "The Survival of Social Work Units in Host Organizations," *Social Work* 31 (September 1986): 342.

59. Joel Fleishman, "Self-Interest and Political Integrity," in Joel Fleishman, Lance Leibman, and Mark Moore, eds., *Public Duties: The Moral Obligations of Government Officials* (Cambridge: Harvard University Press, 1981), pp. 67–77.

60. Eugene Bardach, *The Skill Factor in Politics,* pp. 204–206, 216–220.

61. Jansson and Simmons, "Survival of Social Work Units," p. 341.

62. Matthews, *Hardball,* pp. 207–209.

63. Ibid., pp. 203–204.

64. J. McIver Weatherford, *Tribes on the Hill* (New York: Rawson, Wade, 1981), pp. 87–111.

65. Matthews, *Hardball,* pp. 194–211.

66. Noel Tichy, *Strategic Change: Technology, Politics, and Culture* (New York: Wiley, 1983), pp. 69–94.

67. Weatherford, *Tribes on the Hill,* pp. 20–24. Also see Tom Peters and Nancy Austin, "MBWA (Managing by Walking Around)," *California Management Review* 28 (Fall 1985): 9–34.

68. Matthews, *Hardball,* pp. 21–33.

69. Ibid., pp. 59–73.

70. Kanter, *Men and Women of the Corporation,* pp. 181–184.

71. Weatherford, *Tribes on the Hill,* pp. 87–111.

72. Ibid.

73. Ibid., pp. 250–253.

74. See how a social movement led to legislative reform in Wyoming in William Whitaker, "Organizing Social Action Coalitions: WIC Comes to Wyoming," in Maryann Mahaffey and John Hanks, eds., *Practical Politics: Social Work and Political Response* (Silver Spring, MD: National Association of Social Workers, 1982), pp. 136–158.

75. See Frances Piven and Richard Cloward, "New Prospects for Voter Registration Reform," *Social Policy* 18 (Winter 1988): 2–15.

76. Kanter, *Men and Women of the Corporation.*

77. Ibid., pp. 158–160, 196–197.

78. Ibid., pp. 196–197.

79. Linda MacNeilage and Kathleen Adams discuss various strategies in *Assertiveness at Work* (Englewood Cliffs, NJ: Prentice Hall, 1982).

80. Jansson and Simmons, "Survival of Social Work Units," pp. 339–340.

81. David Mechanic, "Sources of Power of Lower Participants in Complex Organizations," *Administrative Science Quarterly* 7 (December 1962): 349–364.

82. Michael Lipsky, *Street-Level Bureaucrats: Dilemmas of the Individual and Public Service* (New York: Russell Sage Foundation, 1980), pp. 13–18.

Suggested Readings

Building Personal Credibility

Richard Emerson, "Power-Dependence Relations," *American Sociological Review* 27 (February 1962): 31–40.

Bruce Jansson and June Simmons, "Building Department or Unit Power within Human Service Organizations: Empirical Findings and Theory Building," *Administration in Social Work* 8 (Fall 1984): 41–50.

Bruce Jansson and June Simmons, "The Ecology of Social Work Departments: Empirical Findings and Strategy Implications," *Social Work in Health Care* 11 (Winter 1985): 1–16.

Christopher Matthews, *Hardball: How Politics Is Played* (New York: Summit Books, 1988).

Networking

Rosabeth Kanter, *Men and Women of the Corporation* (New York: Basic Books, 1977), pp. 129–163, 181–197.

Noel Tichy, *Strategic Change: Technology, Politics, and Culture* (New York: Wiley, 1983), pp. 69–94.

J. McIver Weatherford, *Tribes on the Hill* (New York: Rawson, Wade, 1981), pp. 87–111, 250–253.

Working with Task Groups

Milan Dluhy, *Building Coalitions in the Human Services* (Newbury Park, CA: Sage, 1990).

Paul Ephross and Thomas Vassil, *Groups That Work* (New York: Columbia University Press, 1988).

Irving Janis, *Victims of Groupthink* (Boston: Houghton Mifflin, 1972).

John Tropman, Harold Johnson, and Elmer Tropman, *The Essentials of Committee Management* (Chicago: Nelson-Hall, 1979).

The Nature of Power

Peter Bachrach and Morton Baratz, *Power and Poverty* (New York: Oxford University Press, 1970).

Varieties of Power

John French and Bertram Craven, "The Bases of Social Power," in Dorwin Cartwright and Alvin Zander, eds., *Group Dynamics: Research and Theory* (New York: Harper & Row, 1968), pp. 259–269.

Lewis Froman, *The Congressional Process: Strategies, Rules, and Procedures* (Boston: Little, Brown, 1967).

Christopher Matthews, *Hardball: How Politics Is Played* (New York: Summit Books, 1988).

Hedrick Smith, *The Power Game: How Washington Works* (New York: Ballantine Books, 1988).

A Defense of Politics

Eric Schattschneider, *The Semisovereign People* (New York: Holt, Rinehart & Winston, 1960).

Using Power from Internal Vantage Points

Burton Gummer, *The Politics of Social Administration: Managing Organizational Politics in Social Agencies* (Englewood Cliffs, NJ: Prentice Hall, 1990).

Bruce Jansson and June Simmons, "The Survival of Social Work Units in Host Organizations," *Social Work* 31 (September 1986): 339–344.

Using Power from External Vantage Points

Donald deKieffer, *The Citizen's Guide to Lobbying Congress* (Chicago: Chicago Review Press, 1997).

Power Resources of Direct-Service Staff

Michael Lipsky, *Street-Level Bureaucrats: Dilemmas of the Individual and Public Service* (New York: Russell Sage Foundation, 1980).

David Mechanic, "Sources of Power of Lower Participants in Complex Organizations," *Administrative Science Quarterly* 7 (December 1962): 349–364.

The Problem of Assertiveness

Rosabeth Kanter, *Men and Women of the Corporation* (New York: Basic Books, 1977), pp. 158–197.

Linda MacNeilage and Kathleen Adams, *Assertiveness at Work* (Englewood Cliffs, NJ: Prentice Hall, 1982).

Stanley Milgram, *Obedience to Authority* (New York: Harper & Row, 1975).

Ethical Issues in Politics

Chauncey Alexander, "Professional Social Workers and Political Responsibility," in Maryann Mahaffey and John Hanks, *Practical Politics: Social Work and Political Responsibility* (Silver Spring, MD: National Association of Social Workers, 1982), pp. 22–25.

George Brager, Harry Specht, and James Torczyner, *Community Organizing,* 2nd ed. (New York: Columbia University Press, 1987), pp. 316–339.

Joel Fleishman, "Self-Interest and Political Integrity," in Joel Fleishman, Lance Liebman, and Mark Moore, eds., *Public Duties: The Moral Obligations of Government Officials* (Cambridge: Harvard University Press, 1981), pp. 52–92.

10

Developing Political Strategy

POLICY PREDICAMENT	The conservative governor of Virginia, George Allen, decided to transfer the Virginia Department of Aging—a freestanding agency—to another department of government. Policy advocates for older people quickly decided that this transfer would have grave implications for the department. What political tactics could such policy advocates as social work professor Robert Schneider use to block the governor's strategy? We discuss these strategies in Policy Advocacy Challenge 10.1.

We have discussed the nature and varieties of power. Now we turn to how policy advocates use their power resources to create political strategy in agency, community, and legislative settings. *Political strategy* is a sequence of actions and verbal exchanges that advocates believe will increase the likelihood that a proposal will be enacted. We discuss the following in this chapter:

- How to establish objectives and positions
- How to gauge who supports and opposes specific policies
- The importance of situational and contextual factors to policy strategy
- How we build alternative scenarios to select and revise political strategy
- Seven recurring steps in strategy building

Establishing Some Objectives

To develop intelligent strategy, policy advocates first have to answer this question: Why am I participating in the political process? Then they must decide which side they are taking and the degree and kind of policy changes they seek.

Determining a Position

Strategists must first decide whether to do the following:

1. Initiate their own proposal (an affirmative position)

2. Change others' proposals (an amending position)
3. Oppose others' initiatives (an opposing position)
4. Assume no role (a bystander position)

These choices are important because they commit the strategist to certain obligations and risks. (See Policy Advocacy Challenge 10.1.) People who initiate their own proposals have to invest considerable time in research, discussion, meetings, and negotiations and may expose themselves to criticism along the way. They have an advantage, however: Their ideas are likely to figure prominently in ensuing policy deliberations.

POLICY ADVOCACY CHALLENGE 10.1 *BLOCKING THE GOVERNOR'S ABOLITION OF THE DEPARTMENT OF AGING* *Robert Schneider, D.S.W., Professor, School of Social Work, Virginia Commonwealth University*	In 1994, the conservative governor of Virginia, George Allen, was implementing with a vengeance his promise to taxpayers to reduce the size of state government. One particular target was the Virginia Department for the Aging (VDA), which was a freestanding agency with its own commissioner and board of advisers. The governor and his Secretary of Health and Human Services (HHS), Kay Cole James, announced in September that by the end of the year, they would transfer this department into another department, the Department of Medical Assistance Services (Medicaid), all in the name of efficiency and eliminating duplication, of course. The VDA would lose its freestanding status, its commissioner would be reduced to an assistant director, the advisory board would be gone, control of the budget would shift to the Medicaid commissioner, and decision making on behalf of the aging would be buried deeper in the state bureaucracy.

As a 10-year member of VDA's board and its chairperson from 1985 to 1987, I read this announcement with grim uneasiness. Governors have every prerogative to make administrative shifts to improve state service delivery, and political pressure can be largely ignored. But this action was going to reverse years of effort to improve the status of the VDA. Several of us had worked perseveringly to upgrade this unit from an office on aging in another department to an independent department with its own budget, decision making, commissioner, and board. It would disappear for the most part with this plan. But what could I do? How could we stop this highly popular governor? The odds seemed slim to zero.

After a day or two of pondering and stewing, I got on the phone and called four other former chairpersons of the VDA's Governor's Advisory Board. Saying that there must "surely be something we can do," I suggested a meeting in Richmond the next week. When we met, we all agreed that we had to take action at least to delay this decision. A certain spirit of shared concern and determination evolved, and from then on, we became known as the Gang of Five.

Remember now, that this meeting was in early September, and a final recommendation from the governor was going to be made in November. How should we proceed? Here is what we did. First, we called on two very experienced veterans of state politics and human services administration to ask for advice. We met with them the following week, and from this meeting, we decided to delay the decision by insisting that some public comment period be allowed for citizen input. Public feedback is a very crucial process in Virginia, but this governor ignored it whenever possible. But the chances he would stop his decision were still unlikely, so we devised a backup plan. This strategy would go to the heart of the issue; that is, it would kill the decision in November by influencing the panel of decision makers, the Virginia Joint Commission on Health Care (JCHC), a legislative committee of the General Assembly of Virginia that made recommendations on all matters pertaining to health. The governor's proposal would first have to pass this group, and we believed that if we had any chance at all, this was the place not only to delay, but to kill the proposal.

While writing to the governor and his secretary to delay the proposal for public comment, we began other tactics. Those of the Gang of Five who knew members of the JCHC were asked to contact them and explain the consequences of the governor's proposals. One of us was an extremely close friend of the commission's senior Democrat. The Gang called on me to write our concerns into a statement that we could circulate far and wide. After consulting with the other four members, I drafted a two-page document outlining the issues, the potential effects of the new proposal, and some action steps that individuals or groups could take. I also began organizing a communication system so that we could write or phone all of the members of the JCHC, the key leaders of the Aging Network (a loosely organized group of policy advocates), the area agencies on aging, and the media.

We quickly discovered that there was little enthusiasm for the governor's proposal among the members of the JCHC. The Secretary of Health and Human Services also found out, and asked us to meet with the commissioner of the Medicaid department. In mid-October, the Gang of Five walked into the commissioner's office armed with the written analysis and other research, particularly around budget issues, and met with him and his well-prepared staff for two hours. They offered us some minor changes, such as retaining *aging* in the name of the agency, and promised us that the new assistant director would have full access to all decision making. We insisted that they show us how their proposal would improve the services for the older people of Virginia. Our argument was based on an opposite view, that, at no cost savings for taxpayers, much of the progress and the improvement of services for the aging would suffer significantly. At that meeting, we sensed that they were afraid of us and what we might be able to do, since there was already a rumor (not unfounded) that we were organizing a mass rally of older Virginians for the November JCHC meeting. We declined their offers and left our documents with them to study.

By this time, our confidence was rising, and support from the Aging Network was in evidence, even though much of it was quiet and almost secretive since many feared retribution. We wrote letters to the JCHC members and outlined the dangers of the shift. We called and met with them. Several regional agencies organized vans and buses of their clients to come to Richmond in November. However, we discovered that at the JCHC meeting, there would be time for comments only from commission members, not from others in attendance.

Through contacts with friends of the commission's chair, I asked, the night before the meeting, for the opportunity to speak to the commission. The next morning, in a room filled with older Virginians, the discussion opened with the Secretary of HHS outlining the reasons for the governor's proposal. The chairman of the commission, asking for clarification, caught my eye, and asked if I would be kind enough to explain the point. This gave me the chance to make my speech and outline our Gang of Five's contentions. Interestingly, I was the only speaker from the gallery that morning. The commission wanted other points clarified and delayed a decision until its December 27, 1994, meeting.

(continued)

(10.1   continued)

While we had at least won a delay, we were not overconfident. We would be prepared for the December 27 meeting and also decided to go on with planning a mass rally in mid-January, just after the opening of the annual session of the General Assembly. The lieutenant governor, unlike the governor, agreed to speak at noon at our rally on the capitol grounds. Our efforts turned to mobilizing hundreds of seniors to come to Richmond in the winter. We decided to piggyback on an already scheduled Senior Day planned by the VDA to begin at 10 A.M. We sent invitations to agencies, individuals, associations, groups, legislators, and others to meet with us at noon *after* their earlier session in a nearby church, St. Paul's. We designed bright orange three-inch stickers saying "SOS" (Support Our Seniors) and distributed about 4,000 of them. We also planned for many to come to the December 27 meeting.

However, the JCHC canceled its meeting on December 27 and rescheduled it for a week before our planned rally in January. Consequently, we had to alert all of our contacts of this change and hope that they would make the difficult adjustments in transportation and preparation. In early January, the JCHC met, facing a sea of bright orange dots in the gallery and changed the agenda to deal first with the governor's proposal. Saying, "I see many of you are here for the obvious—let's get this item finished first," the chairman asked the commission members for comment. A few minor questions later, a nearly unanimous vote rejected the proposal. The secretary then spoke and acknowledged the vote, saying that she disagreed with it but would respect the decision. The chairman then suggested to the audience that those who wished to leave could do so. Orange dots began disappearing through the doors.

We followed up a few days later with our mass rally. It was great fun to see another sea of orange dots come out of St. Paul's church and the VDA's morning meeting, where the secretary again spoke and acknowledged the defeat of the governor's proposal. They all headed across the street to the Bell Tower, where the Gang of Five held its rally with 500 to 600 older Virginians. The lieutenant governor spoke eloquently about services to the aging. We were thrilled and amazed at what had happened, remembering our bleak prospects only three months before.

Much has happened since 1994 and 2002. Virginia Governor George Allen has become U.S. Senator George Allen. Virginia Secretary of Health and Human Services Kay Cole James has become Director of the Office of Personnel under President George W. Bush. The Governor's Advisory Board to the Department for the Aging has become the Virginia Council on Aging with half the previous membership. The Virginia Department for the Aging has a new Commissioner, Dr. Ann McGehee. The Department lost its responsibility for long-term care policy development and planning to the staff of the Joint Commission on Health Care. Republicans have taken control of the House and Senate for the first time in more than 100 years. The Gang of Five keeps an eye on the department and stands ready to act . . . as it almost did when the current commissioner recently scheduled the Governor's Conference on Aging to coincide with the Jewish High Holiday of Rosh Hashanna.

Exercise: After reading this case, discuss the following questions:

What objectives did Robert Schneider and his allies establish early in their crusade?
What group or coalition took the lead in fighting the governor?
What initial strategy, as well as backup strategy, did the Gang of Five develop?
How did Robert Schneider get the chance to speak at the commission meeting?
Why was securing a delay important?
How did the Gang of Five mobilize pressure from multiple sources?

Unlike those who initiate proposals, policy advocates who agree generally with the initiators' position confine themselves to amending the proposal to advance their preferences for specific changes.

It is easier in some respects to block proposals than to develop them, because opposers need only pinpoint their flaws. Opposers may be perceived merely as naysayers, however, who lack constructive alternatives; they may also be accused of opposing changes only because they benefit from the existing policies.

Strategists may adopt a bystander role because they believe they lack the power to influence the outcome, because they want to save their political resources for a future issue, because they believe their involvement in deliberations will antagonize one or both sides in the controversy, or because they expect to assume a mediating role later.

Strategists' roles often depend on their analysis of a proposal's prospects. If they are extremely bleak, for example, an advocate may be reluctant to initiate a proposal; similarly, an advocate may not try to obstruct a proposal that has attracted widespread support. However, policy advocates sometimes oppose objectionable policies or initiate proposals in the face of overwhelming odds, because they believe fundamental principles are at stake or because they want to convince some segment of their constituency of their wholehearted support.

At national and state levels of government, the leaders of the two major parties must frequently decide which issues to champion, which ones to oppose, and which ones to leave alone. They realize, of course, that the leaders of the opposing party must make the same kinds of choices, because both parties want a competitive advantage in forthcoming elections. (See Policy Advocacy Challenge 10.2.)

POLICY ADVOCACY CHALLENGE 10.2

FINDING INFORMATION ABOUT NATIONAL POLITICAL STRATEGY

Stephanie Davis, Research Librarian, University of California, Irvine

Political parties must strategize constantly to make their stance on issues known to the population in order to gain votes and win elections. One strategy is to gain endorsements from an organization, a specific political party, or other politicians in order to swing supporters' votes to a certain candidate. One example of this is the 2001 mayoral race in Los Angeles between James Hahn and Antonio Villaragosa. Each candidate had a long list of endorsements from community organizations, state officials, non-profit organizations, and civil service organizations. Making this type of information known to voters is just one strategy for gaining votes.

More can be learned about political strategy in the form of party platforms, agendas, policy issues and educational information on the following Web sites of political parties in the United States. While there traditionally have been two major parties in the United States, others are gaining ground.

(continued)

(10.2   continued)

- Democratic National Committee www.democrats.org/index.html
- Republican Party www.rnc.org/
- Green Party www.greenpartyus.org/
- Libertarian Party www.lp.org/organization/
- Reform Party www.reformparty.org/

❖ ❖ ❖

Exercise: Visit the Web sites above and compare each party's stance on your research topic.

Selecting the Extent of Policy Changes

Policy advocates must decide whether to seek major or incremental changes, a choice that is often difficult. A policy practitioner may believe that a particular group or program needs major changes that are not politically feasible, or that will require large investments of time and energy.[1] Political realities contribute to this choice; if there is strong opposition to an initiative, for example, policy practitioners may decide to settle for relatively modest changes in existing policy. In some cases, a policy practitioner's aim is only to educate people about a problem, because people must believe that a problem exists before they will support policy changes.

Selecting a Time Frame

Policy advocates often ask the following: Do we want specific changes to be enacted in the short term (during an upcoming meeting, the present year, or the present session of a legislature), or will we accept an extended time frame?[2] Selecting a time frame depends on both the distribution of power and the practitioner's policy objectives; when the power distribution is unfavorable to a proposal, for example, it is difficult to enact it immediately, no matter how skillful its proponents. However, people with a long-term perspective encounter the challenge of maintaining interest in an issue without immediate tangible results.

Grounding Strategy in Current Realities

Political strategy must be firmly linked to existing realities, including power distribution, contextual factors, situational realities, impending developments, and the setting.

The Power Distribution

Kurt Lewin, the noted social psychologist, pioneered the concept of force field analysis to assess the distribution of power in specific situations.[3] To obtain a rough estimate of the support for a proposal, Lewin suggests enumerating persons by name and indicating the strength of their support or opposition in numeric terms, say, from 1 (weak support or opposition) to 10 (strong support or opposition), as illustrated in Figure 10.1,

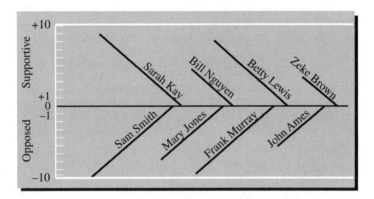

FIGURE 10.1   **Support of and opposition to a measure**

where the line lengths correspond to the strength of opposition or support. The preponderance of opposition to the policy in Figure 10.1 is shown by the number and length of the lines beneath the horizontal line compared with the lines above it.

A detailed evaluation of the strength of support and opposition for a specific policy proposal would require considerable information. First, we must know the relative power of a person to shape policy on a specific issue. The chair of a committee that is considering a proposal, for example, often has more power than any other member of the committee. Second, we need to estimate the salience that specific individuals attach to an issue. Someone who has strong convictions about an issue and is well positioned to affect policy, for example, may not become involved because he believes it falls within someone else's purview or because he is more interested in other current issues.

William Coplin and Michael O'Leary have developed a simple system for scoring the distribution of power and sentiment on an issue.[4] For example, a family of four must consider two issues: whether to ask Grandmother to move into the house after a recent illness and whether to allow the 18-year-old son, Sam, to own his own car. The two parents (Mary and Frank) and the two children (Sam and Diane) have decided to reach these decisions democratically but, as we know policy making does not usually occur on a level playing field. Assume that we know the family well enough to construct Table 10.1, which represents the sentiment, salience, and power of each of the family members. (The initials M, F, S, and D stand for the mother, Mary; the father, Frank; the son, Sam; and the daughter, Diane.)

First, we give each person a score for his or her sentiment on the two issues (extending from -10, very negative, to $+10$, very favorable). Table 10.1 shows that Mary strongly favors allowing her mother to live in their home (her score is 10), whereas Frank opposes the move (his score is -5). The children are mildly supportive (their scores are 2 and 4). All family members support allowing Sam to have a car, having scores of 4, 2, 10, and 8; predictably, the two children support this policy more strongly than either of their parents.

Second, we score each person with respect to the salience, or importance, that they give each issue on a scale from 1 (low salience) to 10 (high salience). Both parents attach considerable importance to each of the issues; hence, their scores of 8 on the issue of Grandmother and 7 on the issue of Sam's car. The children attach much

TABLE 10.1   **Estimating the distribution of sentiments, salience, and power**

	Issue 1: Grandmother				Issue 2: Car			
	M	F	S	D	M	F	S	D
Positions on the issues (-10 to $+10$)	10	-5	2	4	4	2	10	8
Salience (1 to 10)	8	8	3	4	7	7	7	7
Power to influence the outcome of this issue (1 to 4)	3	3	1	1	3	3	2	1
Totals for each participant (multiply the numbers down each column)	240	-120	6	16	84	42	140	56
Grand total for each issue (add the totals for each person)		142				322		

more importance to the issue of the car (they both score a 7), while attaching less importance to Grandmother's residence in their home (their scores are 3 and 4).

Third, we estimate the family members' relative power to influence choices on a scale from 1 (low power) to 4 (high power). The parents have far more power than the children; thus, they score a 3 on each issue, while the children score a 1 or 2 on each issue.

To obtain an overall reading of the distribution of sentiment, salience, and power, we multiply each person's scores on each issue. Mary's score is 240 ($10 \times 8 \times 3$) on Issue 1 and 84 ($4 \times 7 \times 3$) on Issue 2; Frank's scores are -120 ($-5 \times 8 \times 3$) on Issue 1 and 42 ($2 \times 7 \times 3$) on Issue 2. The two children have considerably higher (more favorable) scores of 140 and 56 on Issue 2 than on Issue 1, where their scores are 6 and 16.

Now, we total the participants' scores on each issue. Because a higher score indicates a more favorable prognosis for a proposal, it appears that Sam is more likely to have a car ($84 + 42 + 140 + 56 = 322$) than is Grandmother to be asked to move into the family home ($240 + -120 + 6 + 16 = 142$). Table 10.1 shows that a single negative score for a powerful participant (father or mother) markedly decreases the likelihood that a specific proposal will be approved.

A numbers approach to force field analysis may seem far-fetched, but politicians in legislative bodies sometimes use this kind of numeric analysis, crude and imperfect as it may be, to determine the prognosis for pieces of legislation.[5] If a proposal has an extremely low or unfavorable score, policy practitioners may decide the situation is hopeless, unless they can develop strategy that will enable them to change the sentiment, alter the salience, or modify the power of those who oppose their proposal.

Moreover, identifying the important participants, as well as their sentiment, salience, and power, helps policy practitioners develop strategy.[6] The data in Table 10.1 suggest several strategy options. Assume that Mary wants Grandmother to move into her home. She may try to bring Frank to at least a neutral sentiment, she may hope to reduce the salience he attaches to the issue, or she may try to isolate him from the decision-making process, thus reducing his power to influence the outcome. She may also seek to alter the children's sentiment, salience, and power, perhaps by promising them support for the car in return for their support on the Grandmother issue. Table 10.1 does not include coalitional power, but Mary may increase her power by forming a coalition with her children. She may also try to add new participants to the struggle.[7] Perhaps she will persuade Grandmother to make an impassioned plea to Frank or will secure the family physician's support. To convince Frank that other people will share in entertaining and caring for Grandmother, Mary may enlist the support of other relatives.

Force field analysis does carry a danger. Others' positions might be falsely judged. Misreading evidence may lead advocates to commit two kinds of errors: refraining from pursuing a proposal that could be enacted and promoting a proposal that cannot be enacted.

These errors in calculating sentiment, salience, and power may be compounded by another kind of error: We may assume that the current distribution of sentiment, salience, and power will remain constant in the future. In fact, they often change during deliberations. Indeed, the political strategy of effective policy advocates may transform a bleak and seemingly hopeless situation into a positive one. Our discussion of some of Mary's options suggests how strategists can modify existing realities.

Despite these cautionary notes, force field analysis is far from useless. Without efforts to gauge our support and opposition, we may blindly commit ourselves to proposals that are not politically feasible. In addition, estimating the difficulty of getting a proposal enacted allows us to estimate the time and political resources required. It is best to go into battle with our eyes open to the realities that we confront.

Identifying Contextual Factors

Although knowing a policy's relative support and opposition is useful, we need to know also why people take certain positions and how they are likely to act when an issue enters policy deliberations. Analyzing participants' past stances during deliberation, vested interests, and cohesion of likely opponents and proponents allows a more accurate prediction of people's likely actions than does merely estimating their current position.

Past Stances

Many issues may have been deliberated previously. The responses of decision makers, interest groups, and the general public to policies depends on their recollections or accounts of the prior deliberations.[8] Deliberations are more likely to be conflictual, for example, when an issue has previously been associated with ideological polarization, as illustrated by the controversy that arises whenever Congress considers national health insurance, gun control, or abortion. Indeed, many politicians avoid such issues because they do not want to become embroiled in controversies among their constituents or in an extended legislative battle with an uncertain outcome. In other organizations, too, participants may avoid reintroducing issues or policies that are associated with prior controversy.

Policy advocates sometimes erroneously conclude that the controversies associated with an issue will continue. After Congress defeated President Clinton's national health measure in 1994, many people thought no health reforms could be enacted for years, but Clinton managed to get Congress to approve a measure to fund health coverage for more than 5 million uninsured children in 1997. Indeed, skillful policy advocates try to offset the negative effects of past stances by emphasizing developments that now make a change more feasible. Clinton's proposal was strengthened, for example, by his argument that, with the exodus of hundreds of thousands of single-headed families from the welfare rolls after the welfare reforms of 1996, many children would be medically uninsured.

Vested Interests

People often base their position on an issue on their own interests,[9] which they fear a policy will harm. Politicians may worry, for example, that a certain policy will antagonize some of their constituents or enable the other party to expand its constituency or obtain an electoral advantage. An executive of a social agency or a government bureaucracy may fear that a proposal will shift resources or program responsibilities to rival agencies, impose controls or regulations on their activities, or diminish their revenues. Alternatively, people may support a policy because they believe it will enhance their power, prestige, or resources.

It is difficult to predict how people will calculate the impact of a policy on their interests. A politician may not know how her constituents will respond to a proposal, may mistakenly assume that her constituents will support or oppose it, or may not realize that losses of support in one quarter will be offset by gains in another. Skillful strategists try to predict a position's positive effects on the interests of those people whose support they hope to gain. For example, supporters of the day-care proposal in 1988 asserted that politicians who opposed the proposal risked losing a large share of the female vote.[10]

Cohesion of Likely Opponents and Proponents

Although we can sometimes calculate with considerable precision specific individuals' positions on an issue or policy, our analysis is incomplete if we fail to examine their relationships. For example, evenly balanced support of and opposition to a proposed policy should end in a stalemate. The proponents may still win, however, if their close working relationship allows them to evolve a strategy and to work together to implement it, while their opponents remain disunified. Moreover, if leaders with knowledge, commitment, political expertise, and considerable power support a specific proposal, it is more likely to be successful; successful leaders are also adept at assembling and maintaining supportive coalitions.

Situational Realities

Situational realities often shape the course of policy deliberations. In legislative settings, for example, the success of proposals is often influenced by coming elections, the balance of power between the contending parties, rivalries among powerful legislators and among members of the two legislative chambers, the budget, changes in leadership, the other proposals vying for attention, and the time remaining in a legislative session.[11]

These kinds of situational factors influence decision-makers' interest in a proposal and the extent of the conflict associated with it. When national elections are imminent, for example, politicians of both parties begin to jockey for position; they want to take conspicuous positions that will consolidate their existing support and also draw some of their opponents' constituents to their side. Liberal Democrats from northern cities may support social programs and publicly oppose conservative initiatives, such as efforts to rescind regulations that promote affirmative action. Conservatives not only promote issues that will solidify their traditional support but also advance social measures that will attract some Democrats to their cause. By the same token, impending elections may make all politicians avoid issues offering no advantage or fraught with significant political risks. For example, some liberal Democrats who normally support the federal financing of abortions may avoid this divisive issue in an election year.

Personal and institutional rivalries also influence efforts to initiate proposals. Legislative committees may jealously guard their jurisdiction over certain issues; and, when they hear rumors that another committee is developing a proposal, may hurriedly frame their own proposal. This kind of rivalry may exist between committees within a legislative chamber or between rival committees in the two chambers, for example, the House Economic and Educational Opportunities Committee and the Senate Committee on Labor and Human Resources. In the politics of health reform early in the Clinton administration, for instance, various legislative committees prepared rival proposals.

Situational factors also influence the political process in other organizations, where neither elections nor party rivalries exist. Nevertheless, the succession of leaders, internal institutional and personal rivalries, tensions between the board and the staff, budget realities, and changes in external funding can significantly influence the politics of specific proposals.[12] The institution of new leadership, for example, creates a fluid political situation in which individuals and factions take positions concerning issues on the policy agenda and seek support for them. Indeed, theorists contend that many major changes in organizational policies occur after changes in leadership.[13]

Institutional and personal rivalries pervade most organizations as different factions and units vie for scarce resources, promote their views about where the organization should be heading, and seek recognition for their respective programs. As in legislative settings, these rivalries sometimes influence positions on specific proposals; one person may oppose a rival's initiative simply because the rival proposed it or may initiate a proposal to beat this rival to the punch. Institutional rivalry is invited by the structure of organizations divided into units that have overlapping jurisdictions and that all seek funds from the organization's limited budget.[14] Competition often exists, for example, among the nursing, psychology, and social work units within hospitals as they vie for larger functions and budgets.

Predicting Future Developments

As we have noted, calculating a policy's support may lead us to believe that political interaction is static and should be analyzed only once. In fact, people constantly change their positions on measures as supporters, opponents, and bystanders interact and as events unfold. A person who is neutral about a policy proposal, for example, may become solidly opposed when a proponent uses an unethical power maneuver to push the proposal through. As this example illustrates, strategy may be difficult to formulate, because people's positions on specific issues change during the give-and-take of the political process.

The political process also shapes strategies. Supporters of a measure may decide that they need only spirit a measure quietly through a legislative committee and onto the floor of Congress to secure its enactment. However, if they learn that their opponents plan to attack the measure in emotional terms and publicize it in the mass media, they may quickly adopt a more militant strategy. Indeed, theorists have developed a body of knowledge called *game theory* that examines how people respond to opponents' tactical maneuvers.[15] Because people change their positions during the political process, effective practitioners have to revise their strategy in response to both anticipated and unexpected events.

Adapting Strategy to the Setting

Skillful policy advocates realize that they have to adapt their strategy to the setting. We discuss later in this chapter, for example, how agency politics differ from legislative politics. However, there are many types of agencies, including those with a win-win and team-building atmosphere, and others with more conflictual relationships among staff or units. Two legislative committees may have entirely different norms and operating procedures. If the members of the House Economic and Educational Opportunities Committee are accustomed to wide-open conflict between liberals and conservatives, for instance, the members of the House and Senate Appropriations Committees have traditionally prided themselves on quiet, private deliberations, in which they seek behind-the-scenes solutions to budgetary issues.[16] Policy practitioners must adapt their tactics to such idiosyncrasies.

Building Scenarios to Construct Political Strategy

Thus far our discussion has been oriented toward both the future (setting objectives) and the present (examining the current realities germane to policy deliberations). Political strategy allows us to link the present with the future by identifying likely actions that will help policy advocates obtain their policy preferences.

Developing Alternative Scenarios

Policy advocates sort through a series of political options much as a quarterback considers the possible plays to use in a tight situation. Indeed, creative strategists run through successive what-if scenarios in which they explore whether various actions or statements may help them obtain their policy preferences.[17] Imagine three what-if scenarios. In Scenario 1, the policy advocate asks, "What would happen if I made a *single* presentation to a decision maker, suggesting a course of action?" This presentation might involve a request that a problem be taken seriously enough to be placed on a committee agenda, or a suggestion that a policy option be seriously considered. In some cases, this single presentation (a modest strategy) will suffice, particularly if the practitioner correctly assesses the current environment as supportive.

Policy advocates often develop at least two additional scenarios. Scenario 2's strategy is somewhat more ambitious; perhaps the single presentation will be coupled with discussions with key decision makers to make them more sympathetic to a proposal.

Scenario 3 is even more ambitious; it may involve creating a coalition, cultivating a constituency, coupling presentations with many personal discussions, allocating specific roles and tasks to a range of people, and mixing internal pressure with external pressure. (See Video Clip 10.1.) An example of an ambitious strategy occurred in the early 1990s. A coalition of organizations, in which the National Organization for Women was a central participant, developed a legislative proposal that would allow employees to obtain unpaid leave from work following the birth of a child, because of a parent's illness, or because of the death of a family member or close relative. NOW's members not only had personal liaisons with legislators and government officials but also exerted extensive external pressures on congressional members through letter writing and articles in the mass media.

VIDEO CLIP 10.1

DEVELOPING POLITICAL STRATEGY

In viewing video clip 10.1, consider the following. Susan Hoechstetter, Legislative Liaison of the National Social Work Research Center in Washington, DC, discusses her strategy for securing funds from Congress for this center. Did she anticipate bipartisan support? What kinds of external pressure did she hope to place on Congress?

We contrast the three preceding scenarios with an improvised one. In some cases, policy advocates decide not to formulate a strategy, but to seize opportunities as they arise.[18] At an opportune moment, they may inject an idea into committee discussions, a staff meeting, or a conversation with an official in their organization. Improvisational strategies are sometimes useful when policy advocates lack the time or knowledge of the situation to develop more refined strategies. However, unlike the three preceding strategy scenarios, improvisational strategies do not enable the policy advocate to mobilize and use power resources systematically.

Policy advocates need not invest major resources in this preliminary development of strategy scenarios because they need only the broad outlines of strategy at this point. In effect, they ask: Does this issue now require a major investment of resources and time, or should we address this issue with a modest or improvisational strategy?

Selecting a Strategy

Pragmatic considerations and stylistic preferences shape the selection of strategy. Policy advocates review strategy options in light of the realities we have discussed in this chapter. If their force field analysis suggests that there is extraordinary opposition to their proposal, for example, they may select an ambitious, complex strategy that requires a significant investment of time and energy. However, they must also consider the limits of their resources and time. Accordingly, they often seek a strategy that will allow their measures to follow a path of least resistance.[19] If a proposal can be enacted with a relatively simple strategy that requires few resources and little time, most policy practitioners will select it. Even when they fear a more ambitious one is needed, they may select a relatively modest strategy because they lack time or they place a higher priority on another issue.

Policy advocates' strategy choices are also influenced by their stylistic preferences. Some of us state our positions directly, whereas others discuss them in private deliberations. Some people like to precipitate conflict by advancing controversial positions, and others serve as mediators. Some initiate policies; others prefer to amend or oppose proposals.

Different styles have advantages and disadvantages. Mediators facilitate compromises, but are sometimes accused of failing to take a solid position. Champions of ideological positions initiate proposals for bold changes but sometimes lack the compromise skills necessary for enactment. Persons who select only sure winners or who avoid controversial issues are seen as lacking courage or leadership.

Revising the Strategy

The preceding discussion fails to capture the fluid nature of devising strategies. People cannot make strategy without anticipating how possible opponents will act, but their original predictions of who will support or oppose a specific policy may be incorrect. Perhaps the opponents are more cohesive and bold than was originally assumed, or perhaps they are less effective, and the supporters will find their work easier than they expected.

Interventions devised at the beginning need to be revised as events unfold, as new configurations of support and opposition develop, and as the opponents' strategies change. During revision, strategists encounter the same challenge that confronted them initially: how to capitalize on and strengthen the sources of support for their policy and how to offset or neutralize the opposition.

During this process, the proposal itself may go through changes that require new strategies. In legislative settings, for example, proposed legislation is modified in the give-and-take of committee deliberations, in floor debates, and during negotiations among proponents of the bill, and legislators and their aides.[20]

Seven Recurring Steps in Strategy

We have discussed various factors that policy advocates must consider when they develop strategy, such as the need to establish objectives, to select the extent of policy changes, to select a time frame, to examine the distribution of power, to identify contextual factors, to examine situational factors, to construct alternative scenarios, and to develop strategy. With this as a backdrop, we can now discuss seven recurring steps (see Box 10.1) that policy advocates take when they develop strategy, even if they do not take these steps in any particular order. (In Chapter Eleven, we illustrate these steps in legislative, organizational, and community settings.)

BOX 10.1   Seven Steps in Formulating and Implementing Strategy

> *Organizing a team or coalition*
> - How will proponents organize a leadership team that will develop and coordinate strategy?
> - To the extent resources are needed, whether money or supplies, how will they be obtained?

BOX 10.1   *(continued)*

- To the extent a division of labor is required, such as committees or leaders focusing on specific tasks, how will it be worked out?

Establishing policy goals
- What do proponents wish to achieve?

Specifying a proposal's content and getting early sponsors
- What minimal features or content should the policy proposal contain?
- On what points can proponents negotiate or compromise?
- Can early sponsors be found, such as key legislators, who will support the proposal?

Establishing a style
- What level and scope of conflict will proponents seek?

Selecting power resources and framing strategy
- What kinds of person-to-person, substantive, decision-making, process, and context-shaping power resources will be used?
- Who will use these power resources and in what situations?

Implementing strategy
- How is the strategy to be put into action?
- When may it be necessary to improvise?

Revising the strategy
- How should the game plan be revised in light of the opponents' strategies?
- What new events or background factors suggest a change in strategy?

Organizing a Team or Coalition

Particularly in an ambitious project, policy advocates need to organize themselves into a coherent unit. As events unfold and opposition emerges, it is important that a proposal's proponents develop a common strategy so they will not disintegrate in the face of conflict or give out contradictory messages, and they will implement strategy effectively. They can either establish a new group or work with an existing advocacy group.

As we discuss in Chapter Twelve with respect to task groups, coalitions, and networks, proponents need to address at the outset issues of coordination, leadership, building constituencies, resolving conflict, dividing labor, and communication. They must continue to attend to these issues as events unfold. People may lose interest or become disenchanted with the cause, disagreements may develop about strategy, some people may think others are seeking the limelight, and some may become restive after setbacks.

Establishing Policy Goals

Early in the process, policy advocates have to establish policy goals within the context that they encounter. Do they want basic change or incremental change? Who are the likely proponents and opponents? Will the proposal meet major resistance or be widely accepted?

Specifying a Proposal's Content and Getting Early Sponsors

Policy advocates aim ultimately to have their proposal enacted, but they often must ask: Precisely what proposal? They have to decide what points of a proposal are most important to them and resist efforts to change or delete them. If they are willing to compromise excessively, they risk ending up with nothing, but if they are too rigid or dogmatic, no proposal at all may be enacted.

Early in the process, policy advocates need to find sponsors who will agree to support the proposal. If possible, such sponsors should be influential people who sit on key committees or hold important positions.

Establishing a Style

To be effective, a strategy needs an overarching style. Will behind-the-scenes and non-conflictual deliberations suffice, or is more conflictual and publicized interaction advisable? Of course, the style may change: If a low-conflict approach is unsuccessful, policy practitioners may wish to use a higher-conflict approach.

Selecting Power Resources and Framing Strategy

Decisions must be made about who will use which power resources in which situations. If several people are involved in a project, they may divide the responsibilities for talking with specific people, making presentations, doing research, compiling lists of supporters, and other functions. For example, people seeking policy changes in an agency may decide the following: Joe will propose a place on the next staff meeting agenda to discuss modifying the intake procedure; Mary will comment on the inadequacies of the existing procedure at the staff meeting; Tom will make some comments that support Joe and Mary; Elise will suggest forming a task force to devise a new policy. Moreover, this group might decide to approach some staff members before the meeting to get support for the policy change. Similarly, a coalition of groups seeking a change in legislative policy might assign specific research to one group, ask another group to approach important legislators, and ask still another to compile a mailing list that can be used later in a letter-writing campaign.

Implementing Strategy

Having devised a strategy, policy advocates must implement it skillfully. They must use the full range of policy practice skills (interactional, political, and analytic) to carry out their strategy over an extended period. Skillful advocates sometimes have to deviate from their planned strategy when circumstances require improvisation.

Revising the Strategy

Policy advocates who hold rigidly to a strategy often imperil their success. They may have made miscalculations in devising their strategy, such as underestimating the strength of the opposition or the opponents' counter strategy. Unanticipated events also shape deliberations and may require a modification of strategy.

Chapter Summary

What You Can Now Do

Political strategy puts power resources to use. You are now equipped to do the following:

- Develop objectives and positions at the outset
- Ground strategy in current realities by doing a force field analysis that includes persons' positions, contextual factors, situational realities, and likely future developments
- Build alternative scenarios to select and revise strategy
- Use seven steps in building strategy including organizing a team or coalition or working through an existing advocacy group, establishing policy goals within a context, specifying a proposal's content and getting early sponsors, establishing a style, selecting power resources and framing strategy, implementing strategy, and revising the strategy

We are now prepared to see in the next chapter how policy advocates put political strategy into action in legislative, agency, and community settings.

Notes

1. Ron Dear and Rino Patti discuss the need for compromises in policy making in "Legislative Advocacy," *Encyclopedia of Social Work,* 18th ed., vol. 2 (Silver Spring, MD: National Association of Social Workers, 1987), p. 37.
2. George Brager and Stephen Holloway, *Changing Human Service Organizations* (New York: Free Press, 1978), pp. 107–128.
3. Kurt Lewin, *Field Theory in Social Science* (New York: Harper & Row, 1951).
4. William Coplin and Michael O'Leary, *Everyman's Prince* (North Scituate, MA: Duxbury, 1976), pp. 7–25.
5. Stephen Frantzich, *Computers in Congress* (Beverly Hills, CA: Sage, 1982), pp. 248–250.
6. Coplin and O'Leary, *Everyman's Prince,* pp. 20–25, 170–175.
7. Eric Schattschneider, *The Semisovereign People* (New York: Holt, Rinehart & Winston, 1960), pp. 1–19.
8. See the discussion of organizations' traditions, objectives, and ideology in Brager and Holloway, *Changing Human Service Organizations,* pp. 57–66.
9. Brager and Holloway discuss the role of persons' tangible interests in shaping their position in *Changing Human Service Organizations,* pp. 85–92.
10. Julie Kosterlitz discusses feminist pressure in "Not Just Kid Stuff," *National Journal* 20 (November 19, 1988): 2934–2939.
11. See John Kingdon, *Agendas, Alternatives, and Public Choices* (Boston: Little, Brown, 1984), pp. 152–170.
12. See Yeheskel Hasenfeld, *Human Service Organizations* (Englewood Cliffs, NJ: Prentice Hall, 1983), pp. 43–49.
13. See Perry Smith, *Taking Charge* (Washington, DC: National Defense University Press, 1986), pp. 17–26.
14. Samuel Bacharach and Edward Lawler, *Power and Politics in Organizations* (San Francisco: Jossey-Bass, 1980).
15. Thomas Schelling, *The Strategy of Conflict* (Cambridge: Harvard University Press, 1960).

16. Richard Fenno, *The Power of the Purse* (Boston: Little, Brown, 1966), pp. 193–195.
17. See Schelling, *The Strategy of Conflict.*
18. Eugene Bardach, *The Skill Factor in Politics* (Berkeley and Los Angeles: University of California Press, 1972), pp. 188–189.
19. Brager and Holloway, *Changing Human Service Organizations,* pp. 140–141.
20. Bardach, *The Skill Factor in Politics,* pp. 183–194.

Suggested Readings

Gauging Political Feasibility

William Coplin and Michael O'Leary, *Everyman's Prince* (North Scituate, MA: Duxbury, 1976).

Understanding and Predicting Conflict

Morton Deutsch, *The Resolution of Conflict: Constructive and Destructive Processes* (New Haven, CT: Yale University Press, 1973), pp. 124–152.

Developing and Implementing Political Strategy

Eugene Bardach, *The Skill Factor in Politics* (Berkeley and Los Angeles: University of California Press, 1972), pp. 183–240.

Ron Dear and Rino Patti, "Legislative Advocacy: Seven Effective Tactics," *Social Work* 26 (July 1981): 289–297.

Case Studies of Legislative Politics

Jeffrey Birnbaum and Alan Murray, *Showdown at Gucci Gulch* (New York: Random House, 1987).

Eric Redman, *The Dance of Legislation* (New York: Simon & Schuster, 1973).

Policy Practice in Legislative Settings

Donald deKieffer, *The Citizen's Guide to Lobbying Congress* (Chicago: Chicago Review Press, 1997).

Willard Richan, *Lobbying for Social Change* (New York: Haworth Press, 1996).

Politics in Agency Settings

Burton Gummer, *The Politics of Social Administration: Managing Organizational Politics in Social Agencies* (Englewood Cliffs, NJ: Prentice Hall, 1990).

Politics in Community Settings

Kimberly Bobo, Jackie Kendall, and Steve Max, *Organizing for Social Change: A Manual for Activists in the 1990s* (Washington, DC: Seven Locks Press, 1991).

Putting Political Strategy Into Action

<table>
<tr>
<td>POLICY
PREDICAMENT</td>
<td>Millions of workers across the nation constitute the so-called working poor. Often working near and just above the minimum wage, they lack resources to escape poverty. To remedy this situation for some workers, policy advocates across the nation decided to launch a grass-roots campaign in scores of cities to persuade city councils and mayors to require a "living wage" for persons hired by firms that were reimbursed by public contracts. Professor Manny Gale, Emeritus Professor of Social Work and Gerontology at California State University in Sacramento, helped develop such a campaign in Sacramento. (See Policy Advocacy Challenge 11.2 on page 361.)</td>
</tr>
</table>

We have provided, thus far, an overview of strategy no matter what the setting. Whether policy advocates work in legislative, community, or agency settings, they have to take the seven strategy steps described in Box 10.1 on pages 340-341. They have to organize a team or coalition (or tap into an existing one), establish policy goals within the context of a specific setting, specify a proposal's content, establish a style, select power resources and frame, implement, and revise strategy. Yet different settings also provide specific challenges, so we now discuss political strategy in legislative, agency, and community settings. No matter the setting, there are task groups such as committees, advocacy groups, coalitions, and networks to work with.

We discuss in this chapter how advocates can do the following:

- Organize a campaign to secure the enactment of a specific legislative proposal
- Use an array of interventions that puts pressure on legislators
- Organize or participate in an effort to change an agency policy
- Organize or participate in a community-based effort to change a community policy
- Work with task groups to seek policy changes in legislatures, agencies, or communities

Strategy in Legislative Settings

Policy advocates sometimes work to get a specific piece of legislation enacted—an ambitious undertaking in light of the sheer number of measures that legislators consider during any given session.[1] Or they perform certain tasks in a project organized by other advocates, such as letter-writing campaigns. Even participation in a broader effort, however, requires an understanding of the legislative process, so we analyze political strategy in legislative settings on two levels in this chapter: We discuss how to organize projects to get legislation enacted, and we discuss an array of specific tasks that policy advocates can undertake within them. (*Specific activities* that policy advocates can undertake within legislative projects are described in Box 11.1).

BOX 11.1   Specific Activities That Policy Advocates Can Undertake within Larger Projects

> Testifying before a legislative committee
> Lobbying specific legislators in person
> Writing a letter to a legislator as part of a larger campaign
> Telephoning a legislator's office about a specific measure (or organizing a
>   phone tree)
> Writing a letter to a newspaper about a specific measure
> Participating in a demonstration about a specific measure
> Alerting a legislator to a specific issue or problem in the human services
> Raising funds for a specific advocacy project

Organizing Legislative Advocacy Projects from Scratch

Organizing a Team or Coalition

Policy advocates need an organized group that will spearhead the drive toward enactment of a legislative proposal. It may be an existing group, such as an advocacy group; a coalition of groups established to secure legislation; or the NASW. This group needs leadership, such as a strategy committee that will pull together research materials and devise a master strategy. If an advocacy group is leaderless, its members will probably march in different directions and give out conflicting messages, undermining the group's effectiveness.[2]

An organized group is needed especially in legislative settings because legislatures are complex organizations with participants who make their living by supporting *and* opposing legislative proposals. To succeed in this environment, an advocacy team must operate with considerable efficiency. The team has to create a unified and effective strategy to keep its proposal from being lost among the hundreds of measures on the legislative agenda. If the proposal is controversial, like many that would redistribute resources or services to oppressed populations, it is likely to encounter opposition that can be overcome only by effective strategy.

A stifling or overly centralized team will be counterproductive because the collaborators need the freedom to be innovative and to use their distinctive strengths. But many good projects founder because proponents fail to set up a central leadership that will identify the key tasks, allocate these tasks to team members, and monitor the expeditious completion of the tasks.

Early in the process, proponents need to identify their allies without ruling out possible allies too aggressively; strange bedfellows often rally to an issue. Advocates should have a big-tent philosophy, to the extent this is possible, while also recognizing likely foes from their past records and prior statements.[3] (They are not actual foes until they have taken action against this specific proposal.) Some groups or persons may agree to participate, but only on terms that are unacceptable to the proponents, such as demanding unacceptable provisions in the proposal.

Early in the process, policy advocates also should compile a *resource book* that includes the existing law, legal memoranda from attorneys who have been consulted, likely opponents, likely allies, congressional contacts on key committees (both aides and legislators in both supporting and opposing camps), civil servants from administrative agencies that will be affected by the proposal, and a set of key issues.[4] The organization's team has to know who the key players are. Once proposed legislation is introduced, it is immediately referred to a committee, and based on tradition, advocates should be able to predict how their proposal is likely to be routed. Then they need to analyze which members of the committee are likely to support and oppose the proposal.

Because it contains sensitive information, this resource book (actually, a spiral notebook divided into sections) should not be disseminated beyond the key leaders of the coalition. (If a list of likely foes is widely seen, for example, they may become real foes.)

Establishing Policy Goals in a Legislative Context

At the inception of their work, policy advocates must decide what kinds of policy changes they seek. Do they want to develop new legislation or amend an existing piece of legislation? Do they want to increase funding for a specific program, or do they want to change the administrative regulations that guide the implementation of an existing program? (We discuss these questions in more detail in Chapter Thirteen.) Do they seek relatively modest changes or more ambitious reforms? To what extent are they willing to compromise with likely opponents of their proposal to increase the likelihood of its enactment?

Specifying a Proposal's Content and Getting Early Sponsors

The first rule of legislative lobbying is to do your homework. Advocates have to write a *policy brief,* which comprises an analysis of the existing law, their proposal, why they want to change the existing policy, and the likely objections to their proposal (with rebutting responses).[5] (This policy brief should also be kept in a spiral notebook, separated into sections.) Advocates must know their issue so that they can state concisely (a) what they are concerned about; (b) how their issue affects other areas, such as likely costs and effects on other programs or laws; (c) an array of possible remedies with their likely costs and implementation problems; (d) an initial proposal (not yet in the form of a legislative bill) that addresses the problem; and (e) the likely arguments of opponents.

Most legislators are lawyers, so advocates need to have expert legal opinions early in the advocacy process. Sometimes, they commission a legal memorandum from an experienced law firm (for a fee that is negotiated in advance) to outline the existing law as interpreted by the courts and to tell them how other laws would be affected by the implementation of their proposal.[6] (Alternatively, as we discuss later, advocates can get expert advice from staff assistants to legislators, members of legislative committees, or civil servants.)

The policy brief should contain the likely objections of opponents of the proposal, as well as rebutting arguments. This rebuttal section is pivotal: As a project unfolds, advocates and their allies have to stand together with contrary formulated arguments to rebut the opposition. They do not want different members to give different arguments and different data when the proposal reaches the legislative process or when members of the mass media ask questions about it. Moreover, policy advocates may sometimes decide that they must conduct sit-ins or other demonstrations to draw attention to an issue that legislators have decided to ignore.

We can distinguish between the policy brief that advocates have developed for their own internal use, and proposals they subsequently present to legislators and others, which are often one- or two-page documents that state very succinctly the purpose, rationale, and content of a proposal. Since legislators and others are very busy, it is essential that documents that reach them be brief. Great care must be taken to avoid jargon and excess verbage.

Advocates must make key contacts early in the policy process to secure commitments to the general thrust of their project, even though they have not yet drafted a specific piece of legislation. Later, they will try to get some legislators to sponsor their legislation by agreeing to put their names at the top of the legislative proposal.

Establishing a Style

Legislative advocates usually have an out-front, assertive style. They have to draw attention to their proposal by making contact with many legislators, including those who are on the committees that will consider their proposal.

Personal lobbying, letter writing, and press coverage are often more effective than demonstrations.[7] Protests sometimes incite the opponents of a measure or lead to incidents that make the change effort controversial, although protests may be effective if they are part of a larger strategy.

Policy advocates must decide whether or not they want to assume a relatively nonconflictual style. If they seek only modest changes in existing policy that they believe will attract widespread support, they might seek a relatively nonconflictual political process and a narrow scope of conflict. By contrast, some policy advocates might decide that considerable conflict is necessary to secure the enactment of a controversial reform that pits conservative legislators against liberal ones. In such a situation, they might broaden the scope of the conflict by seeking media coverage and by encouraging many groups to pressure legislators.

Selecting Power Resources and Framing Strategy

Once advocates have finished their research and put together a resource book, they have to develop a *strategy book* that lays out their tactics for the entire campaign. Like the resource book, this material should be kept confidential.[8] It should specify the following:

1. *Press representation.* This task should be done by people who can effectively speak for the legislative proposal. Also to be decided are who will issue press releases and who will be the contact persons if the press need additional information.

2. *Legislators to be contacted,* particularly on the committees likely to hear the legislative proposal. Advocates should also list the key aides of legislators and their personal phone numbers, as well as legislators who are likely to be friendly to the legislative proposal even if they are not on the key committees. Advocates should do a complete analysis of the voting records of these legislators on similar pieces of legislation; this information is available from such lobbying organizations as Americans for Democratic Action and the AFL-CIO's Committee on Political Education. They also should do an analysis of their home districts, making a page for each legislator, that will later serve as briefing material for the advocates who lobby the legislators. For each legislator, advocates should note whether they or their allies have special links with them, whether they know people who live within their constituencies, and whether specific arguments are likely to be particularly persuasive with them.

3. *A committee to spearhead a letter-writing campaign,* to decide when letters will be sent, what their substantive content will be, and who will send them. As with legislative testimony, the advocates need to put forth a consistent argument with legislators.

4. *An initial plan for a blitz of the legislature.* A large group will make appointments with an array of legislators and their staff to push the issue on specific prearranged days. The plan should discuss when this will occur, who will participate, and which key legislators should be targeted.

So far, the advocates have only identified a specific problem and a proposed remedy, but they haven't drafted a specific legislative proposal. Nor have they lined up legislative sponsors.

Implementing Strategy

Implementing a strategy skillfully requires adherence to the conventions or protocols of legislative politics regarding lobbying, testifying, using the mass media and writing letters.

Approaching legislative staff   At numerous points during their work, policy advocates talk with legislative committee staff who number roughly 7,500 in the Congress alone. They must devote considerable time to discussions with legislative staff; indeed, they will probably spend more time with them than with the legislators themselves. Most legislators rely on their staff to make recommendations about key issues—and often scuttle measures when lobbyists have failed to brief their staff.[9] In light of the sheer number of bills submitted to legislatures (20,000 are submitted to the Congress each year), legislators must depend on their staff in this way.

We have already discussed that the policy brief developed for internal use by advocates must be condensed into a brief format so that legislators and others can quickly understand its rationale and substance. For example, a two- to three-page document that also might contain appendix materials is useful.

Advocates should realize that each legislator's office is like a small agency. The legislator often has a personal secretary who makes appointments; an administrative assistant; legislative assistants who specialize in such areas as domestic policy, foreign policy (in the case of the Congress), and liaison to committees on which the legislator sits; a press aide; and so-called case workers who manage constituent relations.

Advocates usually approach the chief staff person first, sometimes known as an administrative assistant or a senior legislative assistant. These aides are gatekeepers for legislators and political strategists, and they are usually more interested in a proposal's political merits than in its substantive merits. Advocates must convince this aide that the legislator's support of their issue will bring him or her substantial political gain, through positive public relations, press releases welcoming the legislator's support, and well-publicized events in the legislator's district to show his or her support for the proposal and the support of key constituency groups. Advocates should be even-tempered but appropriately assertive in their discussions, and they should not oversell their proposal by making inflated claims. (Advocates should remember that in most cases, they are talking with seasoned political professionals who are very well versed in legislative politics.) If the administrative assistant likes their proposal, a legislator's support is often likely, though details are often worked out with lower-level staff who have substantive expertise in the proposal area. These aides are called legislative assistants.

In discussions with legislative assistants, advocates can focus more on the substance of their proposal than on its political merits. In these discussions, advocates give information about the proposal and its merits, and ask for advice. If legislative assistants like the proposal, they can often convince the administrative assistants—and the legislators themselves—to support the proposal.

At some point, advocates will work with a legislator's press aides, such as by drafting a press release for them that announces the legislator's support for the proposal. (Advocates usually schedule appointments with administrative assistants or press aides, through the legislator's personal secretary.)

Working with committee staff   Proposals are processed by legislative committees, which have their own staff, usually appointed by the senior members of the committee. (Nearly 7,500 committee staffers work in the federal legislature; they are powerful participants in the legislative process.) Some of these staff are appointed by members of the majority party and some by members of the minority party. Since they are technically versed in specific areas, advocates should focus with them on the actual provisions of a proposal.[10] Advocates should seek meetings, perhaps over lunch, with committee staff who are responsible for the topic of the proposal; they should brief them and ask them what further information they need, offering to get it for them promptly. Advocates will probably need to keep in touch with key committee staff on a weekly basis or more frequently. They should also consult with staff members from the opposing party. Legislators' personal staff often defer to committee staff members' expertise.

Thus far, advocates probably do not have an actual legislative proposal, but simply a general position or a rough draft of a legislative proposal. At this point, to get help with the proper wording of the proposed legislation, advocates should ask for expert advice from the legal counsel of the legislative committee, the committee staff, or a legislative assistant of a friendly legislator who has sufficient expertise to help them in the drafting effort.

Policy advocates need sponsorship and support if their bills are to be enacted. They must find legislators who will agree to place their names as sponsors (or introducers) at the top of the legislation. Advocates should seek numerous sponsors from both political parties and sponsors who are highly placed in the legislative chambers, such as the presiding office, the majority whip, and the chairpersons of the committees that will examine the proposed legislation.[11] Of course, as we have already discussed, a legislator's agreement to sponsor a bill is not an agreement to invest considerable energy in its enactment, although advocates hope that their discussions with legislators and their aides will convince them to commit their personal resources to it.

Advocates also should seek formal support from the head of government—the governor, president, or mayor—and from the director of the department or agency that will implement the legislation. Of course, their support cannot always be obtained, as many liberal advocates have discovered when they confronted conservative administrations.

Lobbying legislators   *Lobbying* legislators is having personal discussions with them or their aides to elicit support for a bill. In this effort, advocates should use the background material on legislators in their resource book and their strategy book. (See Video Clip 11.1.)

VIDEO CLIP 11.1

HOW TO LOBBY

In viewing Video Clip 11.1, consider the following. Professor Ron Dear is the social work profession's top authority on lobbying, having spent many years lobbying the state legislature in Olympia in the state of Washington.

•What are some personal qualities of good lobbyists?
•Why do legislators *need* lobbyists?
•Do lobbyists need large networks of contacts to be successful?

Through the legislator's appointment secretary, an advocate makes an appointment at least a week in advance for no more than 15 minutes. Advocates should be certain that legislative assistants are also asked to be present, to avoid the appearance of going over their heads. The legislative assistant should be briefed before the meeting. (As we noted earlier, some legislators will dismiss a project if their legislative assistants have not been briefed—and they themselves usually expect to have been briefed by their legislative assistants before they meet with an advocate.[12]) If possible, advocates should include in their delegation someone from the legislator's home district.

On their arrival, advocates should first talk with the legislative assistant, introducing him or her to their delegation and bringing additional briefing materials. When advocates enter the legislator's office, they should cordially introduce their delegation, praising the help they have received from the legislative assistant even if they have received little assistance. (They may need the assistant's further help later.) They should give the legislator a one- or two-page summary of their issue and briefly go over its main points, stressing the political gains the legislator will receive in his or her constituency from his or her support. Appendix materials can accompany the summary or can be provided later on request. Advocates should never bully legislators or make outlandish claims; they should present their case succinctly and with appropriate assertiveness.[13] Advocates should specifically ask the legislator to support their proposal and should keep their comments short, not exceeding 15 minutes unless the legislator lengthens the session. Do not get sidetracked by extraneous issues, and keep the legislator on the topic if he or she tries to shift the subject. Each member of the delegation should leave a business card. If the legislator asks questions to which they do not know the answer, the advocates should offer to get the answers to him or her promptly.[14] Remember, your reputation for honesty is one of your most important power resources in legislative settings—even though many people think most legislators are double-dealers, and not to be trusted.

The follow-up to the meeting should include short thank you notes to the legislator and to individual staff members, briefly restating the basic points made in the meeting.

Advocates should not be awed by legislators, even those with considerable reputations. Instead they should view the meeting as a service because it gives the legislator a chance to enhance his or her reputation by supporting their issue, and provides the legislator with facts and arguments that can be used to support the issue.

Branching out to reach allies   Advocates need an array of allies to support their projects,[15] including government agencies and other interest groups. Most government agencies have their own lobbyists, so their support of an advocacy proposal often means added clout with the legislature. Advocates should ascertain which agencies are most likely to help them by gauging which agencies' budgets, responsibilities, or prestige will be enhanced by the proposal, and which agencies are currently working in the area of the proposal. In their discussions with civil servants or politically appointed agency staff, advocates should emphasize that their proposal is intended to help the agency do its job even better. At some point in the legislative process, some agencies may issue a formal position on the advocates' proposal; if this position is supportive, the advocates should work closely with the agency's legislative liaison office to enlist its aid.

Advocates establish some allies when they form their team or coalition. They should then approach other interest groups that share the objectives of their project. Careful ground rules must be established: Advocates want the support of other groups, but they do not want loose cannons that take positions, make arguments, and use tactics that are divergent from those of the original team. The team cannot excessively muzzle or restrain its allies, but establishing some clearance and review methods will coordinate the collaboration. While endorsement by myriad groups looks impressive, advocates most want as allies groups that will commit time, resources, and public support. Endorsements should include permission to use allies' names publicly.

Advocates can sometimes persuade legislators to write letters to their colleagues supporting the advocates' position. These letters may be very effective, especially when they come from respected or powerful legislators. (Several letters can be written or a number of legislators can sign a single letter.)

The blitz   Policy advocates often decide to invade the legislature with a concentrated all-out mobilization of resources. A blitz takes many weeks of planning. Appointments for three- or four-person delegations to crucial legislators must be made weeks in advance; a master schedule of the visits must be devised; and delegations must have fact sheets on the proposal as well as information on the legislators they will visit.[16] At the appointment, the delegation presents arguments for its proposal and asks the legislator about his or her questions or concerns. After the blitz, the legislators' questions must be answered promptly—and members of delegations must send personal thank you notes to the legislators. The leadership team reviews the feedback received by the delegations to gauge which legislators are supportive, uncertain, or opposed.

Getting legislation introduced   A sponsoring legislator introduces the advocates' proposal into the legislative process, so it is referred to a legislative committee. The chairperson of that committee then refers it to a subcommittee that schedules hearings on the proposal. Whether these hearings are scheduled at all, as well as their timing, is critical. Hearings on a proposal that are delayed to the end of a legislative session receive the required committee report so late that action cannot be taken by the full legislature.[17] Roughly two-thirds of bills introduced in Congress receive no hearings at all. The chances that early hearings will be held on a bill increases when the committee chairperson cosponsors it or when it is actually introduced by the incumbent administration. So advocates need to approach the chairperson of the legislative committee immediately after their proposal has been introduced. They can also ask their other congressional supporters to request that the chairperson schedule early hearings. In a few cases, their congressional supporters will decide that their measure should be reassigned to another committee or should even be reported from the committee by means of unusual parliamentary tactics that will bypass committee members who oppose it.

Testifying   Once hearings are scheduled, advocates should make certain that representatives of their group or coalition are invited to testify, by getting friendly committee staff or staff of legislators to recommend them. Advocates should make clear that they want to testify and that they will keep their testimony brief. Sometimes they ensure a chance at testifying by offering a well-known person, but they should be certain that celebrities are well briefed and use arguments that the advocates' team has assembled.

The protocol for legislative testimony is simple. Advocates submit a brief written statement several days before their testimony. In the first two pages or so, the rationale, focus, and substance of the proposal is presented so legislators can quickly understand it. (Appendix materials that provide further detail can be attached.) This statement must be carefully written so that it reads well and also contains detailed information and data, often in the appendix, that cannot easily be given in a speech. It gives a fuller exposition of the advocate's position and is intended to be read by legislators and their aides. However, the statement cannot be read at legislative hearings, where testifiers are expected to speak only for about 10 minutes. Advocates should list their main points, making their testimony dramatic and spontaneous so that it captures the committee's attention, perhaps by using specific cases as illustrations. Friendly legislators may prompt some committee members to ask questions that will elicit the strong points of the proposal or that will undermine the arguments of opponents. Advocates should be prepared for friendly as well as hostile questions from legislators; ideology and political interests often shape legislators' responses. If asked hostile questions, advocates should stand their ground, stick to their key arguments and data, and not volunteer information that goes beyond the questions asked. Advocates want to be seen as principled people with a well-reasoned case.[18] (See Video Clip 11.2.)

Candor and honesty are highly valued in legislative hearings. If advocates do not know the answer to a question, rather than bluffing, they should say they will find the answer and send it in writing to the committee.

Using the mass media   The mass media can often help policy advocates reach a broad audience that will, in turn, place pressure on politicians to take action. Advocates have several options.[19] A press conference that makes their case for a proposal may be scheduled on the same day as a blitz or the first legislative committee hearing. (See Video Clip 11.3.)

VIDEO CLIP 11.2

HOW TO USE THE MEDIA

In viewing Video Clip 11.2, consider the following. Ron Dear, Associate Professor at the School of Social Work of the University of Washington, discusses how to use the media in policy advocacy.

Of course, advocates must first get the attention of the mass media, which are besieged by people who want coverage. Advocates must make their story appear dramatic and relevant to larger social issues. They should establish personal links with key reporters in the print media, radio, and television, giving them full information about their issue and why it is important.[20] (Some reporters will be less friendly than others, and some critical stories about their project may appear if their issue is controversial.) To get reporters to come to a news conference, send written materials announcing it to reporters with whom you have established contacts and to others. You can also target the mass media in pivotal politicians' districts. If, for example, the chair of a legislative committee has bottlenecked a proposal, allies from an advocacy group in her district might call a press conference to pressure her into supporting the legislation.

Policy advocates sometimes use demonstrations to pressure legislators and to get coverage from the mass media. This tactic may not be as effective as lobbying legislators directly, but it will dramatize an issue and make clear that a substantial group is interested in it. Like legislative blitzes, demonstrations must be organized with care to prevent unnecessary altercations with police and to achieve maximum effect.[21]

Another tactic is writing guest editorials to be sent to the editorial offices of newspapers, radio stations, and television stations. Such editorials should not exceed 800 words and are more likely to be published if well-known persons write them and if they convey a dramatic, well-written message. Advocates can also write letters to the editors of periodicals, stating their central points briefly and dramatically. (See Policy Advocacy Challenge 11.1.)

Orchestrating telephone and letter-writing campaigns   Campaigns to call or write the offices of legislators may use the membership lists of community or professional groups. Letter writers should be provided with suggested themes, but not with form letters: legislators consider individualized letters more credible than standardized letters.[22]

**POLICY
ADVOCACY
CHALLENGE 11.1**

***WRITING EFFECTIVE
"LETTERS TO THE
EDITOR"***

*Ronald B. Dear, D.S.W.,
Associate Professor,
School of Social Work,
University of
Washington*

These are the ten tips I offer my students when I give them the assignment of writing a letter to the editor of a newspaper or other periodical. These tips can also prove useful when writing letters to legislators and other public officials.

1. *Start with your reason for writing.* Be specific about the issue to which you are responding; for example: "I agree with your editorial of October 15 on the necessity of family leave policy, but you seem to have concluded. . . ." You do not need to state the name of the periodical or, if you are writing to a newspaper, the section in which the article or editorial appeared—the editor will know.

2. *Be timely.* Write immediately when you see something to which you wish to respond. You are most excited and concerned at that point. Also, people quickly forget editorials, columns, and letters. Don't respond to yesterday's news or issues. A fine letter, sent too late, will never get published.

3. *Brevity is important.* Your letter should be no longer than one page, 200 to 250 words. Longer letters do, of course, get published occasionally, but they are the exception rather than the rule. To make your letter more readable, divide it into several short paragraphs rather than one long one.

4. *Get to your point right away.* Don't ramble. This is no time for a mystery. You are responding to something. Why? Make it clear.

5. *Address only one issue or topic.* Too many issues and topics make the letter confusing and raise the question about what it is, exactly, you are writing about.

6. *Tone.* Make it terse. Punchy. Humorous, if possible. Be provocative, but always be civil. Give strong opinions. Use logical, lively writing. Editors look for challenge, especially of their views. They like differences of opinion to be well stated.

7. *Give reasons for your views.* Be very specific and, when appropriate, use factual information. However, when you cite dates and facts, make sure they are correct; for example: "Recent poverty data, as cited in the New York. *Times* on October 2 . . ." or "The *U.S. Statistical Abstract* 1996, p. 412, shows that most elderly are not poor."

8. *If you have expertise on the subject, say that you do*—for example, "I have been a CPS worker for the past 12 years and. . . ."

9. *If you have personal (as opposed to professional) experience that is relevant, state it*—for example: "I am a mother with three children, all in Seattle public schools, and I was appalled by the recent article on the upcoming levy."

10. *Be constructive as to what you think should be done.* You have commented and perhaps criticized. What would you do?

Finally, make sure you include your work and home phone numbers. Editors will always verify a letter before they publish it.

Effective letters are short, rarely exceeding two pages, that quickly get to the point; they describe the issue and the advocate's organization or interest in it, discuss the current law and the proposed changes in it, urge positive action, and make clear that the legislator's position will be closely followed in their home district.

Revising the Strategy

Advocates must revise their initial strategy at various points during their campaign because a campaign for an issue is an evolving phenomenon shaped by changing events. For example, other groups and politicians often advocate rival measures. In such cases, policy advocates must try to influence the rival measures when their own measures are stymied. Many other factors can also necessitate changes in strategy. For example, expected opposition or support might not materialize or might increase, external events (such as a budget shortfall) might intrude, or a parliamentary obstacle might emerge or be removed.

Strategy in Agency Settings

The seven strategy steps listed in Box 10.1 also are relevant to organizational settings. Here, too, policy advocates must develop a strategy that will enhance the achievement of their policy objectives.

Organizing a Team or Coalition

Policy advocates often want to obtain changes in agencies' policies as they work within them or as they monitor them from a funding agency. As in legislative settings, policy advocates need to assemble a team or coalition, even if it is loosely constructed, from among people with similar values, people from specific units or programs, members of informal groups or associations, union leaders, or people from different levels in the agency's formal organization.

Establishing Policy Goals in the Organizational Context

Policy advocates are involved in an array of policy goals. One is the extent to which they will respond to policies that descend on them from external sources, such as legislatures, government agencies, insurance companies, and the courts. Their responses include deciding not to seek funds from certain sources (thus avoiding specific policies), seeking external funding from programs whose policies they enthusiastically support, and seeking external funding from programs whose policies they partially accept. When they do accept funds, agency staff have to decide whether to comply with the policies that accompany the funds. They may have various amounts of discretion. For example, a not-for-profit agency that accepts funds for services to teenage mothers who receive welfare may strictly enforce the coercive policies of the welfare authorities or may soften the edges of these policies by not reporting some information to the welfare authorities or by taking other evasive actions.

Shaping informal policies is an important activity in social agencies. (In Chapter One, we stated that the shared beliefs and norms of staff constitute one form of social policy.) When they believe that current informal policies are having a negative effect, staff members can modify them by trying to modify the organization's culture through educational techniques, the use of consultants, and direct interventions with colleagues. They can also shape informal policies by promoting the hiring of people whose policy preferences concur with their own.

Policy advocates may also try to influence who oversees specific programs, where services are provided, what budget allocations specific programs receive, and what kinds of funds the agency seeks from external funders. In each of these cases, a policy advocate shapes the agency's policies by influencing their implementation and budget choices rather than by trying to change official agency policies.

Agency staff can try to shape official policy at the highest levels of the agency, such as its mission, formal policies, and budgets, or they can concentrate on policies in specific agency units or programs, even bypassing higher-level staff when they believe they will receive more favorable responses at the unit or program level. (Recall that the student intern in Policy Advocacy Challenge 9.2 decided with her preceptor not to bring her innovation to high-level staff until it had been implemented as a pilot program.)

Astute tacticians analyze an issue's political economy. When doing force field analysis, they ask whether a specific policy will deter clients or attract a steady stream of clients and resources to the organization. They also note how it will enhance the agency's reputation, flow of clients, support from funding sources, or support from accrediting agencies. Because executives often favor maintaining staff morale, reducing internal conflict, and providing quality services, tacticians can also emphasize these kinds of positive consequences of a specific policy proposal.[23] Recall how the student intern in Policy Advocacy Challenge 10.2 planned to argue that developing group services for the children of institutionalized parents would increase referrals to the clinic and its prestige in the community.

Skillful tacticians view an organization's *formal attributes*—meaning its hierarchy and division of labor—as both constraints and opportunities. As a constraint, hierarchy intimidates persons who believe that their superiors will oppose a policy change. In organizations that lack a team-building atmosphere, some persons understandably fear that they may lose a promotion, a pay increase, or even the job by supporting even relatively small changes that top officials do not favor. Where intimidation and fear exist, support for proposed policy changes may be significantly reduced. When social service organizations are unionized (many public and nongovernmental agencies have unions), lower-level staff may be emboldened to support policy changes, though many unions restrict themselves to bread-and-butter issues, such as employees' wages and working conditions.

Hierarchy also provides opportunities. Astute tacticians can defuse the formal organization's negative aspects by finding allies for a proposed change within the higher ranks of administration. (The student intern in Policy Advocacy Challenge 10.2 hoped to defuse opposition to her proposal by obtaining Mr. Jones's support, since other staff deferred to him on issues relating to outpatient services.) In rarer instances, they can use top officials' opposition to a suggested change to rally lower-level staff against these top officials, a tactic trade unions often use. This tactic must be used with caution, however, because it may merely entrench higher-level officials' opposition to a proposal and may lead to recriminations.

The division of labor is a constraint when it fragments organizations into competing units, causing members of one unit to oppose policy reforms that may benefit other units. When this win-lose ethos prevails, a policy practitioner may find it difficult to establish broad-based support for a change in existing policies. Indeed, the student intern in Policy Advocacy Challenge 10.2 feared that the director of training, Ida Brown, would oppose the innovation because it had come from Mr. Jones, a person she viewed as a rival. Divisions into separate units also can provide rich opportunities for coalitions if policy advocates can devise proposals that appeal to persons with different perspectives and interests, perhaps framing a proposal so that various units will have part of the action. The staff members of the unit that initiates a proposal might agree to a concession to another unit in return for its support.

Because organizations tend to have scarce resources, policy reformers must usually place *budget implications* at the fore in their force field analyses. A policy proposal's prognosis is usually bleak if it will cost the organization considerable funds and has little long-term prospect of generating offsetting funds from fees or external funders. Since it was unclear whether the student intern's innovation in Policy Advocacy Challenge 10.2 would generate fees or resources from funders, she probably should have devoted more energy to examining its fiscal implications.

When examining a proposal's budgetary implications, policy advocates need to consider fee-generating possibilities: whether external funders may be interested in funding it, whether the start-up costs will be offset by revenues once the innovation is institutionalized, and whether an inexpensive pilot phase is possible.

Policy changes that advance the important central goals of the agency (i.e., the *agency mission*)—or at least goals that the top management values—probably have a better chance than changes that are seen as irrelevant to these goals.[24] The student intern's innovation appealed to Mr. Jones in Policy Advocacy Challenge 10.2 precisely because he viewed it as furthering his commitments to community mental health and to outpatient services. When considering an issue's relationship to the agency's mission, policy advocates should refer also to the agency's context: Perhaps a proposal is not congruent with an agency's current mission, but it represents an innovation that addresses emerging community needs or issues that specific funders have prioritized.

It is easy to forget that policy advocates can obtain support for some proposals simply by emphasizing their relevance to beneficence or clients' well-being. As we discussed in Chapter Two, the hallmark of professions is their expressed ethical interest in helping clients. When conducting force field analyses, then, a policy advocate should ask what kinds of evidence will show that a specific proposal advances clients' well-being. Expert opinions, feedback from clients, evaluators' findings, and social scientists' work can buttress the case that a proposal will help clients. (The student intern could have strengthened her case for her innovation by finding evaluative or theoretical literature showing that her innovation would significantly help children.)

Recall our discussion in Chapter Four of *boundary spanners,* who derive power from their ability to lead an agency to sources of funds and referrals that will enhance its survival. Strategists strengthen support for a proposal when they can show that it will bring new funds and referrals or will enhance the agency's prestige in the wider community.

An advocate must gauge the *informal relationships* among organizational participants when assessing a proposal's potential support. When we conduct force field analyses to examine agency employees' separate opinions, we may ignore important relationships among agency staff members. People often take cues from others whom they respect, so convincing a single pivotal person often brings many other persons' support. Policy advocates need to be able to understand long-standing patterns of association and deference in their agency when they try to predict a proposal's outcome.[25]

Using *intermediaries,* which we discussed in Chapter Ten, is particularly important in the politics of organizations. A policy advocate who is a direct-service worker often seeks higher-level intermediaries' support for a proposal, so that other employees will follow their superiors' leads. It also is useful to seek the support of intermediaries in other units of the organization, because some people defer only to the superiors in their own units.

Policy advocates should not reach premature conclusions about the feasibility of a specific policy proposal; even when the outlook is bleak, support may be gained for a proposal if it is framed correctly and if process tactics (such as timing and the use of intermediaries) are chosen well.

Specifying a Proposal's Content

Policy advocates have to frame a proposal that specifies what they want to change in light of their objectives and the political realities—and whether they want merely incremental or larger shifts in policy. They can work on many fronts when participating in their agency's politics—changing official or informal policy, policy on implementing and budget choices, policy at higher levels of an organization, or policy in specific units.

Establishing a Style

Legislators are used to open, protracted, and public conflict among the members of different parties and persons with different ideologies. Indeed, they use conflict over specific issues to prove that they represent their constituents' interests better than the members of opposing parties do. In contrast, organizations' staff members tend not to want ongoing, protracted conflict, partly because staff members have to work together every day to implement agency programs. (Some leaders of organizations actively quell conflict to preserve their own power and preferences, to emphasize win-win decision-making processes, or to enhance the implementation of agency programs.)

If the politics of organizations tend to be more muted than the politics of legislatures, they can still be highly conflictual. Burton Gummer speculates that organizations are most likely to be politicized when they have scarce resources; when there is considerable internal conflict over the priority of different programs; when staff members have different service approaches or philosophies, such as different treatment methods; and when there is conflict between units, programs, or departments. He also notes that most organizations have at least some of these features.[26]

Style must be tailored to the setting and the issue. A frontal attack that polarizes the agency should be chosen only after all other alternatives have been weighed. Of course, conflict is usually unavoidable when major changes are sought that will infringe on the values and interests of key members of the organization.

Consensus-building efforts such as retreats, the use of external consultants who devise collaborative strategies, or group exercises that encourage full discussion of specific issues, frequently meet with considerable success. These devices are also used, however, to promote the views of a specific faction, as when executives use external consultants as "hired guns."

Selecting Power Resources and Framing Strategy

An array of strategy options exists in organizations:

Option 1. A direct-service worker decides to implement (or not to implement) a policy without consulting anyone. (We discussed issues of autonomy in Chapter Ten.)

Option 2. A social worker decides, much like the student intern in Policy Advocacy Challenge 9.2, to begin a pilot program with the support of her supervisor before seeking high-level policy clearance.

Option 3. A social worker decides to organize a broad-based coalition within his organization to seek a specific policy change. He decides to use a confrontive, polarizing style of politics, even though he realizes that the outcome is uncertain and that he risks alienating high-level officials.

Option 4. A social worker decides to develop a program innovation, but only after consulting extensively and striking deals with several people that result in extensive modifications of her original proposal.

Option 5. A social worker decides to change staff members' informal norms because she decides that they harm certain kinds of clients by giving them misdirected services. She persuades a high-level official to bring in an external consultant to give the staff technical training in new approaches to service delivery.

Option 6. A social worker sets up a task force to seek a collaborative win-win solution to a problem in an agency. She believes that a collaborative planning project will produce a better solution than a conflictual approach.

Option 7. Convinced that a proposal will be accepted only if it has the executive director's support, a social worker uses her supervisor as an intermediary to seek the executive director's approval for her proposal.

Option 8. Despairing of any other approach, a social worker settles on whistleblowing, taking an issue directly to the mass media in hopes that external pressure on the agency will make its officials remedy some of its staff members' unethical behavior.

Option 9. A policy advocate does not take an active role in developing a proposal but waits until a strategic moment to place pressure on people to modify the proposal. She uses her negotiating and mediating skills to develop a compromise proposal.

Revising the Strategy

As in legislative settings, strategists must often change their strategy as events unfold, investing greater political resources when they encounter more opposition than they had predicted, revising a proposal in response to a budget shortfall, or taking advantage of the fact that the expected opposition has not materialized.

Developing Strategy in Community Settings

Policy advocates in community settings try to change policies of community institutions or governmental agencies.

Organizing a Task Group

Whether they seek policy changes in legislatures, agencies, or communities, policy advocates usually work with groups, such as task groups, coalitions, and networks. So virtually any serious effort to change policy requires policy advocates to develop and use group-process skills. Sometimes they form new groups, such as a group dedicated to achieving a specific policy change. Sometimes they work with existing groups, such as an existing task group or committee, coalition, or network.[27]

There has been a veritable explosion of nongovernmental organizations at the national, state, county, and city levels that champion the needs of persons with special problems (such as blindness, breast cancer, and dyslexia) and out-groups (including women, Latinos, and refugees). Some groups focus on a population with a specific problem, for example, helping women obtain employment in the building trades or seeking greater assistance for Latinos with AIDS. All policy advocates need to find out, before they become fully engaged in an issue, what groups already exist to deal with that issue. In some cases, policy advocates start a local organization or initiate a coalition that pools the resources of several agencies and groups.

POLICY ADVOCACY CHALLENGE 11.2

THE SACRAMENTO LIVING WAGE CAMPAIGN

Emanuel Gale, Emeritus Professor of Social Work and Gerontology, California State University at Sacramento

The Sacramento campaign is part of a national movement addressing issues of low-wage workers who are struggling for economic survival at below Federal poverty guidelines.

The dramatic changes during the past 25 years, including globalization, mega-mergers, de-industrialization, exporting of jobs, the increase in temporary jobs, the necessity of mothers to work, and the decline in incomes—have negatively affected the economic security of working families.

"Free Trade" agreements, NAFTA, WTO and IMF, are exploiting developing nations and enriching corporations and banks, at the expense of working families at home and abroad.

The widening gaps in incomes since 1975, have been documented by federal and state sources. The U.S. Bureau of Labor Statistics data, analyzing real wages in the U.S., demonstrate that average hourly wages peaked in 1973. Despite economic expansion, wages in 1998 were 13 percent below 1973.

A report of the Legislative Analyst's Office, "California's Changing Income Distribution" (Aug. 2000) reviewed the average adjusted gross income by percentile of taxpayers—1975–1998. The report documented that the bottom quintile lost 24.8 percent in purchasing power while the top quintile gained 66.3 percent.

Living Wage Campaigns

The first living wage ordinance was enacted in Baltimore in 1994. Since then, 65 communities have adopted similar ordinances. In California, 14 cities have joined the movement, including Los Angeles, San Francisco, San Jose, Oakland, Santa Cruz and Santa Monica.

The ordinances apply to entities receiving financial assistance, e.g. service contracts, tax breaks, loans, grants or land. Included generally, are contracts over $25,000 per year, or city assistance over $100,000 per year.

(continued)

(11.2   continued)

The central provisions incorporate wages, benefits, worker retention, responsible bidders, temporary workers and super-session by collective bargaining agreements.

While it is recognized that the ordinances cover a relatively small number of workers, campaigns are important to establish a community precedent re wages and benefits.

The Sacramento Campaign

1. Planning—Several key individuals, representing labor, community organizations and key faculty from CSU Sacramento, met early in 2000, to review issues in Sacramento. There was general agreement that there were serious economic problems for working families in Sacramento, the capital of the largest and wealthiest state in the nation. There was also agreement to explore the concept of a living wage campaign.

   The planning for the campaign included identification of key areas of work—research, mobilizing a broad coalition of organizations, planned community events, a draft ordinance, and contacts with elected city officials.

   A Steering Committee has met regularly to plan and coordinate the living wage campaign.

2. Research—Original research was not necessary because of extensive information that was already available. The essential task was to pull together information about Sacramento that presents an accurate picture of the city and California.

   This included data of household incomes, rentals, health insurance, child care and transportation. Also available was the meaning of low wages, including Federal Poverty Guidelines ($7.03/hr mom and two kids, $8.50/hr for a family of four) and the State's minimum wage. The California Budget Project, the Sacramento County Children's Report Card and the Self-Sufficiency Standard, documented the income necessary for a mother and two children to maintain a basic standard of living.

3. Organizing—People volunteered to target organizations in the community for support of the campaign. These organizations included labor, community groups and the faith communities. Materials were developed describing the movement across the nation, the general concept of the living wage and data about Sacramento.

   During a six month period from 2000–2001, more than 60 organizations had endorsed the campaign, including key representatives from the faith communities.

4. Community Events—The kickoff of the campaign was a Forum on Poverty in Sacramento in November 2000, attended by 325 people. The panel included three committed City Council persons, and religious and community leaders. The program included presentation of data, testimony from working people and responses from the panel.

   The next planned events were similar forums targeted in key City Council districts. The local Council persons were invited to attend and most did. The focus was to demonstrate that there was community support for the living wage campaign.

   In May 2001, a major community rally was held in Cesar Chavez Plaza, across the street from the City Hall. More than 500 people attended, and called upon the City Council to endorse the living wage.

In September 2001, a fundraising dinner attended by 300 people, generated $7,000.

5. Draft Ordinance—A small group, including several volunteer attorneys, reviewed ordinances from around the country and California, and agreed upon the central principles to be included in the Sacramento ordinance. The central feature designated the living wage to be $10/hr, including family health benefits or $12.84/hr, without benefits. The health proposal is unique to Sacramento since ordinances around the nation and California only include the worker. Data to determine the cost of health insurance was derived from the recent Kaiser Family Foundation survey of California employers.

The attorneys have drafted the ordinance which has been submitted to the City Manager and his staff for review.

6. Political Process—Initial meetings were held with two City Council persons who, it was believed, would support the Sacramento Living Wage Campaign. They were receptive and agreed to provide leadership.

Meetings were also held with the City Manager, who is a key player in the City. The Mayor and City Council members are all part-timers, which gives the Manager power on policy decisions.

The City Manager also raised concerns about surrounding cities in the metropolitan area. With sales tax revenues an important revenue source, there is bitter competition among cities. Assemblyman Darrell Steinberg has introduced AB 680 to address the issue of revenue sharing.

Materials were developed for the City Council. Contacts were made with each of the other Council persons to present the proposal. A meeting was scheduled with the Mayor's Chief of Staff, preparatory to a meeting with the Mayor. Regrettably, despite 12 formal and informal requests, the Mayor has refused to meet. The conclusion is that she harbors strong feelings against the Labor Council, because of its support of her opponent in the last election.

As of this date, there are three committed Council persons and two likely supporters. Five votes are necessary to pass the ordinance.

There have been several meetings with members of the Sacramento Chamber of Commerce to inform them of the effort. While they have not adopted a negative position, their view is that the living wage would be a job killer.

There has been a delay in the process because of resistance by the Mayor and the City Manager. It has taken almost a year, to get agreement to have an independent study of the potential financial impact of the ordinance.

Conclusion

The Sacramento Living Wage Campaign has been a significant effort because it has:

1. Focused attention on addressing the struggles of working families.
2. Been effective in organizing a broad coalition of more than 60 organizations, supporting the campaign. It has also involved key faculty and students in a significant community campaign.

(continued)

(11.2   continued)

3. Enabled the spotlight to focus on the problems in Sacramento, i.e. wages, poverty, child care, affordable housing and transportation.
4. Focused attention on the political process and challenges, in enacting a living wage ordinance.

There is an invalid assumption that research, data and logic will determine social policy by themselves. What's needed is effective organizing so policy advocates can pressure policy makers to make humane policies!

Exercise:

1. How does this case illustrate how policy advocates often need grassroots organizing skills?
2. What challenges did the policy advocates encounter when forming a coalition?
3. How did the organizers "coopt" and involve public officials?
4. What interests do you think would likely oppose enactment of living-wage legislation at the city or county level?

Policy advocates need skills in working with *task groups,* which focus on producing or influencing something external to the group itself. In contrast to groups for treatment, therapy, and education, task groups do not emphasize members' personal growth or learning.[28] Among the remarkable range of policy-related task groups[29] are those that concentrate on making and enacting policies, including the boards of agencies, legislative committees, and legislatures.[30] These groups often rely on policy recommendations from feeder groups, such as deliberative committees, subcommittees, study groups, or commissions that develop recommendations and forward them to decision-making entities.[31] Some of these groups are ongoing, such as an agency's program committee or the Select Subcommittee on Children and Youth in Congress. Executives and political leaders also establish ad hoc groups to study specific problems and make recommendations.

Other task groups specialize in implementing policies.[32] Assume, for example, that a county mental health and substance abuse agency develops a new program for students in the school district and establishes an ongoing oversight committee to suggest policy changes when the new program is not realizing its objectives. Ongoing coordinating committees are created as well to promote the communication and policy development of various agencies.

Additional groups are set up for a variety of purposes. Many committees that staff can and should join exist in agencies to examine specific issues. Unions have become a potent power source in the human services system by mobilizing vast numbers of employees in public and nonprofit agencies.[33] Community organizations, like those modeled on the theories of Saul Alinsky, represent specific neighborhoods.[34] Many groups with varying amounts of power and resources serve as advocates for specific populations and institutions. Social movements spawn many groups with an overarching purpose, usually to advance the needs of a specific segment of the population, including advocacy groups for people who are homeless or people with AIDS.[35] Many national social movements have local affiliates, such as chapters of NOW or civil rights organizations. As we discuss later, coalitions merge the resources and power of member groups.[36]

Why develop task groups?   Task groups are more effective than individuals who try to shape policy on their own.[37] For example, individuals who pool their ideas are apt to reach more well-considered solutions. Pooled resources, effective leadership, and pooled policy practice skills also result in more effective efforts to mobilize pressure for reform.[38] Highly placed officials often form task groups to avoid accusations of excluding various interests from their deliberations. (Sometimes, they control the membership of such a task group to be sure it approves only their preferred options.) Some executives also try to increase political support for specific measures by appointing blue-ribbon committees; such groups can give legitimacy to a policy because their members are influential persons.

Policy Advocates' Roles in Task Groups

Advocates participate in task groups as leaders, staff, or members. A *leader* is comparable to an orchestra's conductor or a football team's coach. The leader facilitates the group's work by helping to define its mission and acquire resources like funds and staff. He or she expedites the group's ongoing work by developing agendas and presiding at meetings, and helps shape the group's structure and membership by setting up subcommittees and a nominating process and by intervening at specific points to promote members' participation and decision making. As facilitators, leaders prevent or diminish excessive internal conflict and dysfunctional processes, such as scapegoating specific members. Besides the president or chair of a group, other leaders, such as treasurers and secretaries, perform important logistical tasks.

Staff expedite the work of the group. As expediters, they collect information, assemble materials, perform secretarial functions, and attend to logistical details to allow others to concentrate on developing ideas and taking specific actions. Between meetings, they often help the group's leaders plan upcoming sessions and accomplish specific tasks.[39]

The staff's role, however, places limits on their interventions within a group. Because they are background facilitators and expediters, rather than members or leaders, they must exercise considerable circumspection and restraint. They are apt to refrain from speaking when they disagree with the group's decisions, preferring to influence decisions more discreetly.[40]

Members of task groups provide ideas, perform specific tasks, give the group power by linking it to other interests, lead subgroups, provide resources, and sometimes assume leadership after a period of apprenticeship. While leadership is crucial, few task groups are successful without motivated and active members.[41]

What Successful Task Groups Need

Many task groups are highly successful in establishing and realizing their objectives through their deliberations and activities. Other groups flounder, split, procrastinate, or dwindle to nothingness, as many of us know from experience.

Theorists and researchers have identified several factors that contribute to a task group's success: the group's mission, leadership, developmental needs, procedures, structure, deliberative and interactional processes, and staff and resources.

The Task Group's Mission

Successful groups develop a mission that defines their objectives or goals. Although the mission often changes later on, the members should decide what they want to accomplish during the early stages of the group's existence. Several dangers exist. A group may establish unrealistic expectations, such as hoping to enact a major piece of legislation quickly. When it cannot accomplish this objective, the members' morale and the leaders' reputation may suffer. Another danger is that the group may fail to reach a consensus about its objectives, so that different factions and members have different expectations. In some cases, overt expectations clash with hidden ones, as when leaders possess personal agendas that they do not share with members.

The mission also includes agreements about procedural matters, such as the frequency of meetings, the way leaders are selected, and the group's size and its relationship to external bodies. Groups that do not agree on these matters and their major goals encounter controversies and misunderstandings.

The Task Group's Leadership

Skilled group leaders walk a tightrope. They should be directive and assertive, but should not dominate; they should encourage dissenting perspectives, yet prevent excessive or destructive conflict; they should perform tasks well, but be able to delegate; they should represent the group to the external world, yet not seek excessive personal credit; and they should emphasize the group's objectives, but not neglect the group members' social and emotional needs. Unskilled leaders may be domineering, passive, confrontational, dictatorial, or self-promoting.

A skilled leader understands the group's developmental, structural, and process needs and develops strategies to address them. At one point, a leader might encourage the group to engage in relatively unstructured brainstorming and, at another, to reach closure on a topic.

Effective leaders value democracy. They give members a considerable role in shaping the group's decisions, and they keep the group from engaging in the scapegoating of members who legitimately dissent.

The Task Group's Developmental Needs

Groups evolve through time as they strengthen their mission, engage in deliberations, and accomplish tasks. In early phases, they must agree on their mission, leadership, and procedures and form realistic expectations. During the middle phase, they update their mission, develop and implement procedures, experience successes that give them a sense of momentum, and set up a division of labor that involves the members fully in the group's activities. In later phases, some groups should disband when they are no longer needed, whereas others should regenerate by revising their mission and seeking new members. Some groups do not progress through these stages of development. For example, not having established a mission, some groups keep returning to the question: Why do we exist? Other groups fail to change their mission as events unfold. Some groups continue to exist after accomplishing their original mission.

The Task Group's Procedures

Some people falsely equate leadership and group effectiveness with agendas, minutes, and bylaws, which are merely procedures. Procedures do serve a useful purpose.[42] Agendas allow anticipation of and planning for the future. Minutes provide a history that the group can review to ascertain how it has evolved and what new tasks it might undertake. Bylaws provide mechanisms for selecting leaders, replenishing membership, dividing tasks among officers and subcommittees, and handling funds.

The Task Group's Structure

Task groups must organize internally, establishing subcommittees or ad hoc groups to facilitate a division of labor. They have to decide how large they should be to accomplish their mission and to increase their political clout. They have to examine their relationships with other groups: Do they wish to merge with them, participate in coalitions, or maintain independence?

These kinds of structural issues pose significant challenges. A group that splinters into numerous committees, for example, may lack direction, but a group that is too centralized may fail to delegate responsibilities to its members. A group may lose its identity if it merges with other groups or joins coalitions, but it may lack clout if it remains isolated.[43]

The Task Group's Deliberative and Interactional Processes

To be productive, groups need modes of interaction that allow their members to examine options, to assess the group's strengths and weaknesses, and to make informed choices and develop strategies to implement them. Positive interaction occurs in an open atmosphere where members believe that they are free to contribute ideas, that dissent is permissible, and that their ideas will be taken seriously, and where brainstorming precedes final decisions.[44] Moreover, group members need to respect each other and the deliberative process and to honor the group's decisions.

Deliberations are stifled or abbreviated when leadership and group processes do not favor dissent, brainstorming, and democratic procedures. Social psychologist Irving Janis suggests that groups succumb to "groupthink" when they move too rapidly to unanimous positions, scapegoat dissenters, and do not fully consider the strengths and weaknesses of their positions.[45] Intolerant leaders, membership that fails to represent a variety of perspectives, and truncated deliberations contribute to groupthink.

Janis, Robert Bales, and other researchers suggest that a group should progress through a series of stages when considering issues: (a) brainstorming options in a risk-taking and tolerant atmosphere,[46] (b) carefully and gradually reducing these options to a revised list, and (c) only after extensive consideration of the options' strengths and weaknesses, formulating a final position. This movement from large numbers of options to final choices occurs only when group members feel free to take risks and when the group tolerates internal dissent.

The Task Group's Staff and Resources

Groups that engage in complex work need staff and resources to accomplish logistical tasks, provide technical assistance, and facilitate the group's work. Staff may come from institutions, such as agencies, or may be volunteers. Resources may come from institutions, the membership, special events, private donors, or corporations or foundations.

Just like low-budget lobbyists, groups that lack resources or staff are at a marked disadvantage compared with richer groups. Of course, resources and staff do not guarantee success, and groups with few resources may accomplish a great deal.

Forming Coalitions

Coalitions are temporary associations created to consolidate power in support of a specific issue, such as a piece of legislation. (We discuss ongoing associations, called *networks,* in the next section.)

Why are coalitions needed by policy practitioners seeking policy reforms for oppressed populations? As Policy Advocacy Challenge 9.3 shows, those who represent the poor, the powerless, or the stigmatized have an uphill battle; powerful interests and public apathy or opposition often impede social reforms. Moreover, powerful groups have coalitions of their own, such as coalitions of trade associations, agricultural interests, and tax-cutting groups.

Coalitions are different from many task groups, bringing together representatives of separate organizations to seek common action. The representatives agree to share the costs and labor of their common endeavor in a form of division of labor. When seeking the enactment of a piece of legislation, for example, one member group of a coalition may handle mailings, another the lobbying effort, and another the organization of a phone bank to telephone legislators at critical intervals.[47]

The success of a coalition depends on some of the same elements discussed under "What successful task groups need." As Milan Dluhy suggests, for example, successful coalitions need the leadership of a small executive council that meets frequently and invests considerable energy in planning and overseeing the activities of the coalition. A single person can spearhead a coalition, but a coalition obtains power through the combined efforts of its member organizations. Coalitions must share the credit for their work, or the members will resent the publicity that a single person or organization receives.[48]

The members of a coalition must define its goals and mission at the outset. Do they seek the enactment of a single piece of legislation, continuing pressure on legislators (or agencies), the education of the public about a social problem or the needs of a population, the development of innovative programs, or some combination of these and other goals? They have to decide as well when to disband the coalition or whether to transform it into an ongoing association. (See the following discussion of networks.)

Having developed a mission, the coalition's leadership needs to divide the labor. The leading group should establish subcommittees to focus on tasks such as research, lobbying, developing a phone bank, obtaining funds, and doing public relations (including creating a newsletter and reporting events to the mass media). The central leadership group could perform the coalition's real work, but establishing committees encourages broader participation. (The chairpersons of the committees often sit on the central leadership council.) With a division of labor established, the leadership council meets regularly to monitor the committees' work and to coordinate a strategy for accomplishing the coalition's work.[49]

The leaders of coalitions have to decide what groups to enlist. It is easier to form coalitions of like-minded persons and groups because they are more apt to agree on policy and strategy. An advocate who wants to get more funding for child welfare in a local jurisdiction, for example, can form a relatively homogeneous coalition of children's advocates, social work leaders, and children's institutions. Coalitions that represent more heterogeneous perspectives are more challenging to form and maintain because they find it more difficult to arrive at a consensus on goals and strategy, but they sometimes have more clout because their members can appeal to different kinds of legislators, agencies, and citizens. For example, if the local chamber of commerce joins the child welfare coalition, although its leaders may not share some of the assumptions of children's advocates, they may be able to convince some moderate or conservative politicians to support the funding increases sought.

Establishing Networks

While coalitions are usually temporary alliances that end when they have accomplished their purpose, policy practitioners also establish ongoing networks of persons and organizations. These networks regularly inform their members of pertinent legislation, increase their members' political awareness, and foster the members' participation in the political process.[50] Indeed, Rand Martin's organization, the AIDS-oriented Lobby for Individual Freedom and Equality, is a network, an ongoing organization with a governing council.

Assume that persons interested in state child welfare reform want a mechanism for sharing information about legislation, hearing about program innovations in different counties, and keeping abreast of national legislation. Envisioning their network as an ongoing organization with agency affiliates and individual members, they set up an executive council that establishes a division of labor, central offices, and a newsletter. This committee would schedule occasional meetings and workshops to supplement the newsletter. Like a coalition, this executive council also mobilizes the pooled efforts of its membership to support or oppose important pieces of legislation.[51]

Addressing Dysfunctional Group Processes

Some task groups are highly productive and others are less effective. Indeed, policy advocates sometimes have to use group process skills to improve a task group's functioning.

The degree to which advocates can intervene depends on the position they hold in the group, that is, whether they are staff members, leaders, or group members, whose different roles were described earlier.

Despite the constraints and opportunities that are provided by these different roles, all participants can diagnose or anticipate specific problems. When a task group or coalition loses momentum, the problem usually lies with a failure to develop a coherent mission, inadequate leadership, flawed internal processes, inadequate procedures, flawed structures, an inadequate process of deliberations, or insufficient resources. To diagnose which of these is the problem, we observe the group's operations from the vantage point of our role in the group. We often form our judgments as well from the complaints of other participants. We may also base a diagnosis on such developments as poor attendance and failure to achieve specific tasks.

Having diagnosed the problem, a participant in a task group, often along with others, needs to evolve a corrective strategy, such as having behind-the-scenes discussions, developing ideas during group deliberations, assuming some leadership functions, using power, mediating, directly assuming specific tasks, using humor, and seeking the advice of persons outside the group.

In meetings, members can promote more efficient deliberation in many ways, for example, by asking, "Don't we need to spend more time discussing this idea?" "Isn't it time to reach closure?" "Can we couple this idea with one that was suggested earlier?" or "Is there a different way to look at this problem?" They can also suggest procedures for considering ideas, such as breaking up into smaller groups to seek solutions to a problem.[52]

Even group members who are not leaders can sometimes assume leadership functions. For example, when a leader appears to be pressuring the group toward premature closure on an issue, a group member or a staff member can keep the discussion open by asking to hear more on the subject. Persons adept at parliamentary tactics sometimes use them to inject new perspectives and delay decisions. And between meetings, members may contact leaders directly to add issues to the agenda or to give their opinions on procedural, process, or structural matters. Of course, members and staff risk alienating leaders or erroneously usurping the leaders' functions if they do not use discretion.[53]

As in any collectivity, participants in groups have power resources, like expertise. When disagreements arise about specific issues or even about the group's leadership, processes, or structure, participants may use these power resources to shape decisions.[54] Group members also sometimes try to influence other members between meetings.

Group members need to use their power resources with discretion and without overriding the normal deliberative group processes. Excessive use of power resources can turn a group into a miniature legislative body whose members substitute threats, coercion, and parliamentary maneuvers for deliberation. At the same time, however, the use of power resources sometimes overcomes stalemates, stops destructive activities such as scapegoating, or makes beneficial changes in the group's leadership.

We discussed the use of mediation in Chapter Eight. Mediation may be the best solution when groups become polarized into competing factions.[55] Mediators can help group members identify their common values and can suggest structural or process strategies that will diminish conflict, such as bringing in a neutral facilitator. They also can identify compromises that will appease both parties to a conflict.

Effective persuaders often inject humor into their deliberations to ease tension, relax group members, and encourage the group not to take itself too seriously.[56] Humor can sometimes help in discussing specific group problems, as when a leader says, "At the rate we're proceeding, all the legislators we know will be dead before we come up with a bill."

Participants in groups or subcommittees sometimes take the bull by the horns and volunteer to do difficult or conflict-producing tasks that other members have shunned. When a subcommittee completes a task or develops a position on a difficult issue, for example, all its members have a sense of accomplishment and momentum.

Establishing Policy Goals in the Community Context

As in legislative settings, policy advocates must decide whether they will settle for incremental policy changes or whether they want major changes. This choice is, in turn, linked to estimates of likely support or opposition to the policy change. In some cases, an entire community will rally together for or against specific policies—and encounter scant opposition from the institutions they are challenging. In other cases, the community is polarized into competing groups. In still other cases, community groups encounter powerful entrenched interests that will not easily yield.

Specifying a Proposal's Content

Policy advocates can address an array of community issues: They may want a school to help dropouts or provide condoms to students; a zoning board to approve a halfway house for mental patients in a specific neighborhood; the city to fund an innovative program; an agency to establish a new program to serve a population that is underserved; or the community to help in an agency's operations, as through adding community residents to its board.

Community-based policy advocates may create community forums or community planning projects to solicit ideas from residents about community improvements. In one instance, a social worker helped a community group obtain volunteer architects who, after many community meetings, developed a housing plan for the neighborhood. As this community group met with city officials, it persuaded them to allocate substantial funds to a housing-development project in liaison with federal officials.

Establishing a Style

Changes in community policies can sometimes be achieved without extensive conflict, such as when city officials concur with a recommendation by a community group. On less contentious issues, a policy advocate might develop a collaborative win-win process. To assuage community residents, for example, she might initiate certain safeguards to gain their support for a proposed halfway house. She might convene a meeting of the community residents to develop these safeguards, such as establishing a 10 P.M. curfew for the residents of the halfway house.

Controversies arise when the interests of institutions or powerful officials are threatened, or when a community is divided into competing factions. When a coalition supported the placement of a welfare office in its neighborhood, for instance, it was countered by a powerful group that opposed the office on the grounds that it would lower property values and bring criminal elements into the community. When a community is polarized or when advocates encounter entrenched interests, advocates need skill in mobilizing community groups, developing coalitions, and working with the mass media.

Selecting Power Resources and Framing Strategy

As in legislative settings, policy advocates in communities have to create a campaign to achieve their policy goals. Their strategy may include delegations to community leaders and administrators, petitions, letter-writing campaigns to local officials, demonstrations, stories in the mass media, community forums, and litigation. As it takes these actions, the campaign's leadership must try to sustain and build community support for its position.

Revising the Strategy

Relatively minor and noncontroversial policy changes can sometimes be achieved with modest effort. When a community campaign runs into significant and unexpected opposition, the leadership team has to review its options and perhaps embark on a more extended and ambitious effort.

Chapter Summary

What You Can Now Do

You are now equipped to do the following:

- Use the seven steps in political strategy in legislative, agency, and community settings, including organizing a team or coalition, establishing policy goals, specifying a proposal's content, establishing a style, using selection power resources and framing strategy, implementing strategy, and revising strategy
- Participate in advocacy to secure enactment of policy proposals, such as by helping to devise a resource book, policy brief, or strategy book; working with staff of legislators or legislative committees; getting sponsors; getting, legislation introduced, testifying, and raising funds
- Participate in advocacy to put external pressure on legislators, such as by helping to organize blitzes or demonstrations, use the mass media, organize letter-writing campaigns, and lobby
- Work with or organize advocacy projects in specific agencies to secure approval of specific policies
- Work with or organize advocacy projects in communities to secure approval of specific policies
- Work with or organize such task groups as coalitions, committees, task forces, and networks

Having discussed how we implement political strategy in specific settings, we turn in the next chapter to tactics to change the composition of government, since it is difficult for even the most skillful policy advocates to secure policy changes if they cannot find responsive legislators, heads of government, or civil service appointees. We shall note, as well, that some social workers also run for political office.

Notes

1. My discussion of strategy in legislative settings relies heavily on Donald E. deKieffer, *The Citizen's Guide to Lobbying Congress* (Chicago: Chicago Review Press, 1997). While former Congresswoman Pat Schroeder praises the book in her

preface, she adds a cautionary note that strategy prescriptions must be made with care because "members of Congress don't all react the same way."

2. deKieffer, *The Citizen's Guide,* p. 24.

3. Ibid., pp. 17–20.

4. Ibid., pp. 21–23.

5. I draw the term *policy brief* from Willard Richan, *Lobbying for Social Change* (New York: Haworth Press, 1996), pp. 155–182.

6. deKieffer, *The Citizen's Guide,* pp. 20–21.

7. Ibid., p. 31.

8. Ibid., pp. 27–35.

9. Ibid., pp. 89–103.

10. Ibid., pp. 105–113.

11. Ron Dear and Rino Patti, "Legislative Advocacy: Seven Effective Tactics," *Social Work* 26 (July 1981): 289–297.

12. deKieffer, *The Citizen's Guide,* pp. 105–113.

13. Marilyn Bagwell and Sallee Clements, *Political Handbook for Health Professionals* (Boston: Little, Brown, 1985), pp. 136–156.

14. Ibid., pp. 136–156.

15. deKieffer, *The Citizen's Guide,* pp. 115–121.

16. Ibid., pp. 147–155.

17. Ibid., p. 75.

18. Karen Haynes and James Mickelson, *Affecting Change: Social Workers in the Political Arena,* 2nd ed. (New York: Longman, 1986), pp. 76–78.

19. Bagwell and Clements, *Political Handbook,* pp. 216–234. Also deKieffer, *The Citizen's Guide,* pp. 37–49.

20. deKieffer, *The Citizen's Guide,* pp. 39–40.

21. Ibid., pp. 63–71.

22. Bagwell and Clements, *Political Handbook,* pp. 189–194.

23. D. J. Hickson et al., "A Strategic Contingencies Theory of Organizational Power," *Administrative Science Quarterly* 16 (June 1971): 216–229.

24. Ibid.

25. Rosabeth Kanter, *Men and Women of the Corporation* (New York: Basic Books, 1977), pp. 129–163.

26. Burton Gummer, *The Politics of Social Administration* (Englewood Cliffs, NJ: Prentice Hall, 1990), pp. 25–26.

27. John Tropman, Harold Johnson, and Elmer Tropman, *The Essentials of Committee Management* (Chicago: Nelson-Hall, 1979), pp. ix–xiii.

28. Paul Ephross and Thomas Vassil, *Groups That Work* (New York: Columbia University Press, 1988), p. 1.

29. Tropman, Johnson, and Tropman, *Essentials of Committee Management,* pp. xiii–xiv.

30. Ibid., pp. 179–186.

31. Ephross and Vassil, *Groups That Work,* pp. 16–18, 22–24.

32. Tropman, Johnson, and Tropman, *Essentials of Committee Management,* pp. 196–203.

33. Dennis Chamot, "Professional Employees Turn to Unions," *Harvard Business Review* 54 (May 1976): 119–127.

34. Saul Alinsky, *Reveille for Radicals* (New York: Vintage Books, 1969).

35. Herbert Simons, *Persuasion,* 2nd ed. (New York: Random House, 1986), pp. 253–261.

36. Samuel Bacharach and Edward Lawler, *Power and Politics in Organizations* (San Francisco: Jossey-Bass, 1980), pp. 48–69, and George Brager, Harry Specht, and James Torczyner, *Community Organizing,* 2nd ed. (New York: Columbia University Press, 1987), pp. 193–200.

37. Robert Bales and Fred Strodtbeck, "Phases in Group Problem Solving," in Dorwin Cartwright and Alvin Zander, eds., *Group Dynamics: Research and Theory* (New York: Harper & Row, 1968), pp. 380–398. Also see David Sink, "Success and Failure in Voluntary Community Networks," *New England Journal of Human Services* 7 (1987): 25–30.

38. See Bacharach and Lawler, *Power and Politics in Organizations,* pp. 48–69; Brager, Specht, and Torczyner, *Community Organizing,* pp. 193–200; and Eugene Bardach, *The Skill Factor in Politics* (Berkeley and Los Angeles: University of California Press, 1972), pp. 215–230.

39. Tropman, Johnson, and Tropman, *Essentials of Committee Management,* pp. 5–23. For a compilation of literature on leadership, see Ralph Stogdill, ed., *Handbook of Leadership: A Survey of Theory and Research* (New York: Free Press, 1974).

40. Tropman, Johnson, and Tropman, *Essentials of Committee Management,* pp. 38–48.

41. Ibid., pp. 24–37.

42. Ibid., pp. 63–139.

43. Ephross and Vassil, *Groups That Work,* pp. 84–87, 166–183.

44. Irving Janis, *Victims of Groupthink* (Boston: Houghton Mifflin, 1972).

45. Ibid.

46. Bales and Strodtbeck, "Phases in Group Problem Solving."

47. Milan Dluhy, *Building Coalitions in the Human Services* (Newbury Park, CA: Sage, 1990), pp. 53–57.

48. Ibid., pp. 59–63.

49. Ibid., p. 62.

50. Ibid., p. 52.

51. Marilyn Bagwell and Sallee Clements, *A Political Handbook for Health Professionals* (Boston: Little, Brown, 1985), pp. 189–194.

52. Ephross and Vassil, *Groups That Work,* p. 164.

53. Tropman, Johnson, and Tropman, *Essentials of Committee Management,* p. 45.

54. There is surprisingly little discussion of the positive uses of power in committees and task groups. Power is usually viewed as destructive of group processes.

55. Jay Folberg and Alison Taylor, *Mediation* (San Francisco: Jossey-Bass, 1984).

56. Ephross and Vassil, *Groups That Work,* pp. 158–159.

chapter 12

Engaging in Ballot-Based Policy Advocacy

We discussed in the previous chapter how policy advocates influence the positions and votes of incumbent legislators and heads of government by lobbying or pressuring them. In this chapter, we discuss how policy advocates help determine who gets elected in the first place, because it stands to reason that advocates will have greater success if more public officials possess ideologies and perspectives that favor social justice. Ballot-based policy advocacy seeks to change the composition of government so more public officials will want to advance social justice. Policy advocates also want to influence the electorate to support (or oppose) specific propositions that are placed on the ballot by others or by themselves. We discuss the following in this chapter:

- Why ballot-based policy advocacy is so important to policy advocates
- How political campaigns are waged and the roles policy advocates can play
- How some policy advocates can run for office themselves
- How policy advocates can indirectly help progressive candidates
- How policy advocates can influence outcomes of elections
- How policy advocates can seek the enactment or the defeat of propositions

Why Ballot-Based Policy Advocacy Is Important

Persons who are interested in social justice must often turn for assistance to public policies enacted by municipal, county, state, and federal jurisdictions—and therefore must depend on the legislatures and heads of government (such as mayors, governors, and presidents) to enact enlightened ones. Public officials possess extraordinary resources and power compared with the private sector. (See Policy Advocacy Challenge 12.1.)

POLICY ADVOCACY CHALLENGE 12.1

VOTING AND ELECTORAL POLITICS

Stephanie Davis, Research Librarian, University of California, Irvine

Is the Electoral College a fair process for selecting our national leaders? This has always been a controversial topic, but after the last presidential election, debate surrounding the fairness of the Electoral College process became heated across the country. Complicating the debate is the fact that election laws are made at the state level, and not all states have standard or even similar laws. This inconsistency can have a huge impact on national elections as we learned in the 2000 presidential election.

Exercise: Using the sites below, investigate how your state voted in the last two or three presidential elections or a past congressional election and answer the following questions:

- Which political party had the majority of votes in your state?
- What was the gender and age breakdown of votes?
- What kind of funding did the candidates receive?
- How does the winning candidate/political party impact your research topic?

United States Electoral College

   www.nara.gov/fedreg/elctcoll

Project Vote-Smart

   www.vote-smart.org

OpenSecrets.Org

   www.opensecrets.org

Center for Voting and Democracy

   www.fairvote.org

U.S. Census Bureau: Voting And Registration

   www.census.gov/population/www/socdemo/voting.html

An excellent print source can be found in your library: *America Votes: A Handbook of Contemporary American Election Statistics.* (CQ Press, published annually since 1956.)

From 1931 to 2000 for example, the federal government spent roughly $56 trillion in direct outlays, and another $12.8 trillion just since 1968 in indirect spending through tax concessions to individuals and corporations. Federal and state authorities have enacted an enormous number of regulations in recent decades that protect out-groups from discrimination, prohibit specific unsafe working conditions, redistribute monies from more affluent to less affluent groups such as through the Earned Income Tax Credit and the food stamps program, and finance the bulk of secondary education and a large part of post-secondary education. Countless other victories were achieved by advocates who pressured high-level public administrators, like the heads of human service agencies in state and federal governments, to issue administrative regulations that precluded discrimination against out-groups in specific programs or that increased outreach to eligible persons not using important programs.

Policy advocates were able to achieve these policy victories only because they found key legislators, heads of government, and high-level public administrators sympathetic to their causes—or willing to be persuaded. Imagine working for social justice measures pertaining to African Americans, for example, in southern jurisdictions in eras preceding the enactment of federal civil rights legislation in the mid 1960s—or working for legislation affirming the right of women to have access to birth control in the era preceding the heroic work of Margaret Sanger at the beginning of the 20th century. Sanger was jailed on numerous occasions merely for speaking publicly about birth control.

Yet even in the modern era, policy advocates have to battle to increase the number of persons in public office who really care about the plight of oppressed populations. When Republicans swept both chambers of Congress in 1994 under the leadership of Newt Gingrich, for example, policy advocates found their access to political leaders to be severely limited compared with preceding years. With Congressional Republican leaders pledging to downsize the federal government radically and to rescind a host of government regulations, supporters of pro-choice, affirmative action, and scores of other issues found it difficult to get their measures before legislative committees—much less approved by legislative chambers. (Although a large cadre of relatively liberal Republicans had existed in the Congresses of the 1960s and 1970s, they had been largely replaced by conservative Republicans by the 1994 Republican landslide.)

Policy advocates also find their success diminished when relatively conservative heads of government are elected, as illustrated by the presidential election of 2000 when Republican George W. Bush bested Democrat Al Gore. Bush quickly translated his campaign promises into legislative proposals, such as getting a $1.35 trillion tax cut enacted, proposing significant increases in military spending, and favoring "faith-based" social programs—not initiatives that many policy advocates favored. (While Gore was relatively moderate, he had sought a tax cut of only $250 billion, which would have left considerable funds in government coffers for improvements in Medicare, public school reforms, and other domestic reforms—funds that no longer existed when the Congress slashed taxes so deeply.) Bush's appointees to high-level administrative posts, moreover, meant that policy advocates were less likely to obtain administrative regulations to their liking. Instead of the relatively liberal Donna Shalala (Clinton's Secretary of Health and Human Services), they now dealt with the relatively conservative Tommy Thompson, the former Republican governor of Wisconsin, who became Bush's Secretary of Health and Human Services.

The election of Bush over Gore also had major consequences for the federal judiciary. By appointing scores of relatively conservative attorneys to judicial posts, Bush hoped to influence judicial rulings for decades to come on such issues as abortion rights, affirmative action, separation of church and state, gay rights, and devolution of federal powers to the states.

We need to be careful about overstating the effects of elections on policy choices. Politicians often vote for measures that seem dissonant with their ideological views. Those who strongly oppose big government, often support, for example, such popular programs as Medicare and Medicaid, because many of their constituents benefit from them. Presidents and governors sometimes appoint justices who they think will make certain kinds of rulings only to find they go in contrary directions.

By the same token, however, we should not understate the importance of the composition of legislatures and heads of government to the policy-making process. In a two-party system, the party that wins a majority in a state or federal legislative chamber has an extraordinary advantage over the other party. If it can persuade its members to vote as a bloc (or if it can attract some votes from the other party), it wins many majority votes. The majority party in a chamber controls the chairs of legislative committees and a majority of the committees' members—so it can determine which bills get onto committees' agendas and which bills are approved by committees. The party that wins governorships and the presidency also has an extraordinary advantage. Heads of government often control or shape what issues are placed on legislatures' agendas. They can veto measures they do not like and can shape public opinion through their access to the mass media.

The two major parties differ significantly in the modern era in their positions on social reforms. At the federal level, for example, a majority of Democratic legislators are far more likely than a majority of Republican legislators to support an array of social-reform issues. In 1992, for example, Congressional Democrats supported packages of liberal issues 75 percent of the time, compared with only 18 percent of the time by Congressional Republicans. This ideological schism between the two parties stems in part from their different constituencies. Democrats are more likely than Republicans to come from urban districts, eastern and middle-west northern industrial states, inner-city districts, and relatively liberal suburban districts whereas Republicans are more likely to represent rural areas, western states, southern states, and relatively conservative suburban districts. Republicans are more likely to represent relatively affluent voters.[1] Democrats receive a higher percentage of votes from female, African American, Latino, gay men, lesbians, and disabled voters than Republicans. Although both parties contain liberal, moderate, and conservative legislators and voters, the Democratic Party has had larger liberal and moderate contingents than the Republican Party, particularly from the early 1980s onward. Moreover, while both parties get huge contributions from special interests, Democrats are far more likely to receive funds from trade unions and Republicans get more from corporations. (Trade unions tend to favor more social-reform measures than corporations.)[2] It is accurate, then, to say that significant differences exist in parties' ideology, constituencies, sources of money, and positions on issues.

These group differences, which predispose Democrats to be somewhat more supportive of social-justice issues than Republicans, ought not blind us, however, to certain political realities. Specific Democratic or Republican legislators often deviate from party norms, so some Democrats are very conservative and some Republicans are moderate or quite liberal in their voting patterns. Individual Democrats or Republicans can deviate from party positions on specific issues, such as a Republican who champions the right to abortion or a Democrat who opposes this position. (These deviations can be caused by personal experiences, fear that they will otherwise alienate important blocks of voters, or contributions from special interests.) Contributions from special interests influence the votes of members of both parties, so some Democrats vote against relatively liberal measures because they received campaign contributions from corporate or other sources.[3]

We should not overstate the extent the Democratic Party is committed to social justice, even if Democrats as a group are more likely to support a policy-advocacy agenda. The party has always had a big tent that included liberal, moderate, and conservative voters and public officials. Even in the heyday of the 1960s, when President Lyndon Johnson developed the Great Society with strong Democratic majorities in both chambers, many southern Democrats opposed civil rights measures and other reforms. Its liberal base of support eroded somewhat in the three and one-half decades following 1968 as populations expanded in sunbelt states and in the suburbs where voters tended to be more conservative than in the traditional liberal base of big-city enclaves and northern industrial states. A majority of U.S. voters resided in suburbs by the late 1990s. Wanting to contest Republicans for southern states and suburbs, Democratic leaders increasingly endorsed the argument that the party had to swing to the middle to be successful—with less emphasis on positions favored by trade unions and persons of color. This movement toward the center occurred dramatically during the two-term presidency of Bill Clinton, who favored coopting many Republican issues such as fighting crime, "ending welfare as we know it," cutting federal deficits and debt, protecting military spending, and placing less emphasis on traditional liberal issues like affirmative action. Critics contend that this swing toward the middle, while sometimes enhancing Democrats' political fortunes, has also diminished their commitment to social justice on key issues.[4]

Critics of the two major parties, such as Ralph Nader, the Green Party's presidential candidate in 2000, contend that both parties have been corrupted by the influence of monies contributed to them and their candidates by special interests. Members of both parties have been showered with contributions from corporations, pharmaceutical companies, HMOs, highway contractors, military contractors, the mass media, and many other groups.[5] If some of these funds have gone directly to candidates, others of them—so called soft money—have gone to the parties, who use them to support issue-based ads in particular races. These issue-based ads, in turn, are usually used by the two parties to support their candidates, such as by saying "support the candidate in this race who wants to raise the minimum wage" (a Democratic issue) or who "doesn't favor excessive gun control" (often a Republican issue).[6] While neither of the two major parties assertively backed campaign finance reform to curtail soft-money contributions to political parties, its prospects suddenly improved in 2002 when Enron, the huge energy corporation, filed for bankruptcy after giving huge resources to politicians. Campaign finance legislation was finally enacted in March 2002.

We have discussed the importance of the run-off or culminating elections for candidates, but we should not forget the importance of primary elections.[7] Each of the major parties has a primary election to determine which candidate will represent it in the ensuing partisan election. (In nonpartisan elections, such as for school boards, a first vote for all the candidates who seek a specific seat is followed by a run-off between the two candidates who received the most votes—assuming no one got a majority of the votes in the initial election.) Primary or first elections are very important to policy advocates because the initial batch of candidates in both partisan and nonpartisan elections often differ markedly from one another. A relatively conservative Democrat might, for example, oppose a relatively liberal Democrat in a primary election—just as two Republican candidates might differ markedly from one another in their views on social policy.

Policy advocates sometimes support so-called third parties, such as the candidates endorsed by the Green Party in congressional and presidential elections of 2000. Green Party candidates were considerably more radical than candidates from the major parties on domestic, environmental, and international fronts. By providing an alternative to the existing parties, third parties have the potential to push established parties to become more progressive. And some progressives hope that a third party might displace one of the major parties, providing voters with a truly progressive alternative.

Third parties also present a dilemma for policy advocates because the United States has a winner-take-all system rather than a system of proportional representation as in many European nations. In winner-take-all elections, only the party that gets a majority vote wins an election; in proportional representation seats are allocated on the basis of the percentage of votes that a party receives. So third parties in the United States get seats only when their candidate gets more votes than either of the candidates from the major parties—a daunting task because the third-party candidate has to convince huge numbers of Republicans and/or Democrats to shift parties. A Green Party in Italy would get 10% of the seats in a legislature if it got this share of the vote in parliamentary elections—rather than no seats, which would be the case in the United States if Green Party candidates got 10% of the vote nationally but failed to get more votes from other parties in specific elections.

The history of third parties in the United States is not encouraging to them. The last time a third party supplanted one of the two major parties occurred in the late 1850s when the Republican Party, under the leadership of Abraham Lincoln, took the place of the Whig Party. Relatively liberal third parties, such as the Green Party, also risk diverting votes from Democratic candidates—thus making the victory of Republican candidates more likely. (Far fewer Republicans than Democrats voted for Green Party candidates in the elections of 2000.) So a major debate took place among progressives in the 2000 elections—one that pitted natural allies against one another. (See Policy Advocacy Challenge 12.2.)

POLICY ADVOCACY CHALLENGE 12.2

HOW TO VOTE IN THE 2000 PRESIDENTIAL ELECTION?

Al Gore and George W. Bush were selected as presidential candidates by the Democratic and Republican Parties, respectively, in summer 2000. It seemed a classic face-off between a relatively liberal and a quite conservative candidate. Having been vice president under president Bill Clinton for eight years and running for the presidency during a period of economic growth, many prognosticators believed Gore would win this election.

Ralph Nader complicated matters for Gore, however. A longtime consumer advocate with impeccable reformist credentials, Nader accepted the nomination of the fledgling Green Party—a party clearly to the left of the Democratic Party and far to the left of the Republican Party. On a host of issues, Nader took positions to the left of Gore. He championed living wage legislation, cuts in military spending, efforts to end slave labor in third-world countries, and massive increases in spending to avert pollution.

Clear differences existed, as well, between Gore and Bush. Bush wanted massive tax cuts at a time when budgetary surpluses were appearing after nearly 20 years of government deficits. Gore wanted only modest ones to allow greater domestic spending and to preserve the fiscal integrity of Medicare and Social Security. Bush wanted modest increases in federal spending on education, and Gore wanted greater spending. Bush wanted no campaign finance reform; Gore favored new limits on contributions. Bush wanted only modest measures to increase patient rights, but Gore wanted substantial measures.

Liberals faced a dilemma. If they voted for Nader in states that were closely contested by Gore and Bush, they risked inadvertently giving Bush a victory he would not otherwise have had. If the national race was close—and it was widely predicted to be razor thin—Nader votes might allow Bush to gain a majority of Electoral College votes that he would not otherwise receive.

What should liberals have done under these circumstances?

Policy Advocacy in the Electoral Process

The composition of legislatures and the selection of heads of government are determined by tens of thousands of political races each year in local, state, and federal jurisdictions. These include both partisan races, usually dominated by members of the two major parties, and nonpartisan races, such as in many city council, mayoral, school board, and judicial contests.

If Luciano Pavarotti described opera singing as "controlled screaming," electoral contests can be called "controlled conflict." Elections are conflicts that result in winners and losers based on vote tallies—conflicts where candidates use a variety of power resources to influence members of the electorate. Candidates know this is a win-lose conflict waged in a relatively brief time period. They know the final arbiters of these conflicts are voters and their votes. Yet elections represent controlled conflict because they are fought according to rules established by local, state, and federal authorities—rules that govern campaign finance and ballot procedures.

Developing Population Profiles

Astute candidates carefully analyze the voters in their districts long before ballots are cast.[8] Drawing upon data from previous elections, as well as polling data of their own, candidates estimate at the outset how close the election is likely to be. Some candidates realize they have little chance of winning, for example when they encounter a popular incumbent or when they run in a district where political opinion runs counter to their own beliefs and record. (A Democrat running in a strongly Republican district may realize she has an uphill battle at best.) In other cases, candidates may decide at the outset that they have a chance of winning, but that their races are likely to be closely fought. In still other cases, candidates may decide that they are favorites to win—or even that the election is theirs to lose. And in some cases, outcomes are exceedingly difficult to estimate.

When gauging their chances, candidates' odds of winning increase in the following circumstances:

- They are incumbents rather than challengers because incumbents have many advantages, including name recognition, support from persons and groups who have benefited from policy actions they have taken in prior years, and an ability to raise money from those persons and groups who like to back a likely winner.[9]
- They have considerable name recognition in their electoral district, quite apart from whether they are incumbents.
- They run in a district where a strong majority of voters share their political and ideological preferences. Democrats who face Republicans in districts with strong

Democratic tendencies are far more likely to prevail than Democrats in strong Republican or conservative districts.

- They can find early endorsers who have considerable standing in the district, whether influential people, newspapers, or other public officials.
- They can anticipate support from relatively large blocs of voters because of their ethnicity or race, their occupation (such as being an auto worker in a district with large numbers of blue-collar workers), their religion (such as being Catholic in a district with many Catholics), or their gender (such as being a female candidate who can strongly appeal to large numbers of female voters).
- They are able to raise significant resources compared with likely opponents, whether monetary resources or help from volunteers. The mass media, mailings, and campaign research—which cost money—are invaluable to candidates.[10]
- They are fairly certain they can turn out specific blocs of voters in a contest that will probably have a low turnout, such as an election for a school board seat. If a contestant in a school board election has the support of the teachers' union—and opposing contestants do not— her chances increase because the union will probably help turn out school personnel and contribute volunteers who will persuade other voters to turn out.

Of course, it is important that candidates not be excessively fatalistic even if they lack some of these advantages. Underdogs do win electoral contests. Favored candidates often make mistakes or take their reelection for granted. As many candidates have discovered, a defeat in a specific election is often followed by victories in subsequent contests for the same seat or for other seats.

Candidates often develop voter profiles of their districts that identify blocs of voters who fall into at least four categories: probable strong supporters, probable strong opponents, probable swing voters whose support may be gained relatively easily, and probable swing voters who are tough prospects.[11] To these groups, we can add voters whose voting patterns are virtually impossible to predict. They also need to decide the likelihood that members of these various groups will actually vote, since it does no good to have strong support from voters who fail to turn out.

In developing voter profiles of their districts, candidates often make informed guesses based on party affiliations, demographics, and group affiliations. (See Video Clip 12.1.)

VIDEO CLIP 12.1 *DEVELOPING CAMPAIGN STRATEGY FOR A RACE OF REP. ESTEBEN TORRES*	In viewing Video Clip 12.1, consider the following. Professor Ramon Salcido, M.S.W., D.S.W., Professor, School of Social Work, University of Southern California, discusses how he and Representative Esteban Torres developed strategy that ultimately led to Torres's victory at the polls.

African American or Latino candidates often can assume, for example, that voters with their ethnicity will favor them over other candidates, though they cannot assume complete support or that these voters will turn out to vote. Candidates of major political parties usually can assume that they will receive an edge from voters in their parties. Male and female voters may receive additional support from their gender groups. Other affiliations also can help some candidates, such as their religion, occupational group, and age.

Challengers can make informed estimates about incumbents by dissecting voting patterns from prior elections. Using census and voting data, they can discover in which precincts and with what demographic, racial, and political groups they ran strong or weak. Armed with this information, they can pinpoint their opponents' areas of strength and vulnerability.[12]

This population profile—which can be refined using poll and focus-group data—is vital to candidates. It allows them to estimate whether the election is likely to be closely contended, a landslide, or somewhere in between. If the election looks like it will be closely contended, candidates realize that they will have to invest great effort and resources in the election. The prospect of a landslide election is heartening to candidates who believe they will prevail, but disheartening to candidates who fear they will be on the losing end. In some cases, so many uncertainties exist in the population profile that candidates cannot make even tentative predictions—meaning they must gather more information as the race proceeds so they can devise intelligent strategy.

The population profile also is critical to candidates because it tells them where to channel their scarce resources. Candidates will not want to spend a lot of time speaking to voters who are certain to oppose them. Although they want to devote sufficient time and resources to encourage likely supporters to vote on election day, they do not want to allocate too many resources to them as compared with swing voters who might be converted through advertisements and personal outreach. (If they dissipate their scarce resources on certain supporters and opponents, they risk losing closely fought elections if opponents capture most of these swing voters.)[13]

Even if the prognosis is bleak or uncertain, candidates still may decide to run. Perhaps they want to gain name recognition for a future run for the same post or another one. Maybe they want to educate voters about a specific issue. Or they may want community recognition to advance personal business or professional interests.

As candidates proceed with their analysis of likely voting behaviors of specific groups, they place this analysis over a precinct-by-precinct map of the electoral district. This allows them to decide where to target their mailings, precinct walking, advertisements, and telephone banks. If a candidate wants to reach Latino voters in specific communities, for example, she might seek endorsements from Hispanic leaders; run media spots on radio and television, and in newspapers likely to be heard or read by Hispanic persons in these precincts; and recruit Hispanic volunteers to help with door-to-door visits and distribution of leaflets at local supermarkets. She also might try to get party officials to fund voter registration projects in these precincts.

Using Power Resources to Persuade Voters

Having identified the kinds of voters they want to prioritize—and even their geographic location—candidates need to convince voters to support them and to turn out on election day. They have numerous tools at their disposal. (See Table 12.1.) Indeed, astute candidates use all of these resources as part of their strategy. (See Video Clip 12.2.)

VIDEO CLIP 12.2	In viewing Video Clip 12.2, consider the following. Laura Chick, M.S.W., Controller of the City of Los Angeles, discusses why social workers possess skills that make them good campaigners. Chick won several races for the City Council of Los Angeles and became the first woman to win a seat in a city-wide race in the history of Los Angeles when she became the Controller of Los Angeles in 2000.
WHY SOCIAL WORKERS MAKE GOOD CANDIDATES	

TABLE 12.1   Power resources for influencing voters' views and actions

1. Using One-by-One Retail Power Resources
   a. Personal door-to-door visits in precincts or at special events
   b. Visits by surrogate volunteers door to door or at special events
   c. Distribution of leaflets to voters at neighborhood or other locations
   d. Working the crowd at local or other events
2. Using the Media
   a. Political advertisements in radio, television, and newspaper outlets
   b. Appearances on radio and television outlets
3. Interacting with Opposing Candidates
   a. Participation in organized debates
   b. Participation in organized forums for candidates
   c. Responses to opponents' positions in media advertisements
4. Developing Positions on Issues
   a. Articulation of a set of campaign promises that tell voters what policies a candidate will use in forthcoming elections
   b. Positions on specific issues
   c. Introduction of new issues
5. Demonstrating Positive Personal Characteristics
   a. Convincing voters through personal conduct and by citing one's past resume that a candidate possesses such desirable characteristics as integrity, diligence, fiscal discipline, and compassion
6. Conducting Negative Attacks on Opponents
   a. Attacking their positions on specific issues
   b. Attacking their personal qualities, such as by citing their prior activities
7. Getting Out the Vote
   a. Convincing supporters that they will suffer negative consequences if they fail to vote
   b. Election day visits by campaign volunteers to voters to persuade them to vote (and even to provide them with transportation to the polls)
8. Securing Endorsements
   a. Getting endorsements from influential citizens, groups, and public officials from the electoral district
   b. Getting endorsement from influential citizens, groups, and public officials from outside the electoral district
   c. Getting endorsements from newspapers, radio stations, and television stations
9. Convincing Other Potential Candidates not to Run
   a. Talking up ones campaign before it begins to convince other potential candidates not to run
10. Seeking Support from Party, Trade Union, and Other Organizations

Using One-on-One Power Resources

Candidates need to make personal contact with many voters in a laborious one-on-one strategy. Through these contacts, candidates make voters believe that they have positive personal traits such as a concern for the voters' problems, high levels of energy, and an ability to listen. They can elicit suggestions or input about specific problems or policies. They can share their positions with voters to assure them that they care about their concerns. They can organize a sequence of local meetings, in homes, churches, and community agencies, that allow them to present positions and solicit inputs from voters. When supplemented by campaign literature that highlights their accomplishments, positive personal traits, and campaign promises, candidates build grassroots momentum.

Using the Media

Name recognition is an extraordinarily valuable asset in political campaigns because many voters select names on ballots that are familiar to them—and they are more likely to listen to their messages. The media enhances the name recognition of candidates, whether through paid advertisements, personal appearances, coverage in news stories, or endorsements.[14]

Interacting with Opposing Candidates in Public Forums

Debates with opposing candidates are often important campaign events. They allow candidates to clarify their views and to distinguish them from opposing candidates; demonstrate they have a command of the issues; and place opponents on the defensive by questioning their positions or records.

Debate strategy needs to be carefully planned. Candidates need to anticipate likely positions and arguments of opponents, including how they might attack their own positions or records. They need, as well, to decide what issues to prioritize and what supporting arguments to use.[15]

Developing Positions on Issues and Demonstrating Positive Personal Qualities

Voters' decisions about who to support are shaped by many factors. In a two-person race, voters make their decisions by evaluating both candidates in terms of perceived positive and negative attributes, making an overall ranking of each candidate, and then selecting the candidate with the highest ranking. Each voter does the following:

- Decides what attributes are worth considering for each candidate, both positive ones and negative ones
- Decides what weight to give each attribute for each candidate
- Ranks each candidate on each attribute
- Decides, on balance, which candidate ranks the highest—and (if he or she votes) votes for that candidate

To illustrate this process, assume a voter decides that the following attributes are important when comparing two candidates: honesty, correct positions on three pivotal issues (abortion rights, promoting good schools, and supporting patient rights), and a successful track record in public service. The voter goes through a mental process that we can simplify with a hypothetical example. Suppose a voter ranks each candidate, say from -10 to $+10$, on each of these attributes and then selects the candidate with the highest score after weighting the relative importance of each attribute. In our hypothetical example our voter selects candidate B, with her positions on schools and, especially, her "positive track record" swinging the balance. (See Table 12.2.)

TABLE 12.2   A voter's perception of two candidates

Issues	Candidate A Rank × Weight	Candidate B Rank × Weight
Honesty (weight of 1)	1 × 1 = 1	−1 × 1 = −1
Pro Abortion Rights (weight 5)	10 × 5 = 50	8 × 5 = 40
Pro Schools (weight 2)	5 × 2 = 10	10 × 2 = 20
Pro Patient Rights (weight 1)	−5 × 1 = −5	8 × 1 = 8
Positive Track Record (weight 3)	−5 × 3 = −15	10 × 3 = 30
TOTAL	+41	+97

This example illustrates the tactical challenge faced by each candidate—assuming that large numbers of voters shared, roughly, the perspectives of this voter. Candidate A could try to enhance her positive scores on some attributes, paying particular attention to ones weighted heavily by the voter—such as a positive track record. Or she might try to increase negative scores of her opponent by challenging his record on issues where he scores heavily with voters, such as abortion rights, schools, and positive track record. She might say that he has shifted his stand on abortion rights, has not consistently supported schools, and has many blemishes in his previous track record of public service. Or she might try to add new issues to the list of issues on which she thinks she will score more positively than her opponent. Perhaps she decides to add environmental pollution to the list or adding recreational space to our community. Or she might try to change voters' weighting of specific issues by contending that honesty (now weighted only 1) is the most important attribute voters should consider, perhaps adding some serious questions about her opponent's honesty.

A fluid situation often exists in campaigns.[16] At point 1, a candidate selects specific issues for top priority but then adds issues or puts different emphasis on some existing ones as the campaign unfolds. Sometimes she makes these changes in response to her opponent, wanting to counter his charges, locate vulnerabilities in his positions, or change the topic when she believes he is scoring points against her on specific issues. Sometimes she makes these changes in response to polling data or focus groups that suggest that different issues or different emphases on existing issues will allow her to gain ground. Sometimes candidates discover that certain lines or arguments draw a sympathetic response from particular audiences, leading them to emphasize them. Or, conversely, they may drop or de-emphasize issues or arguments that draw a weak audience response.

Candidates need to develop a set of campaign promises early in the campaign[17] that distinguish them from opponents. They give voters a sense that they will deliver results during their term of office rather than being inactive or ineffective. These campaign promises need to be carefully considered because candidates can assume that opponents will attack them and may contend that they are not feasible (such as overly costly) or that they are ill-advised, too numerous, too vague, or too few. Sometimes opponents might say that a candidate's campaign promises are contradictory, such as when a candidate proposes a costly new program but also promises to cut the budget or cut taxes.

Campaign promises are often linked, of course, to candidates' analysis of their electoral district. They want campaign promises that will mobilize likely supporters and appeal to some swing voters, and they want issues that will increase voter turn out.

Conducting Negative Attacks on Opponents

All candidates face a dilemma: whether to emphasize positive arguments or to make negative attacks on their opponents.[18] Take our example of candidates A and B in Table 12.2. Believing that she trails her opponent, candidate A could emphasize her accomplishments and positions regarding the various issues, as well as her own positive track record and honesty. Or she could attack her opponent's positions and, even more negatively, attack his character. Were she effective in doing this, some of Candidate B's positive numbers in Table 12.2 might diminish or even be converted to negative numbers. If she converted her opponent's position on having a positive track record from +30 to –50, for example, she would nearly catch up to him in the overall ratings.

However, negative attacks sometimes backfire. Candidate B might accuse Candidate A of running a negative campaign rather than discussing the real issues. Ethical issues exist, as well. (See Policy Advocacy Challenge 12.3.)

POLICY ADVOCACY CHALLENGE 12.3

WHEN TO BE NEGATIVE AND WHEN TO BE POSITIVE

Most candidates face an ethical dilemma during their races. Knowing that voters are often less likely to vote for candidates with strong negatives on such personal traits as honesty, consistency, integrity, and diligence, they can often rapidly rise in polls by attacking opponents' personal traits. Sometimes they can find evidence of malfeasance, corruption, dishonesty, and lack of attention to citizens' needs (in the case of incumbents). When solid evidence is lacking, however, they can gain substantial advantage by making vague references, making allegations without credible evidence, or insinuating negative traits.

Why the temptation to go negative? Substantial polling data suggests that negative attacks can be efficient in lowering voters' opinions of opponents. Negative information is often effective in putting doubts into voters' minds about specific candidates. When used in television ads, negative messages are often particularly effective because they can be conveyed through vivid images—such as pictures of opponents in the company of unsavory people. Some candidates rationalize negative attacks by contending they merely want to beat their opponents to the punch. Yet considerable evidence shows that negative ads can backfire—or not be as effective as positive "advocacy" ads.[19]

What's lost in mud-slinging campaigns is intelligent discussion of important issues that ought to be the basis for deciding who wins and who loses. Negative ads often feature untrue or simplistic allegations that are not buttressed by facts.

So what should a candidate do in the following cases?

- She lags in the polls and believes her only hope is to attack her opponent's character.
- She wants to have a positive campaign, but finds her opponent has initiated a negative campaign against her.
- She believes her opponent lacks integrity and is dishonest, but lacks hard evidence to prove it.

Getting Out the Vote

Nonvoters shape election results as powerfully as voters, as a simple example suggests. Assume that 100,000 voters support Candidate A—and 80,000 of them turn up at the polls. Assume that 125,000 voters support Candidate B—but only 75,000 of them actually vote. In this example, the least popular candidate wins the election only because Candidate B could not get more of his voters to actually vote.

This result is not unusual. As Frances Piven and the late Richard Cloward discuss, voters in lower economic strata are considerably less likely to vote than relatively affluent Americans, regardless of their ethnicity.[20] (See Policy Advocacy Challenge 12.4.) Since persons of color are disproportionately poorer than affluent Americans, they are considerably less likely to vote than Caucasians. So candidates with particular popularity among the less affluent members of our society and persons of color, start electoral races with a significant disadvantage—unless they can entice their supporters to vote or can find offsetting support among more affluent persons. This is often not an easy task. While voter registration procedures have been greatly simplified across the nation to encourage registration, many poorer Americans still are not registered—and those who are registered, vote in far fewer numbers than other voters. (Voters can now register when they obtain drivers' licenses and in many public agencies.)

POLICY ADVOCACY CHALLENGE 12.4 *WHY IS VOTING RELATED TO SOCIAL CLASS?*	Identify some alternative explanations why low-income Americans are far less likely to vote than relatively affluent Americans. Be certain to include several kinds of factors in your discussion. These may include the following: A. Factors related to registration B. Factors related to mindsets or attitudes of low-income persons regarding the political process stemming both from historical and present-day experiences C. Factors regarding the two major parties, such as • Kinds of issues put forward by the two parties • Extent the major parties prioritize voter registration in low income areas • Extent candidates offer voters real choices • Extent candidates follow through on promises D. Would you favor paying people to vote—a practice widely used in European nations where citizens of all social classes vote at extraordinary levels?

Candidates can increase voter turnout by targeting populations and precincts having low turnouts with personal (or volunteer) contacts, leaflets, and advertisements. They can seek endorsements from leaders of low-turnout communities and populations. They can highlight the significance of the election to persons who would not normally vote and mount voter registration drives in areas where eligible voters are not registered. They can orchestrate election-day activities, such as contacting voters by telephone and, in some cases, transporting them to the polls.

Securing Endorsements

Endorsements often carry considerable weight in elections—assuming they come from persons and organizations that are respected by the candidates' natural supporters and swing voters.[21] Candidates often vie for endorsements from newspapers, party leaders, public officials, and community leaders—endorsements that candidates often feature on their campaign literature and in their personal appearances. They also compete for the support of Political Action Committees (PACs), which channel funds to candidates from trade unions, interest groups, and professional associations like the National Association of Social Workers.[22] (We discuss NASW's PAC later in the chapter.)

Endorsements can take the form of public statements by organizations and people. In addition, an endorsement can be an agreement to be listed on invitations and advertisements as sponsors of campaign functions, such as fund-raising events or important speeches.

Candidates obtain endorsements in several ways. They often emanate from prior friendships or working relationships, such as when a candidate has worked with specific public officials on previous occasions. Candidates often meet personally with potential endorsers and work hard to convince them that they will be effective public servants on issues that are important to the endorsers. Candidates often must convince endorsers that they have a good chance of being elected. They might provide them with electoral data that demonstrates that they have considerable support in their district and that likely opponents are vulnerable.

Convincing Other Potential Candidates Not to Run

Considerable jockeying for position occurs before each election as persons decide whether to run for specific offices.[23] It is to the advantage of a candidate not to encounter a crowded field in primary contests—and not to encounter opponents in primary or final contests who possess widespread support and resources. Potential candidates cannot stop others from running, but they can try to discourage them by showing them that they will mount formidable campaigns. They can announce their intentions to run far in advance of the election to make clear that they will be serious contenders. They can talk to potential candidates in their own party to make clear their intention to run and to suggest that "if we beat up on each other in the primary, our likely opponent will have an easier time winning." They can approach campaign donors and seek early commitments as a way of showing potential candidates that they will have considerable resources. They can seek early endorsements from community leaders and public officials.

By starting early to build support and a campaign organization, candidates may also discourage some potential—and formidable—candidates from entering a race.

Gaining Support from Party, Trade Unions, and Other Groups

Candidates should assertively seek resources from organizations whose issues and perspectives are consonant with their own. Parties have resources to contribute to candidates, though they give priority to elections where they believe they can pick up seats. Unions distribute funds through their PACs to candidates who support union and union-backed issues. The National Association of Retired Persons not only contributes funds through its PAC, but sometimes organizes elderly volunteers to work in specific campaigns. As we discuss later, issue-oriented groups sometimes run advertisements during campaigns that take positions on specific issues like gun control and offer support for candidates who agree with these positions. (Supports from external groups become more important as candidates seek higher-level seats in county, state, and federal jurisdictions.)

Finding Resources

Resources have become increasingly important to campaigns as the cost of advertising has risen dramatically, whether in newspapers, television, radio, or mailings.[24] The funds spent on campaigns for high-level offices in the United States have become truly remarkable and troublesome. Several points should be considered at the outset. The amount of resources required for a campaign escalates as candidates seek higher or more visible seats. A race for a school board slot or a host of local positions is relatively inexpensive, but the cost rises for some county seats, most state-level seats, and all federal seats. Indeed, social workers who want to enter the electoral process almost always begin with local races that require relatively few resources as compared with high-level races. As they build a track record in initial offices, they develop contacts and reputations that allow them to raise larger sums in subsequent races for higher-level posts.

While extremely important in many races, resources are not, by themselves, a guarantor of victory as billionaire Ross Perot discovered in 1992 when his massive resources yielded him a distant third-place finish in the presidential race. Some candidates succeed even when greatly outspent by opponents, such as Senator Ross Feingold (D-Wisconsin) who won the U.S. senatorial race in 2000 after rejecting many sizeable contributions from wealthy donors and PACs.[25] Yet considerable evidence demonstrates that large imbalances in resources usually favor its more affluent candidate.

Resources pose troubling ethical issues in the United States because some candidates, regardless of their merit, obtain much greater resources than competing candidates. For example, incumbents can raise resources much more easily than most challengers—and wealthy individuals can underwrite their own campaigns. Some special interests, such as corporate entities, can contribute much more than others, such as groups representing disadvantaged and oppressed populations. Federal, state, and local legislation limiting the so-called hard money that candidates can raise is often circumvented by soft money spent by political parties and special interests on media advertising for specific issues. Precluded from giving more than a certain amount of money to individual candidates, for example, the National Rifle Association has given huge resources to parties and individual candidates that oppose control of guns. These ads help the candidate who opposes control of guns even when that candidate is not named in advertisements. Similarly, the major political parties can place issue-oriented ads in local races that favor their candidates—as can many other groups with deep pockets.[26] (Such tactics were partially limited by the enactment of federal campaign finance legislation in March 2002.)

The quest for resources has other troubling aspects. To the extent candidates devote more and more time to finding resources, they have less time to research and discuss issues. Even incumbents must devote considerable time to fund-raising while in office.

Yet resources are a fact of life in campaigns—and candidates for any office must devote considerable effort to raising funds so their opponents cannot buy their way into office.[27] Candidates need to estimate roughly what their opponents are likely to spend in a particular race so they can possess similar, if not greater, resources. Resources are needed to hire campaign staff, to hire political consultants, to advertise in the mass media, to produce campaign literature, and to make mailings. The cost of a 30-second ad in prime time on local television can range from $1,500 to $8,000 depending on the size of the market, though less expensive ads can be purchased on cable TV and radio, and in newspapers. Imagine the prospect of seeing your opponent appear frequently in these media outlets in the weeks preceding an election when you could not afford any of them.

Other campaign costs also exist. Consultants who can provide important information about the local electorate and campaign strategy are costly. Campaigns sometimes use advertising firms to craft their ads—firms that use focus groups and sophisticated electronics to fashion ads that will be effective. Bumper stickers, yard signs, and billboard ads are costly to print, install, and dismantle. Direct mail is very expensive. Campaigns sometimes use professional polling firms to get baseline data at a campaign's outset and tracking data as the campaign proceeds. Even a sample of 400 people can cost more than $10,000 each time data is collected.

Still another reason exists for trying to find resources. Absent them, candidates must perform some tasks that they might otherwise be able to turn over to staff. When candidates try to accomplish these tasks themselves, they have less time to devote to personal interactions with the electorate and to public appearances.

Every candidate gives priority to the recruitment of a resource that costs little but is worth its weight in gold: volunteers.[28] As they walk precincts, leaflet at highly frequented places in the community, or operate phone banks, volunteers operate as surrogates for candidates. Many of them, after brief training, are highly effective in these roles—often making the difference between winning and losing a campaign. Volunteers are also ambassadors of good will in the broader campaign with their extended families and with acquaintances. Candidates sometimes have the good fortune to find volunteers with technical skills like the ability to use computer technology to identify specific precincts or groups of voters. Many successful candidates are even more likely to give post-election access to volunteers than to contributors because they realize they donated their personal time and energy to the campaign rather than merely signing a check.

Creating a Campaign Organization

Campaign organizations are unlike most organizations because they are time-limited and have a single purpose: to gather as many votes as possible for candidates in a matter of several months. Everything about them is dedicated to this urgent task.

Candidates exist at the top of the organizational chart, but they differ widely in the actual roles they assume during the campaign. Some candidates delegate very little—making the key decisions and overseeing their implementation. Other candidates place extraordinary reliance on their staff and consultants, basically following their advice with respect to strategy and implementation decisions. No single style is best because the capabilities of candidates, staff, and consultants vary widely. Experienced candidates who possess political instincts often can and should play a more central role than candidates who lack these attributes. Problems occur when candidates who lack political instincts and savvy make too many decisions—as Ed Rollins recalls when discussing George Bush, Sr.'s lackluster campaign in 1992 when he was bested by Bill Clinton.[29] Falsely assuming that his popularity from winning Desert Storm would carry over into this election, Bush ignored domestic issues even when warned by Rollins and other advisers that this decision could cost him the election. When Clinton's staff adopted the motto, "it's the economy stupid," they set the stage for a landslide victory over Bush.

The size and sophistication of a candidate's staff depends on the resources she can raise. In a campaign with extensive resources, staff could include a campaign manager, consultants, a director of research (polling and focus groups), a director of public policy, a media director, a recruiter and supervisor of volunteers, and a fund-raiser. In smaller campaigns for local seats, candidates may have virtually no staff—or may hire part-time consultants to help them with specific tasks. In some cases, candidates for local seats rely heavily on key volunteers with expertise in specific topics.

Because their work is so time-limited, effective campaign organizations are highly focused, work as a close team, and are highly motivated to succeed. While internal differences may emerge in the heat of the contest about strategy, effective campaign organizations quickly resolve them so they can develop a united strategy. Above all, effective campaign organizations believe in their candidates—and put everything on the line to try to get them elected.

Developing Campaign Strategy

Strategy Options at the Outset of a Campaign

We have already discussed many elements of campaign strategy. Even before a primary contest begins, and before a final contest or a run-off contest occurs, candidates need to do the following:[30]

- Conduct an analysis of the electoral population in their districts to ascertain what groups and geographic areas are in play.
- Link this analysis to the development of an initial set of positions and campaign promises. They may decide what issues to select and what kinds of positions to take initially with respect to them. They may decide what issues to avoid because they believe them to be unimportant or because they work to the advantage of opponents. With respect to some issues, they may decide not to commit themselves to a position or to leave the position relatively vague.
- As they are doing this analysis, they need to examine strengths and weaknesses of likely opponents, both in terms of their electoral support and in terms of their likely or stated positions on issues. Campaigns are competitions—and candidates cannot compete if they fail to analyze opponents' positions.
- Raise funds, recruit volunteers, seek endorsements, and develop a campaign organization.

• Set priorities by deciding what expenditures of time and effort will yield the highest return in terms of issues, geographic portions and populations of the electoral district, campaign advertisements in the media, campaign appearances, and priorities in phone banking and distribution of leaflets. The selection of priorities lies at the heart of campaign strategy; resources must be targeted at activities that will yield results, rather than scattered to many low-yield undertakings.

• Develop a master calendar of events, activities, and expenditures that build toward the final vote—whether the primary or the final or run-off election. Candidates cannot expend most of their resources in the early phase of a campaign, because they need to intensify their personal appearances, advertising, and outreach as the campaign nears its culmination—the final vote. Resources have to be rationed in the early and middle phases to allow an upsurge in the final phase. The early and middle phases must not be neglected, however, because candidates want to build momentum as they go.

• Develop an aggressive absentee ballot campaign so that votes of absentee supporters are counted.

Strategy During the Mid-Phase of a Campaign

Little is set in concrete as the campaign unfolds. Polls and focus groups will show that some issues and positions are not resonating with citizens in the geographic areas or populations that the campaign targets. New issues may arise, as well, from unexpected developments in the community, region, or nation—such as a sharp economic downturn or a crisis in local schools.

Strategy must often be changed to counter tactics of opponents.[31] Campaigns are like chess matches because each side develops strategies to offset or counter their opposition. As campaigns progress, candidates need to do the following:

• Analyze their opponents' strategy. Try to understand how the opponent answered the same questions they addressed in the early phase of their campaigns. (See the previous list.)

• Ask whether they need to strengthen their outreach and advertising to specific geographic areas or populations in light of their opponents' activities. Perhaps, for example, they discover through focus groups that opponents are making inroads on groups they had given high priority.

• Ask whether they should concentrate on new groups of voters who they had prematurely written off. Perhaps a focus group will suggest that certain kinds of swing voters are now up for grabs, whether because opponents have failed to try to reach them or have made serious errors in trying to reach them.

• Decide how to change the selection of issues and the positions on issues in response to opponents selection and positions. Perhaps candidates need to offset or counter opponents' positions on specific issues if they seem to be gathering support from important parts of the electorate.

• Decide whether, when, and where to engage in public debates or forums with opponents. Candidates must decide how many public debates or forums to attend. If they are strong frontrunners and are not skilled debaters, they may want fewer of them—although excessive avoidance of debates or forums can work to the opponents' advantage. Persons who are long shots and good debaters will want more debates and forums to enhance their name recognition.

 • Decide on an advertising strategy in the context of opponents' advertising strategy and how the campaign is progressing. There often is no need to advertise in areas that are already supportive of candidates, but advertising is very important if candidates lack name recognition (as compared with opponents), if opponents are aggressively advertising to specific populations that candidates had targeted, or if candidates are running behind in polls. If opponents are hoarding their advertising funds for a last-minute blitz, candidates may want to retain much of their advertising resources to counter that blitz.

 • Decide to what extent positive versus negative messages should be included in advertisements and personal statements in the context of opponents' ads and statements. Many candidates have found that they suffer electoral damage if they do not quickly counter opponents' negative statements, but negative ads and statements sometimes can backfire.

End-game strategy   Campaigns gather intensity as candidates approach the final vote. They ask two questions: what last minute strategies have the most potential for persuading key voters to change their minds and what will make them turn out to vote? In some cases, of course, elections have already been decided by the last two weeks, but others still hang in the balance. Candidates need to do the following:

 • Select final issues and positions that will change swing voters minds
 • Make the case to supporters that they need to turn out
 • Place as many ads as the campaign budget allows in strategic places
 • Mount an assertive get-out-the-vote drive on election day

Conducting Issue-Oriented Campaigns

During the Progressive Era at the start of the 20th century, reformers in the various states placed legislative proposals directly on the ballot, allowing citizens to bypass the state legislature. If supported by a majority of citizens, such propositions become law by referendum.

As policy advocates soon discovered, however, this option was a mixed blessing. If social reformers could get some of their ideas on the ballot, so could conservatives and special interests. When Proposition 13 was enacted in California in 1979, for example, it set off a wave of similar propositions in other states that slashed property taxes so markedly that many social programs had to be cut. Yet policy advocates have successfully supported the enactment of an array of measures of their own, such as ones dedicating revenues from marriage licenses to programs to stop child abuse and proposals to safeguard rights of gay men and lesbians.

Policy advocates must work on two fronts: They initiate propositions, and they battle those that others have initiated that they do not like. To initiate a proposition, they must draft it, campaign to secure enough signatures from registered voters to qualify it for the ballot, and raise funds for advertising and direct-mail efforts. If their proposition seeks to raise taxes, to establish major new programs, or to regulate powerful interests like gun dealers, they can expect considerable opposition from offended interests and conservatives.

Whether they support or oppose a specific proposition, policy advocates must use strategies similar to those used by candidates for office. They have to build a campaign organization that raises sufficient funds for a potent advertising campaign to be mounted. They need to recruit volunteers to distribute leaflets at shopping centers and other community sites, and they must enlist speakers who can make public appearances. They need strong liaison with editorial staff and reporters of newspapers so they get supportive coverage and endorsements of their positions. Since many propositions are on statewide ballots, they must decide which geographic areas in the state should be top priority.

Making Issue Campaigns and Electoral Politics Intersect

We noted earlier that electoral politics are sometimes influenced by issue campaigns. When propositions are on the ballot, candidates' positions on these propositions can shape elections' outcomes as well as the popularity of incumbents. When Republican Governor Pete Wilson endorsed Proposition 187 in 1994, which severely restricted the rights of undocumented immigrants, including their right to health care and use of public schools, his popularity plummeted. Many Republican candidates subsequently lost key elections, allowing Democrats to gain the governorship and both chambers in California. Policy advocates can influence the outcomes of elections, then, by working on propositions—or on issue-oriented campaigns to secure specific legislation—in certain jurisdictions. They can assertively attempt to get politicians to state their positions on these issues in hopes that grassroots support for them will influence the outcome of key issues. (See Policy Advocacy Challenge 12.5.)

POLICY ADVOCACY CHALLENGE 12.5 *SMOKING OUT THE POSITIONS OF A CONSERVATIVE* *Anneka Scranton, M.S.W., Ph.D., Clinical Professor, School of Social Work, University of Southern California*	Along with several other child advocates, I attended a League of Women Voters candidate forum in the fall of 1996. We were trying to flush out a radical right-wing candidate for the California State Senate. We had discovered that Phil Hawkins, as an assemblyman, had voted for corporal punishment in school. We therefore submitted several questions about this issue. After several questions, Hawkins became overtly angry. He vehemently endorsed spanking and even held up caning in Singapore as admirable discipline. Having got his enthusiasm for caning on video, we sent clips to the media and wrote numerous letters to the editor. Mr. Hawkins was handily defeated by a progressive family and child advocate who has become a leader on this issue in the State Senate: Betty Karnette.

Exercises:

This case presents an interesting alternative to mud slinging: getting candidates to reveal their true beliefs by asking well-designed questions, and then sending these responses to the media.

When policy advocates do attack the motivations or character of an opposing candidate, do they act ethically?

What limits or boundaries should be placed on such negative attacks?

Is it true that candidates who do not resort to such tactics are usually defeated?

In some cases, issue-oriented organizations, such as the AFL-CIO, gun control organizations, the American Association of Retired Persons (AARP), and the National Association for the Advancement of Colored Persons (NAACP) target key electoral districts several years before specific congressional and presidential contests.[32] Their goal is to build a cadre of members who care deeply about specific issues that are relevant to their groups, including, in the case of unions, raising the minimum wage, improving work-safety policies, and expanding medical insurance to uninsured workers. They develop leaders in their membership, who then hold meetings and forums for other members. In the case of the NAACP, the organization mounts aggressive voter registration projects among African Americans. When the elections near, they identify the candidates who support their issues and work to help them by giving them resources, running issue-oriented ads, publicizing their endorsements, walking precincts, running phone banks, and distributing leaflets. Indeed, these examples tell us that campaigning begins long before many elections occur.

These tactics are not unique to relatively liberal groups. The Moral Majority, an umbrella term for conservative groups that include many fundamental protestant churches, was instrumental in electing scores of conservative candidates in the 1980s and 1990s by using precisely these kinds of tactics.

The nexus between electoral politics and issue-oriented organizations is unlikely to disappear. Issue-oriented organizations realize that they cannot obtain policy successes if some public officials do not share their perspectives. By getting involved in grassroots organizing that intersects with electoral politics, issue-oriented groups send a message to legislators and heads of government: support some of our issues or we will build grassroots pressure against you in the next round of elections.

Participating in Electoral and Issue-Oriented Campaigns

Policy advocates can assume major roles in political campaigns as well as ballot propositions—and some run for office as we discuss subsequently. As volunteers, policy advocates can do the following:

- Work inside the campaigns of specific candidates performing myriad tasks, such as organizing and working on phone banks, precinct walking, distributing leaflets, helping with focus groups and data gathering, and helping to prepare policy positions on important issues
- Work on campaigns for or against specific propositions
- Work with specific issue-oriented organizations as they build grassroots and membership support for specific issues and as they try to link such support to electoral campaigns
- Work on voter registration, absentee ballot, developing forums, and get-out-the vote drives (See Policy Advocacy Challenge 12.6.)

**POLICY
ADVOCACY
CHALLENGE 12.6**

*HOW STUDENTS
CAN GET INVOLVED
IN POLITICAL
CAMPAIGNS*

*Ramon M. Salcido,
D.S.W., Associate
Professor, School of
Social Work, University
of Southern California*

*Jolene Swain, M.S.W.,
Field Coordinator,
University of Southern
California*

Background

The electoral project was conceived by the authors as a school of social work project to heighten awareness of the importance of voting and participating in the 1996 presidential election. The goal was to organize several activities that would result in students' participating in the election. The time frame for the project was four months. The activities included (1) voter registration, (2) an absentee ballots effort, (3) a forum rally, and (4) a get-out-the-vote drive.

The authors (a policy instructor and a field educator) initially took the lead in forming a planning committee, since students did not yet have the experience in organizing for an electoral campaign. Moreover, both authors had worked closely during the summer with both the national and the state NASW political action committee. The policy instructor also organized seven policy instructors and the field educator in the school to provide support to the students and to act as a link with the field agencies. A steering committee was organized, consisting of three student organization officers, four student volunteers, and the authors. The committee met once a week to do the planning and co-ordination. Once the plan had been developed, the students took charge of implementation. Officers of the student organization, elected by students to represent them in the school's governance, met with the dean, presented the plan, and received approval.

Role of Student Organization

The school's student organization became the key in implementing the electoral drive, contacting students and informing them of coming events. On September 10, 1996, the student organization sent a memo to every student, announcing the electoral campaign and giving key dates for voter registration training, the forum rally, and the availability of information kits. Similarly, a memo was sent to interested agencies to inform them of the voter registration drive, to encourage them to support students in the field to initiate voter registration activities, and to invite them to participate in the forum rally.

Activities

Voter registration   Several tasks are involved in voter registration activities. The first step was to obtain large numbers of mail-in voter registration forms from the county office of the registrar (election office). The second was to train the members of the steering committee and other students about how to register voters—and then to use this knowledge to register other students to vote. Eleven students were trained and promptly registered 32 other students to vote. Moreover, students registered 123 voters at seven field agencies.

Absentee ballots   The next activity was to have students participate in an absentee ballot effort. The faculty person contacted the county election office and obtained information

(continued)

(12.6   continued)

on absentee ballot procedures, and two student members went to the county elections office to be trained on how to do absentee balloting. On September 30, 1996, the student organization sent another letter to each student, giving information on the steps in absentee voting, a request form for an absentee ballot, and a county number to call for information. A total of 420 information letters were sent to all students of the school. Student feedback informed us that the absentee ballot drive allowed many students to vote by mail during midterm. From an informal count by the policy instructors, it is estimated that about 30 percent (129) of the student body voted by absentee ballot.

Organizing a forum   A forum was organized to provide information on all of the state ballot measures, including the so-called Civil Rights Initiative (a proposition that proposed to eliminate affirmative action in California), to inform participants of NASW's position and endorsed candidates, and to stress the importance of social workers' being part of the political process.

The forum was publicized in many ways. For example, the dean sent a memo to all students and faculty two weeks before the event. Policy instructors also emphasized the importance of the forum and encouraged students to participate as part of a class assignment. The student body president served as master of ceremonies. Forum speakers included a state Cal-PACE person, who spoke about the state initiatives; a representative of a political action committee concerned with persons with disabilities, who spoke about the impact of the so-called Civil Rights Initiative on clients; and a Los Angeles City Council person (Laura Chick, M.S.W.), who spoke about the importance of voting and getting others to vote. The state NASW Cal-PACE and National PACE provided the forum with a list of NASW-endorsed candidates and information on the ballot initiatives. An attempt was made to be educational and nonpartisan. After the presentations, political district maps were displayed, and students were asked to locate their geographic location and identify their political representatives. Sign-in sheets showed a total of 82 students, 3 clients, 6 faculty, and 9 field instructors.

Get-out-the-vote drive   One week before Election Day, the student organization sent letters to students reminding them to vote and asking them if they wanted to participate in any NASW-targeted races. A total of 120 students were personally contacted. About 62 students volunteered to work at NASW-targeted races, as well as in the effort to defeat the proposition that proposed to end affirmative action.

Suggestions

This kind of campaign project is only one of many possibilities for student participation in political campaigns. Other experiences could include participation in one NASW-targeted race as a school project, voter registration initiatives that include registering clients at field education sites, and students' organizing phone banks in a get-out-the-vote effort on Election Day. Our experience suggests the importance of (1) knowing the dates for voter registration completion and absentee ballots; (2) being familiar with the laws concerning electoral activities in the academy; (3) getting an endorsement from the dean; (4) realizing that students have time constraints; and (5) including in the planning field instructors representing social work training sites.

This case example of student involvement raises a number of interesting questions:

- Should schools of social work involve students in the electoral process?
- Should schools and fieldwork agencies engage in voter registration drives?
- Do policy courses motivate students to become involved in the electoral process?

Policy advocates can also work with a political action committee (PAC), such as NASW's PAC, which is called PACE. Because nonprofit organizations may lose their tax-exempt status if they engage in partisan politics, many of them have created these spin-off PACs. For example, the NASW formed PACE, its political action arm, in 1976. PACE solicits its funds from members of NASW, who make small annual contributions to PACE with their annual membership fee unless they choose not to—or who make contributions any time of the year to national or chapter NASW PACE. One-half of membership fee contributions are used at the national level and one-half are given to state chapters. PACE keeps these funds in a separate account from the funds of NASW and has its own board of directors.

The national unit of NASW PACE endorses candidates for federal offices, and chapter units in each state endorse state and local candidates and collaborate with the national unit on federal elections. PACE currently has 46 chapter PACE committees. NASW PACE also trains and mobilizes NASW members to vote and volunteer for endorsed candidates, funds field organizers in certain prioritized races, and lets members know how elected officials voted on issues tracked by NASW.

NASW PACE endorses candidates on the following criteria:

- Issues that candidates support or oppose
- Viability of the campaign in terms of money raised and name recognition
- Relationship to the social work community
- Leadership positions of candidates if they are incumbents
- Whether they come from an underrepresented group such as a racial minority group

NASW PACE staff interview candidates either in person or on the phone to obtain this information. PACE then determines the kind or kinds of support it will give, which can include a letter of endorsement, a financial contribution, publicity in NASW publications, volunteers, fundraisers, and photo opportunities.

PACE has grown steadily. It endorsed many candidates in the 2000 elections and contributed considerable resources to them. NASW PACE has identified 150 social workers who hold elected offices at all levels of government, including six in federal positions that include Senators Barbara Mikulski (D-Maryland) and Debbie Stabenow (D-Michigan) and Representatives Susan Davis (D-California), Barbara Lee (D-California), Ciro Rodgriguez (D-Texas), and Ed Towns (D-New York).

Deciding to Run for Office

Reasoning that they want to make policy decisions themselves, some policy activists run for office. (See Policy Advocacy Challenge 12.7.)

POLICY ADVOCACY CHALLENGE 12.7

MY CITY COUNCIL CAMPAIGN

Victor Manola, M.S.W., Ph.D., Director of the Field Education Department, Department of Social Work, California State University at Los Angeles

It was the case that led me into politics. I just started working for child protective services when I received Brenda's case. Brenda had just given birth to her sixth child, who had a positive toxicology screen for cocaine and her five other children were in foster care. After a lot of hard work, Brenda had completed a drug treatment program and moved into a two-bedroom apartment with all six of her children.

Soon thereafter, I read that an initiative was going to be on the ballot that would sharply decrease AFDC payments in the state. I knew that Brenda used a large part of her AFDC check to pay her rent. I feared that any cuts in her AFDC payment would force Brenda and her newly reunited and very fragile family back down the road of substance abuse and child neglect.

I became very angry and I knew that I had to act. I decided to work on the campaign to defeat that initiative. Thankfully, we defeated that initiative, but the political onslaught on our clients—the poor, the undocumented, the oppressed—continued.

After working on political issues since then, I became frustrated with elected officials who had no idea how to address the needs of our clients. In the policy classes that I taught, I tried to convince students that social workers should be proactive, instead of reactive; making the policies, instead of reacting to policies. Well, I finally convinced myself! I knew that, when the time was right, I would run for office.

I discussed my intentions with my wife, friends, and colleagues, all of whom were very supportive of my decision. I did not have much experience in electoral politics. So, I decided to get involved in my city.

I started attending community events and city council meetings. I began writing letters to the editor to local newspapers. One editor liked my letters so much that she asked me to write a weekly column. As a result of my networking with city officials, I accepted an appointment to the city's planning commission, dealing with zoning and land use issues within the city.

In my two years on the commission, I've voted on issues ranging from affordable housing for seniors and granting permits to adult day health care centers, to upgrading our city parks and improving our commercial district. When I found out that there were three city council seats up in the next election, I knew that I could make a difference.

I called the city clerk to find out how to file to run for city council. After collecting nominating signatures from 25 registered voters in the city and filing papers with the city and with the state's fair political practices commission, I became an official candidate for city council.

It was less than three months until election day and I had a lot of work to do. I began by asking for campaign contributions and volunteer time from family, friends, and colleagues by telephone, in person, and by email. I had social work students walking precincts and phone banking. Besides attending community events, talking to voters, and getting endorsements, I was putting up campaign signs late at night, designing and making copies of my campaign flyers, and preparing voter registration lists for volunteers.

I received endorsements from state and local elected officials, as well as from the California Chapter of NASW, the California Democratic Party, and the Long Beach Press Telegram. The local Lions Club hosted a candidate forum where I used my public speaking skills to my advantage. We had sent out two strong mailers and, going into election day, I felt really positive about my campaign.

On election day, I was a nervous wreck. We went to the polling places to make sure my supporters voted; if not, we called to remind them to vote. That evening, my friends went to city hall to get the vote count, because I was too stressed out. Unfortunately, when the precinct counts came in, my heart dropped—I knew that I would not have enough votes to win a city council seat.

Looking back upon the campaign, I realized, I was not running for one of three open seats against five other candidates, but I was really running for one open seat against four candidates. Two of the seats were being sought by two incumbents (who nearly always get reelected), while the remaining four candidates fought for one seat. The eventual winner of that seat, was a Portuguese man who was supported by a very organized and influential Portuguese community and whose family name was very well known. I came in 4th. I learned the importance of knowing your opponents.

Although I was very disappointed, I believe that my campaign was very successful. Losing a campaign the first time out is not unusual and many influential people from the community have already encouraged me to run again. As a result of my campaign, more people in the community know me now and I have a strong base of supporters from which to build upon for the next election.

While the next election is 1½ years away, I am already beginning to make preparations. I have already been attending city council meetings, community events, and local club meetings, telling people that I am planning to run in the next election. I am learning more about the community and residents' concerns.

Next election, I will put together a campaign committee that will be responsible for running the campaign, so that I can focus on meeting voters. I will raise campaign money early, so that I will have my signs, flyers, and mailers ready to go 3 months before election day. Also, I will ask everyone that I know for campaign contributions. People are generous and they want to see you do well, but they will not give you money unless you ask!

POLICY ADVOCACY CHALLENGE 12.8

CONSIDERING A PUBLIC-SERVICE TRAJECTORY

While many social workers develop outstanding careers "in the trenches" in child welfare, mental health, health, and other organizations, some venture into public-service realms where they interact with legislators, high-level civil servants, and other policy makers. Here are three examples of social workers who branched into public service.

Bio-Sketch: Carol Turner, A.M., Education Advocate, Office of the Mayor, Portland, OR

You can be a good clinician and still decide to go into public service—as my career illustrates. I received training at the University of Chicago in psychiatric social work graduating in 1965. My husband and I moved to Portland, Oregon, where I held clinical

(continued)

(12.8   continued)

positions with non-profit agencies over several decades, in addition to having a small private practice. I was not particularly "political," identifying myself professionally as a clinician.

I was very concerned about public education, however. The Portland School District, which my two children attended, was sorely in need of new leadership and ideas. Somebody asked me one day if I wanted to run for an opening on the school board—something I had not considered before. After making inquiries and deciding I might actually win, I entered a heated race in 1985—and, to my amazement, won the seat.

Since that point, my career has completely changed. I served on the Portland School Board for 12 years where I took part in scores of decisions that shaped policies of the District. For example, I dealt with significant school reform; curriculum development; policies related to prevention—such as alcohol and drug use by students and increasing student, family and community assets; and the impact of gang violence and AIDS on a school district. As chair of the board for three terms, I was intimately involved with making major budget decisions and—the most important work of such boards—hiring a new superintendent. I also served as the president of the statewide association of school board members, in which I worked primarily on funding issues.

In 1997, I was offered a position with the Oregon Department of Human Services and worked in a consultative role with local agencies working on service integration and community development.

I was invited by the Portland Mayor in 1998 to join her staff to give her advice on educational matters. My focus in my five years in this post has been on developing ways that the city can help local school districts be successful in such arenas as stabilizing school funding, increasing volunteerism in schools, expanding after-school programs, leading a community reading initiative and further developing early childhood programs.

I have found my public-service career to be highly fulfilling. I have brought my social work experience and perspectives to the table on many occasions, helping to develop policies and programs that will help youth obtain an array of services that might otherwise not be available to them. Also, such clinical skills as listening carefully and understanding the complexities of human motivation have definitely come in handy in dealing with the pressures from various political constituencies.

So you don't have to be a macro student to get into public service or to run for office. You just have to have a willingness to take some chances and expand your horizons!

Bio-Sketch: Sharilyn Twidwell, MSW, Director of Governmental Relations and Political Affairs for NASW California Chapter

I was a high school teacher in the Boston, Massachusetts, area, and I was tired of running into roadblocks when I and other teachers tried to help students with problems outside their academic life. The mental health worker on our campus was a social worker, and one day when I was complaining to him, he said, "You should look into becoming a social worker so you can actually do something about all this." So I did.

When I entered the MSW program at USC, I was absolutely convinced that I should choose the Mental Health concentration, work as a direct practitioner for about five years (until I was an "expert," hah), and then I would be ready to work in mental health policy. Once I got through the first semester, however, and it was time to make a decision about my concentration, I was torn between the clinical and the macro tracks. I spoke to everyone I possibly could have spoken to, but there was one person in particular who finally changed my mind, and my life, forever.

Dr. Rino Patti sat me down in his office, and we talked about what my ultimate goals were, and what the best path for me might be, and I'll never forget what he said, "Social work needs leaders so badly, Shari. If you feel like you have any inkling towards leadership at all, and I think you do, you would have an incredible path before you in this profession." Something about those words just made sense. I chose the macro concentration called Community Organization, Planning, and Administration (COPA).

My second-year internship was with NASW California's southern California office, where I did various needs assessment and community organization projects, as well as some legislative advocacy work. I also applied for a fellowship with the California Legislature, which I received and accepted shortly after graduating with my MSW. (Applying for this fellowship took some courage because competition is intense to receive it.)

I worked through the fellowship in the capitol building in Sacramento, for a state Assemblywoman named Carole Migden (D-San Francisco), where I became completely addicted to legislative process. I staffed bills for the Assemblywoman that changed the face of California's emancipation process for foster youth, and that increased benefits for registered domestic partners.

At the end of that legislative session, I took the job I hold currently: Director of Governmental Relations and Political Affairs for NASW California. I still cannot believe my luck in having the role models I did throughout my graduate education, and then in the state legislature. They changed my life forever.

Bio-Sketch: Michelle M. Wilson, M.S.W., Program Analyst, National Institute for Occupational Safety and Health, Centers for Disease Control and Prevention

Since the beginning of my career in social work, I have always had a passion and respect for those in macro practice. Early on, I realized that social workers in macro practice play a vital role in the success and survival of any social policy or program. As macro practitioners, we are the advocates, evaluators, organizers, planners, researchers, and change agents for programs that affect people's everyday lives. We bring unique perspectives to the table. We look at things form a systems perspective, advocating and creating change at the macro, mezzo, and micro levels of society.

As I was finishing the second year of my MSW curriculum, I decided to apply for the Presidential Management Intern Program. It was an easy decision, but I had to compete with hundreds of other applicants for a few slots. But I knew that I brought to the interviews unique perspectives stemming from my social work education and internships. My second year field placement was a the Los Angeles County Department of Mental Health, where I primarily focused on program planning and evaluation and policy research surrounding the issue of Institutes for Mental Disease. During my second year of graduate school, I also had the opportunity to work for the United Way of Greater Los Angeles. During this time, I conducted community-based research, looking at the overall development of children in Los Angeles under the age of 6, which has now become a major social issue for Los Angeles County. My drive and passion for becoming a macro

(continued)

(12.8   continued)

practitioner has also been inspired by past professors Rino Patti, Jacquelyn McCroskey, Vince Ornelas, and colleagues Marge Nichols and Jenny Gross, who in their own ways have opened my eyes to the need for macro practitioners and have encouraged me to become a "squeaky wheel" within the public sector.

When I learned that I was successful in receiving a Presidential internship, I chose a two-year internship at the Centers for Disease Control and Prevention (CDC), where I could couple my passion for macro practice and public health. (I had received a B.S. in Applied Behavioral Science and Epidemiology at University of California, Davis.) A job with the U.S. CDC would give me, I decided, the means to become a change agent at the federal level, affecting social policies and programs from the top down. Within my job in the Director's Office at the National Institute for Occupational Safety and Health (NIOSH), I am involved in research analysis, and project planning, strategic planning, performance measurement, policy formulation and analysis, and program evaluation.

Chapter Summary

What You Can Now Do

You are now equipped to do the following:

- Assess candidates' odds of winning seats by analyzing their districts, their name recognition, and other factors, while realizing that many electoral contests are highly unpredictable
- Identify an array of power resources used by candidates to influence voters' views and actions
- Understand the importance of resources for campaigns, while realizing that resources, alone, do not guarantee victory
- Understand what campaign organizations are
- Be able to discuss an array of campaign strategies that arise at the outset, mid-phase, and end-games of campaigns
- Work in issue-oriented campaigns
- Understand how issue-oriented campaigns and electoral politics often intersect
- Be able to participate in various roles as policy advocates during electoral campaigns and issue campaigns
- Work with NASW's PACE
- Consider whether to run for office at some future time
- Understand different public-policy career trajectories

We are now ready to examine in the next two chapters what happens after policies are enacted, when policy advocates participate in policy implementation and assessment.

Notes

1. Robert E. DiClerico, *Political Parties, Campaigns, and Elections* (Englewood Cliffs, N.J.: Prentice-Hall, 2000), pp. 191–250.
2. Robert Biersack, Paul Herrnson, and Clyde Wilcox, *After the Revolution: PACs, Lobbies, and the Republican Congress* (Boston: Allyn & Bacon, 1999), pp. 77–93, 134–143.

3. Bruce Jansson, *The Sixteen Trillion Dollar Mistake: How the U.S. Bungled Its National Priorities from the New Deal to the Present* (New York: Columbia University Press, 2001), pp. 330–333.

4. Ibid., pp. 295–299.

5. Darrell West and Burdett Loomis, *The Sound of Money: How Political Interests Get What They Want* (New York: W. W. Norton, 1998) and Jeffrey Birnbaum, *The Money Men* (New York: Crown, 2000), pp. 3–48. For discussion of campaign finance at the state level, see Joel Thompson and Gary Moncrief, *Campaign Finance in State Legislative Elections* (Washington, DC: Congressional Quarterly, Inc., 1998.)

6. Anne Bedlington, "The Realtors' Political Action Committee: Covering All Contingencies," In Biersack, Herrnson, and Wilcox, *After the Revolution,* pp. 170–183.

7. Gary Jacobson, *The Politics of Congressional Elections* (New York: Longman, 1997), pp. 1–51.

8. Ibid. and Ann Beaudry and Bob Schaeffer, *Local and State Elections* (New York: Free Press, 1986).

9. Jacobson, *The Politics of Congressional Elections.*

10. Thompson and Moncrief, *Campaign Finance,* pp. 99–114.

11. Beaudry and Schaeffer, *Local and State Elections,* pp. 18–37.

12. Jacobson, *The Politics of Congressional Elections;* Beaudry and Schaeffer, *Local and State Elections,* pp. 20–21.

13. Ibid., pp. 20–22.

14. Bruce Newman, The Mass Marketing of Politics: Democracy in an Age of Manufactured Images (Thousand Oaks, CA: Sage Publications, 1999), pp. 71–86; and Karen Johnson-Cartee and Gary Copeland, *Inside Political Campaigns* (Westport, Conn.: Praeger, 1997), pp. 149–184.

15. Public debates assume greater importance as candidates run for "higher" offices in mayoral, congressional, and presidential contests.

16. See Jacobson, *The Politics of Congressional Elections.*

17. Richard Scher, *The Modern Political Campaign* (Armonk, NY: M. E. Sharpe, 1997), pp. 88–111.

18. Kim Kahn and Patrick Kenney, "How Negative Campaigning Enhances Knowledge of Senate Elections," In James Thurber, Candice Nelson, and David Dulio, *Crowded Airwaves* (Washington, DC: Brookings Institution, 2000), pp. 65–95; and Kathleen Hall Jamieson, Paul Waldman, and Susan Sherr, "Eliminate the Negative? Categories of Analysis for Political Advertisement," in Thurber, et. al., *Crowded Airwaves,* pp. 44–64.

19. For a discussion of the pros and cons of negative ads, see Kahn and Kenney, "How Negative Campaigning Enhances Knowledge of State Elections."

20. Frances Fox Piven and Richard Cloward, *Why Americans Don't Vote and Why Politicians Want It That Way* (Boston: Beacon Press, 2000).

21. Beaudry and Schaeffer, *Local and State Elections,* pp. 13, 102–103, 136–138, 169.

22. Biersack, Herrnson, and Wilcox, *After the Revolution,* pp. 1–17.

23. Kim Kahn and Patrick Kenney, *The Spectacle of U.S. Senate Elections* (Princeton, N.J.: Princeton University Press, 1999), pp. 3–29.

24. Gary Moncrief, "Candidate Spending in State Legislative Races," in Thompson and Moncrief, *Campaign Finance,* pp. 37–58.

25. William Cassie and David Breaux, "Expenditures and Election Results," in Thompson and Moncrief, *Campaign Finance,* pp. 99–114.

26. Birnbaum, *The Money Men,* pp. 225–230.

27. David Breaux and Anthony Gierznski, "Candidate Revenues and Expenditures in State Legislative Primaries," in Thompson and Moncrief, *Campaign Finance,* pp. 80–114.

28. Beaudry and Schaeffer, *Local and State Elections,* pp. 187–205.

29. Ed Rollins, *Bare Knuckles and Back Rooms* (New York: Broadway Books, 1996), pp. 216, 264.

30. Beaudry and Schaeffer, *Local and State Elections,* pp. 2–205.

31. Kahn and Kenney, *The Spectacle of U.S. Senate Elections*

32. Robin Gerber, "Building to Win, Building to Last: AFL-CIO COPE Takes on the Republican Congress," in Biersack, Herrnson, and Wilcox, *After the Revolution,* pp. 77–93.

Suggested Readings

Campaigns

Karen S. Johnson-Cartee and Gary A. Copeland, *Inside Political Campaigns* (London: Praeger, 1997).

Richard A. Scher, *The Modern Political Campaign* (Armonk, N.Y.: M. E. Sharpe, 1997).

Political Parties

William J. O'Keefe, *Parties, Politics, and Public Policy in America, 7th ed.* (Washington, DC: Congressional Quarterly Press, 1994).

Robert E. DiClerico, *Political Parties, Campaigns, and Elections* (Upper Saddle River, N.J.: Prentice-Hall, 2000).

Political Consultants

James Thurber and Candice Nelson, eds., *Campaign Warriors: the Role of Consultants in Elections* (Washington, DC: Brookings Institution Press, 2000).

Campaign Finance

Joel A. Thompson and Gary F. Moncrief, *Campaign Finance in State Legislative Elections* (Washington, DC: Congressional Quarterly Inc., 1998).

Campaign Advertising

James Thurber, Candice Nelson, and David Dulio, eds., *Crowded Airways: Campaign Advertising in Elections* (Washington, DC: Brookings Institution, 2000).

Connections Between Issue and Electoral Politics

Megan Twohey, "Gunfights at the State Corrals," *National Journal* (2000), pp. 2376–2377.

Hedrick Smith, *The Power Game: How Washington Works* (New York: Ballantine Books, 1996).

Political Action Committees

Robert Biersack, Paul Herrnson, and Clyde Wilcox, *After the Revolution: PACs, Lobbies, and the Republican Congress* (Boston: Allyn and Bacon, 1999).

Political Strategy

Kim Kahn and Patrick Kenney, *The Spectacle of U.S. Senate Campaigns* (Princeton, N.J.: Princeton University Press, 1999).

Gary Jacobson, *The Politics of Congressional Elections* (New York: Longman, 1997).

Voting Behavior

Frances Fox Piven and Richard Cloward, *Why Americans Don't Vote and Why Politicians Want It That Way* (Boston: Beacon Press, 2000).

Marketing in Politics

Bruce Newman, *The Mass Marketing of Politics* (London: Sage Publications, 1999).

Troubleshooting and Assessing Policies

Having enacted policies, policy advocates must now turn to the implementation of enacted policies. This is a critically important part of policy advocacy because many meritorious policies are inadequately implemented. We discuss policy advocacy strategies during implementation, which we call troubleshooting, in **Chapter 13.**

Equally important is the assessing (or evaluation) of implemented policies, which we discuss in **Chapter 14.** We need to know if specific implemented policies are working. If not, we need to renew our work as policy advocates to secure changes in existing policies to provide a better outcome.

chapter 13

Troubleshooting Policies

<table>
<tr>
<td>

**POLICY
PREDICAMENT**

</td>
<td>

Social workers in a large metropolitan hospital often come across patients who are unaware of their ability to complete a living will, an advance directive, or a durable power of attorney for health care. (These procedures allow patients to state their medical preferences in advance of medical emergencies so that they will not receive unwanted medical treatments when they are terminally ill, unconscious, or incompetent to make medical choices.) Frustrated, they may approach the admissions desk, where the admissions clerk reassures them that all patients receive notification of their rights at the time of admission, as required by the Patient Self-Determination Act of 1990. (Though enacted in 1990, even now the act is only partially implemented.)

Assume you are a social worker who doubts that this policy is being implemented in your hospital. You believe that patients' right to make choices about their health care is violated by such nonimplementation. What do you do?

After discussing policy implementation (or nonimplementation) in general terms, we shall return to the case of the Patient Self-Determination Act, to demonstrate that policy advocates can make a difference during policy implementation.

</td>
</tr>
</table>

Someone who says that a policy exists only on paper suggests that the enacted policy has little effect on the implementers, such as the direct-service staff of a social agency. When people say that direct-service staff members only halfheartedly implement a policy, they suggest that staff members honor it only marginally. Implementation is vital to policymaking; without it, official policies are meaningless.

This chapter provides a framework for understanding policy implementation, including alternative strategies that policy advocates can use to improve the implementation of policies. We discuss the following in this chapter:

- The importance of implementation to policy practice and policy advocacy
- A systems approach to implementation

- The importance of interorganizational processes to implementation
- How implementation is often powerfully shaped by contextual factors
- How some innovations are more difficult to implement or have a bleaker prognosis than others
- How policy advocates have many options for improving the implementation of innovations
- How policy advocates must sometimes sabotage specific policies
- How policy advocates must draw on a range of skills to improve implementation

A Framework for Implementing Policy

We can conceptualize policy implementation by means of a systems diagram that includes (a) policy innovations, (b) oversight organizations and staff, (c) primary implementing organizations, (4) implementing processes within specific agencies, (d) interorganizational processes, (e) external pressures on implementers, and (d) the evaluation of policy outcomes. (See Figure 13.1.) This systems framework is useful because it allows us to track

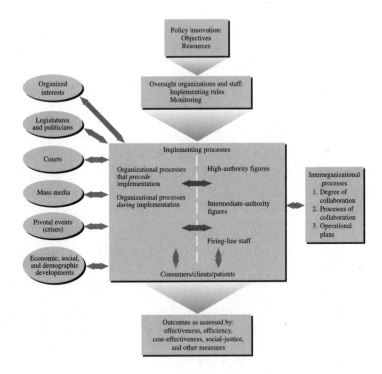

FIGURE 13.1   Implementation action system

a policy from its enactment to its final outcome and to place it in its political, economic, and legal context throughout its implementation. It allows us to identify and analyze the action system that springs into place once a policy innovation is enacted.

When policy innovations are established by Congress and then pass through the states to local agencies, the action system may be quite complex. Such a policy innovation may emanate from a major piece of legislation that contains multiple objectives. In many other cases, the action systems are quite simple, as when an agency adopts a simple innovation that is quickly and easily implemented.

No matter how complex an implementation action system is, policy advocates can use their understanding of implementation to improve it so that the new policy will achieve its objectives. No group is better positioned to reform implementation than social workers, because they know firsthand how specific policies are, or are not, implemented. (See Policy Advocacy Challenge 13.1.)

POLICY ADVOCACY CHALLENGE 13.1

USING THE WEB TO LEARN ABOUT TROUBLESHOOTING: THE WATCHDOGS— INVESTIGATIVE AGENCIES AND THINK TANKS

Stephanie Davis, Research Librarian, University of Southern California, Irvine

Once a policy is implemented, the effect of the policy needs to be assessed. There are several places on the web that you can find evaluations, reports, studies, editorials and other information on the impact of policies. Government agencies, community groups, think tanks and non-profit organizations all fulfill this purpose.

Resources:

- General Accounting Office www.gao.gov
- RAND www.rand.org
- National Institute for Research Advancement (NIRA): World Directory of Think Tanks www.nira.go.jp/ice/tt-info/nwdtt99

Exercise: Visit the GAO and RAND Web sites to become familiar with the mission and the political perspective of each organization. Next, visit the NIRA's World Directory of Think Tanks, and compare and contrast at least three other think tanks listed in the directory, including international think tanks.

Policy Innovations

Policy innovation (i.e., newly enacted legislation or proposals for new programs in agencies), at the top of the diagram in Figure 13.1, is the starting point for implementation. Many kinds of policy innovations exist. Some are simple, such as a new policy that modifies an agency's intake services in a minor way. Others are highly complex, such as the Personal Responsibility and Work Opportunities Act of 1996, which contained myriad items pertaining not only to single heads of household, but also to disabled persons, legal immigrants, and food stamps. The legislation wanted not only to get recipients off welfare rolls, but also to get them into employment. It wanted to free the states to establish their own programs, but to exert specific federal controls over them, such as setting minimum time schedules for reducing the welfare rolls. Some policy innovations require the collaboration of many people and agencies; others can be implemented by relatively few persons and one agency. Some policy innovations involve only a single task, such as changing intake procedures; others involve a sequence of tasks. To stimulate jobs in the inner cities, for example, we would need to lure industry into the cities, provide job training, improve the education system, and repair the infrastructure. Some policy innovations require vast amounts of resources, but others need few resources. Some are mandated by higher authorities and are highly detailed; others are vaguely defined. Some policies are relatively noncontroversial, and others are opposed by powerful interests. Some innovations require implementers to make only modest changes in their traditional practices; others demand sweeping changes.[1]

Some social policy innovations, we should remember, are not programs like Head Start or TANF, but regulations. Regulations include rules governing work safety, requirements that cigarette companies not market their products to teenagers, laws protecting confidentiality of patients and clients, laws prohibiting child labor, the federal minimum wage law, laws requiring states to provide abortions in the first trimester, regulations regarding public loitering (that apply to homeless persons), regulations regarding the licensing and training of social workers and other professionals, regulations governing affirmative action, and regulations giving patients certain rights when using health maintenance organizations. These regulations are often controversial, such as those regarding abortion and affirmative action. Some regulations are rigidly enforced; others are not. So regulations become a critical part of policy advocacy as advocates take positions on them, try to influence whether they are enforced, and (in some cases) try to amend or end them.

Even this cursory discussion suggests that some policies are simpler to implement than others. A straightforward change in an agency's intake procedure that requires few resources and that the executive director has defined precisely can usually be implemented without much difficulty. Contrast this simple change with an ambitious, nationwide effort to make sweeping reforms in the child welfare system. We can hypothesize that innovations become more difficult to implement when they require major changes from the status quo, when they require many institutions to collaborate, when they are costly, when a sequence of tasks must be accomplished, when they are controversial, and when they ask implementers to discard their traditional practices.

Policy innovations also become more problematic when they contain *internal contradictions* and *flawed strategies*.[2] Assume, for example, that a policy innovation seeks ambitious changes in existing programs but allocates only minimal resources. This internal contradiction is illustrated by the Family Support Act of 1988 and the Personal Responsibility and Work Opportunities Act of 1996. In each case, the policy innovations sought sweeping changes, such as the elimination of welfare as we know it and the employment of large numbers of welfare recipients, but the resources allotted to these sweeping goals were modest.

It is easy to overlook the actual substance of policy innovations when predicting their fate. A policy is likely to be unsuccessful if it proposes ill-conceived strategies, as illustrated once again by the Family Support Act of 1988 and the welfare reforms of 1996.[3] The legislation proposed giving jobs to many women on welfare when well-paying, blue-collar jobs were in sharp decline and when women had minimal access to unionized jobs in the trades, such as plumbing and carpentry. Moreover, many studies revealed that most female welfare recipients had educational deficits; indeed, many of them had not even completed high school. Both the Family Support Act and the 1996 welfare reforms proposed lifting numerous welfare recipients into jobs without addressing these fundamental economic and educational realities, proposing only modest training, educational, and day-care remedies. (An economic upturn in the late 1990s, remarkable in its scope and duration, proved to be a lucky break for the 1996 reforms, since many TANF recipients found jobs, although they often were relatively low-paying ones.) The legislation did not acknowledge that the net economic condition of many women might deteriorate if they lost access to Medicaid, public housing, and food stamps, even after obtaining low-paying jobs. By requiring the states to contribute a considerable share of the training and education costs, the legislation overlooked many states' budget deficits, which restricted the resources available for these training and educational programs. While the Family Support Act had some effect on reducing the welfare rolls, many critics assessed the rapid reductions in the rolls in the year following enactment of the welfare reforms in 1996 as resulting from the booming economy that ensued following its passage. Moreover, as discussed in Chapter Six, many people feared that hundreds of thousands of recipients would take low-paying jobs that would leave them considerably poorer than they had been on the AFDC rolls.[4] Their predictions were partly borne out, though many former recipients graduated from minimum-wage jobs to ones that paid between $7 and $10 per hour.

Even before a policy innovation has been implemented, then, we can estimate the likelihood that it will be actualized during the implementation process. (See Table 13.1.)[5] Of course, we may be pleasantly surprised when our estimations prove to be excessively pessimistic, just as we may be disappointed when our estimations are too optimistic. Of course, many worthy projects have an uncertain prognosis, so we should not abandon them but redouble our efforts to make them work effectively.

Once the implementation of policy innovations begins, a battle over priorities often ensues. Different people give priority to some of the provisions and place less emphasis on others. Success for different persons or groups means the achievement of different objectives. Indeed, as the 1996 reform legislation moved toward full implementation in the summer of 1997, the protagonists had already staked out positions. People like Newt Gingrich emphasized reducing the welfare rolls and curtailing federal expenditures on welfare. More liberal politicians did not want to reduce the rolls at the expense of placing women in jobs (public or private) that consigned them to unacceptable poverty or

TABLE 13.1 The prognosis for the implementation of specific policies

Characteristics of the policy innovation	Positive prognosis	Less positive prognosis
1. Extent to which collaboration is needed	Relatively little	Extensive
2. Extent to which a lengthy sequence of tasks is needed	Short	Long
3. Amount of resources needed	Few	Considerable
4. Extent to which policies are clear	Clear	Vague
5. Extent to which large change from the status quo is needed	Little	Major
6. Extent to which innovation is controversial	Noncontroversial	Controversial
7. Extent to which internal contradictions exist in the innovation	Few	Many
8. Extent to which the theory and assumptions behind a policy innovation are flawed	Not flawed	Flawed

unsafe working conditions.[6] (Since the legislation kept some federal rules but gave the states wide latitude, the battles over the implementation of welfare reform occurred at both the federal and the state levels.) At the federal level, President Clinton's administration made key rulings instructing the states to require the minimum wage in public service jobs—a ruling strongly protested by some conservatives who believed it coddled former recipients.[7]

Policy innovations carry not only objectives or goals with them, but usually resources. As discussed in Chapter Four, public policies are funded by the authorization and appropriation processes of federal, state, and local governments. Authorizations put a maximum on the resources that can be allocated to specific policy innovations, and appropriations determine the actual amounts, which are often far lower than the authorization level. Policy advocates need to prioritize the appropriations process if they want the resources to match the intentions or goals of many policies.

Oversight Organizations and Staff

In the case of publicly funded programs, oversight agencies are public funding agencies, such as the federal Department of Health and Human Services, specific state agencies, county-level agencies, and municipal agencies. In the case of privately funded programs, oversight agencies include foundations, the United Way, the Jewish Federation, and other private entities that provide funds to nongovernment agencies.

Oversight agencies are critically important to the implementation of policy. They have clout over agencies because they provide them with resources, which they can withdraw if they believe the agencies are not performing adequately. They often monitor programs that they fund, though the degree of monitoring varies widely. Monitoring may include periodic visits, analysis of program statistics, and audits of budgets. They may provide constructive technical assistance to help agencies better accomplish specific tasks.

With respect to programs established by legislation, public oversight agencies often establish *administrative regulations,* that is, rules governing the implementing process that were not defined in the original legislation. (Recall from Chapter Nine that legislation is often vague regarding many facets of programs, partly because legislators do not anticipate implementing details or because they wish to avoid conflict by simply leaving them out of the legislation.) These administrative regulations, which define many intake, service, budget, and other details of publicly-funded programs, have the force of law. Not only are executives and staff required to know about them, but they can suffer legal penalties if they violate them. (See Policy Advocacy Challenge 13.2.)

POLICY ADVOCACY CHALLENGE 13.2

FINDING AND READING ADMINISTRATIVE REGULATIONS

To find federal administrative regulations online that are contained in the *Federal Register* from 1994 to the present, go to www.access.gpo.gov then click on "access to government information products and go to the federal register." You can search by keywords, enabling law, and issuing agency.

Policy advocates not only need to know about administrative regulations: they need to try to influence their content. They are aided in this undertaking by the fact that oversight agencies are required to publicize proposed regulations before they are enacted, to hold public hearings about them, to invite written comments, and to take public sentiment into account before they issue the final versions. In other words, policy advocates can make certain that the oversight agencies receive input from citizens and agencies before they finalize or change administrative regulations.

In the case of policies that are initiated within agencies and funded from an agency's own resources, the executives and the agency board assume responsibility for oversight. They decide the content of intake, service, and other policies—and decide what funds to allocate to specific programs.

Oversight organizations often use purchase-of-service contracts when giving funds to specific agencies. These contracts are often awarded in the course of a bidding contest where agencies are asked to say what they would charge for a specified amount of services. Oversight organizations sometimes select a specific agency to provide services, rather than using a bidding contest, when they establish that only that agency has the competency to provide a specific service.

These contracts are a critical part of the implementing process, because they define the amount of services to be provided, such as 2,000 hours of counseling services or after-school services to 250 children. The contracts often establish minimum standards, like the qualifications of staff and the parameters of service. (The after-school services might specify tutoring and recreational components.) An evaluation component is often attached to contracts, where providers must develop an evaluative mechanism to gauge client satisfaction and outcomes. Contracts impose specific auditing and budget provisions.

These contracts have burgeoned in the 1980s, 1990s, and the first years of the 21st century as government agencies have turned increasingly to nongovernment agencies (NGOs) to implement an array of services. For-profit agencies have become dominant players in many jurisdictions, even running the bulk of welfare reform services. Indeed, most nongovernmental agencies now receive the bulk of their funding from these kinds of contracts.

Contracts therefore have become a central part of the implementing process. Because often they define standards and content of services, as well as fund them, they should be viewed as policy documents. Sometimes, they contain provisions that detract from quality services, such as contracts that specify unrealistic goals in light of the funding they provide for specific projects. And sometimes bidders are awarded contracts primarily because they gave low bids and not because they possessed the competence to provide quality services.

Primary Implementing Organizations

Once a policy is launched, its fate hinges on the beliefs and actions of various people and groups. We emphasize *evolving* beliefs and actions of decision makers, executives, staff, and clients when we discuss implementing processes, because these beliefs may shift as implementation takes shape.

The beliefs, interpretation, and mind-sets of those directly involved in the implementation shape its evolution. Direct participants include high- and intermediate-authority figures, firing-line staff, and consumers.[8]

High-authority figures can choose to fully support a policy with verbal, financial, and time resources, or they can ignore a policy, neglect to address it, or actively oppose it. When analyzing the success or failure of a policy's implementation, we often examine the sort of leadership that is exerted in its behalf. Leaders' values, commitments, and priorities often influence whether they will lend their prestige, authority, time, and resources to a policy's implementation. When executives believe that a policy is unwise or intrusive, they are more likely not to enforce some of its goals or provisions. By contrast, when executives like an innovation, they may monitor its implementation, invest their own political capital to ensure its success, allocate resources to it, and ask staff members to go the extra mile.

Intermediate-authority figures, such as supervisors and administrative staff, are critical participants in implementation because theirs is a mid-level position between executives and line staff. When they favor a policy, they will report to higher-level executives any problems or issues they see in its implementation, and they will carefully monitor line staff to be certain that they implement the policy. In their proximity to line staff, they can be troubleshooters who help overcome barriers to implementation, whether in logistics or in the skills or orientations of line staff. If they dislike an innovation, they can sabotage it by opposing it or by failing to address implementation barriers.

We discussed in Chapter Nine (pp. 304–309) the considerable autonomy of *firing-line staff.*[9] When staff members have considerable discretion, we must examine their perspectives. How do staff members understand a policy? How committed are they to its implementation? Do they have enough technical training to understand and implement it? Is the agency's informal culture supportive of the policy? If the staff are unionized, do the union leaders support the policy, or do they attempt to hinder its implementation?

The political scientist Michael Lipsky invented the term "street-level bureaucrats" to describe firing-line staff who are critical of the implementation of any policy. Direct-service workers can both implement and sabotage policies. If they fully understand and support a policy and are given technical supports in implementing it, if the agency's informal cultural is consonant with it, and if supervisors skillfully assist them in implementing it, the prognosis for its implementation rises considerably. The converse is true, as well. As Lipsky suggests, the power of firing-line staff is often augmented by their relative autonomy. What they do with specific clients, patients, or consumers, for example, is largely beyond the earshot of agency supervisors and directors, not to mention external monitors. So they have considerable latitude, which they can use to implement or to ignore a specific policy directive. Their personal views are often reinforced, or even shaped, by the informal policies and norms of other staff.

We should not overstate the autonomy of firing line staff, however. Some of their activities can be closely monitored, such as what eligibility standards are used during intake, how many persons they serve, and what kinds of referrals they make.

Although usually ignored in the burgeoning literature on implementation, *consumers* profoundly shape the course of implementation. For example, high-level officials, wanting to get homeless people off the streets, may fund a project in which outreach workers attempt to persuade homeless people to enter shelters. Even if the workers implement this policy diligently, they will fail if large numbers of homeless people refuse to enter shelters, either because they see the outreach workers as unwelcome authority figures or because they believe the shelters are inferior to life on the streets. Indeed, social marketing theory, discussed in Chapter Six, suggests that consumers will reject programs whose benefits do not seem to offset the costs and risks associated with them. If consumers perceive the time and effort involved in using services as greater than the actual benefits received, they are likely to refrain from using a program. If they do use a program, they decide how much effort to invest in it and what kinds of advice or directive to heed or not to heed. Even in the case of involuntary use of programs, such as when a person is required to attend a counseling program by a court, consumers can decide whether merely to make perfunctory appearances or whether to invest themselves in it.

We have discussed each layer of staff as though it was independent of the others. In fact, interactions between different layers of staff powerfully influence the course of implementation. In organizations where lower-level staff like their leaders, for example, an innovation is likely to be taken seriously if the organization's leaders support it. But the converse is likely in organizations where the leaders are not highly regarded. Consumers also pick up cues from firing-line staff. If they sense that staff do not favor an innovation, they may be less likely to participate in it. Organizational processes that precede an innovation often provide valuable clues to whether and how prime organizations, and their collaborators, will implement a policy innovation.

Before implementing a specific policy innovation, organizations have *standard operating procedures* that their staff members have evolved, such as techniques for reaching their clientele, organizing waiting lists, addressing their clients' needs, and making referrals. These standard operating procedures may prove to be well suited to a particular innovation, but they also may frustrate its implementation by being contrary to the procedures needed to implement a new policy.[10]

As discussed in Chapter Four, organizations also have missions, that is, goals that define their approach to specific problems as well as their priorities. When a mission is congruent with a policy innovation, staff and leaders are more likely to implement it. But a mission can also deter implementation. Take the case of a school district that is asked by higher authorities to cut the dropout rates of its students by engaging in aggressive outreach programs and intensive counseling. If the staff in some schools view students' attrition as outside their central mission of providing educational services to students who do attend classes, they may not invest energy in this new policy.

Organizations' patterns of resource allocation may profoundly shape a new policy's fate. If an agency has had to make numerous budget cuts before initiating a costly policy, its officials and staff members may not support its implementation. If they have given higher priority to other kinds of activities in their budget, they may be unwilling to shift resources to a new policy.

Interorganizational Processes

As implementation unfolds, prime implementing organizations are often joined by *collaborating organizations* that perform tasks, provide services, and otherwise interact with the prime implementers. (See Policy Advocacy Challenge 13.3.) Sometimes, these collaborations are planned, or are even mandated in the policy innovation itself, such as when policies require case management services, referral systems, or even the merging of several different agencies to provide a specific service. In other cases, collaborations emerge accidentally or serendipitously as the prime implementers undertake their work. Perhaps a child welfare agency develops links with local schools even though the legislation does not require these links.

POLICY
ADVOCACY
CHALLENGE 13.3

*CROSSING
ORGANIZATIONAL
BOUNDARIES*

*Patsy Lane, M.S.W.,
Director, Department
of Human Services, City
of Pasadena*

As City Child Care Coordinator, my primary job was to implement the city child-care policy adopted by the mayor and the city council. The goal of this policy is to expand the supply, quality, affordability, and accessibility of child care throughout Los Angeles, by working with city staff in various departments, elected officials, consumers, employers, providers, developers, and others who affect child care in Los Angeles.

Since the policy did not approve any mandates for child care, one focus of this work involved trying to find incentives to get planners, land developers, and builders to include child care as they designed and built workplaces and residential communities. In order to find opportunities for such incentives, I had first to become familiar with the permit and approval process for property development in Los Angeles. After meeting with city staff in several departments that issue such permits and approvals and learning how the process works, we sought input from people from the development community about problem areas in the process and possible opportunities for improvements or changes that might offer incentives. There were lots of suggestions that were not "do-able" because of financial, regulatory, or political constraints, for example, to eliminate or greatly reduce city fees or eliminate steps in the review process. However, one area (among several) that seemed possible involved long delays in securing sewer permits. We found that the city sewer system was very close to capacity, so new building projects had to wait until sewer capacity became available (generally because of the demolition or elimination of an old property) before getting the sewer permit—often a delay of several months. On further investigation with the department responsible for issuing sewer permits, we learned that the city's elected officials had approved a set-aside of a small percentage of the available sewer for "priority" projects to add developments that include space dedicated to licensed child care for at least a minimum number of children. Thus, developments like new office buildings, condominium or apartment buildings, and business parks could save up to several months of waiting (which to date had cost both time and money) by including dedicated space for licensed child care.

Outcome

Within the first three months of implementation, there were some four project applications under the new child-care setaside for sewer permits—as opposed to only four major commercial or residential developments proposing to include child care in the prior year.

Lessons Learned

Among the many lessons learned on this project, the primary ones include the following:

- Sometimes, to accomplish a social policy goal, one must step out of one's "comfort zone" (i.e., the social service world) and understand that field's process, players, practices, and so on to find opportunities for implementing the original goal.
- Looking for such opportunities requires learning more than one perspective. In this case, we reviewed both the official city permit process (walking it through from start

(continued)

(13.3   continued)

to finish) and the customer's experience with that process. Without those perspectives, we might have created an incentive that would be opposed by staff and/or elected officials, or one that had no value to the customer and therefore would not increase licensed child-care space in L.A.

- Sometimes, you have to look and learn in very unexpected areas. As a social worker, I never envisioned having to learn all about how sewer permits are issued—but I'm very glad I did!

Whether interorganizational linkages develop among organizations charged with helping specific clients or consumers is a fascinating issue in implementation. Everyone realizes that clients, patients, and consumers often need assistance from many kinds of agencies and programs—such as children nearing age 18 who are about to be released from foster care. They often need job training, educational counseling, specialized counseling or substance-abuse services, housing, a supportive network of friends, and resources. Yet getting interorganizational collaboration is often no easy matter. As Catherine Alter discusses, it can be associated with such costs or difficulties (for a specific agency) as delays in solutions due to problems with communication, loss of autonomy, conflict over goals and methods, and loss of resources and time.[11] On the other hand, interorganizational collaboration can result in better services for clients, sharing costs, learning new technologies, finding innovative solutions, and gaining resources.

Interorganizational collaborations include a spectrum from relatively incidental, for example occasional interactions of two agencies in providing services to specific clients, to integration, where two or more agencies actually merge. Clearly, the incidental collaborations are simpler to put in place, such as joint referral systems and collaboration on modest projects. Even with these simple collaborations, staff from the two (or more) agencies must establish communication, develop common approaches, and trust one another. As collaboration becomes more ambitious, such as when agencies develop major programs jointly, it is more difficult to orchestrate. Such collaborations require extensive negotiations to decide who does what and how resources are shared. They can excite considerable fears by staff in all agencies involved, such as whether one agency will take undue resources or credit or will contribute equal effort. In more ambitious projects, some kind of joint governance is needed to allow decisions to be made as joint projects evolve.

The most ambitious interorganizational collaborations are called service integration, where actual merger occurs, whether programmatically or budgetarily. In such cases, clients or consumers are not aware that separate agencies even existed. Such ambitious collaborations are relatively rare in the human services because they end the autonomy of specific agencies.

Interorganizational collaborations are often frustrated by fragmentation in funding from high-level sources. Look at our example of foster children nearing emancipation at age 18.[12] Since child welfare, education, health, and counseling agencies receive their resources from different oversight agencies, no mechanism exists for pooling their funds to serve specific populations like this. The funds that come to these agencies have different eligibility standards, and the agencies have different missions so, except for the child welfare agency, they are unlikely to focus on this population.

Case management is nor a panacea for spanning organizational boundaries—precisely because it is usually not a joint program but a one-way referral system that lacks resources to purchase services. When cases are referred to other agencies by a case manager absent resources, they often are given less priority than are cases in which funders provide resources.

Interorganizational collaborations remain, then, at the frontier of human services. They often arise from the determined efforts of staff at the grassroots level rather than from high-level edicts. While little data exists, we can surmise that some interorganizational collaborations improve the well-being of clients when compared with single-agency services, precisely because they provide a fuller set of services that address various needs in tandem.

Implementing Processes

Once a policy innovation is in place, we want to analyze the organizational processes that follow its initial implementation. The following questions can determine whether internal implementing processes have been initiated that will support the innovation:[13]

- Is the policy innovation clearly communicated and explained to implementing staff so they are familiar with its goals and provisions?
- Does role clarity exist so that implementing staff know who has responsibility for what?
- Is someone charged with overseeing the implementation of the policy innovation at its outset and in ensuing time periods? And does she or he have the authority and expertise to engage in troubleshooting when snafus develop?
- Is in-service training provided to staff who lack skills needed to implement the innovation?
- Is implementation of the policy innovation built into staff promotion and performance review?
- Do staff receive bonuses or other rewards for additional work on the innovation?
- Are new staff hired to perform key tasks in the innovation?
- Do executives in the primary organizations demonstrate real leadership, carefully monitoring the innovation and troubleshooting its implementation?
- Does the prime organization allocate new resources to the policy innovation when they are needed or seek them from external sources?

When few of these internal actions and processes accompany the implementation of a policy innovation, the prognosis for effective implementation declines.

We also want to analyze implementation processes that are (or are not) initiated across organizational boundaries, particularly when a policy innovation's objectives require collaborations with other agencies and the community:[14]

- Are collaborative relationships with external organizations fashioned in a timely manner?
- Are outreach and community education initiated to the extent that a policy innovation's objectives require these activities?

Policy innovations sometimes specify collaboration among primary organizations and other organizations. An educational establishment, for example, may be required to involve health agencies providing family-counseling information to teenagers. Increasingly, federal and foundation grants favor projects that propose collaborations. Whether and how these collaborations actually develop will have important ramifications for a policy innovation.

Accidental or serendipitous collaborations may also emerge. As an agency implements a policy innovation, it may have to depend on other organizations for certain tasks or services that are essential to the policy innovation.

Interactions between primary organizations and oversight agencies also figure prominently in implementation processes. To what extent do these oversight agencies actually monitor the work of the primary organization?[15] Do they provide technical assistance?

Implementation of policies is a dynamic process. Policies in action are different from written policies because they are shaped by this dynamic process. All social workers are part of this process, whether they are firing-line staff, supervisors, or administrators—or whether they work in the governmental or private-funding agencies that provide resources and regulations to implementers in the first instance.

The Context of Implementation

The context of implementation adds another overlay of factors and forces that can powerfully shape how specific policies are implemented. (See the various factors on the left side of Figure 13.1.) Implementation never occurs in a vacuum.

The implementation of many policies is closely linked to ideology and partisan politics. Remember that chiefs of government agencies are political appointees who usually reflect the viewpoints of the heads of government who appointed them. On such issues as substance abuse, family planning, health care, welfare, homelessness, juvenile delinquency, and social security, real differences exist between leaders of the two major parties—differences that are reflected in their appointments to agencies that administer policies in these areas.

We should not forget the role of courts, who frequently make rulings that influence the implementation of specific policies. Indeed, an entire field of administrative law exists that contains rulings on administrative procedures, rights of recipients, policies concerning commitments, and interpretation of statutes.

When a policy innovation is enacted, powerful contextual factors assist—or impede—its implementation. For example, the Adoption Assistance and Child Welfare Act of 1980 proposed a major overhaul of the child welfare system. Before its enactment, many people were alarmed by the dramatic increase in the number of children placed in foster care because of their parents' alleged abusive behavior or neglect of basic needs. (The number of children in foster care had risen from 177,000 in 1961 to more than 500,000 in 1979.) The framers of the act wanted to reduce dramatically the number of children in foster care by inducing local child welfare departments either to reunite children with their natural parents or to place them with adoptive families.[16] To secure this change, they did the following:

- Required child welfare departments to provide additional funds to the child welfare system to hire social service staff to give services to natural families

- Required each state to have a tracking system to monitor each child's progress so that no children became lost in the foster care or institutional system
- Required each state to have external reviewing bodies (either the courts or administrative bodies) assess each child's progress
- Mandated a case review after a child had been in foster care for 6 months and again at 12 months to make sure that caseworkers had planned permanent arrangements, either by reuniting children with natural families or placing children with adoptive parents
- Mandated a formal review at 18 months to ensure that the permanency plan had been implemented, meaning that the child had either been returned to the natural parents or adopted
- Increased subsidies for adoptive parents, hoping that many African American and Latino parents would decide to adopt minority children, who, along with teenagers, had proved most difficult to place with adoptive parents

The act seemed an ingenious solution to a vexing problem. As child welfare authorities were soon to learn, however, this policy innovation (actually a set of innovations) would prove not to be a panacea. Indeed, by the late 1990s, foster care caseloads approached levels that had existed in 1980 before the legislation had been passed.

The problem resided partly in contextual factors that, singly and in tandem, frustrated the work of child welfare departments. *Negative factors* in the nearly two decades after the enactment of the 1980 legislation included the following:

- Top administrators of child welfare in state and county positions were so preoccupied with responding to child-abuse and child-neglect cases that they lacked time to give intensive services to children or natural families.
- Rigid hierarchies in social services precluded top officials' communication with low-level staff.
- In light of allegations that many children had been harmed when prematurely returned to their natural parents, many high-level administrators emphasized child removal, rather than efforts to improve the parenting skills of natural parents.
- The unions representing direct-service and clerical staff emphasized pay, fringe benefits, and workloads, rather than service-related issues.
- Many legislators did not believe that powerful constituents supported major improvements in child welfare programs.
- State legislatures and county boards of supervisors did not fund child welfare services sufficiently to allow caseloads to be reduced, because of local tax revolts and the absence of political or community constituencies concerned about child welfare.
- Institutions that received funds for children who stayed with them had economic incentives not to return children to their natural families or to place them with adoptive families.
- Because of declassification, in which many local and state governments removed professional training requirements from specific jobs, many supervisors and direct-service staff in child welfare departments lacked training in social work. Lacking treatment skills and concepts, they could not easily perform the complex tasks required by the new legislation.

• Many natural parents viewed the child welfare staff and juvenile court as adversaries that primarily wanted to take their children from them. Because direct-service staff were so burdened with child removal and investigation, they had scant interaction with natural parents. (Increasing numbers of natural parents obtained attorneys.)

• Many parents neglected their children because they lacked sufficient financial resources—a problem that worsened with the growing economic inequality in the United States in the 1980s and 1990s. Thus, many children were insufficiently fed and clothed. Moreover, poverty contributed to some abusive behavior by exacerbating intrafamilial tension. Yet no system existed in child welfare agencies for providing job training or employment referral for parents.

• Innovative services, such as residential centers where troubled families can reside while receiving counseling, did not exist in most localities.

• Child welfare agencies often had few collaborative relations with schools, job-training agencies, or health services, so they could not develop innovative partnerships that might allow some natural families to surmount their economic difficulties.

• An epidemic of infants who were born drug-addicted occurred in the 1990s, leading to an infusion of hundreds of thousands of infants into the child welfare system. (Addicted newborns were often automatically placed in foster care soon after birth.)

• As child welfare agencies did reunite many children with their natural families, some of them were again abused or neglected, leading to widespread popular and political opposition to reunification. (Indeed, by the late 1990s, the pendulum had swung back to the extensive use of foster care!)

• While the welfare reforms enacted in 1996 were in their infancy in the late 1990s, some critics feared that they would exacerbate poverty among single-headed households as mothers were forced to take low-wage jobs, thus creating even more neglect and child abuse.

• Large numbers of adoptive parents for minority children, teenage children, and children with physical and mental problems did not emerge, even with adoption subsidies.

Of course, these negative contextual factors were somewhat offset by *positive ones*. Indeed, we can guess that, had the Adoption Assistance and Child Welfare Act of 1980 not been passed, far greater numbers of children would have entered and remained in foster care. Positive factors included the following:

• Because rapid increases in foster care became extraordinarily costly to local and state governments, they wanted to make the system more efficient.

• Subjected to litigation and adverse publicity stemming from scandals, such as ill-advised placement decisions and poor foster care, many officials and staff in child welfare departments wanted to reform their services.

• Finding it difficult to recruit foster care parents or adoptive parents, particularly for handicapped, ethnic, and adolescent children, many state and local officials were eager to cooperate with legislation to decrease the numbers of children in foster care and to promote adoptions.

- Many juvenile-court justices wanted to assume a more active role in reviewing cases and promoting permanent arrangements.
- Attorneys had increasingly publicized and defended natural families' rights to due process in court proceedings. This development made juvenile courts and child welfare staff less inclined to remove children quickly from their natural families.
- African American and Latino communities had developed considerable interest in same-race adoptions, rather than transracial adoptions, thus enlarging the pool of adoptive parents in ethnic communities.
- By the late 1990s, many local child welfare agencies had developed partnerships with an array of local agencies—and had even begun to subcontract with them to help natural families remain intact.

The Adoption Assistance and Child Welfare Act illustrates that major policy innovations are rarely panaceas for complicated problems like child abuse and child neglect. They must battle an array of contextual factors that exacerbate the problems they seek to solve. If positive contextual factors outweigh negative ones—and if negative ones do not gather momentum as time passes—the prognosis for implementation improves.

As shown in Figure 13.1, many kinds of contextual factors may affect implementation. In the case of public policies, legislatures and politicians watch implementers carefully, sometimes holding oversight hearings when they want to examine problems that have come to their attention. Litigation is sometimes initiated to question specific decisions by implementers or to question provisions in legislation. The mass media sometimes cover facets of implementation, whether through positive stories that discuss successes, or through negative stories that highlight failures. Crises and pivotal events sometimes shape the course of implementation, such as wrongdoing by implementers or incorrect decisions that adversely affect the lives of clients. (Numerous stories in the mass media about children being reunited with natural families only to be abused or neglected again powerfully undermined the basic premise of the Adoption Assistance and Child Welfare Act that large numbers of abused and neglected children should be returned to their natural families.) Economic, social, and demographic developments also influence implementation, as the problem of addicted babies mentioned earlier suggests with respect to the 1980 legislation.

As these factors pressure implementers, so also do organized interests, such as unions, professional associations, and interest groups. As the welfare reforms of 1996 were implemented, for example, governors and their directors of welfare as organized into the American Public Welfare Association assumed powerful roles. Organized interests will support or oppose specific changes in the federal legislation based on their own experiences with its implementation. Leaders of professional groups like the National Association of Social Workers will seek to soften implementation so safeguards and exemptions are provided for women who cannot find work or who can only find work that does not meet their family's survival needs.

Actual Outputs: The Evaluation of Implemented Policies

The framers of policy innovations want them to achieve specific goals, such as social justice, fairness, effectiveness, and cost-effectiveness, but it is not always easy to evaluate outcomes objectively. We often rely on reports and statistics from those who actually implement a policy to ascertain whether it has been implemented. However, agencies and providers may slant these data in order not to jeopardize continued funding from higher officials. Program evaluations that assess policies' implementation require considerable time and resources to complete, as well as the cooperation of the agencies that implement the policy. (We discuss program and policy evaluation in more detail in Chapter Fourteen.)

Perceptions of program outcomes, whether based on empirical studies, secondhand reports, or informal observations, often become an important part of a policy's context. When some legislators believe that implementing staff have not complied with existing policy, they may cut the funding of a program or try to modify the original legislation to make the official policy more precise. For example, at many points in the last three decades, conservative politicians have sought to tighten welfare programs because they believed that agency staff were not enforcing the work requirement provisions. Believing in the summer of 1997 that the Democrats, President Clinton, and some local officials wanted to soften the work requirements of the welfare reforms of 1996, Speaker of the House Newt Gingrich pledged legislation to tighten welfare reform. Of course, people's preexisting orientations often shape which evidence they choose to emphasize or ignore when they consider a program's outcome. These orientations also shape the interpretations people place on evaluations. When viewing a study that suggests a program has achieved modest results, someone who initially opposed it may argue that the glass is half empty, while someone who supported it may declare the glass to be half full.

Reforming the Implementation Process

Our discussion thus for may falsely suggest that various forces determine a policy's fate once it has been initiated. In fact, implementation processes evolve in the months and years after an innovation has been enacted. While some policy innovations are poorly implemented in their initial phase, implementation may improve markedly as leaders and staff take corrective action, whether because they favor the innovation or because they are pressured by external authorities. Innovations ultimately succeed or fail not because of abstract forces but because of the actions or inactions of implementing staff.

Policy advocates have several options when they want to improve implementation. They can target one or more of the facets of implementing action systems that we portrayed in Figure 13.1. (See Box 13.1.)

BOX 13.1   **Reform Options for Policy Advocates During Implementation**

1. Changing the policy innovation itself: its content, its objectives, or its funding
2. Changing the activities or nature of oversight organizations: their administrative regulations or their monitoring
3. Naming different agencies or adding new agencies to be primary implementing agencies, or requiring new collaborations by these agencies
4. Changing the internal or external implementing processes of primary implementing organizations
5. Modifying the context
6. Influencing the evaluations of policy outcomes

Amending the policy innovation   Policy advocates can amend the original policy innovation. In the case of legislation, they can offer amendments or even seek to annul it. Legislation is not written in stone. In subsequent legislative sessions, policy advocates can convince legislators that they made some mistakes in the original version. Advocates often find it difficult to reopen the original legislation for amendments in the years immediately following its enactment, because legislators, having developed the legislation through elaborate compromises, are reluctant to reopen Pandora's box. Moreover, some legislators may argue that a specific problem must be addressed by changes in the administrative regulations, not in the legislation itself or by changes in the implementation processes. However, if they can make a good case that the legislation was fundamentally flawed, advocates can get changes in the original legislation by following the strategy guidelines discussed in Chapter Twelve. As one example, the Adoption Assistance and Child Welfare Act of 1980 was modified several years after its initial passage to allow adopted children to retain their eligibility for Medicaid. Advocates hoped that this amendment would encourage people to adopt children with disabilities or children with other health problems.

Modifying policies of oversight agencies   Policy advocates can try to change the administrative regulations that guide implementation, as when the Clinton administration required that minimum wages be paid to welfare recipients placed in public workfare programs. Advocates can also seek greater or improved monitoring of implemented programs. They can try to alter the content and nature of specific purchase-of-service contracts so they have better goals, policies, and funding.

Modifying the choice of primary implementing organizations   Policy advocates can modify the choice of agencies charged with implementing a policy innovation, for example, by adding new agencies, withdrawing contracts or funds from some agencies, or promoting new partnerships.

Intervening in implementing processes   Policy advocates can intervene in implementing processes in various ways, such as by insisting that the policy innovation be communicated more forcefully to staff, that in-service training be provided, and that staff be rewarded (or punished) as they do (or do not) implement the program.

Intervening in interorganizational processes   Policy advocates can try to enhance interorganizational collaboration to foster more effective services. They might seek specific negotiated agreements between organizations that promote specific kinds of collaboration, or they might agree to share resources to create a joint project. They might decide also to institute exchanges of technical knowledge.

Modifying the context   Policy advocates can try to modify the context by offsetting negative factors and strengthening positive ones. If they publicize problems or faults in the implementation of a policy, for example, they can build pressure on implementers from the outside, such as activating an advocacy group that demands corrective action. They also might draw the attention of the media to flawed implementation or develop task forces that try to solve specific implementation problems in a collaborative fashion, such as an interorganizational task force.

Influencing the evaluation of a policy's outcomes   Advocates should seek evaluations of a policy's implementation. When the genuine accomplishments of a policy's implementation are not understood, policy advocates can publicize its achievements to the mass media, to legislators, and to citizens. When evaluation suggests negative outcomes, advocates should ascertain whether they stem from defects in implementation or in the policy itself.

Working for enhanced funding   Some meritorious policies fail to be implemented because insufficient resources are allocated to them. In this case, advocates can put pressure not on the implementers, but on the funders, such as county or state legislators or public officials, or federal legislators.

Whistle-blowing   When fraudulent or illegal activities occur during implementation—or when the well-being of clients, patients, or consumers is violated—social workers should engage in whistle-blowing if other remedies do not work.

Do Policy Advocates Ever Sabotage Policies?

We have assumed, so far, that policy advocates usually want to enhance the implementation of policy innovations. But what if policy advocates dislike a policy innovation, such as some of the reforms set in place by the Personal Responsibility and Work Opportunities Act of 1996?

This situation is both similar to and different from whistle-blowing, which we discussed in Chapter Nine. Distressed by wrongdoing in organizations, such as fraud or other illegal activities, whistle-blowers divulge information to outsiders. In the sabotaging of policies, however, policy advocates themselves take actions to subvert an existing policy. They can openly defy it, try to subvert it surreptitiously (perhaps by not implementing it in certain cases), or logjam it by creating logistical snafus that render it difficult to administer. Consider the case of the Medicare policy requiring older patients to be discharged rapidly after surgery. Assume that a social worker believes that this policy sometimes harms older patients who have experienced considerable physical or mental trauma in the wake of surgery. An inventive social worker could contend that a shortage of beds exists in convalescent homes (when no such shortage exists), obtain a physician's statement that medical complications preclude discharge (when, in fact, patients with similar medical assessments frequently are discharged), "lose" the required paperwork to delay discharge, or coach the patient to demand nondischarge, hoping this insistence will intimidate medical officials.

Is such sabotage ethical? Outright and continuing sabotage of official policy represents substantial risks and ethical dilemmas for social workers in specific settings. If a social worker is hired to implement the welfare reform of a specific state and cannot in good conscience enforce its provisions, she or he could be dismissed or even prosecuted for knowingly violating the law. In such cases, social workers may have to resign and work against the policy as policy advocates on the outside. Yet bending the rules for specific individuals often is ethically permissible. In such cases, social workers pit beneficence against compliance, deciding in egregious cases to help clients escape specific provisions that threaten their well-being. Who is to doubt that some older patients do need a delay in discharge after surgery, when immediate discharge threatens their well-being? To those who say that social workers play God in such cases, policy advocates can reply, "But doesn't professional training and experience equip us to determine when clients' well-being is endangered?" Moreover, in some cases, policy advocates do not violate existing policy but take advantage of loopholes or ambiguities in it that do allow for exceptions.

A Case Example of Implementation: The Patient Self-Determination Act of 1990

On November 5, 1990, President George Bush signed the Patient Self-Determination Act (PSDA) into law as part of the Omnibus Budget Reconciliation Act of 1990. The act was sponsored by Senators John Danforth (R-Missouri) and Patrick Moynihan (D-New York) and by Representative Sandor Levin (D-Michigan). This act's implementation illustrates concepts in Figure 14.1 and Box 14.1.

The Policy Innovation

The PSDA was the first federal legislation to address patient decision making concerned with medical treatment at the end of life.[17] It was an effort to readjust the balance in the relationship between health care consumers and providers, intending "to empower people to take part in decisions that affect the duration and condition of their life."[18] Within PSDA, an advance directive is defined as a "written instruction such as a living will or durable power of attorney for health care recognized under state law and relating to the provision of such care when an individual is incapacitated."[19] The PSDA directly affects any hospitals, skilled-nursing facilities, home-health agencies, hospice organizations, and health maintenance organizations serving Medicare and Medicaid patients. Under the provisions of the act, these facilities are required to inform patients (adults aged 18 and older) of their rights to refuse treatment and to prepare advance directives. Specifically, the facilities are required to develop and maintain written policies and procedures describing (a) an individual's rights under state law to make decisions about his or her medical care, including the right to accept or refuse medical and surgical treatment; (b) an individual's rights under state law to formulate advance directives, such as a living will or a durable power of attorney for health care, when the individual is incapacitated; (c) the policies and procedures that the institution has developed to honor these rights; (d) a policy and procedure for documenting in the patient's medical record whether she or he has an advance directive; (e) a policy against discrimination in admission, treatment, or setting up conditions based on the existence or lack of an advance directive; and (f) a program of education about the act for the institution's staff, patients and their families, and the wider community.[20]

The act requires providers to present two documents to patients: a summary of the Patient Self-Determination Act and a description of the facility's policies concerned with patients' rights.[21] These two documents are to be made available at the following times: when a patient is admitted to a hospital or to a skilled-nursing facility as an inpatient; when an individual is admitted to a nursing home as a resident; when an individual comes under the care of a home-health agency; and when an individual begins to receive care from a hospice program. The PSDA does not override state laws that permit providers to decline to comply with an advance directive when they find it conflicts with their religious or moral beliefs, as long as the patient has been informed of their position.[22]

Context of the Patient Self-Determination Act

The PSDA can be seen as affirming rights and principles that have their "roots both in common law and constitutional law dating back to the late 19th century."[23] These rights involve choice concerning the kind of health care individuals wish to receive. However, few individuals exercised these rights. In addition, medical advances blurred the line between life and death to such an extent that an increasing number of individuals were being held hostage to technology and entered a suspended state between life and death.[24] Circumstances changed with the consumer rights movement of the 1960s and 1970s. Patients became more aware of their rights as consumers of medical care—and began to assert these rights increasingly.[25] These events provide the backdrop for the emergence of PSDA. Four additional factors played a major role in the inception of PSDA: advances in medical technology, increased legal action concerning patient self-determination, changes in the political climate, and support by professional organizations.

Advances in medical technology   The U.S. health care system is characterized by an unyielding dedication to and focus on acute care and curative interventions driven by the latest technological advances in health care. The use of life-sustaining technology has resulted in high medical costs and growing confusion about the line between life and death, with an increasing number of individuals suspended in a "'living death,' technically alive but incapable of thinking, knowing, feeling, and responding."[26] In 1993, the American Medical Association estimated that daily, "approximately 10,000 individuals are in a persistently vegetative state or an otherwise permanently unconscious state and are maintained by tube feeding,"[27] placing an immense emotional and financial burden on families and society. The use of medical technology has been complicated by the fact that individuals increasingly spend their last days in institutions rather than at home.[28] The American Medical Association estimated that 70% of Americans will be involved in decisions concerning life-sustaining treatment for themselves or a family member.[29]

Legal action concerning patient self-determination   The courts assumed a significant role in highlighting the need for legislation addressing patients' rights. Before the 1970s, court interventions were minimal, decisions were not consistent, and decisions were ambiguous regarding the right of an individual to refuse medical treatment.[30] Subsequent decisions consistently affirmed the competent patient's right to refuse medical treatment, even if it remained unclear how to determine the wishes of patients who were deemed incompetent.

Three cases were particularly instrumental: those of Karen Ann Quinlan (1976), Mary O'Connor (1988), and Nancy Cruzan (1990). In the Quinlan case the "New Jersey Court held that an individual's constitutional right to privacy outweighed the state's interest in preserving life, and therefore, the life sustaining measures could be withdrawn."[31] This decision confirming the desire of Karen Ann Quinlan's family to withdraw life-sustaining supports for their comatose daughter substituted their judgment on her behalf.

In the O'Connor case in October 1988, the New York State Supreme Court ruled that "life-sustaining treatment must be given unless there is 'unequivocal evidence' that the patient would have chosen to refuse it."[32] This ruling came even though O'Connor worked in an emergency room and had stated on several occasions that she did not want life support, though she had never made specific reference to her wishes regarding a feeding tube. Mary O'Connor died in August 1989 with a feeding tube still in place.[33] This decision fostered widespread support of policies that would encourage people to make their wishes explicit through such vehicles as advance directives.

Highlighting the confusion regarding what constitutes adequate evidence is the Cruzan case. Nancy Cruzan was involved in a car accident that left her in a coma in 1987. After aggressive treatment options had been tried, it emerged that she would remain in a persistent vegetative state (PVS), where she could not chew, swallow, or respond, even though she probably did not experience pain or suffering. Able to breathe, patients can remain in this condition indefinitely as long as nutrition and hydration are provided. As her condition worsened, Cruzan's parents wanted to remove the feeding tube to end her life, but Missouri law required "clear and convincing" evidence of a patient's wishes before such actions. The case proceeded through the Missouri court system as lower courts ruled that such evidence was unavailable. The U.S. Supreme Court ruled against the Cruzans in June 1990, indicating that "due process did not require the state to accept the substituted judgment of close family members without substantial proof that their views reflected those of the patient."[34] However, the Court did not determine exactly what constituted "clear and convincing" evidence of a person's wishes, with the justices urging the development of procedures that would facilitate the documentation of patients' wishes and the delegation of decision-making authority.[35] With new testimony from Cruzan's former coworkers about statements she had made regarding not wanting to be kept alive, the Cruzan case returned to the Missouri courts. Nancy Cruzan died on December 26, 1990, after the Missouri courts allowed nutrition to be removed. This dramatic case aroused broad support for federal policies to promote advance directives.[36]

Changes in the political climate   The political setting for PSDA is interesting as it had bipartisan authorship. Not surprisingly, the two authors of the PSDA (Senators Danforth of Missouri and Moynihan of New York) came from the states where the Cruzan and O'Connor cases had taken place. The issue cut across party lines, since members of both parties had had personal experiences with life-sustaining treatment. Moreover, self-determination is a right that is widely supported by politicians in both parties.

Bipartisan support was also based on the fact that advance directives can save considerable money. A significant portion of health care expenditures occurs during the last few months of life. In fact, 40 percent of Medicare expenditures on patients during their last year of life occur during their last month of life, a percentage suggesting huge savings from the termination of heroic measures for terminally ill persons.[37] It is therefore not surprising that PSDA was passed as part of the Omnibus Budget Reconciliation Act, a deficit reduction measure.[38] Of course, the potential cost-saving aspect of the act presented possible ethical problems: Was the primary motive behind PSDA to increase patient self-determination or to decrease health care costs? And would some patients be pressured to terminate treatment even when they desired it?

Professional support for the PSDA   The PSDA was supported by many professional and advocacy organizations, including the National Association of Social Workers, the American Hospital Association's Society for Hospital Social Work Directors, the American Medical Association, the American Academy of Neurology, Concern for Dying, the Society for the Right to Die, and the Hemlock Society.[39]

Unfortunately, however, this strong support by professional health care workers has not often translated into implementation, because many health care workers do not adhere to the provisions of PSDA in their daily work.

While PSDA has the potential of advancing patient self-determination, its promise has been compromised by several barriers to its successful implementation. Let's return to concepts in Figure 14.1 and Box 14.1 to examine why PSDA has had mixed implementation.

Oversight Organizations

The secretary of the Department of Health and Human Services (DHHS) is responsible for a national education campaign to inform the public about PSDA, to distribute information to organizations that are Medicare and Medicaid providers, and to help the states develop information to present to patients.[40] Given their relatively passive role, which emphasizes the dissemination of information, the succession of secretaries of the DHHS have not been active advocates for PSDA—and have failed to put monitoring and enforcement policies in place. Nor have the states—also vested with disseminating information to PSDA providers—assumed leadership with respect to PSDA, mostly letting the health care providers develop their own policies with scant technical assistance or enforcement.[41]

Implementing Processes

Many physicians have been reluctant to inform citizens about advance directives—or to comply with them. Many believe that the Hippocratic oath requires them to offer treatment to patients even when their health has a minimal chance of improving. To these doctors, even initiating a discussion of patients' rights and certainly complying with patient wishes to stop curative treatment are perceived as conflicting with beneficence.[42] Some doctors fear that a discussion of withholding life-sustaining treatments will delay their patients' recovery.[43] Doctors are also concerned that a discussion of advance directives might contribute to an adversarial posture by patients toward physicians, reducing the patients' faith in the doctors' curative powers.[44] Many doctors are uneasy, moreover, about discussing death with their patients, since they are schooled in preserving life.[45]

Many physicians are reluctant even to honor the patient's desires stated in advance directives. Palliative care, which aims to make terminal patients comfortable rather than to cure them, has long been devalued in a profession that concentrates on curative measures. Indeed, caregiving has traditionally been devalued in Western medical culture and associated with the less prestigious professions of nursing and social work.[46] Thus, many doctors do not implement patients' wishes even when they are clearly stated in advance directives.

PSDA implementation is also impeded by the culture of many medical institutions. Many physicians and medical staff view providing information about advance directives as a legal issue that is outside the scope of medical services.[47] This orientation makes them see PSDA as an irritating distraction from their primary work rather than an integral part of it.

Since the act requires only that information be disseminated to patients at intake, it would seem that intake procedures could be easily modified to enhance implementation. While most health organizations have added information about advance directives to the intake process, the burden of intake paperwork often results in the mere addition of information about advance directives to the pile of other forms already given to patients. Moreover, many nurses and clerks are disinclined to discuss advance directives because the intake procedure is emotionally charged for many patients and their families, and is characterized by pain and fear.[48] Intake workers often fear that patients, already stressed by illness, cannot be cognitively receptive to information about advance directives. So, many intake workers take a minimalist approach to the implementation of PSDA, merely passing forms to patients and checking boxes rather than engaging patients in a discussion of advance directives. By taking this minimalist approach, they undermine the objective of PSDA to educate patients about their rights and to promote patients' self-determination.

Staff who do favor extended discussions with patients about advance directives, and scrupulously honoring patients' wishes, are often placed on the defensive in this atmosphere. Some social workers and nurses are torn between organizational norms and their desire to advance patients' self-determination.[49]

Implementation of PSDA also is impeded by medical administrators' belief that it negatively affects their budgets, because organizations must bear the costs of developing, producing, and disseminating PSDA information to patients. When staff devote time to discussing advance directives with patients, they are drawn away from other tasks. Some medical administrators may even fear that a reduction of medical services to terminally ill persons will diminish their revenues from Medicare, Medicaid, or private insurance.

Of course, some positive economic incentives promote the implementation of PSDA. Medical institutions that receive fixed payments for the medical care of patients, such as members of health maintenance organizations, gain financially as heroic treatments for terminally ill persons are curtailed. The families of terminally ill persons, often financially devastated by these treatments, also have an economic incentive to curtail them.

Moreover, compliance with PSDA is mandatory for any institution receiving Medicare or Medicaid funding. If institutions do not comply, they may risk their Medicare or Medicaid funding, even though the act does not specify enforcement provisions other than loss of funding in the case of noncompliance.[50] (No organization has had Medicare or Medicaid funding withdrawn as a result of noncompliance.)

The lenient approach of federal administrators has given the organization administrators a covert message concerning the importance of the policy. In turn, this attitude is passed down to the line staff—doctors, nurses, social workers, and clerical staff—who have their own internal hierarchy. The result of this lack of accountability has been that each discipline, and sometimes each individual, interprets the requirements of the policy and its importance differently, fostering misunderstandings among patients, physicians, and other medical staff. Many patients believe physicians are responsible for initiating a discussion of advance directives, whereas many physicians believe patients should initiate such discussion.[51] Aggressive compliance with both the letter and the nature of the law has often been restricted to institutions where an administrator has vigorously asserted the policy because of her or his own individual values and motivations. The result has been extremely different responses to the policy in different organizations.[52] This inconsistency has further frustrated implementation of the law when patients are transferred between facilities. Organizations do not necessarily transfer records regarding advance directives with the patient. Thus, a patient may wrongly think that he or she does not have to worry about discussing advance directives in the new institution because he or she has already declared his or her wishes elsewhere.

Sometimes the relatives, loved ones, and persons named by patients to be decision makers when they are incompetent hinder the implementation of PSDA. Even when patients have clearly stated their desire to have heroic treatment withheld, relatives who do not feel comfortable with the advance directive may intervene and seriously impede the process of fulfilling the patient's wishes.[53] Simply by questioning the medical staff, relatives raise doctors' fears of malpractice suits, causing them to provide heroic treatment.

The likelihood of noncompliance with patients' wishes is increased by the fact that there has never been successful litigation against individuals or organizations who implemented family wishes to prolong life against a patient's wishes.[54] By contrast, extensive litigation has been brought against physicians who stopped heroic treatment, sometimes even when the patient had requested this action in an advance directive. Without pressure from the courts, physicians are likely to continue overriding patient wishes. Advocacy organizations, such as the American Civil Liberties Union, must champion the rights of incompetent patients whose explicit wishes are overridden by relatives and physicians.

Perceptions of Policy Outcomes

Unfortunately, evidence suggests that the PSDA has not been implemented as intended. A 1996 national survey of 650 home health care directors found that only 67 percent of the agencies complied with the PSDA requirement that they make available to clients their policies on advance directives and life-sustaining treatment decisions.[55] This finding was consistent with that of an earlier study by the Medicare Advocacy Project in Los Angeles County that only 65 percent of hospitals and 33 percent of skilled-nursing facilities provided written materials concerning advance directives.[56] In facilities where policies do exist, patients may still not receive adequate information to facilitate self-determination. A study of one hospital indicated that only 57 percent of patients had received written materials on advance directives and, of those patients, only 55 percent reported having read the brochure.[57] Even if there is formal compliance by giving patients brochures, the intent of the legislation is often violated by not engaging patients in discussions to ensure that the brochure is read and understood. Furthermore, two-thirds of doctors who receive reports of patients' wishes about life-sustaining care do not even look at the reports.[58]

Of course, the defects in the implementation of PSDA ought not to obscure the real gains. Some providers do comply with the PSDA's requirements. And even limited compliance is better than the situation that existed before PSDA, when advance directives were seldom discussed with patients except by a few avant-garde institutions and providers.

Advocates' Options for Reforming the Implementation of PSDA

Following are summaries of a variety of strategies for improving the implementation of policy innovations that apply not only to PSDA but to other policies.

Changing the Content of the Policy

A basic problem with PSDA is that it provides only a minimum standard, requiring only superficial notification about advance directives by giving patients printed materials at intake.[59] What is needed is bolder legislation that covers patient education and patient rights more explicitly.

- Policy advocates can insist that physicians initiate discussions of advance directives in their offices rather than when emergency care is required.[60] This timing would greatly reduce the anxiety and urgent nature of the discussion. It would also answer the criticism that providing information regarding advance directives has become an administrative rather than a medical task, which undermines the serious nature of the topic. This fact was highlighted in a survey of patient reactions to the PSDA: The patients revealed a desire to discuss advance directives earlier in the treatment process.[61]

- Policy advocates can ask the states to provide a legal waiver, that is, to respect the legal documentation of an individual's state of residence when its advance directives, living wills, or durable powers of attorney differ from those used in states where an individual currently lives. When people travel or move to a new state, they often find that the forms used in their first state of residence are not honored in the new state.

- Educational programs that involve patients in meaningful discussions of advance directives should be required in all health care institutions. It simply does not work merely to give patients brochures without also involving them in a discussion of the purpose of advance directives. There is some evidence that educational intervention programs are successful. In one such study, an intense intervention carried out by a social worker with patients, their families, and their health care proxies resulted in 71 percent of the subjects (all of whom were 65 years or older) completing advance directives, a considerably higher rate than the average completion rate of 15 percent.[62]

Changing the Context

The PSDA's implementation has been impeded by widespread public ignorance about advance directives.

- Policy advocates can insist that the federal government, as well as health providers, launch an aggressive advertising campaign similar to the one developed in 1997 to promote the donation of organs and tissue. Advertising spots during prime time on major channels, as well as on radio stations, should invite citizens to complete advance directives—and should give toll-free numbers so people can call for more information and counseling.

Changing Actions of Oversight Agencies

To improve implementation of the PSDA, policy advocates can seek changes in the administrative regulations to clarify several ambiguous points. They also can improve high-level monitoring of the PSDA's implementation, and they can seek the following:

• Clearer guidelines regarding who should initiate such discussions in the hospital setting. A coordinated effort among physicians, nurses, ethics committees, social workers, and clergy would provide optimal coverage. While physicians must be involved to some degree because advance directives involve medical issues, other staff should be empowered to initiate discussion, which should be approached as an ongoing dialogue rather than a one-time discussion.[63]

• Increased monitoring by the administrators of Medicare and Medicaid funding. A potential solution to pulling Medicare and Medicaid funding was offered by A. Capron, who called for the federal government to "reward physicians and other care providers who encourage advance planning."[64] Providing financial incentives has the potential to encourage implementation more effectively than the current mechanism, which is nothing more than an empty threat.

Changing Implementation Processes

Even in the early part of the 21st century, health staff in many institutions remain unclear about the implementation of the PSDA. Policy advocates can do the following:

• Request vigorous efforts to educate health care providers about their potential role in the process. To the extent that they are unwilling to initiate discussions with patients because of their personal discomfort with discussing death or medical complications, they need assistance in surmounting these personal fears. Social workers can play an important role by acting as catalysts in the implementation of the act in their health care setting.

• Make the documents given to patients more readable. The current forms tend to be in legalistic language that is difficult to understand.[65] The average reading standard of the documents is at the 11th-grade level, but most Americans read well below this level.[66] Current documents discriminate against persons who are unable to read documents, especially those who speak English as a second language. (The poor reading skills of many patients also highlight the responsibility of health care workers to discuss this issue with patients rather than simply supplying them with written information.)

• Require health care providers to tailor written materials and verbal discussions to cultural diversity. Individuals from certain cultures—for example, the Navajo or Chinese American cultures—view discussions of death as unlucky.[67] In the Chinese American culture, "suggesting that the patient might become mentally confused or incompetent activates feelings of shame on the part of the patient."[68] Staff education and training efforts should highlight the possibility of such culturally based reactions. In addition, outreach and education programs in culturally diverse communities can ease the confusion and provide an opportunity for advance directives to be beneficial. When advance directives are being discussed, ethnic and racial minorities often misinterpret the motives of medical staff, believing they want to save money. In addition, a study of African Americans revealed the belief that they will receive less care if they complete an advance directive.[69] Education efforts aimed at ethnic and racial minorities—as well as the general public—are necessary to allay such fears, such as reframing advance directives as an opportunity to exercise personal rights rather than an effort to curtail medical services.

    • Encourage the appointment of health care proxies to surmount the often vague or ambiguous instructions that patients place in their advance directives. (Health care proxies are persons empowered by patients to make decisions for them when they become incompetent.)

Improving Interorganizational Collaboration

It would seem at first glance that few opportunities exist for interorganizational collaboration with respect to this policy. Hospitals could, however, develop some innovative collaborations, such as with clergy and the legal community. Perhaps patients would be more open to signing advance directives if they viewed this policy not primarily as a medical one, but as a moral and legal one. Consultation with the clergy and/or lawyers might expose them to different perspectives. Concerning persons of specific ethnic groups, it might make sense to connect with grassroots groups to see if they could facilitate problem solving around this issue.

Securing Evaluations of Policy Outcomes

To the extent that the PSDA is making a difference by curtailing the use of heroic treatment for terminally ill people, policy advocates should obtain data that demonstrate its effectiveness. To the extent that it is not meeting its objectives, policy advocates should obtain data demonstrating its ineffectiveness, using this information to secure support for the kinds of reforms in implementation that have just been discussed.

Participating in Community-Based Advocacy Projects

Once the administrative regulations have been issued and the program is operating, policy advocates can often exert external pressure on policy makers. For example, the Medicare Advocacy Project in Los Angeles conducted research on whether the PSDA was being effectively implemented. By disseminating data to the mass media, this project pressured local, state, and federal officials to improve PSDA's implementation.

Chapter Summary

What You Can Now Do

You are now equipped to do the following:

• Analyze whether specific policy innovations are being implemented
• Diagnose why specific policies are not implemented by using a systems framework
• Initiate strategy to improve implementation

Policy advocates also can use data, such as from program evaluations, to check on the merits of specific implemented policies, as we discuss in the next chapter.

Notes

1. Robert Montjoy and Laurence O'Toole, "Toward a Theory of Policy Implementation," *Public Administration Review* 39 (September–October 1979): 465–476.

2. Jeffrey Pressman and Aaron Wildavsky, *Implementation* (Berkeley and Los Angeles: University of California Press, 1974).

3. Ibid.

4. Mary Jo Bane, "Welfare as We Might Know It," *American Prospect* (January–February 1997): 47–55.

5. Laurence O'Toole and Robert Montjoy, "Toward a Theory of Policy Implementation," *Public Administration Review* 44 (November/December 1984): 491–503.

6. Richard Berk, "Gingrich Promises to Fight Clinton on Welfare Law," *New York Times* (August 23, 1997): 1, 9.

7. Jason DeParle, "White House Calls for Minimum Wage in Workfare Plans," *New York Times* (May 16, 1997): 1.

8. Mary Ann Scheirer, *Program Implementation: The Organizational Context* (Beverly Hills, CA: Sage, 1981).

9. Michael Lipsky, *Street Level Bureaucracy* (New York: Russell Sage Foundation, 1980).

10. Yeheskel Hasenfeld, "Implementation of Social Policy Revisited," *Administration and Society* (February 1991).

11. Catherine Alter, "Interorganizational Collaboration in the Task Environment." In Rino Patti, ed., *The Handbook of Social Welfare Management* (Thousand Oaks, CA: Sage Publications, 2000), pp. 283–302.

12. Jane Waldfugel, "The New Wave of Service Integration," *Social Service Review* (September 1997): 463–484.

13. Scheirer, *Program Implementation.*

14. John O'Looney, "Beyond Privatization and Service Integration," *Social Service Review* (December 1993): 40–54.

15. Bruce Jansson, "The Political Economy of Monitoring: A Contingency Perspective," in Harold Demone and Margaret Gibelman, *Services for Sale* (New Brunswick, NJ: Rutgers University Press, 1989), pp. 343–359.

16. For an overview of the strategy, see Congress, House, Ways and Means Committee, Subcommittee on Public Assistance, *Hearings on Amendments to Social Services, Foster Care, and Child Welfare,* 96th Cong., 1st Sess., March 1979, pp. 22–157.

17. C. Soskis and T. Kerson, "The Patient Self-Determination Act: Opportunity Knocks Again," *Social Work in Health Care* 6 (1992): 1–18.

18. F. Rouse, "Patients, Providers, and the PSDA," *Hastings Center Report* (September–October, 1991): p. S2.

19. N. Paridy, "Complying with the Patient Self-Determination Act: Legal, Ethical and Practical Challenges for Hospitals," *Hospital and Health Services Administration* 38 (1993): 291.

20. Soskis and Kerson, "The Patient Self-Determination Act," pp. 4, 6.

21. Ibid.

22. J. Luce, "Physicians Do Not Have a Responsibility to Provide Futile or Unreasonable Care If a Patient or Family Insists," *Critical Care Medicine* 23 (1995): 760–766.

23. M. White and J. Fletcher, "The Patient Self-Determination Act: On Balance, More Help Than Hindrance," *Journal of the American Medical Association* 266 (1991): 410.

24. R. Cranford, "A Hostage to Technology," *Hastings Center Report* (September–October 1990): 9–10.

25. W. Pinch, P. Miya, K. Boardman, A. Andrews, and P. Barr, "Implementation of the Patient Self-Determination Act: A Survey of Nebraska Hospitals," *Research in Nursing and Health* (1995): pp. 59–66.

26. Soskis and Kerson, "The Patient Self-Determination Act," p. 3.

27. Paridy, "Complying with the Patient Self-Determination Act," p. 288.

28. Ibid., pp. 287–296.

29. Ibid.

30. Ibid.

31. Ibid., p. 289.

32. B. Lo, F. Rouse, and L. Dornbrand, "Family Decision Making on Trial: Who Decides for Incompetent Patients?" *New England Journal of Medicine* 322 (1990): 1228.

33. Ibid., pp. 1228–1232.

34. Soskis and Kerson, "The Patient Self-Determination Act," p. 5.

35. Ibid., pp. 1–18.

36. Ibid.

37. E. Emanuel and L. Emanuel, "The Economics of Dying," *New England Journal of Medicine* 330 (1994): 540–544.

38. H. Osman and T. Perlin, "Patient Self-Determination and the Artificial Prolongation of Life," *Health and Social Work* 19 (1994): 245–252.

39. Soskis and Kerson, "The Patient Self-Determination Act," pp. 1–18. Also L. Emanuel, M. Barry, J. Stoekle, L. Ettleson, and E. Emanuel, "Advance Directives for Medical Care—A Case for Greater Use," *New England Journal of Medicine* 324 (1991): 889–895.

40. Rouse, "Patients, Providers, and the PSDA," pp. S2–S3.

41. Paridy, "Complying with the Patient Self-Determination Act," pp. 287–296.

42. Osman and Perlin, "Patient Self-Determination," pp. 245–252.

43. J. La Puma, D. Orentlicher, and R. Moss, "Advance Directives on Admission: Clinical Implications and Analysis of the Patient Self-Determination Act of 1990," *Journal of the American Medical Association* 266 (1991): 402–405.

44. K. Davidson, C. Hackler, D. Caradine, and R. McCord, "Physicians' Attitudes on Advance Directives," *Journal of the American Medical Association* 262 (1989): 2415–2419.

45. A. Kott, "Findings of RWJF Study on Dying Prompt Education Campaign to Stimulate New Approaches," *Advances* 1 (1996): 3.

46. Paridy, "Complying with the Patient Self-Determination Act," pp. 287–296.

47. Rouse, "Patients, Providers, and the PSDA," pp. S2–S3.

48. H. Silverman, P. Tuma, M. Schaeffer, and B. Singh, "Implementation of the Patient Self-Determination Act in a Hospital Setting," *Archives of Internal Medicine* 155 (1995): 502–510. Also Soskis and Kerson, "The Patient Self-Determination Act," pp. 1–18.

49. Osman and Perlin, "Patient Self-Determination and the Artificial Prolongation of Life," pp. 245–252.

50. Paridy, "Complying with the Patient Self-Determination Act," pp. 287–296.

51. La Puma, Orentlicher, and Moss, "Advance Directives on Admission," pp. 402–405.

52. Soskis and Kerson, "The Patient Self-Determination Act," pp. 1–18.

53. Ibid.

54. Osman and Perlin, "Patient Self-Determination and the Artificial Prolongation of Life," pp. 245–252.

55. J. Davitt and L. Kaye, "Supporting Patient Autonomy: Decision Making in Home Health Care," *Social Work* 41 (1996): 41–50.

56. S. Risdon, V. Flack, and G. Dallek, *Implementing the Patient Self-Determination Act (PSDA): A Survey of Selected Hospitals and Skilled Nursing Facilities in Los Angeles County* (Los Angeles: Medicare Advocacy Project, 1993).

57. Silverman et al., "Implementation of the Patient Self-Determination Act," pp. 502–510.

58. S. Brink, "The American Way of Dying," *U.S. News and World Report* (December 4, 1995): pp. 70–75.

59. White and Fletcher, "The Patient Self-Determination Act," pp. 410–412.

60. Paridy, "Complying with the Patient Self-Determination Act," pp. 287–296. Also L. Emanuel, "PSDA in the Clinic," *Hastings Center Report* (September–October 1991): S6–S7.

61. M. Pfeifer, J. Sidorov, A. Smith, J. Boero, A. Evans, and M. Settle, "The Discussion of End-of-Life Medical Care by Primary Care Patients and Physicians," *Journal of General Internal Medicine* 9 (1994): 82–88.

62. M. Luptak and C. Boult, "A Method of Increasing Elders' Use of Advance Directives," *The Gerontologist* 34 (1994): 409–412.

63. Paridy, "Complying with the Patient Self-Determination Act," pp. 287–296.

64. A. Capron, "The Patient Self-Determination Act: Not Now," *Hastings Center Report* (September–October 1990): 35–36.

65. Soskis and Kerson, "The Patient Self-Determination Act," pp. 1–18.

66. Silverman et al., "Implementation of the Patient Self-Determination Act," pp. 502–510.

67. J. Carrese and L. Rhodes, "Bioethics on the Navajo Reservation: Benefit or Harm?" *Journal of the American Medical Association* 274 (1995): 826–829. Also L. Fung, "Implementing the Patient Self-Determination Act (PSDA): How to Effectively Engage Chinese-American Elderly Persons in the Decision of Advance Directives," *Journal of Gerontological Social Work* 22 (1994): 161–174.

68. Fung, "Implementing the Patient Self-Determination Act (PSDA)," p. 167.

69. Silverman et al., "Implementation of the Patient Self-Determination Act," pp. 502–510.

Suggested Readings

Theoretical Perspectives on Implementation

Erwin Hargrove, *The Missing Link: The Study of the Implementation of Social Policy* (Washington, DC: Urban Institute Press, 1975).

Yeheskel Hasenfeld, "Implementation of Social Policy Revisited," *Administration and Society* 22 (February 1991): 451–479.

Robert Montjoy and Laurence O'Toole, "Toward a Theory of Policy Implementation," *Public Administration Review* 39 (September–October 1979): 465–476.

Carl Van Horn and Donald Van Meter, "The Implementation of Intergovernmental Policy," in Charles Jones and Robert Thomas, eds., *Public Policy Making in the Federal System* (Beverly Hills, CA: Sage, 1976).

Models of Interorganization Collaboration

John Fleischman et al., "Organizing AIDS Service Consortia: Lead Agency Identity and Consortium Cohesion," *Social Service Review* (December 1992): 501–534.

John O'Looney, "Beyond Privatization and Service Integration," *Social Service Review* (December 1993): 40–54.

Privatization and Links to Informal Systems

Charles Hoch and George Hemmens, "Linking Informal and Formal Help: Conflict along the Continuum of Care," *Social Service Review* (September 1987): 434–447.

Julie Kosterlitz, "Unmanaged Care?" *National Journal* (December 10, 1994): 2903–2907.

Lester Salamon, "The Marketization of Welfare: Changing Nonprofit and For-Profit Roles in the American Welfare State," *Social Service Review* (March 1993): 16–39.

Structural-Political Perspectives on Implementation

Jeffrey Pressman and Aaron Wildavsky, *Implementation* (Berkeley and Los Angeles: University of California Press, 1974).

Political-Economy Perspectives on Implementation

Eugene Bardach, *The Implementation Game* (Cambridge, MA: MIT Press, 1977).

Micro or Agency Perspectives on Implementation

Yeheskel Hasenfeld, "The Implementation of Change in Human Service Organizations," *Social Service Review* 54 (December 1980): 508–520.

Mary Ann Scheirer, *Program Implementation: The Organizational Context* (Beverly Hills, CA: Sage, 1981).

Staff Perspectives on Implementation

Michael Lipsky, *Street-Level Bureaucracy* (New York: Russell Sage Foundation, 1980).

Ethical Issues in Policy Implementation

Sissela Bok, "Blowing the Whistle," in Joel Fleishman, Lance Liebman, and Mark Moore, eds., *Public Duties: The Moral Obligations of Government Officials* (Cambridge: Harvard University Press, 1981), pp. 204–220.

Robert Goodin, *Reasons for Welfare: The Political Theory of the Welfare State* (Princeton, NJ: Princeton University Press, 1988), pp. 184–223.

Donald Warwick, "The Ethics of Administrative Discretion," in Fleishman, Liebman, and Moore, *Public Duties,* pp. 93–127.

14

ASSESSING POLICIES

**POLICY
PREDICAMENT**

Concerned that many adolescents were being incarcerated for substance abuse, juvenile offenses, and psychiatric problems, a clinical psychologist pioneered an alternative approach that relied heavily on M.S.W.s. His innovation, which he called multisystemic family treatment (MST), proposed to keep the adolescents at home, but to involve them and their parents in a far-reaching program of family therapy. But how was he to convince policy makers and judges that this approach was superior to incarceration in terms of both cost and effectiveness? The psychologist's approach is discussed in Policy Advocacy Challenge 14.2.

In a sense, the policy-assessing task represents both the ending and the beginning of social policy practice. People often regard policy assessment as the final step in the policy-making process; having had a policy proposal enacted, they wish to determine whether it has been a success. However, assessment is also the beginning of policy practice. When our assessments of existing policies suggest that they are flawed, we are motivated to develop, enact, and implement policies to change them.

The technical aspects of assessment often mask its critical similarities to other topics we have discussed, such as policy debates and analysis. To demystify assessment, we will not discuss it in highly technical terms, although we will identify some technical issues. Instead, we will analyze its fundamental logic and its similarities to policy debates and analysis. We will discuss traditional, quantitative approaches to evaluation, as well as qualitative methods. Moreover, we will argue that assessment is an enterprise that all of us can become involved in, even if we lack the technical skills to assess a specific policy formally.

Assessing Policies

Policy advocates engage in advocacy to improve the well-being of citizens, but they cannot know if their work has been effective without examining the actual impact of specific policies on citizens and society. To discuss whether their work has led to policies that are effective, they must engage in policy assessment (or evaluation). We discuss the following in this chapter:

- Similarities among policy analysis, policy debates, and policy assessment
- Tools for countering criticism
- Obstacles that evaluators confront
- The importance of using evaluation results
- Both quantitative and qualitative modes of evaluation
- How policy advocates use and interpret data

The Fundamental Logic of Policy Assessment

Policy practitioners often want to know whether an existing policy is flawed or meritorious, not just as a matter of idle curiosity, but because the answers have important implications for a number of people and institutions. A policy that harms (or at least fails to help) its intended beneficiaries would be widely regarded as dispensable. A policy that helps consumers but absorbs unacceptable amounts of resources is likely to be criticized by those who wish to use the resources more efficiently. A policy that helps some people but discriminates against others—for example a policy that helps the male victims of a social problem, but provides little help to its female victims—would be widely regarded as an unfair or inequitable policy that needed revising.

Policy assessment, then, requires examining relationships between implemented policies and their effects. Assessment forces us to ask how, if at all, the world is different because a specific policy exists, and what, if any, difference it would make if we removed or modified the policy. (See Policy Advocacy Challenge 14.1.)

POLICY ADVOCACY CHALLENGE 14.1

USING THE WEB TO LEARN ABOUT POLICY ASSESSMENT

Various Web sites are germane to policy assessment.

General Accounting Office   The GAO is the investigative arm of Congress. Charged with examining matters relating to the receipt and disbursement of public funds, it performs audits and evaluations of government programs and activities. It is the most widely respected resource for the identification and comparison of policy options.

www.gao.gov

Center for Budget and Policy Priorities   This is a research and policy institute that offers analysis of government program implementation. Included in the center's work are budget, tax policy, food programs, labor, welfare, housing, and Medicaid issues.

www.cbpp.org

(continued)

(14.1   continued)

John F. Kennedy School of Government at Harvard University   One of the most prestigious entities of policy analysis, this site not only assesses current national policy, but also offers substantive resources.

ksgwww.harvard.edu

The Urban Institute   One of the foremost think tanks in the United States, the UI analyzes multiple arenas of policy from its formulation to its implementation. It is a highly respected organization and offers publications, educational resources, and the full texts of most of its reports.

www.urban.org

To illustrate our discussion of assessment, we will consider an example: A jurisdiction devised and implemented policies to help the natural parents of children whom the courts had removed because of abuse or neglect, hoping that these enhanced services would allow more families to be reunited, would decrease costs by abbreviating foster care, and would enhance the children's well-being. When examined in this fashion, policy assessment is not very different from any other kind of assessment. Direct-service practitioners who examine their work critically often wonder whether an intervention will improve the well-being of specific clients or will be counterproductive. They also wonder whether the sum of their interventions over a specific period has improved their clients' well-being.

Similarities Between Assessing and Analyzing Policy

Chapter Seven, where we examined the fundamental logic of analytic reasoning, gives a head start toward the understanding of policy assessment. Assessment and analysis are strikingly similar. The decision-making matrix discussed in Chapter Seven, Table 7.3, is similar to the policy assessment matrix in Table 14.1. To illustrate the use of this matrix, we will consider a jurisdiction that provides special services to the natural parents of children the courts have removed from the family. We will imagine an employee of the jurisdiction's bureau of child welfare who has been hired to assess the new program. She is thinking through how she will approach this evaluation.[1]

The policy assessment matrix (Table 14.1) describes the policy innovation (in this case, special services for the natural parents) and one or more policy alternatives (the typical services provided to natural parents under these circumstances). People who assess policies usually want to compare an enacted policy with something else because such a comparison gives them some standard for evaluation. If our policy assessor could not make comparisons, she might wonder whether providing special services to the natural parents was an improvement over providing relatively few services.

As she wrestles with evaluating the new policy, the practitioner asks, "On what criteria (outcomes) do I wish to compare the two policy alternatives?" At first glance, this would seem to be a relatively simple decision, but she soon realizes that she must choose from a number of possible measures of outcomes. She could look at the following:

TABLE.14.1   Policy assessment matrix

Policy alternatives	Evaluative criteria		
	Rates of reunification	Cost per case during the first 18 months	Children's developmental well-being
1. Special services to natural parents			
2. The existing situation: the provision of relatively few services			

1. The costs of the new policy
2. The effects on the parents and families
3. The effects on the children
4. The implications for staff and juvenile courts
5. The effects on the foster parents

Of course, as she adds more criteria or outcomes, her work becomes more difficult, because each new criterion requires more data. After discussing this problem with many people, she finally selects three criteria: the effects of increased services to natural parents on (a) the rates of reunifying children with their natural parents; (b) the average cost of each case during the first 18 months, which includes the taxpayers' costs for providing services, paying foster parents, and paying for litigation in juvenile courts; and (c) the children's developmental status at the end of 18 months.

Why did the policy practitioner select three measures of outcome, rather than only one? She knew that many legislators and government officials were particularly concerned about the relative costs of the new policy experiment and whether the costs of providing special services would be partially or completely offset by the reduction in the numbers of children in foster care placements or in subsidized adoptions. Indeed, some legislators had originally resisted the policy because they doubted that it would save funds. One conservative legislator called it "another scheme by do-gooder social workers to get more money to fund their pet projects."

The practitioner also wants to check the rates of reunification of families that received and did not receive the special services. Many people want families to be reunified because they believe that long-term or permanent removal of children from their natural families detracts from children's well-being. Surely, the practitioner reasons, we should obtain information about whether special services increase the likelihood of family reunification.

She realizes, however, that an analysis of costs, as well as rates of reunification, may yield an incomplete and even misleading evaluation of the new policy. In a phenomenon known as *goal displacement,* implementers mistake secondary goals or objectives for the most important ones. Unlike some legislators, many social workers are concerned about the ultimate effects of policies on their clients' well-being; if public authorities use the services to save money on foster care, they may easily forget that some parents will not provide a healthy environment even after they have received intensive services. In other words, a potential exists for harming some children in order to save money. Moreover, praiseworthy as reunification may often be, the practitioner discovers when searching the existing literature that no research has definitively shown that reunification is in the child's best interests.[2] Some children thrive in foster care that provides the emotional support that the natural home lacks.

The researcher chooses three measures of outcomes, then, to obtain a clearer picture of the new policy. She realizes, of course, that she may discover mixed outcomes; the new policy may save the taxpayers money, for example, but may not have advantages over the existing policy in serving children's developmental needs.

Similarities Between Policy Assessment and Policy Debates

Assume that three years have passed, so the evaluator has enough data to assess the outcome of the policy innovation. Assume for the moment that her original evaluations suggested that the special services had indeed reduced child welfare costs by a small but significant amount. The jurisdiction had spent an average of $7,000 on each child in the special services program, but it had spent an average of $9,500 on each child in the regular program, for foster care and other services.[3] Moreover, some increases in reunification had occurred; 27 percent of children had been reunified with their parents in the special services program, but only 19 percent had been in the regular program.[4] To the practitioner's surprise, however, after three years, the children in the special services program had not achieved higher scores than the children in the regular program on several measures of child development.

We have invented these findings, but they illustrate well some dilemmas that program evaluators often encounter. When subjected to rigorous, quantitative evaluations, many policies reflect either no gains or relatively modest changes.[5] Of course, the relatively modest changes sometimes occur in a negative direction; in this case, for example, the children in the special services program could have scored somewhat lower than other children on developmental measures.

We can conjecture why many policy innovations do not produce the marked changes that their framers intended. Because many factors shape people's behavior and development, such as their prior experiences, their economic condition, and the persons with whom they associate, programs in the human services cannot be expected to transform the lives of clients, patients, and consumers dramatically and quickly.[6] The instruments that researchers use may also fail to capture some important dimensions of human behavior.

Whatever the reasons, policy assessments often fail to provide definitive evidence about a program's merits. Indeed, assessments sometimes meet with considerable controversy because the evaluator and others may disagree in their interpretations of the findings. A noted researcher, Donald Campbell, provocatively suggests that program evaluation should be regarded as a form of "argument," and that the program evaluator should make a good case that others may contest.[7] In this context, policy evaluators become like debaters, who must defend their arguments.

The similarities between assessment and policy debates are illustrated by our policy practitioner's mixed findings when she evaluated the child welfare programs. Let us assume that she concluded her work by saying, "On balance, my findings suggest that the special services program should be enlarged so that it covers all children whom the courts remove from their natural homes because of their parents' abusive or neglectful behavior." Let us also assume that some conservative legislators strongly contested this proposal, doubting that "hiring a lot more social workers to provide intensive services to the natural parents will really cut our costs."

The ensuing debate between the policy evaluator and the conservative politicians could involve several dimensions, or axes.[8] First, the evaluator and conservative politicians could debate whether the glass is half full or half empty. Are the cost reductions and increased rates of reunification sufficiently large to justify continuing and enlarging the special services program? No scientific method exists for resolving this dispute, because people derive their positions from their values. Conservatives who opposed the special services program at the outset and who are suspicious of social workers are likely to insist on a higher standard of evidence than are persons who favored the program at the outset. Indeed, we have already noted that many new policies make, at best, marginal improvements over the existing ones; thus, evaluators often encounter this magnitude-of-change argument.

Conservatives might also question the time frame of the research by asking whether 18 months is enough to reveal whether the special services program is truly effective. "How do we know," one of them asks, "that some of the children who have been reunified with their parents will not have to be placed in foster homes again in the near future?" The evaluator responds that "18 months is long enough to allow reasonable inferences." However, this dispute cannot be easily resolved because values often shape one's position; a skeptic is likely to want a stricter standard of proof, such as a study that follows a policy's beneficiaries for a longer period.

People could also question the practitioner's weighting of the criteria she used in evaluating the program. Someone might say, for example, "The special services program may save some funds and may somewhat increase the rate of reunification, but I think that the children's well-being ought to be the prime consideration. On this objective, the data do not seem to demonstrate an improvement over the regular program." This argument does not question the program's superiority in some respects, but its emphasis is on a specific objective. Here, too, individual values and perspectives influence responses to evaluative information. Someone who favors the program from the outset, for example, might be willing to deemphasize a negative finding and emphasize more positive ones. A cost-conscious conservative who initially opposed the special services program might now support it because it appears to reduce costs. A child development expert, who initially supported the innovation, might now oppose it because it fails to improve children's scores on child development tests.

As the practitioner presents her findings, she may encounter some questions about the accuracy of her data. "How do we know," someone may ask, "whether your findings are truly accurate? Maybe the children and families you chose for the special services program did not have problems as severe as those of other children and families." Someone else may ask, "How do we know that you did not select particularly talented and motivated social workers to staff the special services program?

Maybe the program's success stemmed from their skills, rather than from the special services program itself." Someone else may ask whether the child development instruments used to measure the children's well-being provided accurate information about the children's self-esteem.

Tools for Countering Criticism

In Figure 14.1, we summarize barriers to evaluation that we have already discussed. In addition, evaluators are often asked whether a program's successes are attributable to factors other than the intervention itself. This kind of criticism is, to say the least, damaging to evaluators' credibility because it undermines the veracity of their assertions, as a simple illustration suggests. Suppose that a direct-service counselor who runs a for-profit clinic claims remarkable success rates in treating depression but lacks systematic evidence. Critics may question this entrepreneur's claims by asking how he knows that his clients' "miraculous recoveries" did not result from the normal course of life events (many persons mature out of their problems) rather than his intervention. Background events, such as an improving economy or an enhanced marital situation, may have caused his clients' improvement. Critics might accuse him of selecting only certain types of clients, whose prognosis was particularly promising, so that his rates of improvement seem extraordinary. They may also call his measures of his clients' well-being flawed, because they made it falsely appear that his clients were depressed in the first place or had recovered from depression under his care.

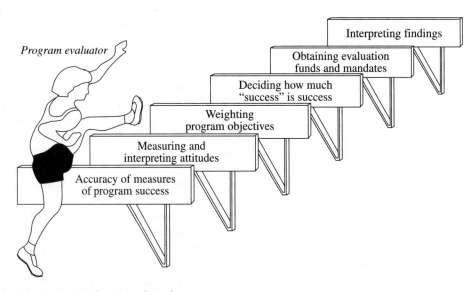

FIGURE 14.1   Evaluator's obstacle course

Every evaluation has a design, a sampling and assignment strategy, instruments or measures, and statistics.[9] These allow our program practitioner to minimize the various threats to her findings.

An evaluation *design* describes the researcher's strategy in obtaining comparisons between the so-called experimental group (the beneficiaries of a specific policy or program) and the control group (persons not receiving benefits from the program). We will contrast three designs to illustrate our evaluator's options. We can place them on a continuum, extending from relatively simple (or nonrigorous) to relatively complex (and rigorous).

In a *correlational design,* the evaluator analyzes not a new project, but projects that have already been implemented. Assume, for example, that our evaluator of the special services program had found local officials unwilling to approve the program. Also assume that the child welfare agency has maintained excellent records of all cases for the past 10 years, including detailed records of the number of visits child welfare staff have made to the natural parents of children removed by the courts. The evaluator might examine the services' effects on reunification rates by studying past cases. Why not, she might ask, compare cases in which parents received extensive services with cases where minimal services were provided to see if people who received intensive services had higher reunification rates?

At first glance, this evaluative strategy seems brilliant, because the case materials for evaluation already exist. As she ponders the issue, however, the evaluator soon realizes that the criticisms that greeted the claims of the depression clinic could also be leveled at her findings, even if they showed a dramatic positive relationship between the intensiveness of services and the rates of reunification. Might these higher reunification rates have been caused not by the intensive services, but by social workers' selection of primarily stable, well-functioning families for intensive services because they liked to work with that clientele? The evaluator would be unable to eliminate this possibility. In addition, certain events, such as an improving economy, might have influenced reunification rates independently of the services the families received. The evaluator would encounter even more formidable research problems if she sought to examine the effects of the services on the children's social and psychological functioning. Because the cases are in the past, she cannot administer special tests to the children, nor are the case records likely to yield accurate rankings of the children on social and psychological functioning.

Indeed, *forward-looking research*—that is, research that analyzes current phenomena—is less subject to external criticism than correlational research, because evaluators can limit the factors that may provide alternative explanations for their findings. Our researcher might begin her project by selecting a random sample of all children who have been subjected to child abuse during, say, a three-month period. By using a random sample, she decreases the likelihood that the children and families in her evaluative study have characteristics different from those of other abused children and their families. As the children enter her sample during the three-month period, the researcher randomly assigns them either to a control group, which does not receive special services, or an experimental group, which does receive the services. Random assignment decreases the likelihood that characteristics of the children and their families, rather than the effects of special services, will cause the differences in outcome between the control and experimental groups.

When the evaluator controls the experiment, she can administer tests directly to the participants to measure the social and psychological outcomes. She might use instruments whose questions have been empirically tested for the accuracy of the data they yield. Or she might observe the children in their homes or at school to assess their social functioning. Contrast this direct measurement of the children's functioning with having to rely on information in case records.

Statistical techniques allow our investigator to examine whether her successful results could have occurred by chance, rather than because of the special services themselves. Statistical tests allow our evaluator to make definitive statements, such as, "There is only one possibility in a hundred that the special services could have improved reunification rates this much if chance were the explanation."

Evaluators want, therefore, to reduce the likelihood of *rival explanations* that critics can use to question their conclusions. In the case of the special services program, one can hear a conservative asking, "How do we know that the special services themselves were responsible for higher reunification rates and not some other factor, such as 'creaming' by social workers who gave services to relatively stable or well-functioning families?" The evaluator is likely to feel more confident in her findings if she can respond that she has used specific design, sampling, assignment, instrumentation, and statistical procedures to decrease the likelihood that rival explanations account for the program's positive outcomes.

We have noted that it is beyond the scope of this discussion to examine the many design, instrumentation, and sampling techniques in forward-looking studies. The research literature explores alternative designs, such as experimental and quasi-experimental designs; several sampling techniques, such as random sampling and stratified sampling; and a host of instrumentation or testing options, including questionnaires and observational techniques.[10]

If highly rigorous studies eliminate rival explanations, why are they not routinely used to assess programs' effectiveness? As the rigor of evaluations increases, so do their costs and the amount of time it takes to conduct them. Evaluators must be versed in the details of research and must have time—often many years—to devise and implement complex studies. Programs are constantly evolving, dynamic entities; therefore, evaluation must capture the essence of what is happening. It also is not usually practical to implement as many controls as are required for a truly rigorous research project. Moreover, some evaluation techniques raise ethical questions. In the case of the special services program, for example, the evaluator might ask whether she could ethically deny special services to the families randomly placed in the control group.

We should not discount the role of politics in failing to commission sophisticated assessments of programs, ignoring certain findings, or biasing of designs or interpretations that protect special interests.[11] Advocates of new policies promote their likely benefits and successes to secure their enactment; few politicians or officials will support policies that seem likely to fail. An evaluation of an enacted program poses risks to the advocates of the program, the staff members involved in the program, and the program's beneficiaries, because the evaluation may suggest that the program has not brought the benefits that its advocates predicted. The special services program achieved only modest cost reductions, modest increases in reunification rates, and no improvement in the children's social and psychological functioning. Such mixed findings, which are typical of evaluative research, cast doubt on the innovation and make the interpretation of the findings problematic. As we noted earlier, it is difficult to determine what magnitude of success is required to support the continuation of a program. Moreover, evaluators are trained to hedge even their positive findings, as in noting limitations in their methodology that may render their findings somewhat suspect.

Political considerations often influence the interpretations of technical data. In fact, conflicting study results are often found, depending on who has commissioned the evaluation. When a program receives unfavorable scores, people can question the data's validity and demand a new study or contend that the unfavorable score suggests terminating the program. They also may assert that, while the program has received low scores on the criteria used in the study, it might receive higher scores on criteria not used in the study. Alternatively, they may maintain that the unfavorable score is not sufficiently strong to merit terminating the policy. To make matters still more complicated, someone may argue that an unfavorable score emanates not from a program's intrinsic defects, but from the lack of enough funding to allow it to function properly.

The production of data, then, sometimes inaugurates a period of controversy during which conflicting parties vie with one another in interpreting the findings. While people who favor a program will also favor interpretations that support it, people who dislike it may seize on negative findings to urge its termination.

Before we lambaste officials and staff who do not routinely use rigorous policy evaluations, then, we should recognize that evaluations often occur in a politicized context, require significant investments of resources and time, and sometimes pose ethical dilemmas. We also should recognize that because of technical flaws in evaluation methodology, findings are not immune to criticism. Indeed, as can be seen in Figure 14.1, which summarizes the points made in the preceding discussion, evaluators encounter many obstacles during their work, each one of which can make their findings controversial, even to experts highly trained in technical procedures.

Barriers to the Use of Policy and Program Evaluation

In 1990, a small gathering of top program evaluators convened to discuss the problems of using evaluation. The evaluators were concerned that, even when good program evaluation is being carried out, policy decision makers often do not use the results.[12] To combat this lack of use, Michael Patton suggests that evaluation focus on "intended use by intended users."[13] He states that it is crucial to get people involved in the process of evaluation in order to increase their stake in the results and the likelihood that they will use the results. If policy makers are involved in framing the evaluation questions, for example, they may be more likely to find the results relevant and to use the research.

Additional barriers to use occur if there is a particularly strong ideology (for instance, opposition to drug use) or a strong vested interest (such as the National Rifle Association) favoring one particular outcome. These very powerful groups may either impede or promote the use of program evaluation, depending on whether the outcome supports their viewpoint.

Policy advocates face two challenges, then: to ensure that good policy evaluation occurs and to ensure that its findings will actually be used by decision makers. (See Policy Advocacy Challenge 14.2.)

**POLICY
ADVOCACY
CHALLENGE 14.2**

*OVERCOMING
POLICY RESISTANCE
TO A PROMISING
INNOVATION*

*Scott Henggeler, Ph.D.,
Director, Family Services
Research Center, Medical
University of South
Carolina*

Scott Henggeler, Director of the Family Services Research Center and a clinical psychologist at the Medical University of South Carolina, developed multisystemic family treatment (MST) to address the needs of "difficult-to-serve" populations such as juvenile offenders, substance abusers, and children facing psychiatric hospitalization.

Currently, many juvenile offenders and juvenile substance abusers are incarcerated, at extraordinary cost to the public. Most of those who are not incarcerated receive minimal treatment, such as brief counseling or outreach.

Alarmed by this punitive treatment of these adolescents and the high recidivism rates of traditional juvenile justice services, Henggeler developed an innovative, comprehensive, alternative treatment and service strategy: MST.

The ultimate goal of MST is to empower families to build ecologies that promote health and well-being. These principles are congruent with the ongoing political and economic forces in health care reform that advocate the use of cost-effective and clinically effective treatments.

Policy makers, government officials, judges, and law enforcement officials were initially skeptical at Henggeler's desire to implement MST. They were concerned about its costs, its ability to ensure public safety, and rates of recidivism.

To persuade critics of the merits of MST, Henggeler initiated rigorous evaluations of it. Initially, Henggeler evaluated the efficacy of multisystemic therapy compared with standard community interventions in the treatment of inner-city offenders. Results showed that adolescents exposed to MST had decreased behavior problems and associated less frequently with deviant peers. In addition, they were more involved in family interaction and communication and enjoyed better relationships with their mothers. In contrast, families that received standard community treatment demonstrated no positive change and showed deterioration in affective relations.

This early success led to funding for three subsequent randomized trials of MST with violent and chronic juvenile offenders and their families (Borduin et al., 1995; Henggeler, Melton, & Smith, 1992; Henggeler, Melton, Brondino, Scherer, & Hanley, 1997). Together, findings from these studies further supported the capacity of MST to improve family relations and youth psychosocial functioning. Perhaps more importantly, findings showed that MST reduced long-term rates of rearrest and incarceration of violent and chronic juvenile offenders, and reductions in incarceration produced cost savings. Hence, the family- and community-based MST program was able to reduce criminal activity at reduced cost to funding agencies.

Good treatment design and sound methodology have played a key role in enhancing respect for the efficacy of MST. Intensive quality-assurance mechanisms to enhance treatment fidelity are strong components of MST and are major tools to counter prospective criticism. Quality-assurance mechanisms, such as therapist collaboration, weekly consultation with MST experts, weekly on-site clinical supervision by a doctoral-level mental health professional with expertise in providing family-based services, and quarterly booster training, contribute to MST's success by ensuring the multisystemic focus of the therapists' intervention strategies and enabling the therapist to attend closely to treatment process and outcome.

Another factor that counters criticism is the rigorous methodology employed throughout the evaluation studies of MST. Judges agreed to random assignment of youth in the clinical trials. Standardized instruments are utilized in assessment. The power of statistical analysis is enhanced by the large number of participants in the studies. And outcomes are evaluated from multiple perspectives, including those of the parent, the child or adolescent, the school, the MST therapist, and archival records for rearrest and out-of-home placement.

A further strength of MST is that it has been developed systematically, building on the information gained from previous research studies. This empirical base has not only enabled Henggeler and colleagues to blunt possible criticism but has also laid a solid foundation for dissemination of the model.

Henggeler and his colleagues, through their scientific investigations, have successfully documented and demonstrated MST's long-term clinical efficacy in treating serious antisocial behavior in adolescents. The evidence of MST's success and its demonstrated cost-effectiveness has garnered support for its implementation. For example, MST programs that treat 1,500 youths per year have recently been developed in 11 states and in Canada. The political approbation of multisystemic therapy has contributed to the gradual shifting of perspectives from a punitive stance to a more hopeful and preventive focus.

This case raises intriguing questions about the relationship between research and politics. For Scott Henggeler to get his promising innovation adopted, judges and policy makers in local jurisdictions must agree to divert adolescents from incarceration to community-based treatment. Law-and-order justices, as well as some politicians who have run on anticrime planks, are likely to oppose his proposal even when shown convincing evidence that it reduces crime and substance abuse when compared with alternative strategies.

Exercises: What strategies in addition to empirical research and the dissemination of his findings might Henggeler consider to secure adoption of his innovation?

How does this case illustrate the relationships among different policy tasks, such as policy assessment, problem analyzing, proposal writing, and policy enacting?

When deciding what criteria to stress with conservative politicians, what outcome measures ought Henggeler to stress? *Hint:* How might he discuss his project's outcomes differently with an audience of clinicians as opposed to conservative politicians?

Borduin, C. M., Mann, B. J., Cone, L. T., Henggeler, S. W., Fucci, B. R., Blaske, D. M., & Williams, R. A. (1995). Multisystemic treatment of serious juvenile offenders: Long-term prevention of criminality and violence. *Journal of Consulting and Clinical Psychology, 63,* 569–578.

Henggeler, S. W., Melton, G. B., Brondino, M. J., Scherer, D. G., & Hanley, J. H. (1997). Multisystemic therapy with violent and chronic juvenile offenders and their families: The role of treatment fidelity in successful dissemination. *Journal of Consulting and Clinical Psychology, 65,* 821–833.

Henggeler, S. W., Melton, G. B., & Smith, L. A. (1992). Family preservation using multisystemic therapy: An effective alternative to incarcerating serious juvenile offenders. *Journal of Consulting and Clinical Psychology, 60,* 953–961.

Qualitative Evaluations

Many researchers have become disenchanted with traditional, quantitative policy evaluations. They doubt that structured questionnaires capture consumers or implementers' attitudes toward the quality or nature of the services they receive or provide. These researchers wonder whether evaluators, often based in consulting firms, develop simplistic criteria for assessing services without consulting consumers, clients, or providers to determine their perspectives. Often relying on single sources of data, such as scores on standardized instruments, evaluators may fail to gather data from several sources, including direct observations and open-ended interviews. Some researchers believe that evaluators should spend some time as participant observers in a project before they develop a research strategy; doing so could make them better informed about a program.[14]

Moreover, some researchers contend that new techniques are needed to evaluate programs in sensitive areas like child abuse, spousal abuse, drug use, AIDS, sexual deviance, and mental illness. People who are affected by these problems are often unwilling to share their perceptions on questionnaires or even to cooperate with researchers.[15]

A feminist critique of traditional evaluations has also emerged. Though this critique lacks unity, feminist evaluators have attacked what they call the myth of value-free scientific inquiry. They ask researchers to acknowledge openly their biases and beliefs related to gender, race, sexual orientation, and socioeconomic class. Some evaluators want a greater dialogue between researchers and their subjects rather than interrogation in an interview. Feminist researchers have developed new devices for collecting data, such as visual imagery, group diaries, drama, conversation, textual analysis, associative writing, genealogy, and network tracing. Like other advocates of qualitative research, many feminist evaluators favor triangulation, in which data are collected from three sources (such as questionnaires, in-depth interviews, and observations) and synthesized to yield a fuller understanding of a project.[16]

Critics of traditional, quantitative evaluations want more attention to be devoted to the context of a program. We have discussed, for example, how a program's effectiveness can be shaped by many external factors, such as the blighted neighborhoods where clients often live, unemployment, and poor schools. Or the implementing staff may have such onerous working conditions that they cannot provide the services planned at the inception of a program. Evaluators who do not examine such factors may wrongly attribute the failure of a program to the helping techniques the staff used rather than to the staff's working conditions or the clients blighted neighborhoods.[17]

Qualitative evaluations, then, make use of various techniques and include multiple sources of data. In addition, qualitative evaluators often use more criteria to evaluate policies and generate their methodology during interactions among researchers, providers, and clients.[18]

While some evaluators and researchers believe that qualitative and quantitative methods are mutually exclusive, evaluators are increasingly combining the two methods to yield findings that provide a better understanding of program dynamics than either approach can provide by itself.

Policy Advocates' Use of Data

Advocates who seek policy reforms for oppressed groups and powerless populations need to evaluate current policies. In some cases, they need to collect and use data like the Children's Defense Fund and other advocacy groups do. Their data may include program statistics describing the kinds of persons who use specific programs, thereby revealing whether programs are reaching their intended beneficiaries. They may seek data about whether programs are achieving specific goals, for example, whether the Head Start program improves children's nutritional and health status. When program administrators lack information on vital points, advocates can pressure them to develop research projects to collect data.

Policy advocates also need to participate in the politics of evaluative projects. For example, when evaluating research showing that a workfare program for female welfare recipients has effectively diminished the welfare rolls, advocates should ask whether the program has also led to long-term improvements in the women's economic well-being, as opposed to merely putting them into low-wage jobs without fringe benefits. Because evaluators of programs choose criteria that reflect their values, advocates should also assert their values.[19]

Why All Social Workers Should Assess Policies

We have discussed the technical challenges of policy evaluation at considerable length, as well as the important role of technically trained evaluators. This discussion may suggest that only experts can assess policies. In fact, all social workers can assess policy, even when they lack training in research. They can participate in arguments about research findings, cite research, use theory based on their practice wisdom, and draw on their moral standards. Furthermore, they can generate relevant and realistic questions and hypotheses based on the intimate understanding of problems they have gained through their practice experience.

Even when they do not produce research findings themselves, social workers can participate in critical discussions of the evaluation of specific projects. Social workers can critically examine evaluators' choice of criteria, methodological choices, instruments, and interpretations of findings. Indeed, in some cases, social workers should vigorously challenge evaluations that appear ill advised, such as those that prematurely suggest the abandonment of a meritorious program.

Social workers can draw on others' research as they evaluate specific programs. For example, when assessing a social program that lacks a bilingual staff, they can cite research that examines whether non–native-speakers use services when no translators are available. Social workers also can adapt suggestive findings from other settings and programs when evaluating programs. We can infer, for example, that findings about having a bilingual staff when providing refugees with health services may also apply to other services that refugees receive.

When evaluating programs, social workers should draw on their professional wisdom, as well as on theory drawn from the social and human sciences. Empirical research is not available to inform the vast majority of decisions and policies in the human services; if we limited ourselves to empirical research, we would be silent on most issues! When we confront policies that conflict with our professional wisdom or with widely respected theories, we should draw on those sources to criticize the policies.

In the 1960s, many people thought consumers should have decision-making control in social agencies and schools. Of course, consumers can make mistakes, but we should solicit their perspectives on specific policies. Even when citizens' opinions are not systematically surveyed, social workers can inject their perspectives into debates about programs. When people with AIDS in a major city demanded special wards devoted to their problems, their preferences influenced hospital officials to create such wards.

Persons can support or oppose policies on purely moral grounds. Some programs can be defended on moral grounds when there is no empirical evidence of their effectiveness. For example, we can support hospice programs for those who are terminally ill because they provide caring, humanistic services to people suffering devastating trauma. An empirical finding that hospices save the government money by reducing the time people spend in hospitals would provide an additional justification, but we can defend the hospice program exclusively on moral grounds. Glenn Tinder argues:

Consequences do not count, at least not decisively (when defending social programs). If someone restores a lost wallet to the owner, we do not ask how the money it contained will be spent in order to determine whether this was an appropriate act. If someone helps save a friend from unemployment and poverty and the friend later dies of drink, we do not conclude that the original assistance was unwise. Indeed, a strict sense of justice is apt to be severely indifferent to consequences.[20]

Policy evaluation need not be reserved for technical experts. All of us can make important contributions, and we can use many kinds of arguments to support or oppose policies. Indeed, assessing policies is the starting point for assuming leadership in the human services system.

Chapter Summary

What You Can Now Do

You are now equipped to do the following:

- Use policy assessment data in policy debates
- Analyze the relative merit of specific research findings in the context of the research design and instruments used to develop them
- Propose both quantitative and qualitative approaches to assessing programs
- Understand why some policy assessments become embroiled in controversy

Notes

1. Michael Wald suggested this example in his article, "Family Preservation: Are We Moving Too Fast?" *Public Welfare* 46 (Summer 1988): 33–38.
2. Ibid.
3. These are hypothetical numbers.
4. These are hypothetical numbers.